KNOWING TOO MUCH

KNOWING TOO MUCH

Why the American Jewish Romance
with Israel Is Coming to an End

NORMAN G. FINKELSTEIN

OR Books
New York • London

© 2012 Norman G. Finkelstein

Published by OR Books, New York and London.

OR Books is a new type of publishing company that embraces progressive change in politics, culture and the business of publishing. We sell our books worldwide, direct to readers. To avoid the waste of unsold copies, we produce our books only when they are wanted, either through print-on-demand or as platform-agnostic e-books. Our approach jettisons the inefficiencies of conventional publishing to better serve readers, writers and the environment. If you would like to find out more about OR Books please visit our website at **www.orbooks.com**.

First printing 2012.

All rights reserved. No part of this book may be reproduced or transmitted in any form or by any means, electronic or mechanical, including photocopy, recording, or any information storage retrieval system, without permission in writing from the publisher, except brief passages for review purposes.

Library of Congress Cataloging in Publication Data:
A catalog record for this book is available from the Library of Congress

British Library Cataloging in Publication Data:
A catalog record for this book is available from the British Library

ISBN 978-1-935928-77-5 paperback
ISBN 978-1-935928-78-2 e-book

The typeface in which this book is set is Amalia. Typeset by Wordstop Technologies, Chennai, India.

*To Maren Hackmann-Mahajan,
editor extraordinaire*

Once it was easy, when everyone had their head in the sand and didn't understand the situation. There are still people who want to talk only about Exodus *and "the only democracy in the Middle East," but younger Jews, students, grew up on other stories, and they have a very tough conflict between the Israel they know and their sense of Jewish ethics.*
Rabbi Shira Milgrom[1]

I learned at Hebrew school that Israel was the "land of milk and honey" where Holocaust survivors had irrigated the deserts and made flowers bloom. . . . It was only after I went to college, met Muslim friends, and enrolled in a Middle Eastern history and politics course that I was challenged to reconcile my liberal, humanist worldview with the fact that the Jewish state of which I was so proud was occupying the land of 4.4 million stateless Palestinians, many of them refugees displaced by Israel's creation.
Dana Goldstein[2]

TABLE OF CONTENTS

Acknowledgments		xi
Introduction		xiii
	PART I: LIBERAL *ANGST*	
1/	Love Me, I'm A Liberal	5
2/	Irreconcilable Differences	19
	PART II: IT'S NOT EITHER/OR	
3/	A New Religion	35
4/	This Land Is My Land	45
	PART III: UPDATING *EXODUS*	
5/	Hair-Raising Screams	97
6/	Human Rights Revisionism	123
7/	Masters of War	155
8/	A Conspiracy So Immense	183
9/	Israel Versus The World	203
	PART IV: MIRROR IMAGE	
10/	History by Subtraction	253
Conclusion		299
Appendix		305
Notes		355
Index		451

ACKNOWLEDGMENTS

I am grateful for the Unz Foundation's support, and for the assistance of Jelle Bruinsma, Noam Chomsky, Chance Lunning, Daniel Macmillen, Frank Menetrez, Feroze Sidhwa, Jamie Stern-Weiner, Eugenia Tsao, and Gregory Whitfield. Alex Nunns of OR Books lent a golden touch during the final stages of editing.

INTRODUCTION

Recent surveys strongly suggest that American Jews are "distancing" themselves from Israel.¹ The data do not however yield a single causal factor for this estrangement. Judging by these surveys as well as the historical record, the interplay of a trio of factors—ethnicity, citizenship and ideology—have shaped the contours of the American Jewish relationship with Israel.

One can observe these factors at play in poll findings of Jewish opinion. When asked in a 2009 J Street survey to name "the single biggest reason" they support Israel, the most frequent replies of American Jews divided into the three classes of ethnic belonging ("I am Jewish and Israel is the Jewish homeland"), state loyalty ("Israel is an American ally in the Middle East and strengthens our national security interests"), and ideological affinity ("Israel is a democracy which shares my values"). Or, when asked whether a notorious anti-Arab politician joining the Israeli cabinet would affect their feelings towards Israel, fully one in three American Jews replied on the basis of ideology that it "weakens my personal connection to Israel because [his] positions go against my core values."²

It is not always clear however which factor is the operative one. Polls show that a decisive majority of American Jews oppose Israeli settlement expansion.³ But is this because successive U.S. administrations have been at loggerheads with Israel over the illegal settlements, or because settlement-building violates the liberal precept of respecting international law and resolving conflicts peacefully?[4]

The bedrock of the American Jewish bond with Israel is kinship: the attachment of an ethnic group to "its" ethnic state. Although their support of Israel does not spring automatically from this primal connection, American Jews plainly would not be as supportive in the absence of an ethnic link. The high rate of intermarriage among American Jews in recent years has diluted the impact of this blood tie and consequently attenuated the connection of many American Jews to Israel.[5]

Both celebrants and critics of the American Jewish romance with Israel typically depict the ethnic factor as the only operative one. Jewish neoconservatives claim that they adopted the neoconservative creed in significant part because its unconditional support for Israel was "good for the Jews," while in their bestseller, *The Israel Lobby and U.S. Foreign Policy*, John J. Mearsheimer and Stephen M. Walt take for granted that Jewish neoconservatives support Israel largely because they are Jewish. But American Jews have been equally protective of their hard-won rights and attendant secular success in the United States. Their support of Israel has consequently fluctuated depending on the state of U.S.-Israeli relations. Fearful of the "dual loyalty" charge that has historically haunted the Jewish people, American Jewry has put Israel at arm's length whenever relations between Washington and Tel Aviv have been tenuous and drawn closer when official ties have been stronger.

Jewish neoconservatives are a case in point. Liberal Jewish intellectuals who were resolutely indifferent to Israel in their youth mutated into neoconservative lovers of Zion not because of an idealistic devotion to kith and kin but because of an opportunistic devotion to power and privilege. Like many a sacred awakening, the one Jewish intellectuals experienced after the June 1967 war, when they "discovered" their roots and homeland, also netted them sizable profane benefits, when—coincidentally—Israel became an American strategic asset. Their new love affair with Israel was shot through with as much poignancy as a decision to reunite with an estranged relative after he has won the lottery.

The lineaments of the American Jewish relationship with Israel have also been molded by liberal ideology. A pair of allegiances distinguish American Jews from fellow Americans: their markedly greater support of liberalism and of Israel. Indeed, these commitments have effectively defined what it means to be Jewish in America. "For many American Jews," Steven M. Cohen observed in his classic anatomy of the contemporary Jewish scene, "politics—in particular pro-Israel and liberal activity—have come to constitute their principal working definition of Jewishness."[6] The interaction between these twin commitments, and in particular the tension between them, is the focus of this book.

For a long while "pro-Israel and liberal activity" appeared perfectly compatible. Israel was conceived among enlightened Americans as an offspring of their own nation-building experiment, a place where rugged settlers had also transformed wasteland into a democratic oasis. But in recent years it has proven increasingly difficult to marry support for Israel with liberal values. In an essay published already some 15 years ago, the eminent American Jewish sociologist Nathan Glazer vividly captured this budding conflict:

> Liberals want to spend money on schools and housing projects rather than arms; but American sophisticated arms may defend Israel. They want to give aid to poor nations; but Israel, not a poor nation, engrosses a huge share of the American aid budget. They want to support democracies, and Israel is a democracy, but one in which the rights of a very large part of the population, Arabs within Israel and the occupied territories, are scarcely models of the rights people expect to have in a democratic society.... Liberals in this country support the strict separation of church and state and the equality of religions before the law, but they support a state in which one religion holds primacy and is backed by state power. They are against the conquest of territory by force but support a state that has doubled its size through force and over time has shown less and less inclination to give up its

conquests. The measures Israel uses to put down the [first] intifada, when resorted to by other democracies . . ., raise an outcry among liberals; in the Israeli case, the outcry is muted.

Glazer went on to speculate that in defense of Israeli policies, American Jews would eventually shed their "anachronistic" liberal sensibility.[7] Some poll data lent support to Glazer's prediction: American Jews have embraced policies such as a strong military that buttressed Israel but contradicted liberalism.[8] However, the overarching tendency has been the reverse of what Glazer anticipated. The robustness of their liberalism has caused American Jews to loosen their bonds with Israel.

A raft of recent studies has chronicled the incipient breakup of liberal Jewish support for Israel. They spotlight how a sequence of political developments in Israel—the accession to power of right-wing parties and politicians, the 1982 invasion of Lebanon, the repression of the first Palestinian intifada, the impasses in the "peace process"—have created rifts in the American Jewish community and concomitantly alienated liberal Jewish opinion from Israel.[9]

This book takes a different tack. It traces the gradual shift in *perception* of the Israel-Palestine conflict, in effect, the knowledge shift from fiction to fact, that has rendered support for Israel on the basis of liberal values increasingly untenable. A 2011 Gallup poll of American public opinion unsurprisingly found "liberals the least supportive of Israel of any group." Although more than 60 percent of Americans generally expressed greater sympathy for Israel than the Palestinians, the percentage fell to under 50 percent for liberals.[10]

The perceptual shift that now casts Israel in a harsher light takes multiple forms and is visible in multiple forums. Respected scholars and human rights organizations have confirmed and deepened the findings of prior, mostly maligned critics of Israel. Additionally, the broad consensus in the legal-diplomatic community for resolving the Israel-Palestine conflict puts the onus on Israel for the failure to achieve peace.

INTRODUCTION

Whereas Israel's critics in the past had to rely on marginalized sources, they can now quote unimpeachable authorities to make the case against Israeli policy. For every apologetic study by a Michael Oren on the history of war and peace in the Middle East, one can now cite a critical Israeli strategic analyst such as Zeev Maoz; for every book and blog entry by a Jeffrey Goldberg whitewashing Israel's human rights record, one can now cite critical publications by authoritative human rights organizations such as B'Tselem, Human Rights Watch and Amnesty International; for every legal-diplomatic justification of Israeli intransigence put forth by an Alan Dershowitz or a Dennis Ross, one can now quote the International Court of Justice or a reputable Israeli diplomat such as Shlomo Ben-Ami. Although reportage will not be directly treated in this book, it might also be noted that for every hackneyed piece by the *New York Times*'s Ethan Bronner and Thomas Friedman, one can now cite the courageous and deeply informed dispatches of *Haaretz* reporters Gideon Levy and Amira Hass.

In fact the vast preponderance of mainstream historical scholarship, human rights reporting and legal-diplomatic opinion upholds impressive standards of objectivity. The findings of this body of work, more often than not sharply critical of Israel, have entered the public debate, and willy-nilly these critical conclusions have seeped into the consciousness of American Jews, who are highly educated and tapped into the broad currents of liberal culture. An indication of these compound developments is that American Jews with relatively higher levels of education tend to be more alienated from Israel.[11]

Still, the pages of this book depict an incomplete, on-going process, a trajectory. Many propagandistic works, and outright frauds, still gain wide currency in the United States. Regrettably, even respected university presses and human rights organizations now and again put out studies of dubious value. A significant portion of this book will be devoted to dissecting such misinformation and disinformation, as a practical demonstration of the process described here.

Because Israeli propaganda no longer monopolizes public discourse, and enough of the truth, even if still only a small fraction of it, has become known, Israel can no longer count on the blind support of American Jews. Nowhere is the shift more palpable than on American college campuses. During the past couple of decades this writer has lectured widely across the U.S. on the Israel-Palestine conflict. Confident of their convictions, Israel's youthful defenders used to pack the audiences and form long queues after the talks to pose hostile questions. But in recent years fewer and fewer of them venture to show up; once boisterous and sure-footed, their presence is now barely audible. Only a handful of diehards are willing to suffer the embarrassment of making the "case for Israel" in public.

Not even the massive proliferation of centers, programs, and endowed chairs devoted to Judaic Studies, Holocaust Studies, Israel Studies, and Anti-Semitism Studies has managed to turn the critical tide of campus opinion. Israel's supporters allege that anti-Semitic (or self-hating Jewish) professors have hijacked Middle East Studies departments and brainwashed students. In reality it is not the scholarship but the facts that are "biased," and what is now being taught is what serious research shows. Not for the first time the messenger is being blamed for the bad news.

It is improbable, however, that American Jews will ever become wholly indifferent to Israel's fate and future. Polls show that regardless of ideological affiliation the primal attachment of American Jewry to Israel stays constant. What differs according to political hue is support for Israeli *policies*: those American Jews calling themselves liberal refuse to back Israeli initiatives antithetical to liberal values.[12]

True, as Israel moves steadily and inexorably to the right, more American Jews will likely grow alienated from it. A small portion will not shy away from publicly denouncing Israel while a larger portion—not wanting to air dirty laundry in public, but also not wanting to defend the indefensible—will lapse into silence. Indeed, a significant percentage of younger American Jews has already expressed indifference to the prospect of Israel's destruction. But even among those Jews most alienated from Israel a residual sentiment of blood-belonging persists, just as it did in the past among Jews wedded to assimilation. "A chain holds them fast to Judaism," the spiritual

Zionist Ahad Ha'am famously observed, mocking these Jewish assimilationists. "Try as they will to conceal it, seek as they will for subterfuges to deceive the world and themselves, it lives nonetheless; resist it as they will, it is a force at the center of their being."[13]

If Israel does, or appears to, confront an existential crisis where its physical existence is literally at stake, American Jewry will almost certainly rally, and *should* rally, to its defense. The physical destruction of any society is a criminal act and sane people will contemplate such a prospect with horror. Should such an eventuality loom large, the near-totality of American Jews will rise to Israel's defense because the elemental compulsion of blood—not to mention the fear, however irrational, that they might be next—will make itself felt; because their own liberal values will spur them into action; and because it is hard to conceive that the U.S. government will stand in their way.

The political upshot for the present moment is that if American Jews are to be won over, the terms set forth for resolving the Israel-Palestine conflict must be aligned with liberal values. Otherwise, however enlightened their convictions and however estranged they might feel from Israel, most American Jews will not actively speak out against it. In other words, it must be shown to American Jews that the choice between Israel's survival and Palestinian rights is a false one; that it is in fact Israel's denial of Palestinian rights and reflexive resort to criminal force that are pushing it toward destruction; that it is possible to resolve the Israel-Palestine conflict so that everyone, Israeli Jew and Palestinian Arab, can preserve their full human dignity; and that such a settlement has been within reach for decades, but that Israel—with critical U.S. backing, largely because of the Israel lobby—has blocked it.

It must be shown to American Jews that what is being asked of them is not more but also not less than that they be consistent in word and deed when it comes to the people of Palestine. If it can be demonstrated that the enlightened values of truth and justice are on the side of Israel's critics, then it should be possible—the evidence is already there—to strike a resonant chord among American Jews that goads them into action.

PART I

LIBERAL *ANGST*

In the course of nearly a century American Jews have demonstrated an enduring commitment to liberal values. Even after achieving worldly success, they resisted the gravitational pull of the conservative pole on the political spectrum. In recent years the liberal ethos of American Jews has been put to a new test. When they first embraced Israel after the June 1967 war, the Jewish state appeared to embody the highest and best in Western civilization: it was the "Light Unto the Nations." But much more is now known about Israel's actual human rights, historical and diplomatic record. This voluminous dossier, assembled by unimpeachable authorities, many of them Israeli and Jewish, cannot be reconciled with the liberalism of American Jewry. Forced to choose between Israel, or the tug of kinship, and liberalism, or the tug of ideology, many American Jews have stayed true to the belief system that has brought them so many earthly blessings, and distanced themselves from a state that has become an embarrassment.

1/ LOVE ME, I'M A LIBERAL

In recent times Jewish neoconservatives have bedecked themselves in the mantle of Israel's staunchest supporters. But those Jews thickening the ranks of American Zionism after the June 1967 war, when support for Israel among American Jewry surged, were preponderantly liberal in outlook. It could not have been otherwise because—whether judged by party affiliation, self-identification, or stance on salient socioeconomic issues—most American Jews have historically placed themselves in the liberal-Democratic camp. Only African-Americans have voted Democratic and self-identified as liberals in greater numbers.

Ever since the 1932 presidential election, when Franklin D. Roosevelt won 82 percent of the Jewish vote (in 1944 it reached an astonishing 90 percent), American Jews have consistently and overwhelmingly voted for Democratic candidates. Such a voting pattern made perfect sense during the Great Depression when Jews constituted a mostly poor immigrant population and FDR's New Deal held out hope and promise in the Jewish ghetto. But already by the mid-1940s American Jews had climbed to the upper rungs of the socioeconomic ladder.[1] It is periodically predicted that Jews will abandon the working-class, liberal Democrats and flock to their more "natural" nesting place among prosperous, conservative Republicans.[2] However, even the emergence of the high profile Jewish neoconservative movement failed to make a significant dent in Jewish support for the Democratic Party.

In contemporary surveys nearly three in four American Jews (versus one in two non-Jews) have consistently labeled themselves Democratic, while nearly 50 percent of American Jews (versus 30 percent of non-Jews) have consistently located themselves at the liberal end of the political spectrum. Many Jews have responded in public opinion polls that liberalism is inherent in and integral to their Jewish identity.[3]

On the socioeconomic issues that define the liberal-conservative divide in American society—school prayer and tuition tax credits for parochial schools; abortion, women's and gay rights; domestic social spending; civil liberties; rights of African-Americans—Jews have generally supported liberal positions in large percentages, and in much larger percentages than non-Jews. The significant exceptions are that neither Jews nor non-Jews are especially supportive of government spending that specifically targets the poor; Jews are not significantly more liberal than non-Jews on issues pertaining to African-Americans, while on affirmative action they are in fact less liberal; and both Jews and non-Jews overwhelmingly support capital punishment.[4] "The departures from the pattern of disproportionate Jewish liberalism," one leading commentator observes, "hint at a selective erosion of liberalism wherever Jewish group interests are at stake."[5]

Many scholars have pondered the paradox of why American Jews remain steadfastly liberal and Democratic despite their increasing affluence and enviable professional status. Indeed, Jews have become by a wide margin the wealthiest ethno-religious group in the United States.[6] In the words of the familiar quip, how has it come to pass that Jews earn salaries of Episcopalians but vote as if Puerto Ricans?[7]

A myriad of hypotheses have been put forth to account for this persistence of Jewish liberalism. Inasmuch as children oftentimes inherit the values of their parents, Jewish liberalism would constitute a generational holdover or residual factor from bygone days when Jews dreamt of, and belonged to leftist organizations advocating, a more just and egalitarian society.[8] If not every Jewish radical in the 1960s was a "red diaper baby," more than a few had worn pink diapers. Jews as a group have also attained levels

1/ LOVE ME, I'M A LIBERAL

of education that typically correlate with a more liberal-secular outlook,[9] and have also gravitated towards "words and ideas" professions,[10] and reside in upscale urban and suburban communities, where a liberal-secular cast of mind is the norm.

In addition, however much Jews might now prosper and be integrated in American society, they still remain an identifiable, historically persecuted minority, carrying all the insecurities and other psychological baggage that burden such a stigmatized status, and still retain an attachment to a group identity that, whether because of nostalgia, pride or spiritual reward, they are unwilling wholly to part with. Consequently American Jews still embrace a liberal ethos that has championed the rights of oppressed minorities, and a political party that has enabled them both to thrive and preserve a vestige of their Jewish identity.[11]

If compelled to choose, most American Jews will not hesitate deciding between, on the one hand, the left-liberal ideology that in the not-so-distant past promoted the emancipation of Jews and underpinned the coalition that defeated Hitler, and, on the other, the conservative ideology that rejected the civil rights of Jews and was, if not the direct precursor of Nazism, nonetheless too close to it for Jewish comfort. It is also no contest for American Jews if forced to choose between, on the one hand, the inclusiveness of the Democratic Party's "interest groups" and "identity politics"—some of which Jews no doubt disdain, but some of which (trade unionism, African-American and women's rights) individual Jews inspired and led—and, on the other, the exclusiveness of the Republican Party's Christian fundamentalist and nativist leanings, which fill most Jews with suspicion if not dread.

A fixation on "The Holocaust" in American Jewish culture has exacerbated the atavistic insecurity of American Jews by inculcating group paranoia. A lucrative and tendentious Holocaust industry propagandizes that lurking in the heart of even the gentlest of gentiles is a homicidal anti-Semite and that concomitantly even where diasporic Jews feel most safe and secure they still face imminent danger.[12] This orchestrated hysteria increases the attraction of Israel as the last refuge in the event of a "second Holocaust," and consequently blind support of Israeli policies, however reactionary. Yet, the contrived insecurity of American Jews has, paradoxically, also reinforced their self-perception as a persecuted minority and consequently their liberalism.

Beyond historical and sociological factors, it has also been suggested that a peculiarly "Jewish" element accounts for a fair portion of this liberalism. It is said to spring from the Judaic tradition of charity (*Zedakeh*), which would explain Jewish support for the welfare state, and a Judaic tradition that valorizes earthly pleasures, which would explain Jewish support for sexual rights.[13] However, doubt has been cast on the actuality of this factor because the Judaic notion of charity begins and ends with other *Jews*; Jewish tradition regards homosexuality as an abomination and women's liberation barely less so; and the most religiously observant Jews (in both the Diaspora and Israel) are as a rule the least liberal.[14]

Regardless of how one accounts for this persistence of liberalism, the fact remains that its values have molded the *Weltanschauung* of American Jews. These values include inter alia the rule of law and equality under the law, human rights and international organizations, and the peaceful resolution of conflicts.[15]

When the romance of American Jews with Israel began after the June 1967 war these liberal values appeared also to be Israeli values. The Jewish state was said to encompass the highest and best in American liberalism: the "Light Unto the Nations," the torchbearer of Western Civilization and an oasis of democracy in the benighted East. American Jews did not have to choose, ideologically, between dual and divided loyalties.[16] But the era of the "beautiful" Israel has now passed, it seems irrevocably, and the disfigured Israel that has replaced it is a growing embarrassment to Jews weaned on liberal values.

Many unsavory truths about Israel can no longer be denied or dismissed. The record of the Israeli-Arab conflict documented by respected historians belies the cowboys and Indians version popularized in the likes of Leon Uris's *Exodus*. The record of Israeli human rights violations compiled by

1/ LOVE ME, I'M A LIBERAL

respected organizations cannot be reconciled with Israel's vaunted commitment to "purity of arms." The record of deliberations in respected judicial and political bodies casts doubt on Israel's avowed commitment to a peaceful resolution of the conflict.

In subsequent chapters of this book we will take a closer look at what this record shows. The point to be made here is that Israel today is not so much a worse place, or behaves worse than before, but rather that the reality of Israel has finally started to catch up with its image. However, this broad generalization also requires some qualifications. To rationalize their change of heart, Israel's erstwhile liberal supporters in the American Jewish community are wont to say that Israel is no longer the place it once was. "For those of us with memories of earlier days, memories of the kibbutz and the Histadrut, memories of Israel before it became a client state of America," a veteran American Jewish liberal writer mourned, "there's been biting disappointment."[17] This notion of a lapsed Israel does contain some truth, if less than widely supposed.

It would be obtuse to deny that after the June 1967 war Israel became a less inspirational place. The enlightened social experiments and egalitarianism that sprang from the founding generation's idealism, and which were, rightly, admired by progressive-minded foreigners, mostly became a thing of the past. The "new" Israel that emerged after, and was largely a by-product of, the June 1967 war came to bear fainter and fainter resemblance to the Zion of the liberal Jewish imagination. The irony is, the fascination of American Jews with Israel's socialist utopia began just on the point of its vanishing.

Between 1967 and 1973 some 60,000 American Jews "moved to the Jewish state ... to create an idealistic Jewish homeland," many doing a stint on a kibbutz in order to experience the spiritual high of Israel's austere collective life.[18] But today's Israel resembles much more the fantasyland of right-wing free-market zealots. It has moved from being among the most egalitarian countries in the Western world in terms of income distribution to the least egalitarian in the West except for the U.S., and its gaps in income distribution are now among the widest in the world.[19]

As distribution of wealth has grown more inequitable, Israel's political life has unsurprisingly grown more squalid. Whatever one's opinion of the Zionist project, it is nonetheless a fact that Zionist leaders of the founding generation were motivated principally by an ideal to which they subordinated personal comfort and that they sought power principally to realize this ideal. It is not hard to understand why many left-leaning Jews, for whom Lenin and the Bolsheviks incarnated revolutionary virtue and ruthlessness, would also come to admire the élan, resourcefulness and ruthless singleness of purpose of David Ben-Gurion and the socialist Zionists. But it is also hard not to notice the chasm separating the selflessness of the founding generation from the personal corruption of the current batch of Israeli leaders.

"Once, the top priority [of Israeli politicians] was the state, then nothing, then the party, and only in the end personal gain," an octogenarian veteran of the Zionist movement recently rued. "Today, the priorities are arranged as me first, then nothing, some more nothing, then the state." And "the fact is that all the politicians then ... died poor."[20] In the face of the spectacular and often grotesque scandals, ranging from financial theft to moral turpitude, nowadays daily wracking the Israeli political establishment,[21] it is a sobering juxtaposition that in 1976 Prime Minister Yitzhak Rabin was forced to step down from office merely because his wife had kept open a U.S. bank account.

Even as recently as 1996 international agencies ranked Israel a highly transparent, corruption-free society. But among the 36 formal democracies annually surveyed in the Israeli Democracy Index for political corruption (first place being least corrupt), Israel has dropped significantly in recent years from 14 to 22 (beside the likes of Estonia), while recent polls have found that 75-90 percent of the Israeli public believes that the political sphere is rife with corruption, and some 40-50 percent believes that "to reach the top in today's politics in Israel you have to be corrupt."[22]

The flipside of the escalating political corruption is the diminishing confidence of the Israeli public—and increasingly of Jews abroad—in the wisdom and integrity of its country's leaders. In recent years some 70 percent of Israeli respondents agreed with the statement, "A politician does not tend to take into account the view of the ordinary citizen," whereas only 39 percent held this opinion in 1969;[23] half and more agreed that Israeli leaders are mostly or solely out for personal gain; and about 70 percent agreed that politicians today are inferior to those in the past.[24] Indeed, who would gainsay that a civilizational abyss separates hyper-eloquent former Israeli foreign minister Abba Eban, who achieved a triple first at Cambridge University, from current foreign minister Avigdor Lieberman, who achieved his fame as a Moldovan nightclub bouncer? In tandem with a loss of faith in their political class, ordinary Israelis have also lost faith in the collective ideal of self-sacrifice and public service, which once captivated Israel's admirers abroad. Whereas 64 percent of Israelis responded in 1981 that the interests of the country as a whole ranked above their personal interests, only 28 percent were primarily committed to the greater good of society in 2008.[25]

As Israeli society gives freer rein to unfettered capitalism and Israeli politicians *pari passu* sink deeper into the mire of corruption, authoritarian and right-wing tendencies, which are anathema—or at any rate, an embarrassment—to liberal American Jews, have gained momentum in Israeli society. Nearly two-thirds of Israelis in recent years have responded affirmatively to the statement, "A few strong leaders can be more useful to the country than all the discussions and the laws."[26] A 2010 poll found that more than half of Israelis agreed with the statement, "Israel's overall situation would be much better if less attention were paid to democratic principles and more to maintaining law and order," and nearly 40 percent agreed with the statement that in light of its current crises "democracy is not suited to Israel."[27]

The souring on liberal norms in Israel has resulted in a contraction of the space available to articulate these norms. Up to nearly 60 percent of Israelis surveyed in recent years agreed that a "speaker should be forbidden to express sharp criticism of the State of Israel in public."[28] In terms of press freedom, among 36 formal democracies Israel in recent years ranked 27-31 (last place being least free) beside the likes of Bulgaria; in Freedom House's tripartite division of "free," "partly free" and "not free" press, Israel in 2009 fell for the first time into the "partly free" category;[29] and in the Reporters Without Borders Annual Index of Press Freedom, Israel ranked 93 among 175 countries (last place being least free) in 2009 just below Guinea-Bissau, and 86 among 178 countries in 2010 just below Serbia.[30]

The ascension of right-wing forces in Israel fuels, and is fueled by, growing social intolerance. American Jews have been weaned on, and benefited from, the values of secularism and church-state separation, and more than half do not belong to a synagogue, do not participate in Jewish communal life and are taking the route of intermarriage. The broad support in Israel for an intrusive State in matters of religion cannot but discomfit many of them. A 2007 survey found that some 60 percent of Israelis believed that the State should "make sure that public life in the country is conducted according to Jewish religious tradition,"[31] while in recent years fully 40 percent of Israeli respondents said that a couple should *not* "be allowed to marry in any way they wish."[32]

Whereas the historical role many Jews played in the struggle for racial tolerance is a point of pride among American Jewry,[33] nowhere has Israeli intolerance grown uglier than in interethnic relations. True, 80 percent of Israelis polled in recent years supported the generic proposition that "all must have the same rights before the law, regardless of political outlook." Only about half of Israeli Jews, however, have supported equality of rights between Arabs and Jews.[34]

The prevalence and depth of bigotry among Israeli Jews can be gauged by their readiness to curtail Israeli Arab rights. A 2007 poll found that only 22 percent of Israeli Jews supported allowing Arab parties and ministers to join the government, while a 2009 poll found that fully three in ten Israeli Jews believed that Arab citizens should be denied the right to vote, four in ten believed that Jewish citizens should have more rights than non-Jewish citizens, and eight in ten believed that a Jewish majority should be required "on decisions fateful to the country." These findings point, in the words of the Israel Democracy Institute, to "broad support for the idea of denying political rights to Israel's Arab minority."[35]

A 2010 survey found that almost two-thirds of Israeli Jews supported making citizenship conditional on swearing an oath of loyalty to Israel as a democratic, Jewish and Zionist state—although "if this exclusionary proposal is accepted, the right to full citizenship will be denied to many who enjoy it today, since they will not be able to make the required declaration without lying about their true beliefs"; more than two-thirds of Israeli Jews opposed family reunification of Israeli Arab citizens' immediate relatives living abroad—although "many states recognize [this] as a basic human right"; more than half of Israeli Jews would support greater State funding for Jewish than Arab communities; and one-third of Israeli Jews supported the incarceration of the Arab population in wartime.[36]

The racism contaminating Israeli society at large has also infected branches of the government and bureaucracy. "This past year has seen a wave of racist statements, bills and initiatives threatening the freedom of expression and freedom of political activity of the Arab minority, as well as their right to their language and culture," the Association for Civil Rights in Israel (ACRI) reported in 2009. "Also threatened have been some of the Arab minority's most basic rights—to equality, education and employment—as well as their very citizenship." "For large sectors of the Jewish population and their elected officials," ACRI concluded, "Arab citizens of this country seem to be entitled to equality and safeguarding of their rights only on condition that they abandon their national identity, culture, language and historical heritage."[37] Even egregious American Jewish apologists for Israel like Anti-Defamation League director Abraham Foxman have felt compelled to denounce some of this racist legislation because it violated the core liberal value of "freedom of speech."[38]

The poisonous state of race relations in Israel is further captured in polls measuring the visceral feelings and social preferences of Israeli Jews. A 2007 survey by the Israeli Center against Racism found that one in two Israeli Jews feels "fear" when hearing Arabic spoken in the street, four in ten feel "discomfort," and one in three feels "revulsion" or "hatred." In addition, three in four Israeli Jews said that they would not agree to live in the same building as Arabs, six in ten were not willing to have Arab friends visit their homes, and more than half supported separate recreational facilities for Arabs and Jews.[39] A 2010 poll found that, if forced to choose, Israeli Jews would prefer a mentally ill to an Arab neighbor.[40]

The ideal among broad swaths of Israeli Jewish society, however, would be not a quiescent Arab minority but an Arab-free Israel. In the past two decades fully 50-70 percent of Israeli Jews have supported the use of State inducements to rid the Jewish state of its Palestinian citizens.[41]

In light of these findings it should not surprise that among 27 countries with vulnerable minority populations Israel ranked 27th (worst) in economic discrimination and 26th in political discrimination.[42] Likewise, among 36 formal democracies Israel has consistently witnessed the most or among the most acute levels of religious/national/ethnic tension.[43] Put simply Israel strongly resembles the American South in the Jim Crow era—in fact Social Affairs Minister Isaac Herzog explicitly compared Israeli racism to "Alabama in the 1940s"[44]—but with Israeli Jews figuratively on the opposite side of the barricade from American Jewish liberals who went down South to join the desegregation struggle.

The distribution of population along the political spectrum points up both the pronounced rightward drift of Israeli society, and the incongruence of Israeli society with the significantly liberal American Jewish milieu. The Israeli political spectrum in recent years is almost a reverse image of its American Jewish counterpart: roughly speaking, 50 percent of Israelis situate themselves right and 25 percent left of center,[45] whereas 50 percent of American Jews situate themselves left and 25 percent right of center.[46]

"By voting disproportionately for their country's first African-American president, American Jews maintained their traditional prominence in helping the U.S. overcome its racist past," an Israeli commentator shrewdly observed, while "in contrast, Israel's eighty-percent Jewish majority has just voted [February 2009] in unprecedented numbers for several overtly—even proudly—racist political parties, whose campaigns incited against Israel's 1.2 million Arab citizens." "When it comes to core democratic values," the commentator concluded, "American and Israeli Jews are headed in diametrically opposite directions."[47] Even when his national approval ratings had dipped in 2010, Barack Obama still remained very popular among American Jews, whereas a majority of Israelis held a negative opinion of him.[48]

One concrete political repercussion of these reverse trajectories was the reaction to Avigdor Lieberman's mooted appointment: one in three American Jews responded that their support for Israel would diminish if he became a senior cabinet member without disavowing his racist beliefs because "Lieberman's positions go against my core values."[49] "The current Israeli government [of Benjamin Netanyahu] has become a source of embarrassment to many liberal American Jews," the editor of the largest circulation Jewish newspaper in the U.S. recently lamented. "Most American Jews want to feel proud of the Jewish State, not frustrated or ashamed. It doesn't help when they read of settlement growth, the flotilla debacle, Foreign Minister Lieberman's hard-line comments about Israeli Arabs and other issues, or that the Knesset conducted inquiries into the funding sources of NGOs, or that the Chief Rabbinate is increasingly rigid on matters of marriage, divorce and conversion."[50]

Although, as the data just presented suggest, Israeli society has coarsened in recent years, and a rift has consequently opened up between it and American Jewry, it can easily be exaggerated just how much the new Israel differs from the purportedly halcyon days of its golden past.[51] Consider the treatment meted out to the indigenous Palestinian population by the "first Israelis."

The founding fathers of Zionism were scarcely immune to racist stereotyping of Arabs, which ran the gamut from the paternalistic when the natives sat passive to the virulent when they grew restless.[52] Insofar as the Zionist conquest of Palestine strongly resembled other colonizing enterprises, it would have been odd if these settlers did not also exhibit a colonial mentality.[53] And, insofar as Zionist leaders set as their goal the creation of an overwhelmingly Jewish state in a place that was overwhelmingly not Jewish, they could only realize their goal through colonial-style ethnic cleansing. As leading Israeli historian Benny Morris put it, "transfer was inevitable and inbuilt into Zionism."[54]

In the course, and under the cover, of the 1948 war, the goal was largely achieved: some 750,000 Palestinians were forced into exile amidst calculated Zionist mayhem and massacre, while 150,000 remained in place. After the war the founding generation committed numberless ghoulish atrocities against mostly unarmed Palestinian refugees seeking to return home.[55] Those Palestinians who managed to escape expulsion and stayed behind were methodically stripped of their land and possessions by the newly born Jewish state, which still hoped eventually to rid itself of them, and stripped of many of their basic rights as they were placed under military rule until 1966.[56]

In the popular imagination Ariel Sharon came to incarnate the evil and rot eating away at the socialist Zionist dream of Ben-Gurion's generation because of the many atrocities to which he was personally party. But in fact Ben-Gurion "did not just like" Sharon, he "positively adored" him, according to Moshe Dayan, because Sharon "embodied the character of the Israeli Jew of his dream—a man of integrity."[57]

Right after the June 1967 war the founding Zionist generation routinely tortured Palestinian detainees in the occupied West Bank and Gaza Strip.[58] Although Israeli torture still goes on, it became less severe and pervasive after 1999 (when Israel's High Court of Justice issued a partial ban) than it had been during the heyday of American Jewry's romance with Israel.[59] Or, consider this: although Israel killed far fewer civilians during its attacks on Lebanon in 2006 and Gaza in 2008-9 than during its 1982 invasion of Lebanon, and Israel's pretexts for launching an attack were arguably stronger (if still flimsy) in 2006 and 2008-9 than in 1982, American Jews were much more divided during the recent Israeli aggressions.[60]

If American Jews have grown more critical of Israel, it is by and large not because Israel has become a qualitatively worse place. Rather, it is because much more is now known about the record of Israel's interactions with its Arab neighbors, there is broad consensus on what this record shows, it is much more difficult to pretend not to know this record, and it is no longer possible to reconcile Israeli behavior documented in this record with core liberal values.

"My generation of American Jews was raised to view the Zionist project through... rose-colored glasses," historian Jonathan Sarna lamented. "Now, though, that dream, which had more to do with the lofty visions of American Jews than with the sordid realities of the Middle East, lies shattered beyond repair."[61] If the romance of American Jews with Israel is coming to an end, it is because they now know too much.

2/ IRRECONCILABLE DIFFERENCES

The accumulation of evidence casting Israel in a harsh light has now reached critical mass. For a long while Israel attempted to deflect and dilute the impact of these damning facts by wielding the twin swords of The Holocaust[1] and The New Anti-Semitism.[2] It was claimed that Jews could not be held to conventional moral-legal standards after the unique suffering they endured during World War II and that criticism of Israeli policy was motivated by an ever-resurgent hatred of Jews. However, neither of these weapons any longer intimidates.

Once criticism of Israel emerged in the mainstream of public opinion, the charge of anti-Semitism proved much less credible. It was one thing to falsely allege back in the 1970s that a dissident pacifist such as Reverend Daniel J. Berrigan was an anti-Semite. Few people knew enough about him to judge one way or the other.[3] It is quite another thing, however, to allege that criticism of Israel by a recognizable public figure such as Jimmy Carter is spurred by Jew-hatred. Who believes it?

Meanwhile, promiscuous use of The Holocaust as a weapon has inevitably dulled its edge. Surveys of public opinion in recent years show that large percentages believe "Jews talk too much about the Holocaust." Ironically Israel's supporters have adduced this finding to prove the pervasiveness of anti-Semitism[4]—which will no doubt cause people to think, rightly, that Jews also talk too much about anti-Semitism.

As a result of Israel's diminishing ability to shield itself from legitimate criticism, its international standing has plummeted. The estrangement of American Jews from Israel is an integral part and the culmination of this much broader process.

Israel won many adherents in the West after its lightning victory in June 1967, while the handful of vocal dissenters belonged to the marginal Left.[5] But in recent years it has been reduced almost to the status of a pariah state. A 2006 survey by the National Brands Index (NBI) of "25,903 online consumers across 35 countries about their perceptions of those countries" found that "Israel's brand is by a considerable margin the most negative we have ever measured in the NBI, and comes at the bottom of the ranking on almost every question . . . by a long margin. . . . There is nowhere that respondents would like to visit less than Israel. . . . Israel's people were also voted the most unwelcoming in the world."[6]

A 2003 poll of the European Union named Israel the biggest threat to world peace.[7] A 2007 British Broadcasting Corporation (BBC) global poll of attitudes toward 12 major nations found that Israel had the most negative image; a 2008 BBC poll ranked Israel second from the bottom (slightly above Iran); a 2009 BBC poll found that "the largest number of countries—19 out of 21—gave negative ratings to Israel"; a majority of respondents in a 2010 BBC global poll believed that, alongside Iran and Pakistan, Israel exerted a mainly negative influence on world affairs—even North Korea's influence was viewed negatively by fewer respondents.[8] An intriguing conclusion from the BBC polls is that, except for the United States, in countries where the governments are most "pro"-Israel, the Israel lobby is most powerful, and "pro"-Israel propaganda is most pervasive—Australia, Canada, France, Germany and Britain—the respective populations hold *overwhelmingly negative* opinions of Israel.[9] This finding suggests how out of step these governments are with popular sentiment, how potent the Israel lobby is in many of these countries, and how ineffectual the "pro"-Israel propaganda has become.

Unsurprisingly Israel's treatment of the Palestinians has come under harsh public scrutiny. A 2008 survey of global opinion named Israel the

2/ IRRECONCILABLE DIFFERENCES

biggest obstacle to achieving peace in the Israel-Palestine conflict. Meanwhile a 2011 poll of 19 countries found that in every country either a plurality or a majority of respondents supported U.N. recognition of a Palestinian state.[10] A pair of polls in 2011 found that more Europeans believed "Israel's oppression of Palestinians" was a bigger obstacle to peace than "Palestinian terror attacks," and 40 percent and more of European respondents believed that "Israel is conducting a war of extermination against the Palestinians."[11]

The simmering global discontent with Israel reached a boiling point of outrage during the Israeli invasion of Gaza in 2008-9. Large popular protests throughout Western Europe dwarfed in size demonstrations supporting Israel. Even in traditional bastions of official support such as Canada and Germany, disapproval of the Gaza assault and broader Israeli policy reached significant levels.[12] "The increased and brutal frequency of war in this volatile region has shifted international opinion," the British *Financial Times* editorialized a year after the Israeli assault, "reminding Israel it is not above the law. Israel can no longer dictate the terms of debate."[13]

Israel's international standing slipped yet another notch after its 2010 assault on the humanitarian flotilla heading towards Gaza to breach the illegal blockade.[14] Only some 20 percent of the respondents in countries ranging from France to Sweden expressed a favorable opinion of Israel in polls taken after the attack, while fully 40 percent of Norway's population supported a boycott of Israeli products, and the Methodist Church of Britain called on its congregants to "support and engage with th[e] boycott of Israeli goods emanating from illegal settlements."[15]

Jewish communities around the world have not been immune to the spreading skepticism. A 2007 *Economist* feature story, "Second Thoughts about the Promised Land," reported that although "most diaspora Jews still support Israel strongly . . . their ambivalence has grown." In places such as Britain, there is a "very low level of enthusiasm and commitment to Israel among pretty much all the middle-to-younger members," while in Germany and Russia thriving independent centers of Jewish life outside Israel's "gravitational pull" have emerged.[16]

Dissenting Jewish voices have begun to coalesce in the West challenging the hegemony of official Jewish organizations that parrot Israeli propaganda.[17] In the course of Israel's 2008-9 attack on Gaza, ad hoc Jewish groups and Jewish-initiated petitions deploring the invasion proliferated, while even Jews prominent in communal life publicly criticized Israel, albeit in muted language.[18] As Tel Aviv stood poised to launch the ground offensive after a week of relentless aerial attacks, a group of Britain's most distinguished Jews, describing themselves as "profound and passionate supporters" of Israel, expressed "horror" at the "increasing loss of life on both sides" and called on Israel to cease its military operations in Gaza immediately.[19]

The overall picture and trends are perhaps not as clear-cut in the United States but they still merit notice. Judging by poll data it can broadly be said that Americans have consistently viewed Israel favorably[20] and have sympathized much more with Israel than with the Palestinians.[21] But Americans have also overwhelmingly supported an evenhanded U.S. approach to the Israel-Palestine conflict,[22] a sizable minority believing that Washington tilts (or tilts too much) in favor of Israel;[23] a robust majority of Americans "think Israel is not doing its part well in making efforts to resolve the conflict";[24] and Americans have on occasion supported the use of sanctions to rein in Israel.[25] Significantly, a majority of Americans have also supported a two-state settlement on the June 1967 borders—i.e., a full Israeli withdrawal from the territories it occupied in the June war.[26]

"The polls show . . . that support for Israel" among Americans "is broad but it is not very deep," M. J. Rosenberg, director of policy analysis for the Israel Policy Forum, observed. "This phenomenon can be seen almost every day in 'Letters to the Editors' columns. Every time an op-ed about Israel appears, especially if it is critical, there are a slew of letters to the editor. Most support the Israeli position. And almost without exception, they are written by Jews. That vast [non-Jewish] majority out there which supposedly is so supportive of Israel virtually never chimes in."[27]

The support among Americans for Israel is not only thin but also *relatively* weak. A 2007 Anti-Defamation League (ADL) poll found Americans

2/ IRRECONCILABLE DIFFERENCES

much more favorably disposed towards Britain and Japan than Israel, while their favorable opinion of Israel only approximated that of India and Mexico. Nearly half of the respondents believed that the U.S. should work with "moderate" Arab states "even at the expense of Israel."[28] A 2010 Gallup poll found Americans much more favorably disposed towards Canada, Britain, Germany and Japan than Israel, while their favorable opinion of Israel only approximated that of India (one in four Americans had a negative opinion of both countries).[29]

In keeping with global trends, the most recent surveys suggest that American support for Israel is on precipitous decline. A 2009 poll by the U.S.-based Israel Project found that American voters calling themselves supporters of Israel plummeted in just nine months from 70 percent to 50 percent, while voters believing that the U.S. should support Israel dropped from 70 percent to 45 percent.[30] A 2010 Israel Project poll found that whereas 60 percent of Americans believed the U.S. should support Israel in 2009, it had fallen to 50 percent a year later. "The section of the American public where Israel is most rapidly losing support," Israel Project pollster Stanley Greenberg observed, "is among liberal Americans who align themselves with the Democratic party."[31] In other words, support for Israel is on sharp decline precisely in those political milieus where Jews tend to cluster.

A 2010 Zogby poll found that a plurality of Americans supported the Palestinian right of return, the evacuation of Israeli settlements built on Palestinian land, and Washington getting "tough with Israel," while more than half wanted Washington to get "tough with Israel" if settlements kept expanding.[32] A 2011 BBC poll noted a significant shift in American opinion of Israel's influence in the world: "the U.S. public is now divided rather than favorable in its rating. While positive ratings have remained quite stable since 2010 (43 percent), negative ratings are up by ten points (41 percent)."[33] When Palestinian President Mahmoud Abbas made a bid for Palestinian statehood at the United Nations in 2011, President Barack Obama, both houses of Congress, both major political parties, and the mainstream media vehemently opposed him. Yet, polls consistently showed that a large plurality of Americans supported the Palestinian initiative.[34] One key conclusion from all these poll findings is that, whatever might have been true in the past, it can no longer be tenably claimed that the President and both houses of Congress near-unanimously support Israel because of overwhelming popular support.

The shift in American opinion also shows up in the polling data on recent outbreaks of armed hostilities in the Middle East. Although Hezbollah has been relentlessly demonized in the U.S. media, half or more of Americans held Israel and Hezbollah equally to blame for the 2006 Lebanon war and supported a (more) neutral U.S. stance.[35] And although Hamas has also been demonized, only about 40 percent of Americans approved of Israel's 2008-9 invasion of Hamas-controlled Gaza.[36] A poll taken after the 2010 Israeli attack on the flotilla headed for Gaza found that despite Israeli denials nearly 60 percent of Americans believed that Gazans were suffering a humanitarian crisis (more than 40 percent believed that Gazans were starving), while under 35 percent supported the Israeli attack and only 20 percent "felt support" for Israel even after it announced that the blockade would be eased.[37]

In light of the overwhelming support Israel commanded in the conventional media and among elected officials during the Lebanon, Gaza and flotilla crises, it cannot be stressed enough just how astonishing these poll findings are. Beyond registering the end of reflexive popular American support for Israel, they suggest the extent to which Americans have come to rely on alternative sources of news information. But it is also true, and telling, that, in the wake of these recent bloody assaults, harsh criticism of Israel began to creep into mainstream news outlets such as *60 Minutes*, as well as the op-ed pages of the *Wall Street Journal* and the *New York Times*. Even former *New Republic* editor and influential conservative blogger Andrew Sullivan entered the fray slashing away at Israeli policy.[38]

In another sign of the times, a 2010 poll by the Chicago Council on Global Affairs found that a majority of Americans opposed U.S. military support for Israel if it bombed Iran's nuclear facilities and a war between them ensued; fewer than half of Americans supported siding militarily with Israel even if it were the victim of unprovoked aggression by a neighboring state; and only one-third of Americans believed that Israel was "very important" to the United States.[39]

The ambivalence towards Israel verging on disaffection has been most visible in the progressive sectors of American society, running the gamut from the liberal denominations to the liberal icons. The Presbyterian Church USA, the World Council of Churches, the United Church of Christ and the United Methodist Church have all supported initiatives including corporate divestment to force an end to Israel's occupation.[40] At its 2010 convention the Presbyterian Church USA called for "withholding of U.S. government aid to the state of Israel as long as Israel persists in creating new West Bank settlements," and for the U.S. to leverage its aid, making it "contingent upon Israel's compliance with international law and peacemaking efforts."[41]

The widely respected former U.S. president and Nobel peace laureate Jimmy Carter has placed himself in the forefront of those criticizing Israeli policy. A 2006 book by him, provocatively titled *Palestine Peace Not Apartheid*, deplored Israeli policy in the occupied Palestinian territory and put the onus for the impasse in the peace process squarely on Israel.[42] The sincerity of Carter's convictions cannot be seriously doubted, but he is also at heart a politician highly attuned to public opinion. He almost certainly calculated, rightly, that his book would gain a wide audience because popular sentiment was shifting. Although Carter came under ferocious attack by the Israel lobby—he was alleged to be a plagiarist, in the pay of Arab sheikhs, an anti-Semite, an apologist for terrorism, a Nazi sympathizer,[43] and a borderline Holocaust denier[44]—his book still landed on the *New York Times* bestseller list and stayed there for months, reportedly selling several hundred thousand copies in hardback. And although snubbed by Brandeis University's president, Carter still received standing ovations from the student body when he came to speak at the historically Jewish institution. (Half the audience walked out when Harvard's Alan Dershowitz rose to answer Carter.)[45]

After the 2008 Israeli attack on Gaza another liberal icon, Bill Moyers, rebuked Israel on his popular public affairs program *Bill Moyers Journal*, albeit in a context that also took Hamas to task: "By killing indiscriminately the elderly, kids, entire families, by destroying schools and hospitals, Israel did exactly what terrorists do." Like Carter, Moyers immediately came under fire from the Israel lobby. He too managed to stand his ground and, as fellow liberals rose to his defense, walked away unscathed after the fusillade of slanders.[46]

But what about the notably liberal American Jewish community? Although perhaps less dramatic, their steadily declining support for Israel is also hard to miss. A 2005 survey by respected Jewish pollster Steven M. Cohen found that "the attachment of American Jews to Israel has weakened measurably in the last two years . . ., continuing a long-term trend."

> Respondents were less likely than in comparable earlier surveys to say they care about Israel, talk about Israel with others or engage in a range of pro-Israel activities. Strikingly, there was no parallel decline in other measures of Jewish identification, including religious observance and communal affiliation. The survey found 26 percent who said they were "very" emotionally attached to Israel, compared with 31 percent who said so in a similar survey conducted in 2002. Some two-thirds, 65 percent, said they follow the news about Israel closely, down from 74 percent in 2002, while 39 percent said they talk about Israel frequently with Jewish friends, down from 53 percent in 2002.
>
> . . .
>
> Israel also declined as a component in the respondents' personal Jewish identity. When offered a selection of factors, including religion, community and social justice, as well as "caring about Israel," and asked, "For you personally, how much does being Jewish involve each?," 48 percent said Israel

matters "a lot," compared with 58 percent in 2002. Just 57 percent affirmed that "caring about Israel is a very important part of my being Jewish," compared with 73 percent in a similar survey in 1989.[47]

A 2007 American Jewish Committee poll found that 30 percent of Jews felt "fairly distant" or "very distant" from Israel; a 2008 J Street poll found that nearly half of American Jews talked about Israel only "a few times a year" (26 percent), "hardly ever" (16 percent) or "never" (3 percent); and a 2010 Brandeis University poll found that only 33 percent of Jews felt "very much" connected to Israel while the other 67 percent felt only "somewhat" (30 percent), "a little" (23 percent) or "not at all" (14 percent) connected.[48]

The shifting opinion of American Jews could also be gauged by their reaction to the 2008-9 Israeli assault on Gaza. A 2009 poll of American Jews found that 47 percent strongly approved of the Israeli assault but—in a sharp break with the usual wall-to-wall solidarity—53 percent were either ambivalent (44 percent "somewhat" approved or "somewhat" disapproved) or strongly disapproved (9 percent). Seasoned observers of the American Jewish scene such as M. J. Rosenberg pointed to a "post-Gaza sea change." Except for "the more conservative segment of the pro-Israel community," he noted, "there was little show of support for this war. In New York, a city where crowds of 250,000 have come out for 'solidarity' rallies in the past, only 8,000 came to Manhattan for a community demonstration on a sunny Sunday." On the other hand, a motley collection of dissenting Jewish groups—American Jews for a Just Peace, Jews Say No, Jews against the Occupation—vigorously denounced the Gaza attack.[49]

"In the long run," Steven Cohen has predicted, a "polarization in American Jewry" will ensue: "a small group growing more pious and attached to Israel, while a larger one drifts away."[50] In fact Orthodox Jews, who constitute just ten percent of the American Jewish population, already stand out at the annual Salute to Israel parade in New York City in their overwhelming numbers, fervor and ideological ferocity.[51]

A harbinger of things to come is the pervasive and pronounced alienation from Israel among the subgroup of younger American Jews. "For too many young Diaspora Jews that I meet," Israeli opposition leader Tzipi Livni lamented, "Israel is not the source of pride or inspiration that it was for their parents' generation."[52] Her concern was not off the mark. A 2006 American Jewish Committee poll found that among American Jews under 40 fully one-third felt "fairly distant" or "very distant" from Israel; a 2007 Jewish Identity Project poll found that among Jews under 35 fully 40 percent registered a "low attachment" to Israel (only 20 percent registered a "high attachment") while, astonishingly, less than half responded affirmatively to the statement, "Israel's destruction would be a personal tragedy"; and a 2010 Brandeis University poll found that only about one quarter of Jews under 40 felt "very much" connected to Israel.[53]

A 2008 study by the Jewish People Policy Planning Institute warned that "many" U.S. college and university campuses "have become hotbeds of a virulent new strain of anti-Semitism that ... threatens the legitimacy of the Jewish state."[54] The contagion appears to have spread to the Jewish student body as well. On the nation's campuses support for Israel has now largely been confined not only to Jewish students but also to the Zionist faithful gathered in the Hillels. "Jewish college students are clearly less attached to Israel than in previous generations," a study commissioned by Jewish advocacy organizations reported. "Many have ambivalent or negative feelings toward Israel, especially in relation to the current conflict. . . . Israel is losing the battle for the hearts and minds of this cohort."[55]

The younger generation of liberal Jewish public intellectuals in the blogosphere have also given voice to deep skepticism. During the 2008-9 Israeli assault on Gaza and the subsequent 2010 Israeli assault on the humanitarian flotilla, these bloggers let loose an unprecedented barrage of criticism targeting Israel. The symbolism could scarcely be missed. Whereas the previous generation of liberal Jewish intellectuals—such as moral philosopher Michael Walzer, Harvard law professor Alan Dershowitz, and *New Republic* publisher Martin Peretz—climbed on board the Zionist bandwagon while in their youths, the generation of youthful Jewish intellectuals now making their names—such as *Salon.com* blogger Glenn Greenwald, *Think Progress* blogger Matthew Yglesias, and *Mondoweiss.net* blogger Philip Weiss—has been jumping off it.[56]

But the most spectacular defection among the younger generation of Jewish intellectuals took place in the heart of the establishment. In a 2010 manifesto-cum-declaration of independence that reverberated throughout the American Jewish community, Peter Beinart portended in the pages of the *New York Review of Books* the coming demise of American Zionism and pinned culpability for its untimely death on the American Jewish establishment. The liberal ethos of American Jews could no longer be reconciled with Israeli policy, Beinart contended, and when forced by apologetic American Jewish leaders to choose between them, American Jews have opted to keep faith with their homegrown values: "For several decades, the Jewish establishment has asked American Jews to check their liberalism at Zionism's door, and now, to their horror, they are finding that many young Jews have checked their Zionism instead."[57]

What created such a stir was not so much the article's thesis, which could hardly stake a claim to originality, but *who* was proclaiming it and *where* it was being proclaimed. Beinart is a former senior editor at the staunchly "pro"-Israel *New Republic* and an Orthodox Jew; the *New York Review of Books* is the bellwether of American intellectual, and American Jewish intellectual, opinion.[58] The skeptic might suppose that this spectacle was less a case of "seeing the light" than of trimming the sails to take full advantage of new tailwinds, but either way Beinart's high profile defection signaled the further decomposition of American Zionism, this time at its hard core.[59]

Soon after Beinart made his big splash, the Jewish editor of the influential *New Yorker* magazine, the pages of which are periodically filled with puff pieces for Israel, abruptly filed for separation. In a spontaneous—or was it calculated?—outburst David Remnick told a Hebrew daily that Israel's "status of an occupier" has been "happening for so long" that "even people like me ... can't take it anymore."[60] Shortly thereafter Remnick reported in his own *New Yorker* that back in the "late nineteen-nineties" he had broken bread with Benjamin Netanyahu's father, a right-wing ideologue and professor. "I am not sure that I have ever heard more outrageously reactionary table talk," he recalled. "The disdain for Arabs, for Israeli liberals, for any Americans to the left of the neoconservatives was chilling."[61] One couldn't but wonder why it took Remnick fully ten years to report this scoop: Was it another straw in the wind, or Remnick's shameless opportunism? Probably both.

It has now come to such a pass that even Israel's diehard apologists can barely rise to its defense. In a keynote address at Israel's Bar-Ilan University in 2006, Dershowitz had to concede that "Israel's human rights record" was "hardly stellar."[62] "The truth is that Israel is neither a shining moral paragon nor a pariah state to be condemned," Foxman limply answered its critics. "Israel is a 'normal' country."[63] Foxman and perennial Israel apologist Elie Wiesel have even taken to publicly rebuking Israel for its failure to pursue peace.[64]

"I'm not under the impression that Israeli occupation is kind and sweet," Martin Peretz, probably Israel's most rabid supporter in times past, "dryly" told *Haaretz*. "But bad things happen everywhere, all the time."[65] It is doubtful a new generation of American Jews can be inspired by the slogan, "Israel: Not the world's only human rights violator."

Fretting over Israel's increasing international "delegitimization," an influential Israeli think-tank speculated that "the Jewish world is growing more distant from Israel" because "a growing number of Jews do not have enough historical knowledge."[66] The reverse would appear to be closer to the truth: they know too much. We will scrutinize this new, rapidly expanding body of knowledge in Part III of this book. But we will look first at the evolution of state-to-state relations between the United States and Israel, and in particular how they have affected American Jewish support for Israel in the past and are likely to affect this support in the future.

PART II

IT'S NOT EITHER/OR

Three factors have historically shaped the contours of the American Jewish relationship to Israel: ethnicity, citizenship, and ideology. Of these three, ideology is currently a dynamic element. The widely observed decline in support for Israel among American Jews is significantly a result of the unavoidable clash that comes when liberal principles are tested against a growing awareness of Israel's actions.

In the past, however, citizenship—the loyalty of American Jews to the country where they live—was the driving force. In fact American Jews initially distanced themselves from Israel because the creation of a Jewish state threatened to revive the "dual loyalty" bogey that had undermined the citizenship status of Jews in the past. If American Jews had embraced Israel too warmly, it could have put in jeopardy their hard-won gains in the United States.

After the June 1967 "Six-Day" war, when Israel became an American "strategic asset," support for Israel no longer threatened the standing of American Jews. It was now safe for American Jewry to be "pro"-Israel, and a personal investment in Israel yielded rich dividends. Thus began the American Jewish romance with Israel.

But what about the present? It has recently been argued that Israel no longer constitutes an American asset and in fact has become a liability. Were this the case, American Jews probably would again become circumspect in their support of Israel. But a close examination of the diplomatic record suggests that, on critical points, the "national interests" of Israel and the United States still mostly intersect. It is therefore unlikely that American Jews will distance themselves from Israel in order to secure their domestic standing. If ideology is currently a dynamic factor in shaping the American Jewish relationship to Israel, then citizenship is largely a static factor.

Still, the interests of Washington and Tel Aviv do diverge on the secondary issue of the Israel-Palestine conflict. The U.S. has no obvious stake in Israel's colonization and annexation of Palestinian territories. Quite the contrary, it is in the American interest to rein in Israel and resolve the conflict diplomatically. If supporting the Israeli occupation becomes a major political burden for Washington, as it might if the Arab Spring ushers in governments responsive to popular opinion, a serious rift could open up between the United States and Israel. For their part American Jews would almost certainly align themselves with the country in which they not only live but have also experienced, as Jews, unprecedented prosperity and recognition.

3/ A NEW RELIGION

"We see the unhistorical and anti-historical character of bourgeois thought most strikingly," Hungarian philosopher Georg Lukács once observed, "when we consider *the problem of the present as a historical problem.*"[1] This failure to see the present as history also distorts contemporary accounts of American Jewry's relationship to Israel. The tacit assumption underlying most of this literature is that Jews have always and naturally embraced Israel out of ethnic solidarity. In fact, once it was established, American Jews only rallied around Israel after such support no longer threatened their interests and also promised rewards.

It is now largely forgotten how recent the American Jewish romance with Israel is. Having struggled to make a new life in the United States, the Jewish community was not about to jeopardize its hard-won material gains in the here and now for the sake of distant relatives who could offer them next to nothing in return. Blood might be thicker than water, but more often than not it is thinner than egotistical calculation.

"The overriding concern of the American Jewish community," a prominent authority notes, "always had been to demonstrate its undivided allegiance to the United States."[2] As barriers to Jewish assimilation in the U.S. rapidly fell away after World War II and opportunities for power and privilege opened up—"Suddenly things were possible," Jewish neoconservative Irving Kristol later reminisced, "that seemed utterly impossible"[3] —the pressures to prove one's patriotism proved ever greater because the stakes were so much higher.

Unsurprisingly American Jews reacted warily to the founding of a state that not only claimed to speak for them but also claimed their primary allegiance. When the newly declared State of Israel came under attack in May 1948, although American Jews overwhelmingly supported its creation, still only a minority expressed a deep interest in the Jewish state's fate as it hung in the balance.[4]

After its establishment Israel's first prime minister, David Ben-Gurion, impoliticly declared that the duty of Zionists living abroad was "to assist the State of Israel in all conditions and under any circumstances . . . whether the government to which the Jews in question owe allegiance desire it or not." Israel's birth in effect created a concrete, institutional basis for the age-old canard of "dual loyalty." It was the "dual-loyalty nightmare" become real life.[5] Israeli foreign minister Moshe Sharett noted that after Israel's creation American Jewish elites experienced "uninterrupted anxiety." Its foreign policy orientation in the Cold War was most worrisome. Israel's ruling Mapai party was avowedly socialist, and the main opposition Mapam party pro-Soviet.[6]

In this fraught political context it is no cause for wonder how marginally Israel figured in American Jewish life after its founding. Except as a sentimental object of charity, it pretty much dropped from sight. Few heeded the pleas of Israel's leaders to make *aliyah* (settle in Israel).[7] In an authoritative 1957 survey, sociologist Nathan Glazer reported that Israel "had remarkably slight effects on the inner life of American Jewry."[8]

A seminal American Jewish Committee study published just before the June 1967 war found that "the character of Jewish life and institutions . . . is not permeated with Israel"; that "involvement based on intense and continuing ties with Israel is limited"; and that "a mere 17 per cent . . . are affiliated with Jewish organizations whose major focus is the State of Israel."[9] "The Jewishness of Jewish youth can still be reached," Elie Wiesel told the Israeli newspaper *Haaretz* in April 1967, "but not through Israel. Perhaps through the problems of Jews in Russia. Perhaps through questions about the Holocaust. Not through Israel."[10]

American Jewish intellectuals across the political spectrum stood especially aloof. Detailed studies of the lively New York Jewish intellectual milieu through the mid-1960s barely refer to Israel.[11] "Israel is not mentioned... at all in Saul Bellow's new novel *Herzog*," an irritated Israeli envoy reported back to Prime Minister Levi Eshkol in February 1967, "even though its Jewish protagonist spends three hundred pages prattling on about an array of spiritual, social and political problems from all corners of the world." Bellow would later become an egregious apologist for Israel.[12]

When Israel invaded Egypt in 1956, American Jewry gave "less than unequivocal support," Norman Podhoretz rued a few months afterward in the Zionist publication *Midstream*, while the intellectuals among them—"at least indifferent and at most hostile to Zionism"—openly deplored the attack. After speculating on the reasons behind this lack of solidarity, Podhoretz concluded that American Jewish intellectuals should embrace Israel because "in some very important human way they were personally implicated" in its fate.[13]

It might be supposed that once Podhoretz became editor-in-chief of *Commentary*, the flagship periodical of organized American Jewry, its pages would have reflected his avowed attachment to Israel. In fact they did not. During the first year of Podhoretz's tenure, which began in 1960, *Commentary* featured 99 articles, of which just two dealt even tangentially with Israel, while of the 57 articles featured in the six month run-up to the June 1967 war again just a couple dealt at all with Israel.[14] In one of these, a 1960 essay on "The Legacy of Henrietta Szold," Midge Decter concluded that "no one really knows what Zionism means anymore." Decter was Podhoretz's spouse and, like her husband, she later became a strident neoconservative defender of Israel.

The Israel-themed articles published in *Commentary* during this period of Podhoretz's stewardship consisted by and large of eminently forgettable human interest, historical and travelogue pieces, while only a handful touched on topical political issues, and even these few were not wholly supportive of Israeli policy. Cautioning Israel to "submit its new reactor to international controls as soon as possible," a 1961 *Commentary* article on "Israel and the A-Bomb" concluded that "an Israeli atomic bomb would be a terrible thing . . . because it would show that nothing at all has been done to prevent the spread of that weapon." To look back at *Commentary* during these years is to stumble upon many surprises. A 1961 book review by Lucy Dawidowicz, who later became a high priestess of the Holocaust religion and an arch apologist for Israel, denounced both the "massacres" resulting from Israeli "state policy" at "Deir Yassin, Kibya, and Kafr Kassem," and the "professional [Israeli] fundraisers" in the U.S. who "helped to create an atmosphere in which the destruction of the Warsaw Ghetto becomes something to be exploited for the raising of money." One might be forgiven the odd thought that Dawidowicz was railing against a Holocaust industry.

Only five Israel-related pieces during Podhoretz's editorship before June 1967 were lead articles in the respective issues. He himself did not publish a single article on Israel, although he did contribute memorable essays such as "My Negro Question—and Ours" and "Hannah Arendt on Eichmann." In fact Podhoretz's famous memoir *Making It*, published just before the June war, made only one fleeting allusion to Israel.[15]

In his indifference to Israel, Podhoretz was typical of his generation of American Jewish intellectuals. An April 1961 *Commentary* symposium, "Jewishness and the Younger Intellectuals," posed a series of questions to 31 "promising Jewish intellectuals" on the meaning of their Jewish identity, the last of which was "Do you feel any special connections with the State of Israel?" Only two respondents avowed a deep (if not uncritical) attachment to Israel, while most briefly expressed a "sympathy" for Israel against the threat of its Arab neighbors coupled with reservations about Israel's politics and ideology. Fully a third of the respondents either did not bother to answer the Israel question or expressed indifference or hostility toward Israel.

Often scathing in their criticism, these up-and-coming Jewish intellectuals variously denounced Israel for its "nationalistic and militaristic

3/ A NEW RELIGION

fervor" and its "rigid position on the Arab refugees," its "racial bigotry, political machinations and . . . excess of nationalism," its "chronic, aggressive insecurities," and its "notion of manifest destiny." Still others proclaimed, "I no longer feel any commitment to or personal sympathy with [Israel]"; "I am anti-Zionist. Jewish chauvinism is no less despicable than other kinds of chauvinism—and more despicable than many, since it is based on racist ideology. . . . In the dispute between Israel and the 900,000 Arab refugees it has driven from their lands, I support the Arabs"; "My landscape is not Israel. My troubles are American troubles." This last curt dismissal came from Barbara Probst Solomon, who later lent her name to Joan Peters's 1984 "pro"-Israel forgery *From Time Immemorial*.[16]

One gets the strong impression that, had Israel not figured in the questions, few of these Jewish intellectuals would have mentioned it. This suspicion is borne out by another symposium sponsored by the American Jewish Committee just before the June 1967 war, "Jewish Identity Here and Now," in which just three of the 31 "best minds in the Jewish community" even mentioned Israel, two of these three only to deny its relevance.[17]

The now largely forgotten turning point came in June 1967 when, as Podhoretz put it in his companion memoir *Breaking Ranks*, Israel became "the religion of the American Jews."[18] By the 1980s "nearly half" of Podhoretz's literary output "focused on the dangers posed to Israel," and "he probably did more than anyone else to keep the survival of Israel at the forefront of public debate," while *Commentary* "became the foremost Zionist publication in the world."[19] The obvious question is, What happened?

A clue can be found in the above-mentioned 1957 article by Podhoretz analyzing the alienation of American Jewish intellectuals from Israel. The Jewish state, according to him, represented narrow, sectarian "interests as a Jew," whereas Jewish intellectuals found inspiration in transcendent values such as Truth and Justice. Thus, American Jewish intellectuals rallied around the heroic Hungarian revolt against Soviet totalitarianism, whereas Israel's mundane turf wars with its neighbors left them cold. Recalling the exalted phraseology that Jewish intellectuals invoked to depict events in Hungary, Podhoretz wrote:

> It is difficult to imagine that anything Israel might accomplish in her struggle with the Arabs could be celebrated as having "achieved the status of the symbolic and the exemplary." In the realm of the "symbolic and exemplary"—as these words are used by intellectuals in contemporary political discourse—Israel is simply not that important; Israel exists in the realm of the politics of interest, where questions of relative justice are involved, but never, as in the realm of "pure," "disinterested" politics, world-shaking issues of Historical Justice. Historical Justice has become a term in the cataclysmic language for forces and classes and economic systems, and in that language there is not even a vocabulary in which to talk about Israel.

A Judeo-centric identity in the U.S. analogously "still meant parochialism, whereas to be an American meant to occupy a key position on the front lines of the great battle of our time" against the Communist menace.

After its shattering victory in the June 1967 war, Israel was effectively annexed to the "great battle of our time." It became the U.S.'s "strategic asset" in the Middle East against alleged Soviet proxies and, consequently, an object of the lavish, lofty rhetoric that Podhoretz mistakenly assumed Israel could never evoke. American Jews could now embrace and celebrate Israel because Israel now subserved American interests;[20] not just Jews but Americans of all stripes embraced and celebrated it. If the jubilation of American Jewry ultimately sprang from familial loyalty and pride, these hitherto dormant feelings only became manifest, and could only become manifest, because Israel now acted in concert with and aggrandized *Pax Americana*.

The idea of a Jewish state was rooted in the Zionist tenet of eternal Jewish alienation from the gentile world. But after the June 1967 war Israel paradoxically facilitated the assimilation of American Jews. It was Jews who

3/ A NEW RELIGION

now stood on the front lines in Israel defending America, even Western Civilization, against Soviet totalitarianism and kindred retrograde forces. Whereas before the June war Israel constituted for American Jews a liability conjuring the bogey of dual loyalty, it was now a boon connoting super loyalty as Israeli Jews fought and died to protect U.S. national interests. And, unlike American GIs in Vietnam, Israeli fighters managed both to vanquish the enemy[21] and deliver their blows while—or so it seemed—maintaining "purity of arms."

"The Israel of American Jews ... was for centuries a mythical Zion, a Zion that reveals more about American Jewish ideals than about the realities of Eretz Israel," historian Jonathan D. Sarna has perceptively noted. "All of the historic American Jewish images of Israel ... spoke to the needs of *American Jews* and reflected *their* ideals and fantasies rather than the contemporary realities of Jewish life in the land of Israel" (his emphases). The projection of Israel as "a 'model state' cast in the image of America served not only to defuse the sensitive issue of dual loyalty," Sarna further observed, "it actually worked to strengthen the position of America's Jews by permitting them both to bask in the reflected glory of those engaged in building the state and to boast of their own patriotic efforts to spread the American dream outward."[22] In short, the operative factor in the American Jewish love affair with Israel has always been not fidelity but utility.

After the June war opinion polls of American Jewry showed that "ninety-nine out of every hundred Jews expressed their strong sympathy with Israel."[23] And unsurprisingly, American Jews conjured an "Israel" to accommodate and aggrandize their domestic agenda. It came to serve as an all-purpose utility item satisfying the needs of the Jewish community as a whole and its variegated constituent parts. In effect Israel also became a "strategic asset" of American Jews. Above all else it now was a source of Jewish self-esteem, not least because Israeli fighters expunged the blot of the scrawny *shtetl* Jews who "went like sheep to slaughter" during the Nazi holocaust. Although Israel had fought at least as impressively in 1948 and 1956, American Jews could not *kvell* about those military victories because

Israel was not yet a firm U.S. ally. Israel also now became a stage on which American Jews projected and played out racist and chauvinist fantasies of revenge and triumph over the goyim.

Israel came to incarnate for American Jewish intellectuals the high cause of Truth, Justice *and* the American Way, to which they could now assert a unique connection by virtue of blood lineage. Joining the Zionist club was a prudent career move for Jewish communal leaders who could then play the role of key interlocutors between the U.S. and its strategic asset. Israel's alleged existential vulnerability served as a useful pretext for politically ambitious Jews to champion American military power on which Israel's survival supposedly hinged.[24] The criticism directed at Israel and American militarism by the political left also supplied a pretext for Jews on the make to repudiate their youthful flirtations with radicalism: didn't such extremist talk jeopardize Israel's security?[25]

The most zealous of these newly minted supporters of Israel were the Jewish liberals who metamorphosed into right-wing neoconservatives. It has been said that solicitude for Israel "pushed" them "to the right."[26] In fact this new generation of upwardly bound Jewish intellectuals eyeing the fruits of power and privilege latched onto Israel because they were *already* turning right. Reinventing oneself as a "Zionist" eased the slide across the political spectrum toward greater respectability. It was yet another instance of the "politically useful—the classic neoconservative category."[27]

These gung-ho Zionists did not even subscribe to the Zionist tenet that Jews had no future in the gentile world. On the contrary, they converted to Zionism because it facilitated their acceptance in the United States.[28] In one peculiar sense, however, it might be said that they did embrace Zionism. Although Zionism was predicated on the notion that assimilation was neither possible nor desirable in gentile nations, its goal of "normalizing" the condition of Jews by creating a state for the Jewish nation *was* a form of assimilation. The expectation was that if Jews would never be accepted as bona fide members of other nation-states, they would nonetheless be able to take their rightful and equal place in the family of nation-states. Like Zionism,

3/ A NEW RELIGION

Jewish neoconservatism was ultimately a form of assimilation; indeed, in their insatiable lust for American power and American privilege, they were the ultimate assimilationists.

A fringe benefit of this born-again Zionism was that it cloaked base opportunism in the noble principles of protecting a beleaguered nation and being faithful to one's people. The flipside of "supporting Israel"—which no longer needed support—was "fighting the good fight" against anti-Semitism—which no longer posed a threat. The American Zionist theatrical played itself out on a stage crammed full of villainous phantoms.

In the neoconservative script, "the United Nations was anti-Semitic, the Third World was anti-Semitic, the Communists were anti-Semitic, affirmative action was anti-Jewish if not anti-Semitic, several prominent liberal black leaders were anti-Semitic, the New Left was anti-Jewish and probably anti-Semitic, and vast sectors of the left might as well be anti-Semitic, having decided that Jews were no longer victims, and sided with the terrorist enemies of Israel." The one gentile group supposedly not tainted by anti-Semitism was the avowedly anti-Semitic right-wing Christian evangelicals, who got a free pass from Jewish neoconservatives because they were "the best friends of Israel."[29]

In the phantasmagorical universe of these Lovers of Zion, defending Israel was even heralded as a singular act of bravery. "Throughout the 1970s and beyond," a Jewish neoconservative memorialized, "Podhoretz's mission to provide a pro-Israel voice in the intellectual community was difficult, considering the lack of support for Israel in the intellectual community."[30] In reality there was probably more criticism of Stalin on his central committee in the post-purge 1930s than criticism of Israel among American intellectuals in the 1970s.

4/ THIS LAND IS MY LAND

In the last chapter it was shown that American Jews kept Israel at arm's length until the June 1967 war, when it became Washington's strategic asset in the Middle East. It has been argued in recent years that Israel ceased serving American interests after the end of the Cold War and instead has become a burden for Washington. The alleged divergence between Washington's continuing support for Israel and its real strategic interests has been attributed to the baleful influence of the Israel lobby.

The most widely cited version of this argument is *The Israel Lobby and U.S. Foreign Policy*, by John J. Mearsheimer of the University of Chicago and Stephen M. Walt of Harvard University's Kennedy School of Government.[1] Their initial article in the *London Review of Books* caused a storm[2] and their book, published under the distinguished Farrar, Straus and Giroux imprint, was a bestseller.

In the book's most sensational charge, and the one that garnered it the most attention, Mearsheimer and Walt contended that the lobby has so skewed Washington's foreign policy that, acting on Israel's behalf, it even caused the George W. Bush administration to attack Iraq in 2003 although the war did not serve American interests.

The premise of Mearsheimer and Walt's analysis is that the core interests of Washington and Tel Aviv no longer overlap. They acknowledge that Israel did constitute a "strategic asset" during the Cold War because it "helped contain Soviet expansion in the region." However, they maintain that since the collapse of the Soviet empire it has become a "strategic liability."[3]

The future relationship of American Jews to Israel partly hinges on the points at issue. If the analysis of Mearsheimer and Walt were correct, it would only be a matter of time before more fissures opened up in the relationship between American Jews and Israel. However ferocious its bark, no domestic lobby jeopardizing pivotal American interests could long withstand the pressures to back off exerted by elite groups and their ramified circuits of power. Should a contest of wills ensue between the Israel lobby and American elites, it would inevitably trigger a revival of the "dual loyalty" charge that American Jews dread and on which they remain vulnerable. Rather than risk their hard-won gains in the United States, experience suggests that American Jews would distance themselves from Israel in the event of a conflict of interests.

It might be supposed that, even if Israel did become a major liability, those many American Jews occupying strategic posts in the polity and economy would put a brake on any concerted elite action targeting Israel's domestic pressure group. But it flies in the face of historical experience that these privileged Jews would jeopardize American interests, of which they themselves are prime beneficiaries, in order to shield the lobby of a foreign power—even one composed of "family" members—from which they draw no benefits.

It happens however that the probability of a clash pitting American Jewish supporters of Israel against basic U.S. interests is fairly remote. Contrary to Mearsheimer and Walt's contention, Israel remains a strategic asset as it projects and protects American power in a region of critical importance to the United States. A conflict of interests does exist, however, between the U.S. and Israel on the secondary issue of resolving the Israel-Palestine conflict, and here the Israel lobby exerts considerable influence over policymaking in Washington. It is quite likely that on this local issue conflicting interests will put an ever-greater strain on U.S.-Israeli relations, making American Jews feel increasingly uneasy, and this process could be accelerated by recent developments including the Arab Spring.

But the core interests of Washington and Tel Aviv still mostly intersect. The analysis of Mearsheimer and Walt, which rests on the premise that Washington's primary objective in the Middle East during the Cold War was checking the Kremlin, overlooks continuities in American foreign policy that straddle the Cold War and the concomitant overlap of U.S. and Israeli strategic aims in the region.

At the dawn of the Cold War the U.S. National Security Council detected "little danger that the Soviet Union will take aggressive military action against the Middle East." The "major threats to Western interests," it continued, lay "in the growing instability within the Middle Eastern states" that sprang from "the nationalist aspirations of the Middle Eastern states—accompanied and intensified by the desire to end what they regard as unjust exploitation," and from the "discontent of the peoples of the area with their social and economic conditions—a fact which weakens the grip on power of the ruling classes and which therefore weakens the ability of the West to maintain stability in these states by working through the ruling classes." Undeniably the Kremlin exploited and fanned these seething frustrations in the hope of strategic gain but the root of the problem was internal: if the Arab people resented the Western powers it was because these powers propped up regimes oppressing them.

The National Security Council, doubting it was feasible to "maintain and defend Western interests in the area in the 19th century fashion," counseled instead "the establishment of a new basis and a new kind of relationship with the Middle East states ... in harmony with their basic interests," and the channeling of well-nigh inevitable "social revolution ... to insure friendliness to Western power."[4] This advice however went unheeded. Like the rhetorically high-minded postwar British Labor government, the U.S. ultimately followed in the footsteps of the old colonial powers, casting its lot with the pashas not the peasants and countering where it could not contain popular upheaval.

If Washington coddled Tel Aviv after the June 1967 war, it was because of the shattering blow inflicted by the Israeli military on those "nationalist aspirations" in the Arab world that had threatened the "ability of the West to maintain stability . . . by working through the ruling classes." The interests of Tel Aviv and Washington converged on toppling Egyptian President Gamal Abdel Nasser, who galvanized the region's hopes and dreams. A 6 June 1967 CIA assessment of Israel's objectives concluded that its "immediate and primary . . . war aim is destruction of the center of power of the radical Arab Socialist movement, i.e., the Nasser regime."[5]

A decade of touch-and-go diplomacy with Nasser also convinced Washington that the Egyptian upstart had to go. After its provision of food aid to Egypt failed to yield political dividends, the John F. Kennedy administration despaired of weaning Nasser from his radical nationalism. The Egyptian leader could not be nudged or budged from his agenda which included "driving the British out of the Arabian peninsula, the reduction of U.S. influence in the area, [and] the elimination of the Jordanian and Saudi regimes."[6] Kennedy consequently resolved to "rely more on [the U.S.'s] traditional regional partners, the Arab conservatives, and its would-be regional ally, the Jewish state,"[7] while Lyndon B. Johnson's administration proceeded further along the path cleared by him.[8]

A memorandum dated 4 June 1967—one day before the war began—by Johnson's special assistant, Walt W. Rostow, points up the near-perfect strategic overlap between Washington and Tel Aviv on the eve of the Israeli attack. "[T]he situation in the Middle East is that the radical nationalism represented by Nasser, while powerful at the moment . . ., is waning," Rostow minuted. "Just beneath the surface is the potentiality for a new phase in the Middle East of moderation. . . . *But all this depends on Nasser's being cut down to size.*"[9] After the Israeli strike it was mission accomplished: the Egyptian leader's humiliating defeat and his death soon thereafter signaled "the end of pan-Arab nationalism"[10] and Egypt's eclipse as a regional power. Slowly but ineluctably Cairo was drawn into the American orbit alongside Israel and reduced to a second-rate power.

The mutual U.S.-Israeli interest in preempting the emergence of autonomous regional powers in the Middle East such as Nasser's Egypt existed independently of the threat posed by Soviet expansionism, and the end of the Cold War has not diminished this joint interest. Just as the respective, and overlapping, strategic agendas of Washington and Tel Aviv have stayed constant despite the demise of Communism, so they have also stayed constant despite the demise of Nasserism. Whereas in an earlier era insurgents opposing Western imperial hegemony rallied under the banner of Arab nationalism, in recent times they have rallied under the banner of Islamic fundamentalism. And, whereas in an earlier era Israel was said to be on the front line battling the Communist-Nasserite hordes, now it is said to be on "the front line of the Western world in its civilizational battle with Muslim and Arab fundamentalist, obscurantist forces."[11] But the stakes have not changed: Who will dominate the fate and future of the Middle East?

Today this question is most often posed in relation to Iran, while the answer to it highlights the commonality of interests between Washington and Tel Aviv. Their conflict with the Islamic regime ultimately springs from the exigencies of geopolitics rather than ideology: Iran's age-old ambition to be recognized as a—or *the*—regional hegemon versus the determination of the U.S. and Israel to foil its ambition and preserve their regional preeminence.[12] Many informed Israelis freely acknowledge that beneath the apocalyptic rhetoric this mundane rivalry constitutes the core of the conflict: "However ideological and Islamic, everything Iran was doing was nationalistic, and even similar to the Shah" (Eliezer Tsafrir, former head of Israeli intelligence in Iran and Iraq); "What the Iranians want is to have the U.S. recognize them as a regional superpower in the Middle East" (Israeli Gen. Amos Gilad); "What had been for the Shah an ambition built on nationalism was for his successors a parallel ambition built on an Islamist radicalism that often simply served as a thin disguise for nationalism" (Barry Rubin, director of an Israeli international affairs think-tank).[13]

If Iran seeks to acquire nuclear weapons, and if the U.S. and Israel oppose Iran going nuclear, it is the reckoning of rational interest that impels both sides. Those who have sounded the tocsin that the "mad mullahs" in Tehran would not be susceptible to the calculus of deterrence if they acquired nuclear weapons surely know better; in fact, it is *because* they know better that they fear Iran's acquisition of such weapons. The ever-calculating leaders of Iran covet earthly blessing much more than eternal bliss. The hope in Tehran and the dread in Tel Aviv and Washington is that an arsenal of nuclear weapons will increase Iran's regional clout.

"Tehran certainly wants nuclear weapons; and its reasoning is not illogical," Reuel Marc Gerecht, a former CIA expert on the Middle East and the leading neoconservative authority on Iran, observed already prior to the 2003 war on Iraq.

> Iran was gassed into surrender in the first Persian Gulf War [of 1980-88]; Pakistan, Iran's ever more radicalized Sunni neighbor to the southeast, has nuclear weapons; Saddam Hussein, with his Scuds and his weapons-of-mass-destruction ambitions, is next door; Saudi Arabia, Iran's most ardent and reviled religious rival, has long-range missiles; Russia, historically one of Iran's most feared neighbors, is once again trying to reassert its dominions in the neighboring Caucasus; and Israel could, of course, blow the Islamic Republic to bits. Having been vanquished by a technologically superior Iraq at a cost of at least a half-million men, Iran knows very well the consequences of having insufficient deterrence. And the Iranians possess the essential factor to make deterrence work: sanity. Tehran or Isfahan in ashes would destroy the Persian soul, about which even the most hard-line cleric cares deeply. As long as the Iranians believe that either the U.S. or Israel or somebody else in the region might retaliate with nuclear weapons, they won't do something stupid.

The actual fear of American policymakers, Gerecht suggested, was not the terminal insanity but the tactical lucidity of an Iran in possession of these weapons:

4/ THIS LAND IS MY LAND

A nuclear-armed Islamic Republic would of course check, if not checkmate, the United States' maneuvering room in the Persian Gulf. We would no doubt think several times about responding to Iranian terrorism or military action if Tehran had the bomb and a missile to deliver it. During the lead-up to the second Gulf War [of 1991], ruling clerical circles in Tehran and Qom were abuzz with the debate about nuclear weapons. The mullahs ... agreed: if Saddam Hussein had had nuclear weapons, the Americans would not have challenged him. For the "left" and the "right," this weaponry is the ultimate guarantee of Iran's defense, its revolution, and its independence as a regional great power.[14]

"The problem," as two influential policy analysts more recently put it, "is that a nuclear Iran, an Iran capable of a nuclear weapons breakout very quickly, even if deterrable, will cast a shadow over the region. Its capacity to coerce will affect the behaviors of others. . . . Iranian concerns will be given greater weight and ours will be given less."[15]

The denial of strategic overlap between the U.S. and Israel not only causes Mearsheimer and Walt to misread the historical record, but also mars their political analysis of recent events. Consider the Israeli assault on Lebanon in summer 2006. If the George W. Bush administration supported Israel's attack, it was because of geostrategic not electoral calculation. The offensive "provided Israel the extraordinary opportunity to demonstrate its utility" to Washington, Charles Krauthammer reflected at the time. "A defeat of Hezbollah would be a huge loss for Iran."[16]

Whereas Israel launched the invasion primarily to undo the damage done by Hezbollah's rout of it in 2000, the Bush administration hoped the murderous Israeli assault would "weaken Iran's spreading influence"; "stick it to the Iranians who had brazenly intervened in Iraq and Syria and were assisting the terrorist cells operating against the American army"; and, by "neutralizing" Hezbollah's fighting capabilities, prepare the ground for an attack on Iran.[17] The 2006 war marked in conception if not execution a near perfect synchronization of interests: a victory over Hezbollah would "put an end" to Iran's "challenge to America and Israel's regional dominance."[18]

Mearsheimer and Walt contrarily allege that it "did not make strategic sense for the Bush administration to back Israel's disproportionate response," and then infer that the lobby must have coerced Washington.[19] The Israeli defeat undoubtedly was, as they put it, "a major setback for the United States," but losing a war (both Tel Aviv and Washington underestimated Hezbollah) surely does not prove the absence of a rational strategic motive for initiating or lending support to it.

Straining to prove that the U.S. supported Israel because of the lobby, Mearsheimer and Walt assert that Washington knew *beforehand* such an offensive was "doomed to fail."[20] But it is not shown how the Bush administration knew this;[21] it is not shown that the Bush administration supported the war despite knowing this; and it is not shown why Israel itself would have launched the offensive if it was manifestly a "fool's errand" (their expression). In fact Vice-President Dick Cheney was emphatic, even as the U.S. was coming under intense pressure to rein in its ally, that "We need to let the Israelis finish the job."[22]

Beyond the military prowess that it displayed to striking effect in June 1967 Israel has offered other unique advantages to the United States. It is the only stable and secure base of U.S. power in the Middle East. The "moderate" Arab regimes on which the U.S. also relies might for all anyone knows fall out of Washington's control tomorrow. Such a nightmare scenario played itself out in 1979 after immense American investment in the Shah of Iran, and might play itself out yet again in Egypt and the Gulf if the revolts currently sweeping the Arab world are not crushed or co-opted.

But Israel was to a significant degree a creation of the West and since 1967 has been in every respect—culturally, economically, politically—in thrall to the United States. Although Arab ruling elites have also been in the American pocket Israel is unique in the degree of *popular* support Washington can count on there. Israel's pro-American orientation represents the will not just of its leaders but also of its people. Come what may in the realm of party or even extra-party politics, it is inconceivable that Israel's pro-American orientation will deviate.

The rationale behind Britain's issuance in 1917 of the Balfour Declaration and its support for the subsequent Zionist colonization of Palestine has carried over to the American strategic partnership with Israel. In 1922, Zionist leader Chaim Weizmann queried a British official why the British supported Zionism despite Arab opposition. Didn't it make more sense for the British to keep the Palestine mandate but drop support for Zionism? "Although such an attitude may afford a temporary relief and may quiet Arabs for a short time," the official replied, "it will certainly not settle the question as the Arabs don't want the British in Palestine, and after having their way with the Jews, they would attack the British position, as the Moslems are doing in Mesopotamia, Egypt and India." Another British official declared in 1938 that, however much it provoked the ire of Arabs, the support Britain lent Zionism was prudent policy because it established in the midst of an "uncertain Arab world a . . . well-to-do, educated, modern community, ultimately bound to be dependent on the British Empire."[23] In other words, after the Zionists the British would inevitably be next, so it made sense to support Zionism as a potent buffer and shield.

Despite the overlap of core interests between Washington and Tel Aviv since 1967, it has been argued, most recently by Mearsheimer and Walt, that American foreign policy has been skewed by the Israel lobby. In fact, however, with the notable exception of the Israel-Palestine conflict, it is unlikely that U.S. policy in the Middle East would significantly differ in the absence of an Israel lobby.

The notion that machinations of Israel's domestic lobby undermine U.S. national interests has a long history, predating Mearsheimer and Walt. President Harry S. Truman's support for the partition of Palestine in 1947 used to be held up as Exhibit A of the Israel lobby's baleful influence on

U.S. foreign policy, while President Dwight D. Eisenhower's opposition to the British-French-Israeli attack on Egypt in 1956 was Exhibit A of enlightened U.S. policy in defiance of the Israel lobby. The popular rendering of both these historical episodes, however, is highly misleading. The thrust of Washington's policy did not in fact diverge from its basic trajectory during either of them.

The conventional wisdom is that Truman supported the U.N. Partition Resolution in November 1947, then rushed to recognize Israel in May 1948, because of high-handed American Zionist lobbying, and that consequently Truman compromised critical American interests in the Arab world.[24] Incontestably Truman coveted the Jewish vote as well as Jewish financial support—both of which were regarded as vital for a Democratic presidential aspirant—and U.S. diplomatic backing for the Zionist movement appeared to be the quid pro quo for securing them.[25]

But American diplomatic options as the conflict in Palestine unfolded were few and none was attractive. In the judgment of Truman's personal advisors such as Clark Clifford, as well as most historians who have in recent years sifted through the documentary record, his support of partition and immediate recognition of Israel made the best of a bad situation.[26] It cannot be known with certainty whether domestic or foreign policy calculations figured uppermost in Truman's mind, but he almost certainly did not consciously jeopardize U.S. interests because of pressure from the Israel lobby.

The Truman administration focused in the Middle East on the intertwined issues of protecting U.S.-based oil companies (primarily Aramco in Saudi Arabia), maintaining the flow of Middle East oil to Western Europe (which was dependent on it for postwar recovery), and checking Soviet expansionism. Additionally, although the U.S. needed only minimal amounts of Middle East oil to service its economy, domestic shortages were anticipated in the near future.

The oil lobby, alongside members of the State Department, Truman's cabinet and the armed services, predicted that Washington's diplomatic support for the Zionists would trigger Arab cancellation of U.S. oil concessions (the Arab "trump card"), an Arab oil boycott, or Arab defection to the Soviet camp.[27] In actuality such dire scenarios were remote because the Arabs themselves depended heavily on revenues from oil exports to the West. "Their need of us," presidential advisor Clifford scoffed, "is greater than our need of them."[28]

An Arab summit in 1946 approved strong reprisals in the event of Western support for Zionism. Those plans, however, were neither publicly revealed nor practically implemented, while Arab summits in late 1947 and early 1948 called for only token gestures of defiance "that fell a long way short of the threatened oil boycott."[29] Despite their incendiary anti-Zionist rhetoric most Arab leaders were prepared to acquiesce in Palestine's division.

Dependent as he was on U.S. oil royalties for 90 percent of his kingdom's revenues, Ibn Saud was not about to sacrifice his pipeline to America on the Palestine altar. The Saudi king confided to U.S. envoys in 1946 that he was "talking big because everyone else is . . ., but in the end Palestine will not affect my relations with the Americans," and right after the partition vote he reiterated that "although the other Arab states may bring pressure to bear on me I do not anticipate that a situation will arise whereby I shall be drawn into conflict with friendly Western powers over this question."[30] In fact Ibn Saud not only did not cancel U.S. oil concessions but in late 1949 he even allowed these oil companies to expand their operations.

Truman did however harbor well-grounded fears that American military intervention on behalf of the Jewish state "would jeopardize the national interest."[31] He could not muster sufficient U.S. combat troops to fight a war in Palestine, and Americans (including a majority of Jews) opposed such a military intervention. What was more, because of teeming popular outrage in the Arab world, the deployment of American troops to enforce partition or merely provisioning Israel with American weapons would have forced otherwise reluctant Arab leaders to strike out against the United States.

Accordingly Truman ruled out U.S. troop involvement in the Palestine conflict and imposed an arms embargo on the entire region. Zionist leaders pled that the embargo was doubly unfair: Arabs still received arms shipments from the British, and Jews were fulfilling whereas Arabs were defying the U.N. mandate. In the meantime key presidential advisors such as Secretary of State George Marshall, probably relying on U.S. intelligence assessments, predicted in early May that if interstate armed hostilities ensued the Zionists could not "hope to hold out."[32]

After the outbreak of interstate war on 15 May 1948 the Israeli foreign minister prioritized the newly born state's acquisition of arms as "a matter of life and death."[33] But despite intense Zionist lobbying Truman refused to lift the embargo. When the military fortunes of the Palestinian Jewish community "appeared to portend defeat" in early 1948,[34] the U.S. had already turned a deaf ear to David Ben-Gurion's "plea for 'international force'" to implement partition, and "even refused an Israeli request for armored plate to protect passenger buses against the Arabs' armed attacks."[35] When forced to choose between a vital U.S. interest and the very survival of the nascent Jewish state, and even after Eleanor Roosevelt personally weighed in exhorting him to lift the embargo (if only in order to secure the Jewish vote), Truman reflexively put the American interest first.[36]

It is an article of faith among critics of the Israel lobby that President Eisenhower and his trusted Secretary of State John Foster Dulles set Washington's policy in the Arab world on a more enlightened course by resisting the lobby's blackmail tactics.[37] The climax of their novel approach is said to have come in 1956-57 when, in rapid succession, Nasser nationalized the Suez Canal Company; Britain, France and Israel jointly plotted and then launched an invasion to topple him; and Eisenhower, on the eve of a presidential election and despite potential Jewish retaliation at the polls, forthrightly denounced the tripartite aggression and then compelled a full withdrawal of the invading armies.

In its relations with both the Arab world and Israel the Eisenhower administration did proceed more cautiously than prior and subsequent U.S. administrations because the economic stakes were so high and the political scene so turbulent.[38] The Middle East possessed the "greatest known petroleum reserves," the National Security Council underscored in 1953, which were "vital to the United States and the rest of the free world," and U.S.-based companies had major investments in these reserves.[39]

To protect these interests the U.S. had to avoid riding roughshod as it had in the past over Arab popular opinion. Nasser, who rose to power in the early 1950s, and the nationalist surge he tapped into appeared to be potent political forces. Even the ultra-conservative Saudis were electrified and intermittently struck a militant pose. The "basic reason for our Mid East trouble," Eisenhower concluded, "is Nasser's capture of Arab loyalty and enthusiasm throughout the region."[40]

Early on Washington still harbored hopes that Nasser could be neutered and detached from the Soviets through diplomatic finesse and economic inducements. The U.S. endeavored to purchase the Egyptian president's allegiance through wheat subsidies, support of the Aswan Dam project and multilateral loans, while Nasser himself opportunistically coaxed the U.S. to help him undermine Arab regimes that he alleged to be pro-Soviet.

But the basic trajectory of U.S. policy during the Eisenhower years retraced past practice. It sought on the one hand to subordinate and supplant the former colonial powers (via the "Open Door" policy) and on the other to preserve intact its alliances with reactionary Arab elites and the corrupt regimes sustaining them, albeit while paying lip-service to the necessity of reform.[41] To inoculate the region against the Nasserite and Soviet contagions, Eisenhower and Dulles relied on deliberate use of the carrot of economic and military assistance and, when their control appeared to be slipping, the stick of subversion and military intervention.

The essence of the so-called Eisenhower Doctrine, promulgated in 1957, was "to preserve conservative Arab regimes and to stem the growth of Arab nationalism while avoiding . . . completely abandoning Israel."[42] Then in its heyday, Arab nationalism had to be placated, and as a result Israel was leaned on harder than in subsequent years.[43] But except for such nuances—mostly circumstantial in nature and springing from the regional power disequilibrium set off by Nasserism—the policies pursued by Eisenhower did not break new ground. On the contrary he "did not so much alter the legacy of the previous administration as pursue the logic of its policies."[44] Even at the peak of their deference to Arab nationalism during the Suez crisis in October 1956, Eisenhower and Dulles hewed closely to the well-trodden path of prior U.S. administrations.

In early 1956 British Prime Minister Anthony Eden resolved that "Nasser must be got rid of" because, in the words of a senior advisor, "the maintenance of Britain's position in the Gulf would depend on its success or failure in countering the Egyptian drive for revolutionary leadership of the Arab world." (Besides being wholly dependent on Middle East oil, the British feared that Nasserism would stir up anti-colonial passions among their African dependencies.) Operational planning to topple the Egyptian leader began after Nasser announced in July 1956 his intention to nationalize the Suez Canal Company. Britain informed the U.S. that it "had taken a firm considered decision to break Nasser and to initiate hostilities at an early date for this purpose."[45] In August it started colluding with France,[46] in September France began colluding with Israel, and in October the trio of powers jointly planned the attack that commenced at the end of October.

The reservations in Washington throughout the ensuing crisis were pragmatic rather than principled, qualified rather than absolute. It sympathized with the "objectives" of the European imperial powers but disagreed with their modus operandi. Eisenhower and Dulles counseled against prematurely deposing Nasser, advocating instead the use of diplomacy before making resort to force.[47] Otherwise, Washington feared, the operation would carry a colonialist taint, which in turn would simultaneously radicalize the Arab world—possibly triggering a suspension of oil shipments and catapulting to power a yet more extremist leader—abet Soviet expansionism, and mire the belligerents in an interminable occupation.

"[Nasser] embodies the emotional demands of people of the area for independence and slapping the White Man down," Eisenhower cautioned, and an attack "might well arouse the world from Dakar to the Philippine Islands against us."[48] Additionally, the White House looked askance at an unprovoked military action by Western powers that both diverted attention from Soviet repression in Budapest (the Hungarian revolt began in late October and the Soviets invaded in early November) and undermined the president's reelection bid in November (Eisenhower was running on a peace platform). Eisenhower also did not take kindly that Israel might have deliberately timed its attack to intimidate him with a potential loss of the Jewish vote if he did not fall into line.[49]

Nonetheless Dulles was "in agreement" with the British "throughout the Suez crisis" on "the removal of Nasser." Upon learning of British resolve to eject him, Dulles advised Eisenhower that if diplomacy failed to clip Nasser's wings, "more drastic action" should be taken. After Nasser nationalized the Suez Canal Company, Dulles again remonstrated, "Nasser must be made to disgorge his theft ... by international means, not by force," but "if it is then necessary to act, world opinion would give greater support," and "the United States Government did not exclude the use of force if other methods failed."[50]

Once "peaceful means of resolving the difficulty" with Nasser were exhausted, Eisenhower told British officials, "the use of force might become necessary." He too wanted to "bring Nasser down," but gradually. In a memorandum to Dulles he objected to British and French saber-rattling but only on the practical grounds that "this was not the issue upon which to try to downgrade Nasser," and, on hearing of CIA plans to "topple Nasser," he demurred only because at that moment it would "inflame the Arab world."

"The British having gone in should not have stopped," Dulles told Eisenhower, "until they had toppled Nasser," and he confided to the British that, although disagreeing with their methods, he "deplored" that they "had not managed to bring down Nasser." In the meantime Eisenhower decried Nasser as an "Egyptian Mussolini" (Dulles and the British also likened him to Hitler) who could become "a danger to our welfare"; White House officials spoke of "our ultimate objective of peacefully eliminating Nasser"; and State Department officials immediately embarked on plans to "isolate Egypt" and "undermine Nasser."[51]

The true colors of the Eisenhower administration revealed themselves in its covert agenda. While publicly denouncing the tripartite aggression against Egypt, U.S. intelligence agencies, in cahoots with their British counterparts and neighboring Arab states, were repeatedly plotting the violent overthrow of the radical-nationalist regime in Syria. In fact the U.S. opposed the tripartite aggression partly because a coup in Damascus that it timed for the end of October had to be aborted.[52] In the bigger picture Eisenhower approved on taking office Operation Ajax that in 1953 overthrew the popular reformist government in Iran, dispatched troops to Lebanon in 1958 to tilt the balance in the civil war towards Washington's preferred victor, and contemplated armed interventions (jointly with the British) throughout the Middle East including Saudi Arabia and Kuwait.

To bring home the Israel lobby's malign influence, past critics typically juxtaposed the Truman against the Eisenhower administration. But it appears doubtful that U.S. policy in the Middle East would have significantly differed in the absence of the Israel lobby. Although Truman solicited the support of American Zionists he never jeopardized critical U.S. interests, while Eisenhower never ceased supporting pro-Western reactionary Arab regimes even as he appeased Arab nationalism and leaned on Israel.

"Many policies pursued on Israel's behalf," according to Mearsheimer and Walt, "now jeopardize U.S. national security," and "this situation . . . is due primarily to the activities of the Israel lobby."[53] But the authors are also at pains to stress that, except for its "extraordinary effectiveness," the Israel lobby "is no different from [other] interest groups."[54] Their caveat, however, is not persuasive.

Although many lobbies promote agendas detrimental to the interests of most Americans, of no other lobby can it be said that it acts at the behest of a foreign power *and* exercises "an almost unchallenged hold on Congress" *and* rams through policies "wreaking havoc on a region of considerable strategic importance to the United States."[55] The resonance of accusations

4/ THIS LAND IS MY LAND

leveled against the Israel lobby is plainly more sinister than bemoaning farm subsidies or lack of gun-control legislation. Mearsheimer and Walt might not technically be charging treason—Israel is not an enemy state—but their indictment of the Israel lobby as the de facto agent of an inimical foreign power carries the same sting.

The authors concede that the case they mount "seems to invoke the specter of 'dual loyalty,' which was once a common anti-Semitic canard in old Europe." They tactically sidestep this potential minefield by entering another caveat: "Americans who work to influence U.S. foreign policy in ways that benefit Israel almost always *believe* that the policies they favor will benefit the United States as well."[56]

Yet, judging by the arsenal of quotes Mearsheimer and Walt marshal, it can easily be inferred that the American national interest is at most an afterthought for leading figures in the Israel lobby: "I devote myself to the security of the Jewish state" (Malcolm Hoenlein, Executive Vice Chairman of the Conference of Presidents of Major American Jewish Organizations); "The Presidents' Conference and its members have been instruments of official Israeli policy" (Alexander Schindler, past chairman of the Presidents' Conference). The authors themselves flatly declare that the lobby's raison d'être is to shape U.S. foreign policy "in a pro-Israel direction," and to assure that it "advance[s] Israeli interests" and "backs Israel *no matter what.*"[57]

It is also ultimately immaterial if members of the Israel lobby have managed to delude themselves.[58] Isn't it commonplace for the domestic agents of an enemy power to believe that the victory of that power would also be a blessing for the domestic population? The bottom line is that in the opinion of Mearsheimer and Walt the lobby *objectively* serves Israeli at the expense of American interests: "no ethnic lobby has diverted" U.S. foreign policy "as far from what the American national interest would otherwise suggest."[59] In other words, and notwithstanding their multiple caveats, Mearsheimer and Walt *are* asserting that the Israel lobby is if not in thought then in deed disloyal. That does not make their contention wrong; it simply illuminates the stakes if their contention is right.

In fact Mearsheimer and Walt are partly right. If the Israel lobby has not subverted American policy in the Middle East as a whole, its ruthless tactics in support of the Israeli occupation have subverted American policy on the secondary issue of the Israel-Palestine conflict. However one configures the elusive notion of "national interest," it is hard to make out how Washington benefits from Israel's occupation and de facto annexation of Palestinian lands, whereas its support of these policies has come at the price of alienating public opinion in the Arab-Muslim world and making itself a likelier target of terrorist attacks.

Already right after the June 1967 war American policymakers feared the political fallout from Israel's territorial aggrandizement but failed to rein it in because of the lobby. Although gleeful over Israel's trouncing of Nasser, the Johnson administration looked askance at Israel's refusal to withdraw to the 4 June 1967 borders. Secretary of State Dean Rusk forewarned that "Israel's keeping territory w[ou]ld create a *revanchism* for the rest of the 20th century," while an advisor of his minuted that "growing Israeli territorial appetites ... put Israel and us on divergent courses."[60] But Washington refrained from pressuring Tel Aviv almost certainly because of the lobby.

The official U.S. position on Jerusalem, for example, was that it "never recognized unilateral action by any of the States in the area." In addition U.S.-based oil companies warned that "the effects in the Arab countries of our abstention" on a July 1967 U.N. resolution condemning Israel's creeping annexation of East Jerusalem would be "devastating." Nonetheless U.S. ambassador to the U.N. Arthur Goldberg counseled that "we should not shift our position of abstention" because "the Jewish community here would be up in arms if we switched." In keeping with Goldberg's advice the U.S. repeatedly abstained on U.N. resolutions censuring Israeli incorporation of East Jerusalem.[61]

Special Consultant to the President McGeorge Bundy concluded that a "generous settlement" with Jordan would even serve "Israel's own long-term interests," and that "if we use our full influence, we can greatly affect the readiness of the government of Israel to move in this direction." But it

4/ THIS LAND IS MY LAND

was "not clear," he mused, "whether we are ready to apply our full influence in this direction, in the light of the depth and strength of the feelings of the people of Israel and of their supporters in the United States."[62]

Special Assistant to the President Rostow counseled Johnson that Israel's continued occupation of Arab territories "works against us in the Arab world," yet attempting to force an Israeli withdrawal "back to 4 June borders ... could lead to a tangle with the Israelis."[63] According to a National Security Council memorandum, the "professional levels of our government" doubted—rightly, as it turned out—that "the President will be willing in an election year to exert the kind of pressure on Israel that would be necessary to restore" the prewar borders.[64]

The Israel lobby also strong-armed the Johnson administration into backpedaling on the final language of U.N. Security Council resolution 242. During the initial U.S.-U.S.S.R. parleys after the June war on a U.N. General Assembly resolution, Washington explicitly supported language calling for full Israeli withdrawal to its prewar borders in return for Arab renunciation of belligerency against Israel. In a meeting with Soviet Ambassador Anatoly Dobrynin on 9 July 1967, Ambassador Goldberg proposed a General Assembly resolution demanding, "Without delay, withdrawal by Israel from territory occupied by them," and then elucidated the underlying principle as "no state could continue to maintain forces on territory other than its own."[65]

On 20 July 1967, Goldberg presented two alternative texts to Soviet Foreign Minister Andrei Gromyko, each of which unequivocally affirmed the principle of a full Israeli withdrawal: (1) "Affirms the principle under the UN Charter of . . . Without delay withdrawal by the parties to the conflict of their forces from territories occupied by them in keeping with the inadmissibility of the conquest of territory by war"; (2) "Affirms the principle that conquest of territory by war is inadmissible under the UN Charter, and consequently that the withdrawal by the parties to the conflict to the positions they occupied before June 5, 1967 is expected."[66] However, as Special Consultant Bundy reported to President Johnson on 11 August, "the Israelis have never liked the particular formulation that emerged from Arthur's talks with the Russians and . . . Arthur may be afraid that the Friends of Israel may try an end-run to the White House."[67]

On 16 August the Israeli Foreign Office "challenged" the proposed U.S. draft that was coauthored with the Soviets. It homed in on the "phrase relating to the 'inadmissibility of conquest of territory by war,' etc." Convinced of Israel's "right to hold such territory," the Foreign Office went on to "forthrightly" warn that if American demurrals "persist . . . we could be on [a] collision course," and that Israeli leaders were "prepared to pull out all the stops available to them."[68]

When deliberations shifted from a General Assembly to a Security Council resolution in late 1967, Washington again conveyed to Tel Aviv that a "reasonable formulation" would be "withdrawal from all territories occupied by it," while Israeli Foreign Minister Abba Eban stood firm that Israeli troops "will not withdraw from all the territories they had occupied."[69] But at the eleventh hour the U.S. did a volte-face: it no longer backed explicit language in the resolution calling for full Israeli withdrawal.

In a dramatic 3 November 1967 meeting, the Soviet First Deputy Foreign Minister V. V. Kuznetsov pointedly asked Rusk "why the United States had retreated from the position it apparently held early this summer when it supported . . . the two draft resolutions prepared and agreed to by the U.S. and Soviet delegations" that explicitly called for full Israeli withdrawal, and "Does the United States favor withdrawal of Israeli forces to the positions held before June 5?"[70]

The compromise language crafted by Britain's U.N. ambassador Lord Caradon that became U.N. Security Council resolution 242 reflected this abrupt retreat by Washington. Although if taken in its totality 242 did still call for full Israeli withdrawal,[71] and although Washington officially still supported full Israeli withdrawal,[72] the language in 242's withdrawal paragraph gave Israel some wiggle room. If not for threats emanating from the Israel lobby, it strains credulity that the U.S. would have backed off in the Security Council from its own considered and consolidated position, creating a linguistic breach in 242 that Israel henceforth exploited with considerable élan.

The Israeli occupation has not jeopardized a vital American strategic interest. The Arab oil states have pursued policies consistent with their own parochial needs, including intimate ties with Washington, regardless of Israel's treatment of the Palestinians and regardless of virtually unqualified American support for Tel Aviv. True, Israeli repression and American backing of it have provoked popular resentment in the Arab world.[73] But the Arab regimes have not experienced internal unrest or been destabilized because of the blind support their benefactor in Washington gives Israel.[74] It is even arguable that the corrupt Arab leaders prefer that the conflict fester so as to deflect popular discontent away from them. However, if democracy takes root in parts of the Arab world after the Arab Spring, then the new regimes might aggressively challenge American support of Israeli repression because of popular indignation.

The open support lent by the U.S. to Israeli repression has spurred terrorist attacks targeting American citizens.[75] But, real as its outrage is over the terrorist attacks climaxing in September 11, Washington is also not blind to the silver lining: just as political elites exploited the real crimes of Soviet leaders during the Cold War, so they can once again exploit the War on Terror to rationalize military intervention abroad and imposition of a national security state at home. It is the art of what Mao Tse-tung used to call "turning a bad thing into a good thing."

If the Israeli occupation had proven more trouble than it was worth Washington would almost certainly have forced Israel to withdraw. No lobby, however well-heeled and well-connected, could long resist a concerted White House campaign marshalling and mobilizing the full gamut of resources at its disposal, including the patriotic invocation of critical *national interests*, and the unspoken subtext of *dual loyalty*.

Still, it would be foolish to deny that Israeli expansionism has been an irritant to successive American administrations. If the U.S. has not compelled Israel to terminate the occupation, it is because of the efficacy and ruthlessness of the lobby. Were it not for the pressures exerted by the lobby in the electoral arena and on public opinion, Washington might well have joined the international consensus supporting a full Israeli withdrawal and Palestinians would have been spared much suffering. Whereas Israel's options are few if finally ordered to pack up and leave, Washington will not order Tel Aviv to withdraw until and unless the occupation becomes a major liability for it. The overall impact of the Israel lobby has been to raise the threshold that would trigger a forceful American reaction.

Ironically Mearsheimer and Walt provide, if only indirectly, the most compelling proof that the Israel lobby is not so powerful. After detailing the depths of Israel's dependence on American largesse,[76] they go on to observe that despite this thralldom "Israel is not in the habit of taking orders from any U.S. leader when its vital interests are at stake."[77] Is it then credible that the most powerful nation on Earth could be coerced into surrendering *its* vital interests by the lobby of its very own dependency? "Israel was heavily reliant on U.S. support and aid both economically and militarily," a recent head of the Israeli Mossad soberly observed, "and it was unthinkable that it could act independently on a matter of vital U.S. global interest."[78]

"The bulk of the lobby," according to Mearsheimer and Walt, "is comprised of Jewish Americans who are deeply committed to making sure that U.S. foreign policy advances what they believe to be Israel's interests."[79] They tick off a formidable list of American Jews both reputed to be "strongly committed to Israel" and occupying strategic posts in Washington and the media.[80] They then proceed to the dual assumptions that these Jews actively promote Israel's agenda and—although never quite explicit on this point—that it is ethnic solidarity that induces them.[81] Mearsheimer and Walt appear to regard these inferences as so self-evident as to make proof of them largely unnecessary.[82]

It is an open question whether professions of ethnic solidarity should be taken at face value. Such inner tuggings surely play a part among Jews at the pinnacle of American power, but they are a bit part in a much larger drama. It has already been shown that American Jewish elites only embraced Israel after it became politically expedient. In the calculus of personal ambition blood loyalty proved a low priority. It is unclear then why Jewish power-holders would now advance the agenda of a foreign power from which they themselves derive few tangible benefits, and one which, leaving them exposed to the combustible charge of dual loyalty, jeopardizes their hard-won professional gains. Doesn't tribal faithfulness presuppose a degree of idealism belied by the opportunistic somersaults in their résumés? In fact American Jewish elites are no more invested in Zionism than the Jewish neoconservatives among them were once invested in Trotskyism.

The Jewish neoconservatives figure at the very top of Mearsheimer and Walt's charge sheet. They are cast as the arch Israel-firsters. But even to denote them "neoconservatives," as if they were ideologically wedded, ennobles run-of-the-mill opportunism. The founding fathers of neoconservatism such as Irving Kristol rode the Marxist wave in the 1930s. When this wave crested after World War II they joined in the liberal anti-Communist witch-hunt of the 1950s. Their "shift right was almost inevitable," according to ex-neoconservative Francis Fukuyama, "because the capitalist United States intervened against Nazi Germany and played a key role in its defeat." He confuses Hollywood with history; the war was lost by the Nazis and won by the Soviets on the eastern front.[83] On Fukuyama's logic the precursors of neoconservatism should have become diehard Stalinists.

The neoconservatives then rode the New Left wave in the early 1960s. When it crested in the mid-1960s, they again joined in the Establishment backlash to it. Podhoretz declared "open warfare" on the New Left "even as the 'enemy' was *already in decline*"; "it was just about then . . . that the neoconservative offensive against the 'enemy' gathered steam," and "*Commentary* began what looked like a systematic assault."[84]

As the spectrum of "respectable" opinion in the U.S. shifted steadily rightward, the Jewish neoconservatives galloped yet more swiftly, eventually crossing the Rubicon from the Democratic Party to the Republican

Party. If they did not stop at the left or center of the political spectrum but regrouped on the right pole, it was because of the defensive reflexes of paranoid *arrivistes*, who have sweated so hard to obtain a seat at the master's table and consequently grow anxious at the slightest jolt to the social order. But it also bespoke the patriotic gratitude of egomaniacs: how could the system possibly be in need of repair if it enabled the best and brightest—*them*—to rise to the top?

The lurch rightward of Jewish neoconservatives additionally betrayed a cast of mind, an atavism, harking back to the glory days of their Bolsheviki youth: a pride in amoral ruthlessness, and a penchant for polemical purity and faux-populist elitism. In a style reminiscent of Leninist vanguard politics, for example, Irving Kristol would "one minute . . . turn to the mass of people as the repository of good sense; in the next he declare[d] them a selfish and unrestrained 'urban mob' and decadent to boot."[85]

The nebulousness of the neoconservative creed perfectly suited its purveyors. Its axioms, according to one camp follower, included these nuggets of profundity: "life is infinitely complex," "man can be good, but man can also be evil," and "man is a social animal." "Consistency to principles," he continued, "often demands that manifestations of those principles must be altered." Or, as Kristol put it, "Life is too complicated to be encompassed by the human intellect, with the result that there are moments when it is wrong to do the right thing." Translation: hypocrisy is a virtue, not a vice. In the application of this last axiom, neoconservatives proved wholly consistent.

Thus, neoconservatives pushed for the 2003 U.S. attack on Iraq on the pretext of wanting to export democracy and recast the Arab-Muslim world. It made no difference that according to another of their doctrinal dictums "people should beware of plans and blueprints to remake society [because] such strategies will inherently be blunt and external, whereas human problems are nuanced and usually derive from internal sources." Still, it would be unfair to place responsibility for the ensuing debacle in Iraq at the doorstep of the neoconservatives because above all else they espoused—wasn't this plain as day in the build-up to the attack?—"the restraining influence of prudence and the humility that informs it."[86]

If as a philosophical creed it is vacuous, as practical politics, and beneath the patina of coolness and complexity, neoconservatism amounted to little more than another apologetic for power and privilege. The "preoccupation and paramount concern" of the neoconservatives is "social stability" and the "reassertion of authority"; the wielders of this authority are to be made "secure in the power and prerogatives they enjoy." In their polemical outpourings neoconservatives have decried dissident social movements and chastised the "underclass," extolled the virtues of unfettered capitalism and tight-fisted social welfare policies, and discredited even the mildest reform of the status quo by "tracing its 'logic' so as to link it to various expressions of extremism."[87] The only intellectual challenge posed by neoconservative policy prescriptions is distinguishing them from humdrum reactionary dogma.[88]

In light of their checkered careers, malleable doctrine and self-aggrandizing politics, it defies belief that Jewish neoconservatives would cast overboard their homegrown, made-in-America earthly pleasures for the sake of Zionism. The only "ism" to which these courtiers of power are in thrall is careerism. Although posturing as embattled outcasts "speaking inconvenient truths," in reality they revealed "an astute feel for politics and culture," as they put a "finger to the wind and tacked rightward."[89] The policy agenda they championed was "congenial to powerful forces, probably *the* powerful forces in American life.... Neoconservatives will not wither for want of well-heeled patrons."[90]

Should the interests of Washington and Tel Aviv collide, and should Jewish neoconservatives have to choose between their cushy seats of power in the U.S. and support for their tribe in Israel, who can doubt that, just as they turned on a dime in the past when the lure of "making it" proved irresistible, many of them would without a moment's hesitation—indeed on this or that contrived "principle"—betray kith and kin?

Jewish neoconservatives sing Israel's praises primarily because it advances American, and consequently their own, interests. But beyond this,

Israel's reflexive preference for violence over diplomacy has warmed the cockles of neoconservative hearts. It has been a love affair made, if not in heaven, then in a Merkava tank.

The core of Israeli security doctrine, according to strategic analyst Zeev Maoz, is periodic resort to disproportionate firepower. It originates in the premise that "Arabs understand only a language of force," and hence Israel "must demonstrate every so often that it is strong and able and willing to use force." Maoz goes on to say that "one almost never hears in Israeli strategic circles that perhaps the reliance on military force as the principal (or even the only) instrument of policy is fundamentally misconceived."[91]

It is arguably the case that the Arab states only came around to acquiescing in Israel's existence after they suffered a string of military defeats. However, Tel Aviv insists not only on its being accepted but also on regional supremacy. Still, here too, the underlying belief is that if the Arabs sense Israeli weakness, they will attempt to overrun it. The result is a self-fulfilling prophecy: the Arabs allegedly will only accept Israel if it dominates them, but in fact they will never accept such subordination, and will periodically use force to free themselves. It is a recipe for perpetual war that a priori rules out the possibility of harmonious relations anchored in mutual interests and based on equality. It should also be noticed that Israel itself only understands the language of force. For example, it withdrew from the occupied Sinai only after Egypt's unexpectedly impressive military performance in the October 1973 war,[92] and from occupied south Lebanon only after Hezbollah's protracted guerrilla war. Israel will also almost certainly not withdraw from the West Bank and Gaza unless the Palestinians force it, although force does not have to mean military force; nonviolent civil resistance can also be an unstoppable force.

In any event, echoing their Israeli ideological bedfellows, neoconservative Charles Krauthammer counsels, "If you want to win the hearts and minds of Arabs, you have to grab their balls and squeeze hard," while neoconservative Michael Ledeen advises, "Every ten years or so, the United

States needs to pick up a small crappy little country and throw it against the wall, just to show we mean business."[93]

Since the collapse of the Soviet empire neoconservatives have fixated on "the Middle East and military power, most of all the use of military power in the Middle East."[94] This Middle East-centric militaristic mindset does not however trace back to a solicitude for Israel except insofar as its combatants, weapons and intelligence facilitate U.S. hegemony in a critical region. If tribal loyalty were the primary impetus, one would be hard-pressed to explain why *as a general rule* proponents of maximal American force in the Middle East sing paeans to the Jewish state.

Mearsheimer and Walt acknowledge that among the bona fide members of the Israel lobby one can count many "prominent gentiles" such as John Bolton, William Bennett, Jeane Kirkpatrick, George Will, and James Woolsey.[95] However, they make no attempt to, and within their framework cannot, account for such support. It clearly does not stem from either ethnic solidarity or fear of the lobby's retribution, and it cannot be said to spring from the irrationalism behind Christian fundamentalist support. If the likes of Bolton and Bennett cleave to Israel, it must be because they embrace its militant ethos and on their cold calculation the Jewish state serves American interests. And if the likes of Jewish neoconservatives such as Paul Wolfowitz and Douglas J. Feith cleave to Israel, isn't it because their cost-benefit analysis also yields this bottom line and they too identify with its militarism?

It is true that the truculent policies promoted by Jewish neoconservatives resemble those emanating from Israel. But this still does not prove that they are acting at Israel's behest. Mearsheimer and Walt suggest otherwise. They point to "two broad options" for countering Iran's "growing power": the use of force—which according to them is "favored by the Israeli government and its key American supporters"—and diplomacy—which according to them "is more consistent with the American national interest."[96] They might be right to prefer diplomatic engagement, but if Jewish neoconservatives recoil from this option, it is not because they are advancing Israel's agenda but because they *always* and *everywhere* prefer the big stick.

The identical deductive error mars Mearsheimer and Walt's broader policy analysis. They do not dispute that the U.S. has vital interests in the Middle East and that in pursuit of these interests it must "project power into the region." They part ways with neoconservatives not on this agreed-upon end but rather on the most effective means to achieve it: "America would be best served if it abandoned regional transformation and adopted a strategy of offshore balancing."[97] The advocacy of "regional transformation" scarcely demonstrates, however, an indifference to American interests. It might be an error of strategic judgment, but it is not *prima facie* evidence of fealty to a foreign power.

On a related note, Mearsheimer and Walt plausibly maintain that the Israel lobby's hawkish agenda has been "directly hurtful to Israel" and that "Israel would have been better off" if the U.S. had reined in the lobby. They also observe that "AIPAC and other hard-line groups have occasionally backed more extreme positions than those favored by the Israeli government," and as a result the lobby has sabotaged a diplomatic settlement and incited violent confrontation.[98] But they never pause to explore the paradox lodged in these insights: If American Jewish elites are so beholden to Israel, why do they abet policies detrimental to it, even to the point of ostracizing and slandering Israeli dissenters who labor for a just peace? Might it be that Israel's welfare is not their only, or even primary, motive?

Undoubtedly many American Jews have thrown their political weight behind Israel's militarization partly because they themselves have internalized the ethos that Arabs/Muslims only understand the language of force and Israel only fights defensive wars. But the embrace of an Israeli Sparta by American Jews also springs from their titillation at playing the part of "tough Jews."[99] Regardless of motive—whether it be concern or conceit—the fact remains that the support lent by American Jews to a militarized Israel is cost-free. Although pretending to chutzpah as they unreservedly back Israel, American Jews pay no personal price so long as Israel does Washington's bidding, whereas Israelis pay the costly price of interminable war. Feigning tribal service, American Jews practice tribal sacrifice.

4/ THIS LAND IS MY LAND

Is it, finally, too cynical to speculate that some American Jews might actually prefer a besieged Israeli garrison state doing Washington's dirty work, an Israel that is useful to America and therefore useful to them, instead of an Israel living harmoniously with its neighbors that would not only be useless to Washington but potentially at odds with it? "The Jewish establishment in America needs Israel only as a victim of a cruel Arab attack," veteran Israeli journalist Danny Rubinstein once wrote. "For such an Israel, one can get support, donors, money."[100]

The most sensational item on Mearsheimer and Walt's charge sheet alleges that the disastrous decision of the Bush administration to invade Iraq in 2003 was orchestrated by the Israel lobby. In both the positive and negative public reception of their book this allegation garnered the lion's share of attention and provoked the most controversy. It was only because the war went so badly, however, that the charge gained traction.

If the optimistic prewar scenarios had panned out, and on better planning they arguably might have, Operation Iraqi Freedom would have been hailed as a boon to our national interest, and a book linking it to the Israel lobby would have barely been noticed. "Iraq did not always look like the blunder it has turned out to be," Mearsheimer and Walt observe. "For a few short months in the spring of 2003, the United States appeared to have won a stunning victory, and there was little need for Israel's defenders to deny responsibility for the war."[101] In other words, the evidence they marshal constitutes an accusation only because of the war's faulty execution. Those lobbying for an attack perhaps demonstrated incompetence, but not disloyalty.

Although they variously qualify its culpability,[102] Mearsheimer and Walt nonetheless pin on the Israel lobby the preponderance of blame for Bush's decision to attack.[103] And, while carefully noting that a bigger percentage of American Jews than the general population opposed the war,[104] they nonetheless depict the Iraq war as largely orchestrated by Jews (if not all Jews) and driven by Jewish interests.

Mearsheimer and Walt copiously document that Israel's leaders and population, on the one hand, and AIPAC and organized American Jewry, on the other, wholeheartedly supported the war.[105] But although the Israel lobby was a major cheerleader—for which it deserves major condemnation—the fact remains that it was not a major player in the actual decision-making process. Mearsheimer and Walt themselves seem to concede that Israeli leaders did not start beating the drums of war until *after* the Bush administration had come close to resolving on an attack.[106] "Israel's endorsement was hardly the only reason why the United States went to war," they more cautiously argue elsewhere, "but to say that Israel did not encourage it is wrong."[107] True enough; but to "encourage" a war is not the same as being its prime mover.

In the first- and second-hand accounts of the prewar behind-the-scenes debates of the Bush administration, Israel barely gets a passing mention. A handful of scattered references to Israel crop up in Bob Woodward's *Plan of Attack* mostly in the context of its being a possible retaliatory target for Saddam Hussein. The Bush administration invoked Israel's vulnerability as justification for an attack, according to Woodward's reconstruction, only after the decision had effectively been taken and mainly to drum up public support.[108] In *The Fall of the House of Bush* respected journalist Craig Unger depicts Cheney as the driving force behind the decision to attack Iraq, and oil and domestic politics as his primary incentives.[109]

In his insider memoir *Against All Enemies* former counterterrorism director Richard Clarke lists "Israel's strategic position" as merely one among five "motivations" of the Bush administration.[110] In her memoir *No Higher Honor*, Condoleezza Rice, who was National Security Advisor in the Bush administration, does not list, or even allude to, Israeli security as the, or even a, motive behind the attack.[111] In his memoir *Known and Unknown*, Donald Rumsfeld, who was Secretary of Defense in the Bush administration, also does not list, or even allude to, Israeli security as the, or even a, motive behind the attack.[112] In his memoir *In My Time*, Dick Cheney, who was Vice-President in the Bush administration, also does not list, or even allude to, Israeli security as the, or even a, motive behind the attack.[113] If the Israel lobby played such a critical role in the decision to attack Iraq, how was it able to so effectively cover its tracks? One could understand why Cheney et al. might want to conceal that oil was the impetus behind the attack but it is unclear what motive they would have to conceal the Israel lobby's role.

To hammer home the Israel lobby's culpability Mearsheimer and Walt single out Israeli intelligence reports hyping Saddam's weapons of mass destruction (WMD).[114] But, however much it echoed and reinforced U.S. intelligence, the misinformation (or disinformation) Israel passed on does not appear to have significantly influenced the Bush administration. In his self-exculpating memoir *At the Center of the Storm* former CIA director George Tenet did what he could to slough off personal responsibility for the false U.S. intelligence that Saddam possessed WMD, but not once does he point an accusatory finger at Israel.[115] Although Rumsfeld also does not shy away from pinning blame on others for what went wrong in Iraq, and although he alleges that U.S. evidence of Iraqi WMD had been corroborated by foreign intelligence services, he does not fault Israeli intelligence or even list it among the erroneous corroborators of U.S. intelligence.[116] Nor does Cheney fault Israeli intelligence or list it among the erroneous corroborators.[117] Nor does Rice.[118] The only plausible explanation for this across-the-board silence is that Israeli intelligence really was irrelevant.

It is beyond dispute that Jewish neoconservatives pushed long and hard for an attack on Iraq. But were they, as Mearsheimer and Walt purport, the war's "driving force" and "chief architects"?[119] Of the six self-styled Vulcans (dis)credited with leading the country to war—Richard Armitage, Dick Cheney, Colin Powell, Condoleezza Rice, Donald Rumsfeld, Paul Wolfowitz[120]—only Wolfowitz fits the Jewish neoconservative profile. And Wolfowitz himself is a most unlikely mole.[121]

The archetypal trimmer, Wolfowitz "moved from job to job under Presidents Nixon, Ford, Carter, Reagan, and Bush," and "never allowed his intellectual or moral passions to get too far out ahead of professional prudence."[122] His does not appear to be the temperament of someone who would be ideologically in thrall to a foreign power, or any power save his own ego.[123] On the contrary, Wolfowitz's obvious muse is Henry Kissinger. When Israeli Prime Minister Golda Meir requested Washington's assistance in the 1970s to facilitate emigration of Russian Jewry, Kissinger counseled President Richard Nixon, "if they put Jews into gas chambers in the Soviet Union, it is not an American concern."[124]

Every reconstruction of the 2003 war places Cheney and Rumsfeld at the helm of the decision-making process.[125] But this duo "were not known as neoconservatives before their tenures,"[126] and Jewish solidarity plainly was not their thing. (Israel rates only passing mention in Cheney's memoir,[127] and even less mention in Rumsfeld's.) How then could the Israel lobby have spearheaded the attack on Iraq? To finesse this glaring factual gap Mearsheimer and Walt insinuate that Jewish neoconservatives occupying second-tier positions such as Lewis "Scooter" Libby had duped Cheney and Rumsfeld.[128]

It cannot be doubted that Jewish neoconservatives inflated the threat posed by Saddam. But the claim that they managed to trick Cheney and Rumsfeld into serving Israeli and risking American interests strains credulity. How is one to explain Rumsfeld's avowed support already in *1998* for "regime change" in Iraq?[129] The scenario conjured by Mearsheimer and Walt becomes yet more of a stretch in light of their guiding premise that the neoconservative agenda, of which the attack on Iraq was the ineluctable climax, *manifestly* did not serve American national interests. How could Cheney and Rumsfeld have missed this? Many unflattering things might fairly be said of Cheney and Rumsfeld, but gullible and naive are not among them.[130] Mearsheimer and Walt "asked one to believe the unbelievable," Norman Podhoretz persuasively rejoined: "that strong-minded people could be fooled by a bunch of cunning subordinates, whether Jewish or not, into doing anything at all against their better judgment, let alone something so momentous as waging a war, let alone a war in which they could detect no clear relation to American interests."[131]

4/ THIS LAND IS MY LAND

The more one works through the logic of Mearsheimer and Walt's sensational claim, the more questions it raises and the less it convinces. Why did Cheney and Rumsfeld fill senior positions in their respective staffs with de facto foreign agents, many of whom they had come to know intimately from many years of joint service in government?[132] Where was Cheney and Rumsfeld's outraged indignation after the war when it became known that Jewish neoconservatives had misled them into sanctioning a catastrophic attack in the service of a foreign power?

In his memoir Rumsfeld does not spare Colin Powell, Condoleezza Rice and many other members of the Bush administration harsh criticism,[133] but he utters not a single word critical, and quite a few words in praise, of the Jewish neoconservatives in the Bush administration.[134] In his memoir Cheney also does not spare Powell, Rice and many other members of the Bush administration harsh criticism,[135] but he also utters not a single word critical, and quite a few words in praise, of the Jewish neoconservatives in the Bush administration.[136] If, as Mearsheimer and Walt contend, Libby played the most dastardly role of all, it is surely cause for wonder why, in his memoir, Cheney reserved his most generous encomium for Libby: "my chief of staff, Scooter Libby, [was] one of the most competent, intelligent, and honorable people I have ever met."[137]

Far from being dupes of neoconservative palace intrigue, the key players in the Bush administration chose to "believe" what it suited them to believe. Those who were open to knowing that Iraq had already eliminated its WMD stockpile would have known it—or, at the very least, would have known that no conclusive evidence of Saddam possessing WMD existed. "Why didn't anybody say anything before the war [about how weak the intelligence on WMD was]?," a former CIA official rhetorically asked. "I did. And I can tell you it was hard, because nobody wanted to hear it, and they made it very clear that they didn't want to hear it."[138]

Those who wanted to believe (or wanted others to believe) that Saddam possessed WMD did not need to be manipulated by the neoconservatives. Cheney was among those who did not need convincing that Saddam possessed WMD, and did not want to be convinced otherwise: "Cheney repeatedly, personally, and vigorously pressed analysts to rethink or recalibrate judgments that Iraq was not a pressing security threat."[139]

Cheney and Rumsfeld did not only partake of the "belief" of Jewish neoconservatives that Saddam posed a mortal danger. Their own "American nationalist" strategic vision also largely coincided with the neoconservative agenda.[140] And like neoconservatives, Cheney and Rumsfeld believed that U.S. support for Israel did not spur anti-American terrorism, but rather was "simply ... another rationale for the continuing jihad," and an "excuse" used by jihadis to "rally support, recruits and financing."[141] The broad conceptual overlap is testament not to Cheney and Rumsfeld's blindness or stupidity but rather to their shared basic assumptions.

"The debate on why the U.S. invaded Iraq has been over-sophisticated," veteran Middle East correspondent Patrick Cockburn has observed. "The main motive for going to war was that the White House thought it could win such a conflict very easily and to its own great advantage. . . . Few governments can resist the temptation to fight and win a war that will boost their standing at home."[142] Mearsheimer and Walt also suggest that straightforward calculations and incentives of the sort Cockburn enumerates induced the Bush administration to attack and observe that "Those who favored war believed that toppling Saddam would convince other rogue states that America was simply too powerful to oppose and compel these regimes to conform to U.S. wishes instead."[143] But isn't it then gratuitous to evoke and inject a supplementary factor in order to account for the Bush administration's decision to attack, let alone to recast this shadowy factor as the primary one?

The speculation that a band of Jewish neoconservatives had hijacked U.S. foreign policy appeared even less plausible in the light of postwar developments. The "pro"-Israel agenda of the neoconservatives could decisively shape prewar deliberations, according to Mearsheimer and Walt, because they had managed to staff high-level positions in the Bush administration and carried with them a prepackaged master plan "at a time when both the president and the vice president were trying to make sense of an unprecedented disaster that seemed to call for radically new ways of thinking about international politics."[144]

However, Mearsheimer and Walt additionally contend that, if the Bush administration balked at negotiations with Iran and leaned toward the military option right through the end of 2006, the Israel lobby was to blame.[145] But by then most of the key Jewish neoconservatives had already left the Bush administration and the initial shock of September 11 had long worn off. The consistency of Bush administration policy from the heyday of the Jewish neoconservatives' influence, when they occupied strategic posts and had a prepared agenda, to well beyond their ignominious departure suggests that the prewar input of neoconservatives did not decisively shape White House decision-making.

The inference that Jewish neoconservatives beat the war drums at Israel's behest also lacks plausibility. To begin with, Mearsheimer and Walt themselves concede that neoconservatives pushed for an attack on Iraq even before Israel came on board supporting it.[146] Their reasoning also and again suffers from fatal factual and logical flaws. To deduce from the benefits Israel stood to gain that Jewish neoconservatives pressed for war at Israel's bidding, it needs to be shown that when confronting other hostile powers they acted differently. Otherwise, they might have pushed for an attack simply because war is their default option. And in fact the bellicosity of neoconservatives has not been confined to any one time or place.

In foreign affairs these "consistently right-wing" hawks advocate the "maximal use of American power" in support of American unilateralism, and despise, in Irving Kristol's words, the "cesspool of treaties, conventions, and alliances that the foreign policy establishment piously accumulated through its quest for a 'world community.'"[147] Mearsheimer and Walt themselves acknowledge that neoconservatives "extol the virtues of American hegemony" and "believe that military force is an extremely useful tool for shaping the world in ways that will benefit America."[148] But this would suggest that the militant neoconservative agenda in the Middle East is shaped by factors beyond Israel's security and wouldn't drastically differ in its absence.

Consider the collection of foreign policy prescriptions, *Present Dangers*, edited by leading neoconservatives Robert Kagan and William Kristol in 2000. The hallmarks of neoconservatism according to the editors and a contributor include "a strong commitment to vigorous American global leadership, to American power," and "the will to create and maintain a sufficient military force and the will to use that force when necessary."[149] To justify the aggrandizement of American power, the volume's contributors point up its ethical foundation and the fortunate coincidence that the whole of humankind benefits from it: "American foreign policy is infused with an unusually high degree of morality" (Kagan and Kristol); "The kind of enterprise in which the nation is engaged . . . is not directly to rule others, but to maintain a civilized world order" (James W. Ceaser); "[T]he history of American involvement abroad has been characterized by its generosity and humane acts. . . . America is not interested in territorial conquest, subjugation of others, or world domination. . . . [O]ur self-interest as a great power will be inextricably linked to mankind's universal interest in life, liberty and the pursuit of happiness" (William J. Bennett).[150] These sentiments, even if patriotic humbug, still point to an expansive outlook on the whys and wherefores of American power, the underpinning and engine of which is military force, and of which neoconservative policy in the Middle East is just a subset.

Whereas Mearsheimer and Walt posit that neoconservatives must have pressed for war to further Israeli interests, in reality their militant agenda was easily explicable not only within the bigger picture of American power in which neoconservatives situated the attack on Iraq, but even within the mainstream framework of American foreign policy. "The fact of the matter," Fukuyama observes, "is that the key principles of neoconservatism . . . are deeply rooted in a variety of American traditions," and are "widely shared . . . across the spectrum of American political life."[151]

"More than any of the other dramatis personae in contemporary Washington," policy analyst Andrew J. Bacevich observed in 2005, "Wolfowitz embodies the central convictions to which the United States in the age of Bush subscribes . . ., in particular, an extraordinary certainty in the righteousness of American actions married to an extraordinary confidence in the efficacy of American arms."¹⁵² Yet, it is hard to make out a distinctly neoconservative, let alone *Jewish* neoconservative, inflection in Wolfowitz's programmatic musings. His itemization of a sound foreign policy barely rises to the banal: "strengthen the liberal democratic-free market consensus including the global free-trade regime"; "maintain and strengthen the alliance structure of the liberal democratic states"; "deal effectively with rogue states and minor disturbers of the international order"; "maintain the U.S. leadership role, including its military pre-eminence."¹⁵³ Who in the American foreign policy establishment would quarrel with these signposts? The mark of distinction of neoconservatism is not critical but merely diacritical: an accent on force as against diplomacy.¹⁵⁴

Iraq had to be subjected to regime change, according to one prominent Jewish neoconservative, "because a rehabilitated Saddam is eloquent testimony to our inability to persevere in an effective policy."¹⁵⁵ The neoconservatives "believed that removing Saddam would improve America's and Israel's strategic position," Mearsheimer and Walt reasonably argue, "and launch a process of regional transformation that would benefit the United States and Israel alike."¹⁵⁶ But then they did not lobby for war despite American interests let alone solely on Israel's behalf, while their solicitude for Israel might just as well have sprung from its utility to Washington.

It might still be wondered why Jewish neoconservatives unconditionally back Israel in its local conflict with the Palestinians. After all, the U.S. not only has no real stake in the colonization of Palestinian lands, but Israeli expansionism has also persistently irritated it. It partly goes back to the neoconservatives' fixation on force and in particular their internalization of the first premise and guiding prejudice of Israeli policy. If Arabs only understand the language of force, then it must be banged into them by force who's in charge, and that their resort to force won't get them anywhere. It is well and good should Israel decide of its own volition and in its own good time to make "concessions." But if Palestinians succeed in wringing their rights despite Israel's will, the wrong message will be transmitted to the Arab world, including where the U.S. does have strategic interests.

But Jewish neoconservatives also give wholehearted backing to Israel against the Palestinians *because* no major American interests are at stake. Then the bonds of blood do come into play. If they do not stand to lose anything, then Jewish neoconservatives *will* stand by "their own." It even lends them an aura of nobility as they cast their lot with kith and kin in an Israel "under siege" and jointly do battle with a phantom anti-Semitism. And what could be more fun than heroically beating up on enemies who are either defenseless or nonexistent? Still, if ethnic solidarity plays a role in the politics of Jewish neoconservatives, the fact remains that they attach first priority to American interests and would be the first to abandon Israel if a major clash pitted it against the fount of their earthly blessings.

The inconsistency in such behavior is more apparent than real. Jewish neoconservatives reached out to their distant Israeli relatives after identifying with the Jewish state promised deliverance of material benefits and ego gratification. They also projected onto Israeli Jews their own sense of ethnic superiority validated by the extraordinary success story of American Jewry. It was a blood solidarity born of and built upon the simple proposition that Jews are better. If the Jewish state was special, it was because the Jewish people were special; and if the Jewish people were special, American Jews were the most special of all; and who among American Jews was more special than the Jewish neoconservative *wunderkinder*?

If an individual's group identity commences with "I" and "me," culminates with "my success" and "my superiority," and perpetually oscillates between these poles, is it really cause for wonder how tenuous such a sentiment of collective belonging is? The real surprise would be if these self-absorbed and self-aggrandizing Jewish neoconservatives did *not* bail out at the first sniff of trouble.

A critical factor molding relations between American Jews and Israel is the state-to-state relationship between the two countries. If these state relations fray or turn sour American Jews, fearing that the dual-loyalty bogey might resurface, will distance themselves from Israel.

It has been suggested in recent years, most forcefully by Mearsheimer and Walt, that since the collapse of the Soviet empire Israel no longer serves American interests and the "special relationship" with it has become on balance a liability. If the alliance has nonetheless persisted, it is allegedly because of the Israel lobby and, concomitantly, if the U.S. attacked Iraq in 2003, it was not because the Bush administration believed it would serve the U.S.'s interests, but because the lobby—in particular Jewish neoconservatives occupying strategic posts in the administration—manipulated it.

In fact the overarching American goal in the Middle East has been to preempt developments that might jeopardize its regional preeminence. This objective straddles and persists despite the end of the Cold War. In a bygone era it was pursued under the banner of fighting "radical Arab nationalism" while in the present day it is pursued under the banner of fighting "radical Islamic fundamentalism." Not just Washington but Tel Aviv too has invested in damming insurgent regional currents. Their interests have historically overlapped. After Israel shattered Nasserism in the June 1967 war, it became a strategic asset of the U.S. and an ally in the next great battle against Khomeinism.

The decision to attack Iraq did not deviate from this pattern. Both the Bush administration and Israel calculated that toppling Saddam would herald a reassertion of American power after September 11 exposed its weakness, and that an overwhelming attack would intimidate into submission regional rivals. Mearsheimer and Walt's supposition that the Bush administration acted at Israel's behest lacks cogency. They say that the war did not serve Washington's interests because of its disastrous outcome. But if the war had gone according to plan, who among ruling elites would have disputed its wisdom?

Mearsheimer and Walt infer that Jewish neoconservatives put Jewish interests first because neoconservatives profess love for Israel. But the résumés of these neoconservatives attest that their first love is self-love and their own comfort takes priority over the welfare of distant relatives. Their power and privilege ebbs and flows with the fortunes of the American not Israeli state. If Jewish neoconservatives exhorted the Bush administration to attack, it was because they believed that toppling Saddam would aggrandize American, hence their own, interests. They championed resort to force in the face-off with Iraq because everywhere and always they brandish the big stick.

But whereas the broad regional interests of Washington and Tel Aviv overlap, Israeli colonization of Palestinian territories does undermine American interests. And if the U.S. lends Israel near-blanket support on this local issue, it is because of the ruthlessness and efficacy of the Israel lobby.

It was earlier stated that the future relationship of American Jews to Israel partly hinged on the analysis presented by Mearsheimer and Walt. If their argument held up, American Jews would inevitably recalibrate their support for Israel. However, because the core strategic interests of Washington and Tel Aviv continue to largely overlap, it is unlikely that American Jews will forsake Israel from fear of the "dual loyalty" bogey.

Still, it would be mistaken to conclude that the "dual loyalty" bogey has been laid to rest. In fact American Jews tend to tread cautiously in areas of friction between Washington and Tel Aviv. We have already seen that their support for Israeli settlement expansion, which successive American administrations have sharply criticized, is lukewarm at best.[157] If the Arab Spring ushers in democratic governments responsive to popular opinion, or Europe more aggressively pursues a diplomatic settlement based on the international consensus, it will exacerbate relations between Washington and Tel Aviv, and concomitantly between American Jews and Israel.

4/ THIS LAND IS MY LAND

Even in the absence of a conflict of core interests between Washington and Tel Aviv, the potency of the "dual loyalty" bogey can still be glimpsed. Polling data illustrate the prudence of American Jews when support for Israel might jeopardize their domestic standing. Consider Washington's confrontations with Iraq in 2003 and subsequently Iran. In both instances Israeli leaders and the Israeli public overwhelmingly favored a U.S. attack,[158] and in both instances Israel analogized the danger threatening them to a Nazi-like genocide.[159] Nonetheless American Jews in both instances proved remarkably unresponsive.

Just on the eve of the 2003 Iraq war American Jews were divided down the middle on launching an attack whereas among Americans in general a clear majority supported it.[160] In the war's aftermath, of all religious denominations American Jews consistently registered the greatest skepticism regarding the wisdom of the attack, although a majority of Israelis continued to support it.[161] Moreover, a solid majority of American Jews in 2007 opposed a U.S. attack on Iran to preempt its acquisition of nuclear weapons,[162] despite Tel Aviv's doom and gloom prophecies that "Iran is more dangerous than Nazism, because Hitler did not possess a nuclear bomb, whereas the Iranians are trying to perfect a nuclear option" (Shimon Peres), and "Iran is Germany, and it's 1938, except that this Nazi regime ... wants to dominate the world, annihilate the Jews" and "also annihilate America" (Benjamin Netanyahu).[163]

The relative reticence of American Jews to sanction the use of military force springs partly from their liberal sensibility. In the liberal-Democratic Party milieu of most American Jews the Iraq war was much less popular than among Americans in general. But this factor does not in itself provide an exhaustive explanation. "The greater opposition to the war [in Iraq] is not simply a result of high Democratic identification among U.S. Jews," a Gallup pollster reported, "as Jews of all political persuasions are more likely to oppose the war than non-Jews who share the same political leanings."[164] Indeed, if Jews harbor a primal loyalty to Israel the finding should have been the reverse—a *lesser* Jewish opposition across the political spectrum because Israel's safety was allegedly also at stake in the Iraq war.

A plausible explanation for this poll result is that American Jews have opposed the Iraq war and an attack on Iran not just on ideological but also on prudential grounds. They fear that these wars might trigger an anti-Semitic spasm at home if it appears as if they were fought on Israel's behalf and then go awry. Before and right after the Iraq war, and just as the Bush administration stood poised to attack Iran, prominent voices inside the American Jewish community counseled that Jewish support for these wars, egged on by Israel but costing American blood and treasure, should not be too conspicuous lest it provoke a domestic backlash against Jews.[165] The hysterical Jewish reaction to Mearsheimer and Walt's *The Israel Lobby* was one index of this fear that they might be scapegoated.[166]

This hypothesis gains credence in light of longitudinal poll results showing that the gap between Jewish opposition and overall American opposition to the war steadily widened—from a 9 point margin (2003-04) to an astonishing 25 point margin (2005-07)[167]—as "mission accomplished" degenerated into a military quagmire and it did appear as if Jews were being blamed. The opposition of American Jews to military actions supported by Israel was yet more remarkable because major American Jewish organizations toed the bellicose Bush-Israeli line on both Iraq and Iran,[168] and stigmatized antiwar protesters as guilty of Chamberlain-style appeasement and anti-Semitism.[169] When their own welfare is at stake American Jews ignore not only Israel's existential pleas but also the counsel of their communal organizations.

Recent developments in the Middle East will perhaps cause the policy gap between Washington and Tel Aviv to widen and concomitantly the love affair of American Jews with Israel to further cool. The debacle in Iraq might incline future American administrations to reassess the reflexive Israeli strategy of maximal force. The Israeli army's dismal performance during its 2006 offensive against Hezbollah, compounded by the bungled Israeli commando operations in Dubai and against the Freedom Flotilla in 2010, strongly suggests that Israel's martial prowess has entered a phase of inexorable decline.[170] These developments will almost certainly cause

Washington to reevaluate Israel's utility as a surrogate for American force in the region.

The revolts that began sweeping the Arab world in 2011 will probably have contradictory effects on U.S.-Israeli relations. The loss of dependable dictatorships in places like Egypt, coupled with the ricketiness of the client regimes that manage to survive the whirlwind, might cause the U.S. to rely more heavily on Israel as the only stable and secure base of American power in the region. On the other hand, although protesters did not initially dwell on the Israeli connection, hatred of Israel is widespread and rising to the surface. The popular attacks on the Israeli embassy in Cairo in 2011 and the championing by Turkish Prime Minister Recep Tayyip Erdogan of the Palestinian cause suggest that the Israel-Palestine conflict might soon cease to be a "local" irritant for the U.S. and instead be elevated to one impinging on core American interests. If this round of popular upheaval brings into office democratic regimes that are more responsive to public opinion, the pressure exerted on Washington by the Arab-Muslim world to break with Israeli intransigence will qualitatively augment. The confrontations between Washington and Tel Aviv over settlement expansion will grow more acute and as a consequence American Jews will further distance themselves from Israeli policy.

Some rumblings can already be felt in the U.S. policy establishment. A 2005 Pew poll found that a majority of American opinion leaders perceived support for Israel as a "major reason for discontent with the U.S." around the world.[171] The enormous interest generated by Mearsheimer and Walt's book also presaged a shift in elite opinion. Both authors are among the leading American theorists in international relations. In a dramatic volte-face deep inside the policy establishment, influential military analyst Anthony H. Cordesman delivered a scorching commentary after Israel's 2010 assault on the humanitarian flotilla. Spotlighting Israeli actions that were turning it into a "strategic liability," Cordesman, who had hitherto been one of Israel's staunchest supporters, put Tel Aviv on notice "that it has obligations to the United States" and must become "far more careful about the extent to which it test[s] the limits of U.S. patience and exploits the support of American Jews."[172] A succession of prominent figures in the defense establishment, including General David H. Petraeus[173] and Secretary of Defense Robert Gates,[174] also publicly weighed in on the damage inflicted by Israeli policies on American interests in the Middle East.

As the debate on Palestinian statehood unfolded at the United Nations in 2011, and Washington, threatening to exercise its veto (again) on Israel's behalf, found itself more diplomatically isolated than ever before, the influential Center for Strategic and International Studies released a report that pointed to an impending clash of basic interests between Washington and Tel Aviv. "Nearly every U.S. president has made some link between resolving the Arab-Israeli conflict and broader U.S. interests in the Middle East," it concluded. "But never have the stakes of failure to execute the policy been so high for the United States. . . . [T]he U.S. national security establishment increasingly sees the Arab-Israeli conflict as a source of regional instability and fuel for the fire of anti-Americanism in the broader Middle East."[175] In perhaps another harbinger of things to come, a 2011 Brookings survey of "the next generation of American leaders" found that they had "the strongest mixed sentiments regarding China, Russia, Mexico, Saudi Arabia, India and Israel (and the Palestinian Territories)."[176]

But if American Jews break away from Israel, it will be not only because supporting Israel in the face of Washington's clashes with it might revive the dual loyalty bogey. It will also be because Israeli warmongering cannot be reconciled with values that most American Jews hold dear. Israel was the only country in the world except for Kuwait where not just the government but also overwhelmingly public opinion supported the U.S. attack on Iraq.[177] Israel was the only country in the world that publicly denounced the U.S. National Intelligence Estimate finding of late 2007 that Iran had suspended its nuclear weapons program, and the Israeli public was the only one in the world that overwhelmingly supported a U.S. military strike against Iran.

"Most Americans," Malcolm Hoenlein of the Conference of Presidents of Major American Jewish Organizations lamented, "see Israel as a dark and militaristic place."¹⁷⁸ Liberal American Jews, many of whom came of age intoning *Give peace a chance*, have predictably looked askance at those who want to give war another *and* another *and* another chance. It surely has not enhanced Israel's appeal to the children of the "Age of Aquarius" that among 140 countries surveyed it repeatedly ranked the fourth most violent.¹⁷⁹ And young American Jews, many of whom tap into the idealistic currents in world politics, could not have been pleased in 2011 when Israel chastised the Barack Obama administration for not sufficiently backing Hosni Mubarak against the Facebook and Twitter revolutionaries gathered in Tahrir Square.

"The Jews of Israel comprise perhaps the most sympathetic group toward [George W.] Bush in the entire world," the chief U.S. correspondent for *Haaretz* observed in early 2007.

> On the other hand, American Jews constitute one of the least sympathetic groups. A vast majority of them oppose Bush. Indeed, many really loathe him. . . . [B]efore the presidential election two years ago, Bush was clearly preferred by Jewish Israelis over his rival, John Kerry. But the Jews of America voted en masse for Kerry. Some American Jews have a hard time digesting a reality in which an Israeli prime minister can stand at Bush's side and describe the war in Iraq as an achievement.¹⁸⁰

Israeli Jews most resemble American white evangelical Protestants and Mormons in their mutual preference for a militaristic foreign policy. One would be hard-pressed to name two groups with whom American Jews have less in common and, in the case of evangelicals, a group whom American Jews dread more.¹⁸¹ The gap in mindset between American Jewry and Israelis on war and peace and kindred issues verges on an abyss.

PART III

UPDATING *EXODUS*

The central argument of this book is that American Jews can no longer reconcile their liberalism with what they have come to know about the Israel-Palestine conflict. Up until recent times a near-perfect overlap existed between popular bestsellers, on the one hand, and academic studies, on the other. In fact most scholarship on the Israel-Palestine conflict could be described with only slight exaggeration as *Exodus* with footnotes. But now a huge chasm has opened up between these genres. Whereas popular literature still generally casts Israel as the embodiment of liberal values or, at a minimum, in basic harmony with them, academic research increasingly casts Israel in a much harsher light.

In order to provide a rounded picture of this paradoxical phenomenon the next five chapters survey it from multiple interrelated perspectives. Three critical dimensions of the Israel-Palestine conflict are scrutinized: the human rights, historical and legal-diplomatic records. In each case, a recent popular bestseller, which in essence repackages the standard Israeli narrative on which generations of American Jews have been weaned, is juxtaposed against the critical findings of current scholarship. The focus is on the hard cases where Israel has appeared least vulnerable to criticism: its "purity of arms" in combat, its "no choice" wars, and its "tireless" search for peace. In addition, the bestselling authors sampled in this book are drawn from milieus shaping public opinion where each of them, respectively, is a prominent fixture: media (Jeffrey Goldberg), academia (Michael Oren), and politics (Dennis Ross). Even where Israel's case seems to be strongest, and even where the writer making Israel's case commands authority, the scholarly evidence suggests that a defense of Israel can no longer sustain serious inquiry.

To be sure, the popular and academic representations of the Israel-Palestine conflict depicted in this book are not always at odds with each other. Inevitably, the popular literature must make the occasional bow to what scholarship has copiously documented: it can no longer be asserted that Egyptian President Gamal Abdel Nasser intended to attack on the eve of Israel's first strike in 1967; that Israel has maintained a "liberal" occupation in the West Bank and Gaza; that the failure to achieve peace has been entirely the Palestinians' fault. Still, it must be remarked just how disingenuous the bestselling literature *is* and how impervious it has been to the findings of academic research.

If popular literature on the Israel-Palestine conflict has had to make some concessions to serious scholarship, it is also true that even in the most lofty precincts of academia and the human rights community, fraud and hypocrisy are a persistent problem. Two particularly egregious examples will be examined presently. Much work still remains to be done in order to sweep this field clean of the rubbish that litters it; indeed, unless vigilance is maintained the garbage rapidly accumulates.

If the popular literature critically analyzed in this book has reached a broad public, it might be wondered how American Jews have escaped its influence. It puzzles yet more because most Jews would probably prefer the congenial storyline of these apologetic bestsellers over the discomfiting conclusions of academic research. The first and most obvious point is that the popular literature *does* still exert a potent influence on Jewish opinion. The enduring ambivalence of even the most liberal Jews regarding Israel attests to this impact. It is also the case, however, that the mythologies propagated in the popular blockbusters no longer monopolize public debate; that the findings of academic scholarship have willy-nilly crept into the public debate; and that the highly literate American Jewish population tends to frequent precisely those milieus where serious scholarship finds an audience and carries weight.

It might finally be asked, if the popular literature systematically misrepresents crucial aspects of the Israel-Palestine conflict, how does it manage to garner plaudits in the dominant media? The fact is that in highly politicized disciplines these media tend to promote—whether it be through book reviews, news articles, or talk shows—pseudo-scholarship that serves an ideological agenda.[1] The exact modalities and mechanisms of the mainstream media's policing function might be elusive, while any such delineation would easily be susceptible to the caricature of a conspiracy theory, but the practical outcome cannot be open to serious dispute. It is child's play to draw up a list of books that fall into this category of ballyhooed-but-bogus scholarship,[2] just as it is child's play to draw up a list of groundbreaking scholarly studies that have been systematically ignored by leading media outlets. Many of the studies cited in these pages fall into the latter category.

5/ HAIR-RAISING SCREAMS

During the first decades of Israel's occupation of the West Bank and Gaza Strip, its violations of Palestinian human rights attracted little attention. When critics sought to expose these abuses, they had to rely on the research and testimony of a handful of courageous but politically marginal Israelis[1] and their Palestinian clients and colleagues, all of whom could be, and were, ignored. In recent years, however, Israel's egregious human rights record has come under critical scrutiny by respected organizations and as a result Israel can no longer evade public reproach. Consider torture.

Right from the onset of the occupation Israel tortured Palestinian detainees.[2] But until the 1990s and despite a wealth of corroborative evidence, respectable opinion treated Israeli torture gingerly and, when broaching the topic, discreetly steered clear of using the locution *torture*. For example Amnesty International currently acknowledges that Israel "routinely" ill-treated and tortured Palestinian detainees since 1967.[3] But back in its 1979 "Report and Recommendations . . . to the Government of the State of Israel," Amnesty merely stated that "there is sufficient *prima facie* evidence of ill-treatment of security suspects in the Occupied Territories . . . to warrant the establishment of a public inquiry," while in its influential 1984 study *Torture in the Eighties* Amnesty cautiously signaled having "continued to receive reports of ill-treatment" in Israeli prisons of "some Palestinians from the Occupied Territories arrested for security reasons."[4]

A sharp reversal occurred after the inception of the first Palestinian intifada in 1987. On the one hand, the ill-treatment and torture of Palestinian detainees reached epidemic levels and, on the other, the newly founded Israeli human rights organization B'Tselem (Israeli Information Center for Human Rights in the Occupied Territories) exhaustively documented Israel's torture of Palestinian detainees.[5] Then, human rights organizations in the West began, finally, to fulfill their mandate when it came to Israel. It would appear that they exposed Israeli use of torture and other human rights violations only when it was no longer tenable to ignore what was happening and, having the protective moral cover of an *Israeli* human rights organization, they no longer needed to.

Once it openly criticized Israel, the human rights community unsurprisingly came under vicious attack.[6] However, it commanded sufficient stature and resources to aggressively defend itself and, in the current climate of skepticism towards Israel, the smear campaigns backfired. Thus, after Human Rights Watch (HRW) copiously documented Israel's "war crimes" during its summer 2006 attack on Lebanon,[7] Harvard law professor Alan Dershowitz alleged, "When it comes to Israel and its enemies, Human Rights Watch cooks the books about facts, cheats on interviews, and puts out predetermined conclusions that are driven more by their ideology than by evidence." Abraham Foxman of the Anti-Defamation League accused HRW of "immorality at the highest level," and HRW executive director Kenneth Roth of resorting to a "classic anti-Semitic stereotype." *New Republic* editor Martin Peretz declared that "this Human Rights Watch libel has utterly destroyed its credibility."[8] In the past this illustrious trio would almost certainly have had the last word. Not anymore. The respected *New York Review of Books* published a comprehensive rebuttal by Aryeh Neier, president of the Open Society Institute, disposing of all the allegations against HRW, and deploring that in the United States "time and again, rational discussion is precluded by charges of anti-Semitism against anyone with the temerity to criticize Israeli policy or practice."[9]

5/ HAIR-RAISING SCREAMS

Even scathing criticism of Israel that was once confined to the margins has spread to the respectable mainstream. Just a short while ago any comparison of the Israeli occupation to apartheid in South Africa elicited hysterical denunciations. Although the evocation of apartheid in the title of his book *Palestine Peace Not Apartheid*[10] did initially put Jimmy Carter on the defensive, it is much more telling how many prominent personalities and institutions can now be cited in support of him. The lengthy roster of those making the apartheid analogy in the context of Israel's occupation includes: former Israeli Attorney General Michael Ben-Yair; former Israeli ministers of education Shulamit Aloni and Yossi Sarid; former deputy mayor of Jerusalem Meron Benvenisti; former Israeli Ambassador to South Africa Alon Liel; veteran Israeli journalist Danny Rubinstein; South African Archbishop and Nobel Laureate for Peace Desmond Tutu; "father" of human rights law in South Africa John Dugard; B'Tselem; The Association for Civil Rights in Israel (ACRI); and the *Haaretz* editorial board.[11]

The absurdity of the attack on Carter becomes even clearer when it is remembered that Israeli Prime Minister Ariel Sharon himself was obsessed with the apartheid model and reportedly opined, "The Bantustan model was the most appropriate solution to the conflict."[12]

In the face of voluminous and damning evidence, it is no longer possible to mount a credible defense of Israel's human rights record. Although the popular literature still whitewashes this record, it is ultimately half-hearted because so much is now known and the authority of Israel's human rights critics is unimpeachable. A recent book by one of the most influential American apologists for Israel illustrates these points.

The recipient of numerous journalism awards, Jeffrey Goldberg has in recent years been a staff writer for *The New Yorker* and currently writes for *The Atlantic Monthly*. Whereas just a few years ago he was an authoritative, if clearly biased, interpreter of Israel in the liberal American print media and on the internet, as Israeli policy became increasingly impossible to defend, he rapidly degenerated into an unabashed hack and, outside the circuits of power, an object of derision even, maybe especially, among many liberal Jews.[13] Still, he remains the object of lavish public attention, his every utterance circulating at split-second speed throughout cyberspace, and—most troubling—his core reportorial competence taken for granted.

On its surface his acclaimed 2006 book *Prisoners: A Muslim and a Jew across the Middle East divide*[14] seamlessly and engagingly interweaves the memoir of an American Jew's enchantment and subsequent disappointment with Israel, on the one hand, and the reportage of a tough, knowing journalist covering the Middle East beat, on the other. Its main interest, however, is as a sophisticated work of ideology. On a political level it registers the limits of what is currently permissible to acknowledge in popular literature on the Israel-Palestine conflict, while on a personal level it registers the limits of what an enlightened believer in the faith can admit to himself. More broadly it signals the eclipse of liberal American Jewry's love affair with the Jewish state, itself integral to an incipient larger American estrangement from Israel.

Prisoners should not and cannot simply be dismissed as a Zionist propaganda tract. Like most successful ideological enterprises, and giving the book credit where due, much of *Prisoners* rings true. Goldberg knows the lay of the land and is attentive to the fluctuating moods of its inhabitants. Eschewing Thomas Friedman's formula in *From Beirut to Jerusalem*[15] (a book to which *Prisoners* bears obvious comparison), Goldberg does not quote a Fouad Ajami here and a Rabbi David Hartman there to lend credence to his prepackaged opinions, but rather speaks from the authority of some personal knowledge.

Goldberg made *aliyah* in the 1980s and lived on a left-wing kibbutz, served as a military policeman at the Israeli prison Ketziot during the first intifada (1987-1993), and reported from the occupied Palestinian territory during the Oslo years (1993-2000) and the second Palestinian intifada (2000-2006). He attached himself to one Palestinian from Gaza in particular named Rafiq Hijazi, the odyssey of this personal friendship mirroring and humanizing in *Prisoners* the larger drama unfolding in the Holy Land.

Goldberg depicts as an extraordinary feat his forging of a personal bond with a Palestinian, and commentators have reacted in tones of hushed awe. Yet, although such a relationship between Jew and Arab might have raised eyebrows a few decades ago, in the real world it is by now a commonplace. It is still cause for consternation among American pundits, however, that a Jew might be coming for dinner at a Palestinian home (or vice versa).

Although appalled by Goldberg's half-truths and misrepresentations, informed readers will probably also find themselves nodding in agreement with, and in appreciation of, the nuance of his insights. In skillful, subtle and luxuriant prose he captures the mutations in Palestinian attitudes towards Israel and the "peace process," from the anger and hope of the first intifada to the naive generosity of spirit of the Oslo years to the abject embrace of suicide bombings and fundamentalist Manichaeism during the second intifada.

Like many others (this writer included) Goldberg tests the possibility of bridging the chasm separating The Arab and The Jew through the artifice of personal engagement, experiencing the exhilaration of authentic connection intermingled with fears of betrayal verging on, but not quite reaching, paranoia. It is not an altogether implausible worry when Goldberg suddenly drips with sweat fantasizing that the gift he is transporting to Washington from his Palestinian friend might actually be a time-bomb.

And yet it is precisely because Goldberg seems to know his subject, and knows how to convey its truth to the reader, that, depending on one's take, the cynicism of his bad faith and faux innocence or the thick-headedness of his refusal to see what's right before his eyes (probably both) not only rankles but enrages. For it must be said that *Prisoners* is a wretched book that, for all its willingness to acknowledge ugly realities about Israel's occupation, albeit realities that can no longer be concealed, nonetheless reiterates and, because of the seeming openness, revivifies the old pernicious myths and threadbare clichés sustaining the occupation.

The reader is also never quite sure whether Goldberg intends his book to be an objective these-are-the-facts account of the Israel-Palestine conflict, one which should be judged according to the ordinary criteria of accuracy and logical coherence, or whether he intends it to be a subjective this-is-how-I-felt account, the misrepresentations and incoherencies being, as it were, inclusive of the story of how a decent and intelligent person can still get things dead wrong and think mutually contradictory thoughts. In other words, is the book primarily about the Israel-Palestine conflict or is it primarily about Goldberg? Such a confusion is perhaps inevitable in a work that wants to be both memoir and reportage, although the suspicion lingers that the "authenticity" of a humanly flawed personal voice might also be a device to rationalize otherwise gross factual and moral lapses.

Ultimately, even if not simply propaganda, *Prisoners* leaves behind the foul odor of a party tract because so many of its framing propositions have been refuted in widely available and irreproachable scholarly and documentary sources. The more one knows, the less it convinces, but it must also be said that, even if one is convinced, the book contains so many disquieting facts and observations, that those taken in by Goldberg's subtle alloying of fact with fiction will still leave the book largely disillusioned with Israel. Put otherwise, although *Prisoners* clearly belongs in the category of popular, propagandistic literature, it still had to incorporate enough of the unarguable record to be credible, but in making this accommodation to the reality, and when so much of this squalid reality is now known, it undercut its own propagandistic function. It is just not possible any longer anywhere—except perhaps among the born-again crazies, Jewish and Christian—to purvey the mythologies of yesteryear in a form that both convinces the faithful and keeps the faithful convinced. The old, immaculate myths won't persuade Jews, while the new, warts-and-all myths won't inspire them.

The heart of Goldberg's book is his stint during the first intifada as a military policeman in Ketziot (Ansar Three), an Israeli prison for Palestinian detainees situated in the Negev desert. It is in Ketziot that Goldberg befriends his Palestinian alter ego Rafiq, and Ketziot also serves as the metaphor for his larger claim captured in the book's title that Israelis and Palestinians are both prisoners of the occupation.

Tens of thousands of Palestinians, Goldberg reports, were arrested during the first intifada for both violent and nonviolent offenses.[16] Elsewhere Goldberg observes that "habeas corpus . . . is not a cherished value of Arab security services"[17] but, on his evidence, it does not appear to be much of an Israeli value either. He notes that "many of the prisoners" in Ketziot were "so-called administrative detainees. They had been put in jail without charge and without trial, by military order, for six-month terms, renewable at the discretion of a military judge, who did what the Shabak [Israel's internal security police] told him to do. . . . The administrative detainees included many of the intellectuals and lawyers of the Palestinian national movement."[18] Amnesty reported that the number of Palestinians held in Israeli prisons during each of the first years of the intifada hovered around 25,000, of whom 4-5,000 were administrative detainees.[19]

"Ketziot was a kind of appalling joke," Goldberg writes, a miniature of the equally "absurd occupation."[20] Palestinians were "allowed to organize their lives, even their political lives, more or less as they chose," he says, and "sometimes, it seemed as if we weren't running a prison, but a vast arts-and-crafts workshop."[21] In its annual reports, however, Amnesty described conditions at Ketziot as "harsh" throughout the intifada, although reporting some improvement in 1990, when Goldberg joined the prison staff. Goldberg does acknowledge that it was not all fun and games, noting the "systemic cruelty" of Israel's ban on family visits—"Some of these men, many with children, did not see their families for two and three years"—and that "the harsh climate was in itself a form of cruelty."[22]

Goldberg also alludes to those Israeli prisons which had a meaner reputation than Ketziot, such as Dahariya and Gaza Beach camp (Ansar Two). It is instructive to juxtapose Goldberg's description of Gaza Beach camp (Rafiq had been held there before Ketziot) with that of an Israeli journalist, Ari Shavit, who served there:

Goldberg	Shavit
Here is where young Palestinians were assimilated into the apparatus of occupation, where the Shabak extracted from the Arabs what they could and then trucked them to the desert.... The policy of Ansar Two was consistent: Prisoners being prepped for interrogation were made to stand on the basketball court under the sun for four, or five, or six hours. They were forced to raise their arms, and they were not allowed to sit, or drink. When Rafiq's arms dropped from exhaustion, he was struck.... Rafiq was smacked around a bit [during interrogation].[23]	Most [Palestinians] are awaiting trial; most were arrested because they were throwing stones or were said to be members of illegal organizations. Many are in their teens. Among them, here and there, are some boys who are small and appear to be very young.... The prison has twelve guard towers. Some Israeli soldiers are struck—and deeply shaken—by the similarity between these and certain other towers, about which they have learned at school.... [T]he unjust analogy with those other camps of fifty years ago won't go away.... And I, too, who have always abhorred this analogy, who have always argued bitterly with anyone who so much as hints at it, I can no longer stop myself. The associations are too strong.... Like a believer whose faith is cracking, I go over and over again in my mind the long list of arguments, the list of differences.... But then I realize that the problem is not in the similarity—for no one can seriously think that there is a real similarity—but that there isn't enough lack of similarity. The problem is that the lack of similarity isn't strong enough to silence once and for all the evil echoes, the accusing images. Maybe the Shin Bet [Shabak] is to blame for this—for the arrests it makes and what it does to those arrested. For almost every night, after it has managed, in its interrogations, to "break" a certain number of young men, the Shin Bet delivers to the [soldiers] a list with the names of the friends of the young

(continued)

5/ HAIR-RAISING SCREAMS

men.... [Then] the soldiers ... go out almost every night to the city and ... come back with children of fifteen or sixteen years of age. The children grit their teeth. Their eyes bulge from their sockets. In not a few cases they have already been beaten.... And soldiers crowd together in the "reception room" to look at them when they undress. To look at them in their underwear, to look at them as they tremble with fear. And sometimes they kick them—one kick more, before they put on their new prison clothes.... Or maybe the doctor is to blame. You wake him up in the middle of the night to treat one of those just brought in—a young man, barefoot, wounded, who looks as if he's having an epileptic fit, who tells you that they beat him just now on the back and the stomach and over the heart. There are ugly red marks all over his body. The doctor turns to the young man and shouts at him. In a loud, raging voice he says: May you die! And then he turns to me with a laugh: May they all die! Or maybe the screams are to blame. At the end of the watch..., you sometimes hear horrible screams ... from the other side of the ... fence of the interrogation section, ... hair-raising human screams. Literally hair-raising.... In Gaza our General Security Services [Shabak] therefore amount to a Secret Police, our internment facilities are cleanly run Gulags. Our soldiers are jailers, our interrogators torturers. In Gaza it's all straightforward and clear. There's no place to hide.

It would appear that Goldberg's sketch of Ansar Two effaced more than a few telling details. Incidentally, Gaza Beach was, according to Shavit, "one of the best of all [Israeli] internment camps of its kind."[24]

Goldberg treads cautiously on the subject of Israeli torture of Palestinian detainees. In accordance with recommendations of an Israeli state commission, he reports, "some of the prisoners . . . were, in some sort of limited way, subject to 'moderate physical pressure,' . . . in pursuit of certain types of intelligence—ticking-bomb intelligence."[25] Although recording the cruelty here and there of an aberrant Israeli soldier (almost always a Sephardic Jew)[26] or army unit,[27] and occasionally quoting or paraphrasing a Palestinian detainee as alleging he was tortured,[28] Goldberg himself prudently sidesteps use of the "t" word to describe Israeli practices.

But human rights organizations documented a much starker picture. They concluded that during the first intifada "Palestinians under interrogation were systematically tortured or ill-treated" (Amnesty); "some 85 percent of persons interrogated by the [Shabak] were interrogated by methods constituting torture" (B'Tselem); and "the number of Palestinians tortured or severely ill-treated while interrogated during the intifada is in the tens of thousands—a number that becomes especially significant when it is remembered that the universe of adult and adolescent male Palestinians in the West Bank and Gaza Strip is under three-quarters of one million" (HRW). One police unit "specialized in interrogating at night with methods including severe beatings with wooden sticks and electric shocks" (Amnesty).[29]

To his credit Goldberg notes that "nearly everyone was found guilty in the Gaza military court" and that "the defense lawyers were not allowed to see the evidence collected against their clients."[30] He neglects to mention however that in "many" instances the "primary evidence" used to convict Palestinian defendants was confessions obtained by "torture, or other forms of cruel, inhuman or degrading treatment or punishment" (Amnesty).[31]

It appears that Goldberg does not reckon the standard Israeli interrogation techniques to be torture. When Palestinians use identical techniques, however, he is not at all averse to deploring them as torture. Consider what he calls one of the "many creative methods of torture" used by Palestinian interrogators acting at the behest of the Palestinian Authority during the Oslo years: "In *shabeh*, a prisoner is bound in a kneeling position, his arms pulled back and tied to the ankles. The prisoner is then left hooded for hours. This torture causes hellish pain in the joints, and it stimulates an overwhelming desire to die."[32] Could Goldberg possibly have been unaware that *shabeh* was a routine Israeli form of torture repeatedly condemned in human rights reports?[33]

On a couple of occasions Goldberg mentions that the punishment for even minor infractions at Ketziot was

> twenty-four, forty-eight, or even seventy two hours in solitary confinement, *zinzana*, in Arabic. The *zinzana* was the size of a refrigerator box, into which three, four, five or six prisoners were shoveled. The prisoners were seated on a cold and hard plastic floor, limbs draped over limbs, and they shat in a bucket that was emptied once a day. After a few days in the box, prisoners could no longer stand unaided.[34]

This Israeli method of torture was also repeatedly condemned in human rights reports. Although admitting that he personally sent prisoners to the *zinzana*, and although liberal in his outrage at the "cruelties" of the tortures Palestinians inflicted on each other,[35] Goldberg rejects (albeit obliquely) the implication that he himself might be an accessory to torture, if not a torturer himself. When the Israeli guards needed "someone to go to solitary" for a minor infraction of prison rules, Goldberg recalls at one point,[36] "twenty Arabs immediately volunteered." He processes this episode not as a demonstration of their solidarity and courage[37] but rather as showing that the "Arabs want to be our victim" and "the Geneva Convention . . . said nothing about prisoners who asked to be punished." It is also noteworthy that the "field work" qualifying Goldberg to serve as the leading American interpreter of the Israel-Palestine conflict was his stint as a cog in Israel's machinery of torture.

A supreme failing of Palestinians during the first intifada, in Goldberg's opinion, is that they embraced violence and lacked appreciation of nonviolent resistance. He returns to this theme at multiple junctures, it becoming a mantra of his book. Lamenting that he "had not yet seen" nonviolent resistance among Palestinians, Goldberg typically writes:

> The idea did not seem to exist in their moral vocabulary. It was a shame and a waste that the Palestinians had blinded themselves to the ideas of Gandhi and King. If they hadn't, they might have broken the occupation in a week. In my desire to convince Rafiq that violence was no solution, I asked him once to think about what would happen if ten thousand Palestinian men marched on an Israeli checkpoint, as Gandhi once marched on the salt sea. Imagine, I said, that these Palestinians resisted the temptation to throw rocks and Molotov cocktails, but instead simply sat in the road and blocked traffic, keeping settlers from their settlements and soldiers from their bases. It is quite possible that the Israelis would meet them with violence, just as the British met Gandhi's followers with violence. But the Israelis would stop soon enough. I was sure of that. The Israelis, like the British soldiers of India, could not sustain such one-sided violence. Germans could slaughter the defenseless at close quarters, but not Jews—not most people, especially in front of television cameras. The Israelis would be forced to negotiate with you.[38]

It is surely a curiosity that Goldberg personally witnessed the first intifada yet "had not seen" nonviolent resistance among the Palestinians.[39] "The [first] intifada has thus far been distinguished on the Palestinian side by predominantly nonviolent forms of struggle," a leading American academic specialist on nonviolent resistance observed more than a year into it.

"Considering their lack of preparation for disciplined nonviolent struggle," he continued, "and given the severity of Israeli repression in the form of beatings, shootings, killings, house demolitions, uprooting of trees, deportations, extended imprisonments and detentions without trial, and so on, the Palestinians during the intifada have shown impressive restraint."[40]

It seems that Goldberg managed to miss the ubiquitous boycotts of Israeli goods, tax and commercial strikes, and strike days brutally suppressed by the Israel Defense Forces (IDF), such as the highly publicized nonviolent tax resistance in the Palestinian town of Beit Sahour, and the ensuing six-week-long Israeli siege and pillage of the town. He also managed to miss the hundreds of grassroots mass organizations ("popular committees") displacing Israeli rule nonviolently that sprung up in every sphere of Palestinian life from health and education to agriculture and the judiciary. "They were extraordinarily resilient; whenever their members were arrested, others rose to fill their place," Israeli military correspondents Zeev Schiff and Ehud Yaari recounted. "The fact is that by the spring of 1988, a sprawling network of popular committees was functioning in one form or another in every city, village, and camp, spreading the web of the uprising's machinery to the farthest corners of the territories." Intent on crushing these "seeds of self-government," and using the pretext that they fomented violence, Israel, according to Schiff and Yaari, "outlawed the popular committees and arrested hundreds of their members." It methodically wrecked the practical experiments in nonviolent civil disobedience; for example, "the campaign to encourage self-sufficiency by raising chickens, rabbits and vegetables fell apart when the [Israeli] Civil Administration closed the stations run by the agriculture committees."[41]

The administrative detainees held in Ketziot during the first intifada included "Palestinian leaders who openly supported the peace talks with Israel and dialogue to promote Palestinian-Israeli understanding" (B'Tselem), while Israeli military courts convicted Palestinians on the basis of draconian Israeli military orders that criminalized and made punishable "by up to 10 years' imprisonment every form of political expression in the Occupied

Territories, including nonviolent forms of political activity" (Amnesty).[42] One reason Goldberg did not see any nonviolent resistance is perhaps because he suffered an optical impairment. "She had joined a group of foreigners, advocates of the Palestinian cause, who stood one day against a line of Israeli bulldozers," he writes of the death of American peace activist Rachel Corrie during the second intifada. "She came too close to one and she was plowed under."[43] Just as the Twin Towers came too close to the hijacked airplanes and got plowed under.[44]

Goldberg is precise on the number of "suspected collaborators... killed by their brother Palestinians" during the first intifada,[45] yet he is mute on the balance-sheet for fatalities between Israelis and Palestinians in this period, except that, in his telling, Israelis only used "rubber bullets" or "fired live rounds in the air."[46] His silence is no doubt prudent because "the ratio of Israeli to Palestinian deaths demonstrates unequivocally from where the preponderant violence comes."[47] Between December 1987 and September 1993, 1,124 Palestinians were killed by Israelis as against 75 Israelis killed by Palestinians. In 1988 and yet again in 1989, for example, "over 260 unarmed Palestinian civilians, including children, were shot dead by Israeli forces, often in circumstances suggesting excessive use of force or deliberate killings" (Amnesty). To judge by these figures, Goldberg should perhaps have preached the virtue of nonviolence to Israelis.[48]

During the first intifada "it was illegal to fly th[e] flag," Goldberg reports, while "a Palestinian man holding a rifle would be shot and killed."[49] In fact the official Israeli rules of engagement allowed for the killing of a Palestinian for hoisting the national colors or ignoring an order to halt, while the unofficial or de facto rules of engagement were yet more lax. The few Israelis indicted in connection with Palestinian deaths were convicted on minor charges and received derisory punishments, whereas Palestinians convicted of throwing a stone were handed sentences of up to five years' imprisonment.[50]

Each year of the first intifada thousands of Palestinians were "beaten by Israeli forces" and "many were punitively kicked or struck with clubs or rifle butts," according to human rights organizations. "The victims included people who refused to clear roadblocks or delete graffiti, or who were suspected of having thrown stones. Many suffered severe injuries, particularly fractures" (Amnesty). More than 50,000 Palestinian children required medical attention in the first years of the intifada due to "indiscriminate beating, tear-gassing and shooting" (Save the Children).[51] In his distillation of these atrocities Goldberg reports that the daily routine of Israeli soldiers "consisted of chasing rock-throwing children."[52] He recalls having sympathized with the "symbolic violence" of these diminutive stone-throwers until he himself was hit by a rock: "There was nothing symbolic about the pain, or the blood that ran down the back of my neck"[53]—which no doubt justified "chasing," as it were, the perpetrators.

Other Israeli tactics that scandalized public opinion also escaped Goldberg's notice. During the first intifada Israel demolished or sealed nearly nine hundred Palestinian homes. Although Israel was the only country in the world (except for Iraq under Saddam Hussein) that legally sanctioned house demolitions as a form of punishment, and although this practice was widely condemned (a former Israeli Supreme Court justice called it "inhuman"),[54] it merits not a single mention in Goldberg's putatively definitive account. He does however manage to devote several emotive pages to his "shock" at the alleged rape of a Palestinian teenager in Ketziot, which "sent me back to a persistent question: If this is what they do to their own people...."[55] Israel's indiscriminate killing, torture and beating of Palestinians and the demolition of their homes evoked no such soul-searching, for the understandable reason that in his reckoning it never happened.[56]

It is an abiding conceit of Goldberg's book that, locked in mutual fear and suffering comparable deprivation, Israelis and Palestinians were equally prisoners of Ketziot, and accordingly the occupation: "we were both trapped in the same desert," "we were level with the Arabs in so many things—our food came off the same trucks, our tents were all antediluvian, we all coughed up the same desert dust," "we slept on the same kind of beds as the prisoners," "we all ate the same fruit, guards and prisoners alike."[57] He even manages to fish out a former prisoner who is said to have proclaimed "You were *our* prisoners."⁵⁸ So convinced was he of the mutuality of victimhood that it comes as a revelation to Goldberg when he is reminded that, unlike the prisoners, the guards "can go home on leave and then come back again."⁵⁹ One can only imagine Goldberg's epiphany were he capable of registering the "hair-raising human screams," the "severe beatings with wooden sticks and electric shocks," the piles of human corpses, the countless homes demolished.

A most peculiar juxtaposition of Goldberg's book is his singing the praises of gun Zionism to Jews on one page while singing the praises of Mahatma Gandhi and Martin Luther King, Jr. to Palestinians on another. Like many an American Jew, Goldberg first became enamored of Israel on account of its martial prowess.⁶⁰ Recalling his maiden trip to the Holy Land, Goldberg emphasizes that what resonated for him most was

> Jews with guns, and not just .22s but Uzis and M-16s and bigger guns than these, grenade-spitting guns, great barking machine guns. On a bus tour across the Galilee, we drove in the wake of a tank transport, a mammoth truck carrying a dead Jewish tank. A Jewish tank! And Jewish armored personnel carriers! It was a miracle. Enough of thinking and suffering. Let's do some shooting.⁶¹

Goldberg's new-found hero is Ari Ben Canaan of Leon Uris's *Exodus*, a "Hebrew (not, somehow, Jewish) warrior, brave and cold-eyed, who defended Jewish honor." The "lesson of the Shoah," Goldberg comes to realize, is that "it is easy to kill a unilaterally disarmed Jew but much harder to kill one who is pointing a gun at your face," while during target practice at army boot camp he relishes the prospect of avenging the anti-Semites who had ravaged the Jewish people and, allegedly, humiliated him in his youth.⁶²

None of these prideful ruminations, however, prevents Goldberg from expressing revulsion at the teachings of Muslim fanatics, who "build self-esteem" through bloody vengeance, and who embrace a "warrior" Islam opposed to the Christian value of "passive surrender."[63] It is hard to make out the difference between this warrior religion and the one Goldberg himself adopted after discovering Israel. Although intermittently conveying some second thoughts about his initial fascination with violence,[64] Goldberg is far from a convert to passive resistance. When a pacifist interlocutor questions the utility of Goldberg's rifle, his not-very-Gandhian repartee is, "[I]t solves problems.... It protects people from violence,"[65] and while ultimately disavowing force for its own sake, he reports being "still partial to fighting Jews."[66]

It is likewise cause for perplexity that Goldberg never preaches to Israelis (and their American "supporters") the wonders of pacifism. Surely he did not forego the exercise for a lack of need. The IDF has occupied a "unique position" in Israeli society, Israeli military historian Martin van Creveld observes, "comparable, if at all, only to the status the armed forces held in Germany from 1871 until 1945." Israel's founders, he continues, set as their goal "creating a race of warrior-settlers." In the state that emerged, the "greatest compliment anyone could receive was that he was a 'fighter,'" and the "highest praise one could bestow on anything was to say that it was *kmo mivtsa tsvai* (like a military operation)," while after the June 1967 war Israel "had become one huge military laboratory."[67] This does not exactly sound like King's "beloved community."

Zeev Maoz, formerly head of Israel's Jaffee Center for Strategic Studies, describes the IDF as the primary Israeli instrument of national integration and social cohesion, the "key element of national identity." In order to preserve the army's exalted status in Israeli society, as well as to mobilize the population and divert its attention from internal conflicts, Israeli leaders, according to Maoz, have fostered a "siege mentality," promoted "militarism," and preferred war to peace. Indeed, he reports that Israeli leaders have periodically resorted to murderous reprisal raids for the sake of combat training and nurturing esprit de corps, and provoked armed hostilities and carried out targeted assassinations for the sake of testing high-tech weaponry.[68] It is to the ultimate undoing of Palestinians, Goldberg laments, that they "see violence as a panacea" and have "let violence into every corner of their lives."[69] If only they would emulate Israel.

Speaking of the saintly Israelis, Goldberg apparently found this army "joke" so hilarious that he could not resist slipping it in his book:

> Two soldiers, infantry-men in the Golani Brigade, were on patrol in Hebron, getting ready to enforce the six p.m. curfew. The streets were mostly empty already, but one of the soldiers saw an old Arab man hobbling down the lane in the distance. The soldier dropped to one knee, took aim, and fired, taking off the old man's head. The other soldier watched this in shock. "What are you doing?" he cried. "It's not six yet."
> "I know," said the first soldier. "But I knew where that guy lived. He never would have made it home in time."[70]

A real knee-slapper.

Were Palestinians to practice nonviolence, Goldberg contends, Israel would quickly be forced to negotiate. This is allegedly because, like Britons but unlike Germans, Israelis "could not sustain such one-sided violence..., especially in front of television cameras."[71] The basis of Goldberg's faith, however, is unclear. The first intifada was a "mass civil uprising," Schiff and Yaari observed, "not a war... but a challenge posed without weapons."[72] One of Israel's early acts of retaliation was to deport the Palestinian-American pacifist Mubarak Awad of the Center for the Study of Nonviolence. Fully seventeen months into this popular civil resistance "without weapons," and notwithstanding the massive force Israel had already brought to bear to quell it, more than half of all Israelis supported the deployment of still "stronger measures" by the IDF, while "an overwhelming 72 percent...

saw no contradiction between the army's handling of the uprising and 'the nation's democratic values.'"[73]

It is of course possible that if Palestinians had found the inner wherewithal to stay the nonviolent course yet longer in the face of the IDF's brutality, fissures would have opened up in Israeli society, just as, after years of acquiescence in anti-Jewish measures, Germans recoiled at the raw violence unleashed by the Nazis on Kristallnacht.[74] Thus, Israel's liberal, cosmopolitan milieus such as the High Court of Justice have occasionally proven to be sensitive to international opinion. An outpouring of worldwide condemnation caused the Court, for instance, to reverse its prior authorization of torture.[75] If the nonviolent civil disobedience Goldberg counsels is to succeed, however, its practice and the violence being used to crush it must be widely publicized. It is a supreme irony lost on Goldberg that it is precisely his manner of ignoring Palestinian civil disobedience and airbrushing Israeli brutality that has thus far doomed this tactic to failure.[76]

Goldberg's account of the rise of Hamas and the second intifada conforms to the pattern already set. He repeatedly condemns Hamas, and concomitantly Palestinian society, for being "ravaged by a cult of death."[77] The key manifestation of this death cult has been, of course, the suicide bombers. Although Goldberg makes reference to Palestinians killed during the second intifada,[78] the dramatic core of his narrative is these suicide bombings, the deranged perpetrators and the decimated victims.

Goldberg is surely entitled to his outrage at the "bestial manifestations" of Hamas's ideology.[79] But shouldn't he have somewhere mentioned that "Israel's disproportionate response to what had started as a popular uprising with young unarmed men confronting Israeli soldiers armed with lethal weapons fuelled the [second] intifada beyond control and turned it into an all-out war" (former Israeli foreign minister Shlomo Ben-Ami); that the first Hamas suicide bombing during the second intifada did not occur until five months into Israel's relentless bloodletting (Israeli forces fired one million rounds of ammunition just during the first few days of the uprising, while the ratio of Palestinians to Israelis killed during the first weeks was 20:1); and that four times as many Palestinians as Israelis, overwhelmingly civilians on both sides, were killed during the second intifada (4,046 as compared to 1,017 persons)?[80]

Goldberg is appalled by a Hamas leader's "calm unperturbed by the thought of bleeding" Israeli children.[81] He might also have mentioned, but does not, the widely reported counsel of Major General (subsequently Chief of Staff) Dan Halutz to Israeli pilots who dropped a one-ton bomb on a densely populated civilian neighborhood killing nine Palestinian children: "Guys, sleep well tonight. By the way, I sleep well at night, too."[82]

Goldberg is shocked at any imputation of similarity between the deaths of Palestinian and Israeli children: "For God's sake, we don't *try* to kill children."[83] Still, just during the first month of the second intifada, 37 Palestinian children were killed, 18 of them from a "live bullet to [the] head" (Defense for Children International). Fully 811 Palestinian children were killed in the course of the second intifada, which was more than the total number of Israeli civilians killed (711, of whom 109 were children). For the want of trying to kill Palestinian children, it would appear that Israelis were awfully good at it.[84]

In fact unarmed Palestinian demonstrators killed by Israeli soldiers *were* "on many occasions . . . deliberately targeted" (Amnesty), while in other cases these unarmed demonstrators, a large proportion of whom were children, fell victim to "indiscriminate," "excessive" and "disproportionate" use of force. Many of these latter deaths are legally indistinguishable from intentional killings. "Indiscriminate attacks differ from direct attacks against civilians," Israel's leading authority on international law, Yoram Dinstein, observed

> in that "the attacker is not actually *trying* to harm the civilian population": the injury to the civilians is merely a matter of "no concern to the attacker." From the standpoint of LOIAC [Law of International Armed Conflict], there is no genuine difference

5/ HAIR-RAISING SCREAMS

between a premeditated attack against civilians (or civilian objects) and a reckless disregard of the principle of distinction: they are equally forbidden.[85]

Goldberg might also have mentioned, but does not, the notorious case in 2004 of an Israeli captain who fired two bullets at point blank range into the head of a 13-year-old Palestinian schoolgirl while she was lying on the ground already injured, and then, after starting to walk away, turned back to riddle her body with many more bullets, including seven to her head. The officer was subsequently acquitted of all charges, received hefty monetary compensation from the state and a promotion in his rank—clearly because, for God's sake, he did not *try* to kill her.[86]

After recalling the March 2002 Hamas suicide bombing in Netanya, Goldberg ridicules the "credulous members of the American Colony press corps" who, during Operation Defensive Shield that followed the bombing, "accused the [Israeli] army of committing a massacre" in Jenin: "This was the opposite of the truth: The army in Jenin killed the makers of massacres."[87] He might have mentioned, but does not, that Israel did in fact commit "war crimes" (HRW, Amnesty) during its assault on Jenin, including the flattening of large swaths of the refugee camp after the fighting was already over, leaving 4,000 Palestinians homeless. One of the "makers of massacres" killed by Israeli forces was "Kamal Zgheir, a fifty-seven-year-old wheelchair-bound man who was shot and run over by a tank on a major road outside the camp on April 10, even though he had a white flag attached to his wheelchair" (HRW).[88]

Goldberg heaps contempt on Palestinian political leaders who, he alleges, used civilians, including their own children and grandchildren, as human shields to ward off Israeli attacks. Thus he ingeniously manages to invert Israel's policy of targeted assassinations, which constitute a "war crime" (Public Committee Against Torture in Israel), into instances of Palestinian pusillanimity. These Palestinian leaders were "unconstrained by Western notions of chivalric behavior," he continues, "notions [they] assumed, correctly, that Israel would respect."[89] Unsurprisingly Goldberg does not mention that "scores of men, women and children bystanders have been killed and hundreds have been injured in the course of assassinations or attempted assassinations of Palestinians by the Israeli army.... Claims that efforts are made not to harm bystanders are inconsistent with the practice of carrying out attacks on busy roads and densely populated areas" (Amnesty). One-third of the 500 Palestinians killed in the course of Israeli targeted assassinations during the second intifada were civilian bystanders.[90] What's more, Goldberg does not mention Israel's resort to "systematically coercing Palestinian civilians" as human shields (HRW), for example, chivalrously ordering Palestinian civilians to "walk in front of soldiers to shield them from gunfire, while the soldiers hold a gun behind their backs and sometimes fire over their shoulders" (B'Tselem).[91]

The difference between Palestinian and Israeli violence, Goldberg elucidates, "is the difference between action and reaction." Indeed, he expresses indignation when a fellow journalist implies that a Hamas suicide bombing might be retaliatory.[92] According to Maoz, however, Israel made use of targeted assassinations during the second intifada in order to provoke Palestinian retaliation, thereby creating a pretext for its massive resort to force: "On four separate occasions Israel violated an implicit cease-fire that the Palestinians imposed upon themselves by assassinations that caused escalation.... In each of these cases, the Palestinian response was a wave of suicide bombings that resulted in Israeli encirclement of the major population centers, entry into the Palestinian cities and refugee camps, mass arrests, numerous house demolitions, and long curfews of the Palestinian population."[93]

In addition to deploring the Palestinian death cult, Goldberg expresses irritation at the Palestinians' hypersensitivity to their personal dignity: "Ah, yes, humiliation: the Arabs, and their insufferable egos, as fragmented as old bones"; "The smart officers [in Ketziot] understood the importance of providing their prisoners, who came to humiliation so easily, with the simulacrum of dignity."[94] Yet, the prisoners in Ketziot, although having been degraded and tortured, although their relatives had been maimed and murdered, although their homes had been demolished and their lives ravaged—nonetheless these same Palestinian prisoners, according to Goldberg, received him warmly during the Oslo years when he returned to Palestine, swapping stories with him about Ketziot "like old bunkmates from summer" and saying "all the things about peace and compromise that I hoped to hear."[95] "We don't care what people did in the past," a Palestinian leader tells him. "We're not going back to the past."[96] So smug is Goldberg in his disdain of Palestinians clinging to their dignity that he cannot see that perhaps he—Israelis, Jews—might have something to learn from them about forgiveness, notwithstanding the multitudinous horrors and humiliations Israelis have inflicted.

Goldberg's life story reads like the curriculum vitae of the Everyman of American Zionism. His parents were New York City school teachers and union members, liberal Democrats and supporters of iconic farm workers' leader Cesar Chavez. Their hero was Martin Luther King, Jr., although he himself claims to have been "partial to Malcolm X."[97]

Goldberg's home was filled with his grandfather's tales of anti-Semitic Cossacks "as cruel as Pushkin's" and his fearless great-uncle, the only Jew in the *shtetl* who fought back: "Mendel, *my* uncle, was not one to cringe in the face of violence."[98] His Long Island, New York neighborhood was predominantly Irish. He claims to have suffered in this "wasteland of Irish pogromists" relentless anti-Semitic persecution, which was "the forge on which many American Jews build their identities. This is how I built mine."[99] A "red river of anti-Semitism," according to Goldberg, still flows "under the surface of America."[100] It seems that he cannot resist a single silly cliché, however divorced from reality.

In rapid succession Goldberg reports having "drowned" himself "in the literature of the Shoah," which provided the "consolation" that his own persecution "was a minor link in an eternal chain of terror";[101] discovered Meir

Kahane's "specifically Semitic model of self-defense," but then rejected Kahane's message of hate;[102] and embarked on a semi-clandestine "mission" to the Soviet Union, "dodging the KGB" in order to make contact with persecuted Soviet Jews wanting only to "go home" to Israel[103]—even if, in the real world, most of them wanted only to go to the United States. Goldberg eventually decides to drop out of college and leave behind the "dog's life of the Diaspora" where Jews were a "whipped and homeless people"—bear in mind that he's talking about American Jewry *in the 1980s*—for Israel where he finally "felt at home."[104]

During his military service in Ketziot, Goldberg tells readers, fellow Israeli guards disparagingly labeled him a "beautiful soul" because of his otherworldly saintliness.[105] He claims that he "never hit a Palestinian who wasn't already hitting me";[106] that he "did not believe in collective punishment. I found it repugnant;"[107] that because "the Arabs, the prisoners, had no masks" during the Iraqi Scud missile attacks in 1991, "I wouldn't wear a mask";[108] that he "despised the isolation tanks for their cruelty";[109] that he "might have been the only soldier [Rafiq] met who didn't deny the existence of misfortune in Palestinian history";[110] that he was an "enemy of checkpoints and a champion of honor";[111] that he "happened to think a day in which no one died... was a successful day";[112] that the "guilt was rising" in him after he "had been making a show of toughness";[113] that for him "the removal of every last settlement in exchange for peace seems like a bargain";[114] and that "I have not stopped wanting what I have always wanted: security and justice for Israel, and security and justice for Palestinians."[115]

It is child's play to poke fun at the hypocrisy, sanctimoniousness, implausibility and absurdity of Goldberg's testimony. What is most noteworthy, however, is how Goldberg's story ends. He decides that Israel is not the place for him—not because it is too good for him but because he is too good for it. He departs Israel after the epiphany that he's an American after all and that Jews belong in America: that the U.S. is a better place for Jews than Israel. This is not how the journey of the Everyman of American Zionism making *aliyah* is supposed to climax.

5/ HAIR-RAISING SCREAMS

In the course of his sojourn in Israel, Goldberg experiences mounting disillusionment. Prior to coming to Israel he had attended a left-wing Zionist summer camp organized by emissaries from Zion who were exemplars of the New Jew. Once in Israel he made a beeline for its parent kibbutz bursting with the high-minded rhetoric of socialist Zionism, only to be shattered when a kibbutznik tells him: "We get the Arabs to clean up the shit. That's why we have Arabs."[116] After an accumulation of psychic wounds he comes to the "melancholy realization" that

> I was not at home here. It was an awful thing to recognize, but it seemed true: I felt alienated and untethered. Israel was a hard place, filled with hard people. I knew in my heart that I was failing to transform myself into an Israeli, and there were moments when I no longer believed I should have this as my goal. The coarseness of life in Intifada Israel was so bottomless that my disappointment with it was bottomless, too.[117]

On returning to the U.S., Goldberg realizes that he "was proud to be an American" and "was no longer embarrassed to be an American Jew"; that although there were things Israeli that he "still admired, . . . there were American Jewish traits I now had come to appreciate: irony, tolerance, and ambivalence about the possession of physical power and the use of force. These were not, after all, shameful traits";[118] that "America . . . is the greatest country in the history of the earth";[119] that "faith in the absence of almost any hope is the American way";[120] and that America has "certainly become my Promised Land."[121]

Again, it is easy to mock how effortlessly Goldberg discards one bundle of vapid clichés about Israel and trundles forth a new bundle of vapid clichés about the United States. But the more intriguing question is, What accounts for this souring on Israel? Goldberg's audience consists almost entirely of liberal Jews and he counts himself one among them. The pristine image of Israel that once appealed to them is no longer credible. Too much of the reality has become known. Try as he may to deny it, even Goldberg must acknowledge that something's gone seriously awry in paradise. It is consequently no longer possible to reconcile liberal American values with hosannas for Israel. Forced to decide between them, most American Jews will choose the values on which they have been nurtured and which have served them so well. Ultimately, then, Goldberg's book is more elegy than apologia. It is American Jewry's farewell to Israel.

But since his book's publication six years ago, Goldberg himself has not severed his ties with Israel. If anything he has grown yet more rabid in his defense of it. He has carved out a lucrative, high-profile niche for himself in the U.S. as Kol Israel (the Voice of Israel) and, it appears, is not prepared to let go of it. However, the inexorable rightward drift of Israeli society has forced Goldberg into the unenviable position of having to publicly defend the crazed state of Prime Minister Benjamin Netanyahu and Foreign Minister Avigdor Lieberman. But while Goldberg and his ilk continue to be presented as authoritative voices in the establishment media, much of informed liberal Jewish opinion has come to regard them as buffoonish characters inviting ridicule and scorn.

Cracks have now appeared even in the wall of hardcore media support for Israel,[122] further isolating party hacks such as Goldberg, who shrilly defend the evermore indefensible, turning them into caricatures of themselves. Still, to be even minimally credible in a journalistic milieu where so much more is known, where the establishment media are losing their monopoly on what is reported, where critics of Israeli policy no longer fear career penalties if they bluntly confront its defenders—in such a milieu the likes of Goldberg must concede enough of the truth that, even if they themselves hold the fort, they can no longer coax other Jews to join them.

6/ HUMAN RIGHTS REVISIONISM

In recent years the human rights community has demonstrated courage and principle in its documentation of the Israel-Palestine conflict. Its meticulous reports have played a critical role in casting an authoritative light on, and opening the eyes of hitherto blind supporters of Israel to, the injustices that have been committed. In the future these reports will serve as the definitive archival source for historians on a conflict that not only caused so much unnecessary suffering and death but was also saturated with hypocrisy and lies.

The findings of these human rights organizations have probably had the most decisive impact on Jewish opinion because most Jews are liberal, human rights organizations are liberal, and these organizations are significantly staffed by liberal Jews. The fact that the Israel lobby invests so much energy and resources trying to discredit these organizations shows the potential they possess to undermine "the cause."

Still, it would not be accurate to say that the record of human rights organizations has been flawless. Of course, human error is to be expected, but these organizations have also been subject to professional and—especially—financial pressures from Israel's domestic partisans and, lamentably if unsurprisingly, succumbed to them. The damage caused by these periodic regressions, however, has been relatively limited. Because human rights organizations function in a community of kindred souls, most of whom are genuinely committed to the principles they espouse, each watches over, and is being watched over by, the others. Moreover, unlike in the past, when human rights organizations steered clear of the Israel-Palestine conflict and Israel's press releases served as holy writ, the unvarnished truth is now publicly accessible. The practical upshot is that the facts themselves are rarely tampered with.

The accommodations made by human rights organizations to external pressure typically show up in their conclusions, where the law is sufficiently flexible that it can be stretched, albeit often to the breaking point, in order to harden or soften the blow of the findings, whichever is politically more expedient. But even here, because the facts possess a compelling force in and of themselves, it is easy enough to demonstrate that they have been squeezed into, and ill-fit, legally disingenuous conclusions. In other words, the more the facts are repackaged in order to make them appear less "offensive," the more transparent it becomes that the advertising lacks truth.

The reports issued by Human Rights Watch (HRW) on the summer 2006 Lebanon war vividly illustrate these points. The criticisms of HRW set forth in this chapter should not, however, be construed as detracting from the book's heavy reliance on the findings of human rights organizations. Ordinarily such organizations do not apply made-up standards or double standards. Rather, they consistently apply widely accepted and uncontroversial norms drawn from canonical sources of human rights law. Furthermore, the Israeli human rights violations documented in this book have been confirmed by correlating the findings and conclusions of multiple human rights organizations. What makes the Lebanon episode unusual—but, alas, not unique—is how egregiously HRW departed from these well-established norms after it came under political fire from the Israel lobby.[1] Although much progress has been made, it nonetheless remains an on-going struggle to keep human rights reporting on Israel honest.

Human Rights Watch's description of the facts bearing on human rights violations during the 2006 Lebanon war is generally accurate. The surprise would be were it otherwise because, as already noted, human rights organizations do not operate in a vacuum. None can stray too far from the factual record without risking ridicule and ostracism from the human rights community. Indeed, HRW's account of the facts does, on any rational interpretation, paint a damning picture of Israeli conduct during the war, one which could not have pleased Israel's apologists. Even amidst its trimming, hedging and double standards, HRW's reportage on the Lebanon war nonetheless documents Israel's staggering violations of the laws of war and must therefore be reckoned a devastating indictment of Israel from a respected liberal institution.

But HRW failed to draw the obvious conclusions from the facts it presented, conclusions it readily reached with respect to Hezbollah on the basis of weaker evidence. There is thus no escaping the inference that HRW has applied different evidentiary and legal standards to Hezbollah and Israel, the result being that it mitigated Israel's crimes while, in at least some cases, it conjured Hezbollah's out of thin air.

The events triggering the 2006 Lebanon war are well known: Hezbollah's capture of two Israeli soldiers and an ensuing exchange of fire on 12 July 2006 rapidly escalated into full-blown war. Israel anticipated that its offensive (in preparation from as far back as mid-2000)[2] would last a few days, but it dragged on for 34 days until 14 August because of the guerrilla army's stiff and surprisingly sophisticated resistance.

From early on in the war, it was difficult to understand why HRW was not condemning Israel for war crimes in Lebanon, but merely calling on Israel to "investigate" attacks on civilians.[3] It had already issued a statement one week into the war condemning Hezbollah for "serious violations of international humanitarian law and probably war crimes."[4] Coming under intense criticism because of its silence on Israeli conduct,[5] and after international outrage over the Qana massacre,[6] HRW did finally issue a statement on 30 July condemning Israel's "indiscriminate bombing in Lebanon" as a "war crime."[7] On 3 August HRW issued a comprehensive indictment of Israel's assault on Lebanon, *Fatal Strikes: Israel's indiscriminate attacks against civilians in Lebanon*. Predictably the document, highly critical of Israel's conduct during the war, was received with near hysteria by the Israel lobby, which mounted a media smear campaign targeting HRW and its executive director Kenneth Roth.[8]

Several months later, in November 2006, Palestinians gathered nonviolently on the rooftop of and in the street surrounding a Gazan home to prevent Israel's illegal destruction of it. Israel's policy was to give occupants of a dwelling marked for destruction an hour's notice by telephone, a practice that U.N. Special Rapporteur John Dugard condemned as "terrorism by telephone."[9] But HRW, apparently still smarting from the Israel lobby's attack, issued a press release on this Gaza confrontation that suggested the Palestinians, not the Israelis, were committing a "war crime."[10] This attempt to appease its critics was so indefensible and the moral calculus so bizarre that HRW had to withdraw the press release a few weeks later.[11]

In August and September 2007, HRW issued a pair of hefty new reports on the summer 2006 Lebanon war, *Civilians Under Assault: Hezbollah's rocket attacks on Israel in the 2006 war*, and *Why They Died: Civilian casualties in Lebanon during the 2006 war*, that retraced and broadened the original investigation documented in *Fatal Strikes*. A juxtaposition of the new reports against the original shows that the factual findings of *Fatal Strikes* critical of Israel were overwhelmingly confirmed, but the legal conclusions were significantly revised. *Fatal Strikes* had concluded that "in some cases ... Israeli forces deliberately targeted civilians"; that "no cases [were found] in which Hezbollah deliberately used civilians as shields to protect them from retaliatory IDF [Israel Defense Forces] attack"; and that the "pattern of attacks during the Israeli offensive ... indicate[s] the commission of war crimes" by Israel.[12]

The new report on Hezbollah's rocket attacks on Israel, *Civilians Under Assault*, basically reiterated HRW's conclusion in *Fatal Strikes* that Hezbollah had committed "war crimes." But, in striking contrast to *Fatal Strikes*, the new report on Israel's conduct of the war, *Why They Died*, omitted mention that Israel "deliberately targeted civilians," except for a couple of stray, tentative remarks;[13] discovered that in a "handful of cases" it was "probable" that Hezbollah made use of "human shields"; and put Israel's culpability for serious violations of the laws of war in the conditional-subjunctive—for example, *if* an Israeli commander indiscriminately targeted an area knowing civilians were present, *then he would be* guilty of war crimes. HRW's differing assessment of Israeli versus Hezbollah culpability is signaled in the titles of the respective reports, which leave no doubt that Israeli civilians were targeted ("under assault") but are noncommittal about the cause of Lebanese "civilian casualties."

It might be supposed that the revisions in HRW's report on Israel were due either to significant errors it found when retracing its original investigation or to significant new information it uncovered when broadening the investigation. But HRW found only a couple of significant lapses,[14] and those two errors cannot account for HRW's dramatic revision of its conclusions concerning Israeli culpability. The reasonable inference is that HRW revised its conclusions to appease its Israel lobby critics. A careful analysis of the reports sustains that supposition.

An anomaly in the HRW reports should preliminarily be noted. The breakdown of casualties during the war shows:

TABLE 1 CASUALTIES IN THE 2006 LEBANON WAR

	Total fatalities	Civilians (% of total)	Combatants (% of total)
Israelis	160	43 (25)	117 (75)
Lebanese	1,200[15]	1,000 (80)	180-250 (20)[16]

Whether judging by the absolute number of civilians killed or the relative number of civilians to combatants killed, Israel's record would appear to be much worse than Hezbollah's. Indeed more Lebanese civilians were killed during the first two days of the war (55) than the total number of Israeli civilians killed in the entire 34-day conflict.[17] (It is easy to miss the full magnitude of the discrepancy when juxtaposing the respective HRW reports because *Why They Died* is just twice the length of *Civilians Under Assault*.[18]) Human rights organizations also documented that the respective damage to Israeli and Lebanese civilian infrastructure was on a vastly different scale.[19] Finally, HRW reported that Hezbollah fired, mostly in violation of the laws of war, some four thousand cluster submunitions on Israel while Israel fired some four *million* cluster submunitions on Lebanon.[20] These raw figures suggest that it would be highly improbable, if not impossible, that Hezbollah's violations of international law exceeded those of Israel during the 2006 war.

HRW purported to present "strong evidence that some Hezbollah members and commanders were responsible for war crimes."[21] The evidence it adduced fell into two broad categories: (A) Hezbollah's use of "indiscriminate" weapons in "populated settings," and (B) Hezbollah's declared policy of targeting Israeli civilians. Both of those allegations are problematic.

INDISCRIMINATE WEAPONS: A tenet of the laws of war is the distinction between a combatant/military object and a civilian/civilian object, the former being a legitimate and the latter an illegitimate target. HRW alleged that "all of the rockets" Hezbollah fired at Israel were "unguided" and could not be aimed "with enough accuracy to target a particular building or artillery mount";[22] and, consequently, that the firing of these rockets in "populated settings" would in and of themselves constitute "serious violations of the laws of war."[23] It is to be noted that by this standard Hezbollah would still be guilty of war crimes even if every one of its rockets hit combatants or military objects in built-up areas.[24]

HRW never specified the degree of accuracy a weapon used in populated settings must achieve to qualify as lawful. In the absence of such specification, its assertion that the firing of "unguided" rockets by Hezbollah at built-up areas by itself constituted "serious violations of the laws of war" cannot be independently assessed. The standard of precision HRW applied to Hezbollah must however have been stringent. Thus, it condemned Hezbollah's rocket attacks even if a military object was the target and even if the military object was hit because its "inaccurate rockets stood a good chance" of striking a civilian site "just beyond."[25]

HRW did acknowledge that nations possessing state-of-the-art weaponry might be seen as having an unfair advantage over guerrillas armed with relatively primitive weaponry in what it calls "asymmetrical conflict." Such an advantage would in fact be absolute to the extent that "high-tech" weaponry effectively determined the degree of precision qualifying a weapon as discriminate, thereby disqualifying use of any less precise weapon because it is "indiscriminate." In order to avoid criminal indictment, "low-tech" armies must "find alternative ways of waging war" such as "using sniper fire."[26] In the case at hand, as Israel "launched some 7,000 bomb and missile strikes in Lebanon, which were supplemented by numerous artillery attacks and naval bombardment,"[27] Hezbollah could have defended Lebanon, according to HRW, by firing rifles at Israel. It would seem that in an analogous contest fish in a barrel stand a better chance of defending their territory.[28]

Although HRW deplored Hezbollah rockets for being indiscriminate, it also reported that the IDF found complex "range cards" prepared by Hezbollah containing the "precise coordinates of various locations within Israel and the formulas for aiming" rockets (and mortar shells) at them. The fact that one location was designated "Cultural Center, northern Nahariya"[29] apparently attests to the potential for a fine degree of targeting. In addition, to justify its indictment of Hezbollah for deliberately targeting civilian objects, HRW itself provided ample evidence that these rockets *were* able to discriminate between targets. It cited multiple instances of deliberate Hezbollah targeting, such as "the fact that the same hospital [in Mazra] was struck twice on consecutive days suggests that the first strike was no accident," and "the hit on the hospital [in Nahariya] looks intentional when viewed in the context of the many near-misses during the war."[30] At this point it is no longer clear whether HRW was condemning Hezbollah's rockets for deliberate or indiscriminate attacks on civilians/civilian objects, or both simultaneously.

For its part Hezbollah claimed "both the preference and the technical means to direct its fire at military targets," its rockets purportedly having a margin of error of "less than 50 meters."[31] How true this is, it cannot be said.[32] HRW noted that it was barred by Israel from visiting Israeli military sites attacked by Hezbollah, and as a result, it could not ascertain how many Hezbollah rockets hit military targets "or how the number of such attacks compares with the number of rockets that hit civilian areas."[33]

Still, HRW concluded that there can be "no doubt that Hezbollah deliberately or indiscriminately fired rockets at civilians much of the time."[34] The most precise relevant data HRW cited, however, arguably do not sustain this contention. According to Israeli officials quoted by HRW, Hezbollah fired "3,917 rockets, of which 23 percent landed within 'built-up areas,'" while other Israeli sources reported that "of the 4,000-4,500 rockets fired [by Hezbollah], about 900 hit built-up areas, i.e., villages, towns and cities; the remainder landed in 'open areas.'"[35] "23 percent" might be said to constitute a relatively small amount, not "much." In fact, the most revealing conclusion, which HRW ignores, is that Hezbollah rockets overwhelmingly did *not* hit built-up areas in Israel although they indisputably could have been hit if Hezbollah had targeted the heart of these areas.

The results of an exhaustive study by the Arab Association for Human Rights in Israel also undercut HRW's conclusion insofar as it suggested that Hezbollah rocket attacks frequently targeted civilians:

> [The Israeli] Arab towns and villages that suffered the most intensive attacks during the war were the ones that were surrounded by military installations, either on a permanent basis or temporarily during the course of the war. These installations are located at a distance of just 0.5-2 kilometers by air from the civilian community; in some cases the installations

are located inside the town or village. Such short distances are within the margin of error of the rockets fired by Hezbollah. During the war, artillery was launched at Lebanon from many of these installations, and particularly from the temporary installations.

...

Hezbollah declared on several occasions that it was targeting its rockets primarily at military installations inside Israel. Given the findings of the study . . ., there is no reason to doubt that the Arab towns and villages were hit due to their proximity to the adjacent military installations. . . . This assumption is reinforced by the fact that Arab communities that were not surrounded by military installations, including villages close to Israel's northern border, were not hit by rockets, or suffered a lesser degree of damage. Conversely, communities that were surrounded by military installations were hit by rockets, even when these communities were further removed from the Israeli-Lebanese border.[36]

If, as Hezbollah alleged, it fired 8,000 rockets in the course of the war (Israel claimed the actual figure was half as many), and these rockets mostly targeted and hit military sites,[37] it might account for the relatively small number of civilian Israeli casualties. What is indisputable, however, is that HRW's analysis is riddled with apparent contradictions as well as dubious conclusions.

HRW got so carried away in its indictment of Hezbollah that it devoted fully eight pages to tracing the source of Hezbollah's weapons back to Iran and Syria.[38] In its reports HRW has routinely included among its recommendations that countries supplying weapons to violators of the laws of war should cease doing so. But in the case of Hezbollah, HRW inexplicably broadened its mandate to include enforcement of U.N. resolutions calling for the "disarmament of all Lebanese and non-Lebanese militias." It manifestly wanted Hezbollah to be rendered weaponless but, however much such a preference will have resonated with (and placated) its critics, this would appear to be none of HRW's business, while the interjection of it suggests the existence of a political agenda behind the report. If HRW has decided henceforth to incorporate enforcement of U.N. resolutions in its mandate, it is not difficult to think of another country whose routine breach of them HRW should also consider monitoring.

TARGETING CIVILIANS: On 16 July 2006 Hezbollah leader Sayyed Hassan Nasrallah declared that Hezbollah would abandon its undertaking during the conflict's first few days to spare Israeli civilians because, in HRW's paraphrase of him, "it had no other means to compel Israel to cease its attacks on Lebanese civilians."[39] HRW condemned Hezbollah both for a serious violation of the laws of war and for disingenuously justifying these attacks directed at civilians. Neither of HRW's accusations, however, withstands close scrutiny.

HRW asserted that targeting an enemy's civilians in response to attacks on one's own civilians—the technical term being *belligerent reprisals*—is "never permitted" under international law.[40] To support its assertion HRW referred readers to the International Committee of the Red Cross's standard reference work *Customary International Humanitarian Law*. Turning to the cited pages, however, we find that the manual reads: "it is difficult to conclude that there has yet crystallized a customary rule specifically prohibiting reprisals against civilians during the conduct of hostilities." The ICRC opinion reflects the broad consensus among authorities in the field.[41] The point at issue is not the morality of such reprisals but their standing under international law. Although it would surely be difficult to justify ethically belligerent reprisals against civilians,[42] the fact remains that, in this condemnation of Hezbollah, HRW misrepresented international law. (To be sure, in the past HRW also condemned Israel for belligerent reprisals against civilians.[43])

Moreover, it would appear that in the eyes of HRW whatever Hezbollah did was multitudinously illegal. Thus, each statement of Hezbollah that it would target civilians so long as Israel persisted in doing so constituted, according to HRW, not only evidence of criminal intent but also intent "to spread terror," which would also "violate international law, even if the attack is never carried out."[44] To illustrate such intent HRW cited the statement of Nasrallah, "If you bomb our capital Beirut, we will bomb the capital of your usurping entity." It is unclear how this statement in and of itself reveals intention to spread terror and is not, however regrettable, simply a flat declaration of Hezbollah's policy of belligerent reprisals. By contrast HRW found no fault with Israeli leaflets ordering 500,000 south Lebanese to flee their homes and communities as a prelude to Israel flattening the area, apart from the fact that these leaflets were "too general to be helpful and did not provide specific instructions or a time-frame for civilians."[45]

HRW dismissed as "not credible" Nasrallah's assertion on 16 July that prior to that date "we aimed our rocket firing toward military sites only," and that Hezbollah would resort to the extreme measure of targeting civilian objects only "as long as the enemy undertakes its aggression without limits or red lines."[46] To disprove the Hezbollah leader HRW cited a Hezbollah communiqué listing civilian Israeli communities targeted on 18 July, two days *after* Nasrallah's statement.[47] A U.N. Mission to Lebanon and Israel, although also alleging that belligerent reprisals against civilians are illegal, still acknowledged that "Hezbollah's actual conduct was consistent with Nasrallah's public statements" that the rocket attacks were retaliatory.[48] His verbal declarations of tit-for-tat reprisals also echoed Hezbollah's past practice—as HRW had itself shown,[49] and Israeli officials themselves conceded[50]—while HRW adduced no evidence that Hezbollah was targeting Israeli civilians before 16 July.[51] Moreover, Hezbollah clearly relished the prospect of ground combat with the IDF whereas Israel clearly hoped to inflict such massive suffering on the civilian population that it and the government would turn against Hezbollah.[52] (In this respect Israel also acted in conformity with past practice—again, as HRW had shown.[53]) It is also unclear why Nasrallah would freely acknowledge a policy of targeting civilians yet prevaricate about his willingness to desist if Israel reciprocated.

HRW defined the war crime of "human shielding" as the intentional use of civilians to deter an enemy from attack.[54] One critical legal burden of course is to prove intentionality. HRW reported that "throughout the north" of Israel, "fixed military facilities, such as IDF bases, are located next to or in the midst of civilian settlements"; for example, "the Israeli navy has a major training base on the Haifa waterfront, across the street from Rambam Hospital and adjacent to Bat Galim, a neighborhood of low-rise apartment buildings."[55] In addition, "the IDF fired artillery into Lebanon from locations quite near to residential communities."[56] It is also to be noted that Israeli "Arabs in several Galilee towns and villages . . . have protested against the construction or expansion of IDF and defense industry facilities in their immediate vicinity."[57]

Despite the plethora of circumstantial evidence, HRW still gave Israel a clean bill of health on the matter of human shielding: "We found no evidence that Israeli authorities or the IDF intended to use civilians . . . in this fashion."[58] It only posed the possibility ("the question remains") that Israel might have violated the norm in international law of taking all "feasible precautions" not to locate military objects nearby civilians.[59] Yet, although reserving judgment on the specific question of human shielding, the exhaustive study of the Arab Association for Human Rights in Israel did reach the definite conclusion that, having located "military installations close to civilian centers" and thereby "endangered the Arab civilian population and exposed it to the danger that rockets would hit these communities," Israel "violated the specific obligation imposed by international humanitarian law to refrain from locating military installations within or close to civilian centers."[60]

In *Why They Died*, HRW accused Israel of "frequent failure . . . to distinguish between military targets, which can be legitimately attacked, and civilians, who are not subject to attack," and consequently of "reckless indifference to the fate of Lebanese civilians" that "violated the laws of war."[61] Although classifying these attacks as "serious violations of the laws of war,"[62] HRW stopped short of accusing Israel of war crimes. It asserted instead that the indiscriminate killing of Lebanese civilians and massive destruction of Lebanese civilian objects was not intentional but "apparently" the result of "erroneous assumptions." There appears to be an unbridgeable chasm, however, between the incriminating evidence assembled by HRW and its extenuating conclusion.

INCRIMINATING EVIDENCE: "During the vast majority of the deadly air strikes we investigated," HRW reported, "we found no evidence of Hezbollah military presence, weaponry or any other military objective that would have justified the strike," and "in many instances there was no apparent military objective in villages hit by Israeli attacks." In those instances where military targets were in the vicinity HRW concluded that Israeli attacks frequently inflicted disproportionate harm on the civilian population.[63]

Judging by the evidence HRW accumulated of Israel's attacks on Lebanese civilian targets, it might be inferred that Israel deliberately targeted them. When evaluating Hezbollah's conduct in *Civilians Under Assault*, HRW asserted that the absence of evidence of "a legitimate military target in the vicinity" of an attack on civilians should be construed as "suggesting it was a deliberate attack on civilians."[64] Insofar as HRW documented case after grisly case in which there was no Hezbollah activity or military target in the vicinity of a lethal Israeli attack on civilians/civilian objects,[65] the evidence suggests, using the standard HRW itself applied to Hezbollah, that Israel was culpable of repeatedly targeting civilians. Indeed, on this basis (and related ones) an authoritative U.N. Commission of Inquiry concluded that in numerous incidents it investigated Israel "must have known" it was attacking, or "deliberately" and with "clear intent" attacked, or "targeted" and "directly aimed at" civilians/civilian objects.[66] HRW itself asserted that Israel targeted "a large number of private homes of civilian Hezbollah members . . . as well as a variety of civilian Hezbollah institutions such as schools, welfare agencies, banks, shops, and political offices," and that it targeted "densely populated... multi-story residential apartment buildings in areas considered supportive of Hezbollah."[67]

It might also be noted that on the basis of HRW's own analysis the *prima facie* case that Israel deliberately targeted civilians is much stronger than the *prima facie* case that Hezbollah deliberately targeted them: Hezbollah used, according to HRW, low-tech weapons that could not discriminate between civilian and military targets, and therefore were incapable of deliberately targeting civilians, whereas Israel used high-tech weapons that could discriminate between civilian and military targets yet repeatedly hit civilian targets even when no military targets were in the vicinity.[68]

Nonetheless HRW concluded that "strong evidence" existed that Hezbollah committed war crimes, whereas it found no evidence that Israel deliberately targeted civilians and reserved judgment on whether Israel committed war crimes. How can this be?

EXTENUATING CONCLUSION: The apparent reason HRW did not accuse Israel of war crimes is that Israeli attacks on Lebanese civilian targets resulted from a colossal misunderstanding: Israel erroneously assumed that these were legitimate military targets. HRW repeated this argument ad nauseam, subsuming entire sections of *Why They Died* under it:

> Israel assumed that all Lebanese civilians had observed its warning to evacuate villages south of the Litani River, and thus that anyone who remained was a combatant. Reflecting that assumption, it labeled any visible person, or movement of persons or vehicles... as a Hezbollah military operation which could be targeted;[69]

> Throughout the conflict, Israeli warplanes targeted civilian vehicles on roads and homes, apparently assuming them to be Hezbollah military movements;[70]

6/ HUMAN RIGHTS REVISIONISM 137

The chief cause of this wrongful and deadly selection of targets was Israel's assumption that Lebanese civilians had observed its warnings to evacuate all villages south of the Litani River, and thus that no civilians remained there;[71]

Israel's False Presumption of No Civilian Presence and Ineffective Warnings to Evacuate, With Resultant Indiscriminate Bombardment and Indiscriminate Targeting of All Visible Persons or Vehicles in Southern Lebanon or the Beka' Valley as "Hezbollah" [section heading];[72]

Israeli officials often justified their extensive bombardment of southern Lebanon by advancing the erroneous assumptions that (i) all civilians had fled the areas under attack and (ii) only Hezbollah members or their supporters remained in the south and therefore anyone who remained was a legitimate military target;[73]

Israel's assumption that the civilian population had emptied southern Lebanon is especially problematic because Israel's warnings were often ineffective;[74]

Coupled with its wrongful assumption that southern Lebanon had been emptied of its civilian population, the Israeli military also seems to have determined that any vehicular or personal movement in southern Lebanon could be considered the movement of Hezbollah forces, and often targeted vehicles and other movements of persons on that basis;[75]

Attacks on Presumed Hezbollah Targets and Inadequate Precautions [section heading];[76]

> Inadequate Precautions in Attacking Presumed Hezbollah Targets [section heading];[77]
>
> Despite destroying or damaging tens of thousands of homes during its bombing campaign, many of them in precision-guided strikes against presumed Hezbollah targets, Israel failed to kill a single national Hezbollah leader and was unable to destroy or neutralize Hezbollah forces;[78]
>
> Particularly at the beginning of the war, Israel used hundreds of precision-guided bombs to demolish homes where Israeli intelligence must have indicated a Hezbollah target. However, in the vast majority of these cases, Israeli intelligence was plainly wrong: the buildings targeted had no Hezbollah presence or links inside.... This pattern of precision-guided strikes on civilian homes would continue throughout the war, indicating that Israeli intelligence on Hezbollah targets was severely flawed, that the IDF took insufficient action to address the problem, or that the IDF simply stopped caring about civilian casualties after it issued warnings to the civilians to evacuate and wrongfully assumed that those who remained behind were all Hezbollah militants.[79]

Thus HRW artfully reconciled "pinpoint strikes on suspected Hezbollah members' homes and weapons stores" with the singularly odd result that "only civilians" were killed.[80]

However, right after absolving Israel of intentionality and consequently war crimes, HRW conceded that "it is questionable whether Israeli officials really believed the assumption that there were no Lebanese civilians left in southern Lebanon, or simply announced this to defend their actions. Certainly, there is evidence to suggest that Israeli officials knew that their assumption was erroneous."[81] HRW itself cited plentiful evidence that Israel's official pronouncements were purely propagandistic and unlikely to be credited by anyone except the professional hack or willful dupe:

> At the time of the Israeli attacks in southern Lebanon, stories about Lebanese civilians dying in Israeli strikes or trapped in southern Lebanon filled the Israeli and international media. In addition, foreign embassies were in regular contact with Israeli diplomats to request assistance with the evacuation of their nationals caught in the fighting in the south. And in some instances, Israel seemed to know exactly how many people remained in a village.... In addition, Israel must have known from its past conflicts in southern Lebanon that a civilian population is rarely willing or able to leave its homes according to timetables laid down by a belligerent military force.... Israel should have known that significant numbers of civilians would remain in their villages throughout the war.[82]

Furthermore HRW pointed to statements by "Israeli government officials and military leaders" demonstrating that "Israeli forces intentionally blurred the distinction between civilian and combatant," and it concluded from these statements that "Israel's claim that it only attacked military targets rings hollow."[83] It also cited the finding of a postwar IDF internal intelligence investigation that Israel had exhausted its list of potential Hezbollah targets by the fifth day of the war and that subsequently many targets were "created out of nothing."[84] Were any doubts still to linger that Israel's indiscriminate and disproportionate as well as deliberate attacks on civilian targets sprang from official policy, HRW itself cited the statements of Israeli military leaders that they were targeting residential apartment buildings in Beirut.[85] It might finally be noted that of the nearly half of the Lebanese civilian casualties of whom HRW was able to confirm the gender and age, fully sixty percent were women and children and accordingly impossible to confuse with Hezbollah militants.[86]

Although HRW's own findings showed that Israel's attacks on Lebanese civilians and civilian objects were indiscriminate and disproportionate; and although its own findings showed that Israel deliberately targeted civilians and civilian objects; and although its own findings showed that Israel's public avowals of ignorance were not credible; and although it cited the statements of Israeli military leaders proclaiming the intention to target civilians and civilian objects; and although the majority of Lebanese civilian casualties could not possibly have been mistaken for Hezbollah militants—although it had assembled this cumulatively devastating brief, nonetheless HRW refrained from condemning Israel for war crimes. Instead it limited itself to generic, conditional propositions:

> Insofar as the attack is launched knowing that the target should be treated as a civilian under international humanitarian law, those responsible would have committed a war crime;[87]

> To the extent such attacks were conducted with knowledge or reckless indifference to the civilian nature of those being attacked, then those who ordered these attacks would have the criminal intent needed for the commission of war crimes.... And to the extent that senior commanders or officials knew or should have known that war crimes were being committed, and were in a position of authority to stop the attacks or punish those responsible and did not do so, they would be responsible for war crimes as a matter of command responsibility.[88]

The closest HRW came to accusing Israel of war crimes was in the context of documenting Israel's indiscriminate bombing of a civilian neighborhood in Beirut, on the one hand, and the declared intention of senior Israeli military officials to target this neighborhood, on the other. HRW wrote: "Statements by Israeli officials strongly suggest that in launching its massive attacks in southern Beirut, the IDF did not limit itself to Hezbollah military targets, as required by the laws of war. Such statements when by persons in the chain of command may be evidence of criminal intent necessary for demonstrating the commission of a war crime."[89] It will be noticed that in the comparable case of Hezbollah, HRW had no difficulty connecting the dots between explicit statements and consequent actions in order to find that war crimes had been committed.

In another revealing example HRW documented that Israel was targeting clearly marked Lebanese ambulances with missile fire, although "there is no basis for concluding that Hezbollah was making use of the ambulances for a military purpose, and Human Rights Watch is not aware of any allegations by the IDF or in the media that Lebanese ambulances were misused for military purposes during the 2006 war."[90] The corresponding footnote read: "Anyone responsible for deliberately making an ambulance the object of attack would be committing a war crime." Anyone, it seems, except an Israeli: even in this instance HRW did not directly accuse Israel of committing a war crime.

If HRW failed to condemn Israel for war crimes, the reason would appear to be not a lack of evidence but lack of a consistent evidentiary and legal standard.

Throughout the war Israel blamed Lebanon's loss of life and devastation on the Hezbollah tactic of firing from civilian areas.[91] HRW's findings overwhelmingly disputed this alibi:

> On some occasions . . . Hezbollah fired rockets from within populated areas, allowed its combatants to mix with the Lebanese civilian population, or stored weapons in populated civilian areas in ways that violated international humanitarian law. Such violations, however, were not widespread: we found strong evidence that Hezbollah stored most of its rockets in bunkers

and weapon storage facilities located in uninhabited fields and valleys, that in the vast majority of cases Hezbollah fighters left populated civilian areas as soon as the fighting started, and that Hezbollah fired the vast majority of its rockets from pre-prepared positions outside villages.[92]

And again, "in all but a few of the cases of civilian deaths we investigated, Hezbollah fighters had not mixed with the civilian population or taken other actions to contribute to the targeting of a particular home or vehicle by Israeli forces."[93] HRW further reported that "Israel's own firing patterns in Lebanon support the conclusion that Hezbollah fired large numbers of its rockets from tobacco fields, banana, olive and citrus groves, and more remote, unpopulated valleys."[94]

However, in contrast with its original *Fatal Strikes* report, which had found "no cases" of Hezbollah deliberately using civilians "as shields to protect them from retaliatory IDF attack," HRW now concluded that in a "handful of cases" it was "probable"[95] that Hezbollah did not just fail to take every feasible precaution to protect civilians from attack, but made use of "human shields."[96] It will be recalled that human shielding, which constitutes a "war crime" under international law, is the intentional use of civilians to deter an enemy attack. According to HRW a paradigmatic case was Iraqi forces during the 2003 war "confronting coalition forces with women and children as human shields, lining up women and children in front of their vehicles to prevent coalition forces from attacking them, and placing women and children on their vehicles when attacking coalition positions."[97] HRW's example illustrates a pair of features that are likely to be shared by any genuine cases of human shielding:

- The belligerent is *visibly* interposing civilians to deter an attack. If the belligerent conscientiously seeks to make its presence *un*known among civilians, it is manifestly not using civilians for the purpose of deterring an attack on it;

- The belligerent interposes civilians *likely* to deter an attack. If the enemy has a known record of callous disregard for civilians, it manifestly cannot be inferred from the belligerent firing from behind civilians that they were being used for the purpose of deterring an attack.

Consider now the evidence HRW adduced of Hezbollah's probable use of human shields:

(A) *Hezbollah hid weapons in civilian areas.* HRW reported that Hezbollah militants allegedly placed themselves and weapons that they "covered ... with sheets" in an occupied civilian bomb shelter, which "suggests an intent to use civilians as a shield against attack."[98] Yet, doesn't the concealment of the weapons signal that Hezbollah did not intend for Israel to know of their existence and that consequently Hezbollah could not have intended for the civilians among whom these weapons were stored to serve as human shields? Put otherwise, if Hezbollah did not want Israel to know the weapons were in the shelter, it could not have wanted to use the civilians as shields to prevent Israel from targeting them. It is also unclear why Hezbollah militants would have assumed that Israel knew their whereabouts if, according to HRW, Hezbollah's activities were "shrouded in secrecy," which "significantly affected Israel's ability to target Hezbollah from the air."[99]

In addition, the building in which this alleged weapons transfer took place was located in a pro-Hezbollah neighborhood of Beirut (Dahiya), which Lebanese expected to be bombed regardless of its civilian residents and which in fact was bombed, and "Hezbollah fighters and officials evacuated their offices as soon as the conflict began and often warned other occupants in the same building to also evacuate."[100] It would surely be peculiar if Hezbollah intended civilians almost certainly targeted for attack to serve as human shields, and if Hezbollah intended for these civilians to serve as human shields yet planned to and did in fact evacuate the building before the civilians could serve this intended purpose.

(B) *Hezbollah launched rockets in the vicinity of United Nations outposts.* Although acknowledging that "U.N. outposts tended to [be] located on the top of hills, which also happen to be good positions from Hezbollah's military perspective to fire at Israel," and that Israel fired on U.N. outposts with reckless abandon even when no Hezbollah fighters were in their vicinity,[101] HRW still speculated that Hezbollah "chose those locations to launch attacks because the proximity of U.N. personnel would make counterattack difficult."[102] It might be noticed that although Israel located many military objects in the near vicinity of Arab villages in Israel, HRW drew no inference that Israel intentionally used these Arabs as human shields against an attack from Hezbollah, but HRW automatically inferred from Hezbollah's firing adjacent to U.N. observers that Hezbollah was likely using the U.N. personnel as human shields.

The U.N. Commission of Inquiry persuasively maintained that on thirty occasions Israel launched "direct attacks" on U.N. outposts with "no justification," causing multiple injuries and deaths,[103] while on six occasions Hezbollah also aimed "direct fire" at these U.N. outposts, and on 62 occasions "fired their rockets from the close proximity of United Nations positions towards Israel ... using the United Nations positions as shields for the launching of their attacks."[104] However, although scathing in its criticism of Hezbollah (and Israel),[105] the Commission "found no evidence regarding the use of 'human shields' by Hezbollah."[106] HRW did not produce a particle of evidence to dispute this finding of the Commission, which was also HRW's original finding in *Fatal Strikes*.

Shortly after the first anniversary of the 2006 war HRW organized a news conference in Beirut to mark the release of its report *Civilians Under*

6/ HUMAN RIGHTS REVISIONISM

Assault. Lebanese of all political stripes expressed outrage, forcing the conference's cancellation. It is cause for perplexity why HRW did not also call a news conference at Ground Zero on the first anniversary of September 11 to condemn the U.S. for war crimes in Afghanistan. The outside observer gets the distinct impression that HRW was grandstanding to prove its impartiality by provoking a hostile reaction from Lebanese after having come under attack from Israel and its apologists. HRW was apparently of the opinion that if one got attacked by the flat-Earthers at one extreme and the round-Earthers at the other, then it proved that the oblong-Earthers must be telling the truth.

After cancellation of the news conference HRW denounced Hezbollah for orchestrating a smear campaign and denied that it had been "taking sides" in its reports. "The fairness and accuracy of our reporting will speak for themselves," it declared, "whether we hold a press conference or not."[107] Indeed, the fairness and accuracy of HRW's reportage on the 2006 Lebanon war spoke loud and clear.

In February 2008 HRW issued a separate report entitled *Flooding South Lebanon: Israel's use of cluster munitions in Lebanon in July and August 2006*. The report found that Israel dropped as many as 4.6 million cluster submunitions on south Lebanon during the war.[108] It was the "most extensive use of cluster munitions anywhere in the world since the 1991 Gulf war," while relative to the size of the targeted area the density of the attack was historically unprecedented.[109] (Apparently the only reason Israel did not drop yet more cluster munitions was that its stocks had been depleted.[110]) Some 90 percent of these cluster munitions were dropped "during the final three days when Israel knew a settlement was imminent," the U.N. ceasefire resolution having already been passed but not yet gone into effect.[111]

Although finding that Israel committed "extensive violations" of the laws of war,[112] HRW did not go beyond stating that Israel's massive resort to cluster munitions was "in some locations possibly a war crime."[113] HRW reached this minimalist legal conclusion, however, by deploying a double standard in its application of international law and ignoring its own evidence.

Israel's cluster munition attacks on Lebanon were indiscriminate in multiple respects: the inaccuracy of their delivery (or carrier) systems; the "wide dispersal patterns" of such weapons; and the "high dud rates" endangering civilians returning to their homes after the ceasefire.[114] In addition, the saturation use of these weapons in civilian areas multiplied manyfold the inherent dangers posed by them.

INDISCRIMINATE DELIVERY SYSTEM: According to HRW, "none of the cluster munition carriers used by Israel was precision-guided. Only a small number of carriers had any type of guidance mechanism."[115] It should immediately be noticed that HRW accused Hezbollah of war crimes because the rockets it fired at populated settings were "unguided" weapons that could not be aimed "with enough accuracy to target a particular building or artillery mount." Yet the artillery projectiles Israel used to deliver cluster munitions to populated settings were also unguided and could not target a particular building or artillery mount,[116] while the rockets Israel used to deliver cluster munitions were "known to be very inaccurate" and "to compensate for the rockets' imprecision, the order was to 'flood' the area with them."[117] It is unclear why on this basis alone HRW did not also accuse Israel of committing war crimes.

INDISCRIMINATE WEAPON: Apart from the indiscriminate delivery system the cluster munitions themselves are indiscriminate weapons in a double sense: "During strikes they endanger civilians because they blanket a broad area, and when they are used in or near populated areas, civilian casualties are virtually guaranteed"; "They also threaten civilians after conflict because they leave high numbers of hazardous submunitions that have failed to explode on impact as designed—known as duds—which can easily be set off by unwitting persons."[118] The "failure rate for many of Israel's submunitions appear to have averaged 25 percent," which means that as many as one million duds were left behind.[119]

INDISCRIMINATE USE OF WEAPON: Israel's resort to cluster munitions was also indiscriminate by virtue of the sheer density of their use. HRW reported that Israel's cluster attacks "blanketed" both "built-up areas" and "fields," resulting in the "high saturation of towns and villages," and the "systematic 'flooding' of certain villages and populated areas." One Israeli soldier quoted by HRW said, "In the last 72 hours we fired all the munitions we had, all at the same spot, we didn't even alter the direction of the gun."[120]

The HRW report described in vivid detail the macabre scenes that ensued. The "vast majority" of cluster munitions targeted "population centers" such as towns and villages.[121] In the village of Yohmor, "Bomblets littered the ground from one end ... to the other. They were on the roofs of all the houses, in gardens and spread across roads and paths. Some were even found inside houses."[122] In the village of Zwtar al-Sharkiyeh deminers had to remove "2,000-3,000 submunitions" inundating a primary school and its environs, although "Hezbollah had not used the school at any time during the war and there had been no Hezbollah forces anywhere in the town."[123]

Meanwhile, according to a "very conservative" estimate, "submunitions contaminated at least 26 percent of south Lebanon's agricultural land," transforming olive and citrus groves and tobacco fields into "*de facto* minefields." Many fields were simply "abandoned," while desperate farmers continued to work others despite the lethal hazards.[124] From the ceasefire until December 2009 the explosion of duds caused 227 civilian casualties, of whom 35 percent were children.[125]

HRW further reported that "perhaps the biggest challenge" facing demining groups "has been Israel's refusal to provide information about its cluster munition strikes."[126] Although documenting Israel's possession of the crucial information and its simple transferability, HRW never posed the obvious question, *Why did Israel refuse?* Perhaps HRW preferred to evade the equally obvious answer: the postwar civilian deaths from cluster munitions were intentional, making them war crimes, a topic to which we now turn. Before doing so, however, it deserves notice that Israel's refusal to provide the information should itself be seen as a violation of the laws of war, according to which "All feasible precautions must be taken to avoid, and in any event to minimise, incidental loss of civilian life, injury to civilians and damage to civilian objects."[127]

According to HRW, individuals bear responsibility for "war crimes" if they "intentionally or recklessly" authorize or conduct attacks "that would indiscriminately or disproportionately harm civilians." In other iterations HRW defines war crimes as attacks that are "knowingly or recklessly indiscriminate or deliberate"; the "knowing or reckless disregard for the foreseeable effects on civilians and other protected objects"; "deliberate attacks on civilians, as well as indiscriminate or disproportionate attacks when committed with knowledge or reckless indifference to their illegal character"; and "indiscriminately or deliberately" attacking a civilian object "without military justification and with criminal intent."[128] HRW also cited with approval the Israeli legal authority Yoram Dinstein who, as already noted, asserted that under international law "there is no genuine difference between a premeditated attack against civilians (or civilian objects) and a reckless disregard of the principle of distinction" between civilians (or civilian objects) and combatants (or military objects): "they are equally forbidden."[129]

It might be useful for the purposes of this exposition to elucidate further the meaning of "intentional" and "deliberate." In the first place, it should be recalled that, when scrutinizing Hezbollah, HRW stated that the absence of "a legitimate military target in the vicinity" of an attack on civilians should be construed as "a deliberate attack on civilians."

In addition, it merits recalling the International Court of Justice's *Advisory Opinion on the Legality of the Threat or Use of Nuclear Weapons*, which addressed the qualitatively (if clearly not quantitatively) comparable issue of a mega indiscriminate and disproportionate attack having lethal aftereffects.[130] In their respective dissenting opinions, Judge Rosalyn Higgins noted the "legal doctrine of foreseeability, by which one is assumed to intend the consequences of one's actions," and Judge Christopher Weeramantry noted "the well-known legal principle that the doer of an act must be taken

6/ HUMAN RIGHTS REVISIONISM

to have *intended* its natural and foreseeable consequences" (his emphasis).[131] Thus, because a breach of the laws of war such as an indiscriminate or disproportionate attack inevitably and predictably causes civilian suffering and death, it can and should be reckoned deliberate and intentional.

Consider now HRW's description of the Israeli cluster attacks on Lebanon:

> By their nature, these dangerous, volatile submunitions [i.e., the duds] cannot distinguish between combatants and noncombatants, foreseeably endangering civilians for months or years to come;[132]

> It is inconceivable that Israel ... did not know that ... its strikes would have a lasting humanitarian impact;[133]

> Many of the cluster attacks on populated areas do not appear to have had a definite military target. Our researchers ... found only one village with clear evidence of the presence of Hezbollah forces out of the more than 40 towns and villages they visited;[134]

> The staggering number of cluster munitions rained on south Lebanon over the three days immediately before a negotiated ceasefire went into effect puts in doubt the claim by the IDF that its attacks were aimed at specific targets or even strategic locations, as opposed to being efforts to blanket large areas with explosives and duds;[135]

> Cluster munition attacks on or near population centers, like those launched by Israel, give rise to a presumption that they are indiscriminate, as the weapons are highly imprecise with

a large area effect that regularly causes foreseeable and excessive civilian casualties during strikes and afterwards;[136]

Given the extremely large number of submunitions employed and their known failure rates, harm to remaining and returning civilians was entirely foreseeable;[137]

Israel was well aware of the continuing harm to Lebanese civilians from the unexploded duds that remained from its prior use of munitions in South Lebanon in 1978 and 1982;[138]

The paucity of evidence of specific military objectives, the known dangers of cluster munitions, the timing of large scale attacks days before an anticipated ceasefire, and the massive scope of the attacks combine to point to a conclusion that the attacks were of an indiscriminate and disproportionate character;[139]

A senior UN demining official said he had "no doubt" that Israel had deliberately hit built-up areas with cluster munitions, stating "these cluster bombs were dropped in the middle of villages";[140]

Israeli soldiers were well aware of the large numbers of duds their cluster strikes were producing. A soldier said that his . . . commander gave a "pep talk" after a period of heavy fire, saying, "just wait until Hezbollah finds the little presents we had left them";[141]

Given the sheer number of cluster duds on the ground, casualties are unavoidable;[142]

In south Lebanon in 2006, Israel employed a means of warfare that was likely to cause significant harm to civilians—unreliable and inaccurate submunitions used widely and heavily in populated areas. Despite ample past experience of the deadly effects of cluster duds on the civilian population of south Lebanon, awareness of the impending end of the war, and the knowledge that there would be a legacy of unexploded duds creating de facto minefields, the IDF did not refrain from launching these attacks.... The post-ceasefire casualties have to our knowledge all been civilians or deminers, and civilian access to agricultural areas and property has been severely affected. The aftereffects of Israel's cluster strikes were foreseeable by the IDF;[143]

The paucity of evidence of specific military objectives, the known dangers of cluster munitions, the time of large-scale attacks days before an anticipated ceasefire, and the massive scope of the attacks themselves lead to the conclusion that the attacks were of an indiscriminate and disproportionate character;[144]

We found scant evidence that would demonstrate a concrete and direct military advantage with relation to any other possible military objectives, such as attacking fighters, rocket launchers, or strategic locales;[145]

When considering the foreseeable civilian damage that could ensue, the anticipated and soon-approaching end to the armed conflict weighs heavily against Israel's last-minute massive saturation of civilian areas with old cluster stockpiles.... The fact that duds would turn civilian areas into de facto minefields, given the extremely large number of submunitions employed and their known failure rates, was foreseeable—testimony from soldiers (and the reported IDF prohibition of firing cluster munitions into areas it would subsequently enter) indicate that the IDF knew this;[146]

Israel's use of cluster munitions in south Lebanon in 2006 was characterized by extensive and intensive attacks across civilian areas and swaths of territory, leaving an extremely high number of duds that are creating foreseeable deaths and injuries to civilians.[147]

A composite distillation of these HRW statements would read: just before an agreed-upon ceasefire Israel saturated Lebanese civilian areas having no military targets with cluster munitions; the inevitable and foreseeable—in fact foreseen—consequence was that many Lebanese civilians were injured and killed. Nonetheless HRW did not go beyond concluding that Israel's cluster attacks constituted "in some locations possibly a war crime."[148]

In the case of Hezbollah, HRW found that the evidence "leaves no doubt that Hezbollah deliberately or indiscriminately fired rockets at civilians," and consequently that it committed (or such rocket attacks were "strong evidence" of) war crimes. But didn't HRW's own evidence leave no doubt that Israel too deliberately or indiscriminately targeted civilians, and consequently that it too committed (or such cluster attacks were "strong evidence" of) war crimes?

Like HRW, the U.N. Commission of Inquiry found that Israeli cluster attacks were "indiscriminate . . . many towns and villages were littered with the bomblets as well as large tracts of agricultural land," and that "the use of cluster munitions by [the] IDF was of no military advantage." Nonetheless HRW cast doubt on the finding of the Commission that "these weapons were used deliberately to turn large areas of fertile agricultural land into 'no go' areas for the civilian population." It asserted that the Commission "does not explicitly cite the evidence leading to its conclusion of 'deliberate' harm."[149] But HRW itself asserted that the absence of "a legitimate military target in the vicinity" of an attack should be construed as "a deliberate attack on civilians." If the Lebanese civilian areas overwhelmingly lacked military targets; and if a ceasefire was imminent; and if it was well known that the inevitable consequence of saturating civilian areas with cluster submunitions was massive harm to civilians—then how could one possibly conclude that the harm to civilians was not deliberate? Moreover, HRW itself relied on Dinstein's assertion that "there is no genuine difference" between a deliberate attack and an indiscriminate attack.

HRW twice quoted the commander of an Israeli cluster munitions unit saying, "What we did was insane and monstrous."[150] It quoted the U.N. humanitarian coordinator in Lebanon calling the Israeli attacks "outrageous" and the U.N. emergency coordinator calling them "completely immoral."[151] HRW itself deplored them as "shocking and unprecedented."[152]

"Insane and monstrous," "outrageous," "completely immoral," "shocking and unprecedented"—but, alas, HRW could not find "strong evidence" of Israeli war crimes. Incongruously, HRW executive director Kenneth Roth would later declare that, "if you look . . . at the investigation that Human Rights Watch did in southern Lebanon, we were very capable of deeply criticizing Israel and calling things war crimes when they were."[153]

In his dissenting opinion Judge Weeramantry took note of the irony that international law could condemn use of the "dum-dum" bullet yet the International Court of Justice recoiled at condemning use of nuclear weapons: "it would seem passing strange that the expansion within the body of a single soldier of a single bullet is an excessive cruelty which international law has been unable to tolerate since 1899; and that the incineration in one second of a hundred thousand civilians is not." He then goes on to observe:

> Every branch of knowledge benefits from a process of occasionally stepping back from itself and scrutinizing itself objectively

for anomalies and absurdities. If a glaring anomaly or absurdity becomes apparent and remains unquestioned, that discipline is in danger of being seen as floundering in the midst of its own technicalities.[154]

It might also seem passing strange that HRW could find "strong evidence" that Hezbollah committed war crimes by firing several thousand rockets at primarily military targets in Israel, yet after Israel dropped several million cluster submunitions on primarily civilian targets in Lebanon, causing dislocation, death, and contamination for decades to come, the most HRW could find was that in "some" places Israel "possibly" committed war crimes. It cannot be said, however, that the "anomalies and absurdities" in the report resulted from HRW's "floundering in . . . its own technicalities." Rather, they were a by-product of HRW's intentional misuse of legal technicalities in order to mitigate the political impact of its factual findings. However much it might protest otherwise, HRW caved in to a powerful and well-heeled lobby, and thereby set back the cause of truth and justice. Unforgivably, it validated the skepticism of those in the Middle East who question the objectivity of Western human rights organizations. Still, even in this egregious instance Israel and its "supporters" could not have found much solace in the finished product, containing, as it did, so many damning facts.

7/ MASTERS OF WAR

For a long time academic research on Israel's past was essentially a footnoted version of the heroic, official Zionist tale immortalized in Leon Uris's *Exodus*.¹ The political message of this scholarship was that Israel deserved unqualified support. A small body of historiography dissented from the prevailing wisdom but its impact on public discourse was negligible.

During the past couple of decades, however, a voluminous academic literature has accumulated debunking the *Exodus* mythology.² A broad scholarly consensus sharply critical of Israel has crystallized while the once-dissenting narrative, proving closer to the truth, has largely displaced the official Zionist one. Because much of the new "revisionist" history is already widely known, the focus here will be on a few salient points for illustrative purposes.

No aspect of the history of the Israel-Palestine conflict used to be more contentious than the origin of the Palestinian refugee problem. The standard account, put forth by Israeli officials and echoed in the scholarly literature, held that Palestinians fled during the 1948 war after Arab leaders had urged them via radio transmissions to clear the field for invading Arab armies.³

In fact already by the early 1960s Palestinian scholar Walid Khalidi and Irish scholar Erskine Childers, after sifting the archive of Arab broadcasts from the 1948 war, had concluded that no such official Arab exhortations had been issued.⁴ But revelations such as these had little or no impact on the broad public. Beginning in the late 1980s, however, Israeli academics such as Benny Morris concluded after scouring newly opened Israeli archives that the dominant Israeli narrative was false. Most scholars now concur that Palestinians suffered an ethnic cleansing in 1948, although debate continues on the secondary question of whether or not this ethnic cleansing was premeditated.[5]

A recent book by former Israeli foreign minister Shlomo Ben-Ami, who is by professional training a historian, shows just how narrow the historical controversy on the Palestinian refugees has become. The "reality on the ground" during the 1948 war, Ben-Ami writes in *Scars of War, Wounds of Peace*, was "an Arab community in a state of terror facing a ruthless Israeli army whose path to victory was paved not only by its exploits against the regular Arab armies, but also by the intimidation, and at times atrocities and massacres, it perpetrated against the civilian Arab community." Ben-Ami concludes that Israel premeditatedly expelled the Palestinians in accordance with the Zionist "philosophy of transfer" which, he says, "had a long pedigree in Zionist thought," framed David Ben-Gurion's "strategic-ideological" vision, and "provided a legitimate" framework "for commanders in the field actively to encourage the eviction of the local population." Thus, a former Israeli foreign minister situated himself at the pole of the scholarly spectrum most critical of past Israeli policy.[6]

Ben-Ami's conclusions on the Palestinian refugee question are of a piece with his other reflections on the theory of Zionism and the practice of Israel. Although epitomizing the new conventional wisdom among serious scholars, his statements on these topics would have been considered up until recently not just controversial but veritable heresies in American public life. For example Ben-Ami writes that Zionism was partly "a movement of conquest, colonization and settlement . . . that was forced to use the tools of colonial penetration"; that creating a Jewish state in Palestine "implicitly meant evicting and expelling" the indigenous Arab population; that in the "inherently Western-orientated inclination of Zionism . . . Israel could not, some also believed . . . should not, peacefully integrate within the Arab

Middle East"; that an "aspiration [Ben-Gurion] always had was to reshape the map of the Middle East in a way that would guarantee Israel's existence as a hegemonic regional power"; that "the endorsement of partition along the lines of Resolution 181 by Ben-Gurion [in 1947] was essentially a tactical move ... to gain time until the Jews were strong enough to fight the Arab majority"; that there was a "policy of creeping annexation of the West Bank that all the governments, right or left, subscribed to after 1967"; that after the June 1967 war "there was no Israeli peace initiative, and there was no credible and thoughtful response to the initiatives coming from others"; and that "A popular prejudice in Israel about the Arabs is that 'they only understand the language of force.' But this can just as well be said of the Israelis."[7]

If Ben-Ami illustrates how thoughtful Israeli officials have repudiated past mythologies, a juxtaposition of the outpourings of Harvard law professor Alan Dershowitz[8] against the findings of Israeli scholar Zeev Maoz (formerly head of the Jaffee Center for Strategic Studies at Tel Aviv University) illustrates the abyss separating popular apologetics from academic research. Table 1 compares what each has written on the various Arab-Israeli wars.

TABLE 1   ARAB-ISRAELI WARS: FICTION VERSUS FACT

	Dershowitz	Maoz
Balance of forces in Arab-Israeli wars	At great cost in human life ... the ragtag Israeli army defeated the invading Arab armies and the Palestinian attackers [in 1947-1948]. They won in large part because ... the stakes were much greater for them.	In each and every war—including the 1948 War of Independence—Israel enjoyed an overwhelming superiority in terms of both quantitative and qualitative capabilities to the Arab forces that actually confronted it. Israel was never the David in this conflict and the Arabs never played the role of the Goliath.

(continued)

TABLE 1 (continued)

	Dershowitz	Maoz
Origin of the 1956 "Sinai campaign"	On October 29, 1956, in a plan coordinated with Great Britain and France, Israel invaded the Sinai and easily captured it. Although the Suez Canal attack was in reaction to Egyptian provocation, the war ... was largely preventive in nature: It was designed to stop the Egyptians from exercising control over two international waterways and to keep the Egyptian Army from using the largest shipment of weapons it was scheduled to receive from the Soviet bloc.	This war was the result of the persistent drive of Ben-Gurion and [Moshe] Dayan to a second confrontation with the Arabs. The Sinai War was unavoidable because Israel sought every avenue to start a war.... [Gamal Abdel] Nasser helped Israel by providing it with both a strategic pretext (i.e., the Egyptian-Soviet weapons deal of September 1955) and a diplomatic pretext (i.e., the nationalization of the Suez Canal on July 26, 1956) that enabled the collusion with France and Britain. The aim of the war was none of the official reasons given by Israel. Rather, it had been the overthrow of Nasser and the rearrangement of the Middle East.
Origin of the June 1967 "Six-Day" war	Although Israel fired the first shots, virtually everyone recognizes that Egypt, Syria, and Jordan started the war.... After exhausting all diplomatic options and learning that Egypt was preparing an imminent attack..., the Israeli air force attacked.... Arab armies were massing along Israel's border poised to strike.... The only question was whether the Arab armies would be able to strike the first military blow.	Israel's policy had an important impact on the process that led to the Six Day War. Israeli misconduct during border conflict with Syria was to a large extent responsible for the process of escalation that evolved into the May-June 1967 crisis.... The IDF [Israel Defense Forces] command was not too worried about an Egyptian surprise attack.... Most observers seem to agree that Nasser did not want a war.

TABLE 1 (continued)

	Dershowitz	Maoz
Origin of the October 1973 "Yom Kippur" war	The unprovoked attack on Israel was unjustified.... No one disputes that the Egyptians and Syrians ... started the Yom Kippur War.	If there was an unnecessary and avoidable war in the Middle East, the Yom Kippur War was it. This is a prime example of where a little bit of diplomatic foresight and a little less political and military arrogance [by Israel] could have prevented the most severe war in the Middle East since 1948.
Origin of the June 1982 Lebanon invasion	[T]he large-scale long-term occupation of southern Lebanon [was] an effort to prevent terrorist attacks against [Israel's] northern towns and to end the Palestinian Liberation Organization (PLO) presence in Lebanon.... This war was different because it was almost entirely preventive rather than preemptive in nature, designed to strengthen Israel's position in the event of future attacks.[9]	[Menachem] Begin and [Ariel] Sharon ... relied on the Palestinian automatic response to Israeli provocations during the summer of 1981 and the winter and spring of 1982. Their hope was that the Palestinians would react to these provocations in a manner that would provide Israel with a diplomatic pretext to invade Lebanon. There is no question that the Lebanon War was a war of Israeli aggression. Israelis prefer to use the "war of choice" understatement, but the meaning and import of the term are just the same.... The Lebanon War was not really a war about Lebanon. It was part of a grand scheme aimed at creating a new order in the occupied territories designed to perpetuate Israeli occupation of the West Bank and Gaza by destroying the PLO.... The war in Lebanon was not about peace to the Galilee [i.e., northern Israel]. The Galilee was not under threat.... The evidence on PLO operations ... suggests that the PLO was exercising considerable restraint along the border.[10]

The central conclusions of Maoz's authoritative study, *Defending the Holy Land*, which itself is largely a synthesis of the full gamut of relevant monographic literature, also deserve lengthy quotation:

> Israel's war experience is a story of folly, recklessness, and self-made traps. None of the wars—with a possible exception of the 1948 War of Independence—was what Israel refers to as Milhemet Ein Brerah ("war of necessity"). They were all wars of choice or folly.
>
> Israel's decision-makers were as reluctant and risk averse when it came to making peace as they were daring and trigger happy when it came to making war.... [T]he official Israeli decision-makers typically did not initiate peace overtures; most of the peace initiatives in the Arab-Israeli conflict came either from the Arab world, from the international community, or from grass-roots and informal channels.... [W]hen Israel was willing to take risks for peace, these usually paid off. The Arabs generally showed a remarkable tendency for compliance with their treaty obligations. In quite a few cases, it was Israel—rather than the Arabs—that violated formal and informal agreements.[11]

It would be hard to exaggerate how radically these and other scholarly conclusions diverge from what has until recently constituted the conventional wisdom. The violent suppression of Palestinians, far from being an aberration, and Tel Aviv's diplomatic intransigence, far from being a reaction to past vulnerability, have now both been shown to spring from deep-seated tendencies in Israeli history.

Of all the milestones in Israeli history, the June 1967 war has probably played the most pivotal role in rationalizing Israel's current policy, from its refusal to withdraw from Palestinian land—"because the Arabs want to destroy Israel"—to its alleged right not to withdraw—"because the Arabs started the war." Despite—or because of—the fact that academic research has by now debunked these myths and the truth about the war is better known, Israel's most ardent apologists do all they can to keep alive the old David versus Goliath, Good versus Evil story in the public's mind. A book advertised in 2002 as the "most comprehensive history ever published" of the June war is a case in point.

Michael Oren's book, *Six Days of War: June 1967 and the making of the modern Middle East*,[12] enjoyed unusual commercial success in the United States. Although weighed down with nearly a hundred pages of endnotes and bibliography, it immediately leapt to the top of bestseller lists. The *New York Times* lavished unstinting praise on the book ("gripping," "fascinating," "staggering," "masterly," "engrossing," "fabulous," "thrilling," "powerful") in several reviews, while *Newsweek* reported that even President George W. Bush had been greatly influenced by it as he geared up for war against Iraq.[13]

Oren, an American-born Israeli historian, who since mid-2009 has served as the Israeli ambassador to the United States, observed in his introduction that, unlike many other partisan tracts, the account he presents of the June war stood above the political fray.[14] In light of the author's pronounced right-wing biases, were this the case it would surely have been an achievement.[15] But in fact Oren basically reiterates the official Israeli version of the June war. However, to reconcile recently released archival evidence and the latest scholarly research with his apologetic narrative Oren resorts to several distinct, if overlapping, procedures:

- attaching equal weight to a public statement (or memoir) and the hard evidence of an internal document contradicting it
- burying in an avalanche of dubious evidence a critical counter-finding
- minimizing, misrepresenting, or suppressing a critical piece of evidence.[16]

A systematic comparison of Oren's storyline with the known factual record vividly illustrates just how wide the gap has grown between popular literature and serious scholarship.[17]

A massive Israeli "reprisal" raid against the Jordanian village of Samu in November 1966 marked the inception of the crisis that would culminate in the June 1967 war. Although Jordan was taking maximum steps to curb guerrilla infiltration from its border,[18] the IDF methodically razed Samu and killed 18 Jordanian soldiers and civilians (one Israeli soldier died). The assault poisoned inter-Arab relations as Jordan denounced Egypt for sheltering behind the United Nations Emergency Force (UNEF)[19] rather than providing assistance to it.

In early April 1967 long-simmering tensions between Israel and Syria reached a head in a major aerial engagement during which many Syrian planes were downed. In Oren's account, a prime "catalyst" of the June war was Syrian belligerence that culminated in this dogfight: "The calculus of Syrian attacks, whether direct or through Palestinian guerrilla groups, had become overwhelming for the Israelis."[20] It is instructive to take a close look at his account of these direct and indirect "Syrian attacks."

The armistice agreement between Israel and Syria at the close of the 1948 war called for the creation of demilitarized zones (DMZs) along their common border, and an Israeli-Syrian Mixed Armistice Commission (ISMAC). Oren initially states that the DMZs constituted "areas of Israel evacuated by the Syrian army" but then quickly backpedals, designating them areas "over which Israel claimed total sovereignty."[21] The claim, however, lacked international validation.[22] In his account of the periodic armed clashes in the DMZs, Oren occasionally implies that Israel acted the belligerent[23] or that both sides were equally blameworthy.[24] But he overwhelmingly depicts Israel as the innocent victim of Syrian aggression: Israel "thwarted Syria's ... attempts to dominate the D[M]Zs"; "Israel was indeed preparing the groundwork for a reprisal against Syria. . . . At the next Syrian provocation,

Israel would send armored tractors deep into the D[M]Zs, wait for them to be fired on, and then strike back. The provocation was not long in coming"; and so forth.²⁵

In fact independent observers on the scene recalled that—in the words of Odd Bull, chief of staff of U.N. forces in the Middle East—"the status quo was all the time being altered by Israel in her favor," as Arab villagers were evicted, their dwellings demolished, and "all Arab villages disappeared" in wide swaths of the DMZs. Oren frequently quotes from Bull's essential memoir but omits mention of these observations and similar ones by other reliable eyewitnesses.²⁶

Indeed, Oren suppresses what is surely the most revealing source on the root cause of these border clashes. In the course of an interview that created a stir in Israel after its publication Defense Minister Moshe Dayan declared:

> I know how at least 80 percent of all of the incidents there [the Golan Heights] started. In my opinion, more than 80 percent, but let's speak about 80 percent. It would go like this: we would send a tractor to plow... in the demilitarized area, and we would know ahead of time that the Syrians would start shooting. If they did not start shooting, we would inform the tractor to progress farther, until the Syrians, in the end, would get nervous and would shoot. And then we would use guns, and later, even the air force, and that is how it went.... We thought... that we could change the lines of the cease-fire accords by military actions that were less than a war. That is, to seize some territory and hold it until the enemy despairs and gives it to us.²⁷

It was just such a staged provocation in April 1967—an Israeli tractor plowing through a disputed field despite Syrian pleas for compromise—that sparked Israel's "massive employment of the air force" which downed six Syrian planes.²⁸ In Oren's reckoning however the battle ensued after a pattern of "Syrian provocation."²⁹

Prevented from returning home, Palestinian refugees organized commando raids against Israel and, after a February 1966 coup in Syria, the new "radical" regime increased support for them. According to Oren, the "reasons for this upsurge [of Syrian support] were obscure, as inscrutable as the Syrian regime itself."[30] Yet in a statement not quoted by Oren, head of Israeli military intelligence General Aharon Yariv bluntly acknowledged shortly before the June war that Syria backed these Palestinian commando raids "because we are bent upon establishing ... certain facts along the border"—i.e., in retaliation for Israel's land grab in the DMZs.[31]

Oren's narrative is replete with references to these Syrian-backed Palestinian attacks supposedly causing Israel's "security situation" to deteriorate "from worse to insufferable." Thus we read: "Over the course of 1965 ... the armed wing of al-Fatah received Syria's support in carrying out thirty-five attacks according to Israel's reckoning, 110 by Palestinian accounts"; "Over the course of 1966, Israel recorded ninety-three border incidents—mines, shootings, sabotage—while the Syrians boasted seventy-five guerrilla attacks in the single month of February-March";[32] "[in late 1966] eleven guerrilla attacks, most of them from Jordan, ensued in rapid succession—seven Israelis died and twelve were wounded.... Then ... a paramilitary police vehicle struck a mine. Three police were killed, one [was] wounded"; "the first months of 1967 saw some 270 incidents—an increase, Israel acknowledged, of 100 percent.... Al-Fatah issued a series of thirty-four communiqués describing its actions in great detail and praising the courage of its martyrs"; "[during April-May 1967] al-Fatah undertook no less than fourteen operations. Mines and explosives were planted not only on the Israeli side of the Syrian and Jordanian borders, but across from Lebanon as well"; and "[in late May] the IDF's hands were tied; al-Fatah could attack at will."[33]

After these cumulatively overwhelming statistics, it comes as something of a surprise when Oren quotes Moshe Dayan saying in an October 1966 Knesset speech, "There is no major wave of infiltration today. Just because several dozen bandits from al-Fatah cross the border, Israel does not have to get caught up in a frenzy of escalation."[34] Furthermore, shortly after the June war ex-head of Israeli military intelligence Yehoshaphat Harkabi reported that the "operational achievements" of the Palestinian commando raids "in the *thirty* months from [their] debut to the six-day war are not impressive by any standard" (his emphasis). The few successful sabotage operations and few Israeli casualties in that period (a total of 14 civilians, police and soldiers), "did not endanger Israel's national life," Harkabi continued, while "to hide its mediocre results, Fatah inflated communiqués which bore no resemblance to what actually took place."[35]

Oren cites as if credible the Fatah communiqués that bore "no resemblance" to reality, thereby inflating the threat posed to Israel. Elsewhere he mockingly reports that after the June war "in a communiqué issued from Damascus, al-Fatah claimed credit for killing Prime Minister Levi Eshkol with a surface-to-surface missile."[36] One wonders why Oren did not credit this communiqué as well.

In the first weeks of May 1967 Israel's cabinet gave qualified support to an attack on Syria, and numerous Israeli officials openly called for massive retaliation.[37] According to Maoz, Israel "probably redeployed secretly some tank units" as well as troops along the Syrian border, and "a large-scale operation ... may have been in the making."[38] The Soviets apparently got wind of the Israeli cabinet deliberations and conveyed a warning, albeit overblown, to Nasser.

A postwar analysis by a member of the U.S. National Security Council presented this interpretation of Soviet behavior:

> In early May, it is probable that Soviet agents actually picked up intelligence reports of a planned Israeli raid into Syria. I would not be surprised if the reports were at least partly true. The Israeli[s] have made such raids before; they have been under heavy provocation, and they maintain pretty good security (so we might well not know about a planned raid).

> Intelligence being an uncertain business, the Soviet agents may not have known the scale of the raid and may have exaggerated its scope and purpose. Apparently the Soviets warned the Syrians. Whether they deliberately magnified the threat is hard to say. They bear neither the Israeli[s] nor ourselves great love, and there may well have been some element of deliberate exaggeration. However, this was *not* necessarily a calculated incitement to conflict—made out of whole cloth and responsive to a global design. The Soviets did accompany their warnings of Israeli action with advice toward restraint. (emphasis in original)[39]

The most recent scholarly research corroborates these National Security Council speculations. "The Soviet assessment from mid-May 1967 that Israel was about to strike at Syria was correct and well founded," Israeli historian Ami Gluska reports, and "Soviet Intelligence sources must have been aware of this fact."[40] But Oren, purporting that "the reasons for the Russians' warning would remain obscure," offers multiple tortured speculations in the body of the text such as "the tendency of Communist decision-makers to be influenced by their own propaganda on imperialist and Zionist perfidy," and tucks away in an endnote the most obvious, and true, explanation: that Israel was in fact gearing up for such an attack.[41]

Having endured ridicule in the Arab world for standing idly by after both the Samu raid and the downing of Syrian aircraft, Nasser now worried, according to American officials, that "his prestige would suffer irreparably if he failed a third time to come to the aid of an Arab nation attacked by Israel."[42] Consequently he responded in mid-May to the renewed Israeli threats by moving Egyptian troops into the Sinai and ordering the removal of UNEF from Sinai, Gaza, and Sharm-el-Shaykh overlooking the Straits of Tiran.

To dampen tensions on the Sinai border U.N. Secretary-General U Thant proposed (with the support of Israel's closest allies, the U.S. and Canada) that UNEF be repositioned on the Israeli side of the border. Oren defends

Israel's peremptory rejection of U Thant's initiative on the grounds that UNEF "incorporat[ed] contingents from countries hardly sympathetic to Israel" and therefore "would be less likely to stop aggression than to limit Israel's response."⁴³ Oren does not offer a jot of evidence to support this allegation of UNEF's partisanship (there isn't any). Earlier on in his account, however, Oren does concede that "the mere presence of UNEF had sufficed to deter warfare during periods of intense Arab-Israeli friction, to keep infiltrators from exiting Gaza and ensure free passage through the Straits of Tiran."⁴⁴

In addition Oren repeatedly suggests that Nasser's decision to remove UNEF (as well as U Thant's acquiescence in it)⁴⁵ put the Egyptian leader in a position to "threaten" the fragile peace.⁴⁶ It is hard to grasp, however, why stationing UNEF on the Egyptian side of the border preserved peace while stationing it on the Israeli side would not have preserved peace or, put otherwise, why UNEF would have deterred Egyptian aggression on the Egyptian side but not on the Israeli side.⁴⁷ Oren also rapidly disposes of U Thant's stopgap proposal—enthusiastically backed by Nasser (although Oren never mentions Nasser's support), but firmly rejected by Israel—to reactivate the Egyptian-Israeli Mixed Armistice Commission (EIMAC).⁴⁸

After the removal of UNEF from Sharm-el-Shaykh, Nasser announced that the Straits of Tiran would be closed to Israeli vessels and foreign vessels carrying "strategic" cargo to the Israeli port city of Eilat. Although conceding that "few Israeli-flag vessels in fact traversed the Straits," Oren still designates this waterway a "lifeline of the Jewish state" and Eilat a "thriving port."⁴⁹ In reality just five percent of Israel's trade passed through Eilat; the only significant commodity possibly affected by a blockade was oil, which could have been rerouted to the ports of Haifa or Ashdod, and anyhow Israel held in reserve an ample supply of oil carrying it over for many months to come.⁵⁰

Oren reports in profuse detail on the "frightful" news that Egypt had mined the Straits and otherwise forcibly implemented the blockade, only to note later in passing that "the waterway remained mine-free."⁵¹ In fact

Israel already knew right as Nasser declared the blockade that he would allow ships escorted by the U.S. to go through, and after a few days vessels using the Straits passed freely without even being searched: *Nasser had quietly lifted the blockade*.[52] When Nasser expressed willingness to submit the Straits issue to the International Court of Justice "if it could be done speedily," Washington inferred from this caveat that he "anticipated maintaining freedom of passage pending the Court's decision."[53] Privately Israeli officials conceded that an Egyptian blockade of the Straits was "not crucial" but rather a "political symbol," and "secondary," indeed "an opportunity," presumably to justify a first strike.[54]

Reaching Cairo right after the blockade was announced, U Thant elicited a "very significant" (his words) assent from Nasser to a new diplomatic initiative: the appointment of a special U.N. representative to mediate the crisis, and a two-week moratorium on all provocations in the Straits. Israel rejected outright both of U Thant's proposals.[55] Its dismissal of the moratorium proposal rates only a scant mention by Oren, while he does not bother to mention Egypt's acceptance and Israel's rejection of a special mediator. Likewise, Nasser's repeatedly expressed willingness to submit the Straits dispute to the International Court of Justice is dispatched by Oren in a single, negatively charged phrase. Israel also rejected this option out of hand.[56]

Alongside U Thant, the U.S. also tried its hand at mediation in late May and early June. In what Oren describes as "precisely the opening the White House sought," Nasser agreed to send his vice-president to Washington to explore a diplomatic settlement.[57] Just two days before the Egyptian's scheduled arrival, however, Israel attacked. Recalling that the U.S. was "shocked . . . and angry as hell," then-Secretary of State Dean Rusk speculated, "We might not have succeeded in getting Egypt to reopen the straits, but it was a real possibility."[58]

Even *Middle East Record*, a semi-official Israeli compilation, observed after the June war that "a number of facts seem to indicate Abdel Nasser's belief in the possibility of terminating . . . the conflict through diplomacy." It pointed in particular to the Egyptian president's "suggestion" that the

International Court of Justice arbitrate the Straits dispute, his purposeful "vagueness" on the blockade's enforcement, and his "willingness" to revive EIMAC.[59] "Up to the outbreak of the war," Maoz concludes, "Nasser was interested in finding a ladder to climb down from the tall tree he found himself on."[60]

One would never guess from reading Oren, however, that such a "real possibility" existed for a diplomatic settlement of the crisis, if only because the crucial facts enumerated in the Israeli compilation enter just barely or not at all in his uniquely comprehensive and impartial history of the June war.

A major thrust of Oren's account suggests that Israel launched its first strike to preempt an imminent and overwhelming Arab attack. Basing himself on a few self-serving postwar Egyptian memoirs, Oren gives over several pages to "Operation Dawn," which he depicts as a first strike against Israel planned for the end of May by Egyptian defense minister Abd al-Hakim Amer, but aborted by Nasser at the last minute.[61] Even scholars who credit that such an Egyptian attack was in the works typically consign it to a footnote or a phrase. But Oren, citing the same sources as everyone else, turns this ephemeral and inconsequential alleged episode into a centerpiece of his history, thereby magnifying the threat Egypt posed.[62] Fabricating a mammoth speculative edifice on top of an already flimsy evidentiary foundation, Oren professes to divine Nasser's subtle calculations for supporting Operation Dawn, even after conceding that it is debatable whether "Nasser even knew about the plan."[63]

At one point in his chapter on the "countdown" to the June war Oren implies that Nasser had resolved not to attack on the eve of Israel's first strike.[64] This acknowledgment easily gets lost, however, amid supposed indications cited by Oren of an imminent Egyptian attack. For example Oren reports the 4 June Israeli cabinet decision to "launch a military strike aimed at . . . preventing the impending assault by the United Arab Command"; the UNEF commander's surmise that Egyptian troops stood poised for an "offensive"; the renewed hopes of Amer "to launch an air and ground offensive in the Negev"; and the innocent plea of Eshkol on 5 June, which closes the book chapter, that "all Israel strove for was an end to the immediate threat."[65]

In fact an Egyptian assault was almost certainly *not* imminent. IDF intelligence chief Yariv reported at the tail end of May that Egypt would not initiate hostilities before "two or three weeks" and that Egyptian forces in the northern Sinai were in a state of "total chaos." At the crucial 2 June meeting of Israel's security cabinet, IDF Chief of Staff Yitzhak Rabin stated that the Egyptian army was "perhaps in a defensive orientation only."[66]

American intelligence agencies uniformly assessed that Nasser would not attack (see Table 2), while, in the most revealing acknowledgment, Major-General Meir Amit, head of the Mossad, told senior American officials on 1 June that "there were no differences between the U.S. and the Israelis on the military intelligence picture or its interpretation."[67] "The Egyptian build-up in Sinai lacked a clear offensive plan," Israeli scholar Avraham Sela reports, "and Nasser's defensive instructions explicitly assumed an Israeli first-strike."[68]

Oren does not adduce a scrap of evidence refuting the broad scholarly consensus that Nasser did not intend to attack. Even Menachem Begin, a member of the Israeli cabinet in June 1967, later publicly admitted, "The Egyptian army concentrations in the Sinai approaches do not prove that Nasser was really about to attack us. We must be honest with ourselves. We decided to attack him." Oren prudently omits mention of Begin's remarkable testimony.[69]

TABLE 2 U.S. APPRAISALS OF NASSER'S INTENTIONS ON EVE OF 1967 WAR

25 May	CIA Appraisal	In our view, UAR [Egyptian] military dispositions in Sinai are defensive in character....The steps taken thus far by [other] Arab armies do not prove that the Arabs intend an all-out attack on Israel.... In sum, we believe these are merely gestures which all Arab states feel compelled to make in the interests of the fiction of Arab unity, but have little military utility in a conflict with Israel.

TABLE 2 (continued)

26 May	General Earle Wheeler, Chairman, Joint Chiefs of Staff	The UAR's dispositions are defensive and do not look as if they are preparatory to an invasion of Israel.... [T]here was no indication that the Egyptians would attack. If the UAR moved, it would give up its defensive positions in the Sinai for little advantage.
26 May	CIA's Board of National Estimates	Clearly Nasser has won the first round. It is possible that [Nasser] may seek a military show-down with Israel, designed to settle the whole problem once and for all. This seems to us highly unlikely.... The most likely course seems to be for Nasser to hold to his present winnings as long as he can, and in as full measure as he can.[70]

Oren suggests, citing mostly public statements and tendentious memoirs, that Israel's security was rapidly deteriorating and that, on the eve of its first strike, Arab armies posed an "existential threat" (his phrase). Thus we read: "It is now a question of our national survival, of to be or not to be," and "The noose is closing around our necks" (Rabin); "Eshkol now understood that time was not on Israel's side"; "The news in the interim was frightful. Egypt's 4th division had completed its deployment in Sinai"; "[T]he general staff determined that 'every day is a gamble with Israel's survival'"; "Should Egypt attack first, 'Israel has had it'" (Avraham Harman, Israel's ambassador to the United States); "[Israel's] one chance for winning this war is in taking the initiative and fighting according to our own designs. . . . God help us though if they hit us first" (Dayan); "'This is Egypt's greatest hour,' . . . the combined Arab armies could push Israel back to the UN partition lines, or further" (Yariv); and so forth.[71]

Yet, these avowals are flatly contradicted by what intelligence agencies and officials privately conveyed. To judge by these analyses Israel's security was not at risk (and possibly even improving over time), and it was bound to win a quick and easy victory regardless of which side initiated hostilities. Strangely Oren cites portions of this confident internal record in the very same sections where he uncritically quotes the panicky pretenses. He notes that U.S. intelligence predicted "the IDF would win a war in two weeks even if attacked on three fronts simultaneously—one week if Israel shot first," and that Israeli intelligence "agreed entirely" with these American forecasts. Echoing the findings of multiple American intelligence agencies President Lyndon B. Johnson told Israeli representatives at the end of May that "our best judgment is that no military attack on Israel is imminent" and if, against all odds, the Arabs do attack, "you will whip the hell out of them" (see Table 3).

Foreign Minister Abba Eban informed U.S. officials just before the attack that "Israel believed its forces would win and . . . that the balance of power had not been shifted by deployment of the last few days." The U.S. ambassador to Israel reported back to Washington that "[the Israelis] feel they can finish Nasser off." Labor Minister Yigal Allon expressed to the cabinet "total faith in the IDF's ability to beat the Egyptians," Chief of the Central Front Uzi Narkiss dismissed the Arab forces as a "soap bubble—one pin will burst them," and Divisional Commander Ariel Sharon declared, "The army is ready as never before to repel an Egyptian attack . . . to wipe out the Egyptian army." Mossad chief Amit assured Eshkol that "If [Nasser] strikes first, he's finished," and he told U.S. Defense Secretary Robert McNamara that "the war would be over in two days."

Oren cites the foreboding of Quartermaster General Mattityahu Peled, "The Egyptian threat had to be eliminated at once if Israel were to survive." He omits mention however of Peled's subsequent admission that this posture had been a "bluff." Oren also quotes IDF chief of operations Ezer Weizman, "We must strike now and swiftly . . . we must deal the enemy a serious blow, for if we won't other forces will soon join him," and "All the signs indicate that the Egyptians are ready to strike. We have no option but to attack at once."

Oren again omits mention however of Weizman's later acknowledgments that "there was no threat of destruction," and that the Egyptians would have "suffered a complete defeat" even if they "attacked first."[72]

TABLE 3 U.S. ESTIMATES OF BALANCE OF FORCES ON EVE OF 1967 WAR

23 May	Central Intelligence Agency	Israeli *ground forces* "can maintain internal security, defend successfully against simultaneous Arab attacks on all fronts, launch limited attacks simultaneously on all fronts, or hold on any three fronts while mounting successfully a major offensive on the fourth." *In the air*, the judgment is less clear: the Israelis "probably could defeat the Egyptian air force if Israel's air facilities were not damaged beyond repair."
26 May	General Wheeler, Chairman, Joint Chiefs of Staff	[If Egypt attacked first, Wheeler] believed that Israelis would win air superiority. The UAR would lose a lot of aircraft. Israel's military philosophy is to gain tactical surprise by striking airfields first but [Wheeler] believes this is not essential to Israel's gaining air supremacy.
26 May	Central Intelligence Agency	Israel could almost certainly attain air superiority over the Sinai Peninsula in 24 hours after taking the initiative or in two or three days if the UAR struck first. In the latter case, Israel might lose up to half of its air force. We estimate that armored striking forces could breach the UAR's double defense line in the Sinai within several days. Regrouping and resupplying would be required before the Israelis could initiate further attacks aimed at driving to the Suez Canal. Israel could contain any attacks by Syria or Jordan during this period.
2 June	Secretary of Defense McNamara	Secretary McNamara said that the Israelis felt that they could start hostilities now or a week from now and prevail. They believe their capabilities are perishable as time goes on, but Secretary McNamara thought they could delay from 2-4 weeks and still accomplish their military objective.... Secretary McNamara said Israelis think they can win in 3-4 days; but he thinks it would be longer—7-10 days.

(continued)

TABLE 3	(continued)	
3 June	National Security Council	By a delay of one week—28 May to 4 June—the Arabs have made a net military gain if war should now occur. The ultimate outcome ... would be unchanged. Israel would still win. ... If war outbreak were delayed one more week—to 11 June, the Israeli military position would probably deteriorate further, but at a slower rate. ... After 11 June, the military balance would not change until the economic effects of mobilization began to affect military posture. ... I conclude that Israeli concern about delaying a war which they fear is inevitable is based primarily on their concern about a deterioration in their political and diplomatic position rather than on military factors.[73]

Far from panicking on the eve of the June war, the "IDF under Rabin" was, in the words of noted Israeli military historian Martin van Creveld, "at the peak of its preparedness," "confident in its power" and "spoiling for a fight and willing to go to considerable lengths to provoke it."[74] The IDF generals yearned to attack "not necessarily because they felt the country's existence was in danger," Israeli historian Tom Segev observes, "but because they believed it was an opportunity to break the Egyptian army" and "crush Nasser."[75]

The one real Israeli fear was a repetition of the 1956 Sinai invasion when the U.S. handed Nasser a political victory by ordering Israel to withdraw.[76] Echoing former prime minister Ben-Gurion, Eshkol counseled that "Israel should not go to war as long as the United States was opposed," and therefore was "waiting for the green light from the United States." (Eshkol also believed Israel needed more time "to convince the world that Nasser was acting like Hitler.")[77] Once U.S. officials de facto gave their blessing to an Israeli first strike at the end of May and early June, an Israel brimming with confidence unleashed its war machine.[78]

"It is doubtful whether [Eshkol] believed that Israel's existence was truly in danger and equally doubtful that he was convinced Egypt would attack," Segev concludes. "He knew what the army knew: that even if Egypt had attacked, Israel would win."[79]

The preponderance of evidence points to the conclusion that Israel did not fear an imminent Arab attack when it launched a first strike. It is accordingly inaccurate to denote Israel's 1967 blitzkrieg "preemptive."[80] Even if international law does make provision for preemption, this war was nevertheless illegal. The best case that can be made for Israel is that it launched the first strike on 5 June because it feared that eventually the balance of forces would tip against it or that the casualties it sustained would over time drastically increase.[81] It must be said however that American intelligence estimates—which Israel seconded—did not anticipate a dramatic deterioration in Israel's military position in the short term, while international law clearly, and with good reason, prohibits "preventive" war based on unknowable future contingencies.

In fact the primary impetus behind Israel's first strike was to preserve the "credibility" of its "deterrence."[82] The practical import of this seemingly technical notion, which repeatedly cropped up in internal Israeli debates during the build-up to the war,[83] was fleshed out by Sharon. He admonished those hesitant to attack that Israel was losing its "deterrence capability . . . our main weapon—*the fear of us.*"[84]

The challenge confronting Tel Aviv was that Nasser had dared to defy its prerogative to dictate the rules of the game. Israel rejected any diplomatic settlement short of Nasser's complete capitulation because he—the Arabs—needed a timely reminder that what Israel says goes. Otherwise, the Arab world might no longer automatically acquiesce in Israeli diktat. "To respond diplomatically to the crisis," Maoz explains, "would kill Israel's deterrence, even if diplomacy succeeded in defusing the crisis and returning the status quo ante."[85] But if Israel were to inflict a "resounding blow" on Nasser, Chief of Staff Rabin predicted, it would transform the entire Middle East: Israel's "deterrence capability" would be restored, and Arabs would again snap to attention when it issued a command.[86]

Oren contends that the sole objective of Tel Aviv in the June war was "eliminating the Egyptian threat and destroying Nasser's army." Israeli leaders had not "planned or even contemplated," according to him, the conquests of the Sinai Peninsula, Gaza Strip, West Bank and Golan Heights. In formulations strikingly reminiscent of Benny Morris's account of the origins of the Palestinian refugee problem ("born of war, not by design"), Oren avows that the Israeli offensives had been "determined less by design than by expediency," and by "the vagaries and momentum of war, far more than by rational decision making." In fact, just as Morris's formulations apologetically distorted the dynamics of the 1948 expulsions, so Oren's formulations apologetically distort the dynamics of the 1967 conquests.[87]

Many contingencies shaped the particular course of Israel's offensives: Arab resistance (or the lack thereof), international public opinion, U.N. diplomacy, Soviet threats and American responses, and so on. There also was neither tactical nor strategic consensus among Israelis on exactly how to proceed with the offensives. For example, despite internal pressures Dayan temporized on conquering the West Bank and Golan Heights apparently because, attaching top priority to the Egyptian Sinai, he dreaded a multifront war.[88]

In addition Tel Aviv preferred pretexts—however flimsy and, if need be, fabricated—before going on the offensive. On the Egyptian front it alleged that Nasser's bellicosity justified a first strike,[89] while on the Jordanian and Syrian fronts it pointed to armed hostilities. Oren dramatically reenacts the Jordanian attack: "Two batteries of the American-made 155-mm 'Long Tom' guns went into action, one zeroing in on the suburbs of Tel Aviv.... The Jordanians gradually escalated the fighting, ... introducing 3-inch mortars and 106-mm recoilless rifles.... Arab Legion howitzers launched the first of 6,000 shells on Jewish Jerusalem."[90] But according to the balance-sheet of a respected Israeli military historian, King Hussein of Jordan responded to Israel's first strike against Egypt with "two symbolic thrusts," and a "few" artillery shells and air attacks (against Israeli airfields) because "he had no choice but to do something, all the while hoping to avoid serious retaliation." And, for all his purple prose depicting a "massive" Syrian artillery barrage here and a "Syrian thrust" there, Oren himself seems to concede that Israel desperately sought the "right pretext" to attack Syria, and that Syrian hostilities were largely symbolic (to ward off the accusation that "Syria was willing to fight to the last Egyptian").[91]

In fact Israel intended to launch assaults against Jordan and Syria even if a casus belli were wanting. "Let's be honest with ourselves," Rabin declared after Nasser's announcement of a blockade. "First we will attack Egypt; then we will also attack Syria and Jordan." At the end of May, the IDF high command prepared to "attack and then occupy the West Bank and to shift its priorities from Egypt, then Syria, then Jordan, to Egypt, then Jordan, then Syria," according to Segev, and "none of them assumed that the IDF would wait for a Jordanian attack."[92]

Although a plurality of circumstantial factors came into play during Israel's offensives, Oren's assertion that these offensives were not "planned or even contemplated" is patently false. Quite the contrary, with external constraints temporarily in abeyance, internal differences provisionally resolved and just barely credible pretexts in hand, Israel implemented, albeit hesitantly and in piecemeal fashion, long-incubating plans to conquer the Sinai, Gaza Strip, West Bank and Golan Heights.

Ironically Oren himself copiously documents that Israel contemplated and meticulously prepared for these offensives over many years. He reports that on the southern front "contingency plans" had been developed after conquering the Sinai in 1956 "for moving tanks over desert wastes that were widely believed insurmountable"; that on the eastern front "the dream of completing the War of Independence and freeing the Land of Israel" had "guided" the "military planning" of "all" Israeli commanders, and "a drawer full of plans" had been developed to "knock out Jordanian artillery concentrations on the West Bank and lay siege to East Jerusalem"; and that on the northern front an "array of contingency plans for dealing with Syria" had been developed "from a limited assault on the Golan ridge ... to ... conquering the entire Heights," and "to conquer[ing] the enemy's capital [Damascus] within eighty hours."[93]

Even as Oren claims that Israel had not "even contemplated" anything beyond neutralizing the Egyptian military threat, he reports that in the weeks leading up to the June war (and, on the Jordanian and Syrian fronts, before hostilities actually broke out), different IDF commanders expected to "conquer Gaza"; "strike Egypt, and then we'll fight Syria and Jordan as well"; "advanc[e] into Sinai and ... to the Jordan headwaters in the north and the Latrun corridor leading to Jerusalem"; "advance westward to al-Arish and, time permitting, beyond in the direction of the Canal"; "take care of the Syrians"; "eliminate the Egyptian army and ... seize the initiative on other fronts as well"; "get to the Canal and to Sharm al-Sheikh"; "eliminat[e] the Jordanian air force even without provocation"; and "take Jenin" in the West Bank. With his eye riveted on conquering "all of the Sinai Peninsula," Dayan declared in early June, according to Oren, that "Our success ... will be judged not on the number of Egyptian tanks we destroy ... but on the size of the territory we'll seize."[94]

Oren uncritically quotes Allon's avowal that "Israel sought no territorial gain."[95] But he ignores Allon's publicly stated agenda just before the attack: "In case of a new war, we must avoid the historic mistake of the War of Independence and, later, the Sinai Campaign. We must not cease fighting until we achieve ... the territorial fulfillment of the Land of Israel."[96] Oren also reports that just after the June war Allon "led" the cabinet ministers urging retention of the occupied territories.[97] It seems Allon did not exactly undergo, as Oren's account suggests, an overnight conversion.

The planning and prospects for the June offensives reflected Israel's persistent territorial *desiderata*. From just after the first Arab-Israeli war many Israeli leaders lamented the IDF's failure to conquer the West Bank and Gaza Strip. During the 1956 Sinai invasion they envisaged annexing these territories as well as the Egyptian Sinai.[98] June 1967 was a replay of October 1956, except this time with Washington on board.[99]

Oren himself reports that Weizman was said to have proclaimed Israel's "right to Hebron and Nablus and all of Jerusalem"; that Narkiss "regretted Israel's inability to seize the West Bank and Jerusalem in 1948" and conceived the June war as an "opportunity to rectify Israel's failure in 1948, a miraculous second chance," declaring at a postwar briefing that "Central Command fulfilled its natural aspirations and established Israel's borders on the Jordan"; that "shortly before the outbreak of hostilities" Rabin exhorted troops on the Jordanian front to "complete what we were unable to finish" in 1948, and "many" officers "shared that sentiment"; and that already on the third day of the war Israel envisaged retaining the West Bank, Gaza and the Sinai.[100]

Oren uncritically quotes Eshkol's assertion, "Of course, we don't want a centimeter of Syrian territory." But he himself repeatedly acknowledges that Eshkol "went a little crazy" coveting the headwaters of the Jordan river in the Golan,[101] while Moshe Dayan, in a postwar interview not quoted by Oren, stated with "absolute certainty" that the primary motive behind Israel's seizure of the Golan was not Syrian shelling but "good land for agriculture ... lust for that ground."[102]

Segev confirms that Israel's conquests hardly came as an unanticipated surprise. He reports that well before the June 1967 war Eshkol contemplated "a possible expansion of Israel's borders"; that Rabin (then IDF deputy chief of staff) recommended to Eshkol that "if the opportunity arose" the "ideal boundaries of Israel ... would follow the Jordan River, the Suez Canal, and the Litani River in the north"; that "a few of the generals who believed that Israel should expand its borders discussed taking over the West Bank" and "the idea that the IDF might actively seek to expand Israel's borders came up repeatedly"; and that "much admired" labor movement leader Yitzhak Tabenkin avowed, "Anywhere war will allow, we shall go to restore the whole of the country's integrity," which was "also the approximate position of Menachem Begin, leader of Herut."

The "compromise position" of the IDF a few months before the June war, according to Segev, was that it "accepts the current situation, but would welcome an opportunity to change the status quo to create a new and more comfortable one," while by early May the IDF General Staff had resolved, and planned accordingly, that the impending war "would be unlike the first, with all its flaws, including the failure to occupy the West Bank and the Old City."[103]

According to Oren, Israel's territorial conquests during the June war "came about largely through chance": they just happened.[104] To judge by the historical record, however, they were just *waiting to happen*.

In his introduction to *Six Days of War*, Oren states that the objective of his book was to reconstruct the June 1967 war so that it would "never be seen the same way again." In fact he merely repeats the same old, tired Israeli apologetics. To be sure, because he pretends to be a serious historian, Oren could not entirely omit what the available documentary record and academic research now show. His book consequently often reads as if Oren wrote it in a schizophrenic state, denying in the second breath what he reluctantly conceded in the first.

It would appear that the real purpose of Oren's book is to reclaim the world of Israeli heroism and innocence that inspired American Jewry after the June war. The imagery of an embattled Israel launching a preemptive strike when the only options were—in Abba Eban's emotive phrase at the United Nations—"to live or perish" has also served as the bedrock historical rationale for its occupation of Palestinian land and diplomatic intransigence. Famed moral philosopher Michael Walzer listed Israel's "preemptive" strike as one of a handful of unambiguous cases of self-defense in the twentieth century ("one about which we can, I think, have no doubts"), while Harvard law professor Alan Dershowitz cast the June 1967 war as *the* paradigm of legitimate preemption.[105]

But the Manichean world to which Israel's apologists beckon is now lost and gone forever. The new generations of American Jews might not be familiar with every arcane historical detail on, say, the June 1967 war, but in college, at public forums, on the internet and in learned periodicals many have discovered that not only might shades of gray predominate over black-and-white, but that often what their parents' generation believed was black-and-white turns out to be white-and-black. Those of us who grew up cheering the cowboys and jeering the Indians in the movies also experienced such an epiphany in the 1960s when a new generation of historians turned our world upside down, or right side up.

8/ A CONSPIRACY SO IMMENSE

A central premise of this book is that current academic scholarship on the Israel-Palestine conflict has achieved impressive levels of objectivity, that this historical record is better known, and that consequently more and more people are able to see through the propaganda from which Israel has benefited for so long. The battle, however, is far from over. Full-fledged "pro"-Israel frauds masquerading as scholarship still get published by distinguished university presses and still gain praise in the academy. But these hoaxes also provide backhanded validation of the argument in this book: the foundations of the official Zionist narrative have been so completely shattered that attempts to restore Israel's pristine image must rely on preposterous inferences and speculations.

A prime example is the recent book *Foxbats over Dimona: The Soviets' nuclear gamble in the Six-Day War* by Isabella Ginor and Gideon Remez.[1] Although both authors hail from Israel, the book was largely an American phenomenon: Yale University Press published it, and the praise it garnered came largely from American experts. It bespeaks the persistent aberrations of American intellectual culture when it comes to the Israel-Palestine conflict.

Ginor and Remez conjure a highly provocative theory. The June 1967 war marked, according to them, the climax of a manifold Soviet conspiracy to destroy Israel's nuclear weapons program.[2] Additionally they allege that not only the Soviets but also the Arabs, Americans and Israelis have participated in a "cover-up" of this conspiracy for the past 40 years, until their own "laborious sleuthing"[3] unearthed nuggets of information and connected the dots.

The core argument of *Foxbats* is fairly straightforward. Beginning in the early 1960s the Soviet Union began to panic that Israel was on the verge of producing nuclear weapons at its Dimona reactor. The Soviets and their Arab client states lacked, however, a legitimate pretext for launching a preemptive strike. In search of a credible alibi the Soviets plotted with Arab leaders to lure Israel into attacking first and then planned to destroy the Dimona reactor in a counterattack, which the U.S. would acquiesce in because Israel was the aggressor. This minutely orchestrated conspiracy worked perfectly until the climactic moment of 5 June 1967 when the unanticipated destructiveness of Israel's first strike eliminated the possibility of an effective reprisal. It was, in the authors' phrase, an "inept conspiracy."[4]

It would be hard to exaggerate the magnitude of their alleged revelations. It is not just that no evidence of such a conspiracy has surfaced in the vast documentary record on the June 1967 war and that it has eluded the attention of scores of trained scholars who have pored over this record. What is yet more remarkable, not one of the co-conspirators in this multitudinously ramified Soviet plot has yet stepped forward to bear witness to it.

After the June war the Egyptian leadership fell out in mutual recriminations over culpability for the military debacle, but no one pinned blame on a Soviet plot. After President Anwar Sadat expelled the Soviet Union from Egypt in 1972 and castigated it while realigning with the U.S., he did not use this ripe occasion to expose the Soviet plot, and neither did any of the Egyptians who subsequently wrote memoirs of the war. After the Soviet Union imploded in 1989 and a lucrative cottage industry sprung up of ex-Communists testifying to the countless perfidies (real and imagined) of the Soviet era, none of the conspirators stepped forward to expose this Soviet plot. And the authors never make clear what motives the U.S. and Israel might have had in perpetuating the cover-up.[5]

8/ A CONSPIRACY SO IMMENSE 185

Still, it cannot be ruled out a priori that new pieces of evidence might have turned up that compel a revisiting of the historical record. The authors do and do not make such a case. They concede that they have not found a "smoking gun" such as a transparently incriminating archival document. Rather, they claim to have amassed an "astonishing number of facts"[6] which *if properly contextualized*—this is the crucial point—provide ample proof of a Soviet conspiracy. Insofar as the validity of their book stands or falls on this alleged new evidence, there appears to be no alternative except to go through the salient pieces they adduce one by one.

It might as well be said at the outset that the book does not contain a scrap of evidence to support the claim of a vast Soviet conspiracy and cover-up. If one discounts the breathless prose that introduces each new "disclosure"; the hysterical italics used to embellish banal statements; the "special" techniques resorted to for decoding documents; the reliance on anonymous and otherwise dubious sources; the speculative propositions of what "could," "may," "might," "must have" and "possibly" happened, which then mysteriously metamorphose later in their book into dead certainties; and the outright mangling and misrepresentation of source material—if one discards all this dross what remains of their allegedly tantalizing evidence can barely fill a thimble. The authors compare their "prodigious" labor of "setting straight the historical record" to a "10,000-piece jigsaw puzzle, of which we receive a random five pieces in the mail every week."[7] To judge by the evidence adduced in their book, it appears that they were inundated with junk mail.

The authors point to multiple motives behind the Soviet conspiracy. To begin with, "at least part of the Soviet leadership" allegedly wanted to liquidate Israel. The authors cite an "affidavit" presented to them by a "former Soviet officer" who claimed to have overheard Minister of Defense Andrei Grechko declare in 1967, "The 50th year of the Great October Socialist Revolution will be the last year of the existence of the State of Israel." Moreover, the Soviets were allegedly hoping for a "dramatic deed" to mark the Soviet anniversary. As evidence, the authors cite KGB operatives who allegedly "stressed the importance of 'active measures' for commemorating the anniversary."⁸

Were this not proof enough of the Russians' dastardly designs, the authors also quote an "unnamed Soviet diplomat at the United Nations" who "appeared to betray this preoccupation in an inverted form by 'saying they would...*not* get involved in a war on their 50th anniversary'" (authors' emphasis).⁹ This piece of evidence attests to a perfidious Soviet plot because Communists say the opposite of what they mean. Likewise, when Soviet Foreign Minister Andrei Gromyko told Israeli Foreign Minister Abba Eban that because "Israel does not aspire to surround and crush the USSR, the Soviet Union has no reason to fear Israel or to harbor hostility toward it," Eban "must have taken it as a very serious warning" because Gromyko said it with a "grin."¹⁰ Presumably, if he had said it with a grimace, Israel could have rested easy.

The overarching Soviet motive however was allegedly to prevent Israel from acquiring nuclear weapons. It is not a matter of dispute that from the early 1960s Israel's nuclear program had alarmed the Kremlin, as well as Arab capitals and even Washington. The only pertinent evidence would have to show that this dread impelled the Soviets to plot an attack on Israel. The authors do indeed purport to have discovered a "sensational document" that "utterly surprised" them in a recently published "official collection of Soviet diplomatic papers."¹¹ They quote this incriminating portion of it:

> Memorandum of the Department for Middle Eastern Countries of the Ministry of Foreign Affairs of the USSR on Israel's Intent to Possess Atomic Weapons
> 23 February 1966
> Top Secret
> On 13 December 1965, one of the leaders of the Israel Communist party, Comrade Sneh, informed the Soviet Ambassador in Tel Aviv about his conversation (9 December 1965)

with the adviser to the prime minister of Israel, Gariel, in which the latter declared Israel's intention to produce its own atomic bomb.[12]

The authors surmise (on scant evidence, but it hardly matters) that "Gariel" must have been head of Israeli intelligence Isser Harel, and they then proceed to assert that "the magnitude, motives, and consequences of Harel's disclosures appear to be of historic proportions." It is hard however to make out why.

It is purported that because "Gariel" said that Israel was "*developing* an atomic bomb and *intended* to arm itself with such a weapon, the main news for Moscow must have been not the Israeli intent but the fact that it had *not yet been realized*, and that a window of opportunity still existed to prevent its fruition" (authors' emphases). But it would only have been "news for Moscow" if Israel's intention had in fact been realized and the window had been closed; the intention itself was already common knowledge. Moscow seems hardly to have imputed "enormous significance" (as the authors claim) to the "news," for their official reaction quoted later in the book was Soviet-era boilerplate: "Tell Comrade Sneh that in Moscow there is full confidence that Israel's Communists and other progressive forces, who correctly assess the gravity of certain Israeli circles' extremist policy, will in case of need be capable of recruiting broad masses in the country against such a policy."[13]

The authors repeatedly stress that Soviet spies had infiltrated Israel's nuclear program and that, between them and Soviet spy satellites, the Kremlin was privy to the "actual nature of Israel's 'textile plant' at Dimona" and "had excellent intelligence on Israel's nuclear progress."[14] What then could be the "historic" import of "Gariel's" declaration? Sneh was a high-profile Israeli Communist and, according to the authors, at the time was suspected by Israelis of being a Soviet spy. Why then would the Soviets attach any special significance to what Israel's chief spy would openly declare to a suspected Soviet spy? The authors indirectly answer this question by speculating that

Harel "might" also have been a Soviet spy.[15] They do not speculate on whether Harel "might" have assassinated JFK.

Seemingly aware that their "sensational" document reporting the "disclosures" of "Gariel" and the Soviet reaction to it barely rise to the banal, the authors try a different tack. The fact that it says nothing is immaterial, they explain, because it could not have been otherwise: "It would be precisely the most important, forceful, and potentially fateful operational decisions that would *not* be recorded" in a Soviet document "so, whether and how the USSR's leadership decided to respond, politically or militarily, to Harel's disclosure cannot be expected to appear in any document—certainly none that is likely to be released anytime soon" (authors' emphasis).[16] On this premise the wonder is why the authors did not just cite blank sheets of paper.

A turning point in the Soviet plot allegedly took place in December 1966 at a Central Committee plenary meeting, although "remarkably the published version of this conclave's resolutions made no explicit reference at all to the Middle East." The absence of any evidence poses no evidentiary challenge for the authors because it was "an omission that more probably reflects secret decisions than an actual disregard of this high priority issue in the deliberations."[17] (Mercifully they do not put "secret decisions" in italics.) The plenum's allegedly covert resolutions were then allegedly confirmed a few months later when Soviet party boss Leonid Brezhnev "notified" Polish party boss Wladislaw Gomulka that a "decisive blow" was about to be dealt to U.S. interests in the Middle East, "even at the cost of sacrificing [Egyptian President Gamal Abdel] Nasser." At any rate, this is what Gomulka's interpreter claimed he recalled hearing after his defection to the West several years later, when he also "understood in retrospect" that in June 1967 "Nasser was tempted by the Soviets." Although the authors do not mention it, according to this interpreter's memoir Brezhnev shouted his revelations about Nasser during a break at the opera "and obviously had difficulty finishing his sentence in a logical manner. Even though he was already slightly drunk, he downed several more cognacs." It would appear that many of the disclosures in *Foxbats* come from Russians in a hyperinebriated state.[18]

It is alleged that the Kremlin orchestrated each step in the build-up to the June 1967 war. In February 1966 a radical faction seized power in Syria. Although "there is as yet no direct evidence" of a connection between this coup and the Soviet conspiracy, the authors surmise that "the parallel timing indicates that ... [they] were at least simultaneously undertaken as facets of the USSR's same overall strategy."[19] The Syrians, acting in cahoots with the Kremlin, are then said to have leveled "accusations of aggressive designs" against Israel in order to "precipitat[e] a conflict that might be used to end Israel's nuclear development."[20] But, rather than being pretexts fabricated to justify an attack on Israel, these Syrian accusations were, according to Israeli strategic analyst Zeev Maoz, firmly grounded in reality: "Israel's policy had an important impact on the process that led to the Six Day War. Israeli misconduct during border conflict with Syria was to a large extent responsible for the process of escalation that evolved into the May-June 1967 crisis."[21]

In November 1966 Egypt and Syria signed a defense pact allegedly at the Soviets' behest.[22] Then, "Jordan fell into line" after Israel was apparently duped—exactly how it is not made clear—into launching a bloody retaliatory raid against a Jordanian village and, as a result, "King Hussein was constrained to go along with the Egyptian-Syrian line."[23]

In April 1967 a border incident between Syrians and Israelis escalated into a major aerial battle during which six Syrian MiGs were downed and Israeli planes circled over Damascus. The authors credit the theory that it was "initiated by the Soviets."[24] But, according to Moshe Dayan, this sort of border incident that climaxed in the dogfight was routinely instigated by Israel.[25]

After a succession of ominous developments it was widely anticipated in May 1967 that Israel was going to attack Syria. The Kremlin then privately relayed to high-level Egyptian officials information it had obtained auguring an imminent attack. The consensus among historians is that the Soviets got wind of the Israeli war plan, although they (or their informants) exaggerated its dimensions.[26] The authors dismiss such an interpretation as "the most far-fetched" and instead contend that the "patently preposterous" and "blatantly bogus" Soviet message was yet one more link in the carefully orchestrated plot.[27] They refute current scholarly opinion by minimizing the importance of one of the official Israeli threats,[28] and by excising from their account the many more official Israeli threats as well as the wealth of other evidence showing that—in the words of Israeli historian Ami Gluska—"the Soviet assessment from mid-May 1967 that Israel was about to strike at Syria was correct and well founded" and "Soviet Intelligence sources must have been aware of this fact."[29]

It is further cause for wonder why the Kremlin would go through the trouble of fabricating a message warning Egyptian officials of an imminent Israeli attack, and circuitously conveying it in secret through multiple emissaries to senior Egyptian officials, if these senior Egyptian officials were themselves co-conspirators in the Soviet plot. The authors speculate that the actual target of the disinformation campaign was "lower echelons in both Moscow and Cairo, who had not been privy to the plan, as well as for external propaganda purposes."[30] But if factotums and outsiders were wholly insulated from the complex and convoluted conveyance of privileged information, it is unclear how they could have been duped by it.

The authors also purport to have unearthed new evidence that the Soviet message to Egypt triggered the plot's implementation.[31] It is a postwar speech by Brezhnev to the Soviet Central Committee, copies of which were found in the East German and Polish party archives. The crucial passage quoted by the authors reads in full:

> In mid-May—and to this I want to draw your attention—reports reached us that Israel was intending to land a military blow on Syria and other Arab states. *The Politburo resolved* to bring this information to the attention of the governments of the UAR and Syria. (authors' emphasis)

8/ A CONSPIRACY SO IMMENSE 191

Homing in on the italicized words, the authors declare: "Seldom does such significance hinge on a single phrase in any document." Indeed, according to them, it provides "verification of a Soviet 'grand design'" that "included the elimination of Dimona." One searches in vain, however, for the grounding in that single phrase for these whopping inferences. The reader might be excused for concluding that this passage confirms from a "startling" source the current scholarly wisdom on the impetus behind the Soviet warning: the Kremlin believed, correctly, that an Israeli attack on Syria was imminent.[32]

After the Soviet warning, Nasser in mid-May sent Egyptian troops into the Sinai. He then called for the removal of U.N. peacekeepers (UNEF) from the Egyptian-Israeli border and announced a blockade of the Straits of Tiran, closing the Israeli port of Eilat to shipping. The consensus among historians is that these last initiatives of Nasser caught the Soviets off guard. Indeed, in a passage of the secret speech that the authors quote, Brezhnev states that these steps "came as a complete surprise."[33]

According to the authors, however, two months earlier in March 1967 the Soviet Politburo had adopted a most precise "plan, of which the eviction of UNEF and the blockade of Eilat were central features."[34] They know this[35] because

- at the end of March, Cairo newspapers reported that Gromyko would meet with Nasser to "discuss the problems of the U.N. peace-keeping forces in Gaza";
- at the end of May an "obviously embarrassed" Soviet official told the American ambassador in Moscow "after a long pause [that] he thought Nasser had acted on his own," and an Egyptian official who conceded "not to be in the know" and who "dislike[d]" both Nasser and the Soviets told this same U.S. ambassador that although the Soviets did not publicly endorse Nasser's moves, it was "not important because Soviets [are] supporting [Egypt] 'in other ways'";

- in his postwar speech Brezhnev stated that *"following* the Egyptian moves" he attempted to "lessen the pressure of the Western powers" (authors' emphasis).

It should be obvious, painfully so at this point, that these scraps do not prove that Nasser was implementing a Soviet or joint plot; in fact, they do not prove anything. To be sure, the authors do adduce one other devastating proof of Soviet culpability:

> It is noteworthy that Nasser cited *party* authority when he stated on 26 May 1967: "I was authorized by the Arab Socialist Union's High Executive to implement this plan [moving forces into Sinai, removing UNEF, and closing the Straits] at the right time. The right time came when Syria was threatened with aggression." (authors' emphasis and interpolations)[36]

Were it not for the authors' singular decoding technique, who would have guessed that "Arab Socialist Union's High Executive" really meant "Soviet Communist Party's Politburo"?

The "conventional narrative," according to the authors, is that at the end of May "the USSR's policy was aimed at deescalating the crisis."[37] But this mistake also springs from the inability of the untutored eye to read Soviet documents. When the Kremlin privately urged restraint on the Arabs, replying with a "resolute 'nyet'" to an Egyptian first strike, and when the Kremlin privately exhorted Israel "not to increase the tension and not to escalate the situation to the point of letting the weapons talk," its real purpose, according to the authors, was to "precipitate a crisis" by luring Israel into a first strike.[38] In other words, the more the Kremlin counseled against war, the more it must be understood to have supported it. One is hard-pressed however to conceive a statement by a Soviet leader that on such a decoding technique would not constitute proof of the Kremlin's nefarious designs.

In another "sensational" revelation, the authors report that at the end of May a double-agent working for Israel conveyed to his KGB handlers Israel's intention to launch a first strike. (It is argued that Israel was hoping such a message would induce the Soviets to pressure Nasser into backing down.) The authors assert that this message "must have been music to the Soviets' ears" and "may have provided the clincher" for them—even if according to the available evidence the Soviets urgently sought to avert war and anyhow, according to the double-agent, the KGB "might not have passed" his tip to Soviet leaders.[39]

It ought not to come as a surprise at this juncture that Nasser's avowals to Soviet leaders at the end of May that Egypt "never will start *first* the armed conflict" (authors' emphasis); to American leaders that he "would wait until the Israelis had moved"; to Jordanian leaders that he "was quite prepared ... in the event the USG [US government] intervened militarily against him to ask for Soviet assistance"—that these unremarkable statements become further evidence of the "grand design" after being plugged into the authors' program.[40]

The centerpiece of the authors' brief is their allegation that Soviet pilots flew state-of-the-art MiG-25s (Foxbats) over Israel's nuclear facility at Dimona just days before the Israeli attack. The authors have said that these Soviet reconnaissance overflights "encapsulate" the book's argument and constitute "Exhibit A" in support of it.[41]

Before scrutinizing the evidence they marshal, it merits first querying what difference it would make even if the allegation were true. These Foxbat flights are said to constitute the linchpin of the Soviet conspiracy. But how? It has already been noted that, according to the authors, through espionage the Soviets were kept fully apprised of Israel's nuclear program at Dimona. The overflights did not then provide vital intelligence, and the authors do not pretend otherwise. Instead, their importance is said to be that they were "a direct display of Soviet military prowess" and accordingly the "ultimate provocation" designed to "create such concern in Israel that it would surely launch a first strike."[42] But the authors simultaneously contend that until now Israel itself was totally unaware of the Foxbat overflights because the Kremlin had so successfully concealed them.[43] What was not known plainly could not have intimidated and provoked. Thus it appears that even if Exhibit A were true its value as evidence of a Soviet plot would still be nil.

But is it even true? The authors focus on the whereabouts of a highly decorated Soviet flying ace named Aleksandr Vybornov.[44] Piecing together an "extraordinary disclosure," and an "unprecedented assertion," and a "momentous contribution," they claim to have irrefutably proved ("we now know") that Vybornov was dispatched by the Kremlin to Egypt just before the June 1967 war in order to ready the "Soviet air intervention" once Israel took the bait, and that he also must have flown the Foxbat over Dimona "that in time brought the crisis to its climax." The one tiny gap in this subplot is that no verifiable evidence places Vybornov in Egypt before the June war and all the verifiable evidence places him in it only after the war.[45]

The references cited by the authors, as well as others not cited by them,[46] state that General Vybornov arrived in Egypt after the June war as part of a high-level Soviet delegation to provide immediate military assistance. Such accounts square with the well known fact that during the War of Attrition (which began shortly after the June 1967 war) Soviet pilots stationed in Egypt did go on military missions. But no credible evidence exists that Soviet pilots actively participated in the run-up to the June war or in the war itself. The authors speculate on this point with many "ifs" and "may haves," but provide no evidence except "rumors," and this "fascinating bit of hearsay": an American seaman told the authors that he was told by his Russian coworker that he (the coworker) was told by one of his Russian "military buddies" that after "many glasses of refreshment" his (the military buddy's) "Air Force friend admitted flying Egyptian planes during the Six-Day War. He did swear all his friends to secrecy, though."[47]

The authors nonetheless maintain that Vybornov must have been in Egypt before and during the June war because: (1) a 1993 article reports Vybornov explicitly stating that he "witnessed the Israeli attack on an

Egyptian airfield," and (2) a pair of reputable sources—Lieutenant Colonel (ret.) David McFarland of the U.S. Air Force and Brigadier General (ret.) Amir Nachumi of the Israeli Air Force—both personally heard Vybornov speak about "his Egyptian exploits."[48]

But the 1993 article does not state or imply that Vybornov witnessed an Israeli attack on an Egyptian airfield. As for the two key informants who, according to the authors, "definitely" and "precisely" pinpointed Vybornov's "Egyptian exploits" during the period "*leading up* to" the June 1967 war (authors' emphasis),[49] McFarland emailed this writer that he did "not know the exact date,"[50] while Nachumi emailed this writer, "I had spoken to Vybronov [sic] indeed. . . . I do not recall anything said by him referring the [sic] the Six Days War."[51]

The authors left no stone unturned in their search for evidence of the Soviet conspiracy. Every lead in every remote Russian provincial local newspaper was tracked down for new clues and "disclosures." Every potential witness, however peripheral, was interviewed. Strangely, however, the authors never bothered to contact Vybornov. It is not as if he was inaccessible. He lived not in a distant Russian town but in retirement in Moscow, mentally lucid and vigorous, while the authors were writing their book.

On 7 March 2008 at this writer's request a Russian translator put several questions to Vybornov, which he answered after first consulting his notes from the period in question. Here's what Exhibit A of "Exhibit A" had to say:

> *Did Soviet leaders send you on a mission to Egypt before the June 1967 war?*
>
> No.
>
> *Did you fly a MiG-25 (Foxbat) airplane on a reconnaissance mission over the Dimona reactor or over any other place in Israel before the June 1967 war?*
>
> No.

> *Did any Soviet pilot go on a reconnaissance mission in a MiG-25 over the Dimona reactor or over any other place in Israel before the June 1967 war?*
>
> No.
>
> *Did you personally witness the destruction of an Egyptian airfield during the June 1967 war?*
>
> No. Nothing even close to this happened.
>
> *Did you go to Egypt before, during or after the June 1967 war?*
> I went to Egypt in July 1967 for one month and a half. I trained Egyptian pilots to fly the MiG-17, MiG-21, and Su-7.

The authors state that because "the Middle Eastern mission was not his main claim to fame," Vybornov "would have little motive to fabricate its incidental mention in his résumé."[52] Their contentions that before the June 1967 war Vybornov went to Egypt in order to prepare an air assault on Israel and that he flew a Foxbat over Dimona must—in light of his categorical denials *and their own reasoning*—be false.[53]

Although they fail to adduce any evidence whatsoever that on the eve of the June war Soviet-piloted Foxbats flew over Dimona, the authors nonetheless proudly proclaim, "When we presented our MiG-25 hypothesis to a former Israeli intelligence officer who specialized in the Soviet military, his response was: 'Of course.'"[54] The corresponding endnote cites an anonymous interview.

Once conclusively proven, the Foxbat overflights become a crucial nexus in the alleged Soviet plot. Here's a typical passage:

> Badran arrived in Moscow on the 25th, with the plan already in hand. Grechko's order to carry out the second sortie over Dimona (as Vybornov specified, it had to be authorized personally and individually by the minister) was issued no later than

the morning of 26 May, while Badran's talks in Moscow were deadlocked. Several hours after the flight was completed and its report was flown directly to Grechko, Nasser was handed the letter that Kosygin dispatched the same day. The flight might have been mentioned in its text, which has never been published, or added orally by Pozhidayev (who was probably informed directly by Vybornov as well), or communicated through Badran. Nasser's compliance with the Soviet request not to strike first by bombing Israel may well have been due at least in major part to this token of the Soviets' continued determination to provoke Israel into a preemptive attack.[55]

The cast of characters and particulars of place and time are of less account than the wondrous new speculations ("might have," "probably," "may well have") that are conjured up on the basis of "the flight"—itself a speculation lacking a particle of proof yet confidently asserted with the definite article. The absence of proof in the first instance of Soviet overflights also does not deter the authors from going on to assert that, although no "direct evidence has emerged yet," nonetheless it is "reasonable to assume that the US military was aware" of them; and does not deter the authors from going on to speculate whether "General Vybornov's mission ... has been suppressed to this day" by Israel.[56] On one point however it would be unreasonable to quarrel with the authors: the Foxbats over Dimona "hypothesis" truly is Exhibit A of the book's substance.

The Kremlin's plot was foiled, according to the authors, because the unanticipated devastation wrought by Israel's first strike preempted a joint Soviet-Arab retaliation. In yet another bombshell, it is alleged that a Soviet mole in Israel "with access to information at cabinet level" had obtained the precise date of Israel's attack.[57] It might be wondered why the Kremlin did not alert its Arab co-conspirators that Israel was poised to deliver a crippling blow and achieve a swift victory, thereby foiling their plot? The authors just barely take notice of this elementary question, while their response once again strains gullibility: at the very last moment the Kremlin botched its finely calibrated plot, failing to take the obvious step of warning Nasser, because of bureaucratic "syndromes that have bedeviled not only the Soviet system."[58]

The authors also allege that the Kremlin's planning for the retaliatory strike included a massive naval invasion of Haifa,[59] strategic bomber attacks and even a nuclear blast,[60] although and alas whether Soviet leaders set the "goal of eradicating Israel . . . remains unanswerable—probably forever."[61]

In the real world Soviet leaders were split over how to react to Israel's surprise attack, some counseling (or rumored to be counseling) military intervention in support of the Arabs.[62] The authors construe any Soviet statement after the attack counseling intervention as proof of the conspiracy, just as they construe any Soviet statement before the attack counseling restraint as proof of the conspiracy. But if the conspiracy phantasmagoria they concocted is stripped away, the handful of credible statements cited by them simply confirm what is already known.

The authors also allege that, although the Soviets were not directly responsible for the Israeli attack on the U.S.S. *Liberty*,[63] "disclosures from US and Israeli records" show that "the circumstances are covered with Soviet fingerprints," indeed "there beckons a seductive but unsubstantiated scenario, in which the Soviets deliberately lured the Israelis into attacking the US ship."[64] If Soviet culpability is not better known, it is because the U.S. and Israel have both been engaged in a cover-up of it.[65] Disappointingly, the authors present no new "disclosures" on the U.S. cover-up of Soviet complicity in 9/11.

Although the absurdity of *Foxbats over Dimona* would be hard to exaggerate, it was nonetheless published by Yale University Press and received rapturous notices from respected scholars. Its publication and reception point up that, when it comes to Israel, the divide between academic research and popular propaganda is not always clear-cut. Even among distinguished publishers that should know better, and despite the vetting process of peer review, sheer fraud can still pass muster and, consequently, Israel's apologists can still, occasionally, find ammunition in the realm of scholarship. The transparent shoddiness of the book, and the ease with which it can be exposed to ridicule, also attest, however, to the difficulty today of mounting a case for Israel in the face of the extant scholarly record.

Here is a book that is truly revisionist, challenging what we thought we knew about the origins and conduct of the Six-Day War, Israel's crushing victory over Egypt, Jordan, and Syria 40 years ago. The exact role played by the Soviet Union has always been murky. The authors work their way through the murk, meticulously using every snippet of relevant information from an extraordinary range of sources.—Lawrence D. Freedman, *Foreign Affairs* (included in its list of outstanding new books)

Ginor and Remez argue in this book that the Soviet Union played a much larger role in the June 1967 Arab-Israeli War than has been recognized previously.... Their argument is based on, among other sources, a careful study of Soviet documents—many of which have only recently come to light—as well as interviews with former Soviet officials and servicemen who participated in the June 1967 events.... I must concur ... with Lawrence Freedman's judgment that Ginor and Remez have presented such a strong case for their argument that "the onus is now on others to show why they are wrong."—Mark N. Katz, *Middle East Journal*

[The authors] offer a plausible explanation for the causes of the war.... The text reads like the solution to a mystery, amassing information from voluminous sources, guiding readers step by step through the argument, and making an intuitively compelling case that must be taken seriously.... It offers a viable, exciting interpretation for others to chew on, with many implications.—Daniel Pipes, *New York Sun*

A unique contribution to the history of the Cold War in the eastern Mediterranean. The authors challenge the predominant view of the

1967 war, and theirs is certainly an original explanation that has been little appreciated if not entirely ignored by Western historians.—David Murphy, former chief of Soviet operations, Central Intelligence Agency

A fascinating, plausible, and hitherto untold tale. The authors demonstrate that the Six-Day War marked a major Soviet political-military defeat comparable to the Cuban Missile Crisis. Carefully researched and reconstructed, fast-paced and well-written, this book represents a major contribution to the history of the modern Middle East.—Dov S. Zakheim, former U.S. Under Secretary of Defense

Ginor and Remez have done an impressive job of information gathering, and they have conducted a comprehensive and in-depth inquiry. There is no question that as a pioneering study presenting issues that need to be reexamined and probed further, this is an important book.—Reuven Pedatzur, *Haaretz*

An ambitious and thoroughly revisionist account of the origins of the Six-Day War. By placing Israeli nuclear ambitions—and the Soviet reaction—as major links in the chain of events, the authors have produced a book that will stand out in the debate about the Cold War and the Middle East.—Odd Arne Westad, co-chair, Cold War Studies Centre, London School of Economics

A well-researched and provocative new look at the background to the 1967 Israeli-Arab war. Its central thesis appears unreal until one assesses the myriad sources and deep documentation that add up to a compelling argument. This book will immediately assume a place of prominence among the must-read sources for understanding the war.—Daniel C. Kurtzer, former U.S. Ambassador to Israel and Egypt, Woodrow Wilson School of Public and International Affairs, Princeton University

This book resolves one of the great mysteries of the Six-Day War, putting the Soviet Union at the center of the drama. Written with a wealth

of documentary evidence, it has all the intrigue of a detective story, and all the pace of a novel.—Sir Martin Gilbert, author of *Israel: A history*

This fascinating new book brings to light new, original research on the origins of the 1967 War. While data and facts are still coming in and skeptics may scoff, the Soviet role now appears to be larger and more intensive than many of us may have realized.—Thomas R. Pickering, Former Under Secretary of State for Political Affairs 1997-2000, Ambassador to Russia 1993-96, Ambassador to Israel 1985-88

Ginor and Remez's book opens a door for further research. Its thesis deserves to be beaten like bushes by hunters outing their prey—and the prey will indeed be trapped, one way or another, at the moment the Russian archives open the relevant files. And if what the authors suggest is true, the Six Day War will end up illumined in a completely fresh light.—Benny Morris, *New Republic*

[A] fantastic book by Isabella Ginor and Gideon Remez, Foxbats over Dimona, *used released documents and amazing research techniques to document the fact that the Soviets were egging the Arabs on to provoke Israel into a war that they could exploit to try to take out the budding nuclear capabilities at Dimona. Hence, the deployment—unprecedented—of Foxbats in reconnaissance missions over Dimona prior to the war.*—Ian Lustick, University of Pennsylvania[66]

The Washington Institute for Near East Policy awarded its 2008 Silver Prize for "nonfiction books on the Middle East" to *Foxbats over Dimona*. The jurors were Jim Hoagland (*Washington Post*), Bernard Lewis (Princeton University), and Michael Mandelbaum (Johns Hopkins School of Advanced International Studies).

9/ ISRAEL VERSUS THE WORLD

A growing consensus in recent years has pinned the blame for the diplomatic impasse on Israel's refusal to withdraw from the Palestinian territory it occupied in June 1967. "Israel's continued control and colonization of Palestinian land have been the primary obstacles to a comprehensive peace agreement," former U.S. president Jimmy Carter concluded in *Palestine Peace Not Apartheid*. "Peace will come to Israel and the Middle East only when the Israeli government is willing to comply with international law ... by accepting its legal borders."[1]

Yet, not too long ago, statements such as Carter's, putting the onus for the conflict's persistence on Israel because of its defiance of international law, would have evoked bewilderment and indignation. True, some distinguished legal scholars early on did point to the Israeli occupation of Arab lands as the primary impediment to peace. "In view of the acceptance in principle of the resolution [242] by the adjacent Arab states except Syria," Quincy Wright observed in 1970, "the major obstacle to progress seems to be the refusal of Israel to do so and to agree to withdraw from occupied territories."[2] In the court of U.S. public opinion, however, the terms for resolving the conflict were still largely in dispute for many years after the occupation began, and Israel's diplomatic posture still commanded widespread support.

Consider the debate over the meaning of U.N. Security Council resolution 242. Although the documentary record made unmistakably clear that it had no title to the conquered territories, Israel still managed to persuade a broad public that 242 conferred legitimacy to its claim on these lands. Thus, in his widely cited publications defending the Israeli occupation, influential legal authority Julius Stone argued[3] that the preambular paragraph of 242 "[e]mphasizing the inadmissibility of the acquisition of territory by war" had been distorted by Israel's enemies.[4] It did not require a full Israeli withdrawal, according to him, because the West Bank and Gaza had been acquired in a defensive war:

> International law forbids acquisition by unlawful force, but not where, as in the case of Israel's self-defense in 1967, the entry on the territory was lawful. It does not forbid, in particular, when the force is used to stop an aggressor, for the effect of such prohibition would be to guarantee to all potential aggressors that, even if their aggression failed, all territory lost in the attempt would be automatically returned to them. Such a rule would be absurd to the point of lunacy. There is no such rule. . . . International law presented no obstacles even to formal annexation by Israel if she were so minded.[5]

Beyond asserting an absolute legal basis for Israel's territorial claim, Stone also alleged that relative to Israel "no other State can show a better title"[6] to the West Bank and Gaza; and that "even assuming that a legal principle concerning self-determination exists and that Palestinian Arabs now qualify for 'national' rights . . ., there already exists in Palestine a state, the State of Jordan."[7] He further purported that Israel's right to East Jerusalem went "beyond that of a merely lawful belligerent occupant to territorial sovereignty";[8] that "far from forbidding the settlement of Jews" in the West Bank and Gaza, international law "contemplates such settlement as a principal objective," and that the Fourth Geneva Convention, which prohibits such settlement, was "totally irrelevant";[9] and that "'return or compensation' is neither a necessary nor a feasible basis of solution" to the Palestinian refugee problem.[10]

In effect Stone concluded that on all the "permanent status" issues of the "peace process"—borders, Jerusalem, settlements, refugees—Israel occupied the legal high ground.

Stone's contentions in fact lacked any legal or historical foundation. It is testament to the potency of systematized propaganda that a pellucid statement as well as a peremptory legal principle such as *the inadmissibility of the acquisition of territory by war* could have been twisted out of shape and turned into an object of heated controversy. Because Stone's arguments have been echoed by Israel's "supporters" for decades in countless venues, and because they still carry some conviction, albeit in much narrower circles, it merits juxtaposing the components of his analysis against the relevant documentary record. Such a comparison brings home just how meretricious the Israeli case has been all along.

STONE: Israel acted in self-defense against Egyptian aggression in June 1967.

THE RECORD: Neither Tel Aviv nor Washington believed that Israel faced an imminent attack when it launched a first strike on 5 June 1967.[11] Still, Stone sought support for his contention in the fact that postwar resolutions at the United Nations branding Israel the aggressor did not garner substantial support.[12]

It is true that at the U.N. General Assembly Fifth Emergency Special Session after the June war,[13] the operative paragraph of a Soviet-sponsored resolution that "Vigorously condemns Israel's aggressive activities and the continuing occupation by Israel of part of the territory of the United Arab Republic, Syria and Jordan, which constitutes an act of recognized aggression" garnered only 36 votes in favor and fully 57 votes against, with 23 abstentions.[14] However, it would appear to be at least as telling that the General Assembly never even contemplated, let alone put to a vote, a resolution branding Egypt (or the Arab states) the aggressor in the June war.

During the debate at the Special Session, member states were divided between those holding Israel guilty, those holding both sides culpable, those deeming it futile or pointless to apportion blame and those refraining from comment (see Table 1). Although dissenting from the Soviet resolution, the U.S. did so not because it held Israel to be an innocent party in the June war, but rather on the grounds that "in light of all the events...that led up to the fighting, it would be neither equitable nor constructive for this Organization to issue a one-sided condemnation" of Israel.[15] *The only country in the world that maintained Israel had acted in self-defense against Egyptian aggression was Israel.*

TABLE 1   STATE RESPONSIBILITY FOR THE OUTBREAK OF HOSTILITIES ON 5 JUNE 1967: SPEAKERS AT THE GENERAL ASSEMBLY FIFTH EMERGENCY SPECIAL SESSION 17 JUNE—18 SEPTEMBER 1967[16]

Country (meeting/paragraph)	Israel	Both Sides	Unknown/ Unimportant	No Comment
Afghanistan (1533/11, 20-24)	x			
Albania (1535/19)	x			
Algeria (1543/88)	x			
Argentina (1537/111-112)			x	
Australia (1542/80)			x	
Belgium (1531/57)			x	
Bolivia				x
Brazil (1540/5)		x		
Bulgaria (1528/30)	x			
Burma				x
Burundi (1542/46)	x			
Byelorussia (1533/47)	x			
Canada (1533/110)		x		
Ceylon				x
Chile				x
Colombia				x
Costa Rica (1542/115-117)			x	
Cuba (1534/106)	x			

TABLE 1 *(continued)*

Country (meeting/paragraph)	Israel	Both Sides	Unknown/ Unimportant	No Comment
Cyprus (1541/71-73)	x			
Czechoslovakia (1527/125)	x			
Democratic Republic of Congo				x
Denmark (1529/74)			x	
Ecuador (1539/10-11)			x	
Ethiopia				x
Finland				x
France				x
Greece				x
Guinea (1534/34, 40)	x			
Honduras				x
Hungary (1534/1, 10)	x			
India (1530/153-168)	x			
Indonesia (1534/94)	x			
Iran				x
Iraq (1537/30-32)	x			
Ireland				x
Italy (1530/127)			x	
Ivory Coast (1540/44)			x	
Japan				x
Jordan (1536/2, 4)	x			
Kuwait (1542/17)	x			
Lebanon (1539/96, 110)	x			
Libya (1543/3-4)	x			
Madagascar				x
Malaysia (1541/61-62)	x			
Mali (1543/115-119)	x			
Malta (1542/94)			x	
Mauritania (1531/6)	x			
Mexico				x
Mongolia (1547/57)	x			

(continued)

TABLE 1 *(continued)*

Country (meeting/paragraph)	Israel	Both Sides	Unknown/ Unimportant	No Comment
Morocco (1537/15-17)	x			
Nepal				x
Netherlands				x
New Zealand (1540/24)		x		
Nigeria (1537/74)			x	
Norway (1536/67)			x	
Pakistan (1531/126, 161)	x			
Peru (1541/15)			x	
Poland (1534/53)	x			
Romania				x
Saudi Arabia (1541/22)	x			
Sierra Leone (1548/5)			x	
Somalia (1538/2-8)	x			
Spain (1539/81)			x	
Sweden (1533/91)			x	
Sudan (1530/37-59)	x			
Tanzania (1530/18)	x			
Thailand (1545/79)			x	
Trinidad and Tobago				x
Tunisia (1543/29)	x			
Turkey				x
Ukraine (1532/19)	x			
United Kingdom				x
United States (1527/33)		x		
Uruguay				x
U.S.S.R. (1526/25-28)	x			
Venezuela				x
Yemen (1536/40, 56-8)	x			
Yugoslavia (1529/81)	x			
Zambia (1538/84-85, 87)	x			

STONE: It is lawful to annex territory conquered in a war of self-defense.

THE RECORD: Prior to as well as immediately after the June 1967 war leading authorities in international law rejected the proposition that a state can acquire legal title to territory in a war of self-defense:

- Ian Brownlie (1963)—"lawful belligerents should not be permitted to act *ultra vires* [i.e., beyond their power] by acquiring territory as a result of a lawful war";[17]
- R. Y. Jennings (1963)—"the suggestion that the State that does not resort to force unlawfully, e.g., resorts to war in self-defense, may still acquire a title by conquest ... is to be regarded with some suspicion. It seems to be based upon a curious assumption that provided a war is lawful in origin, it goes on being lawful to whatever lengths it may afterwards be pursued.... Force used in self-defense ... is undoubtedly lawful. But it must be proportionate to the threat of immediate danger, and when the threat has been averted the plea of self-defense can no longer be available.... [I]t would be a curious law of self-defense that permitted the defender in the course of his defense to seize and keep the resources and territory of the attacker";[18]
- D. W. Bowett (1971)—"there is virtually universal acceptance of the principle ... that states cannot acquire territory by resort to force.... [I]t is impossible to conceive self-defense as justifying the acquisition of title to territory. One can conceive of self-defense justifying the temporary occupation of territory but never the permanent acquisition of title and there is no system or principle of law which conceives of such a thing."[19]

These conclusions have been reiterated in recent scholarly studies. Sharon Korman finds that the U.N. Charter, as well as the League of Nations Covenant before it, "prohibit all acquisitions of territory by force, irrespective of the lawfulness of the cause of war,"[20] while John Dugard finds that "the United Nations expressly refuses to accept the argument that territory may be permanently acquired as a result of action taken in lawful self-defense," and that "large majorities in the General Assembly in support of this principle [prohibiting acquisition of territory by means of the lawful use of force] and the failure of any major power to veto it in the Security Council must surely provide *prima facie* evidence that this principle is part of the international public order and, by implication, a peremptory norm."[21]

Stone further asserted that such a prohibition would be "absurd to the point of lunacy" because would-be aggressors would then know in advance that embarking on territorial aggrandizement entailed no risk of their own territorial loss.[22] International law bars annexation, however, for the same reason that it bars resort to mass executions, forced labor, and deportations against an aggressor: "such measures would . . . involve the concept of collective guilt which is generally considered to be illegitimate."[23] To go by Stone's tit-for-tat reasoning, it would be equally absurd to prohibit the sanction of genocide against a state held culpable of that crime.[24]

STONE: The "inadmissibility" clause was a token verbal gesture by the U.N., the significance of which the Arab states inflated.[25]

THE RECORD: There was "near unanimity" at the Special Session regarding "withdrawal of the armed forces from the territory of neighboring Arab states," U.N. Secretary-General U Thant noted in his annual report, because "everyone agrees that there should be no territorial gains by military conquest."[26] A tabulation of the public statements at the Special Session shows that some states called for Israel's full withdrawal because it was the aggressor, others because international law prohibits the acquisition of territory by war, and still others for both reasons or with no reason given (see Table 2).

9/ ISRAEL VERSUS THE WORLD

TABLE 2 WHY ISRAEL MUST WITHDRAW TO ITS 4 JUNE BORDER: SPEAKERS AT THE GENERAL ASSEMBLY FIFTH EMERGENCY SPECIAL SESSION, 17 JUNE—18 SEPTEMBER 1967[27]

Country (meeting/paragraph)	Israel Committed Aggression	It Is Inadmissible to Acquire Territory by War	Both Reasons	No Reason
Afghanistan (1533/36, 77)	x			
Albania (1535/67)	x			
Algeria (1543/88)	x			
Argentina (1537/119, 128)		x		
Belgium (1531/76)				x
Bolivia (1549/163)		x		
Brazil (1540/6)				x
Bulgaria (1528/30)	x			
Burma (1548/31)		x		
Burundi (1542/65)				x
Byelorussia (1533/77)	x			
Canada (1546/139)		x		
Ceylon (1540/65-67, 70)		x		
Chile (1549/125-126, 131)		x		
Colombia (1538/66, 68)		x		
Costa Rica (1542/122)		x		
Cuba (1534/111)	x			
Cyprus (1541/84)			x	
Czechoslovakia (1527/125)	x			
Democratic Republic of Congo (1548/99)				x
Denmark (1529/71)		x		
Ecuador (1539/21)		x		
Ethiopia (1547/39)		x		
Finland (1549/77)		x		
France (1546/111-112)		x		
Greece (1542/31-32)		x		

(continued)

TABLE 2 (continued)

Country (meeting/paragraph)	Israel Committed Aggression	It Is Inadmissible to Acquire Territory by War	Both Reasons	No Reason
Guinea (1534/48)	x			
Honduras (1546/170)		x		
Hungary (1534/1)	x			
India (1530/172-175)			x	
Indonesia (1534/97-98)	x			
Iran (1530/105-106)		x		
Iraq (1537/36, 39)	x			
Ireland (1538/32, 36)		x		
Ivory Coast (1540/49, 56)		x		
Japan (1549/92)		x		
Jordan (1536/22)	x			
Kuwait (1542/17, 20-21)			x	
Lebanon (1539/112)	x			
Libya (1543/7)	x			
Madagascar (1546/107)				x
Malaysia (1541/59, 61-62)			x	
Mali (1543/146-147)	x			
Malta (1542/104)		x		
Mauritania (1531/40)	x			
Mongolia (1547/58)	x			
Morocco (1537/26)	x			
Nepal (1534/5-6)		x		
New Zealand (1540/28)		x		
Nigeria (1537/80)		x		
Norway (1536/76-77)		x		
Pakistan (1531/140, 161, 168)			x	
Peru (1541/18)				x
Poland (1534/59)	x			

TABLE 2 *(continued)*

Country (meeting/paragraph)	Israel Committed Aggression	It Is Inadmissible to Acquire Territory by War	Both Reasons	No Reason
Romania (1533/136-137)		x		
Saudi Arabia (1541/31)	x			
Sierra Leone (1548/5)		x		
Somalia (1538/29)	x			
Spain (1539/86)		x		
Sudan (1530/83)			x	
Sweden (1533/92)		x		
Tanzania (1530/19-23)			x	
Thailand (1545/80)				x
Trinidad and Tobago (1548/47, 58)		x		
Tunisia (1543/76)	x			
Turkey (1532/11)		x		
Ukraine (1532/42)	x			
United Kingdom (1529/15)		x		
United States (1546/3, 5, 9-10, 32; 1554/91)		x		
Uruguay (1543/85)		x		
U.S.S.R. (1526/82)	x			
Venezuela (1545/44-46, 53)		x		
Yemen (1536/63)	x			
Yugoslavia (1529/83, 97)	x			
Zambia (1538/85-87)	x			

Note: Australia, Italy and the Netherlands used vaguer formulations on Israeli withdrawal in their respective interventions during the debate but then voted for a General Assembly resolution calling for full Israeli withdrawal in accordance with the principle of the inadmissibility of acquiring territory by war.

Every draft resolution submitted for a vote at the Special Session explicitly called for a full Israeli withdrawal.[28] What divided the General Assembly was whether or not full Israeli withdrawal should be made conditional on a termination of belligerency and recognition of Israel by neighboring Arab states. Of the two principal draft resolutions submitted for a vote,[29] the text sponsored by Non-Aligned countries called for unconditional full Israeli withdrawal whereas the text sponsored by Latin American countries called for conditional full Israeli withdrawal.[30] The key withdrawal paragraph(s) in the respective draft resolutions read:

Non-Aligned draft	Latin American draft
1. Calls upon Israel immediately to withdraw all its forces behind the armistice lines established by the General Armistice Agreements between Israel and the Arab countries.[31]	1. Urgently requests: (a) Israel to withdraw all its forces from all the territories occupied by it as a result of the recent conflict; ... 2. Reaffirms its conviction that no stable international order can be based on the threat or use of force, and declares that the validity of the occupation or acquisition of territories brought by such means should not be recognized.[32]

Fully 113 of the 121 member states of the United Nations either supported one of the two draft resolutions put to a vote or expressly supported the principle of full Israeli withdrawal during the General Assembly debate.[33] The U.S. voted for the Latin American resolution and during the General Assembly debate stressed that for a "durable peace" to be achieved "one immediate, obvious and imperative step is the disengagement of all forces and the withdrawal of Israeli forces to their own territory."[34] *The only country in the world that registered any dissent from the principle that Israel must fully withdraw was Israel.* It might also be noted that Israel did not vote against the Latin American resolution but instead only abstained, and that its lone dissent from the full withdrawal principle was couched in the circumspect language, "Sovereign states have the right and duty to fix their permanent frontiers by mutual agreement amongst themselves."[35]

9/ ISRAEL VERSUS THE WORLD

In his statement to the Security Council in late November 1967, Britain's U.N. ambassador Lord Caradon clarified the import of his draft resolution, which was subsequently adopted unanimously as Security Council resolution 242:

> In our resolution we stated the principle of the "Withdrawal of Israel armed forces from territories occupied in the recent conflict" and in the preamble we emphasized "the inadmissibility of the acquisition of territory by war." In our view the wording of these provisions is clear.[36]

Of the fourteen other members of the Security Council, fully ten (Argentina, Brazil, Bulgaria, Ethiopia, France, India, Japan, Mali, Nigeria, Soviet Union) underscored during the vote on 242 the obligation of Israel fully to withdraw in accordance with the "inadmissibility" principle,[37] and three more (Denmark, Canada, United States) had already called for full Israeli withdrawal in accordance with the "inadmissibility" principle during the Special Session. (The credentials of the fifteenth member, Nationalist China, were under challenge in the Security Council as well as the General Assembly and consequently it barely participated.) *Not one of the 15 members of the Security Council registered any dissent from the "inadmissibility" principle in their respective statements during the vote on 242.* Were it not for the "inadmissibility" clause, Lord Caradon would later recall, "there could have been no unanimous vote" for 242 in the Security Council.[38]

Beyond its vote in support of the Latin American resolution and its statements during the Special Session, the U.S. also registered support for the "inadmissibility" clause and/or called for a full Israeli withdrawal in multiple draft resolutions negotiated behind the scenes with the Soviet Union prior to the Security Council's adoption of 242.[39] Apparently succumbing to pressures exerted by Israel and its domestic lobby, the U.S. proposed in early November a draft resolution to the Security Council omitting the "inadmissibility" clause and calling merely for "withdrawal of armed forces from occupied territory," but it garnered little support and was not put to a vote. In its own diplomatic representations, however, Washington adhered to the "inadmissibility" principle in that it consistently interpreted 242 to allow for at most minor and mutual land swaps.[40]

For its part Israel harbored no illusions that the "inadmissibility" clause of 242 called for a full withdrawal, hence its strenuous but ultimately abortive undertakings to expunge the offending words from the resolution,[41] while the Arab states found satisfaction in the knowledge that "the clause on withdrawal, taken together with the clause on the inadmissibility of acquiring territory by war, meant that in principle their point had been conceded."[42]

If any doubts still lingered about the legal and practical import of the "inadmissibility" clause, then proceedings at the General Assembly in 1970 should have dispelled them. In a resolution adopted by consensus, "Declaration of Principles of International Law Concerning Friendly Relations and Co-operation among States in Accordance with the Charter of the United Nations," the General Assembly tersely underlined: "The territory of a State shall not be the object of acquisition by another State resulting from the threat or use of force. No territorial acquisition resulting from the threat or use of force shall be recognized as legal."[43]

If, as Stone alleged, the "inadmissibility" clause in 242 was intended only to bar the acquisition of territory in an illegal war of aggression, and if, as he alleged, the consensus was that Israel occupied the West Bank and Gaza in a lawful war of self-defense, then why did so many states vigorously argue for the clause's inclusion in 242 and why did Israel vigorously argue for its exclusion in the resolution? To judge by Stone's exposition, all the parties suffered from a colossal misapprehension and squandered massive amounts of time and energy because the "inadmissibility" clause was wholly irrelevant.

A perusal of the documentary record unequivocally demonstrates that the case mounted by Israel's defenders to justify its retention of (parts of) the occupied Palestinian territories lacked any grounding in law, opinion or recent history. When Jimmy Carter put the onus on Israel for the diplomatic impasse because of its defiance of international law, he could easily have cited a wealth of evidence to support him.

Still, the sorts of arguments made by Stone used to carry a lot of weight among the broad American public and particularly in liberal circles. But in recent years the fundamental legal-political questions bearing on the Israel-Palestine conflict have been definitively settled, and on each of them the position upheld by Israel has been resoundingly repudiated. Whereas Israel's arguments once persuaded, they now fall flat because the consensus has hardened and concomitantly Israel's defiance of it has grown starker. Although popular propagandistic literature maintains the pretense that the fundamental "permanent status" issues are controversial, the scholarly and documentary sources make plain that they are anything but.

The U.N. General Assembly votes every year on the resolution "Peaceful Settlement of the Question of Palestine." The resolution uniformly includes these tenets:

> Affirming the principle of the inadmissibility of the acquisition of territory by war
>
> Affirming also the illegality of the Israeli settlements in the territory occupied since 1967 and of Israeli actions aimed at changing the status of Jerusalem
>
> Stresses the need for: (a) The realization of the inalienable rights of the Palestinian people, primarily the right to self-determination; (b) The withdrawal of Israel from the Palestinian territory occupied since 1967[44]
>
> Also stresses the need for resolving the problem of the Palestine refugees in conformity with its resolution 194 (III) of 11 December 1948.[45]

The vote on this resolution during the past 14 years is recorded in Table 3.

TABLE 3 U.N. GENERAL ASSEMBLY VOTE ON "PEACEFUL SETTLEMENT OF THE QUESTION OF PALESTINE" RESOLUTION

Year	Vote [Yes-No-Abstained]	Negative votes cast by ...
1997	155-2-3	Israel, United States
1998	154-2-3	Israel, United States
1999	149-3-2	Israel, United States, Marshall Islands
2000	149-2-3	Israel, United States
2001	131-6-20	Israel, United States, Marshall Islands, Micronesia, Nauru, Tuvalu
2002	160-4-3	Israel, United States, Marshall Islands, Micronesia
2003	160-6-5	Israel, United States, Marshall Islands, Micronesia, Palau, Uganda
2004	161-7-10	Israel, United States, Australia, Grenada, Marshall Islands, Micronesia, Palau
2005	156-6-9	Israel, United States, Australia, Marshall Islands, Micronesia, Palau
2006	157-7-10	Israel, United States, Australia, Marshall Islands, Micronesia, Nauru, Palau
2007	161-7-5	Israel, United States, Australia, Marshall Islands, Micronesia, Nauru, Palau
2008	164-7-3	Israel, United States, Australia, Marshall Islands, Micronesia, Nauru, Palau
2009	164-7-4	Israel, United States, Australia, Marshall Islands, Micronesia, Nauru, Palau
2010	165-7-4	Israel, United States, Australia, Marshall Islands, Micronesia, Nauru, Palau
2011	167-7-4	Israel, United States, Canada, Marshall Islands, Micronesia, Nauru, Palau

The weight of this broad General Assembly consensus[46] repudiating Israel's diplomatic posture was enhanced by the landmark 2004 International Court of Justice (ICJ) advisory opinion on the legality of the wall Israel has been constructing in the West Bank.[47] In its statement of the "rules and principles of international law which are relevant in assessing the legality of the measures taken by Israel," the ICJ inventoried these:

> "No territorial acquisition resulting from the threat or use of force shall be recognized as legal"[48]
> "the policy and practices of Israel in establishing settlements in the Palestinian and other Arab territories occupied since 1967" have "no legal validity"[49]

In its complementary deliberations on "whether the construction of the wall has violated those rules and principles," the ICJ found that:

> [B]oth the General Assembly and the Security Council have referred, with regard to Palestine, to the customary rule of "the inadmissibility of the acquisition of territory by war".... It is on this same basis that the Council has several times condemned the measures taken by Israel to change the status of Jerusalem.
>
> ...
>
> As regards the principle of the right of peoples to self-determination,... the existence of a "Palestinian people" is no longer in issue.... [Its] rights include the right to self-determination.
>
> ...
>
> Israel has conducted a policy and developed practices involving the establishment of settlements in the Occupied Palestinian Territory.
>
> ...
>
> The Court concludes that the Israeli settlements in the Occupied Palestinian Territory (including East Jerusalem) have been established in breach of international law.[50]

It warrants noting that *not one of the 15 judges sitting on the ICJ registered dissent from these basic principles and findings*. It can scarcely be said however that they evinced prejudice against Israel, or that it was a "kangaroo court," as Harvard law professor Alan Dershowitz charged.[51] Several of the judges, although voting with the majority, expressed profound, perhaps undue, sympathy for Israel in their respective separate opinions.[52] If the judges were nearly of one mind in their final determination, this consensus sprang not from collective prejudice but from the factual situation: the uncontroversial nature of the legal principles at stake and Israel's uncontroversial breach of them.

Even the one judge voting against the 14-person majority condemning Israel's construction of the wall, Thomas Buergenthal of the United States,[53] was at pains to stress that there was "much" in the advisory opinion "with which I agree." On the crucial question of Israeli settlements he stated: "Paragraph 6 of Article 49 of the Fourth Geneva Convention ... does not admit for exception on grounds of military or security exigencies. It provides that 'the Occupying Power shall not deport or transfer parts of its own civilian population in the territory it occupies.' I agree that this provision applies to the Israeli settlements in the West Bank and that their existence violates Article 49, paragraph 6."

A broad consensus has also crystallized upholding the Palestinian "right of return." Respected human rights organizations "urge Israel to recognize the right to return for those Palestinians, and their descendants, who fled from territory that is now within the State of Israel, and who have maintained appropriate links with that territory" (Human Rights Watch), and "call for Palestinians who fled or were expelled from Israel, the West Bank or Gaza Strip, along with those of their descendants who have maintained genuine links with the area, to be able to exercise their right to return" (Amnesty International).[54]

Some two decades ago Oxford professor of international law Adam Roberts opined that "there is still basic disagreement about what parts of international law are formally applicable to the situation in the [West Bank and Gaza] territories," and international law specialist Antonio Cassese observed that "the question of Palestinian rights is one of the most difficult, controversial, and divisive issues in the present international community."[55] The ICJ advisory opinion coupled with the findings and conclusions of respected human rights organizations demonstrate that this contentious juridical situation no longer obtains. There is now agreement among recognized authorities in international law (excepting the Israeli contingent) on the essential legal principles governing the Israeli occupation and the practical political consequences flowing from these principles.[56] The positions defended by Israel's "supporters" fall well outside this authoritative consensus. Whereas Stone could mount a legal argument defending Israel and still be taken seriously a few decades ago, the legal consensus opposing Israel's occupation is now so robust that this line of defense is no longer open. Instead, apologists for Israel must now resort to pleading the irrelevance of international law or passing over it in silence. A popular account of the "peace process" by one of Israel's staunchest advocates illustrates this point.

Dennis Ross's *The Missing Peace: The inside story of the fight for Middle East peace*[57] exemplifies how Israel's diplomatic posture is only defensible if the broad legal consensus for resolving the conflict is ignored. Upon its release, the book was widely heralded as the definitive treatment of the Israeli-Palestinian "peace process," and a vindication of the role Israel played in it.[58] A close scrutiny of *Missing Peace* reveals, however, that its analysis and conclusions are based on a wholesale repudiation of the widely accepted norms of international law applicable to the conflict.

The "one overriding lesson from the story of the peace process," Ross observes in his prologue, "is that truth-telling is a necessity."[59] The "purpose" of his book as well as the "key to peace," he likewise concludes, "is to debunk mythologies ... to engage in truth-telling."[60] Ross's execution of this debunking and truth-telling enterprise however poses significant problems. His account of the peace process is based almost entirely on his memory and notes. Its authority derives chiefly from the fact that Ross was the "point person"[61] on the Arab-Israeli conflict in President Bill Clinton's administration. (He played the same role until recently in President Barack Obama's administration.) But major discrepancies crop up when his depiction of the historical background to the peace process is juxtaposed against the documentary record. If Ross's history turns out to be a "pro"-Israel apologia where it can be crosschecked, one cannot help but wonder whether his eyewitness account of the negotiations is not also skewed.

A second problem with Ross's "inside story" is that on salient points it differs from the accounts of other key participants. Rather than retread the ground covered by that testimony,[62] the focus here will be on the *premises* grounding Ross's description of what happened and why, and the distortions that spring from them. Those premises show that Ross subordinates the normative framework of rights—i.e., what each side is entitled to under international law—to the arbitrary and capricious framework of "needs." Judging by their respective rights, all the concessions at the 2000 Camp David summit, which is the focus of Ross's book, came from the Palestinian side, none from the Israeli side.

To prove Palestinian culpability for the summit's failure, Ross contrives a standard of needs and appoints himself the final arbiter of what each side needed. If Palestinians emerge from Ross's account as the principal obstacle to peace, it owes not to the factual reality but rather to the rigged framework in which Ross situates the facts. It should of course be borne in mind throughout that Ross merely articulates the consistent positions and biases of successive U.S. administrations. The problems with his book are institutional, not personal.

An overarching theme of Ross's book is that Palestinian terrorism undercut Israeli trust and consequently the peace process. One of the "lessons of the past," Ross somberly observes, is that "Palestinians needed to understand that the consequence of violence and terror would not be Israeli concessions but increasing Israeli demands."[63] His text is dotted with emotive snapshots of this Palestinian scourge, such as "a shooting attack in the heart

9/ ISRAEL VERSUS THE WORLD

of Jerusalem that left four Israelis dead; the kidnapping, heart-wrenching videos, and subsequent death of a dual U.S.-Israeli citizen, Corporal Nachshon Wachsman; and a bus bombing in the center of Tel Aviv that killed twenty-two people and wounded fifty-six."[64] When set against this sanguinary background, who can fault Israel's obsession with security and its frustration with Palestinian leader Yasir Arafat? Benjamin Netanyahu's obduracy at one point in the negotiations, Ross interpolates, was fully justified: "Bibi was clear and on strong footing: he would not make concessions in the face of terror; indeed, even if he wanted to, it was politically impossible."[65]

To be sure, Ross also intermittently alludes to Jewish settler violence[66] and on one occasion refers to an Israeli soldier firing on a crowd of Palestinians as an act of "Israeli terrorism."[67] In addition, he obliquely gestures to official Israeli abuses, but in a context that almost always extenuates them. Thus, "Israeli actions used to prevent Palestinian acts of terror . . . deepened Palestinian resentment and fostered their sense of victimization," and, in the face of escalating "Palestinian rioting," Israel perforce responded with lethal firepower.[68] Although clear-eyed on "Palestinian security forces who had committed acts of terror,"[69] and, although repeatedly deploring Arafat's indirect complicity in terrorism, Ross almost never rebukes the behavior of Israeli security forces, and he dismisses as "ridiculous" Arafat's assertion that "Israel had a revolving-door policy on releases" of its own violent offenders.[70]

The bottom line of Ross's balance-sheet comes through in his praise of Prime Minister Yitzhak Rabin's "seriousness about peace" and restraint, in contrast to Arafat, whom Rabin understandably "held responsible for countless acts of terror. . . . Terror made Arafat an implacable foe for Rabin."[71] "Arafat's greatest travesty as a leader," Ross perorates,

> is that he did nothing to delegitimize those who used violence against the Israelis. Never throughout the Oslo process did he declare that those carrying out terror and violence against Israelis were wrong, were illegitimate, were enemies of the Palestinian cause. . . . When there is a Palestinian leadership

prepared to make clear that there is a legitimate way to pursue the Palestinian cause and an illegitimate way to do so—and violence is illegitimate—peace will no longer be a distant dream.[72]

One hint that Ross's depiction of Palestinian violence might be skewed comes in a footnote buried at the end of the book where the reader learns that many more Palestinians than Israelis had been killed during the Oslo years.[73] In fact human rights organizations painted a very different picture from Ross's of this period.[74] Some 387 Palestinians as compared to 261 Israelis were killed between 14 September 1993 and 28 September 2000.[75] Most of the Palestinian casualties were shot by Israeli security forces. According to Amnesty, the "vast majority" of these deaths were either "unlawful killings" such as "extrajudicial executions" that "showed Israel's contempt for the right to life," or killings "in the context of demonstrations and disturbances" that "could not be justified under international standards." The Israeli human rights organization B'Tselem concluded that "Israel's attitude toward the many killings of Palestinians indicates the shameful disregard it holds for human life."

Whereas Ross ridicules the notion that Israeli perpetrators of violence benefited from "revolving-door" justice, Amnesty reported, "There continues to be impunity for the vast majority of [Israeli] perpetrators of unlawful killings." In one of the rare instances of a conviction, an Israeli military court fined each of four Israeli soldiers "one agora—the equivalent to about U.S. $0.03" for the unjustified killing of a Palestinian. Indeed Israeli soldiers killed fully 1,500 Palestinians from the inception of the first Palestinian intifada in 1987 through the Oslo years. Yet not a single Israeli soldier served prison time.[76]

The enforcement of the law against Jewish settler violence, according to B'Tselem, was no better: "Frequently soldiers who witness acts of violence by settlers against Palestinians make no effort to prevent or put a stop to the incident.... In many cases ... no police investigation at all is carried out.... If any investigation is launched, it almost always ends without anyone being brought to trial." Israeli courts "tend to deal harshly with Palestinians," B'Tselem continued, while "lightening the punishment of Israeli citizens who committed identical crimes." Thus, "for the crime of stone throwing, Palestinians have often been sentenced in military and civil courts to one year's imprisonment, and in certain cases to much harsher punishments," whereas a settler convicted of killing a Palestinian in 1996 was fined one agora.[77] "Israeli settlers who committed acts of violence against Palestinians," Ross himself concedes at one point, "rarely served much, if any, time in jail."[78] In the course of the Oslo years Israel also arbitrarily arrested thousands of Palestinians and held more than a thousand in harsh conditions of administrative detention without charges or trial, systematically tortured and ill-treated thousands of Palestinian detainees, and conducted sham trials of Palestinian detainees in its military courts.[79]

Beyond deploring Israeli misconduct, human rights organizations also condemned the Palestinian Authority (PA) headed by Arafat for pervasive abuses against Palestinians,[80] such as large-scale arbitrary arrests, prolonged detention without charges or trial, widespread use of torture, and extrajudicial executions and unlawful killings. "Neither we nor the Israelis questioned what Arafat was doing internally," Ross reports. "As we would hear often from Rabin, we shouldn't be pressing Arafat on human rights or even corruption."[81] But Tel Aviv and Washington did not just turn a blind eye to these human rights abuses: *they exerted pressure on Arafat and the PA to commit them.*

"One of the meanings of Oslo," former Israeli foreign minister Shlomo Ben-Ami observed, "was that the PLO was ... Israel's collaborator in the task of stifling the [first] intifada and cutting short what was clearly an authentically democratic struggle for Palestinian independence."[82] In particular Israel endeavored to reassign Palestinians the dirty work of occupation. "The idea of Oslo," Israeli "human rights champion" Natan Sharansky unabashedly declared, "was to find a strong dictator to ... keep the Palestinians under control."[83] "The Palestinians will be better at establishing internal security than we were," Rabin explained prior to signing the accord, "because they will allow no appeals to the Supreme Court and will prevent [groups like] the Association for Civil Rights in Israel from criticizing the conditions there.... They will rule by their own methods, freeing, and this is most important, the Israeli soldiers from having to do what they will do." And, speaking later to the Labor Party he reiterated, "If we find a partner for peace with the Palestinians, they will run their internal affairs without the High Court of Justice, B'Tselem, or all sorts of groups of mothers and fathers and bleeding hearts."[84]

The PA's human rights violations, according to Amnesty, were "generally in response to Israeli pressure." "Such pressure is highly potent," Human Rights Watch (HRW) further noted, "due in part to the situation of extreme political and economic dependency in which the Palestinian self-rule entity exists." The irony was not lost on HRW that, whereas Israel denounced the PA's "abuse of human rights and the rule of law . . ., [t]his criticism ignores the relentless demands that Israel made on the PA to prevent attacks against Israelis without reference to the means employed." HRW also cast a harsh light on Washington's tacit support for these Palestinian abuses: "The Clinton administration demanded that Arafat act more decisively to prevent anti-Israel violence, but made no reference to the need for due process, even as the massive, arbitrary round-ups were taking place," and it praised Arafat's crackdown "while remaining largely silent on the tactics used."

The state security courts set up by the PA in 1995 constituted, according to HRW, "the most disturbing feature of the Palestinian judicial system."[85] Trials took place behind closed doors in the dead of night, often lasting just minutes, while judges and defense attorneys were drawn from the ranks of Palestinian security forces and lacked legal expertise. According to Ross, "Rabin urged us not to pressure Arafat on the human rights questions raised by these courts, hardly paragons of due process."[86] In fact Ross's client and patron both bore major culpability for them. "A significant factor in the court's creation was the pressure being placed on the PA by Israel and the U.S.," Amnesty reported. "There is no doubt whatsoever that trials with heavy sentences were demanded and encouraged by Israel and the U.S.," and that both of them "welcomed the first sentences handed down by the State Security Court at trials which so clearly violated international human rights norms."

"I know that there has been some controversy over the security courts," U.S. Vice-President Al Gore declared on one of many such occasions. "I personally believe that the accusations are misplaced and that they [the PA] are doing the right thing."

Besides whiting out Israel's own human rights violations, Ross's one-sided emphasis on Palestinian terrorism distorts the historical record in other ways. Because he ignores the brutality of Israel's occupation, Ross makes Palestinian resort to violence appear wholly irrational. He glosses over not only Israel's indiscriminate arrest, detention, torture and killing of Palestinians during the Oslo years, but also its illegal demolition of more than 1,000 Palestinian dwellings, which left thousands of Palestinians homeless, and its crippling closure policy, which caused soaring levels of unemployment and poverty.

Furthermore Ross makes only fleeting reference to Israel's massive settlement expansion in the occupied Palestinian territory. The settler population increased from 250,000 to 380,000 during the Oslo years, while Israel confiscated, all told, nearly half the land surface of the West Bank.[87] Although the index of Ross's book contains copious page references under the heading *terrorism*, there is not even a listing for *settlements*. Ross's cursory treatment of Israeli settlement policy all the more perplexes because, on the one hand, he lectures, "Negotiations, not unilateral acts, must remain the hallmark of peacemaking"[88] yet, on the other, Israel's settlement expansion during the Oslo years patently constituted a massive accumulation of such unilateral acts.[89] Ross emphasizes that his hero Rabin "made clear that he was determined to shift priorities away from building settlements in the territories."[90] He neglects to mention, however, that settlements expanded more rapidly under Rabin than even under his Likud predecessors.[91]

"There is no moral equivalency between suicide bombers and bulldozers," Ross approvingly quotes Secretary of State Madeleine Albright, "between killing innocent people and building houses."[92] Setting aside that many more Palestinian than Israeli innocents lost their lives, and even granting that there is no moral equivalency between suicide bombers and bulldozers: if you arbitrarily humiliate, arrest, detain and torture a man or members of his family; and if you steal his family's land; and if you drive his family into abject poverty; and if you demolish his family's home—if, after suffering a relentless escalation of abuses and crimes, he strikes out blindly in revenge, is it really cause for shock?

While Ross pontificates from on high against moral equivalency, Ben-Ami homed in on the "fatal symmetry between settlements and terrorism that became the hallmark of the Oslo years." "A tragic and fatal vicious cycle," he further observed,

> was created that neither the Israelis nor the Palestinians were able to halt. The disenchantment mounted among the Palestinian masses. They were hit by Israeli closures, collective punishment, unemployment, economic decline, a humiliating dependence on Israel and the expansion of existing settlements.... Rather than behaving as a modern state bound by, and respectful of, international law, Israel in the territories seemed possessed by an irresistible agrarian hunger that trampled underfoot the natural rights of the occupied population.[93]

One searches Ross's authoritative "inside story" in vain for a remotely comparable acknowledgment.

It is a *point d'honneur* for Ross that he personally lobbied for the Oslo Accord to "contain a clear renunciation of terror and violence from Arafat"; that he personally urged Albright to "come down hard on [Palestinian] terror"; and that he personally "confronted" Arafat to "take action" against terrorism.[94] His passionate sympathy for Israeli victims of criminal violence apparently did not extend to Palestinian victims, however. Judging by his own account Ross never once entreated Israeli leaders to curb their far greater brutality.

The inception of the Middle East "peace process" is generally dated from shortly after the June 1967 war when the U.N. Security Council ratified resolution 242. The phase of the process culminating in the 2000 Camp David negotiations opened in September 1993 when the Oslo Accord was signed. Ross devotes the preponderance of his narrative to the Oslo years (1993-2000).[95] Although Arafat emerges from *Missing Peace* as the arch-villain, Ross grounds the Palestinian leader's culpability in a deeper social pathology.

Palestinians, according to Ross, are in thrall to a victim syndrome. While acknowledging in the book's final pages that they "surely have suffered,"[96] Ross nonetheless diagnoses that "the Palestinians' sense of being victims has ... fostered a sense of entitlement."[97] He peppers the text with many illustrations of this delusional-cum-aggrandizing malady: Palestinians clung to the belief that "They were entitled to the land. It was theirs, and it had been taken"; in Palestinian "eyes" they "were not responsible for what was done to the Jews in Europe," and consequently in their "eyes" accepting "Israel's presence" was a major concession; Palestinians chafed at Israel deciding the pace and parameters of withdrawal because they "believed they were getting what was rightfully theirs," and that "the land is 'theirs'"; Palestinians reacted with "outrage" at settlement expansion because Israel was "absorbing land that they considered to be theirs," "[they] perceived to be theirs" and "they believed was theirs or should be theirs."[98] It so happens however that this Palestinian "sense of entitlement" to the West Bank and Gaza coincided with the letter of the law—the land *was* theirs; and not just "in their eyes" but in those of any sane person, whatever sins Palestinians might be chastised for, perpetrating the Nazi holocaust is not among them.[99]

His Arab interlocutors also failed, according to Ross, to grasp the subtleties of international diplomacy and law. "Palestinians and many in the Arab world continued to see an American double standard," he rues.

> They asked why was Israel permitted to effectively ignore Security Council resolutions while Saddam was forced to comply? They did not see the difference between the Security Council resolutions. Those against Iraq came as a response to Saddam's eradication of a member state of the U.N.; the resolutions required his compliance, not his acceptance. Noncompliance carried sanctions, and led to the use of force against his absorption of Kuwait. The resolutions that Palestinians and Arabs more generally focused on with regard to Israel were resolutions 242 and 338. They were adopted after the 1967 and 1973 wars. They provided the guidelines or principles that should shape negotiations to resolve the conflict between Arabs and Israelis. The terms of a final peace settlement were not established in these resolutions and they could not be mandatory on either side. But drawing distinctions between Security Council resolutions involving the Iraqis and the Israelis was not satisfying. The Arab world generally rejected the idea that Iraq faced pressure to implement Security Council resolutions while Israel did not. They wanted equal treatment. They wanted to portray all Security Council resolutions as having the force of international law. For the Arab world generally, the resolutions were their face-savers. They would resolve the conflict with Israel, but only on the basis of international law, "international legitimacy," as they called it. Here was their explanation, their justification for ending the conflict. If Iraq had to follow international legitimacy, so too, must Israel.[100]

The essence of Ross's exegesis (placed here in italics) poses multiple problems however:

(1) *In its resolutions on Iraq the Security Council focused on breaches of international law requiring "compliance" and carrying "sanctions," whereas in its resolutions on Israel the Security Council focused on "principles" for a settlement requiring "acceptance" and envisaging "negotiations."* In fact the international community long ago reached broad consensus on the principles for resolving the Israel-Palestine conflict. They are embodied in resolution 242 and subsequent U.N. resolutions which inter alia call for a two-state settlement along the 4 June 1967 border and mutual recognition.[101] It is unclear why principles that find overwhelming support in the U.N. require compliance and carry sanctions in the Iraqi but not the Israeli case.

The persistent refusal of Israel to resolve the conflict in accordance with universally validated norms puts its occupation of Palestinian land on an identical juridical footing as Iraq's occupation of Kuwait. "An occupation regime that refuses to earnestly contribute to efforts to reach a peaceful solution should be considered illegal," Tel Aviv University law professor Eyal Benvenisti opines. "Indeed, such a refusal should be considered outright annexation. The occupant has a duty under international law to conduct negotiations in good faith for a peaceful solution. It would seem that an occupant who proposes unreasonable conditions, or otherwise obstructs negotiations for peace for the purpose of retaining control over the occupied territory, could be considered a violator of international law." "The continued rule of the recalcitrant occupant," he continues, should be construed "as an aggression";[102]

(2) *Palestinians and Arabs have focused on resolutions 242 and 338.*[103] In fact they have also demanded compliance and sanctions in the face of Israel's persistent disregard of scores of Security Council and General Assembly resolutions deploring its illegal annexation of East Jerusalem (and the Syrian Golan Heights), its illegal settlement activity in the occupied Palestinian territory, its illegal inva-

sion and occupation of Lebanon (and other Arab countries), and numerous other flagrant violations of international law.[104] If the Arab world has not drawn "distinctions" between these resolutions and the ones targeting Iraq, it is perhaps because there aren't any to be drawn.

In fact Israel falls into a category all its own regarding compliance and sanctions. Because of the U.S. veto—which Ross prudently passes over in silence, and which lies behind the hypocritical "distinctions" in U.N. proceedings—Israel has been shielded from any sanctions, whereas in recent times the Security Council has repeatedly imposed them on member states, often for breaches of international law identical to Israel's.[105] Again, if the Arab world "continued to see an American double standard," this is perhaps because it sees clearly, and if the Arab world demanded "equal treatment" for Palestinians "on the basis of international law," it is not self-evident why this should be objectionable.

Until the breakthrough at Oslo, according to Ross, the principal obstacle to Middle East peace was Arafat's intransigence. The tale he weaves goes like this. "Throughout the 1980s" Washington endeavored to gain Palestinian agreement to U.N. resolutions, but "those efforts typically came to naught as Arafat would hint at being ready to accept 242 and 338 only to retreat into ambiguity." The Palestinian leader instead allegedly maneuvered to "mobilize the international community to get for him what he could not get for himself, ... which would permit the Palestinians to avoid any painful compromises." Arafat finally "crossed the threshold of recognizing Israel's right to exist" in September 1993, signaling "a complete redefinition of the PLO and an acknowledgment of Israel's needs," and in a reciprocal gesture Israel accepted "the PLO agenda, including statehood."

But despite the bountiful goodwill of Israelis, according to Ross, neither the Palestinian people nor their leader underwent an authentic change of heart:

[T]he Palestinians failed not just to transform their day-to-day behavior. Their leader, Yasir Arafat, never went through any transformation at all. Israeli political leaders changed their words; Arafat did not. Rabin and [Shimon] Peres had made a historic choice; Arafat made only a tactical move. He might say Oslo represented a strategic choice; in reality, for him it represented a strategic necessity. Arafat went to Oslo after the first Gulf War not because he made a choice but because he had no choice.... The PLO was in deep financial crisis, having lost its financial base in the Gulf.... Oslo was his salvation. As such, it represented less transformation than a transaction.... [T]here was almost no conditioning of his public for peace. There was never talk of painful compromises for peace. On the contrary, Arafat was telling his public they would get everything, and give up nothing.

Nonetheless Ross finds grounds for optimism in the fact that the 2000 Camp David negotiations, although failing to yield the fruit of peace due to Arafat's recalcitrance, did at long last produce a core consensus for resolving the conflict. "Mutual recognition of Arabs and Israelis proved to be irreversible," he cheerfully reports. "There has been no return to the mutual rejection and denial of the past. Moreover, a *new* consensus emerged among Israelis and Palestinians and internationally as well on the essential requirement for peace; two states, Israel and Palestine, coexisting and living in secure and recognized borders."[106]

This narrative conflicts at nearly every point with the available evidence, and on the rare occasion when Ross gets the facts right, they nonetheless belie his overarching interpretation. An international consensus started crystallizing in the mid-1970s to settle the Israel-Palestine conflict. It called for two states along the 4 June 1967 border and mutual recognition. Israel opposed the full withdrawal component of such a settlement, and consequently the U.S. vetoed Security Council resolutions in 1976 and again in 1980 affirming the international consensus and carrying the support of

Arab states. The General Assembly also overwhelmingly ratified the two-state settlement, but Washington's opposition yet again obstructed any progress. A 1989 General Assembly resolution calling for the two-state settlement garnered the support of 151 member states, while only Israel, the United States and Dominica opposed it.[107]

The documentary record clearly shows that Ross has twice erred: the two-state consensus is not a recent development, and neither Israel nor the U.S. has supported it.

Independent Arab initiatives dovetailed with the consensus at the United Nations. Saudi Arabia unveiled in 1981, and the Arab League subsequently approved, a peace plan based on the two-state settlement.[108] Israel reacted by stepping up preparations to destroy the PLO, which was headquartered in Lebanon.[109]

In his analysis of the build-up to the 1982 Lebanon war, Israeli strategic analyst Avner Yaniv reported that Arafat was contemplating a historic compromise with the "Zionist state," whereas "all Israeli cabinets since 1967" as well as "leading mainstream doves" opposed a Palestinian state. Fearing diplomatic pressures Israel maneuvered to sabotage the two-state settlement. It conducted punitive military raids "deliberately out of proportion" against "Palestinian and Lebanese civilians" in order to weaken "PLO moderates," strengthen the hand of Arafat's "radical rivals," and thereby guarantee the PLO's "inflexibility." However, the PLO refused to react, and thus Israel eventually had to choose between a pair of stark options: "a political move leading to a historic compromise with the PLO, or preemptive military action against it." To fend off Arafat's "peace offensive"—Yaniv's telling phrase—Israel embarked on military action in June 1982. The "*raison d'être* of the entire operation," Yaniv concluded, was "destroying the PLO as a political force capable of claiming a Palestinian state on the West Bank."[110]

In 1988 the Palestine National Council convened in Algiers to formally ratify the two-state settlement. Although asserting that Arafat "crossed the threshold of recognizing Israel's right to exist in 1993," Ross contradictorily concedes that already five years earlier at this conclave Arafat "engineered the PLO's adoption of the Algiers Declaration, which called for a two-state solution to the conflict with Israel. . . . Palestinians were now ready to accept a Jewish state alongside an Arab state."¹¹¹ Meanwhile the Labor-Likud "National Unity" government unveiled a peace plan of its own in 1989. The "basic guidelines" of this Israeli consensus document explicitly barred a Palestinian state in the West Bank and Gaza: "Israel opposes the establishment of an additional Palestinian state in the Gaza district and in the area between Israel and Jordan."¹¹² (The qualifier *additional* refers to the Zionist tenet that a Palestinian state already existed in Jordan.)

The juxtaposition of Arab-Palestinian and Israeli demarches points up that the chief obstacle to a diplomatic settlement was not Palestinian but Israeli resistance to "painful compromises for peace."

Struggling for political survival, the exiled PLO leadership capitulated after the 1991 Gulf War to Israeli diktat. We have already seen that following the first intifada Israel resolved to subcontract the policing of the occupation to Palestinian collaborators. It homed in on "Arafat's men in Oslo" who, according to Ben-Ami, were "far more accommodating than the Palestinians from the territories." Because of the "disarray of the PLO and its financial crisis," and the prospect of its "declining into oblivion," exiled Palestinian leaders were "more amenable" to an agreement that "did not secure vital Palestinian aspirations such as the right of self-determination, an end of Israel's policy of settlements, and an acceptable solution to the issues of Jerusalem and refugees." Meanwhile Israeli leaders "were encouraged to move to a settlement with the PLO," Ben-Ami further notes, "by their perception that the peace process would eventually secure them strategic portions of, and key settlement areas in, the West Bank."¹¹³ Put otherwise, the virtue of Arafat was that he possessed the nationalist credentials of a Nelson Mandela but unlike grassroots Palestinian leaders he appeared desperate enough to play the part of the Bantustan chief Mangosuthu Buthelezi.

"For Rabin, the measure of leadership was a readiness to make difficult decisions," Ross intones. "It was also the measure of seriousness about peace."¹¹⁴ Israeli leaders allegedly evinced such a readiness at Oslo, where

"Rabin and Peres had made a historic choice" offering Arafat "acceptance of the PLO agenda, including statehood," while the Palestinian leader supposedly "made only a tactical move" under duress. It is true that Arafat executed only a tactical adjustment at Oslo, but this adjustment was *not* in his recognition of Israel, which was unwavering. His strategic goal remained a two-state settlement but, because he had no choice, Arafat tactically put off the establishment of a Palestinian state to an indefinite future.

Whereas the "difficult decisions" of Arafat included recognition of the Israeli state, the "difficult decisions" of Israeli leaders *excluded* a Palestinian state. Again, the testimony of Israel's former foreign minister sheds a bright light on *their* "seriousness about peace":

> Rabin was less of a peace architect than some commentators believed him to be. . . . As a matter of fact, neither Rabin nor, especially, Peres wanted the autonomy to usher in a Palestinian state. As late as 1997—that is, four years into the Oslo process when, as the chairman of the Labour Party's Foreign Affairs Committee, I proposed for the first time that the party endorse the idea of a Palestinian state—it was Shimon Peres who most vehemently opposed the idea. . . . A Palestinian state was clearly not within Rabin's priorities either.

After ratifying the Oslo II Accord in September 1995 and just before his assassination in November of that year, Rabin told the Knesset that Israel's desired "permanent solution" would be a "Palestinian entity . . . which is less than a state."[115] Rabin "would have by no means agreed," Ben-Ami observes, "to the kind of compromises that the [Ehud] Barak government was ready to make on Jerusalem and on the other core issues of the conflict."[116]

"Even if [Israeli political leaders] sometimes appear to have changed their policies or appear to have veered to positions diametrically opposite to those previously maintained," a former head of the Israeli Mossad recently observed, "in the final analysis, these often turn out to be tactical moves dictated by short-term considerations rather than genuine changes of heart."[117] A merely "tactical move" on mutual recognition was indeed made at Oslo, but it was Rabin and Peres, not Arafat, who executed it. Once more Ross has turned the historical record upside down.

Because they conceived themselves "as victims," Palestinians felt, according to Ross, that "it was the Israelis who were always required to take the first step or make the first concession in the talks," that "little was required" of them, and that "they were owed much." And, because they allegedly played the role of victim in the peace process, Ross goes on to conclude that "responsibility was not part of the Palestinian political culture."[118] Yet, Palestinians had already taken the "first step" of registering support for a two-state settlement in the mid-1970s and formally recognized Israel at Algiers in 1988 and yet again at Oslo in 1993, although "as late as 1997" Israel's leaders recoiled at the prospect of any kind of Palestinian state.

"Israeli political leaders changed their words," according to Ross, whereas the Palestinian leader engaged in "almost no conditioning of his public for peace. . . . Arafat was telling his public they would get everything, and give up nothing." Yet, judging by public opinion polls at the tail end of the Oslo years, the reverse appears nearer the truth. In 1999 a mere 11.3 percent of Israeli Jews fully supported and another 12.0 percent gave qualified support to a two-state settlement along the 4 June 1967 borders, whereas 52.7 percent of Palestinians fully supported and another 22.3 percent gave qualified support to it.[119]

The tale Ross weaves of the Palestinians' persistent refusal to accept a two-state settlement and the Israelis' forthcoming embrace of it comprises, from beginning to end and in sum, a perfect inversion of the truth.

Ross's analysis of why Camp David[120] failed rapidly gained wide currency. The essence of his explanation is that, whereas Barak made huge concessions, Arafat reciprocated with his "tendency to pocket" and made none. This antagonistic juxtaposition sustains the dramatic tension and forms the connective tissue of Ross's narrative: "the summit was about to collapse. The President [Clinton] had made his best effort, and now so had Barak. Arafat had said no to everything"; "I had had it with [Arafat]. . . . [H]ere at Camp David he had not presented a single idea or single serious comment in two weeks"; "[Arafat] could not compromise or concede in order to end the conflict"; "Palestinians . . . must give up the illusion that Arafat fostered: that they did not have to compromise on land or on refugees or on Jerusalem, and maybe most important, that they did not have to be responsible"; "the Arafat legacy [is] rejecting compromise on the permanent status issues of Jerusalem, refugees and borders."[121]

Both the analysis Ross presents and his allocation of culpability for the political impasse are grounded in a package of "basic trade-offs" that, according to him, each side had to accept if the conflict was to be resolved. These consisted of: "on the western border, the Palestinians get the 1967 lines, but with modifications to take account of the Israeli settlements; on the eastern border, it's sovereignty for the Palestinians, with Israel's security needs met; on refugees, it's the general principle for the Palestinians in terms of reference to U.N. General Assembly resolution 194 (not the 'right of return') and its practical limitation for the Israelis."[122] Discarding one bottom-line after another, Israelis inched toward these necessary "compromises" at Camp David whereas Palestinians acted the spoiler by rejecting them out of hand. Or, so Ross would want readers to believe.

If measured against the consensus of legal opinion, however, each of the "basic trade-offs" Ross delineates required major concessions from Palestinians and none at all from Israel:

- Palestinians must relinquish title to parts of the territory Israel conquered in 1967, although "all these territories (including East Jerusalem) remain occupied territories" (ICJ), to which Israel had no valid title;[123]

- Palestinians must accept the permanence of Jewish settlements, although "Israeli settlements in the Occupied Palestinian Territory (including East Jerusalem) have been established in breach of international law" (ICJ);[124]
- Palestinians must concede restrictions on the right of refugees to return to their homes, although respected human rights organizations "call for Palestinians who fled or were expelled from Israel, the West Bank or Gaza Strip, along with those of their descendants who have maintained genuine links with the area, to be able to exercise their right of return" (Amnesty, HRW).[125]

The framework of necessary "trade-offs" and "compromises" contrived by Ross consists of gains for Israel and losses for Palestinians: after reaching his designated midpoint Israel nets a surplus and Palestinians net a deficit of rights. Beyond this, Ross himself concedes that Palestinians did make "meaningful concessions on three settlement blocs in the West Bank, accepting that the Jewish neighborhoods of East Jerusalem would be Israeli, and agreeing to Israeli early-warning sites in the West Bank," as well as acquiescing in swaps of Israeli territory for Palestinian territory coveted by Israel, and capping the number of Palestinian refugees allowed back. It is not clear how the Palestinians could have both "reject[ed] compromise" *and* offered these "meaningful concessions."[126]

If, according to Ross, the peace process nonetheless collapsed because of Palestinian inflexibility, it is ostensibly because he credits Israel as *more* forthcoming in negotiations. In his representation of the talks on Day 6 of the Camp David summit Ross typically reports that Israel "had made big moves," granting Palestinian sovereignty over three outlying Arab neighborhoods in Jerusalem and 90 percent of the West Bank. But Palestinian negotiators intransigently insisted that Israel first accept the principle of land swaps: "once the principle of swaps was accepted, then [we] could work out the modifications on the border," "the Israelis have needs and we can address them once the principle of swaps is accepted." Ross's account of this session concludes:

> Shlomo, in summing up, had said that he and Gilad had come in the spirit that the President [Clinton] had asked. They came to make a deal, stretching well beyond their instructions. Unfortunately, he said, their Palestinian friends had not come in such a spirit, but he hoped they would consider carefully everything he had suggested and respond in kind. Saeb responded, appreciating the seriousness of the discussion but also claiming that he had gone very far on Jerusalem. He was out on a limb, accepting Jewish neighborhoods in East Jerusalem that most Palestinians considered illegal. Now the two sides should continue their negotiations. Gilad got angry and said this is rock bottom for us. "You think you can just take this as a new floor and negotiate from there. We came to make a deal, not to go into the souk [market]".... In our meeting with the President afterward, I said this is going to confirm Barak's worst fears: he moves in a big way, Arafat pockets it, and he is expected to move again in a way that will definitely go beyond his redlines.... We cannot ask Barak for anything more; the Palestinians have made that impossible.... You have to push [Arafat] back hard and say they moved and you didn't. Enough is enough. You have to say I cannot get you anything unless you move seriously.

Like the Israelis, Ross testily observes, "We too had had enough of the Palestinian unwillingness to negotiate."[127]

Even accepting for argument's sake his account of the Israeli offer, what Ross deems Israel's "big moves" nonetheless fell far short of what Palestinians had a rightful claim on. Would Ross reckon it "big moves" if Arafat recognized Israeli sovereignty over the suburbs of Tel Aviv and 90 percent of Israel's sovereign territory? On the other hand what Ross deems "the

Palestinian unwillingness to negotiate" met, and—in the concessions on Jerusalem and settlements—even surpassed, their legal obligations, while what "Arafat pockets" is what Palestinians were legally entitled to.

One does not recall Ross chastising Israeli leaders for a "tendency to pocket" when they wrested Palestinian recognition of Israel's legally sanctioned borders. A fitter use of the locution would perhaps be that Israel denied Palestinians their internationally sanctioned rights while simultaneously pocketing full recognition from them. "We have recognized Israel and agreed to its demands for secure borders, security arrangements and cooperation and coordination in security matters," a Palestinian negotiator complained after Camp David. "You pocketed this incredible historical concession and made more demands."[128]

The demands of Palestinians appear maximal in Ross's exposition, and their concessions minimal, because he has effaced international law. It is not just "most Palestinians" who consider Israeli settlements in East Jerusalem "illegal"; it also happens to be the consensus of international legal opinion. Palestinian acquiescence in Israel's retention of many of these settlements constituted a major concession, but in Ross's account it does not come across because he dismisses Palestinian title to the whole West Bank as a quirky misapprehension ("in their eyes"). According to Ross, Israel refused to recognize the Palestinian right of return—merely the principle, not even its implementation—because "no Israeli prime minister could be expected to make gut-wrenching compromises on all issues."[129] Such recognition would not signal, however, an Israeli compromise, but rather its bare minimum acknowledgment of a binding legal obligation. The only real compromise would have been if Palestinians forfeited this right at Camp David, which is exactly what they did, if not in principle then in its restricted implementation.

Not one of Israel's "gut-wrenching compromises," whether at Oslo or at Camp David, contained real substance. Israelis might have had to settle for much less than they wanted, but Palestinians had to settle for much less than they were *owed*. Curbing one's desires is a different genre of sacrifice from surrendering one's rights. In disregarding international law Ross obfuscates this crucial distinction and concomitantly the crucial fact that throughout the peace process all the genuine concessions came from the Palestinian side.[130]

Ross does not, however, just ignore international law; he also explicitly repudiates it. Undoubtedly aware that the rights standard is an encumbrance on his tale, Ross substitutes for it the burden-shifting standard of "needs." Once having appointed himself the supreme arbiter of each side's needs, it is child's play for Ross to demonstrate Palestinian culpability: whereas Israeli demands mirrored their needs, Palestinian demands exceeded theirs; *ergo*, Palestinians bore sole culpability for Camp David's failure. The case Ross mounts cannot be refuted. But it is irrefutable because it is rigged: Ross decided that the Palestinians were blameworthy because, on his own and in his infinite wisdom, he decided that what Israel wanted was just what it needed and what Israel offered was all that Palestinians needed.

The critical artifice of Ross's narrative is to shift the framework of the peace process from rights to needs. This factitious framework serves as an analytic device to demonstrate Israeli flexibility and Palestinian intransigence, and as a normative device for justifying a settlement of the conflict that negates Palestinian rights.[131] Consider Ross's representation of the negotiations on Day 5 of the Camp David summit, which climaxed in a widely reported outburst by Clinton against the Palestinian negotiators:

> In response to an Israeli map that showed three different colors—brown for the Palestinian state, orange for the areas the Israelis would annex, and red for transitional areas—Abu Ala was not prepared to discuss Israeli needs unless the Israelis first accepted the principle of the territorial swap and reduced the areas they sought to annex. The President [Clinton] at first tried to reason with Abu Ala, explaining that he could see "why this map is not acceptable to you. But you cannot say to them, not good enough, give me something more acceptable; that's not negotiation. Why

9/ ISRAEL VERSUS THE WORLD

not say the orange area is too big, let's talk about your needs and see how we can reduce the orange area and turn it into brown? If we focus on the security aspect and look at the Jordan Valley, we might discuss the security issues and see if we can reduce the orange area." Shlomo agreed with that approach—thereby signaling that he was open to reducing the orange area, which amounted to close to 14 percent of the total of the West Bank outside of Jerusalem. Abu Ala continued to resist. As he did, and he repeated old arguments about the settlements being illegal and the Palestinians needing the 1967 lines, the President's face began to turn red.[132]

Palestinians appear to be uncompromising because they won't negotiate Israel's needs without prioritizing their own rights. Contrariwise, Israel appears to be reasonable because it is willing to negotiate on the basis of reciprocal needs. Needs against needs: isn't this a fair quid pro quo? Further, Israelis demonstrate flexibility by signaling a willingness to reduce their needs whereas Palestinians demonstrate inflexibility by not budging from their rights. Each party presenting its respective needs, Clinton tries to reason with Palestinians, is the essence of negotiations. The Palestinians stubbornly retort however that each party's needs must be reckoned within and subordinated to their respective rights: if Israel needs more than it is legally entitled to, then it must compensate. But, according to Clinton, this is the wrong language: of rights, not needs. In the face of yet another round of Palestinian irrationality and intransigence, he justifiably explodes.

Whereas Palestinians come across as inflexible in Ross's exposition because they stubbornly cling to the rights framework, one is hard-pressed to name a conflict the negotiations of which were not anchored in reciprocal rights. Was it incumbent on Kuwait to negotiate its occupation on the basis of Iraqi *needs*? Earlier on in his book Ross explains that the U.S. negotiating strategy started from Israeli needs "because the Israelis held the territories, they were on the giving end."[133] Was this how the U.S. conducted negotiations while Iraq held the territory of Kuwait? Or consider Israeli-Egyptian negotiations over the Israeli-occupied Sinai that culminated in a peace treaty. Prior to the 1977 Camp David summit, Israeli leaders asserted that Sharm-el-Shayk was "vital" to Israeli security, Foreign Minister Moshe Dayan famously declaring that he would prefer "Sharm-el-Shayk without peace to peace without Sharm-el-Shayk." Once negotiations commenced Israel maintained that the oil refineries, airfields and settlements it had built in the Sinai constituted irreducible needs, and it bargained hard at Camp David to retain them. But didn't Israel ultimately have to forsake all these "needs" on account of Egypt's legal title to the whole of the Sinai?[134]

Israel appears reasonable because it is willing to negotiate on the basis of reciprocal needs. But doesn't Israel embrace this framework because on the basis of rights it would have to withdraw fully from the occupied Palestinian territory, and make accommodation for the Palestinian right of return? The willingness of Israel to reduce its needs also appears to demonstrate flexibility. But even these reduced needs greatly exceed its rights. Would Ross praise the flexibility of Palestinians if they reduced their needs from 14 percent of Israeli territory to 10 percent of it, and would he then condemn Israel for having "continued to resist" an agreement?

The whole of Ross's narrative on Camp David is squarely embedded in the needs framework or, more precisely, the framework of *Israeli* needs. He reports that on the summit's eve Israel formulated "a basis for success": if Palestinians acquiesced in "modifying the Green Line to take account of... Israel's needs," while Israel made the "concession" of giving Palestinians their eastern border along the Jordan River, it "would mark the end of the conflict."[135] He reports that on Day 1 of the summit the U.S. proposed that the Green Line "would be modified as necessary" to meet Israeli "settlement bloc requirements." Although Palestinians protested that they "needed" the June 1967 border or a land swap as compensation for Israeli needs, the U.S. decided "not to introduce the concept of a swap at this stage," because Palestinian needs did not carry the same imperative: it was merely something they "believed in."[136] During talks preceding the Clinton Parameters of December 2000, Ross reports, Palestinians objected to Ross's advocacy of "Israeli positions that would deny the Palestinians what they needed to sell a deal: clear independence, sovereignty over the Haram, and a just solution of the refugee problem." "I was tough in my response," he continues. "They focused on their needs to the exclusion of the Israeli needs."[137] It will be noticed that in Ross's reckoning Israeli needs systematically trump Palestinian rights, and Palestinian rights are disingenuously put on a par with exorbitant Israeli demands by his affixing the label *needs* on what are in fact Palestinian *rights*.

The "one unmistakable insight from the past about the Arabs," Ross meditates in his conclusion, is that "no Israeli concession can ever be too big."[138] However much Israel gives, the Arabs never "accept that Israel has needs as well—justifying compromise."[139] Except that no Israeli "concession" to Palestinians required a sacrifice of Israeli rights, whereas for Palestinians to satisfy Israeli needs it did require such basic sacrifices. The compromise Israel (and Ross) proposed was not needs for needs but Israeli needs at the expense of Palestinian rights. "The kind of transformation that would make it possible for the Arab world to acknowledge that Israel has needs," Ross laments, "has yet to take place."[140] Translation: Arabs have yet to grasp that Israel's needs trump their rights.

"There can be no deal unless each side is prepared to respond to the essential needs of the other," according to Ross. "Agreements are forged . . . on the basis of reconciling needs."[141] One might be forgiven for concluding however that hitherto diplomatic agreements have been reached on the basis of law and rights. Whereas his own colleagues supported these time-tested criteria Ross rejects them in favor of the allegedly superior standard of needs:

> Aaron was always arguing for a just and fair proposal. I was not against a fair proposal. But I felt the very concept of "fairness" was, by definition, subjective. Similarly both Rob and Gamal believed that the Palestinians were entitled to 100 percent of the

territory. Swaps should thus be equal. They believed this was a Palestinian right. Aaron tended to agree with them not on the basis of right, but on the basis that every other Arab negotiating partner had gotten 100 percent. Why should the Palestinians be different? I disagreed. I was focused not on reconciling rights but on addressing needs. In negotiations, one side's principle or "right" is usually the other side's impossibility. Of course, there are irreducible rights. I wanted to address what each side needed, not what they wanted and not what they felt they were entitled to.[142]

It is not immediately obvious why a rights standard reached by broad international consensus and codified in international law is more "subjective" than a needs standard on which there is neither consensus nor codification. The rights standard was notably uncontroversial on the "permanent status" issues in contention at Camp David. Ross asserts as a flaw of the rights standard that the parties to negotiations typically interpret it differently. But such a difficulty did not arise at Camp David. At one point in the negotiations Clinton erupted at a Palestinian negotiator who invoked international law: "This isn't the Security Council here. This isn't the U.N. General Assembly.... I'm the president of the United States."[143] If Clinton did not want to hear from U.N. resolutions and international law, it cannot be because they lacked clarity. On the contrary, it is likely he fumed at any mention of rights because he knew *exactly* where such talk would lead.

It is surely peculiar that Ross would believe reference to a consensual body of rights is more capricious that his personal arbitration of needs. Leaving aside his tacit premise that the received opinion of many should count for less than the transitory whim of one, it is unclear what qualifies Ross of all people for this role of philosopher-king. Rather, his lengthy affiliation with the Washington Institute for Near East Policy, a think-tank created by the Israel lobby group AIPAC, would seem to cast doubt on his pretenses of objectivity. After leaving the Clinton administration, Ross re-affiliated with the Washington Institute, and became the first chairman of a new Jerusalem-based think-tank, the Jewish People Policy Planning Institute, founded and funded by the Jewish Agency.

In light of how Ross assesses the needs of Palestinians, it does not surprise that he holds them culpable for Camp David's failure. On the eve of the summit he proposed that Israel "symbolically" swap land "as a way to provide the Palestinians with an explanation for the modification of borders."[144] On Day 1 of the summit he determined that Palestinians had merely "symbolic needs" on the eastern border of their future state whereas Israel had "very real and legitimate ... concerns about security."[145] On Day 6 he reasoned that to recoup their losses Palestinians needed only a token regarding Jerusalem, such as an American embassy in a village abutting the city: "That would be a big symbol for Arafat. I said in addition the President could lead an international delegation that Arafat could host and take to the Haram, again symbolizing for the world, especially the Arab world, Palestinian control."[146]

Ross additionally reckoned that Palestinians did not require equal compensation for the territory Israel coveted. Inasmuch as Gaza is one of the most densely populated places on earth, and inasmuch as one aspect of the solution to the refugee problem was that Palestinians would return to the Palestinian state (but not Israel), one might suppose that Palestinians needed at bare minimum full territorial compensation. But Ross decided otherwise when formulating the Clinton Parameters. "I felt strongly about 6 to 7 percent annexation" by Israel, he recalls, "and I was not prepared to lower the ceiling. Nor was I prepared to introduce the idea of an equivalent swap."[147] When even *Israeli* negotiators proposed a smaller percentage of Israeli annexation, Ross reports being "furious"—which conveys some sense of his nonpartisan tallying of Palestinian needs.[148] On refugee repatriation Ross consistently maintained that Palestinians yet again had only "symbolic needs" as against "Israel's practical needs."[149]

The Camp David summit ultimately failed, to judge by Ross's exposition, because Palestinians clung to the absurd illusion that they had real needs.

Had they understood that all they actually needed were symbols Palestinians would have leapt at the generous Israeli offer.¹⁵⁰ The root of the problem again appears to be that incorrigible Palestinian "sense of entitlement": Camp David would have succeeded if only Palestinians grasped that they are not real, actual human beings.¹⁵¹

Upon its publication Ross's narrative was acclaimed as the definitive account of Camp David and the "peace process." It was not long, however, before cracks began to show in this orthodoxy. The era when "pro"-Israeli apologias would completely monopolize the mainstream has passed. A raft of compelling eyewitness and scholarly accounts, many of which have been quoted in this chapter, sharply contested Ross's distribution of culpability for the summit's collapse and the impasse in the "peace process." "If I were a Palestinian," Shlomo Ben-Ami, one of Israel's chief negotiators at Camp David, observed, "I would have rejected Camp David as well," while former director of the Jaffee Center for Strategic Studies Zeev Maoz concluded that the "substantial concessions" Israel demanded of Palestinians at Camp David "were not acceptable and could not be acceptable."¹⁵²

The excision of international law from Ross's account points up the shoddy foundations on which it rests. When juxtaposed against the consensus in representative judicial bodies, human rights organizations and political councils, the partisanship of Ross's narrative stands exposed. The enlightened consensus also constitutes a touchstone for liberal Jewish opinion, which has historically championed the rule of law and revered its institutional infrastructure. In the face of this consensus and Israel's flagrant defiance of it, more and more Jews have lapsed into an embarrassed silence, or entered into open revolt against a state that speaks neither to nor for them.

PART IV

MIRROR IMAGE

The overarching theme of this book is that American Jews are significantly liberal and, because many myths surrounding Israel have been punctured in recent years, Jews can no longer reconcile their liberal convictions with blind support for it. Many American Jews have consequently begun to distance themselves from Israel.

A reverse dynamic has been at play in Israel itself. Whereas American Jewish society remains significantly liberal, Israeli Jewish society has become significantly conservative. It has already been shown that, politically, Israeli Jews are a mirror image of American Jews.[1] One upshot is that liberal Israeli intellectuals seeking to keep pace with Israel's rightward lurch have been forced to abandon their liberal values and, in order to defend policies that are indefensible on the factual record, to reject their own past scholarship. The most (in)famous case is Benny Morris, who is probably the best known historian on the Israel-Palestine conflict and whose work has most contributed to revealing the underside of Israel's history. In recent years Morris has repudiated his own original research in order to shore up Israel's image.

Morris's odyssey from liberal to court historian illustrates from another angle the thesis of this book. Whereas American Jews have clung to liberal values and forsaken Israel, Morris has forsaken these values as he clings to Israel. In both cases, however, the operative factor has been self-interest: American Jews have benefited enormously from liberal ideology and a liberal state; Morris has sought to curry favor with and join the ranks of a state that has become resolutely un-liberal. Morris most resembles the Jewish neoconservatives who discarded their former liberalism when American society drifted rightward and put their talents at the disposal of the new conservative political establishment.

10/ HISTORY BY SUBTRACTION

A large part of this book documents that in recent times a new scholarly consensus has crystallized on the Israel-Palestine conflict that casts Israel in a much harsher light than hitherto. A striking anomaly appears to be the corpus of Israeli historian Benny Morris. Widely acclaimed as one of the leading "new historians," Morris played a critical role in molding the current scholarly consensus. Morris himself took issue with the designation "new historians" on the ground that the original, *Exodus*-like accounts of Israel's past did not constitute genuine history: "Israel's old historians, by and large, were not really historians and did not produce real history. In reality, they were chroniclers, and often apologetic, interested chroniclers at that."[1]

During the past decade, however, Morris has been given to lashing out at, and defending the old orthodoxy against, critics of Israel. It is accordingly a quandary whether to characterize him now as a "new" or "old" historian and—more to the point—whether to treat Morris's output as genuine scholarship or, in his preferred terminology, as belonging to the category of "apologetic, interested chroniclers."

One, as it were, compromise position has been to acknowledge the "stridency and darkness of some of his public pronouncements" while also asserting that Morris's scholarship "makes every attempt at depth and balance."[2] Such a bifurcation is theoretically tenable. For instance

Shlomo Ben-Ami is both a trained historian and a diplomat. In the first half of his book, *Scars of War, Wounds of Peace*,[3] Ben-Ami renders a scrupulous account of Israel's past, but in the second half he replaces his historian's hat with his diplomat's chapeau and produces a largely apologetic account of the 2000-1 peace negotiations where he served as Israel's chief representative.

In the case of Benny Morris, however, the two compartments, professional and political, have never been watertight, the seepage making Morris the historian virtually inseparable from Morris the ideologue. It is nonetheless undeniable that on balance the old Morris *was* a new historian producing serious scholarship.[4] It is equally undeniable that the new Morris has become an old historian churning out "apologetic, interested" tracts.

An unorthodox new historian not too long ago, Morris has in effect reinvented himself in recent times as an orthodox old historian. The process has been incremental, the quantitative degeneration becoming at a certain point qualitative.[5] Although disfigured in ways small and large by ideological bias, Morris's earlier works such as *The Birth of the Palestinian Refugee Problem, 1947-1949*,[6] *Israel's Border Wars, 1949-1956: Arab infiltration, Israeli retaliation, and the countdown to the Suez war*,[7] *Righteous Victims: A history of the Zionist-Arab conflict, 1881-1999*,[8] and *The Road to Jerusalem: Glubb Pasha, Palestine and the Jews*[9] brought to light a wealth of novel information. The body of his subsequent major work, *1948: The first Arab-Israeli war*,[10] preserves a standard of scholarly rigor, but his conclusion crosses the threshold to crude distortion. His most recent volume, *One State, Two States: Resolving the Israel/Palestine conflict*[11]—published incidentally by Yale University Press, which also released the *Foxbats over Dimona* hoax[12]—lacks any redeeming value and reeks of rancid propaganda.

Whereas he did not break new conceptual ground, the old Morris did roam the archives and cull revealing documents on the Israel-Palestine conflict that he then collated into a fresh, compelling narrative of the past. Once an industrious clerk, the new Morris has metamorphosed into a raging kook. In all fairness to him, it is of course arguable that Morris has honestly come to reconsider his former conclusions on the basis of new evidence; to discover that, however deficient their scholarship, the conclusions of the old historians were right after all. The problem is that Morris does not adduce new evidence to support his return to the old orthodoxy, but rather whites out the findings of his own pioneering research. This genre might be called doing history not by accretion but by subtraction.

The conclusion of *Righteous Victims*, Benny Morris's sweeping "history of the Zionist-Arab conflict," opened with a quote from Zionist leader (and Israel's future first prime minister) David Ben-Gurion. The "conflict" with the Arabs, Ben-Gurion said in 1938, "is in its essence a political one. And politically we are the aggressors and they defend themselves." Morris then observed: "Ben-Gurion, of course, was right. Zionism was a colonizing and expansionist ideology and movement. . . . Zionist ideology and practice were necessarily and elementally expansionist." Insofar as "from the start its aim was to turn all of Palestine . . . into a Jewish state," he went on to elaborate, Zionism could not but be "intent on . . . dispossessing and supplanting the Arabs." Or, as Morris formulated it earlier on in his book, "Jewish colonization meant expropriation and displacement" of the indigenous population.[13] These consequences of Zionism, and the Arab resistance they inexorably generated, would figure as signature themes in Morris's scholarly corpus.

A fundamental challenge for Zionism was how to create a Jewish state, which meant minimally a state the population of which was overwhelmingly Jewish, in an area the population of which was overwhelmingly not Jewish. One novelty of Morris's original scholarship was to point up the centrality of "transfer"—a euphemism, as Revisionist Zionist leader Zeev Jabotinsky put it, for "brutal expulsion"[14]—to resolving this dilemma. Insofar as orthodox Israeli historians had treated it, they consigned the idea of transfer to a footnote, downplaying it as incidental to the Zionist enterprise. Thus, Shabtai Teveth purported that the Zionist movement only "here and there" and "briefly" contemplated transfer, while according to Anita Shapira the Zionist movement conceived transfer merely as a "good thing" that it could just as well "do without."[15]

But Morris contended in his groundbreaking study, *Birth of the Palestinian Refugee Problem*, that, on the contrary, from the mid-1930s "the idea of transferring the Arabs out . . . was seen as the chief means of assuring the stability of the 'Jewishness' of the proposed Jewish State,"[16] while in *Righteous Victims* he wrote that "the transfer idea . . . was one of the main currents in Zionist ideology from the movement's inception."[17] In another seminal essay Morris documented that "thinking about the transfer of all or part of Palestine's Arabs out of the prospective Jewish state was pervasive among Zionist leadership circles long before 1937."[18]

In a greatly expanded version of *Birth*,[19] Morris gave over fully 25 densely argued pages to documenting the depth and breadth of "the idea of 'transfer' in Zionist thinking." His conclusion merits full quotation:

> [T]ransfer was inevitable and inbuilt into Zionism—because it sought to transform a land which was "Arab" into a "Jewish" state and a Jewish state could not have arisen without a major displacement of Arab population; and because this aim automatically produced resistance among the Arabs which, in turn, persuaded the Yishuv's leaders that a hostile Arab majority or large minority could not remain in place if a Jewish state was to arise or safely endure.[20]

Thus, in Morris's temporal-logical sequence of the conflict's genesis, Zionist transfer was cause and Arab resistance effect in an ever-expanding spiral. He put forth a sequence of succinct and copiously documented formulations on this crucial point in *Righteous Victims*: "The fear of territorial displacement and dispossession was to be the chief motor of Arab antagonism to Zionism down to 1948 (and indeed after 1967 as well)"; "In the 1880s there were already Arabs who understood that the threat from

10/ HISTORY BY SUBTRACTION

Zionism was not merely a local matter or a by-product of cultural estrangement. 'The natives are hostile towards us, saying that we have come to drive them out of the country,' recorded one Zionist settler"; "[T]he major cause of tension and violence ... was ... the conflicting interests and goals of the two populations. The Arabs sought instinctively to ... maintain their position as [Palestine's] rightful inhabitants; the Zionists sought radically to change the status quo ... and eventually turn an Arab-populated country into a Jewish homeland.... The Arabs, both urban and rural, came to feel anxiety and fear."[21]

In the conclusion of *Righteous Victims*, Morris reiterated that the Arabs' trepidation and ensuing opposition were "solidly anchored in a perception that [Zionist] expansion ... would be at the expense of their people, principally and initially those living in Palestine itself."[22] As Morris originally reckoned it, Arab fear was rational—because transfer was "inevitable and inbuilt into Zionism"—and Arab resistance natural—because it sprang "automatically" from the Zionist goal of transfer. The root of the conflict was accordingly located in a historical clash between Zionism and the indigenous Arab population of Palestine and the historical (if not moral) onus for engendering the conflict was placed squarely on the shoulders of the Zionist movement.[23]

The new Morris however has a very different story to tell. He drastically reduces the salience of transfer in Zionism; locates the genesis of the conflict in "Islamic Judeophobia"; and reckons transfer as a Zionist *reaction* to this Judeophobia and the "expulsionist" tendency inherent in it. Cause and effect have magically been reversed: expulsionist Judeophobia—which is inevitable and inbuilt *into Islam*—is the cause, Zionist transfer—which automatically springs from Islamic Judeophobia—the effect. The onus for engendering the conflict is now placed by Morris squarely on the shoulders of the Arabs, while Zionists are depicted as the innocent victims of a lethal Muslim intolerance towards Jews.

According to this new Morris, transfer initially figured as but a "minor and secondary element" in Zionism; "it had not been part of the original

Zionist ideology"; key Zionist leaders only "occasionally" supported transfer "between 1881 and the mid-1940s"; and "its thrust was never adopted by the Zionist movement . . . as ideology or policy" until the late 1940s.[24] Whereas the old Morris asserted that "the logic of a transfer solution to the 'Arab problem' remained ineluctable" for the Zionist movement, and "without some sort of massive displacement of Arabs from the area of the Jewish state-to-be, there could be no viable 'Jewish' state,"[25] the new Morris alleges that "the Zionist leaders generally said, and believed, that a Jewish majority would be achieved in Palestine, or in whatever part of it became a Jewish state, by means of massive Jewish immigration, and that this immigration would also materially benefit the Arab population."[26]

If Zionists eventually came to embrace transfer, according to the new Morris, it was only in reaction to "expulsionist or terroristic violence by the Arabs,"[27] "expulsionist Arab thinking and murderous Arab behavior,"[28] which were "indirectly contributing to the murder of their [the Zionists'] European kinfolk by helping to deny them a safe haven in Palestine and by threatening the lives of the Jews who already lived in the country."[29] Transfer has inexplicably metamorphosed from an "inevitable and inbuilt" component of Zionism into a response "triggered"[30] by expulsionist Arab threats and assaults, not to mention Arab complicity in the Nazi holocaust.

Indeed, in the narrative frame crafted by the new Morris the indigenous population of a country has metamorphosed into expulsionists. Many cruel and unforgivable things have been said by American historians about our native population, but it took a peculiarly fecund Israeli mind to pin the label "starkly expulsionist"[31] on an indigenous population resisting expulsion. To document this "expulsionist mindset,"[32] Morris cites the testimony of a Palestinian delegation before a foreign commission of inquiry: "We will push the Zionists into the sea—or they will send us back into the desert."[33] Insofar as the Zionists were intent on "transferring the Arabs out," it is unclear how this statement manifests malevolence. Doesn't an indigenous population have the right to resist expulsion?

10/ HISTORY BY SUBTRACTION

The new Morris alleges that "Arab expressions in the early years of the twentieth century of fear of eventual displacement and expulsion by the Zionists were largely propagandistic."[34] He seems to have forgotten that he himself pointed up this fear as the "chief motor of Arab antagonism to Zionism" and that he rationally grounded this fear in Zionist transfer policy. Morris now purports that the Arabs' resistance to Zionism sprang from their thralldom to the notion of "sacred Islamic soil"; was "anchored in centuries of Islamic Judeophobia"; and reached into "every fiber of their Islamic, exclusivist being."[35] After Israel's establishment Ben-Gurion conceded, "If I was [sic] an Arab leader I would never make [peace?] terms with Israel. That is natural: We have taken their country." Morris alleges however that because of his ignorance of the Arab world Ben-Gurion failed to grasp that this rejection of Israel was not "natural" but rather rooted in Islamic "abhorrence" of Jews.[36] Insofar as Morris is not known for his expertise on Islam, and insofar as he used to be known for not speculating a hair's breadth beyond what his sources showed, it might be expected that he would copiously substantiate such gross generalizations. But Morris's elucidation of 14 centuries of an allegedly hate-filled "Muslim Arab mindset" and "Muslim Arab mentality" consists of all of one half paragraph of boilerplate.[37]

Coming to the modern period Morris alleges that "since the fin de siècle, Palestine Arabs had been murdering Jews on a regular basis for ethnic or quasinationalist reasons. . . . Arab mobs had assaulted Jewish settlements and neighborhoods in a succession of ever-larger pogroms."[38] But the old Morris found that it was the very real prospect of Zionist transfer that "automatically produced resistance among the Arabs." Morris appears also to have forgotten what he earlier wrote about Zionist resort to self-serving epithets: "anti-Zionist outbreaks were designated 'pogroms,' a term that belittled the phenomenon, demonized the Arabs, and, in a peculiar way, comforted the Jews—it obviated the need to admit that what they faced was a rival national movement, rather than Arabic-speaking Cossacks and street ruffians."[39] Is this perhaps why Morris now designates Arab resistance "pogroms"?

The new Morris laments that "historians have tended to ignore or dismiss, as so much hot air, the jihadi rhetoric" of the Arabs, and he counters that "the evidence is abundant and clear" that the struggle against Zionism was conceived by Arabs "essentially as a holy war."[40] But the old Morris himself barely mentioned the "jihadi" factor and it was Morris himself who declared that the "chief motor" of Arab opposition to Zionism was not "jihad" but the "fear of territorial displacement and dispossession."

To prove that Palestinian resistance was driven by a jihadi "impulse,"[41] the new Morris cites these statements: a "penitent land seller" swore, "I call on Allah, may He be exalted, to bear witness and swear . . . that I will be a loyal soldier in the service of the homeland"; the mufti of Egypt declared that the Jews intended "to take over . . . all the lands of Islam"; the ulema of Al-Azhar denoted it a "sacred religious duty" for "the Arab Kings, Presidents of Arab Republics, . . . and leaders of public opinion to liberate Palestine from the Zionist bands . . . and to return the inhabitants driven from their homes."[42] It would not however be the first or last time that God and religion were invoked in a patriotic struggle: Stalin rehabilitated the Greek Orthodox Church in the battle against Nazism, Gandhi utilized the Hindu religion at every turn in resistance to British occupation, Bush conscripted a Christian god for homeland security and the War on Terror.

In fact, although the old Morris took note that "the Arab radicalization often took on a religious aspect," and that "increasingly the points of friction with the Zionists were, or became identified with, religious symbols and values,"[43] he nonetheless recognized that the "chief motor" of Arab resistance was fear of displacement and dispossession. The new Morris reports that "even Christian Arabs appear to have adopted the jihadi discourse" of "holy war."[44] But doesn't this contrarily show that, although utilizing the "jihadi discourse" of "holy war," the opposition to Zionism was *not* "anchored in centuries of Islamic Judeophobia"? He purports that, in light of their "expulsionist and, in great measure, anti-Semitic" mindset, "it

10/ HISTORY BY SUBTRACTION

is unsurprising that the Arab mobs that periodically ran amok in Palestine's streets during the Mandate . . . screamed '*idhbah al yahud*' (slaughter the Jews)."[45] Yet, as Yehoshua Porath observed in his magisterial study of Palestinian nationalism, although Arabs initially differentiated between Jews and Zionists, it was "inevitable" that opposition to Zionism would turn into a loathing of all Jews: "As immigration increased, so did the Jewish community's identification with the Zionist movement.... The non-Zionist and anti-Zionist factors became an insignificant minority, and a large measure of sophistication was required to make the older distinction. It was unreasonable to hope that the wider Arab population, and the riotous mob which was part of it, would maintain this distinction."[46] If the Arabs shouted "*idhbah al yahud*," it was because nearly every Jew they encountered *was* a Zionist bent, according to the old Morris, on expelling them.

It is instructive to recall here the old Morris's treatment of the first intifada. He reported that "in the Gaza Strip, Islamic Jihad and other fundamentalists immediately took a leading role," "Hamas was a major component of the rebellion in the Strip and, to a lesser extent, the West Bank," and "from the start the Hamas and Islamic Jihad dominated the rebellion in the Gaza Strip"; that these Muslim fundamentalist organizations espoused "Koran-based hatred and contempt for Jews," intended "to wage a holy war against the Zionist enemy," and "made the destruction of Israel" their "official goal"; and that the intifada commenced as "thousands poured out of the alleys of Jibalya and other Gaza camps for the funerals, shouting '*Jihad, Jihad!,*'" and "fundamentalists . . . had been in the forefront of the demonstrations in December 1987."[47]

Still, Morris was emphatic that "the main energizing force of the intifada was the frustration of the national aspirations" of the Palestinians, "who wanted to live in a Palestinian state and not as stateless inhabitants under a brutal, foreign military occupation."[48] And again, after expatiating on jihadi influences, he cautioned: "But the factors that made individual Palestinians take to the streets and endure beating, imprisonment, and economic privation were predominantly socioeconomic and psychological"—such as the "continuous trampling of the[ir] basic rights and dignity," and their fear that "Israel's settlement policy and its discriminatory economic policies" prefigured "the government's ultimate intent to dispossess them and drive them out and to replace them with Jews."[49]

The old Morris—the pre-propagandist Morris—was able to discern that although Islamic zealots figured prominently in the first intifada and Islamic symbols and texts, even hateful anti-Semitic ones, might have been pervasive, its "main energizing force" was not hoary "Islamic Judeophobia" but the mundane denial of basic Palestinian rights. Even in his account of the second intifada, when the salience of the Islamic component was yet greater and he himself was already given to tirades against jihadis, Morris emphasized that "at base" the revolt resulted from "the state of the Palestinians and the peace process ... the frustrations and slights endured since the signing in 1993 of the Oslo agreement, and more generally since the start of the occupation."[50]

The new Morris alleges that "many observers defined the [1936-39] Arab Revolt as a jihad." He cites the concerns of some Christians that are jotted down in a random "note" of an "unknown" member of the Peel Commission.[51] But Morris omits mention of what the Peel Commission itself found. "The overriding desire of the Arab leaders ... was ... national independence," the landmark Peel Report stated, and "It was only to be expected that Palestinian Arabs should ... envy and seek to emulate their successful fellow-nationalists in those countries just across their northern and southern borders." There was "no doubt," the Report concluded, that the "underlying causes" of Arab-Jewish hostilities were "first the desire of the Arabs for national independence; secondly their antagonism to the establishment of the Jewish National Home in Palestine, quickened by their fear of Jewish domination."

However much the new Morris might like to conscript the Peel Commission for his own ideological jihad, its Report in fact explicitly repudiated the notion that Arab opposition to Zionism was born of primordial hatred:

Nor is the conflict in its essence an interracial conflict, arising from any old instinctive antipathy of Arabs towards Jews. There was little or no friction ... between Arab and Jew in the rest of the Arab world until the strife in Palestine engendered it. And there has been precisely the same political trouble in Iraq, Syria and Egypt—agitation, rebellion and bloodshed—where there are no "National Homes." Quite obviously, then, the problem of Palestine is political. It is, as elsewhere, the problem of insurgent nationalism. The only difference is that in Palestine Arab nationalism is inextricably interwoven with antagonism to the Jews. And the reasons for that, it is worth repeating, are equally obvious. In the first place, the establishment of the National Home [for Jews] involved at the outset a blank negation of the rights implied in the principle of national self-government. Secondly, it soon proved to be not merely an obstacle to the development of national self-government, but apparently the only serious obstacle. Thirdly, as the Home has grown, the fear has grown with it that, if and when self-government is conceded, it may not be national in the Arab sense, but government by a Jewish majority. That is why it is difficult to be an Arab patriot and not to hate the Jews.[52]

Not the sacredness of "Islamic soil," not "Islamic Judeophobia," not an "Islamic, exclusivist being," not a "jihadi impulse," but rather Zionism's "negation" of the indigenous Arab population's right to self-determination and the concomitant Arab fear of Jewish domination—a domination that, according to the old Morris, would perforce result in "transferring the Arabs out": those were "no doubt" and "quite obviously" the roots of Arab resistance to Zionism, according to the Peel Commission, a resistance that was "only to be expected." In fact, according to the old Morris, Zionism "automatically produced" this resistance.

The new Morris gestures at one point to the Palestinians' "expulsionist, or eliminationist mindset."[53] *Eliminationist* was a neologism popularized by the now discredited Holocaust-monger Daniel Jonah Goldhagen to characterize the anti-Semitic German mindset allegedly responsible for the Nazi holocaust.[54] One problem with Goldhagen's thesis was that he could not explain why, if Germans had been afflicted for centuries with an eliminationist Judeophobic mindset, the Final Solution occurred when the Nazis came to power and not long before.[55]

The new Morris has appropriated Goldhagen's neologism but, alas, also the problem that comes in its train. If the "expulsionist, or eliminationist mindset" of Arabs was "anchored in centuries of Islamic Judeophobia," why did it manifest itself after the advent of Zionism whereas hitherto there had been "little or no friction ... between Arab and Jew"? It is of course arguable that the picture painted by the Peel Report was a mite rosy and that the old Morris was closer to the truth when he asserted that historically Jews in the Islamic world were treated with "contemptuous tolerance" (quoting Elie Kedourie). But even so, Morris himself also then acknowledged that "generally the Jews' lot was not a matter of violence," and that "the nineteenth century witnessed a gradual change for the better in the Jews' status."[56]

The violent clashes that commenced at the turn of the twentieth century and then relentlessly escalated, the old Morris understood, marked a qualitatively new development. Zionism was to introduce a unique—indeed, judging by the old Morris, a uniquely toxic—ingredient into the brew of Arab-Jewish relations. Morris pointedly signaled this critical rupture in his volume's subtitle, "A history of the Zionist-Arab conflict, 1881-1999." Contrariwise, a typical propagandist for Israel such as Joan Peters titled her book, "*From Time Immemorial: The origins of the Arab-Jewish conflict over Palestine.*"[57] The conflict was not "immemorial" for the old Morris and fundamentally not a conflict between Arab and Jew, but rather of relatively recent vintage and fundamentally between Arab and *Zionist*. However, the new Morris has discarded his prodigious scholarly apparatus demonstrating the historically specific nature of this "Zionist-Arab" encounter and instead cribbed a vacuous formula and

10/ HISTORY BY SUBTRACTION

hitched it to an ahistorical framework—an "expulsionist, or eliminationist mindset" that was "anchored in centuries of Islamic Judeophobia"—for which he adduces not a scrap of evidence and the heuristic value of which is nil, but which possesses the singular virtue of exonerating Zionism of any culpability for the unfolding Palestinian catastrophe.

The old Morris's account of Israeli treatment of Palestinian civilians during combat and under occupation consisted of both exposé and extenuation. It could not be said that he was an apologist, but it also could not be said that he was wholly free of apologetics. The new Morris, however, carries on like an unabashed party hack. One winces in embarrassment not so much at what he says, which is just plain laughable, but at what he has become.

The old Morris was one of the seminal Israeli historians who debunked many of the myths surrounding the first Arab-Israeli war. For example he documented that contrary to the David versus Goliath myth "the truth ... is that the stronger side, in fact, won," "the Jews ... were better organized, had more men under arms (the Arab armies lacked equipment for some of their troops and others had to be left at home to guard shaky regimes) ... —in short, they were stronger."[58] But in a 180-degree reversal, the new Morris alleges that although Israel won the 1948 war it was "*not* because it had more manpower or more equipment."[59]

To Morris's credit, he was also among the first historians to document Israeli massacres during the 1948 war. Even in his propagandistic conclusion to *1948*, Morris forthrightly observes that "Jews committed far more atrocities than the Arabs." Nevertheless, although reporting that Palestinian Arabs barely fought in the 1948 war, and although providing estimates that 6,000-12,000 Palestinian Arabs were killed in the course of it, he asserts in *1948* that the victims of Israeli atrocities numbered only "some eight hundred," or about 10 percent of all Palestinian deaths.[60] The figure and percentage also seem improbably low in light of Morris's assertion in another context that "the IDF [Israel Defense Forces] has progressively become a 'cleaner' army," and that its record "when it comes to *tohar haneshek* [purity of arms]" was "far better" in the 1982 Lebanon war than in 1948.[61] To judge by authoritative accounts of Israel's "cleaner" war in 1982,[62] premeditated and indiscriminate Israeli atrocities accounted for a large proportion of civilian deaths. Morris's minimization of Israeli atrocities during the 1948 war appears to spring from his persistently tendentious usage of the term. Thus, the old Morris's account of the Zionist army's climactic assault on Haifa in April 1948 depicted "completely indiscriminate and revolting machinegun fire and sniping on women and children," and "hysterical and terrified Arab women and children and old people on whom the Jews opened up mercilessly with fire."[63] Yet even back then, and despite his own evidence, Morris averred that he "found no evidence of any 'atrocity' committed in Arab Haifa during and after its capture."[64]

The old Morris published a remarkably frank account of Israel's conflicts with its Arab neighbors after the 1948 war in *Israel's Border Wars*. He pinned the lion's share of culpability on Israel for the escalation of postwar hostilities that climaxed in its invasion of the Egyptian Sinai in 1956. The basic outline of the story he told (and on which historians now generally agree)[65] went like this. After the armistice agreement was signed in 1949, "Cairo's overriding concern in its relations with Israel was to avoid sparking IDF attacks," "Egypt generally sought tranquility along its border with Israel."[66] But "from some point in 1954," IDF Chief of Staff Moshe Dayan "wanted war, and periodically, he hoped that a given retaliatory strike would embarrass or provoke the Arab state attacked into itself retaliating, giving Israel cause to escalate the shooting until war resulted."[67] The "policy of trapping [Egyptian President Gamal Abdel] Nasser into war" through incremental provocation "was hammered out between Ben-Gurion and Dayan": "because Israel could not afford to be branded an aggressor, war would have to be reached by a process of gradual escalation, to be achieved through periodic, large-scale Israeli retaliatory attacks in response to Egyptian infractions of the armistice."[68]

Nasser reversed his "policy of restraint" after Ben-Gurion and Dayan instigated the "Gaza Raid" in February 1955 that left some 40 Egyptian soldiers dead. It "mark[ed] a clear watershed: Before the raid, Egyptian policy had, with few exceptions, consistently opposed civilian infiltration; after it, while continuing to oppose uncontrolled infiltration, the Egyptian authorities themselves initiated terrorist infiltration."[69] But when Egypt still "refused to fall into the successive traps set by Dayan,"[70] who sought a credible casus belli, Israel colluded with Britain and France to attack Egypt outright.[71]

The old Morris also forthrightly depicted Israeli atrocities in *Border Wars*. Israel killed "perhaps as many as 5,000" Palestinian refugees who infiltrated the state after its establishment. The "vast bulk" ("90 percent and more") of these casualties comprised "unarmed 'economic' and social infiltrators" retrieving their abandoned possessions, harvesting crops they had sown, and reuniting with family members left behind.[72] The Palestinian deaths resulted directly from "state-authorized, or at least, permitted killing of unarmed civilians," the "overall attitude" of Israeli authorities being that "killing, torturing, beating and raping Arab infiltrators was, if not permitted, at least not particularly reprehensible and might well go unpunished."

Under the subheading "Atrocities," Morris gave over several pages of *Border Wars* to delineating the ghoulish deaths inflicted by the IDF, and he also carefully documented the "massacres" Israel committed in Gaza after occupying it during the Sinai invasion, when "Israeli troops killed between 447 and 550 Arab civilians."[73] In addition Morris reported that Palestinian infiltrators killed up to 250 Israeli civilians between 1949 and 1956, but only "a small proportion of Jewish casualties was caused by infiltrators who set out with the intent to kill or injure Jews." He variously attributed "most" of these Jewish deaths to "unpremeditated encounters" and somewhat inconsistently to Palestinian infiltrators "motivated by hatred and, in many cases revenge—revenge for the national and personal wrongs and injuries inflicted during 1948 or during subsequent border incidents."[74]

The new Morris, however, has reversed his causal framework for the 1956 war. He entirely omits mention of the pivotal facts that "from some point in 1954" Israeli leaders "wanted war" and sought to provoke Nasser militarily "until war resulted." Instead we are now told that the build-up to the war began with "terroristic infiltration, certainly from 1954 on, [that] was organized by the Egyptian government"; that the "Israeli raid on Gaza in February 1955 . . . probably had very little to do with the substance of [Nasser's] policies" after the Israeli attack; that "Israel responded" to Egyptian-orchestrated attacks "with retaliatory raids"; and that these Egyptian-orchestrated raids were one of the "very basic casus belli presented by Egypt" that impelled Israel to invade in 1956. Cause—i.e., Israeli leaders "wanted war" with Egypt—has become effect—i.e., "Israel responded" to unprovoked Egyptian-backed attacks; provocation—i.e., Israel attacked Egypt to elicit a pretext for war—has become self-defense—i.e., Egyptian-backed attacks constituted a "very basic casus belli" for Israel. Morris also sanitizes the Israeli record for the 1949-56 period, during which, he now alleges, Israel "almost exclusively" targeted combatants—the thousands of Palestinian infiltrators killed as a result of Israeli "atrocities" vanish from the printed page—while the Arabs alone stand guilty of killing civilians.[75]

In his rendering of Israel's more recent confrontations the old Morris similarly combined revelatory research with recycled apologetics. Consider his account of the 1982 Lebanon war. He candidly reported that Israel "spent the months between August 1981 and June 1982 seeking a pretext to invade Lebanon"; that the PLO "took great pains not to violate the [ceasefire] agreement of July 1981"; that "subsequent Israeli propaganda notwithstanding, the border between July 1981 and June 1982 enjoyed a state of calm unprecedented since 1968"; and that Israel's "broader objective" in the 1982 invasion was "the destruction of the PLO and its ejection from Lebanon," which would leave Israel "a far freer hand to determine the fate of the West Bank and Gaza Strip," and would compel Palestinians to "give up their national political aspirations altogether or look to their fulfillment in Jordan."[76]

Still, the old Morris's account of Israeli armed clashes with Lebanon before, during and after the June 1982 invasion lapsed into state propaganda. In his tally of total Arab casualties during Israel's 1978 invasion of Lebanon

(Operation Litani) "about 300 Palestinian fighters were killed, several hundred wounded, and several dozen captured,"[77] yet Human Rights Watch (HRW) cited the figure for total Arab casualties of "about 1,100 dead, the great majority of them civilians."[78]

The old Morris also repeatedly alleged that during the 1982 Lebanon war Israel was "reluctant to harm civilians," sought to "avoid casualties on both sides," and "took care not to harm Lebanese and Palestinian civilians." Although he acknowledged "the massive use of IDF firepower against civilians" during the siege of Beirut, which "traumatized Israeli society" (luckily Beirutis weren't traumatized . . .), Morris quickly entered the caveat that Israel "tried to pinpoint military targets, but inevitably many civilians were hit."[79] It might be noticed that Morris had a personal stake in putting a humane veneer on Israeli conduct: he personally served in the Lebanon war and participated in the siege of Beirut. In any event the picture painted in authoritative accounts, based on voluminous testimony by unimpeachable sources and witnesses, did not remotely resemble Morris's account of Israeli solicitude for civilians.[80]

It is instructive to juxtapose Morris's rendering against the "war diary" of Dov Yermiya, a veteran Israeli soldier (he was a battalion commander in the 1948 war) and the oldest soldier to serve in the 1982 invasion. In his daily record of the Lebanon war Yermiya inter alia jotted down: "the war machine of the IDF is galloping and trampling over the conquered territory, demonstrating a total insensitivity to the fate of the Arabs who are found in its path"; "a PLO-run hospital suffered a direct hit"; "Thousands of refugees are returning to the city. . . . When they arrive at their homes, many of which have been destroyed or damaged, you hear their cries of pain, and their howls over the deaths of their loved ones"; "The air is permeated with the smell of corpses; destruction and death are continuing. . . . I am ashamed to be a son of this nation, this arrogant, condescending, cruel nation"; "It seems that a solitary Arab sniper fired a round in the direction of our forces. In retaliation—a feast of fire from all our weapons"; "Never have I seen a war such as this. Is this a war, or a huge IDF practice range?";

"This was a picture that reminded me of the death march of the Jews in Auschwitz [an operations officer tells Yermiya after a file of prisoners staggered by]"; "A population overtaken by war could have received urgently needed aid, like powdered milk for babies and children, but . . . we, a merciful people, the sons of merciful fathers, do not allow these vital supplies to be brought to the population"; "They make a numbers game out of the refugees and homeless. The media speak of 600,000. Here [headquarters] they throw around numbers like 200,000 and 400,000. They play with numbers as though they were speaking about birds or insects"; "The district commander announces in his disgusting style: 'Another prisoner stopped smoking today.' Earlier, I had learned that a prisoner who had been beaten and tortured died. . . . The commanders were only concerned that it be written in the death certificate that the prisoner died of a heart attack"; "this is what I ran into every step of the way: despicable actions of humiliation, of striking at women and children who wander, confused and miserable, along the sidelines of the war and its aftermath, not knowing their own souls in their fright, hunger, and thirst"; "firepower had been directed toward the entire camp, without any connection to the degree of enemy opposition, which was highly ineffective and sparse"; "the barrages only hurt the non-combatant population. They caused both killings and the destruction of buildings in a most systematic manner, which . . . was not meant to hurt terrorists, but rather, to eliminate the possibility of the existence of refugees in this camp."[81]

In extenuation of IDF outrages Morris alleged that PLO militants in the refugee camps "fought grimly, occasionally using civilians as human shields." But Yermiya reported that "the story that the civilian population had been held hostage by the PLO, and prevented from responding to the IDF's call to leave the camp . . . was totally unfounded," and that "the PLO demonstrated no significant resistance."[82]

Whereas Morris alleged that "Israel tried to pinpoint military targets" during the siege of Beirut, Robert Fisk in his classic eyewitness account *Pity the Nation* reported: "To call the gunfire indiscriminate was an understatement. It would also have been a lie. The Israeli bombardment of 4 August was, we realized, later, *discriminate*. It targeted every civilian area, every institution in west Beirut—hospitals, schools, apartments, shops, newspaper offices, hotels, the prime minister's office and the parks. Incredibly, the Israeli shells even blew part of the roof off the city's synagogue."[83] Although it is unclear how Morris measured trauma levels in Israel during the terror bombing of Beirut, it can be gauged from numerous opinion polls that overwhelmingly Israeli society supported this brutal war of aggression while it unfolded, and still overwhelmingly believed it was justified in retrospect.[84]

In 1996 during Operation Grapes of Wrath, another of Israel's periodic rampages in Lebanon, Israel shelled the U.N. compound at Qana killing more than a hundred Lebanese civilians taking refuge there. Morris alleged that Israel "accidentally" hit the camp, and that the presence of Lebanese civilians was "unbeknownst" to it.[85] But an exhaustive Amnesty International investigation concluded that "the IDF intentionally attacked the UN compound," and that Israel "must have had knowledge or should have assumed" that the compound was providing shelter for "a considerable number of refugees."[86]

The old Morris's account of the Israeli occupation of the West Bank and Gaza and of the first intifada was only slightly marred by apologetics. To be sure, unlike in the case of the Lebanon war, Morris had no personal stake in whitewashing Israeli conduct. On the contrary he was among the few Israelis who refused on moral grounds to serve in the occupied territories during the first intifada.[87]

Morris forthrightly reported that "the overwhelming majority of West Bank and Gaza Arabs from the first hated the occupation"; that "Israel intended to stay in the West Bank, and its rule would not be overthrown or ended through civil disobedience and civil resistance, which were easily crushed. The only real option was armed struggle"; that "Like all occupations, Israel's was founded on brute force, repression and fear, collaboration and treachery, beatings and torture chambers, and daily intimidation, humiliation, and manipulation"; and that the occupation "was always a brutal and mortifying experience for the occupied."[88] The old Morris additionally pointed up the non-martial character of the first intifada: "It was not an armed rebellion but a massive, persistent campaign of civil resistance, with strikes and commercial shutdowns, accompanied by violent (though unarmed) demonstrations against the occupying forces. The stone and, occasionally, the Molotov cocktail and knife were its symbols and weapons, not guns and bombs."[89]

Although occasionally resorting to exculpating caveats such as "the IDF tried to restrict the use of firearms to life-threatening situations,"[90] the old Morris generally provided a harrowing account of brutal and methodical Israeli repression during the first intifada: "Almost everything was tried: shooting to kill, shooting to injure, beatings, mass arrests, torture, trials, administrative detention, and economic sanctions"; "a large proportion of the Palestinian dead were not shot in life-threatening situations, and a great many of these were children"; "Only a small minority of [the IDF] malefactors were brought to book by the army's legal machinery—and were almost always let off with ludicrously light sentences."[91]

It must be acknowledged that the old Morris shone a harsh light on many dark corners of Israeli treatment of the Palestinians, but it must also be said that the credibility Morris thereby garnered then lent legitimacy to his more propagandistic pronouncements. It is not possible however to detect any saving grace in the new Morris, who spews forth an irrepressible stream of unalloyed hate and lies. Were it not for Morris's past reputation, these morally obscene utterances would have been peremptorily dismissed as the rantings of a crackpot. Many of his statements have already been subjected to critical commentary.[92] The ensuing remarks will focus on ground not already covered.

Most of the new Morris's relevant remarks bear on the second intifada. However, the new Morris's perverse mindset can also be glimpsed in his retrospective commentary. Whereas the old Morris reported that during and right after the June 1967 war hundreds of thousands of Palestinians "fled or were driven from the West Bank and the Gaza Strip,"[93] the new Morris alleges that they "moved" elsewhere.[94] (Did they use *Shalom* or *Shleppers* van line?) Whereas the old Morris depicted the first intifada as "not an armed rebellion but a massive, persistent campaign of civil resistance" against the "occupying forces," the new Morris alleges that the first intifada was a "semi-armed revolt against Israel."[95] Why then did he refuse to serve during the first intifada?

In his account of the first intifada the old Morris made extensive use of the findings of human rights organizations such as the Palestinian human rights organization al-Haq and particularly the Israeli human rights organization B'Tselem.[96] The new Morris totally disregards the findings of human rights organizations as well as critical reportage (much of it Israeli) and critical statements by Israeli officials. He resorts instead to mind-numbing repetition—in a smugly authoritative tone and without adducing a shred of corroborative evidence—of official government press releases.

Thus Morris alleges that during the second intifada Israel displayed "great restraint," "praiseworthy discrimination," "extreme restraint in face of acute provocation," and was "always cautious and restrained"; "Israeli policy was to avoid, so far as possible, harm to noncombatants, and the IDF generally took great operational care to avoid civilian casualties," "Care was taken [by Israel] not to hit collateral targets and non-rioting and non-shooting bystanders," "The Israelis . . . took care, often great care, not to kill civilians"; and "most of the Arabs killed . . . were armed fighters, not civilians." If the picture appeared otherwise, according to the new Morris, it was because of "Western, Arab and Israeli television crews" that "almost never arrived on the scene in time to catch who had started a given firefight," and because gullible "Western journalists," and "Arab and Western press reports" gave credence to the "never-ending torrent of Palestinian mendacity" and particularly to Yasir Arafat's Palestinian Authority, "a virtual kingdom of mendacity," rather than to the "straight, or far less mendacious, Israeli officials."[97]

The documentary record however confutes Morris on all points. The 2001 Mitchell Report found that the second intifada initially consisted of "demonstrations of unarmed Palestinians."[98] The IDF manifested its alleged "extreme restraint in face of acute provocation" (Morris) by firing "in the first few days about 700,000 bullets and other projectiles in Judea and Samaria and about 300,000 in Gaza" (according to Israeli intelligence)—or, as one Israeli officer quipped, "a bullet for every child."[99] The new Morris cannot decide whether to reckon this Israeli display of firepower overreactions "or underreactions."[100]

Human rights organizations copiously documented the ensuing "care, often great care, not to kill civilians" that Israel allegedly showed. Amnesty found that "the majority of people killed were taking part in demonstrations where stones were the only weapon used.... Many persons were apparently killed by poorly targeted lethal fire; others ... appear, on many occasions, to have been deliberately targeted."[101] HRW reported "a pattern of repeated Israeli use of excessive lethal force during clashes between its security forces and Palestinian demonstrators in situations where demonstrators were unarmed and posed no threat of death or serious injury to the security forces or to others."[102]

Although Morris accurately reports that "armed Palestinians, hiding behind or among the rioters, joined in with occasional shots,"[103] HRW still found that "where gunfire by Palestinian security forces or armed protesters was a factor, use of lethal force by the IDF was indiscriminate and not directed at the source of the threat." Furthermore B'Tselem reported that "Palestinians did not open fire in the vast majority of demonstrations. The soldiers responded to these demonstrations by using excessive and disproportionate force, leading to many casualties, including children."[104] Whereas Morris alleges that the IDF was "on order to use live fire only in life-endangering situations,"[105] B'Tselem reported that "regulations apparently enable firing in situations where there is no clear and present danger to life, or even in situations where there is no life-threatening danger at all."[106]

The new Morris purports that during the second intifada "most of the Arabs killed ... were armed fighters, not civilians," and that "by 2004, altogether some four thousand Palestinians—about two-thirds of them armed men—and thirteen hundred Israelis—about two-thirds civilians—had died."[107] But Amnesty, citing this 3:1 ratio, reported, "The vast majority of those killed and injured on *both* sides have been unarmed civilians and bystanders."[108] If Israel appeared not to be exercising "extreme restraint," it was according to Morris because of credulous television crews and Western journalists. He forgets to mention not only credulous human rights organizations, including those based in Israel, and credulous Israeli journalists, but also credulous Israeli officials. For instance, a former head of internal Israeli intelligence publicly declared during the second intifada that "we are behaving disgracefully. Yes, there is no other word for it. Disgracefully."[109] But according to Morris there are other words: "cautious," "restrained"....

The new Morris alleges that Israel's "liquidation policy" during the second intifada consisted of "pinpoint strikes" on "specific local Fatah, Hamas and Islamic Jihad commanders who were suspected of mounting" attacks on Israelis, and it targeted "individual terrorists and their controllers."[110] He forgets to mention that as a result of these so-called pinpoint strikes "scores of men, women and children bystanders have been killed and hundreds have been injured," according to Amnesty. "Claims that efforts are made not to harm bystanders are inconsistent with the practice of carrying out attacks on busy roads and densely populated areas."[111]

Morris goes on to observe that Israel's liquidation policy "was challenged by [Ehud] Barak's left-wing critics; Arab human rights organizations and criticized by the United States."[112] He forgets to mention that not just Arab but international human rights organizations such as Amnesty as well as Israeli human rights organizations such as B'Tselem and the Public Committee against Torture in Israel (PCATI) deplored the political liquidations that—according to them—amounted to extrajudicial executions, PCATI calling the policy a "heinous crime both legally and morally."[113] Morris also forgets to mention that opposition to the liquidations emanated not just from Israeli "left-wing critics," but also from reserve pilots in the Israeli air force who declared in a public letter their refusal to participate any longer in such an "illegal and immoral" policy.[114]

The climax of the second intifada came in April 2002 when Israel invaded West Bank cities during Operation Defensive Shield. Dismissing criticism of the operation as "fantasy or propaganda," Morris (alongside Ehud Barak) alleged that "no army has ever been more discriminating and gone to such lengths to avoid inflicting civilian casualties."[115] Indeed, consider Israel's "discriminating" siege of Jenin refugee camp. Human rights organizations found that "Israeli forces committed serious violations of humanitarian law, some amounting *prima facie* to war crimes" (HRW), and "the IDF carried out actions which violate humanitarian law; some of these actions amount to ... war crimes" (Amnesty).[116]

Whereas Morris alleges that only "several dozen homes" were destroyed in the course of the whole operation, HRW reported that just in Jenin refugee camp "at least 140 buildings—most of them multi-family dwellings—were completely destroyed . . ., and severe damage caused to more than 200 others has rendered them uninhabitable or unsafe. An estimated 4,000 people, more than a quarter of the population of the camp, were rendered homeless because of this destruction." HRW further noted that "the destruction extended well beyond any conceivable purpose of gaining access to fighters, and was vastly disproportionate to the military objectives pursued," while Amnesty reported that "in one appalling and extensive operation, the IDF demolished, destroyed by explosives, or flattened by army bulldozers, a large residential area of Jenin refugee camp, most of it after the fighting had apparently ended."

"I left them a football stadium in the camp," one of Morris's "discriminating" IDF soldiers operating a bulldozer in Jenin chortled. "I wanted to destroy everything," he told an interviewer. "I begged the officers ... to let me knock it all down, from top to bottom. To level everything. ... For three days I just destroyed and destroyed. ... I found joy with every house that came down, because I knew that they didn't mind dying, but they cared for their homes. If you knocked down a house, you buried 40 or 50 people for generations. If I am sorry for anything, it's for not tearing the whole camp down. ... I had plenty of satisfaction. I really enjoyed it."[117]

At least 22 civilians were killed in Jenin refugee camp during Operation Defensive Shield (Morris alleges "five or six"), among them, a "37-year-old paralyzed man was killed when the IDF bulldozed his home on top of him, refusing to allow his relatives the time to remove him from the home," and a "57-year-old wheelchair-bound man . . . was shot and run over by a tank on a major road outside the camp . . . even though he had a white flag attached to his wheelchair" (HRW). Israel not only committed comparable human rights violations and war crimes in Nablus, according to Amnesty, but it also razed "religious and historical sites . . . in what frequently appeared to be wanton destruction without military necessity." It appears that B'Tselem executive director Jessica Montell also fell victim to "fantasy or propaganda" when she censured Israel's "vengeful assault on all symbols of Palestinian society and Palestinian identity" during the operation and the "hooliganism" of "thousands of teenage boys and young men in uniform allowed to run wild in Palestinian cities with no accountability for their actions."[118] In a rare allusion to the findings of a human rights organization the new Morris alleged that "Human Rights Watch and other non-partisan bodies subsequently upheld the Israeli version" of events at Jenin. Taking "strong exception" to his assertion, HRW stated in a public rebuke that "Morris mischaracterizes the findings of Human Rights Watch."[119]

The new Morris chides Western journalists for not crediting the "straight, or far less mendacious, Israeli officials," whom he himself faithfully echoes. But (far too) many Western journalists did defer to them. It was respected *Israeli* journalists who ridiculed Morris's primary source during the second intifada. "The state authorities, including the defense establishment and its branches," Uzi Benziman observed in *Haaretz*, "have acquired for themselves a shady reputation when it comes to their credibility." The "official communiqués published by the IDF have progressively liberated themselves from the constraints of truth," B. Michael editorialized in *Yediot Ahronot*, and the "heart of the power structure"—police, army, intelligence—has been infected by a "culture of lying."[120]

Beyond bamboozling credulous Westerners during the second intifada, "Palestinian spokespeople," according to Morris, orchestrated the "designation of Israeli policies as 'apartheid.'"[121] But the roster of those bracketing Israeli policies with apartheid also happens to include many prominent Israelis.[122] And far from being a recent development, already a quarter century ago knowledgeable Israelis such as Danny Rubinstein had sounded the alarm that Israel was "creating a system of apartheid in the West Bank and Gaza Strip."[123]

Although Arafat indisputably presided over a "kingdom of mendacity," judging by the new Morris's depiction of the second intifada, he has managed to fabricate a kingdom of his own that rivals it.

It is well established and largely undisputed that Palestinians opposed the partition proposals of the Peel Commission in 1937 and the United Nations General Assembly in 1947.[124] Orthodox Israeli historians such as Shabtai Teveth had already conceded that not only the Palestinians but also the Zionist movement in principle opposed the Peel Commission's partition proposal: for Ben-Gurion it was merely "a stage in the longer process toward a Jewish state in all of Palestine."[125] The "new historians" went a step further as they demonstrated that the Zionist movement also opposed in principle the U.N. Partition Resolution assigning the Jewish state 56 percent of Palestine. "The acceptance of partition, in the mid-1930s *as in 1947*," Morris reported, "was tactical, not a change in the Zionist dream."[126] Both prior and subsequent to the passage of the Partition Resolution in November 1947, Ben-Gurion was emphatic that "We want the Land of Israel in its entirety" (May 1947), and that the boundaries assigned Israel in the Partition Resolution were "not final" but subject to revision should the occasion allow (December 1947).[127] When, in 1948, circumstances seemed ripe to achieve these goals, Zionist leaders "embarked . . . on a campaign aimed at a new definition of the borders of their state" (Shlomo Ben-Ami),[128] and by war's end Israel controlled 78 percent of Palestine.

The old Morris brought to bear a wealth of evidence documenting that even after the 1948 war Israel still coveted the remnants of Palestine beyond its control, and more: "A strong expansionist current ran through both Zionist ideology and Israeli society. There was a general feeling, shared by such prominent figures as Dayan and Ben-Gurion, that the territorial gains of the 1948 war had fallen short of the envisioned promised land. *Bechiya LeDorot*—literally a cause for lamentation for future generations—was how Ben-Gurion described the failure to conquer Arab East Jerusalem; leading groups in Israeli society regarded the Jordanian-controlled West Bank with the same feeling"; "Large sections of the Israeli public, including many in its political and military elite . . ., were keen on expansion, optimally down to the Jordan River. . . . Indeed, key Israeli leaders between 1949 and 1956 viewed the Kingdom of Jordan itself as an 'artificial' and 'unnatural' country that could not in the long run survive and would eventually be divided up and absorbed by its more powerful neighbors, with the West Bank going to Israel and the East Bank to Iraq."[129]

In the aftermath of the 1948 war Israeli leaders consequently awaited, surveyed, planned and plotted an "opportunity" that could be exploited in order to expand their country's borders.[130] Once a concrete occasion availed itself in 1956, when Israel colluded with Britain and France to attack Egypt, Ben-Gurion drew up an extravagant blueprint to annex the West Bank, south Lebanon and parts of the Sinai. It was the French, according to the old Morris, who "gently brought Ben-Gurion down to earth."[131]

After Israel invaded the Sinai, the old Morris further reported, Ben-Gurion declared "Israel's historic right to the island of Tiran, which he identified with Yodfat, where a Jewish kingdom had existed in the sixth century A.D. The message was clear—Israel had no intention of withdrawing from Sinai." Alongside other Israeli leaders Ben-Gurion homed in on Gaza and the Sinai as "the cradle of our transformation into a nation and the harbingers of hopes for the future," and as integral to a greater Israel, part and parcel of "the third Jewish kingdom."[132] Although forced by international pressure to withdraw from the bulk of the Sinai, Ben-Gurion still held out the prospect of retaining Gaza and Sharm-el-Shaykh, but Washington demanded a full Israeli withdrawal.[133] "It was an expansionist war," the old Morris concluded, "Ben-Gurion and Dayan hoped it would lead to Israel's occupation and annexation of tracts of Egyptian territory in the Sinai Peninsula."[134]

In a weird throwback to what the Russian revolutionist Leon Trotsky called the "Stalinist school of falsification," the new Morris inters the whole of the historical record that the old Morris so painstakingly exhumed. Although acknowledging that the Zionist leaders' "aim from the start was the conversion of the whole country into a Jewish state," and that they envisaged the Peel Commission's partition proposal "as a springboard for a future expansion of Jewish sovereignty,"[135] the new Morris alleges that by 1947 "the Zionist mainstream, including Ben-Gurion, *internalized* and came to accept the *principle* of partition."[136] He additionally purports that Zionist leaders "full-throatedly hailed the UN partition resolution . . . and endorsed a two-state solution. . . . This time, unlike in 1937, Ben-Gurion's declarations had the ring of sincerity."[137]

But the old Morris reported that "the acceptance of partition, in the mid-1930s as in 1947 was tactical, not a change in the Zionist dream," and none other than Ben-Gurion himself repeatedly avowed right before and after passage of the Partition Resolution that the borders designated for the Jewish state were provisional, not final. The new Morris alleges that Ben-Gurion "was to remain fixed in his advocacy of partition throughout the 1948 War while supporting the limited expansion of Israel at the expense of parts of the areas allotted to the Palestinian Arabs."[138] But by the end of the war the Zionist armies had conquered fully 78 percent of Palestine and, if Ben-Gurion did not also conquer the West Bank, it was not because he had "internalized . . . the principle of partition," but because—as the old Morris reported—such a conquest would have triggered a war with Britain and "burdened Israel . . . with more than half a million additional Arabs."[139]

One cannot but marvel at—or be nauseated by—how the new Morris disposes of inconvenient facts:[140]

- "It is true that on 26 September [1948] he [Ben-Gurion] tabled a motion supporting a renewed IDF offensive in parts of the West Bank ... which ... would have added East Jerusalem, and perhaps the whole of the West Bank, to the Jewish state, but he probably knew in advance that his fellow ministers would reject it, as they did in the vote that afternoon." But if he had "internalized ... the principle of partition," why did Ben-Gurion table the motion in the first place?
- "And later, in March 1949, just before the signing of the Israel-Jordan armistice agreement, when IDF general Yigal Allon proposed conquering the West Bank, Ben-Gurion turned him down flat. Like most Israelis, Ben-Gurion had given up the dream of the whole land and had internalized the necessity, indeed inevitability, of partition." But why then did Ben-Gurion and other Zionist leaders subsequently regard Israel's failure to conquer East Jerusalem and the West Bank as "a cause for lamentation for future generations," and why did Ben-Gurion contemplate annexation of the West Bank during the Sinai invasion?
- "Even Ben-Gurion, who occasionally during the first post-1948 War years toyed with the idea of expansion, in the end always pulled back, his natural caution overcoming his ideological predisposition." But wasn't it the French who "brought Ben-Gurion down to earth" when he put forth his wildly expansionist agenda, and didn't the Americans later coerce him despite his protestations to withdraw from the Sinai and Gaza? The new Morris seems also to have forgotten that, according to him, Ben-Gurion no longer had an "ideological predisposition" to expansion but rather had "internalized ... the principle of partition."

If Israel's borders did not expand between 1949 and 1967, it was not because, as the new Morris alleges, its leaders "preferred the territorial status quo,"[141] but because—however much they longed, and endeavored to exploit any opportunity, for territorial aggrandizement—the status quo proved intractable. That is, until June 1967.

The old Morris was less forthright on Israel's territorial ambitions during the June 1967 war. He reported that "it was not part of Israel's original intentions to conquer the West Bank or parts of Syria"; that "of Israel's political leadership, only Dayan appears to have contemplated, before the outbreak of the fighting, conquering the West Bank"; that "Israel had hoped on the morning of June 5 to confine the war to Egypt"; that "once the fate of the Egyptian army had become clear to the decision-makers, thoughts of offense began to supersede defense in Israeli thinking vis-à-vis the West Bank and East Jerusalem," but "the possibility of conquering the West Bank and East Jerusalem" was tabled by Israeli leaders "without any advance preparation, without working papers, without knowing anything about political or military plans"; and that once King Hussein initiated hostilities on the Jordanian front the IDF "thrust into the West Bank without a clear plan for conquering the territory." The only caveats—in fact, *contradictory* indications—Morris entered in this depiction of Israeli innocence were that some Israeli leaders appeared eager to "exploit to the full" any missteps of Hussein because they lamented Israel's failure in the 1948 war to conquer East Jerusalem and the West Bank; that "IDF planning . . . took into account the possible entry of Jordan and Syria into the war"; and that "from the beginning of the crisis in mid-May, the head of the IDF Northern Command . . . maintained that the war would inevitably spread to the Syrian front and that it would be necessary to capture the Golan Heights."[142]

It might be said in extenuation of the old Morris that research on the June 1967 war was still in an inchoate state when he made these assertions, and that he himself was careful to qualify his account as being based on "the documentation so far available."[143] Nonetheless, he was able to quote influential Labor Party official Yigal Allon from a few days before the June war stating, "In . . . a new war, we must avoid the historic mistake of the War of Independence . . . and must not cease fighting until we achieve total victory, the territorial fulfillment of the Land of Israel."[144] One would be hard-pressed to reconcile statements such as this, cited by Morris, with his concurrent assertions that "it was not part of Israel's original intentions to conquer the West Bank" and that "of Israel's political leadership, only Dayan appears to have contemplated, before the outbreak of the fighting, conquering the West Bank."

In trying to make sense of the old Morris's apologetic depiction, it might be noticed that he has typically deferred to Israeli orthodoxy except when his own personal research proved otherwise, and he has not done original research on the 1967 war.[145] In addition, the old Morris was always more revelatory on historical topics that no longer had a political resonance. He could accordingly be quite candid about what transpired in the course of Zionist settlement through Israel's founding in the 1948 war because Israel's existence has long ceased to be an object of political (or military) contestation.[146] But the Palestinian refugee problem still endures, and its practical resolution is still subject to negotiation, which perhaps accounts for the ten thousand caveats Morris enters on what happened to them in 1948, making it impossible to pin him down: however his position is characterized by others, Morris invariably protests that he has been misrepresented.

As his historical scholarship edged closer to the present, the old Morris became ever more apologetic. His account of the 1967 war barely if at all departed from the orthodox Israeli narrative, virtually none of which holds up in light of current research. The repercussions of the June 1967 war— in particular the occupation of the West Bank and Gaza—are still charged political issues, so Morris, always the most political of historians, has been careful not to let his findings subvert Israel's diplomatic posture.

In any event, Morris's depiction of Israeli innocence on the eve of its territorial conquests in June 1967 cannot be sustained. The cumulative scholarly evidence is overwhelming that Israeli leaders desired and planned to conquer the West Bank and Gaza in the event of a new war and waited only for the opportunity to implement these long-incubating ideological-strategic goals.[147] The new Morris has no problem reconciling this copious documentary record with his allegation that already before 1947 the Zionist leadership had "internalized and come to accept the principle of partition" because he has comprehensively effaced it.

Beyond alleging that Israeli leaders historically supported partition, the new Morris makes the auxiliary assertion that Israeli leaders—at least those affiliated with Labor—have historically supported a "two-state solution"[148] whereas Palestinians have uniformly and right up to the present opposed it. The consensus understanding of the "two-state" solution, which is anchored in the 1947 Partition Resolution, denotes an Israeli withdrawal from the West Bank (including East Jerusalem) and Gaza, and the Palestinian exercise of self-determination and statehood in these territories. It has been ratified by multiple authoritative bodies including the United Nations General Assembly and the International Court of Justice.[149]

Israeli leaders "firmly opposed" a Palestinian state from the start of the occupation, according to the old Morris, and right through the first intifada they "appeared determined that there would be . . . no Palestinian state."[150] In light of the record he himself documented it would be quite the feat if the new Morris could demonstrate that Israel's most influential political figures historically championed a two-state settlement. He meets this daunting challenge by resort to linguistic subterfuge. The two-state settlement is construed by him to denote the partition of Palestine *even if it is at the expense of, indeed negates, Palestinian self-determination and statehood*— or, as he euphemistically puts it, with "Jordan rather than the Palestinian Arabs as the political beneficiary," and "no Palestinian state." Thus, he dubs a "two-state solution" the Zionist leadership's secret negotiations with King Abdullah in 1946-47 to partition Palestine not with the Palestinians but the Hashemite Kingdom of Jordan; he dubs a "two-state solution" the partition of Palestine between Israel and Jordan at the end of the 1948 war; and he dubs a "two-state solution" Israel's Allon Plan formulated after the 1967 war to divide the West Bank with Jordan.[151] Although Morris acknowledges that "even Rabin had not formally endorsed two 'states'"[152]—neither Yitzhak Rabin nor Shimon Peres conceived a Palestinian state emerging from the 1993 Oslo agreement[153]—it does not prevent the new Morris from simultaneously alleging that Labor leaders supported a "two-state solution," because it is of no account to him whether such a solution affirms or aborts Palestinian self-determination.

His rechristening a resolution of the Israel-Palestine conflict that negates Palestinian self-determination as a "two-state solution" enables the new Morris to project as fact a fictitious image of Israeli moderation. In one variant of this fiction, the new Morris alleges, "Traditionally, since 1967, what had divided left from right was the left's willingness to compromise and make territorial concessions for peace and, ultimately, to *agree to a Palestinian state in the West Bank and Gaza.*"[154] But the old Morris showed that the Israeli left was just as opposed as the Israeli right to a Palestinian state.

Morris also alleges that as part of the original 1993 Oslo Accord "Israel agreed to ... enter into negotiations for a final status agreement, covering refugees, borders, Jerusalem, settlements, security, *and Palestinian statehood.*"[155] But Israel did not and could not have agreed to negotiate a Palestinian state because at the time Israeli leaders opposed it. It was not until 1997 that the Labor Party ratified, hesitantly, "the Palestinians' right to self-determination," and did "not rule out in this connection the establishment of a Palestinian state with limited sovereignty." Its platform was silent however on the crucial question of the Palestinian state's borders, and it explicitly stated that "Israel extends its sovereignty over the areas that are major Jewish settlement blocs"[156]—a caveat that in effect preempts the possibility of a viable Palestinian state. The 1999 Likud platform, which is still operative today, "flatly rejects the establishment of a Palestinian Arab state west of the Jordan river."[157]

The old Morris reported that since the mid-1970s Palestinian leaders had been "inching toward moderation" by signaling acquiescence in a two-state solution, notwithstanding intransigent Israeli opposition to it: "The idea of a Palestinian state emerging alongside Israel ... was first implicitly posited at the PNC [Palestine National Council] meeting in 1974"; "the concluding 'Political Statement' [of the November 1988 PNC meeting in Algiers] was moderate and innovative, and therefore historically significant, in content.... It accepted the need for a 'comprehensive political settlement' and direct negotiations with Israel, and posited the convocation of an international conference on the basis of Resolutions 242 and 338"; "Even Arafat's willingness... to go yet further and in effect renounce the Palestinian National Charter—in May 1989 he told French interviewers 'C'est caduc' (meaning 'it is null and void')—failed to get a bite out of Peres and Rabin, let alone [Yitzhak] Shamir"; "PLO moves toward moderation had failed to elicit a matching echo from the Israeli government"; in the early 1990s "the PLO agreed to recognize and make peace with Israel, and to establish a self-governing entity in a small part of Palestine"; on "September 9, 1993, Arafat stated that the PLO 'recognize[s] the right of the State of Israel to exist in peace and security,' 'accepts UN Security Council Resolutions 242 and 338,' commits itself to the peace process and 'to a peaceful resolution of the conflict'"; "On April 24 [1996], the PNC, meeting in Gaza, voted ... to amend the covenant to remove those articles calling for the elimination of Israel."[158] Although he took note of an occasional ambiguity in the Palestinian record that the "Israeli Right" would pounce on,[159] the overarching conclusion of the old Morris's comprehensive history was that already "by 1988 the moderating process had ripened sufficiently for the [PLO] to publicly and formally declare its readiness for a 'two-state solution,' implying acceptance and recognition of Israel."[160]

In yet another awesome feat of historical engineering, the new Morris manages to undo this "moderating process" that climaxed in a "readiness for a 'two-state solution.'" He now alleges that the "Palestinian national movement started life with a vision and goal of a Palestinian Muslim Arab-majority state in all of Palestine—a one-state 'solution'—and *continues to espouse and aim to establish such a state down to the present day*."[161] Those who dare suggest otherwise—including, it would appear, the old Morris—he promiscuously accuses of "mendacity" (Morris's favorite epithet).[162]

In support of his new spin on the historical record, Morris does not so much revise as *reverse* his old findings: "Arafat and company saw 1974 [i.e., the PNC meeting] merely as the acceptance of the need for the elimination of Israel in stages rather than in one fell swoop"; "Many Westerners and some Israelis saw the document [of the November 1988 PNC meeting] as implying acceptance of Israel's existence. . . . But of course it was not"; "Arafat declared [in December 1988] that the PNC accepted Resolutions 242 and 338 as a basis for negotiations—in truth, it had not."[163] *Caveat lector*: Without adducing a scrap of evidence to justify it, the new Morris has just nullified all his old findings.

The new Morris appears to concede that from 1998 the Palestinian leadership formally accepted a two-state settlement.[164] However he then quickly enters the qualification: "Palestinian foot-dragging and squiggling . . . had left many Israelis skeptical. . . . Did their obvious reluctance . . . not hint at the basic untrustworthiness of Israel's 'partners' in peace?" Morris leaves no doubt as to where he comes down. Whatever their formal affirmations, the new Morris avers, "Palestinian Arabs, in the deepest fibers of their being, oppose such an outcome [i.e., a two-state settlement], demanding as they did since the dawn of the national movement, all of Palestine as their patrimony."[165] Alas, he never reveals how he divined what lurks in the "deepest fibers of their being."

But Morris does not stop here. Even if Palestinians formally accept a two-state settlement, and even if "in the deepest fibers of their being" Palestinians accept a two-state settlement, Morris alleges that they *rationally cannot* accept a two-state settlement: "There are good objective reasons why a two-state solution . . . can have little traction even among Palestinians who, in principle, might agree to such a compromise. The division of historic Mandatory Palestine as proposed, 79 percent for the Jews and 21 percent for the Palestinian Arabs, cannot fail to leave the Arabs, all Arabs, with a deep sense of injustice, affront, and humiliation and a legitimate perception that a state consisting of the Gaza Strip and the West Bank (and perhaps large parts of East Jerusalem)—altogether some two thousand square miles—is simply not viable, politically and economically."[166] Let us set to one side that if what Morris says here is true, then Palestinians might have opposed the two-state settlement not because of "Islamic Judeophobia" and "their Islamic, exclusivist being," but because of their "legitimate perception" that such a settlement was manifestly unjust. The bigger problem however is that on Morris's construction Palestinians literally cannot accept a two-state settlement: if they formally accept it, they must viscerally reject it; and if they formally and viscerally accept it, they must rationally reject it. On these terms it is child's play to demonstrate that Palestinians "continue to espouse and aim to establish . . . down to the present day" an exclusivist state in the whole of Palestine. Morris's "proof" is already contained in his premise: Palestinians oppose a two-state settlement because—even if the factual evidence proves otherwise—they *must* oppose such a settlement.

The new Morris's account of the 2000-1 Israeli-Palestinian peace negotiations brokered by the United States[167] hews closely to the largely discredited official narrative propagated by the likes of Dennis Ross. He alleges for example that at Camp David in July 2000 "Israel made a series of proposals, each better than the last, on territory, Jerusalem, the nature of the Palestinian state. Arafat consistently said 'no' and demanded more."[168] The repeated rejection of a two-state offer by Arafat during the 2000-1 negotiations, the new Morris concludes, demonstrated that the Palestinians were "still wedded to the one-state solution and wanted all of Palestine."[169]

The actual facts however speak otherwise. The points of contention in these negotiations included borders, East Jerusalem, settlements, and refugees. It is undoubtedly true that Barak "expressed astonishment and anger at the Palestinian rejection of the most far-reaching Israeli concessions ever offered,"[170] but, as already shown,[171] from the applicable standard of international law *all* the concessions during the 2000-1 negotiations came from the Palestinian side: although legally entitled to the whole of the West Bank and Gaza, Palestinians were willing to cede a small percentage to Israel (as part of a one-to-one land swap); although legally entitled to the whole of East Jerusalem, Palestinians were willing to divide it with Israel; although legally the Jewish settlements had to be dismantled, Palestinians were willing to let Israel retain the bulk of them; although legally the refugees had a right to return and compensation, Palestinians were largely willing to relinquish the right of return.

10/ HISTORY BY SUBTRACTION

In order to capture the logic behind Palestinian rejection of Barak's offer at Camp David, one can do no better than quote Morris himself. "During the 1980s and 1990s," he wrote in 2001,

> the PLO leadership had gradually accepted, or seemed to accept, history's verdict: That Israel, in its post-1948 borders, was there to stay—keeping 78 percent of historic "Palestine." But the PLO wanted the remaining 22 percent, the West Bank and Gaza Strip, regarding this as a modicum of justice. At Camp David Barak had endorsed the establishment of a Palestinian state; but he had proposed that it make do with 84-90 percent of that 22 percent—and to underline his point had insisted that the bulk of the settlers and large concentrations of Jewish West Bank settlements be incorporated into Israel. Also Israel was to control the territory between a greatly enlarged "Jerusalem" and Jericho, effectively cutting the core of the future Palestinian state in two, and giving Israel control of the border crossings between the Palestinian state and Egypt and Jordan. To Palestinians, this was not fair or just.[172]

It cannot be doubted that Morris's biggest obstacle as he endeavors to reintegrate himself with a society gone drunk on self-righteous delusion is his own past sobriety.

Taking yet another tack, the new Morris alleges that even if Palestinian leaders did historically support a two-state settlement, it is "in a practical sense meaningless, since there was, and is, no Palestinian Arab state and none has yet come into being."[173] But one might suppose that an historian of the conflict would find it meaningful whether Israeli or Palestinian intransigence has caused the endless bloodshed. Moreover, hasn't the new Morris devoted the whole of his energies to proving that "Islamic Judeophobia" and the "Islamic, exclusivist being" are the *fons et origo* of the Israel-Palestine conflict?

Instead of focusing on the past, Morris counsels that we direct our attention to Hamas because it is now the dominant presence on the Palestinian political landscape. He quotes at extraordinary length from the notorious Hamas covenant; cautions the naive reader that "Hamas's mindset is deadly serious" (his proof being, "I don't remember a Hamas leader cracking a joke"); and submits that Hamas's ideology and leading role preclude "an accommodation with Israel based on a two-state settlement."[174] Were any doubts still to linger Morris gestures to Hamas's "consistent statements" rejecting a two-state settlement and then reiterates that "Hamas has the virtue of speaking clearly and consistently."[175] Can Morris possibly be unaware that, as the publication of an official U.S. government agency pointed out, Hamas "has, in practice, moved well beyond its charter ... has been carefully and consciously adjusting its political program for years and has sent repeated signals that it is ready to begin a process of coexisting with Israel"?[176]

According to the new Morris, not just Palestinian leaders but the Palestinian public as well has effectively opposed a two-state settlement, whereas "the *overwhelming majority* of Israelis, as opinion polls have consistently shown *for decades*, support partition and a two-state settlement of the conflict."[177] Scrutiny of the available poll data gives keen insight into the trustworthiness of the new Morris as a scholar. An authoritative 1990 Hebrew University poll of Israelis found:

Possible final settlement	% support
Palestinian state in all territories	9.1
Palestinian state in Gaza Strip only	8.9
Territorial compromise and forming a Palestinian-Jordanian state	12.6
Territorial compromise with Jordan without a third state between Israel and Jordan	19.0

Thus, less than 10 percent of Israelis supported the international consensus while, even to judge by Morris's fanciful "two-state solution" that negates

Palestinian self-determination, total support still came to under 50 percent.[178] Israeli support for any variant of a Palestinian state stood at only 21 percent in 1987 and 35 percent in 1993, and even as late as 1999 only 6 percent of Israeli Jews fully accepted and another 18 percent gave qualified acceptance to a Palestinian state on the pre-1967 borders (13 percent and 18 percent respectively for all Israelis including Palestinian citizens).[179] During the second intifada Israeli support for a two-state settlement approximating the international consensus hovered around 40 percent.[180] Yet the new Morris distills from the poll data that the "overwhelming majority of Israelis" have "for decades" supported a two-state settlement.

In another of his signature statistical forays, the new Morris alleges that "the idea of transfer ... vis-à-vis Israel's Arab minority or the Arabs of the occupied territories or both" has been supported "at various times over the past 60 years, especially during Arab assaults on Israel" by "10 to 30 percent of the Jewish population."[181] Yet, the old Morris reported that circa 1950 virtually the "entire nation" of Israeli Jews supported "the expulsion of Israel's post-1948 Arab minority," while during the first intifada, he reported, "one opinion poll indicated that almost half the electorate looked to some sort of transfer solution."[182] Nearly half of Israelis polled during the second intifada supported expelling all Palestinians in the occupied territories and one-third supported expelling the Israeli Arabs, while in the course of the past two decades fully 50-70 percent of Israeli Jews have consistently supported the use of state inducements to rid Israel of its Palestinian minority.[183]

Morris concedes that polls of Palestinian public opinion "have often concluded that most Palestinians, at least in the West Bank and Gaza, support a two-state settlement." But beyond contesting the veracity of such polls Morris alleges that other data belie them: "there is almost complete unanimity among the Palestinians in support of the 'right of return,' the implementation of which would necessarily subvert any two-state settlement"; Palestinians "are equally unanimous in denying the legitimacy of Zionism and Israel," "Israel's Jewishness," and "Israel as a 'Jewish state.'"[184] Morris's real quarrel however appears to be not with Palestinians but international law and enlightened public opinion. The Palestinian right to return and compensation has been repeatedly validated by the United Nations General Assembly and respected human rights organizations such as HRW and Amnesty.[185] Furthermore, the terms of the international consensus for resolving the Israel-Palestine conflict do not require Palestinian recognition of the "legitimacy of Zionism and Israel" (neither Egypt nor Jordan recognized such a "legitimacy" when they signed peace treaties with Israel), while it is hard to reckon how Palestinians can recognize Israel as a "Jewish state" if Jews themselves barely agree on what it means to be a Jew, let alone what it means for a state to be "Jewish."[186]

The new Morris mounts the case that Palestinians have always rejected a two-state settlement and will not be sated with less than the whole of Palestine. Although the allegation is highly dubious it nonetheless piques the curiosity just how he proposes to resolve the conflict. Yale University Press announces on the jacket of Morris's latest book that "he arrives at a new way of thinking about the discord, injecting a ray of hope in a region where it is most surely needed." What is this ray of hope?

Morris alleges that Israel cannot withdraw from the West Bank until "the IDF acquires the technological capability to protect its population centers from short-range missile attacks." But, alas, "it is unclear whether such a system will be operational before 2013 and whether it will be effective"; indeed, the costs involved "could impoverish Israel and render the defensive systems ultimately inoperative."[187] It is difficult to make out the ray of hope, let alone justice, in holding the elementary human rights of Palestinians hostage to Israel's budgetary constraints. Incidentally, do Arabs get to occupy Israel until they can protect themselves against *its* periodic rampages?

But far be it from Morris to despair. His so-called new way of thinking is to revive the Allon Plan "of a partition of Palestine into Israel, more or less along its pre-1967 borders, and an Arab state, call it Palestinian-Jordanian, that fuses the bulk of the West Bank and East Jerusalem and the east bank, the present-day Kingdom of Jordan." Morris does not pretend that Palestinians are likely in the future to acquiesce in a settlement that they have

10/ HISTORY BY SUBTRACTION

forcefully opposed in the past, but ever espying a glimmer of hope he points to a solution: Jordan's "relatively powerful army and security services . . . would provide the possibility of reining in the militants."[188] No doubt Jordan's torture chambers will also come in handy.

It might be supposed that such a "two-state settlement"[189] violates the basic right to self-determination, but the new Morris also sets the naive reader straight on this misapprehension. For, according to him, Palestinians, Arabs, Muslims—"they" are not like "us"; "they" don't attach the value "we" do to human rights. Thus Morris dots his text with these *aperçus*: "Palestinian spokesmen regularly invoked slogans like democracy, majority will, and one man, one vote—catchphrases and norms that, in fact, were completely alien to their history and social and political ethos and mindset"; "Western liberals like or pretend to view Palestinian Arabs, indeed all Arabs, as Scandinavians, and refuse to recognize that peoples, for good historical, cultural and social reasons, are different and behave differently in similar or identical sets of circumstances"; "Palestinian Arabs, like the world's other Muslim Arab communities, are deeply religious and have no respect for democratic values and no tradition of democratic governance."[190]

In his own research on the 1948 war Morris qualifies his every conclusion with a seemingly endless string of caveats. He shows no compunction however about spewing forth gross generalizations about the history, ethos, mindset, culture and society of "the world's . . . Muslim-Arab communities." He possesses no known expertise on the Muslim-Arab world and cites no sources for any of his allegations. Poll data do not support claims of his, such as that Muslim-Arab communities devalue democracy.[191] He appears to have culled his grand insights from *The Complete Idiot's Guide to Orientalist Stereotypes*. After the Egyptian people erupted in revolt against the dictatorship of Hosni Mubarak, Morris knowingly observed that "what Egyptians really want" was "probably" their "material betterment" and "not political freedom and human rights." If Westerners believed otherwise, it was because they "don't know Arabic." As it happens, neither does he.[192]

Lest there be any doubt on the chasm separating "them" from "us," Morris adduces this clincher: "The value placed on human life and the rule of (secular) law is completely different—as exhibited, in Israel itself, in the vast hiatus [sic] between Jewish and Arab perpetration of crimes and lethal road traffic violations. Arabs, to put it simply, proportionally commit far more crimes (and not only ones connected to property) and commit far more lethal traffic violations than do Jews. In large measure, this is a function of different value systems (such as the respect accorded to human life and the rule of law)."[193] Like some crazed xenophobe scratching out his manifesto while holed up in a dimly lit garret, Morris collates in a sprawling endnote an ethnic breakdown of crime statistics obtained from "Chief Inspector Hamutal Sabagh" and "in my possession."[194] But couldn't the data demonstrate not that Arabs are intrinsically different but that like minorities suffering discrimination elsewhere they are more vulnerable to the criminal justice system? The disparity in auto fatalities should according to Morris convince all but "the most disconnected and unrealistic of minds" that Jews couldn't possibly live together with Arabs under one roof. Indeed, knowing what we all know about women drivers, isn't it verily a miracle that men have managed to live with *them* for so long?

It remains to reflect if only briefly and speculatively on the roots of Morris's bizarre transformation from a relatively judicious liberal historian into a ranting right-wing crackpot. Morris proclaims that it was the Palestinians' rejection of Barak's "generous offer" at Camp David and the Clinton Parameters that opened his eyes to their insidious nature.[195] But this explanation does not withstand a moment's scrutiny: the generous offer was largely a myth, while both the Palestinians and Israel accepted the Clinton Parameters with reservations.[196] The collapse of these negotiations was less the context than the pretext for Morris's political epiphany. To make sense of his (d)evolution we must look elsewhere.

10/ HISTORY BY SUBTRACTION

The late Israeli sociologist Baruch Kimmerling once noted Morris's "great arrogance and unique talent for public relations."[197] Morris has always been ambitious and accordingly cautious. While making his name in the academic establishment as a Young Turk, Morris finely calibrated his position on the political spectrum near enough the left pole and far enough from the mainstream Old Guard to draw attention to himself, but not so far to the left that he lost respectability and not so near the Old Guard that he lacked novelty. In the tiny space he carved out, there was room enough only for him, which is just how Morris liked it.

Morris feigned being the only objective historian standing above the political fray and counseled against politicizing scholarship: "The moment the historian looks over his shoulder, begins to calculate how others might utilize his work, and allows this to influence his findings and conclusions, he is well on his way down that slippery slope leading to official history and propaganda."[198] But in fact Morris has himself always calculated the effect of his every word. He would complain of being misunderstood when in fact he was perfectly understood. He alleged that others simplified his complex findings whereas the problem was the complexity not of his positions but of his *positionings*. He would mitigate the impact of each of his politically-charged conclusions with a contrary conclusion, so that he could be claimed by neither side, or so that he could disown both sides and stand alone in splendid isolation. It was a delicate balancing act that often appeared schizophrenic. When crossing swords with an establishment Israeli historian such as Shabtai Teveth, he thrust so forcefully you might mistake him for Palestinian scholar Edward Said, but when Said accurately paraphrased his findings, Morris sounded like Teveth as he chastised Said for being a propagandist.[199]

It seems Morris now aspires to become Israel's court historian. He would not be the first ambitious Young Turk wanting to replace the Old Guard as he gets on in years and they pass from the scene. It is also true that the political left, and the tiny space Morris carved out in its vicinity, barely exists any longer in Israeli life. He could be either a cheerleader like *Haaretz* columnist Ari Shavit, who once wrote a chilling eyewitness account of the Israeli occupation in Gaza,[200] but in latter days justified the 2008-9 Israeli invasion of Gaza,[201] or he could be a marginalized pariah like *Haaretz* columnist Gideon Levy, who was pilloried by what passes today for the Israeli left because he wouldn't abide the invasion.[202]

Morris's ego was palpably too big for the role of marginal pariah, but to become a court historian he had to forsake both his professional calling and political sensibility. It is no longer possible to both be an honest historian and perpetuate the *Exodus* version of Israel's past, and it is no longer possible to defend Israel on the basis of liberal values. To gain entry into the elite tier of Israel's historiographic establishment, however, it has always required recycling the mythical version of Israel's past and staunchly defending the Israeli state. It was therefore predictable and inevitable that Morris, eyeing greener pastures, would jettison his original framework that cast Zionism as the conflict's cause and Palestinian resistance as the effect. But what would he substitute for it?

Morris's first tack in his new role of *fidei defensor* was an ideological throwback to another era. He defended the "overall final good" of a Jewish state by resorting to 19th century social-Darwinist justifications. Thus, he echoed Theodore Roosevelt's rationale for the displacement and dispossession of Native Americans: it is a regrettable necessity of progress that "savage and barbaric peoples" get plowed under.[203] The crudity of this posture was such that Morris came under blistering attack abroad. Even in the retrograde moral climate after September 11, when the virtues of Empire were once again being heralded, this defense of Zionism would not wash: some liberal values have become so ingrained in Western culture that everyone has to make, at any rate publicly, a bow to them. Having no other plausible option, and taking flight from the historical record, Morris reinserted his history in a hoary Muslim anti-Semitism. Far from initiating the conflict, Zionism emerged in his reconfigured narrative as just another chapter in the annals of Arab loathing of Jews, while the Zionist settlers metamorphosed into innocent victims of this immemorial hatred. The root cause of the conflict, according to Morris as he reinvented himself by customizing his history, was and remains to this day "Islamic Judeophobia." His ideological bona fides now in order, Morris stood on the threshold of acceptance.

But Morris had to compensate for the double personal burden of having once been both a conscientious objector in a highly militarized society and a thorn in the side of the militant academic establishment that he now sought to join. Thus he conspicuously placed himself at Defense Minister Ehud Barak's side, and at every opportunity volunteered to serve as a quasi-official emissary of Israeli militarism. In anticipation of its invasion of Gaza, Israel's propaganda agencies geared up for a PR blitz.[204] After Israel launched the attack at the end of 2008 and proceeded to obliterate everything in sight, Morris promptly published an op-ed in the *New York Times* pushing all the right buttons ("many Israelis feel that the walls ... are closing in ... much as they felt in early June 1967") and praising "Israel's highly efficient air assault" on Gaza.[205] Meanwhile, as Israel keeps endeavoring to recruit Washington for an assault on Iran, Morris continues to make the rounds in the West repeatedly warning, Cassandra-like, that if the Americans do not launch a conventional attack Israel would be compelled and justified in launching a nuclear strike to prevent a "second Holocaust."[206]

Still, it has not been so much his personal liabilities as the liabilities of Israeli society that have nudged Morris ever more rightward. To become Israel's court historian he had to keep pace ideologically with it. It is social rather than biographical factors that at bottom account for his political odyssey. If Morris has gone berserk, it is because he aspires to be the official storyteller of a nation that itself has gone over the cliff. His degeneration vividly illustrates that except by resorting to a mishmash of lies and lunacies, deceits and delusions, it is no longer possible for Israel's defenders to justify its policy.

CONCLUSION

This book was conceived in the mid-2000s and largely completed by 2008. Although its publication was unavoidably delayed,[1] this writer did manage to lecture widely on its thrust that a tipping point had been reached: large sectors of the significantly liberal American Jewish community now knew too much of the truth about the Israel-Palestine conflict to continue lending Israel blind support. The argument was skeptically received by audiences and experts alike back then, but just a few years later, as these lines are being written, it has practically passed into conventional wisdom.

Although disagreements persist on exactly why American Jews are "distancing" themselves from Israel, it is largely accepted that in recent years a divide has opened up. Indeed, the poll data sampled in this book probably underestimate the depth of this estrangement because of the traditional reticence of Jews to "air dirty laundry in public," and because of their reluctance to acknowledge that Israel no longer touches them as it once did. The anecdotal evidence on this growing alienation however is hard to miss. Besides the periodic high profile defections of the likes of Peter Beinart and David Remnick, one can point to the profusion of public testimonials by Jews expressing their disenchantment with Israel, the acid criticism of Israel by influential liberal Jewish bloggers, the indifference of Jews on college campuses to "pro"-Israel events, and the small numbers of Jews attending public rallies in support of Israel at moments of crisis or on commemorative occasions.

Judging by the historical record and polling data, a trio of factors will, as in the past, shape the contours of the American Jewish relationship with Israel:

- *Ethnicity*—American Jews have felt a "natural" affinity for a state that identifies itself as Jewish and where many of their Jewish brethren reside. But surveys show that as rates of Jewish intermarriage climb, this sense of ethnic affinity will correspondingly weaken;
- *Citizenship*—American Jews have felt a deep sense of gratitude toward the United States because it is not only where they live, but also where they have experienced a success and prosperity unprecedented in the annals of Jewish history. However, American Jews also carry many of the insecurities typical of a minority group, and in the specific case of Jews, the fear of the "dual loyalty" bogey. Insofar as the respective "national interests" of the United States and Israel come into collision, American Jews have been, and will continue to be, resistant to appearing disloyal—not least for prudential reasons—to their country of citizenship;
- *Ideology*—In the course of nearly a century American Jews have demonstrated an enduring commitment to liberal values and have contributed disproportionately to the vitality of liberal American institutions. In recent years however they have experienced a conflict between fidelity to these liberal values and fidelity to an increasingly illiberal Jewish state.

The focus of this book has been on the ideological rift. It has been argued that in the face of the accumulated documentary record American Jews are no longer able to reconcile Israeli policy with bedrock liberal principles. Except in cloistered Orthodox Jewish communities, and among elderly Jews who have been weaned on Zionist mythology, the human rights, historical, and diplomatic record of the Israel-Palestine conflict can no longer be ignored. To be sure, propagandistic accounts of the conflict still gain wide currency. But unlike in the past, when much of scholarship could fairly be described as *Exodus* with footnotes, a huge gap has now opened up between media-promoted pabulum, on the one hand, and the findings of respected scholars and human rights activists, many of them Jewish and Israeli, on the other. Because it is tapped into the broader intellectual culture, the liberal, highly literate American Jewish community can no longer be unaware, or pretend to be unaware, of the brutal realities of Israeli policy.

Meanwhile, the hitherto reliable tactics of invoking The Holocaust and dismissing the bearers of bad news as anti-Semites (or self-hating Jews) are proving less efficacious as the Holocaust industry increasingly becomes an object of derision,[2] and the number and respectability of these bearers of bad news steadily mounts. Can it be credibly sustained that so many respected Israeli historians and journalists, so many respected legal scholars, judges and human rights organizations, so many forums of world public opinion are all driven by a common and collusive loathing of Jews?

We stand now at a crossroads. Having invested so much in fabricating an illusory Israel, the generation of liberal American Jews who climbed on board after the June 1967 war will probably stay the course. Tempting though it might be, pride and fanaticism prevent them from scurrying off as the ship sinks, not to mention that holding aloft the cause's banner until the bitter end will yet garner them applause. Just as the hacks in the American Communist Party sang the Soviet Union's praises even after it imploded, the likes of Alan Dershowitz will continue to laud Israel's "generally superb" human rights record[3] even after Israelis themselves look back upon on it with shame.

But Israel's egregious practices can no longer be credibly denied and few American Jews, especially among the younger generations, are willing to publicly support them. The reason is not hard to find. A young, liberal and idealistic Jew does not want to have to defend flooding south Lebanon with four million cluster submunitions, or firing white phosphorus shells reaching a temperature of 1,500 degrees Fahrenheit on hospitals in Gaza,[4] anymore than he or she wants to defend the legality of Israeli settlements against the considered opinion of every member of the International Court of Justice. If you are the son of a Rush Limbaugh or the daughter of a Sean Hannity, you might not recoil at such a public posture. But it's just not a Jewish thing.

Twenty years ago Israeli soldiers toured U.S. college campuses to be feted by Jewish students as war heroes. Now, the campus Hillels drag them on tours to persuade Jewish students that Israeli soldiers are not war criminals. Twenty years ago "pro"-Israel Jewish students aggressively interrogated critics of Israel at public events. Now, they sit silently in the audience, or do not even bother to show up. Twenty years ago defense of Israel was *the* Jewish cause on college campuses. Now, Jewish activists fill the ranks of the local Students for Justice in Palestine (SJP) chapters. Twenty years ago campus Jewish organizations relished the prospect of making the case for Israel in the court of public opinion. Now, they machinate behind closed doors to stifle public debate on the Israel-Palestine conflict. Once a banner of pride for American Jewish youth, Israel has now become its albatross.

American Jewry will increasingly have to decide between two mutually exclusive options. The first is to jettison its professed liberal values. In the Israeli context this has been the route taken by the likes of historian Benny Morris. After having gone some distance towards dispelling the mythology and exposing the underside of Israel's founding, Morris has now proceeded to declare, "There are cases in which the overall final good justifies harsh and cruel acts that are committed in the course of history."[5] In an earlier epoch apologists for Stalin's Russia dutifully recited that standby of "breaking eggs to make an omelet." In light of the resilience of liberal culture in the U.S., and the formative role that American Jews have played in its development, the likelihood that many of them will opt for this crude alternative is remote.[6] The more likely scenario is that American Jews will cast Israel adrift. In their hearts and minds the Jewish state will return to the status quo ante the June 1967 war: an occasional object of charity and a rallying-point only in times of existential crisis. But beyond this, Israel will be put out of sight like the slightly *meschugge* aunt confined to the attic because of "what the neighbors might think."

A pair of interrelated practical-political conclusions also flow from the findings of this book. Those working toward a just and lasting peace should, and need only, stick to what the authoritative record shows. The most potent weapons in the struggle for a just peace are Truth—the facts assembled in the scholarly literature and human rights reports—and Justice—the concerted wisdom of representative judicial and political bodies on the parameters for the conflict's resolution. In the face of these weapons American Jews in particular are "defenseless": they can run but they can no longer hide from what the factual record shows, while their liberal consciences, or the fear of appearing hypocritical, will not allow them to sanction the immoral Israeli practices that this unimpeachable record documents.

In addition, because American Jews are susceptible to appeals based on truth and justice, it is not only possible to reach them on a principled instead of a self-interested basis, but that is probably the only basis on which they *can* be persuaded. To try to reach Jews on a narrowly ethnic basis would mean posing the eternal question, "Is it good for the Jews?" Not only is such a question morally problematic but also, for all anyone knows, what Israel has wrought might be "good for the Jews." To try to reach Jews on the basis of American "national interest," it would have to be shown that U.S. and Israeli interests fundamentally conflict. But arguably they don't. To try to reach Jews on the basis of their liberal conscience, however, it would have to be shown that Israeli policy cannot be reconciled with elementary principles of justice. Here, the answer is no longer open to serious dispute. We are therefore in the historically rare position of being able to build a mass movement that appeals not to narrow sectarian or patriotic interests, but to the great universal principles that have brought glory to and elevated humankind.

The end of the American Jewish love affair with Israel will be a boon not only for Palestinians but for Israelis as well. Since the June 1967 war Israel has been a stage on which American Jews have played out their fantasies and a pawn in their pursuit of power and privilege. If Israel has become a crazy state, it is in no small part because of American Jews. By abetting its most retrograde tendencies and freeing it of needful restraints, they have exerted a baleful influence on Israeli society. But American Jews now have an opportunity to right a double wrong: the horror inflicted on Palestine, and the damage caused to Israel. If the liberal conscience of American Jews is pricked and, finally, they do the right thing, the long, dark night might yet soon end.

APPENDIX

In Chapter Ten we saw how a formerly liberal Israeli historian reversed his research findings and reinvented his political identity as he sought to accommodate himself to a state that clings to its founding myths while its political center of gravity drifts ever more rightward. In this appendix we look at how the institutional bastion of Israeli liberalism tied itself in mental knots as it endeavored to reconcile Israeli policy with the opinion of the world's most authoritative and enlightened legal body. It illustrates yet again the impossibility of reconciling support for Israel with liberalism.

ILLIBERAL LIBERALISM

Israel prides itself on governance by the rule of law, while American Jews used to flaunt it as "the only democracy in the Middle East."[1] But human rights organizations have in recent years copiously documented that Israel has committed massive violations of international law in the occupied Palestinian territory.[2] In the division of burdens for perpetuating the occupation Israel's High Court of Justice (HCJ) performs the critical ideological function of reconciling Israel's enlightened avowals with its egregious practices. Whereas human rights organizations have condemned Israel for its gross violation of international covenants on torture, collective punishment, and so forth, the HCJ—which is widely regarded as the institutional bastion of Israeli liberalism—has repeatedly found that Israeli practices fully conform to international law.[3]

The HCJ opinions on the legality of the wall Israel has been constructing in the West Bank marked a continuation and culmination of its rationalizing function.[4] In an advisory opinion the International Court of Justice (ICJ) voted overwhelmingly that the wall's construction in the West Bank violated international law,[5] whereas the HCJ repeatedly upheld the legality of such a wall. Nonetheless, in keeping with its professed respect for the rule of law—in particular, the authority of the ICJ—the HCJ purported that its judgments accorded with the legal norms set forth in the advisory opinion. The disagreement between them, according to the HCJ, bore not on the normative legal framework but rather on the data on which their respective decisions were reached: if the ICJ reached a conclusion diametrically opposed to the HCJ's, it was allegedly because the ICJ was ill-informed regarding the facts on the ground. The upshot of the HCJ decisions was that Israel's construction of the wall in occupied Palestinian territory was both in accord with enlightened international law and consistent with the ICJ advisory opinion.

In fact the HCJ's reconciliation of its rulings with those of the ICJ was disingenuous. Contrary to the HCJ's claim, the factual bases upon which it and the ICJ rendered their respective opinions did not substantively differ. The HCJ was able to sustain the legality of the wall only by blindly deferring to the state's military authority, peremptorily dismissing challenges to it, and by sanctioning flagrant violations of international law, as interpreted by the ICJ as well as all other international bodies. Despite its pious lip-service to the rule of law, the HCJ yet again breached it in the service of raison d'état. In addition, the HCJ decisions on the wall were riddled with internal contradictions. The Court deferred absolutely to the military authority of the state, but also disputed the state's military rationale for segments of the wall, in the process undercutting the basis of the Court's own finding of the military necessity of the wall.

Although the HCJ's opinions on the wall fit into a long-established pattern of lending a cloak of legality to illegal practices, it would be difficult to exaggerate the pernicious consequences of these particular opinions. Apart from the humanitarian disaster it has wrought, the wall, once completed, will fragment the West Bank, cut it off from its hub in East Jerusalem, and deprive it of some of its most productive land and water resources. In other words, it will preempt any possibility of a two-state settlement, condemning Palestine and Israel to endless bloodshed. If all branches of Israeli government and society bear responsibility for this impending catastrophe, the share of the HCJ and especially its revered liberal Chief Justice at the time, Aharon Barak, is relatively larger. Because of its moral authority the HCJ was in a unique position to sensitize the Israeli public. Beyond helping fend off external criticism of Israel's annexationist policies, the HCJ chose to mute the collective Israeli conscience.

On a broader level, and for the purposes of this book, a systematic juxtaposition of the ICJ advisory opinion on the wall against the HCJ judgments confirms the impossibility of reconciling the consensus of enlightened international opinion on the Israel-Palestine conflict with the practices of the Israeli government. The more Israel's liberal High Court endeavored to effect such a reconciliation, the more it tangled itself in intellectual knots and caught itself in flagrant contradictions. If nothing else, the HCJ's desperate performance underscored that one could be both a defender of the rule of law and a defender of Israeli policy only by resorting to sophistry.

The ICJ Advisory Opinion

On 9 July 2004, the International Court of Justice rendered its advisory opinion in response to this request of the United Nations General Assembly:

> What are the legal consequences arising from the construction of the wall being built by Israel, the occupying Power, in the Occupied Palestinian Territory, including in and around East Jerusalem, as described in the report of the Secretary-General, considering the rules and principles of international law, including the Fourth Geneva Convention of 1949, and relevant Security Council and General Assembly resolutions?[6]

The opinion addressed many issues including whether the ICJ had jurisdiction to interpose itself, whether prudentially the ICJ should have interposed itself in this dispute as well as the legal ramifications for Israel and the international community of the ICJ's conclusions. The focus here will be strictly on the ICJ's findings regarding the legality of the wall.[7]

Legal framework

The ICJ first set out the legal framework of "rules and principles of international law" for assessing the legality of the wall. At the head of the list it put the principle, derived from Article 2 of the United Nations Charter and explicitly adopted by the General Assembly in 1970, that "No territorial acquisition resulting from the threat or use of force shall be recognized as legal."[8] Regarding international humanitarian law or the "general laws and customs of war," the ICJ pointed to the applicability of the Hague Regulations of 1907 and, although Israel disputed this, the Fourth Geneva Convention of 1949.[9] The Court also found, despite Israeli objection, that the international human rights covenants to which Israel was party applied within the occupied Palestinian territory.[10]

The factual data on which the ICJ based its opinion were culled from a "voluminous dossier" assembled by the U.N. Secretary-General documenting the wall's construction and its impact on the Palestinian population, as well as from the written submissions of "numerous" participants in the proceedings.[11] Although Israel's submission to the ICJ was limited to issues of jurisdiction and judicial propriety (it refused to cooperate in the proceedings beyond this point), the Court found that "it has before it sufficient information and evidence to enable it to give the advisory opinion."[12]

ICJ findings[13]

The ICJ observed that "the wall's sinuous route has been traced in such a way as to include within [the "Israeli" side] the great majority of the Israeli settlements in the [O]ccupied Palestinian Territory (including East Jerusalem)."[14] The ICJ next recalled the U.N. Security Council's findings that, based on Article 49 of the Fourth Geneva Convention, these settlements "have no legal validity" (March 1979, July 1979) and constituted a "flagrant violation" of international law (March 1980).[15] On this crucial point the Court concluded that "Israeli settlements in the Occupied Palestinian Territory (including East Jerusalem) have been established in breach of international law."[16] Finally, the ICJ voiced concern that, rather than being provisional in nature, the wall might be designed to annex Palestinian land on which the illegal Israeli settlements were built, thereby violating both the U.N. Charter principle that prohibits appropriation of territory by war and the Fourth Geneva Convention prohibition on settlement activity:

> Whilst the Court notes the assurance given by Israel that the construction of the wall does not amount to annexation and that the wall is of a temporary nature . . ., it nevertheless cannot remain indifferent to certain fears expressed to it that the route of the wall will prejudge the future frontier between Israel and Palestine, and the fear that Israel may integrate the settlements and their means of access. The Court considers that the construction of the wall and its associated régime create a "fait accompli" on the ground that could well become permanent, in which case, and notwithstanding the formal characterization of the wall by Israel, it would be tantamount to *de facto* annexation. . . . In other terms, the route chosen for the wall gives expression *in loco* to the illegal measures taken by Israel with regard to Jerusalem and the settlements, as deplored by the Security Council.[17]

The ICJ opinion also considered the wall's construction in light of other provisions of international humanitarian law, specifically:

- The Hague Regulations—Article 43 (occupant's responsibility to "ensure public order"), Article 46 (obligation that private property be "respected"), and Article 52 (conditional right of requisitions in kind and services for the army of occupation);

- The Fourth Geneva Convention—Article 47 ("Protected persons who are in occupied territory shall not be deprived . . . of the benefits of the present Convention . . . by any agreement between the authorities of the occupied territories and the Occupying Power"), Article 49 (prohibition on population transfer and deportation to or from occupied territory, except temporary evacuation of the occupied population for "the security of the population or imperative military reasons"), Article 52 (prohibition on "all measures aiming at creating unemployment"), Article 53 (prohibition on any destruction of property, "except when such destruction is rendered absolutely necessary by military operations").

The ICJ additionally cited the human rights protections of the International Covenant on Civil and Political Rights and the International Covenant on Economic, Social and Cultural Rights, which codified the right to freedom of movement as well as the right to work, health, education and an adequate standard of living.[18]

The ICJ found that construction of the wall had "led to the destruction or requisition of properties" under conditions that violated Articles 46 and 52 of the Hague Regulations and Article 53 of the Fourth Geneva Convention. It also had "imposed substantial restrictions on the freedom of movement," had "serious repercussions for agricultural production," and had "led to increasing difficulties . . . regarding access to health services, educational establishments and primary sources of water," in violation of international human rights law.

Furthermore, the Court found that "since a significant number of Palestinians have already been compelled by the construction of the wall and its associated régime to depart from certain areas, a process that will continue as more of the wall is built, that construction, coupled with the establishment of the Israeli settlements . . ., is tending to alter the demographic composition of the Occupied Palestinian Territory," in violation of Article 49 of the Fourth Geneva Convention.[19]

The Court next considered the special allowances international humanitarian law made for "military exigencies." It found that Article 46 of the Hague Regulations (private property must be respected) and Article 47 of the Fourth Geneva Convention (agreements signed under occupation cannot annul the Convention's protections) were absolute, as was Article 49 of the Fourth Geneva Convention, which prohibited an Occupying Power from settling its civilian population in occupied territory.

Although Article 53 of the Fourth Geneva Convention allowed for the destruction of property "rendered absolutely necessary by military operations," the Court "was not convinced" that the destruction wrought by the wall was unavoidable. In addition, the Court found that, although human rights law also contained qualifying clauses, the exceptional circumstances under which these clauses applied "are not met in the present instance."[20]

The ICJ concluded that neither the wall nor the attendant violations of Palestinian rights could be justified on grounds of military necessity:[21]

> [T]he Court, from the material available to it, is not convinced that the specific course Israel has chosen for the wall was necessary to attain its security objectives. The wall, along the route chosen, and its associated régime gravely infringe a number of rights of Palestinians residing in the territory occupied by Israel, and the infringements resulting from that route cannot be justified by military exigencies or by the requirements of national security or public order. The construction of such a wall accordingly constitutes breaches by Israel of various of its obligations under the applicable international humanitarian law and human rights instruments.[22]
>
> ...
>
> [T]he Court is not convinced that the construction of the wall along the route chosen was the only means to safeguard the interests of Israel against the peril which it has invoked as justification for that construction.[23]

The ICJ voted 14-1 that "construction of the wall being built by Israel, the Occupying Power, in the Occupied Palestinian Territory, including in and around East Jerusalem, and its associated régime, are contrary to international law." Judge Thomas Buergenthal from the U.S. cast the lone negative vote.

Separate ICJ opinions

Fully six of the judges voting with the majority on the Court issued separate opinions. Although several of those judges were critical, sometimes harshly, of aspects of the majority opinion, they nonetheless concurred on its fundamental finding that the wall was illegal. Judges Rosalyn Higgins, Hisashi Owada and Pieter Kooijmans all criticized the majority opinion for lack of balance, and they lamented the paucity of data submitted supporting the Israeli position.[24] Nonetheless Judge Higgins concurred that Israel had violated the provisions of humanitarian law cited in the majority opinion; that "While the wall does seem to have resulted in a diminution on [sic] attacks on Israeli civilians, the necessity and proportionality for the route selected, with its attendant hardships for Palestinians uninvolved in these attacks, has not been explained"; and that "there is undoubtedly a significant negative impact upon portions of the population of the West Bank, that cannot be excused on the grounds of military necessity . . . ; and nor has Israel explained to the United Nations or to this Court why its legitimate security needs can be met only by the route selected."[25]

Judge Owada observed that "it would seem reasonable to conclude on balance that the political, social, economic and humanitarian impacts of the construction of the wall, as substantiated by ample evidence supplied and documented in the course of the present proceedings, is such that the construction of the wall would constitute a violation of international obligations"; that "these [harmful] impacts are so overwhelming that I am ready to accept that no justification based on the 'military exigencies,' even if fortified by substantiated facts, could conceivably constitute a valid basis for precluding the wrongfulness of the act on the basis of the stringent conditions of proportionality"; and that even if it were true that Israel's "sole purpose" in building the wall was to combat terrorist attacks, it "would not be a sufficient ground for justifying the construction of the wall as it has actually been drawn up and implemented."[26]

Judge Kooijmans stated that "The Court is right when it concludes that the available material allows it to give the opinion"; that "Israel by constructing the wall and establishing the associated régime has breached its obligation" under international humanitarian and human rights law; that the "Court's concern that the construction of the wall creates a fait accompli" is legitimate; that "the conditions set out in the qualifying clauses in the applicable humanitarian law and human rights law conventions have not been met and that the measures taken by Israel cannot be justified by military exigencies or by requirements of national security or public order"; and that, although the ICJ should have put construction of the wall to the "proportionality test," the wall would nonetheless have failed the test, because "the ensuing disturbing consequences for the inhabitants of the Occupied Palestinian Territory are manifestly disproportionate to interests which Israel seeks to protect."[27]

It remains to consider Judge Buergenthal's negative vote on the finding that the wall was illegal. Buergenthal did not file a dissenting opinion but rather what he called a "Declaration," in which he was at pains to stress that there was "much" in the advisory opinion "with which I agree." Nonetheless, Buergenthal maintained that the ICJ should not have rendered the requested opinion, and that the "Court did not have before it the requisite factual bases for its sweeping findings."[28] On the latter point Judge Buergenthal specifically argued that, regarding Israel's legitimate security concerns, the Court did not have sufficient information to make an accurate assessment, did not give Israel's submissions sufficient consideration, and did not provide an adequate account of its own reasoning:

Instead, all we have from the Court is a description of the harm the wall is causing and a discussion of various provisions of international humanitarian law and human rights instruments followed by the conclusion that this law has been violated. Lacking is an examination of the facts that might show why the alleged defenses of military exigencies, national security or public order are not applicable to the wall as a whole or to the individual segments of its route. The Court says that it "is not convinced" but it fails to demonstrate why it is not convinced, and that is where these conclusions are not convincing.[29]

As an alternative to the approach of the ICJ majority and without prejudging the outcome of it, Buergenthal recommended, first, assessing whether Israel's right of self-defense could be legitimately invoked against the terrorist attacks; second, assessing whether the wall was a necessary and proportionate response to these attacks; and third, applying these tests in a segment-by-segment scrutiny of the wall's legality.[30]

On these points as well as many others in his declaration, Buergenthal took the identical position as the Israel High Court. There was one crucial exception, however. He explicitly declared the Jewish settlements and, concomitantly, any means to preserve and protect them, illegal under international law:

> Paragraph 6 of Article 49 of the Fourth Geneva Convention ... does not admit for exceptions on grounds of military or security exigencies. It provides that "the Occupying Power shall not deport or transfer parts of its own civilian population into the territory it occupies." I agree that this provision applies to the Israeli settlements in the West Bank and that their existence violates Article 49, paragraph 6. *It follows that the segments of the wall being built by Israel to protect the settlements are* ipso facto *in violation of international humanitarian law*.[31]

This last sentence delivered a crushing blow to the Israel High Court's defense of the wall: not even the declaration of the American judge could rescue it.

First Israel High Court Judgment on the Wall

The Israel High Court rendered two principled opinions bearing on the wall, one shortly before the ICJ advisory opinion and one a year after it. The point of departure of each opinion was the legality of a different segment of the wall.

The first HCJ judgment was delivered on 30 June 2004 in response to this question:

> The Commander of the IDF [Israel Defense Forces] in Judea and Samaria issued orders to take possession of plots of land in the area of Judea and Samaria. The purpose of the seizure was to erect a separation fence on the land. The question before us is whether the orders and the fence are legal.[32]

Although the HCJ occasionally blurred the distinction, this first judgment treated the wall mainly as a means of "preventing the passage of Palestinians into the State of Israel," and not, as in the second judgment, as a means of protecting Jewish settlements in the West Bank.[33]

Sociopolitical context

The Court first sketched the sociopolitical context of its judgment in lengthy, emotive paragraphs chronicling Palestinian "terror attacks" to which Israel had been subjected since September 2000, for example:

> They are directed against citizens and soldiers, men and women, elderly and infants, regular citizens and public figures. Terror

attacks are carried out everywhere: in public transportation, in shopping centers and markets, in coffee houses and in restaurants.

The penultimate sentence in the second of these paragraphs mentioned in passing that "The armed conflict has left many dead and wounded on the Palestinian side as well"—only to be followed, however, by a profusion of yet more paragraphs deploring the Palestinian "terrorists," "terrorist infrastructure," and "terror acts." The Court pointed to these Palestinian terror attacks as "the background behind the decision to construct the separation fence . . . in the Judea and Samaria area, which would make it difficult for terrorists to strike at Israelis and ease the security forces' struggles against the terrorists."[34]

Appraisal

The Court's account of the second intifada omitted mention that Palestinians did not resort to terrorist attacks until after Israel had used massive, lethal and indiscriminate firepower to quell largely nonviolent demonstrations; that fully three times as many Palestinians as Israelis were killed during the second intifada; and that, except for the fatalities on both sides, *all* the victims of the manifold human rights violations documented by human rights organizations—house demolitions, torture, political liquidations, arbitrary detentions, prolonged curfews and closures, denial of medical care—were Palestinians.[35]

It might be argued that, in the context of adjudicating the legality of constructing a wall to ward off terrorist attacks, Palestinian suffering, however real, was beside the point. Yet, apart from such an omission radically distorting the overall context, if the root cause of Palestinian attacks was this brutal Israeli occupation, then, arguably, one alternative to constructing a wall was ending the occupation, especially if and inasmuch as the effect of the wall's construction would be to further brutalize the affected population, provoking yet more attacks. By situating the state's decision to build the wall solely in the context of Palestinian terror attacks, and by ignoring the state's longstanding territorial ambitions, the Court also preempted consideration that the real purpose of the wall might not be military-security but rather political, the terror attacks serving as a pretext for annexation of West Bank land.

Rejection of petitioners' claims

The petitioners from Beit Sourik and other Palestinian villages challenged the wall's route on the grounds of the massive, disproportionate harm it would inflict on them, and the violation attending its construction of their fundamental rights under international law, as well as because the "security arguments . . . disguise the real objective: the annexation of areas to Israel."[36] In addition to Palestinian petitioners, the "nonpartisan" Council for Peace and Security, comprised of "high-ranking" Israeli reserve officers having "background in security," also submitted a "serious and grave" affidavit stating that, although it supported "a separation fence as a solution to Israel's security needs," the proposed route encroaching on West Bank territory was not only unnecessary from a military perspective, but actually exacerbated Israel's security problems.[37] Finally, residents of the Israeli town of "Mevasseret Zion, which was adjacent to the Beit Sourik village," likewise petitioned that "the fence route should be immediately adjacent to the Green Line," on the grounds that the wall's route inflicted undue injury on Palestinian villagers, who, on its account, had already "turned from a tranquil population into a hostile one."[38]

Taking as its departure point that "Israel holds the area in belligerent occupation," the HCJ cited the Hague Regulations and the Fourth Geneva Convention, alongside Israeli administrative law, as the relevant normative framework.[39] It found that "the fence is motivated by security reasons." To support its conclusion the Court adduced this evidence: "[T]he government has emphasized, numerous times," that it is a "security measure," not a "political border"; "The Commander of the IDF forces of Judea and Samaria . . . submitted an affidavit . . . stat[ing] that 'the objective of the security fence is to help contend with the threat of Palestinian terror'"; in an "additional affidavit" the Commander attested that "it is not a permanent fence, but rather a temporary fence erected for security needs." The HCJ opined, "We have no reason not [sic] to give this testimony [of the Commander] less than full weight, and we have no reason not to believe the sincerity of the commander."[40]

In its rejection of petitioners' claims that the real objective of the Israeli government was annexing land, and that "if the fence was primarily motivated by security considerations, it would be constructed on the 'Green Line'" (i.e., Israel's pre-June 1967 border), the Court stated:

> We have no reason to assume that the objective is political rather than security-based. Indeed, petitioners did not carry the burden and did not persuade us that the considerations behind the construction of the separation fence are political rather than security-based. Similarly, petitioners did not carry their burden, and did not persuade us that the considerations of the Commander of the IDF Forces in the area, in choosing the route of the separation fence, are not military considerations, and that he has not acted to fulfill them in good faith, according to his best military understanding.[41]

In addition, citing articles 23 (g) and 52 of the Hague Regulations and article 53 of the Fourth Geneva Convention, the Court found that the seizure of Palestinian land along the wall's route was legal:

> [T]he military commander is authorized—by the international law applicable to an area under belligerent occupation—to take possession of land, if this is necessary for the needs of the

army. . . . He must, of course, provide compensation for his use of the land. . . . [T]he military commander must consider the needs of the local population. Assuming that this condition is met, there is no doubt that the military commander is authorized to take possession of land in areas under his control. The construction of the separation fence falls within this framework. The infringement of property rights is insufficient, in and of itself, to take away the authority to build it. It is permitted, by the international law applicable to an area under belligerent occupation, to take possession of an individual's land in order to erect the separation fence upon it, on condition that this is necessitated by military needs. To the extent that construction of the fence is a military necessity, it is permitted, therefore, by international law. Indeed, the obstacle is intended to take the place of combat military operations, by physically blocking terrorist infiltration into Israeli population centers.[42]

Appraisal

Besides adducing the avowals of the military echelon of Prime Minister Ariel Sharon's government, which are credited at face value, the HCJ never stated *why* it was convinced that the purpose of the wall was security, or *why* petitioners failed to convince that its real purpose was to annex land. Likewise, it never demonstrated the military necessity upon which it justified seizure of private Palestinian land. In fact, as becomes plain further on in the judgment, petitioners literally could not persuade the HCJ that the wall's route was motivated by political rather than military-security considerations. For the Court's bedrock position was that, lacking competence to judge in security matters, it must defer to the state's military echelon, whereas its own domain, according to the Court, was limited to assessing the lawfulness of the military's recommendations. The route of the wall, it stated, raises problems within the realm of military expertise. We, Justices of the Supreme Court, are not experts in military affairs. We shall not examine whether the military commander's military opinion corresponds to ours. . . . So we act in all questions which are matters of professional expertise, and so we act in military affairs as well.

And again (quoting from a prior judgment):

In exercising judicial review, we do not turn ourselves into experts in security affairs. . . . [W]e shall not substitute the discretion of the commander with our own discretion. We shall check the legality of the discretion of the military commander and ensure that his decisions fall within the "zone of reasonableness."[43]

The impossible burden put on petitioners to disprove the government's contention of military necessity was pointed up by the Court's treatment of the affidavit submitted by the Council for Peace and Security, composed of Israeli reserve officers, challenging the military necessity of the route chosen for the wall. It was not disputed that the Council members possessed the requisite competence and information to judge in this matter; and, unlike the military echelon subordinate to Sharon's government, these high-level Israeli officers were not subject to direct political pressures. Yet the position of the Court was that when in doubt, credit the state, not its critics. "The petition before us is exceptional," the Court wrote,

in that opinions were submitted by the Council for Peace and Security. These opinions deal with the military aspect of the separation fence. They were given by experts in the military and security fields, whose expertise was also recognized by the commander of the area. We stand, therefore, before contradictory military opinions regarding the military aspects of the route of the separation fence. These opinions are based upon contradictory military views .... In this state of affairs, are we at liberty to adopt the opinion of the Council for Peace and Security? Our answer is negative. At the foundation of this approach is our long-held view that we must grant special weight to the military opinion of the official who is responsible for security.[44]

Given the importance and universal acceptance of the legal norms that Israel was alleged to have breached, and the narrowness of the "military exceptions" that Israel claimed to be applicable; and given the mutual balancing of judgments by military experts for and against the wall's route; and given the massive harm the Palestinians would suffer due to the wall's construction, on which all sides agreed; and given that the wall's route was determined by an openly annexationist prime minister and his hawkish defense minister;[45] and given the *prima facie* bias of the military commander responsible for security but also subordinate to the ministerial architects of the wall, as against the acknowledged expertise and undisputed nonpartisanship of high-ranking former military and intelligence personnel on the Council—in the light of all these factors and considerations, it would appear that the skeptical testimony of the Council would put a crushing burden on the government to prove its case of military necessity. The contrary position of the Court underscored the peculiarity of its locution that petitioners "did not carry the burden and did not persuade." In fact, the quality and quantity of petitioners' evidence were manifestly of no account: the state's position automatically took precedence.[46]

The Court's resolve to defer to the state on the wall's route could not even be shaken by opposition of residents of the Israeli community adjacent to Beit Sourik and, consequently, on the front line in the event of a terrorist attack. An equally perplexing statement of the Court was this:

We are dealing with two military approaches. Each of them has military advantages and disadvantages. In this state of affairs, we must place the expert opinion of the military commander at the foundation of our decision.⁴⁷

If each of these respective military approaches had both advantages and disadvantages, and considering Israel's hotly contested right to construct a wall in the West Bank, shouldn't the tipping factor have been not which approach was supported by the military commander currently in charge, but rather which approach inflicted less harm on the affected population—in the options at hand, limited versus massive harm?

Finally, notice must be taken of the contradictions in which the Court got entangled. On the one hand, it affirmed the state's position that the wall's route was determined *exclusively* by "the operational-security consideration,"⁴⁸ and that "great weight was given [by the state] to the interests of the residents in the area, in order to minimize, to the extent possible, the injury to them."⁴⁹ But, on the other hand, it highlighted the state's willingness, in the course of trial deliberations, "to allow changes in part of the route"⁵⁰ making the wall less encroaching on the West Bank. In fact, as seen presently, the Court ordered the state to modify the wall's route yet further insofar as the state's proposed course could not be justified on strictly "operational-security" grounds. Does this not suggest that the state's original route for the wall was based on more than "operational-security" exigencies alone, and shouldn't such a finding have called into question the good faith that the Court uncritically attributed to the wall's proponents?⁵¹

Applying the proportionality test

Having convinced itself of the wall's military necessity, the Court proceeded to assess whether it could be legally justified. It found that the legality of the wall must be judged on whether it properly balanced "human rights and the needs of the local population" against "security needs from the perspective of the military commander." To test whether this balance was effected, the Court proposed using the principle of proportionality, according to which "the liberty of the individual can be limited (in this case, the liberty of the local inhabitants under belligerent occupation), on the condition that the restriction is proportionate."[52] Specifically, the Court assessed the legality of the wall by subjecting it to a cumulative three-prong test:

(1) The means used to achieve the stated objective must be "rational" or "appropriate";
(2) The means used to achieve the stated objective must be "least injurious";
(3) The damage caused by the means used to achieve the stated objective must be proportionate to the gain brought about by that means.[53]

The Court found that condition (1) had been met by virtue of the Court's "very ruling" that the wall constituted a military necessity;[54] and that condition (2) had been met by virtue of the state's avowal, and "our very determination that we shall not intervene in that position," that it was the least injurious means to prevent terrorist attacks.[55] However, the Court found that condition (3) had not been met, and urged an alternative route to the one proposed by the state:

> Our answer is that the relationship between the injury to the local inhabitants and the security benefit from the construction of the separation fence along the route, as determined by the military commander, is not proportionate. The route undermines the delicate balance between the obligation of the military commander to preserve security and his obligation to provide for the needs of the local population. This approach is based on the fact that the route which the military commander established for the security fence—which separates the local inhabitants from their agricultural lands—injures the local inhabitants in a severe and acute way, while violating their rights under humanitarian international law....

> These injuries are not proportionate. They can be substantially decreased by an alternate route, either the route presented by the experts of the Council for Peace and Security, or another route set out by the military commander. Such an alternate route exists. It is not a figment of the imagination. . . . [T]he military commander's choice of the route of the separation fence is disproportionate. The gap between the security provided by the military commander's approach and the security provided by the alternate route is minute, as compared to the large difference between a fence that separates the local inhabitants from their lands, and a fence which does not separate the two (or which creates a separation which is smaller and possible to live with).[56]

"There is no escaping," the Court concluded, "a renewed examination of the route of the fence, according to the standards of proportionality that we have set out."[57]

Appraisal

Unlike the ICJ, which found that the wall violated absolute principles of international law and that the extenuations of military necessity did not apply in this instance, the HCJ started from the premise that no absolute principles had been violated and that the relevant standard was proportionality.[58] It claimed to apply a three-prong proportionality test but, in applying the first and second prongs, the Court merely reiterated the position of the state: the wall's route was "rational" and "least injurious" because the state said so. Inasmuch as the results of these two tests were decided *a priori and irrespective of the evidence adduced*, the Court seems to have confused test-administering with rubber-stamping.[59] Moreover, on the "least injurious" test, the Court ignored alternative options proposed by human rights organizations for averting terrorist attacks, such as beefing up the hitherto lax security measures at Israeli checkpoints, through which most of the suicide bombers had entered Israel, and bolstering the Israeli military presence along the Green Line, protection of which had been a low priority for the IDF.[60]

The Court's negative finding in the third subtest, while welcome from the vantage point of human rights, posed yet new problems of internal coherence:

- The state had argued that the proposed route of the wall was least injurious to the local population while still protecting Israel's vital security interests. In the third subtest the HCJ maintained that Israel's vital security interests could still be protected while rerouting the wall so that less injury was inflicted on the local population. But doesn't this mean that, although the Court attested that the state satisfied the second prong of proportionality ("least injurious"), by the Court's own finding in the third subtest it did not?
- The Court's departure point was that it would not second-guess the expertise of the military commander. Yet, by maintaining in the third subtest that, if the wall were rerouted, Israel's net loss in security would be marginal and its vital interests still protected, didn't the Court second-guess the military commander?
- The Court maintained in the third subtest that, in lieu of the state's proposed route, the alternative routings proposed by the Council for Peace and Security should be considered. But why then did the Court automatically defer to the state as against the Council regarding the military necessity of the wall's original route, and regarding subtest one on its rationality?

In deciding on the wall's military necessity, rationality, and least injuriousness, the Court reflexively deferred to the expertise of the state's military commander, even privileging this expertise over that of the military officers in the Council for Peace and Security. Yet in applying the third subtest, the Court disputed this expertise, even siding with the Council for Peace and Security. The Court's negative finding in the third prong of the proportionality test contradicted all its prior positive findings on the necessity, rationality, and least injuriousness of the wall. Finally, although ordering a few kilometers of the wall to be rerouted,[61] the Court nonetheless affirmed that a wall deeply encroaching on the West Bank was legal under international law. The state, far from being dealt a political blow, scored a resounding victory in this case.

Second Israel High Court Judgment on the Wall

The second Israel High Court judgment was issued on 15 September 2005, after deliberating on this question:

> Alfei Menashe is an Israeli town in the Samaria area. It was established approximately four kilometers beyond the Green Line. Pursuant [to] the military commander's orders, a separation fence was built, surrounding the town from all sides, and leaving a passage containing a road connecting the town to Israel. A number of Palestinian villages are included within the fence's perimeter. The separation fence cuts them off from the remaining parts of the Judea and Samaria area. An enclave of Palestinian villages on the "Israeli" side of the fence has been created. Petitioners are residents of the villages. They contend that the separation fence is not legal.... Is the separation fence legal?[62]

This Court judgment was divided into five parts. Because its first two parts, the relevant legal framework and the Beit Sourik case, go over some ground already covered, only the new elements in these parts of the Court's judgment will be considered in this section. It will then go on to evaluate the last three parts of the judgment, in which the Court assesses the ICJ opinion, the repercussions of the ICJ opinion for its own ruling in the Beit Sourik case, and the legality of the wall incorporating the Alfei Menashe enclave.

Incorporating the Jewish settlements

A novelty of the second High Court case was that it directly confronted the legality of the wall to protect not Israel proper, but instead illegal Jewish settlements in occupied Palestinian territory such as Alfei Menashe: "Does the military commander's authority to construct a separation fence also include his authority to construct a fence in order to protect the lives and safety of Israelis living in Israeli communities in the Judea and Samaria area?"[63] The Court responded that "in our opinion, the answer is positive." It grounded this critical finding in both international and Israeli law:

- *The Hague Regulations.* Article 43 gives the military commander authority "to ensure ... public order and safety." The Court inferred from this authority that "the military commander must preserve the safety of every person present in the area of belligerent occupation" and, accordingly, "is authorized to construct a separation fence in the area for the purpose of defending the lives and safety of the Israeli settlers in the area."[64] The Court was as emphatic as it was passionate that this authority obtained regardless of the settlements' legal status:

    It is not relevant whatsoever to this conclusion to examine whether this settlement activity conforms to international law or defies it, as determined in the Advisory Opinion of the International Court of Justice at the Hague. . . . The authority to construct a security fence for the purpose of defending the lives and safety of Israeli settlers is derived from the need to preserve "public order and safety." It is called for, in light of the human dignity of every human individual. It is intended to preserve the life of every person created in God's image. The life of a person who is in the area illegally is not up for the taking. Even if a person is located in the area illegally, he is not outlawed.[65]

Lending further weight to this conclusion, the Court recalled from its prior judgments and the Oslo Accords the allegedly indeterminate legal status of the settlements: "Their legality ... will be determined in the peace treaties which the relevant parties will reach"; "the status of the settlements will be determined in the peace treaty"; "the question of the Israeli settlements in the area will be discussed in the negotiations over the final status";[66]

- *Internal Israeli law.* The settlers were Israeli citizens. The Court inferred from this legal status that the military authority was bound to protect all their citizenship rights: "[T]he constitutional rights which our Basic Laws and our common law grant to every person in Israel are also granted to Israelis who are located in territory under belligerent occupation which is under Israeli control. ... Israelis present in the area have the rights to life, dignity and honor, property, privacy, and the rest of the rights which anyone present in Israel enjoys." However, the Court then entered the caveat that the precise "scope" and "level" of protection to which settlers were entitled differed from that of Israelis living in Israel because "the area is not part of the State of Israel" but, rather, a "regime of belligerent occupation."[67]

Appraisal

The Court maintained that, in light of the military's authority to protect the lives and safety of Israeli settlers, construction of the wall around Israeli settlements could be justified regardless of the legal status of the settlements. The wall served the dual and distinct functions, however, of protecting the lives and safety of the settlers as "human individuals," and protecting their lives and safety *as settlers living in the West Bank*. The position of the Court might have been tenable if the wall were the *only* means available to ensure the settlers' safety, defense of their persons being, as it were, inseparable from defense of their living as settlers. But the lives and safety of the West Bank settlers could equally be protected by evacuating them to Israel and, if necessary, building a wall along the recognized border. If the wall protected both settlers and settlements whereas repatriation could just as well protect the settlers' lives but not the settlements, then invoking the settlers' safety to justify the wall is a red herring—why not just evacuate them?—and the settlements' legality, far from being "not relevant," becomes dispositive: illegal settlements, illegal wall. Thus, concurring in his ICJ declaration that Israeli settlements violated Article 49 of the Fourth Geneva Convention, Judge Buergenthal concluded: "the segments of the wall being built by Israel to protect the settlements are *ipso facto* in violation of international humanitarian law."[68]

The principle at stake would appear to be uncontroversial. If a squatter comes under assault from the property owner, the law would kick in to protect his life and safety, but it would be a queer judicial decision indeed that would uphold the squatter's right, in the name of his "human dignity" and creation in "God's image," to construct a wall around his illegally-occupied parcel of land, further encroaching on the owner's property, and thereby allowing the squatter to reap advantage from his own wrong. Rather than compound one injury against the property-owner by another, isn't it obvious that the judge would protect the squatter by having him escorted off the premises he's illegally occupying?[69]

One might want to argue that the Court did not propose evacuation because it was not a feasible option. Yet, not having canvassed the state or military authority on repatriation (the judgment makes no mention of it in the West Bank context), and given the Court's own insistence that it lacked competence in strategic-military matters, it could not have ruled out this option on feasibility grounds. This option could hardly have escaped the Court's notice: the evacuation of illegal Jewish settlers residing in Gaza, in accordance with the Gaza "disengagement plan," was occurring just as the Court deliberated on this case. In silently passing over the option of evacuation, and under the holy cloak of protecting the settlers' "human dignity" and creation in "God's image," the Court, on its own initiative and in its autonomous capacity, decided to fasten a protective curtain around illegal settlements as well.

To justify construction of a wall surrounding the settlements, the Court further pointed to their allegedly indeterminate legal status. But if the allegedly indeterminate legal status of the settlements justified the wall's construction, how could it be that the settlements' legal status is "not relevant whatsoever" to the wall's legality? On the contrary, the logical correlative of the Court's argument would seem to be: if the legal status of the settlements has been decided, it would be supremely relevant to the wall's legality.

In fact the ICJ, alongside every other authoritative international body, had determined that the settlements were illegal. From this finding, and on the logic of the High Court's own reasoning, it followed that if Israel was building the wall to protect illegal settlements, the wall was "*ipso facto*" (Buergenthal) illegal as well. The Oslo Accords could not be used to trump the international consensus on the settlements' illegality: on the one hand, the Accords explicitly did not speak on questions of legality[70] while, on the other, Article 47 of the Fourth Geneva Convention, cited by the ICJ, states that "Protected persons who are in occupied territory shall not be deprived . . . of the benefits of the present Convention . . . by any agreement between the authorities of the occupied territories and the Occupying Power."

The invocation of internal Israeli law to justify construction of a wall protecting Israeli citizens resident in the West Bank was just as problematic. The Court initially contended that West Bank settlers, being Israeli citizens, had rights identical to those of Israeli citizens living inside the Green Line, which the state was duty bound to protect. But the relevant field of a *citizen's* rights is bounded by the state's territorial borders, while the state's protection of its citizens abroad is proscribed by international law and interstate treaty. To assert that "Israelis present in the area" have all the same rights "anyone present in Israel enjoys" is in effect to annex the occupied

Palestinian territory to Israel. It also effectively grounded the *right* of settlers to reside in this territory: if a basic right of citizenship is the right of place and if an Israeli settler resident in the West Bank had identical rights to an Israeli living inside the Green Line, then a settler's right of place in the West Bank must be on a par with an Israeli citizen's right of place inside the Green Line. The Court accordingly lent legitimacy to the settlements, even if it maintained elsewhere that their legal status was indeterminate, and even if international opinion has uniformly declared them illegal.

The Court, no doubt cognizant of these insoluble contradictions, proceeded to temper its sweeping pronouncements: the "scope" and "level" of rights to which the settlers could lay claim, and which the state was bound to protect, differed from those of an Israeli citizen living inside Israel insofar as "the area" was not part of Israel, and not subject to Israeli law but instead the law of belligerent occupation. But then, the settlers could not possess rights proscribed by relevant international law. Because this body of law speaks unambiguously on the illegality of the settlements and, *ipso facto*, the illegality of the wall, Israel's internal law could not justify construction of the wall to protect the settlers.

Confronting the International Court of Justice opinion

After recounting the substance of the ICJ advisory opinion on the wall, the High Court proceeded to juxtapose their respective conclusions. Striving to align itself with enlightened opinion abroad, and thereby safeguard its place in the community of liberal opinion, the HCJ purported that it and the ICJ shared a "common" normative legal framework:

> The ICJ held that Israel holds the West Bank (Judea and Samaria) pursuant to the law of belligerent occupation. That is also the legal view at the base of The Beit Sourik Case. The ICJ held that an occupier state is not permitted to annex the occu-

pied territory. That was also the position of the Court in The Beit Sourik Case. The ICJ held that in an occupied territory, the occupier state must act according to The Hague Regulations and The Fourth Geneva Convention. That too was the assumption of the Court in The Beit Sourik Case, although the question of the force of The Fourth Geneva Convention was not decided, in light of the State's declaration that it shall act in accordance with the humanitarian part of that convention. The ICJ determined that in addition to the humanitarian law, the conventions on human rights apply in the occupied territory. This question did not arise in The Beit Sourik Case. For the purposes of our judgment in this case, we assume that these conventions indeed apply. The ICJ held that the legality of the "wall" (the "fence" in our nomenclature) shall be determined, inter alia, by regulations 46 and 52 of The Hague Regulations and §53 of The Fourth Geneva Convention. This was also the position of the Supreme Court in The Beit Sourik Case. The ICJ held that as a result of the building of the "wall," a number of rights of the Palestinian residents were impeded. The Supreme Court in The Beit Sourik Case also held that a number of human rights of the Palestinian residents had been impeded by the building of the fence. Finally, the ICJ held that the harm to the Palestinian residents would not violate international law if the harm was caused as a result of military necessity, national security requirements, or public order. That was also the approach of the Court in The Beit Sourik Case.[71]

Finding no substantive disagreement in their respective legal frameworks, the Court concluded:

> The main difference between the two judgments stems primarily from the difference in the factual basis upon which each court made its decision. Once again, the simple truth is proven: the

facts lie at the foundation of the law, and the law arises from the facts (*ex facto jus oritur*).[72]

Appraisal

One notes a pair of glaring omissions in the seemingly exhaustive inventory of shared legal principles that the Court ticks off:

- In its opinion the ICJ repeatedly cited the cardinal principle of international law of the inadmissibility of the acquisition of territory by force,[73] while it designated the West Bank, including East Jerusalem, and Gaza as "Occupied Palestinian Territory"—i.e., the territorial space reserved for "the exercise by the Palestinian people of its right to self-determination."[74] The ICJ thereby explicitly affirmed that Israel had no legitimate title to any of these territories. In the Beit Sourik case, however, the High Court stated only that it was not within the purview of the military commander to redraw Israel's borders: "the military commander cannot order the construction of the separation fence if his reasons are ... motivated by a desire to 'annex' territories to the state of Israel."[75] Unlike the ICJ, it failed to establish that Israel had no legitimate claim on this territory, the sovereignty of which had been definitively resolved. This crucial difference colors every aspect of their respective judgments. Whereas the ICJ uniformly referred to the West Bank as occupied Palestinian territory, the High Court rather referred to "Judea and Samaria" or, treating it as *terra nullius*, "the area."[76] A wall the route of which deeply encroaches on another people's sovereign territory plainly casts a more sinister shadow than a wall the route of which merely traverses a no-man's-land or even potentially the land of the wall's builder;
- In multiple places the ICJ highlighted the illegality of the Jewish settlements. But in the High Court's enumeration of the ICJ's normative principles, all of which the High Court supposedly held in com-

mon, it omitted mention of this fundamental ICJ finding, on which the High Court decidedly did not agree.[77] Indeed, it referred to illegal Jewish settlements benignly as "Israeli communities in the Judea and Samaria area."[78] The case under High Court deliberation hinged, however, on the legal status of the settlements: if Alfei Menashe was illegal, then the wall tracing a path around it was *ipso facto* illegal as well.

Contrary to the High Court's conclusion, the ICJ and the High Court agreed on the essential facts (more on which presently), but disagreed on the normative framework.

Reaffirming the wall's military necessity

Regarding the discrepant factual data, the High Court maintained that the "first difference, and the most important one" between it and the ICJ bore on the military necessity of the wall. The Court first recalled the broad spectrum of evidence it scrutinized in the Beit Sourik case before concluding that the "objective" of the wall was "security-based," not "political." It went on to fault the ICJ for the paucity of data it consulted and for giving Israel's case short shrift:

> The security-military necessity is mentioned only most minimally in the sources upon which the ICJ based its opinion. . . . In Israel's written statement to the ICJ . . ., data regarding the terrorism and its repercussions were presented, but these did not find their way to the opinion itself. This minimal factual basis is manifest, of course, in the opinion itself. It contains no real mention of the security-military aspect. In one of the paragraphs, the opinion notes that Israel argues that the objective of the wall is to allow an effective struggle against the terrorist attacks emanating from the West Bank. That's it.[79]

Accordingly, whereas the ICJ was "not convinced that the specific course Israel has chosen for the wall was necessary to attain its security objectives,"[80] the High Court found that this ICJ conclusion was factually unsupported:

> We need not determine ... who is to blame for this severe oversight.... Whatever the reason may be, the reality is that the ICJ based its opinion on a factual basis regarding impingement of Palestinian residents' rights without the factual basis regarding the security-military justification for this impingement. In contrast, in The Beit Sourik Case, an expansive factual basis was laid before the court.[81]

Appraisal

According to the High Court, its conclusion that the wall's route constituted a military necessity stood on a firmer evidentiary base than the ICJ's opposite conclusion. However, the Court reached its determination by yielding reflexively to the authority of the military commander currently in charge, not after assessing the solidity of the state's evidence. Not even the critical affidavit submitted by acknowledged Israeli military authorities could get the High Court to budge from this absolute deference to the state.

The Court faulted the ICJ for not giving due consideration to the data Israel submitted on "terrorism and its repercussions." But it was not the overall threat posed by terrorism that was at issue; rather, it was the necessity of building a wall that encroached deeply into West Bank territory to meet such a threat. To demonstrate that "the reason behind the decision to erect the fence is a security consideration," the High Court subsequently adduced data and anecdotal evidence that the wall's construction had dramatically reduced terrorist attacks, which "indicate the security importance of the fence and the security benefit which results from its construction."[82] Setting aside how much this reduction in suicide attacks was due to the wall as opposed to a new political environment or other factors,[83] and setting aside how much credibility to attach to state's evidence based on "the interrogation of various terrorists," none of this data proved that rerouting the wall along the Green Line and evacuating the settlers could not have achieved the same objective.

Deeming it a "severe oversight," the Court chided the ICJ for insufficiently deliberating on the military necessity of the wall. If, however, a wall the purpose of which is to protect illegal settlements *ipso facto* violates international law, it is hard to conceive what evidence could be adduced to justify the building of Israel's wall on Palestinian land when its "sinuous route has been traced in such a way as to include . . . the great majority of the Israeli settlements." The ICJ perhaps gave short shrift to the claim of military necessity not because of a "severe oversight" but because it was manifestly an impossible claim to sustain.

Weighing the factual data

Beyond the ICJ's allegedly inadequate data on military necessity, the High Court cited factual inaccuracies in some data relied upon by the ICJ when assessing the damage wrought by the wall. The High Court claimed that "The difference between the factual bases upon which the courts relied was of decisive significance," for slight differences in the weight of the evidence can determine on which side the scale tips when applying the proportionality test: "According to international law, the legality of the wall/fence route depends upon an appropriate balancing between security needs on the one hand and the impingement upon the rights of the local residents on the other. . . . Delicate and sensitive balancing between the two sides of the scale . . . brings about the appropriate solution." To illustrate these principles, the Court pointed to the case of the Palestinian town of Qalqiliya:

On one side of the scale, the ICJ placed the severe impingement of the rights of Palestinians in Qalqiliya. Even if we remove the imprecision of these figures [i.e., the allegedly erroneous data relied upon by the ICJ], the remainder is sufficient to indicate a severe impingement of their rights. On the other side of the scale, the ICJ did not place—due to the factual basis laid before it—any data regarding the security and military considerations. It was not mentioned that Qalqiliya lies two kilometers from the Israeli city of Kfar Saba; that Qalqiliya served as a passage point to Israel for suicide bomber terrorists . . . ; that the Trans-Israel highway . . ., whose users must be protected, passes right by the city; that the majority of the fence route on the western side of the city runs on the Green Line, and part of it even within Israel; that since the fence around Qalqiliya was built . . . terrorist infiltrations in that area have ceased.[84]

The High Court also faulted the data relied upon by the ICJ for its indiscriminateness. The information supplied to the ICJ did not distinguish between the lesser and greater injurious impacts of the wall along its route, compelling the ICJ to render comprehensive judgment on the totality of the wall, whereas a differentiated approach, and deploying a proportionality test, would have shown that some segments of the wall passed legal muster while others did not:

The material submitted to the ICJ contains no specific mention of the injury to [the] local population at each segment of the route . . . [and] contains no discussion of the security and military considerations behind the selection of the route, or of the process of rejecting various alternatives to it. These circumstances cast an unbearable task upon the ICJ. Thus, for example, expansive parts of the fence (approximately 153 km of the 763 km of the entire fence, which are approximately 20%) are adjacent to the Green Line (that is, less than 500 m away). An additional 135 km—which are 17.7% of the route—are within a distance of between 500 m and 2000 m from the Green Line. Between these parts of the route and the Green Line . . . there are no Palestinian communities, nor is there agricultural land. Nor are there Israeli communities in this area. The only reason for establishing the route beyond the Green Line is a professional reason related to topography, the ability to control the immediate surroundings, and other similar military reasons. Upon which rules of international law can it be said that such a route violates international law?[85]

Appraisal

The thrust of this argument is that if the ICJ had at its disposal the accurate and discriminate factual data presented to the High Court, it would not have pronounced the wall (or every section of it) illegal.[86] On multiple levels, however, this inference of the Court was problematic. First, it was not clear that the factual errors in the ICJ dossiers mattered much.[87] Thus, in the example on which it homed in, the High Court itself acknowledged that even if the allegedly erroneous ICJ data on Qalqiliya were corrected, "the remainder is sufficient to indicate a severe impingement of [Palestinian residents'] rights." Moreover, the ICJ did not reach its conclusion after the *relative quantitative* weighing of evidence in a proportionality test, but rather after reaching the *absolute qualitative* finding that the wall could not be justified on grounds of military necessity and breached non-derogable provisions of international law.[88] None of the alleged errors in the ICJ data affected its absolute qualitative findings.

Even if the proportionality test were applied, and on a segment-by-segment basis, it is still highly doubtful whether the wall, or parts of it, would have passed legal muster. For example, applying its proportionality test to the wall segment enclosing Qalqiliya, the High Court justified the wall's construction by juxtaposing the "severe impingements" on its Palestinian residents against these allegedly countervailing military-security factors:

- *Qalqiliya lies two kilometers from the Israeli city of Kfar Saba.* According to the Court's second proportionality test, however, the means used to achieve the stated objective of preventing terrorist attacks must be the "least injurious." Didn't the Court then have to weigh the injury done by a wall enclosing Qalqiliya *versus a wall enclosing Kfar Saba*, either of which could obstruct terrorist attacks? On the contrary, the Court took for granted that if the Israeli and Palestinian communities were within close proximity of each other, and construction of the wall inevitably entailed injury, it was the Palestinian side that must suffer;
- *The majority of the fence route on the western side of the city runs on the Green Line, and part of it even within Israel.* But even if true, it was irrelevant given that the ICJ ruling bore only on those parts of the wall "situated within the Occupied Palestinian Territory."[89] Likewise, the Trans-Israel highway ran entirely inside the Green Line while the section of the wall interposed between the highway and Qalqiliya was built along the Green Line, which means that the ICJ decision did not bear on it;
- *Since the fence around Qalqiliya was built . . . terrorist infiltrations in that area have ceased.* But even if the efficacy of the wall in warding off terrorism was proven, in itself this did not demonstrate that the specific route chosen was the "least injurious" for achieving the stated objective, a wall built along the Green Line perhaps being equally effective.

The Court's complementary, and rhetorically most compelling, claim that segments of the wall encroaching on occupied Palestinian territory could be justified where, on the one hand, neither Palestinian communities nor agricultural lands were affected, while, on the other, the wall's route was dictated by "a professional reason related to topography, the ability to control the immediate surroundings, and other similar military reasons," was equally questionable.[90] The Court never demonstrated that such deviations from the Green Line were based strictly on "a professional reason," and were accordingly the "least injurious" route for the wall. Israeli reserve officers in the Council for Peace and Security, although supporting a wall to prevent terrorism, sharply disputed rationales for deviating from the Green Line such as topographical advantage, arguing that to route the wall on these grounds was not only superfluous but in fact undermined Israeli security.[91] The Court peremptorily dismissed the Council's battery of arguments in its absolute deference to the state.[92] The Court also never explained the odd coincidence that, except for a few kilometers of the wall located inside Israel, all the topographical advantages just happen to be on the Palestinian side of the Green Line, through which 85 percent of the wall wound.

HCJ decision

Although it "shall give the full appropriate weight to the norms of international law" laid out in the ICJ advisory opinion, the High Court found that, because the factual basis of the advisory opinion was flawed, Israel was not bound by its conclusions. The Court first retreaded familiar ground on the military necessity of the wall and its route. Turning specifically to the Alfei Menashe enclave, the Court said it "reached the conclusion that the considerations behind the determined route are security"; that "It is not a political consideration which lies behind the fence route at the Alfei Menashe enclave, rather the need to protect the well-being and security of the Israelis"; and, consequently, that "the decision to erect the separation fence at the Alfei Menashe enclave was made within the authority granted to the military commander."[93]

The Court next proceeded along the lines mapped in its first decision of applying the proportionality test on a segment-by-segment basis. The segment under consideration in this second decision concerned an 11,000 dunam area incorporating Alfei Menashe (population 5,650) and five Palestinian villages (total population 1,200). Located on the "Israeli" side of the wall, the enclave was territorially contiguous with Israel.[94] The court, applying the three-prong proportionality test, made these determinations:

- *The means used to achieve the stated objective must be "rational" or "appropriate."* The Court reported petitioners' contention that the means used was irrational: whereas the stated objective was to prevent terrorism, the wall "creates a reality," according to petitioners,
    > in which hundreds of Palestinians find themselves west of the fence, without any checkpoint or gate between them and the cities of Israel. Therefore, it is difficult to see how the impingement upon the rights of the residents of the villages promotes the security of the State of Israel, of the IDF, or even of Alfei Menashe, none of which are separated from the residents of the villages; au contraire.

    The Court peremptorily dismissed this contention, stating in full: "We cannot accept this argument. The separation fence creates a separation between terrorists and Israelis (in Israel and in the area), and from that standpoint, the required rational connection exists between the objective and the means for its attainment";[95]

- *The means used to achieve the stated objective must be "least injurious."* The Court reported the petitioners' contention that less injurious means could be used to achieve the security of Israelis by building the wall along the Green Line. Rejecting this claim, the Court stated:
    > In their arguments before us, respondents [the State] correctly noted that construction of the separation fence on the Green Line would leave Alfei Menashe on the eastern side of the fence. It would be left vulnerable to terrorist attacks from [Palestinians in the West Bank]. Movement from it to Israel and back would

> be vulnerable to acts of terrorism. Indeed, any route of the fence must take into account the need to provide security for the 5,650 Israeli residents of Alfei Menashe.[96]

Nonetheless, the Court did find that a less injurious route, which protected the Alfei Menashe settlement yet left Palestinian villages outside the wall, was feasible:

> The alteration of the route, which will remove the villages from the enclave, will reduce the injury to the local residents to a large extent. . . . Indeed, based upon the factual basis as presented to us, the existing route of the fence seems strange. We shall begin with the southwest part of the enclave. We are by no means convinced that there is a decisive security-military reason for setting the fence route where it presently is. . . . We shall now turn to the northern and northwestern part of the enclave. . . . [W]e were by no means convinced that it is necessary for security-military reasons to preserve the northwest route of the enclave.[97]

"Thus," the Court concluded, "we have by no means been convinced that the second subtest of proportionality has been satisfied by the fence route creating the Alfei Menashe enclave," because an "alternative route," which would "ensure security with a lesser injury to the residents of the villages," is conceivable;[98]

- *The damage caused by the means used to achieve the stated objective must be proportionate to the gain brought about by that means.* The Court found that, if the wall could be rerouted to exclude the Palestinian villages but still protect Alfei Menashe, the security of Israelis could be achieved without undue injury to Palestinians.

In its final judgment, the Court called on the state to "reconsider the various alternatives for the separation fence route at Alfei Menashe, while examining security alternatives which injure the fabric of life of the residents of the villages of the enclave to a lesser extent."[99]

Appraisal

The Court stated that it "reached the conclusion" that the wall's route creating the Alfei Menashe enclave was determined by military necessity. However, although the Court cited petitioners' arguments contesting this military necessity,[100] it never analyzed these counterclaims and never explicated why they failed to convince. In addition, given the Court's absolute deference to the state on military matters, it could not but have "reached the conclusion" of the state that the wall's route was based on security concerns. It is hard to fathom how the Court could have "reached the conclusion" if the conclusion was foreordained before it was "reached."

The Court then proceeded to apply the three-prong proportionality test. In the means/ends test, it reported the petitioners' claim that the wall was irrational in view of the state's purported objective of warding off terrorist attacks: to carve out the Alfei Menashe enclave in such a fashion as to make it territorially contiguous with Israel allowed hundreds of Palestinians living in villages alongside the Jewish settlement to enter Israel freely. Although the Court itself acknowledged that "The enclave is connected, with territorial integrity, to Israel (with no checkpoint),"[101] it adduced no grounds for rejecting petitioners' argument, merely averring that the wall "creates a separation between terrorists and Israelis," even if it manifestly did not.[102]

The Court next applied the "least injurious" subtest. Significantly, in deliberating on this subtest, the Court explicitly acknowledged that the stakes in its current judgment were the protection of Jewish settlements in occupied Palestinian territory: it did not maintain (as before) that routing the wall along the Green Line was not an option on account of topography, etc., but rather that doing so would have left the Alfei Menashe settlement "vulnerable to terrorist attack." In rejecting petitioners' claim that the wall could be routed along the Green Line, the Court maintained that the settlers merited protection. It overlooked, however, the option of forcibly evacuating them. Indeed, it ignored a pair of options less injurious to Palestinians while fully protecting settlers' rights *as defined by the Court's own case law*:

- *Evacuating the settlers with compensation.* At one point in the Alfei Menashe judgment the Court recalled the Gaza Coast Regional Council case, which upheld the state's right to evacuate the Gaza settlers. It cited from this case a key finding on the contingency of settlers' property rights:

    This property right is limited in scope ... most Israelis do not have ownership of the land on which they built their houses and businesses in the territory to be evacuated. They acquired their rights from the military commander, or from persons acting on his behalf. Neither the military commander nor those acting on his behalf are owners of the property, and they cannot transfer rights better than those they have. To the extent that the Israelis built their homes and assets on land which is not private land ("state land"), that land is not owned by the military commander.... The State of Israel acts ... as the administrator of the state property and as usufructuary of it.

    The Court went on to rule in the Gaza case that it was even within the competence of the state to put a ceiling on the amount of compensation paid out to settlers:

    In determining the substance of the impingement and the rate of compensation, one must take into consideration the fact that the rights impinged upon are the rights of Israelis in territory under belligerent occupation. The temporariness of the belligerent occupation affects the substance of the right impinged upon, and thus also, automatically, the compensation for the impingement.[103]

    Besides being perfectly legal on the High Court's own terms, the practical feasibility of compensating West Bank settlers while evacuating them was enhanced in light of both the expressed willingness of many settlers to voluntarily leave the occupied Palestinian territory in return for compensation[104] and the freeing up of probably billions of dollars for compensation that would otherwise have been squandered on the wall's construction;

- *Ringing the settlements with electronic fences.* Even if, in defiance of international law, the Court sought to protect the settlers while simultaneously enabling them to remain in situ, it still had an option less injurious to the Palestinian population. "Even if Israel does not dismantle the settlements," the Israeli human rights organization B'Tselem observed,

  the contention that the only option to defend the settlements is to situate them west of the barrier is baseless. Most of the settlements will remain east of the barrier. With the objective of protecting these settlements, the Ministry of Defense decided to erect "a new protection system that includes an electronic fence to provide warning [of infiltration], and a staffed central-control room," and to set up "special security areas" surrounding the settlements, where protection would be greater. These same measures can be taken for the settlements that, according to the current plan, will lie west of the barrier. Such action would provide a reasonable solution to the security threat they face and significantly reduce the infringement of the rights of the Palestinians that will occur if the barrier is erected on land within the West Bank.[105]

  In this regard the Court never explained the anomaly that if the state's purpose in constructing the wall was to protect settlers' lives, not to incorporate the major settlement blocs, and if the wall was the only means the state could devise to achieve this objective, then the state must have forsaken to a lethal fate the many tens of thousands of settlers left on the other side, whom it allegedly could not protect yet did not even propose to evacuate.[106]

The Court did conclude, however, that the proposed route of the wall could not be justified on security-military grounds, and recommended repositioning it to exclude Palestinian villages from the enclave. In fact, as Israeli human rights organizations have conclusively shown, the aim of the state's proposed route in Alfei Menashe (as elsewhere) was not security-military but political, to facilitate massive settlement expansion:

> Had the purpose of the barrier been to protect the residents of Alfei Menashe, as Israel contends, and not to promote the expansion plans and to establish new settlements inside Alfei Menashe's jurisdictional area, the barrier could be built along the route of the fence surrounding the settlement. This option would still enable substantial growth of Alfei Menashe, for there is much land inside the fence available for construction.[107]

A major problem arises, however, if not in the High Court's conclusion, then in its rationale. The Court earlier cited these contentions of the state: "[T]here is no justification for altering the Alfei Menashe route. The fence indeed changed the reality of life for the residents of the villages left on the Israeli side of the fence. This stems from the decisive security need to defend the citizens of Israel against terrorist attacks. The injury to the residents of the villages is proportionate, considering the decisive security need to leave the fence where it is";[108] "The obstacle itself provides defense not only to the [Alfei Menashe] community itself, but also to the access roads and to its surroundings. However, the selected route is not the ideal route from a security standpoint. That is the case, due to the duty to protect the conflicting interests of the Palestinian residents."[109]

Thus, the state had testified that the route it proposed was both essential for Israel's security and least injurious to Palestinians while still taking this essential Israeli security interest into account. For the Court to cast doubt on these assertions—"We are by no means convinced. . . . We have by no means been convinced . . ."—it must have repudiated the tenet of its jurisprudence according to which "the Court does not substitute the discretion of the military commander with its own discretion," and "does not examine the wisdom of the [military commander's] decision," but, instead, only passed judgment on the legality of the military commander's recommendations.[110] By impinging on the right of the state to decide on its own, and without appeal to a higher power, the parameters of military necessity, the Court demolished the basis of its own determination that the wall constituted a military necessity.

Security Fence or Permanent Border?

In its advisory opinion the International Court of Justice affirmed the U.N. Charter's principle on the inadmissibility of acquiring territory by war and, accordingly, that Israel had no legal title to any of the West Bank, including East Jerusalem, all of which constituted occupied Palestinian territory. Additionally, there is no dispute that under international law the occupying power must respect private property in occupied territory. Israel's High Court contended that the wall's construction did not violate such strictures—or, at any rate, the latter one, making no mention of the "inadmissibility" principle—because Israel was only *temporarily* requisitioning Palestinian property for reasons of military necessity. "It is worth noting," the Court stated in the second judgment,

> that construction of the separation fence is unrelated to expropriation or confiscation of land. The latter are prohibited by regulation 46 of The Hague Regulations. . . . Construction of the fence does not involve transfer of ownership of the land upon which it is built. The construction of the fence is done by way of taking possession. Taking of possession is temporary. The seizure order orders its date of termination.[111]

And again: "The fence is inherently temporary. The seizure orders issued in order to erect the fence are limited to a definite period of a few years."[112]

The Court did, however, make fleeting reference to the fact that although seizure orders for Palestinian land were technically temporary, "they are renewable."[113] It was just such "inherently temporary" seizure orders, initially issued and repeatedly renewed on grounds of security, that enabled the entrenchment of Israeli settlements in the occupied Palestinian territory. "In the past," B'Tselem reports,

> Israel has used "requisition for military needs" orders as a means to take control of Palestinian land to establish settlements. These lands were never returned to their owners. It is now clear that Israel did not intend to seize the land for a temporary period, but to expropriate it permanently.[114]

In light of this precedent, and combined with Israel's enormous financial investment in constructing the wall, as well as its dismissal of alternative means for protecting Israel (and even the settlers in situ), it would seem arguable that the wall's primary purpose was not security and that Israel did not intend to return the land requisitioned for it but rather that Israel sought to establish a new, permanent border along the wall's "sinuous route" incorporating the "great majority of the Israeli settlements" under the pretext of military necessity.

In its advisory opinion the ICJ voiced concern that "the construction of the wall and its associated régime create a 'fait accompli' on the ground that could well become permanent."[115] Taking note of this ICJ concern, Israel's High Court rejoined that the ICJ lacked a "factual basis" for reaching definite conclusions.[116] Not just the ICJ, however, but also many respected human rights organizations expressed such worries. B'Tselem concluded that the "underlying reason" of the wall's route was "to establish facts on the ground that would perpetuate the existence of settlements and facilitate their future annexation into Israel." Likewise, Human Rights Watch concluded that the "existing and planned route of the barrier appears to be designed chiefly to incorporate and make contiguous with Israel illegal civilian settlements." Likewise, Amnesty International concluded that Israel was building the wall to "consolidate its control over land which is being used for illegal Israeli settlements," and that "the very expensive and sophisticated structure of the fence/wall indicates that it is likely intended as a permanent structure."[117]

The consensus among enlightened opinion notwithstanding, Israel's putatively liberal High Court insisted that the "fence is inherently temporary" because the state said so. Soon after the Court rendered its second judgment, however, the state publicly acknowledged that it had been disingenuous. The wall would serve as "the future border of the state of Israel," then-Justice Minister and current head of Israel's "centrist" Kadima party Tzipi Livni stated in late 2005, and the High Court, in its rulings on the wall, "is drawing the country's borders."[118] In fact, in all the cartographic proposals Israel presented during peace negotiations with Palestinians the past decade, Israel's projected border runs along the route traced by the wall. Following the Justice Minister's announcement, a High Court justice complained that this was not what the state "contended in court."[119]

Were it an independent judicial body and not a rubberstamp for the state, and were its deliberations designed to ferret out truth and not obfuscate it, the High Court would have discerned the wall's real purpose on its own long ago. "You have to be nearly insane to think that somebody uprooted mountains, leveled hills and poured billions here in order to build some temporary security barrier," Israeli journalist Meron Rapoport wrote in *Yediot Ahronot*. "The moment the work began on the fence last August [2002], everyone understood that this was to be the new border."[120] Everyone, it seems, except the justices sitting on Israel's High Court.[121] Former director of the Jaffee Center for Strategic Studies Zeev Maoz has with good cause deemed the High Court "a partner in crime to the policy establishment."[122]

In its July 2004 advisory opinion the International Court of Justice found that the wall Israel was constructing in occupied Palestinian territory could not be justified on grounds of military necessity and that it violated absolute provisions of international law. The vote was 14-1, with even the one judge casting a negative vote, Thomas Buergenthal, concurring that if the purpose of the wall was to protect Jewish settlements, it was *"ipso facto"* illegal under international law.

Israel's High Court of Justice issued two major decisions on the wall. In the first, rendered just prior to the ICJ advisory opinion, the High Court found that the wall constituted a military necessity to protect Israel from terrorist attacks, but that segments of it might inflict disproportionate harm on the local population and consequently would have to be rerouted. The High Court concluded that the wall was a military necessity on the basis of the state's testimony, which the Court held to be unimpeachable, despite compelling argumentation to the contrary. In applying a proportionality test to a segment of the wall, however, the Court disputed the state's claim that the route chosen was necessary. In doing so, the Court undercut its own finding on the wall's necessity, grounded as it was on absolute deference to the state.

After the ICJ advisory opinion the Israel High Court rendered a second decision bearing directly on the legality of building a wall to protect Jewish settlements. The Court justified construction of a wall incorporating settlements on the ground that it would protect the lives and safety of settlers. It failed to notice, however, that the settlers' lives and safety could be equally (and perhaps better) protected by repatriating them to Israel. The High Court also purported that its disagreement with the ICJ related not to the normative legal framework but instead to the empirical facts surrounding the wall's construction. In reality, however, the High Court did not acknowledge bedrock principles of international law, principles that the ICJ emphasized: the inadmissibility of acquiring territory by war and the illegality of establishing settlements in occupied territory. These principles, not a dispute over empirical facts, proved to be dispositive in determining the wall's legality. Finally, the Court found that, notwithstanding concerns registered by the ICJ and human rights organizations, and notwithstanding the weight of accumulated evidence, the wall was "inherently temporary." Not long thereafter, the state acknowledged that the wall and the High Court's rulings on it were tracing Israel's future borders.

The wall Israel has been constructing "compounds the fragmentation of the West Bank by creating non-contiguous enclaves of Palestinian communities and territory which are isolated from each other and from the remainder of the West Bank." It will annex 9.5 percent of the West Bank to Israel, including some 10.2 percent of the total cultivated area. It will "physically separate East Jerusalem"—the hub of Palestinian society— "from the rest of the West Bank," and "already separates Bethlehem from Jerusalem."[123] The consensus of expert opinion is that the wall will preempt any possibility of a viable Palestinian state and, consequently, of a just two-state settlement.[124] The result will be the dismemberment of Palestine and, in all likelihood, endless bloodshed. The white glove of legality that the Israel High Court has drawn over this sanguinary process will be drenched in blood as well.

Beyond the egregious practical repercussions of the Israel High Court's decisions, they attest on an ideological level to the impossibility of reconciling Israeli practices in the occupied Palestinian territory with the rule of law. The High Court—in particular, Aharon Barak—desperately strained to carve out common ground between its opinions and that of the International Court of Justice. But the arguments it contrived were so manifestly unpersuasive that, paradoxically, in essaying to make the best case for Israel's deference to the rule of law, and because Israel's most nimble judicial minds undertook to make it, the High Court ultimately showed just how appalling the chasm has grown between Israeli practices and enlightened legal opinion, and how indefensible these practices have become from the vantage point of liberal values.

NOTES

EPIGRAPHS
1 Noam Sheizaf, "Our Brothers, Ourselves," *Haaretz* (1 April 2011).
2 Dana Goldstein, "Why Fewer Young American Jews Share Their Parents' View of Israel," *Time* (29 September 2011).

INTRODUCTION
1 For full bibliographic references, see Theodore Sasson, Charles Kadushin, and Leonard Saxe, *American Jewish Attachment to Israel: An assessment of the "distancing" hypothesis* (Steinhardt Social Research Institute: February 2008). Although this particular study disputes what it calls the "taken-for-granted" thesis of American Jewish distancing from Israel, it nonetheless concedes that "for those looking for detachment, there is plenty of evidence to be found."
2 *J Street National Survey of American Jews* (28 February-8 March 2009), questions 37, 59.
3 Ibid., questions 60, 61.
4 For survey data connecting Jewish opposition to settlements with liberal ideology, see Theodore Sasson et al., *Still Connected: American Jewish attitudes about Israel* (August 2010), pp. 24-25.
5 Steven M. Cohen and Ari Y. Kelman, *Beyond Distancing: Young adult American Jews and their alienation from Israel* (Andrea and Charles Bronfman Philanthropies: 2007), pp. 13-16. Because much has already been written on intermarriage and its impact on American Jewish life, this topic will not be pursued in these pages.
6 Steven M. Cohen, *American Modernity and Jewish Identity* (New York: 1983), p. 32 (cf. pp. 154-55).

7. Nathan Glazer, "The Anomalous Liberalism of American Jews," in Robert M. Seltzer and Norman J. Cohen, eds., *The Americanization of the Jews* (New York: 1995), pp. 141, 143.
8. Seymour Martin Lipset and Earl Raab, *Jews and the New American Scene* (Cambridge: 1995), p. 161.
9. Steven T. Rosenthal, *Irreconcilable Differences? The waning of the American Jewish love affair with Israel* (Hanover, NH: 2001), Ofira Seliktar, *Divided We Stand: American Jews, Israel, and the peace process* (Westport, CT: 2002). Other sources of contention between American Jewry and Israel reported in these studies include the Jonathan Pollard spy case and Israel's discriminatory definition of *Who is a Jew?*. For surveys gainsaying a nexus between Jewish liberalism and estrangement from Israel, see Sasson et al., *Still Connected*, pp. 10-12, 31.
10. Lydia Saad, "Americans Maintain Broad Support for Israel," *gallup.com* (28 February 2011; http://tinyurl.com/4bsx423).
11. Cohen, *American Modernity*, pp. 162-66; Sasson et al., *Still Connected*, pp. 11, 29.
12. Cohen, *American Modernity*, pp. 162, 166, 167, 170.
13. Ahad Ha'am, "Slavery as Freedom," in Leon Simon, ed., *Selected Essays by Ahad Ha'am* (Philadelphia: 1912), pp. 183-84.

PART I/CHAPTER ONE
1. Lawrence H. Fuchs, *The Political Behavior of American Jews* (Glencoe: 1956), pp. 74-76, 104.
2. Alan M. Fisher, "Realignment of the Jewish Vote," *Political Science Quarterly* (Spring 1979).
3. Steven M. Cohen, *The Dimensions of American Jewish Liberalism* (New York: 1989).
4. Steven M. Cohen and Charles S. Liebman, "American Jewish Liberalism: Unraveling the strands," *Public Opinion Quarterly*, vol. 61 (1997), pp. 417-22. For the checkered history of Jewish support for African-American rights, see Michael E. Staub, *Torn at the Roots: The crisis of Jewish liberalism in postwar America* (New York: 2002), pp. 112-16.
5. Steven M. Cohen, *American Modernity and Jewish Identity* (New York: 1983), pp. 139-43 (quote at p. 143), 151-53.
6. Seymour Martin Lipset and Earl Raab, *Jews and the New American Scene* (Cambridge: 1995), pp. 26-28, 168.
7. The quip originated with American Jewish Committee researcher Milton Himmelfarb (cited by Nathan Glazer, "The Anomalous Liberalism of American Jews," in Robert M. Seltzer and Norman J. Cohn, eds., *The Americanization of the Jews* (New York: 1995), p. 133). For the qualified hypothesis that Jewish voting patterns *do* in fact correlate with perceived economic self-interest, see Lee Sigelman, "'If You Prick Us, Do We Not Bleed?,'" *Journal of Politics* (November 1991).
8. Robert Lerner, Althea K. Nagai and Stanley Rothman, "Marginality and Liberalism among Jewish Elites," *Public Opinion Quarterly* (Autumn 1989).

9 Jerome S. Legge, Jr., "Explaining Jewish Liberalism in the United States: An exploration of socioeconomic, religious, and communal living variables," *Social Science Quarterly* (March 1995), pp. 126, 137.
10 William Spinrad, "Explaining American-Jewish Liberalism: Another attempt," *Contemporary Jewry*, vol. 1 (1990), p. 115; Cohen, *American Modernity*, p. 137 (quote).
11 Lipset and Raab, *Jews and the New American Scene*, pp. 151-52; Cohen, *American Modernity*, pp. 24-25.
12 Norman G. Finkelstein, *The Holocaust Industry: Reflections on the exploitation of Jewish suffering* (New York: 2000; second paperback edition, 2003), pp. 49-50.
13 For the classic exposition of this hypothesis, see Fuchs, *Political Behavior*, pp. 177-203. For a more complex version of this hypothesis, see Geoffrey Brahm Levey, "Toward a Theory of Disproportionate American Jewish Liberalism," in Peter Y. Medding, ed., *Values, Interests and Identity: Jews and politics in a changing world* (Jerusalem: 1995).
14 Charles S. Liebman, "Toward a Theory of Jewish Liberalism," in Donald R. Cutler, ed., *The Religious Situation: 1969* (Boston: 1969), pp. 1037-42, 1046-47.
15 Spinrad, "Explaining."
16 Allon Gal, "Preface," in Allon Gal, ed., *Envisioning Israel: The changing ideals and images of North American Jews* (Detroit: 1996), p. 9.
17 Leonard Fein, "Why Israel is Losing Liberals," *Forward* (13 February 2009).
18 Marc Dollinger, *Quest for Inclusion: Jews and liberalism in modern America* (Princeton: 2000), p. 218.
19 Inequality in Israeli society has doubled since the 1950s, while fully one-fifth of Israeli families and more than one-third of Israeli children live in poverty. Association for Civil Rights in Israel (ACRI), *The State of Human Rights in Israel and the Occupied Territories: 2008 report*, p. 53; Asher Arian et al., *The 2003 Israeli Democracy Index: Measuring Israeli democracy* (Jerusalem: 2003), pp. 7-8; Asher Arian et al., *Auditing Israeli Democracy—2006: Changes in Israel's political party system* (Jerusalem: 2006), p. 34; Asher Arian et al., *Auditing Israeli Democracy—2007: Cohesion in a divided society* (Jerusalem: 2007), pp. 70-71. See the ACRI 2008 report, pp. 58ff. for deterioration in workers' rights, pp. 63ff. for deterioration in the right to health, pp. 69ff. for deterioration in the right to housing.
20 Meirav Arlosoroff, "'Once Politicians Died Poor,'" *Haaretz* (8 June 2008).
21 Jewish People Policy Planning Institute, *Annual Assessment 2008* (Jerusalem: 2008), p. 35; Asher Arian et al., *Auditing Israeli Democracy—2010: Democratic values in practice* (Jerusalem: 2010), p. 31.
22 Asher Arian et al., *Auditing Israeli Democracy—2007*, pp. 20-27, 114; Asher Arian et al., *Auditing Israeli Democracy—2008: Between the state and civil society* (Jerusalem: 2008), pp. 11, 24-27, 59, 80-81, 121-22; Asher Arian et al., *Auditing Israeli Democracy—2009: Twenty years of immigration from the Soviet Union*, pp. 32, 34, 61-62, 119, 120; Asher Arian et al., *Auditing Israeli Democracy—2010*, pp. 46-47, 79, 177, 178. In Transparency International's 2011 "Corruption Perceptions Index," Israel ranked

only 36 (first place being least corrupt) in the world, below Botswana and Slovakia (http://tinyurl.com/6rzjnsf).

23 Asher Arian et al., *Auditing Israeli Democracy—2007*, p. 41; Asher Arian et al., *Auditing Israeli Democracy—2008*, pp. 11, 39, 42, 56-57, 78, 113.

24 Asher Arian et al., *Auditing Israeli Democracy—2008*, pp. 65, 83-84, 121; Asher Arian et al., *Auditing Israeli Democracy—2009*, pp. 61-62, 120; Asher Arian et al., *Auditing Israeli Democracy—2010*, pp. 79, 81.

25 Asher Arian et al., *Auditing Israeli Democracy—2008*, pp. 65-66.

26 Asher Arian et al., *Auditing Israeli Democracy—2007*, pp. 46-47, 110; Asher Arian et al., *Auditing Israeli Democracy—2008*, pp. 83, 119 (the results reported on p. 119 of the 2008 survey do not fully jibe with the findings reported in the 2007 survey); Asher Arian et al., *Auditing Israeli Democracy—2009*, pp. 58, 115; Asher Arian et al., *Auditing Israeli Democracy—2010*, pp. 76-77, 174.

27 Asher Arian et al., *Auditing Israeli Democracy—2010*, pp. 107-8, 183.

28 Asher Arian et al., *Auditing Israeli Democracy—2007*, pp. 38-39, 115 (the results cited in the text of the 2007 survey do not jibe with the results in the table at the back); Asher Arian et al., *Auditing Israeli Democracy—2008*, p. 122; Asher Arian et al., *Auditing Israeli Democracy—2009*, pp. 63, 87. Still, a 2010 poll found that two-thirds of Israelis opposed a law criminalizing media harshly critical of the government (Asher Arian et al., *Auditing Israeli Democracy—2010*, pp. 151-52).

29 Asher Arian et al., *Auditing Israeli Democracy—2007*, pp. 20, 22; Asher Arian et al., *Auditing Israeli Democracy—2008*, pp. 20, 23; Asher Arian et al., *Auditing Israeli Democracy—2009*, pp. 22-25, 35-36, 38.

30 http://en.rsf.org/press-freedom-index-2009,1001.html; http://en.rsf.org/press-freedom-index-2010,1034.html.

31 Asher Arian et al., *Auditing Israeli Democracy—2007*, pp. 74-75.

32 Ibid., pp. 76, 106; Asher Arian et al., *Auditing Israeli Democracy—2008*, p. 122; Asher Arian et al., *Auditing Israeli Democracy—2009*, p. 113.

33 A complete picture would note that Jews living in the South did not support the Civil Rights Movement, while Jews in the North disproportionately supported it only until the early 1960s—that is, before its social repercussions were felt in the big Northern cities where most Jews resided.

34 Asher Arian et al., *Auditing Israeli Democracy—2008*, pp. 46, 115; Asher Arian et al., *Auditing Israeli Democracy—2009*, pp. 87, 113 (chart findings tabulate all Israelis, including Arabs); Asher Arian et al., *Auditing Israeli Democracy—2010*, pp. 82, 84, 139-40, 163, 172.

35 Asher Arian et al., *Auditing Israeli Democracy—2007*, pp. 64-65; Asher Arian et al., *Auditing Israeli Democracy—2008*, p. 115; Asher Arian et al., *Auditing Israeli Democracy—2009*, pp. 65-67, 87, 113 (chart findings on Jewish majority tabulate all Israelis, including Arabs), 118 (chart finding on Jewish rights tabulates all Israelis, including Arabs), 120 (chart finding on Arab vote tabulates all Israelis, including Arabs); Asher Arian et al., *Auditing Israeli Democracy—2010*, pp. 82, 84, 139-41, 172 (almost 70 percent of Israeli Jews oppose Arab parties joining the government; 86 percent of Israeli

Jews support Jewish majority for fateful decisions). For the years 2007-10, on average less than one-third of all Israelis (including Israeli Arabs) supported allowing Arab parties to join the government, and 70 percent supported a Jewish majority for fateful decisions.

36 Asher Arian et al., *Auditing Israeli Democracy—2010*, pp. 121-22, 142-45, 179-80 (see these pages for some caveats on the State funding question).
37 Association for Civil Rights in Israel, *The State of Human Rights in Israel and the Occupied Territories: 2009 report*, p. 2. For pending anti-Arab legislation and discriminatory administrative acts, see ibid., pp. 7, 15-19.
38 Haviv Rettig Gur, "US Jews Discomfited by Rightist Bills," *Jerusalem Post* (27 May 2009).
39 Cited in Association for Civil Rights in Israel, *The State of Human Rights in Israel and the Occupied Territories: 2007 report*, p. 16.
40 Asher Arian et al., *Auditing Israeli Democracy—2010*, pp. 147-49, 185.
41 Asher Arian et al., *Auditing Israeli Democracy—2007*, pp. 68, 107; Asher Arian et al., *Auditing Israeli Democracy—2008*, p. 116; Asher Arian et al., *Auditing Israeli Democracy—2009*, pp. 64, 87, 113; Asher Arian et al., *Auditing Israeli Democracy—2010*, pp. 82, 172. Between 2003 and 2010 some 55 percent of Israeli Jews have on average supported such State inducements.
42 Asher Arian et al., *The 2005 Israeli Democracy Index* (Jerusalem: 2005), pp. 36-37.
43 Asher Arian et al., *Auditing Israeli Democracy—2007*, pp. 21, 31-33; Asher Arian et al., *Auditing Israeli Democracy—2008*, pp. 20-21, 23, 36-37; Asher Arian et al., *Auditing Israeli Democracy—2009*, pp. 46-48; Asher Arian et al., *Auditing Israeli Democracy—2010*, pp. 35, 65.
44 "Social Affairs Minister: Israel today feels like Alabama in the 1940s," *Haaretz* (13 January 2011).
45 Asher Arian et al., *Auditing Israeli Democracy—2007*, p. 117; Asher Arian et al., *Auditing Israeli Democracy—2008*, p. 126; Asher Arian et al., *Auditing Israeli Democracy—2009*, p. 120; Asher Arian et al., *Auditing Israeli Democracy—2010*, p. 178.
46 "J Street National Survey of American Jews" (29 June—3 July 2008); "J Street National Survey of American Jews" (28 February—8 March 2009); "J Street National Survey of American Jews" (17-19 March 2009).
47 Mike Prashker, "Preventing a Schism," *Haaretz* (20 February 2009).
48 "J Street National Survey of American Jews" (March 2010); Natasha Mozgovaya, "Poll: Half of Israeli Jews hold negative views of Obama," *Haaretz* (9 December 2010).
49 "J Street National Survey of American Jews" (28 February—8 March 2009).
50 Gary Rosenblatt, "When Israel Becomes a Source of Embarrassment," *Jewish Week* (8 March 2011).
51 A full discussion of this topic is beyond the scope of the book. Suffice it to say that even the fabled kibbutzim occupied a much larger space in the image of Israel than its reality. At their peak, the kibbutzim were home to only about seven percent of the Israeli population and most of the time, even before the crisis they entered in recent decades, it was nearer three percent.

52 Anita Shapira, *Land and Power: The Zionist resort to force, 1881-1948* (Oxford: 1992).
53 Norman G. Finkelstein, *Image and Reality of the Israel-Palestine Conflict* (New York: 1995; expanded paperback edition, 2003), pp. 88-120.
54 Benny Morris, *The Birth of the Palestinian Refugee Problem Revisited* (Cambridge: 2004), p. 60. See Chapter Ten below.
55 Benny Morris, *Israel's Border Wars, 1949-1956: Arab infiltration, Israeli retaliation, and the countdown to the Suez war* (New York: 1993). See Chapter Ten below.
56 Morris, *Border Wars*, pp. 163-64. Ilan Pappé, *The Forgotten Palestinians: A history of the Palestinians in Israel* (New Haven: 2011).
57 Moshe Dayan, *Story of My Life* (New York: 1976), p. 524; Tom Segev, *1967: Israel, the war, and the year that transformed the Middle East* (New York: 2007), p. 91.
58 Amnesty International, *Combating Torture* (London: 2003), section 2.2; Benny Morris, *Righteous Victims: A history of the Zionist-Arab conflict, 1881-2001* (New York: 2001), pp. 341, 568; Segev, *1967*, p. 517.
59 B'Tselem (Israeli Information Center for Human Rights in the Occupied Territories) and Hamoked (Center for the Defense of the Individual), *Absolute Prohibition: The torture and ill-treatment of Palestinian detainees* (Jerusalem: May 2007).
60 Israel killed 18-20,000 Palestinians and Lebanese, overwhelmingly civilians, during its 1982 invasion of Lebanon; 1,200 Lebanese, overwhelmingly civilians, during its 2006 attack; and 1,400 Palestinians, overwhelmingly civilians, during its 2008-9 attack on Gaza.
61 Jonathan D. Sarna, "Why Are American Jews Abandoning Israel?," *Haaretz* (5 October 2009).

PART I/CHAPTER TWO

1 I use the term Nazi holocaust to denote the actual historical event, and The Holocaust to denote the ideological instrumentalization of that event. See Norman G. Finkelstein, *The Holocaust Industry: Reflections on the exploitation of Jewish suffering* (New York: 2000; second paperback edition, 2003), p. 3 and chapter 2.
2 Norman G. Finkelstein, *Beyond Chutzpah: On the misuse of anti-Semitism and the abuse of history* (Berkeley: 2005; expanded paperback edition, 2008), chapters 1-3.
3 Ralph Blumenthal, "Reverend Daniel Berrigan's Speech to Arabs Stirs a Furor over Award," *New York Times* (16 December 1973); Noam Chomsky, *Peace in the Middle East? Reflections on justice and nationhood* (New York: 1974), pp. 165-72.
4 See the Anti-Defamation League's annual surveys on anti-Semitism.
5 See Isaac Deutscher, *The Non-Jewish Jew and Other Essays* (New York: 1968), pp. 126-52; Maxime Rodinson, *Israel: A settler-colonial state?* (New York: 1973; originally published in *Les Temps Modernes* in 1967); Chomsky, *Peace in the Middle East?*.
6 "Survey: Israel worst brand name in the world," *Israel Today* (22 November 2006).
7 Peter Beaumont, "Israel Outraged as EU Poll Names It a Threat to Peace," *Guardian* (2 November 2003).
8 BBC World Service polls, 2007-2010. On average, 50 percent in countries polled said Israel was having a negative impact and 20 percent said it was having a positive impact. A 2008 Pew poll found that among Europeans nearly half of Spaniards, more than one-

third of Russians and Poles, one-quarter of Germans and one-fifth of French held a negative view of Jews. Although these findings might appear related to Israel's increasingly negative image, Pew pointed to domestic sources of this animus: "there is a clear relationship between anti-Jewish and anti-Muslim attitudes: publics that view Jews unfavorably also tend to see Muslims in a negative light"; anti-Muslim and anti-Jewish opinions are "most prevalent" among "Europeans on the political right" as well as among "older people and those with less education." "Unfavorable Views of Jews and Muslims on the Increase in Europe," *Pew Global Attitudes Project* (September 2008).

9 The 2011 BBC World Service poll found that 20 percent of respondents in Australia held a positive opinion of Israel versus 58 percent negative; in Canada, 23 versus 52 percent; in France, 18 versus 56 percent; in Germany, 15 versus 65 percent; in Britain, 14 versus 66 percent.

10 WorldPublicOpinion.Org Staff, *World Public Opinion on the Israeli-Palestinian Conflict* (1 July 2008); BBC World Service poll (18 September 2011).

11 Middle East Monitor, "European Public Perceptions of the Israel-Palestine Conflict" (January 2011); Andreas Zick et al., *Intolerance, Prejudice and Discrimination: A European report* (Berlin: 2011).

12 Norman G. Finkelstein, *"This Time We Went Too Far": Truth and consequences of the Gaza invasion* (New York: 2010; expanded paperback edition, 2011), pp. 116-19.

13 "Israel's Revealing Fury towards EU," *Financial Times* (13 December 2009).

14 For the illegality of Israel's blockade, and the counterclaims of the Palmer Report, see Norman G. Finkelstein, "Torpedoing the Law: How the Palmer Report justified Israel's naval blockade of Gaza," *Insight Turkey* (Fall 2011).

15 Finkelstein, *"This Time,"* pp. 169-71.

16 "Second Thoughts about the Promised Land," *Economist* (11 January 2007).

17 Martin Hodgson, "British Jews Break Away from 'Pro-Israeli' Board of Deputies," *Independent* (5 February 2007); Ben Weinthal, "German Jews Feud over Criticizing Israel," *Forward* (9 March 2007); Ben Cubby, "Jewish Coalition Calls for Open Debate on Palestine," *Sydney Morning Herald* (Australia) (6 March 2007).

18 Finkelstein, *"This Time,"* pp. 119-20.

19 Peter Beaumont, David Smith and Ben Quinn, "Leading British Jews Call on Israel to Halt 'Horror' of Gaza," *Observer* (11 January 2009).

20 CBS News/New York Times polls covering period 1998-2010 (www.pollingreport.com/israel2.htm); "American Opinion on the Israeli-Palestinian Conflict," *Zogby International* (March 2010).

21 Gallup polls covering the period 1997-2010 (www.pollingreport.com/israel.htm); Pew Research Center polls covering period 2003-09 (www.pollingreport.com/israel.htm); "America's Place in the World 2005: Opinion leaders turn cautious, public looks homeward," *Pew Research Center for the People and the Press* (17 November 2005), p. 97 (polls covering period 1978-2005); Robert Ruby, "A Six-Day War: Its aftermath in American public opinion" (30 May 2007; www.pewforum.org/docs/?DocID=281); Jodie T. Allen and Alec Tyson, "The U.S. Public's Pro-Israel History," *Pew History Center Publications* (19 July 2006). A 2010 WorldPublicOpinion.org poll did find that the percentage of Americans that "sympathize equally" with Israelis and Palestinians

had significantly increased since 2002 and that by 2010 more than half of Americans expressed equal sympathy, while only 33 percent expressed more sympathy for Israel. But 2010 and 2011 Gallup polls found that 63 percent of Americans sympathized more with Israel and that, although this percentage was "statistically unchanged" from 2006-2009, it was still a "near record high" (15-17 percent sympathized more with Palestinians, 20-23 percent favored both sides, neither side, or had no opinion). "Growing Majority of Americans Oppose Israel Building Settlements," *WorldPublicOpinion.org* (29 April 2010); Lydia Saad, "Support for Israel in U.S. at 63%, Near Record High," *gallup.com* (24 February 2010; http://tinyurl.com/ya9xr4x); Lydia Saad, "Americans Maintain Broad Support for Israel," *gallup.com* (28 February 2011; http://tinyurl.com/4bsx423).

22. Gallup polls covering period 1998-2003 (www.pollingreport.com/israel2.htm); Andrew Kohut, "American Views of the Mideast Conflict," *New York Times* (14 May 2002); "Opportunities for Bipartisan Consensus: What both Republicans and Democrats want in U.S. foreign policy," *PIPA/Knowledge Networks Poll* (18 January 2005).
23. CBS News poll, 31 July-5 August 2008 (www.pollingreport.com/israel2.htm); USA Today/Gallup polls covering period 2001-2006 (www.pollingreport.com/israel.htm); The Harris Poll, May-August 2002; The Harris Poll, April-July 2002; Newsweek Poll, 25-26 April 2002. In fact nearly half of *Israelis* believe that U.S. policy favors Israel too much (Allen and Tyson, "The U.S. Public's Pro-Israel History").
24. WorldPublicOpinion.Org Staff, *World Public Opinion on the Israeli-Palestinian Conflict* (1 July 2008).
25. "Poll: Americans supporting cutting aid to Israel," *Reuters* (12 April 2002).
26. USA Today/Gallup polls covering period 1999-2009 (www.pollingreport.com/israel2.htm). The Harris Poll, April-July 2002; ABC News.com Poll, 3-7 April 2002.
27. "Israel's Increased Isolation," *Issue #308* (Washington, D.C., 19 January 2007; www.ipforum.org/display.cfm?id=6&Sub=15&Dis=3). See also Amiram Barkat, "Jewish Leaders Concerned by Trend to Delegitimize Israel," *Haaretz* (10 July 2007).
28. Anti-Defamation League, "American Attitudes towards Israel, the Palestinians and Prospects for Peace in the Middle East: An Anti-Defamation League survey" (19 October 2007).
29. Lydia Saad, "In U.S., Canada Places First in Image Contest; Iran Last," *gallup.com* (19 February 2010).
30. "Poll Shows Dip in American Voters' Supporting Israel," *Jewish Telegraphic Agency* (16 June 2009).
31. Barak Ravid, "U.S. Support for Israel Is Decreasing, New Poll Shows," *Haaretz* (18 August 2010).
32. John Zogby, "American Public Opinion and the Middle East Peace Process," www.bitterlemons-api.org (1 June 2011).
33. 2011 BBC World Service poll.
34. BBC World Service poll (18 September 2011) (45 percent support, 36 percent oppose); Pew Research Center, "Palestinian Statehood: Mixed views, low visibility" (20 September 2011) (42 percent support, 26 percent oppose).

35 ABC News/Washington Post poll (3-6 August 2006; www.pollingreport.com/israel.htm); Los Angeles Times/Bloomberg Poll (28 July-1 August 2006; www.pollingreport.com/israel.htm); USA Today/Gallup poll (21-23 July 2006; www.pollingreport.com/israel.htm); "U.S. Should Be Neutral in Lebanon War" (17 August 2006; www.zogby.com/search/ReadNews.dbm?ID=1159).
36 "Americans Closely Divided over Israel's Gaza Attacks," *Rasmussen Reports* (31 December 2008); "Modest Backing for Israel in Gaza Crisis," *Pew Research Center* (13 January 2009).
37 "Hasbarapocalypse—Leaked Frank Luntz Memo: Israeli public diplomacy in US on Flotilla failed dismally," *Coteret* (5 July 2010; http://tinyurl.com/36c4nmm).
38 Finkelstein, *"This Time,"* pp. 121-23, 173.
39 Chicago Council on Global Affairs, *Constrained Internationalism: Adapting to new realities* (2010). It was ranked fifth in importance well below China, Great Britain and Canada, and between Japan and Mexico. The "favorable feeling" for Israel was significantly less than for Great Britain, Germany and Japan, and fell within a cluster including France, Brazil and South Africa. In striking contrast to the Chicago Council findings, a December 2009 poll by an affiliate of the Israel lobby found that 61 percent of Americans favored U.S. military support for Israel if it bombed Iran's nuclear facilities and a war between them ensued (according to the Chicago Council only 38 percent favored it), and 68 percent supported siding with Israel militarily if it were the victim of unprovoked aggression (according to the Chicago Council only 47 percent supported it). The Israel Project, *December [2009] National Survey*, p. 7. It is hard not to wonder whether the Israel Project findings were calibrated with the Israeli government's declared intention to attack Iran and its lobbying for American support.
40 The Amman Call: Issued at WCC International Peace Conference "Churches Together for Peace and Justice in the Middle East" (18-20 June 2007; www.oikoumene.org/?id=3748); Toya Richards Hill, "GA Overwhelmingly Approves Israel/Palestine Resolution" (21 June 2006; www.pcusa.org/ga217/newsandphotos/ga06124.htm); "United Methodists Urged to Divest from 20 Companies Supporting In a Significant Way Israel's Occupation of Palestinian Land" (21 June 2007; www.neumc.org/news_print.asp?PKValue=165); "Seeking a Just Peace in the Middle East, Synod Adopts Economic Leverage Resolution" (5 July 2005; www.ucc.org/news/seeking-a-just-peace.html).
41 Presbyterian Church (USA), "Breaking Down the Walls—From the Middle East Study Committee" (n.d.; http://tinyurl.com/2949slh).
42 Jimmy Carter, *Palestine Peace Not Apartheid* (New York: 2006).
43 Ezra HaLevi, "Exclusive: Jimmy Carter interceded on behalf of Nazi SS guard" (18 January 2007; www.israelnationalnews.com/News/News.aspx/119732).
44 Deborah Lipstadt, "Jimmy Carter's Jewish Problem," *Washington Post* (20 January 2007).
45 Philip Weiss, "Jimmy Carter's Book Stirs a Critical Debate," *American Conservative* (26 February 2007); David Abel and James Vaznis, "Carter Wins Applause at Brandeis," *Boston Globe* (24 January 2007). See also Hinda Mandell, "Brandeis Students at Odds

over Israel," *Boston Globe* (8 May 2008), reporting the student senate's vote *not* to congratulate Israel on its sixtieth anniversary.
46 Finkelstein, *"This Time,"* pp. 121-22.
47 Steven M. Cohen, "Poll: Attachment of U.S. Jews to Israel falls in past 2 years," *Forward* (4 March 2005).
48 American Jewish Committee, *2007 Annual Survey of American Jewish Opinion* (6 November-25 November 2007); J Street, *National Survey of American Jews* (29 June-3 July 2008); Theodore Sasson et al., *Still Connected: American Jewish attitudes about Israel* (August 2010), p. 9. For criticism of the Sasson study's optimistic spin on the poll data, see Steven Cohen's comments in Gal Beckerman, "Survey Says Young Jews Do Care about Israel," *Forward* (10 September 2010).
49 Finkelstein, *"This Time,"* pp. 123-24.
50 "Second Thoughts."
51 Asaf Shtull-Trauring, "It Might Have Been Wise to Look the Other Way," *Haaretz* (13 June 2010); Rabbi Sidney Schwarz, "Opinion: This is Zionism?," *Haaretz* (7 June 2009).
52 Tzipi Livni, "Time for a New Jewish Conversation," *Jerusalem Post* (12 September 2010).
53 *2006 Annual Survey of American Jewish Opinion*, conducted for the American Jewish Committee by Synovate (25 September-16 October 2006); Steven M. Cohen and Ari Y. Kelman, *Beyond Distancing: Young adult American Jews and their alienation from Israel* (Andrea and Charles Bronfman Philanthropies: 2007); Sasson et al., *Still Connected*, p. 11.
54 Jewish People Policy Planning Institute, *Annual Assessment 2008* (Jerusalem), p. 13.
55 CJP-Jewish Boston Connected, *Israel Advocacy Strategic Planning Subcommittee Final Report* (February 2008), pp. 15-16. See also Michael Paulson, "Push on to Bolster Israel's Image: Calls for reaching out in new ways to young Jews," *Boston Globe* (26 September 2008), and Abe Selig, "U.S. Professors: Support for Israel eroded," *Jerusalem Post* (29 June 2009).
56 Finkelstein, *"This Time,"* pp. 125-28, 178-79.
57 Peter Beinart, "The Failure of the American Jewish Establishment," *New York Review of Books* (10 June 2010).
58 The ground for Beinart was arguably cleared back in 2003 in another manifesto by noted Jewish historian Tony Judt that also appeared in the *New York Review of Books*. Judt asserted that "Israel today is bad for the Jews," and doubted both the viability and the desirability of a Jewish state. The reaction to Judt's essay already suggested back then which way the winds were blowing. When the Israel lobby's pressures led to cancellation of one of Judt's speaking engagements, he became an instant *cause célèbre* in American intellectual circles, while his critics, such as Abraham H. Foxman of the ADL, were derided for "slinging the dread charge of anti-Semitism" and for being an "anachronism." Tony Judt, "Israel: The alternative," *New York Review of Books* (23 October 2003); Mark Lilla and Richard Sennett, "The Case of Tony Judt: An open letter to the ADL," *New York Review of Books* (16 November 2006), "A Statement in Sup-

port of Open and Free Discussion about U.S. and Israeli Foreign Policy and Against Suppression of Speech," *Archipelago* (www.archipelago.org/vol10-12/freespeech.htm); James Traub, "Does Abe Foxman Have an Anti-Anti-Semite Problem?," *New York Times* (14 January 2007).
59 Finkelstein, *"This Time,"* pp. 177-78.
60 Ibid., p. 179.
61 David Remnick, "A Man, a Plan," *New Yorker* (21 March 2011).
62 Daphna Berman, "Dershowitz: Boycotts abet terrorism," *Haaretz* (27 January 2006).
63 Abraham H. Foxman, *The Deadliest Lies: Mearsheimer and Walt, the Israel lobby and the myth of Jewish control* (New York: 2007), p. 91.
64 Orly Halpern, "Foxman, Wiesel Upbraid Israel for Pace of Peace Effort," *Forward* (18 May 2007).
65 Cnaan Lipshiz, "I Don't Care If Our Pro-Zionist Stance Costs Us," *Haaretz* (18 February 2008).
66 The Reut Institute, *Building a Political Firewall against Israel's Delegitimization* (Tel Aviv: March 2010), para. 120.

PART II/CHAPTER THREE
1 Georg Lukács, *History and Class Consciousness: Studies in Marxist dialectics* (Cambridge: 1999) p. 157 (emphasis in original).
2 Jerold S. Auerbach, "Are We One? Menachem Begin and the long shadow of 1977," in Allon Gal, ed., *Envisioning Israel: The changing ideals and images of North American Jews* (Detroit: 1996), p. 335.
3 Murray Friedman, *The Neoconservative Revolution: Jewish intellectuals and the shaping of public policy* (New York: 2005), p. 12.
4 Marshall Sklare and Benjamin B. Ringer, "A Study of Jewish Attitudes toward the State of Israel," in Marshall Sklare, ed., *The Jews: Social patterns of an American group* (Glencoe: 1958), pp. 438-42.
5 Zvi Ganim, *An Uneasy Relationship: American Jewish leadership and Israel, 1948-1957* (Syracuse: 2005), chapter 1 ("The Specter of Dual Loyalty") and pp. 68, 95, 119; "dual-loyalty nightmare" quoted from Auerbach, "Are We One?," p. 349. See also Marc Dollinger, *Quest for Inclusion: Jews and liberalism in modern America* (Princeton: 2000), p. 127. In an earlier era, privileged British Jews had been vociferous opponents of the Balfour Declaration, fearing that the creation of a Jewish state in Palestine would undercut their standing in British society. See Isaiah Friedman, *The Question of Palestine: British-Jewish-Arab relations, 1914-1918* (New Brunswick, NJ: 1992), pp. 23-37, 49, 137-38, 227-43, 259, and Ronald Sanders, *The High Walls of Jerusalem: A history of the Balfour Declaration and the birth of the British mandate for Palestine* (New York: 1983), pp. 314-17, 430, 530-31, 566-67, 598.
6 Ganim, *Uneasy Relationship*, pp. 32, 61; see also Michael T. Benson, *Harry S. Truman and the Founding of Israel* (Westport, CT: 1997), pp. 84, 156, quoting American officials on the proclivity of Jews generally and Zionists in particular for Communism. For British admonitions to the U.S. that "the new state of Israel would become

Communist" and align with the Soviet Union, see Wm. Roger Louis, *The British Empire and the Middle East, 1945-51* (Oxford: 1984), pp. 43-44, 114-15, 538-39, 570.
7 Steven T. Rosenthal, *Irreconcilable Differences? The waning of the American Jewish love affair with Israel* (Hanover, NH: 2001), p. 27.
8 Nathan Glazer, *American Judaism* (Chicago: 1957), p. 114.
9 Marshall Sklare and Joseph Greenblum, *Jewish Identity on the Suburban Frontier: A study of group survival in the open society* (New York: 1967), pp. 7-9, 228-29.
10 Tom Segev, *1967: Israel, the war, and the year that transformed the Middle East* (New York: 2007), p. 110.
11 Alexander Bloom, *Prodigal Sons: The New York intellectuals and their world* (New York: 1986).
12 Segev, *1967*, p. 107. Noam Chomsky, *Towards a New Cold War: Essays on the current crisis and how we got there* (New York: 1982), pp. 299-307.
13 Norman Podhoretz, "The Intellectual and Jewish Fate," *Midstream* (Winter 1957). American Jewry acquiesced in President Dwight D. Eisenhower's ultimatum to Israel in 1956 that it must withdraw from Egyptian territory. "I must tell you that it will be impossible to mobilize to support this posture [of refusal to withdraw]," World Zionist Organization leader Nahum Goldmann warned Ben-Gurion. "If there will be an open dispute between Israel and the United States Government on this point . . . , I foresee great difficulties. . . . What is needed is a step that will prevent an open split with Eisenhower" (quoted in Melvin I. Urofsky, *We Are One! American Jewry and Israel* (New York: 1978), p. 314). Urofsky dubiously asserts that, "Although American Jews agonized over Israeli intransigence, they did not worry about the old charge of dual loyalty," and that they boldly championed Israel's case against Eisenhower (ibid., pp. 314-17). For the demystified record, see Norman G. Finkelstein, *The Holocaust Industry: Reflections on the exploitation of Jewish suffering* (New York: 2000; second paperback edition, 2003), p. 18, and Isaac Alteras, *Eisenhower and Israel: U.S.-Israeli relations, 1953-1960* (Gainesville, FL: 1993), esp. pp. 291-92, "the [Conference of Presidents of Major American Jewish Organizations] would not side with Israel to the extent that it might find itself in open conflict with the administration or public opinion at large." Except for the Zionist Organization of America, Jewish organizations outside the umbrella of the Presidents' Conference such as the American Jewish Committee also fell into line.
14 For the full period of Podhoretz's tenure up to the June 1967 war (February 1960-June 1967), the magazine featured 619 articles of which only 30 dealt in any way with Israel (or Zionism).
15 Norman Podhoretz, *Making It* (New York: 1967), p. 133. The passing reference is to disagreements at the time of Israel's founding between *Commentary*'s first editor and the organized Jewish community.
16 Norman G. Finkelstein, *Image and Reality of the Israel-Palestine Conflict* (New York: 1995; expanded second paperback edition, 2003), p. 22.
17 Lucy Dawidowicz and Milton Himmelfarb, eds., *Conference on Jewish Identity Here and Now* (American Jewish Committee: 1967).

18 Norman Podhoretz, *Breaking Ranks* (New York: 1979), p. 335.
19 Gary Dorrien, *The Neoconservative Mind: Politics, culture, and the war of ideology* (Philadelphia: 1993), p. 184 ("nearly"); Jacob Heilbrunn, *They Knew They Were Right: The rise of the neocons* (New York: 2008), p. 71 ("survival"); Mark Gerson, *The Neoconservative Vision: From the Cold War to the Culture Wars* (New York: 1996), p. 162 ("foremost"). However, in keeping with Podhoretz's overarching allegiance to American power, "his magazine's principal attention was devoted to the Soviet threat" (Dorrien, *Neoconservative Mind*, p. 182).
20 Even when Podhoretz urged Jewish intellectuals in his 1957 article to support Israel against its Arab enemies, he was careful to note that such support of Israel would also serve the American national interest of impeding Soviet penetration of the region.
21 Walter Russell Mead, "The New Israel and the Old: Why gentile Americans back the Jewish state," *Foreign Affairs* (July/August 2008), p. 43.
22 Jonathan D. Sarna, "A Projection of America as It Ought to Be: Zion in the mind's eye of American Jews," in Gal, ed., *Envisioning Israel*, pp. 41-42, 57, 59.
23 Dollinger, *Quest*, p. 202.
24 Friedman, *Neoconservative Revolution*, p. 148; Gerson, *Neoconservative Vision*, p. 165; Heilbrunn, *They Knew*, pp. 134-35.
25 Noam Chomsky, *Peace in the Middle East?: Reflections on justice and nationhood* (New York: 1974), pp. 163-64. For a classic of this genre, see Martin Peretz, "The American Left and Israel," *Commentary* (November 1967). Peretz drubbed gadfly journalist I. F. Stone for alleging a "coerced Arab exodus" in 1948 and for discerning a post-June-war "trend toward chauvinism and militarism in Israel." Then a Harvard instructor and campus radical, Peretz later became editor and publisher of *The New Republic*, which he remolded into the house organ of Cold War liberals and Israel apologists.
26 Heilbrunn, *They Knew*, p. 68; Dorrien, *Neoconservative Mind*, p. 186.
27 Heilbrunn, *They Knew*, p. 221. Another "politically useful" category after the June 1967 war was "The Holocaust," an ideological (mis)representation of the Nazi holocaust. In order to justify their support of Israel and U.S. foreign policy and opposition to "appeasement," Jewish neoconservatives routinely invoked their unique Jewish sensitivity to the Nazi genocide. Thus, Midge Decter recalled that after World War II the Nazi holocaust so enraged her that "I literally did not know what to do with myself.... You might say I became a concentration-camp junkie"; Paul Wolfowitz was "transfixed by the threat of totalitarianism" after "reading about Nazism" in his youth; and on and on. It is even said of Ronald Reagan that "his sympathy for Israel had deeply personal roots: he never forgot that his father bypassed a hotel that didn't admit Jews," and he was "aghast at the Holocaust." Heilbrunn, *They Knew*, pp. 75, 107, 162, 255. These politically convenient memories of Jewish neoconservatives should perhaps be taken with a boulder of salt, while their apotheosis of Reagan should be juxtaposed next to his now largely forgotten declaration at Bitburg cemetery that the German soldiers (including Waffen SS members) buried there were "victims of the Nazis just as surely as the victims of the concentration camps."

28 Steven M. Cohen, *American Modernity and Jewish Identity* (New York: 1983), p. 34. Cohen persuasively argues that because American Zionism has rejected this Zionist tenet it should more properly be called "pro-Israelism" (ibid.).
29 Gerson, *Neoconservative Vision*, pp. 192, 299.
30 Ibid., p. 162.

PART II/CHAPTER FOUR

1 John J. Mearsheimer and Stephen M. Walt, *The Israel Lobby and U.S. Foreign Policy* (New York: 2007).
2 John J. Mearsheimer and Stephen M. Walt, "The Israel Lobby," *London Review of Books* (23 March 2006).
3 Mearsheimer and Walt, *Israel Lobby*, pp. 5, 50-77.
4 "Draft Study by the National Security Council" (27 December 1951), *Foreign Relations of the United States, 1951, vol. V, The Near East and Africa* (Washington, D.C.: 1982).
5 Donald Neff, *Warriors for Jerusalem: The six days that changed the Middle East* (New York: 1984), p. 230.
6 Warren Bass, *Support Any Friend: Kennedy's Middle East and the making of the U.S.-Israel alliance* (New York: 2003), p. 141. The early 1960s witnessed a string of seemingly Nasserite coups in Iraq and Syria, and Cairo's armed intervention in support of a radical coup in Yemen. These developments alarmed the Saudi and Jordanian monarchies, and their principal backer in Washington.
7 Ibid., p. 101. A decision by the Kennedy administration to sell Hawk missiles to Israel marked a rupture in U.S. policy that had hitherto steered clear of such sales to Israel or the Arab states lest it set off a Middle East arms race.
8 Ibid., pp. 249-50.
9 "Memorandum from the President's Special Assistant (Rostow) to President Johnson" (4 June 1967), *Foreign Relations of the United States, 1964-1968, vol. XIX, Arab-Israeli Crisis and War, 1967* (Washington, D.C.: 2004) (my emphasis). See also "Memorandum from the Deputy Assistant Secretary of Defense for International Security Affairs (Hoopes) to Secretary of Defense McNamara" (8 June 1967), ibid.:

> With Nasser removed (or discredited to the point where the Soviets deny him support), the Middle East would probably be relieved, for some years, of the intense and effective extremism that has been constantly stimulated by the Nasser charisma and the UAR [Egypt] political propaganda apparatus. With those removed or seriously discredited, reasonable dealings with individual Arab states on the basis of practical mutual interest would be far more likely for Israel, and also for the U.S.

10 Dennis Ross and David Makovsky, *Myths, Illusions and Peace: Finding a new direction for America in the Middle East* (New York: 2009), p. 56.
11 Ian S. Lustick, "Abandoning the Iron Wall: Israel and 'the Middle Eastern muck,'" *Middle East Policy* (Fall 2008), p. 39.
12 Trita Parsi, *Treacherous Alliance: The secret dealings of Israel, Iran, and the U.S.* (New Haven: 2007); Robert Baer, *The Devil We Know: Dealing with the new Iranian superpower*

(New York: 2008). At times Mearsheimer and Walt strangely suggest that the U.S. alliance with Israel is the principal cause of Washington's friction with Tehran (*Israel Lobby*, pp. 8, 59-60).

13 Parsi, *Treacherous Alliance*, pp. 129, 181, 263.
14 Reuel Marc Gerecht, "Iran: Fundamentalism and reform," in Robert Kagan and William Kristol, eds., *Present Dangers: Crisis and opportunity in American foreign and defense policy* (San Francisco: 2000), pp. 138-39.
15 Ross and Makovsky, *Myths*, pp. 179-82; cf. p. 205. See also Jewish People Policy Planning Institute, *Annual Assessment 2008* (Jerusalem), p. 27.
16 Charles Krauthammer, "Could a Hezbollah Win Destroy the US-Israel Relationship?," *Jewish World Review* (4 August 2006).
17 Amos Harel and Avi Issacharoff, *34 Days: Israel, Hezbollah, and the war in Lebanon* (New York: 2008), pp. 104-5, 255 ("stick it"); Parsi, *Treacherous Alliance*, pp. 15 ("weaken," "neutralizing"), 275-76. According to Harel and Issacharoff, Washington also "viewed the war as an opportunity to dispose of Bashar Assad's regime in Syria" and expressed outrage at Israel's refusal to attack it.
18 Parsi, *Treacherous Alliance*, p. 15.
19 Mearsheimer and Walt, *Israel Lobby*, pp. 306-13, 326-33.
20 Ibid., pp. 9, 314.
21 They conflate what the Bush administration actually knew with what, according to them, it *should* have known.
22 Condoleezza Rice, *No Higher Honor: A memoir of my years in Washington* (New York: 2011), pp. 490-91.
23 Isaiah Friedman, *The Question of Palestine: British-Jewish-Arab relations, 1914-1918* (New Brunswick, NJ: 1992), pp. 305-6.
24 This paragraph and subsequent ones are based on Kenneth Ray Bain, *The March to Zion: United States policy and the founding of Israel* (College Station, TX: 1979); Michael T. Benson, *Harry S. Truman and the Founding of Israel* (Westport, CT: 1997); Michael J. Cohen, *Palestine and the Great Powers, 1945-1948* (Princeton: 1982), Michael J. Cohen, *Truman and Israel* (Berkeley: 1990); Zvi Ganim, *Truman, American Jewry, and Israel, 1945-1948* (New York: 1979); Peter L. Hahn, *Caught in the Middle East: U.S. policy towards the Arab-Israeli conflict, 1945-1961* (Chapel Hill: 2004); Wm. Roger Louis, *The British Empire in the Middle East, 1945-1951: Arab nationalism, the United States, and postwar imperialism* (Oxford: 1984); Aaron David Miller, *Search for Security: Saudi Arabian oil and American foreign policy, 1939-1949* (Chapel Hill: 1980); Benny Morris, *1948: A history of the first Arab-Israeli war* (New Haven: 2008); John Snetsinger, *Truman, the Jewish Vote, and the Creation of Israel* (Stanford: 1974); Evan M. Wilson, *Decision on Palestine: How the U.S. came to recognize Israel* (Stanford: 1979).
25 Except for Woodrow Wilson in 1916, no candidate since 1876 had lost New York State and won the presidency, and the Jewish vote could determine which way New York went. Nonetheless Truman won the New York Jewish vote in 1948 and won his reelection bid while losing the electoral contest in New York State. It is possible however that he won the election because of the Jewish vote in Ohio, California and

Illinois. Truman credited Jewish financial backer Abe Feinberg with making possible the "whistle-stop" tour that clinched his 1948 electoral victory.
26 Truman's pro-Jewish tilt apparently also reflected a humanitarian impulse of his as well as of the American public. An October 1947 nationwide Gallup poll found that 65 percent of those questioned favored partitioning Palestine and only 10 percent opposed it.
27 Louis, *British Empire*, p. 193.
28 Benson, *Harry S. Truman*, p. 113.
29 Cohen, *Palestine and the Great Powers*, pp. 192-94, 318-21.
30 Bain, *March to Zion*, p. 154 ("talking big"); Miller, *Search for Security*, p. 189 ("bring pressure").
31 Cohen, *Truman and Israel*, p. 175.
32 Benson, *Harry S. Truman*, p. 159n33; Morris, *1948*, p. 175.
33 Hahn, *Caught in the Middle East*, p. 54.
34 Morris, *1948*, p. 109; cf. pp. 81, 112.
35 Ganim, *Truman, American Jewry*, p. 150; Cohen, *Truman and Israel*, pp. 174-75.
36 Ganim, *Truman, American Jewry*, pp. 180-81. As it turned out, the U.S.-U.N. arms embargo ultimately worked in Israel's favor. The Zionist leadership had anticipated such an eventuality and arranged for the purchase of weapons from sundry third parties, whereas the Arabs had made no such preparations (Morris, *1948*, pp. 201-2, 206-7, 402-3).
37 This and subsequent paragraphs are based on Isaac Alteras, *Eisenhower and Israel: U.S.-Israeli relations, 1953-1960* (Gainesville, FL: 1993); Irene L. Gendzier, *Notes from the Minefield: United States intervention in Lebanon and the Middle East, 1945-1958* (New York: 2006); Peter L. Hahn, *The United States, Great Britain, and Egypt, 1945-1956* (Chapel Hill: 1991); Hahn, *Caught in the Middle East*; Wm. Roger Louis and Roger Owen, eds., *Suez 1956: The crisis and its consequences* (Oxford: 1989); Ritchie Ovendale, *Britain, the United States, and the Transfer of Power in the Middle East, 1945-1962* (London: 1996); Salim Yaqub, *Containing Arab Nationalism: The Eisenhower Doctrine and the Middle East* (Chapel Hill: 2004).
38 Pro-Western regimes were toppled in Syria in 1949 (albeit with U.S. complicity), Egypt in 1952, and Iraq in 1958. Lebanon and Jordan nearly experienced comparable fates in 1958. In neighboring Iran a nationalist regime came to power in 1951 but was subverted by the U.S. and Britain in 1953.
39 Gendzier, *Notes from the Minefield*, pp. 107, 148.
40 Hahn, *Caught in the Middle East*, p. 242.
41 Gendzier, *Notes from the Minefield*, p. 366.
42 Hahn, *Caught in the Middle East*, pp. 4, 279.
43 In reaction to Israeli cross-border raids and other provocations against neighboring Arab states, the U.S. on its own and in concert with the U.N. frequently censured Tel Aviv for its "merciless severity" (Eisenhower) and its "attitude of the conqueror" (senior American official). Washington was also much less responsive to Israeli requests for weapons transfers. Besides the exigencies of its Middle East policy, the Eisenhower administration was probably less obliging because it was not in thrall

to the Jewish vote, which went overwhelmingly to the Democratic Party. Alteras, *Eisenhower and Israel*, pp. 36, 87 (quote), 88, 95, 101, 105 (quote), 161, 167-78.
44 Gendzier, *Notes from the Minefield*, p. 153.
45 Hahn, *The United States*, p. 201 ("rid of"); Ovendale, *Britain, the United States*, p. 149 ("revolutionary leadership"); Alteras, *Eisenhower and Israel*, p. 191 ("firm").
46 The French calculated that unseating Nasser would deliver a fatal blow to the Algerian independence struggle.
47 Hahn, *Caught in the Middle East*, p. 208 ("objectives"). But Washington was dismissive of Tel Aviv's grievances against Nasser during the diplomatic parleys leading up to the tripartite aggression. Once the crisis broke out Eisenhower used the threat of U.S.-U.N. sanctions, combined with largely token concessions that allowed for Israel's "respectable retreat," to effect an Israeli withdrawal from Egyptian territory, which Ben-Gurion had vowed never to leave. Ibid., pp. 196, 210-20; Alteras, *Eisenhower and Israel*, pp. 246-86 (quote at p. 248).
48 Alteras, *Eisenhower and Israel*, p. 192.
49 Ovendale, *Britain, the United States*, p. 165; Alteras, *Eisenhower and Israel*, pp. 226-27.
50 Ovendale, *Britain, the United States*, p. 151 ("in agreement"); Hahn, *The United States*, pp. 202 ("drastic"), 214 ("disgorge"), 219 ("exclude"). In point of fact even State Department legal experts conceded that Egypt's nationalization of the Suez Canal Company conformed to the letter of the law (Nasser pledged compensation at prevailing market rates), while intelligence officers predicted that Egypt could on its own handle day-to-day operations on the waterway.
51 Hahn, *The United States*, pp. 222 ("bring," "inflame"), 236 ("stopped"), 237 ("deplored"), 238 ("Mussolini"); Robert R. Bowie, "Eisenhower, Dulles, and the Suez Crisis," in Louis and Owen, *Suez 1956*, pp. 199 ("peaceful"), 200 ("downgrade"); Yaqub, *Containing Arab Nationalism*, p. 69 ("objective," "isolate," "undermine").
52 Yaqub, *Containing Arab Nationalism*, pp. 43, 45, 49-50, 52, 155-77.
53 Mearsheimer and Walt, *Israel Lobby*, p. 8.
54 Ibid., pp. 5, 13-14, 150, 161, 165.
55 Ibid., pp. 162, 150.
56 Ibid., pp. 13, 16, 112, 131, 147, 166, 199 (my emphasis).
57 Ibid., pp. 112, 114, 115, 121-26, 146, 150, 334; the last quote comes from John J. Mearsheimer and Stephen M. Walt, *Setting the Record Straight: A response to critics of "The Israel Lobby"* (www.Israellobbybook.com; 2006), pp. 11, 15 (my emphasis).
58 Mearsheimer and Walt, *Israel Lobby*, p. 148.
59 Ibid., p. 8.
60 "Notes of a Meeting of the NSC Special Committee" (14 June 1967), "Information Memorandum from the Assistant Secretary of State for Near Eastern and South Asian Affairs (Battle) to Secretary of State Rusk" (17 November 1967), in *Foreign Relations of the United States, vol. XIX, Arab-Israeli Crisis and War, 1967*.
61 "Action Memorandum from the Control Group to Secretary of State Rusk" (n.d.), "Memorandum from W. Howard Wriggins of the National Security Council Staff to the President's Special Assistant (Rostow), the President's Special Consultant

(Bundy)" (12 July 1967), in ibid.; cf. "Telegram from the President's Special Assistant (Rostow) to President Johnson in Texas" (6 July 1967), "Memorandum from the President's Special Assistant (Rostow) to President Johnson" (13 July 1967), "Memorandum from the President's Special Consultant (Bundy) to President Johnson" (14 July 1967), in ibid.

62 "Paper Prepared by the President's Special Consultant (Bundy)" (18 July 1967), ibid.

63 "Memorandum from the President's Special Assistant (Rostow) to President Johnson" (3 October 1967), ibid.

64 "Memorandum from Harold H. Saunders of the National Security Council to the President's Special Assistant (Rostow)" (17 October 1967), ibid.

65 "Telegram from the Mission to the United Nations to the Department of State" (9 July 1967), ibid.

66 "Telegram from the Mission to the United Nations to the Department of State" (21 July 1967), ibid. U.S. representative Arthur Goldberg stressed during the Fifth Emergency Special Session of the General Assembly convened right after the June war that to reach a "durable peace" the "withdrawal of Israeli forces to their own territory" was an "essential step." See Chapter Nine below.

67 "Memorandum from the President's Special Consultant (Bundy) to President Johnson" (11 August 1967), in *Foreign Relations of the United States, vol. XIX, Arab-Israeli Crisis and War, 1967*. An attachment to this document on the latest draft text of the U.S.-proposed resolution read: "Affirms the principle under the UN Charter of: A. Without delay withdrawal by the parties to the conflict of their forces from territories occupied by them in keeping with the inadmissibility of the conquest of territory by war."

68 "Telegram from the Embassy in Israel to the Department of State" (16 August 1967), ibid. In late August Israel again conveyed to the U.S. that "the heart of the Israeli objection to the joint U.S.-Soviet resolution is its implication that Israel must return to the territories occupied on June 4," and particularly the language calling for "withdrawal from all occupied territories"; "Memorandum of Conversation" (29 August 1967), ibid.

69 "Telegram from the Mission to the United Nations to the Department of State" (26 October 1967), ibid. A secret Israeli cabinet decision in early November opposed "inclusion of words 'all' or 'occupied in the recent conflict'" in a resolution; "Telegram from the Department of State to the Embassy in Lebanon" (12 November 1967), ibid.

70 "Memorandum of Conversation" (3 November 1967), ibid. Right until the eve of the vote on what became Security Council resolution 242, the Soviets fought for inclusion of "all" before "territories" or "withdrawal to positions before June 5" in the withdrawal paragraph; "Telegram from the Mission to the United Nations to the Department of State" (21 November 1967), ibid.

71 See Chapter Nine.

72 The U.S. conveyed to Jordan's King Hussein that it supported full Israeli withdrawal from the West Bank except for minor and mutual border rectifications, while also stipulating that "we cannot guarantee that everything will be returned to Jordan since, of course, we cannot speak for Israel." The U.S. apparently did not inform Israel

that, during its meetings with Hussein, it advocated not only minor border adjustments but "the principle of mutuality" as well. "Telegram from the Mission to the United Nations to the Department of State" (4 November 1967), "Telegram from the Department of State to the Embassy in Israel" (5 November 1967), "Telegram from the Department of State to the Embassy in Israel" (30 November 1968), "Memorandum from Secretary of State Rusk to President Johnson" (n.d.), in *Foreign Relations of the United States, vol. XIX, Arab-Israeli Crisis and War, 1967*.

73 Mearsheimer and Walt, *Israel Lobby*, pp. 68-70.
74 Ross and Makovsky, *Myths*, pp. 25, 29, 86-87, 100-1.
75 Mearsheimer and Walt, *Israel Lobby*, pp. 65-68.
76 Ibid., pp. 23-48.
77 Ibid., p. 270.
78 Efraim Halevy, *Man in the Shadows: Inside the Middle East crisis with a man who led the Mossad* (New York: 2006), p. 59.
79 Mearsheimer and Walt, *Israel Lobby*, p. 115.
80 Ibid., pp. 129-30, 238-39.
81 Although they stipulate that "it is the specific political agenda that defines the lobby not the religious or ethnic identity of those pushing it" (ibid., pp. 115, 132), if not for blood loyalties it would be hard to account for why American *Jews* comprise the "bulk of the lobby."
82 On the rare occasions when Mearsheimer and Walt do adduce substantiating evidence, it appears inconclusive at best. They recall for example that, in the "famous 'Clean Break' report" (1996), Jewish neoconservatives Douglas Feith, Richard Perle, and David Wurmser urged then-incoming Israeli Prime Minister Benjamin Netanyahu to "'focus on removing Saddam Hussein from power in Iraq—an important Israeli strategic objective in its own right.'" Netanyahu "did *not* implement their advice," the authors continue, "but Feith, Perle and Wurmser were soon advocating that the Bush administration pursue those same goals" (ibid., pp. 130, 239; my emphasis). But couldn't this episode also illustrate that it was *not* Israel's interests that they were promoting?
83 Francis Fukuyama, *America at the Crossroads: Democracy, power, and the neoconservative legacy* (New Haven: 2006), p. 17. Until the summer of 1944 the Soviet Union never faced less than 90 percent of the German army, and even after the Normandy landings the overwhelming bulk of the German army fought on the eastern front. Of the roughly 13.5 million German casualties or prisoners during the war, 10 million occurred on the eastern front. The magnitude of the Soviet burden can be judged from the fact that Britain and the United States together on all fronts (including the Pacific) suffered just under 600,000 casualties while the Soviets lost over 11 million on the eastern front. Clive Ponting, *Armageddon: The reality behind the distortions, myths, lies, and illusions of World War II* (New York: 1995), pp. 96, 157-58. The quoted insight of Fukuyama is of a piece with many others in his book, such as: the Bush administration's policy of "regime change" can be traced back to Socrates (p. 28); "Ronald Reagan was an intellectual . . . he saw more clearly than most [the Soviet

Union's] internal contradictions and weaknesses" (pp. 45-46); "concepts like 'revolution,' 'civil society,' 'state'" originated in "fascism and Marxism-Leninism" (p. 73); and "the best way to study the prospects and limitations of strategies for promoting democracy is to look back at historical efforts the United States has undertaken" (p. 131).

84 Peter Steinfels, *The Neoconservatives: The men who are changing America's politics* (New York: 1979), pp. 46-48 (my emphasis).
85 Ibid., p. 248.
86 Mark Gerson, *The Neoconservative Vision: From the Cold War to the Culture Wars* (New York: 1996), pp. 16-18, 25, 253, 354.
87 Steinfels, *Neoconservatives*, pp. 49-69.
88 Fukuyama, *America*, p. 38.
89 Jacob Heilbrunn, *They Knew They Were Right: The rise of the neocons* (New York: 2008), pp. 78, 80.
90 Steinfels, *Neoconservatives*, pp. 12-13 (emphasis in original).
91 Zeev Maoz, *Defending the Holy Land: A critical analysis of Israel's security and foreign policy* (Ann Arbor: 2006), pp. 235, 484-85, 552. To be sure, the belief that natives only understand force is common to all colonizing and imperial societies. See V. G. Kiernan's magisterial study *The Lords of Human Kind: Black man, yellow man, and white man in an age of empire* (Boston: 1968), esp. pp. 152-53, 165, 225.
92 Norman G. Finkelstein, *Image and Reality of the Israel-Palestine Conflict* (New York: 1995; expanded second paperback edition, 2003), chapter 6.
93 Francis Fukuyama, "The Neoconservative Moment," *National Interest* (Summer 2004; Fukuyama renders Krauthammer's notorious quote in sanitized language); Jonah Goldberg, "Baghdad Delenda Est, Part Two," *National Review* (23 April 2002; quoting Ledeen).
94 Stefan Halper and Jonathan Clarke, *America Alone: The neo-conservatives and the global order* (Cambridge: 2004), p. 19.
95 Mearsheimer and Walt, *Israel Lobby*, pp. 132, 240.
96 Ibid., pp. 281-84, 298-305.
97 Ibid., pp. 337-41. They define "offshore balancing" as the deployment of American military power "only when there are direct threats to vital U.S. interests and only when local actors cannot handle these threats on their own."
98 Ibid., pp. 8-9, 12, 17, 18, 112, 127, 228, 273-74, 278-79, 317-18, 336, 352, 355. AIPAC stands for American Israel Public Affairs Committee.
99 Paul Breines, *Tough Jews: Political fantasies and the moral dilemma of American Jews* (New York: 1992).
100 Noam Chomsky, *Pirates and Emperors: International terrorism in the real world* (New York: 1986), pp. 29-30.
101 Mearsheimer and Walt, *Israel Lobby*, p. 262.
102 Ibid., pp. 231, 233, 249, 252-53.
103 They reject all competing explanations such as its being a war for oil. Ibid., pp. 230-31, 238, 253-55.

104 Ibid., p. 243.
105 Ibid., pp. 238-50.
106 In "early 2002," they report, the Bush administration "was thinking seriously about another war against Iraq" while
> Israeli leaders told U.S. officials . . . Iran was a greater threat. They were not opposed to toppling Saddam, however. . . . Once they realized that the Bush administration was countenancing a bolder scheme, one that called for winning quickly in Iraq and then dealing with Iran and Syria, they began to push vigorously for an American invasion. In short, Israel did not initiate the campaign for war against Iraq. . . . But Israel did join forces with the neoconservatives to help sell the war to the Bush administration and the American people well before the president had made the final decision to invade. . . . The Israelis began their efforts in the spring of 2002 a few months before the Bush administration launched its own campaign to sell the Iraq war to the American public. (ibid., pp. 233-34)

And further on: "there is no question . . . that by August 2002 Israel's leaders . . . were encouraging the Bush administration to launch a war to remove [Saddam] from power" (ibid., p. 235).
107 Mearsheimer and Walt, *Setting the Record Straight*, p. 23.
108 Bob Woodward, *Plan of Attack* (New York: 2004).
109 Craig Unger, *The Fall of the House of Bush: The untold story of how a band of true believers seized the executive branch, started the Iraq war, and still imperils America's future* (New York: 2007), pp. 202-3.
110 Richard A. Clarke, *Against All Enemies: Inside America's war on terror* (New York: 2004), p. 265.
111 Rice, *No Higher*, pp. 187, 197.
112 Donald Rumsfeld, *Known and Unknown: A memoir* (New York: 2011), pp. 435-36.
113 Dick Cheney (with Liz Cheney), *In My Time: A personal and political memoir* (New York: 2011). He only mentions Israel in this context as a possible retaliatory target in the event of a U.S. attack (p. 383).
114 Mearsheimer and Walt, *Israel Lobby*, pp. 55, 235-36.
115 George Tenet, *At the Center of the Storm: My years at the CIA* (New York: 2007). Israeli intelligence did attempt to sway CIA analysts but, because of the known Israeli biases, CIA analysts largely ignored their reports (James Risen, *State of War: The secret history of the CIA and the Bush administration* (New York: 2006), pp. 72-73).
116 Rumsfeld, *Known*, pp. 434-35. He lists the foreign intelligence agencies of Britain, Australia, Spain, Italy, Poland and Egypt as corroborating U.S. assessments.
117 Cheney, *Time*, p. 419. He lists British and German intelligence agencies as corroborating U.S. assessments.
118 Rice, *No Higher*, p. 197. She specifically mentions British intelligence as echoing American assessments.
119 Mearsheimer and Walt, *Israel Lobby*, pp. 238, 245.
120 James Mann, *Rise of the Vulcans: The history of Bush's war cabinet* (New York: 2004).

121 Oddly, even Mearsheimer and Walt imply that Wolfowitz was not fully committed to attacking Iraq and that Israeli intelligence had deceived him (*Israel Lobby*, pp. 245, 251).
122 George Packer, *The Assassin's Gate: America in Iraq* (New York: 2006), pp. 26, 115; cf. Heilbrunn, *They Knew*, p. 234.
123 The same can be said, incidentally, of American negotiators such as Dennis Ross and Aaron David Miller, who are also often accused of a transcendent ethnic attachment to Israel. Before dominating Middle East policymaking in the Clinton administration, Ross was a member of Secretary of State James Baker's inner circle and headed policy planning in the reputedly anti-Semitic George Bush Sr. administration. Miller, a colleague of Ross's during the Clinton years, likewise worked for Bush-Baker. It is indicative of Miller's true loyalties (as well as of his desire to protect the self-image of a "proud Jew") that his memoir *The Much Too Promised Land: America's elusive search for Arab-Israeli peace* (New York: 2008) gives over many effusive—one might say, sycophantic—pages to Baker while scrupulously omitting mention of Baker's widely reported aside, "F*** the Jews. They don't vote for us anyway."
124 Adam Nagourney, "In Tapes, Nixon Rails about Jews and Blacks," *New York Times* (10 December 2010).
125 Ian S. Lustick, *Trapped in the War on Terror* (Philadelphia: 2006), pp. 65-66; by most accounts President Bush was outside the loop (ibid., pp. 54-55).
126 Fukuyama, *America*, p. 4.
127 Mostly in the context of Israel's 2007 attack on an alleged Syrian nuclear reactor, which Cheney supported.
128 Mearsheimer and Walt, *Israel Lobby*, pp. 246-47, 250-53.
129 Rumsfeld, *Known*, p. 417.
130 Cheney was "shrewd, a quick thinker, a good arguer, the best I've ever seen," according to Council on Foreign Relations head Leslie Gelb, and apparently "ruthless" as well. "Rumsfeld was one of the smartest people I'd ever met," State Department policy advisor Aaron David Miller recalled. Far from Wolfowitz duping his superiors, "Rumsfeld's deputy Wolfowitz became his loyal front man," and "Rumsfeld cut Wolfowitz out whenever he felt like it," while Cheney held Wolfowitz in near-contempt. Packer, *Assassin's Gate*, p. 44 (Gelb); Miller, *The Much*, p. 24 ("smartest"); Heilbrunn, *They Knew*, pp. 231, 252 ("front man").
131 Norman Podhoretz, *World War IV: The long struggle against Islamofascism* (New York: 2007), p. 64. Even a broken clock is right twice a day.
132 Cheney, Rumsfeld and Wolfowitz all held key national security posts in the Gerald Ford administration (1974-76). Rumsfeld forged an alliance with the neoconservatives as far back as the 1970s. He colluded with neoconservative Richard Perle to undermine Henry Kissinger's policy of détente, joined the neoconservative "Committee on the Present Danger," and worked with Wolfowitz in 1998 on the Ballistic Missile Threat Commission. Cheney was defense secretary and Wolfowitz his policy chief during George Bush Sr.'s term of office, and Cheney lobbied for Wolfowitz to be defense secretary in Bush Jr.'s administration. When Bush gave Rumsfeld

the Pentagon's top job, Rumsfeld selected his long-time collaborator Wolfowitz for the number two position and fellow neoconservative Douglas J. Feith for the number three position in the Defense Department. (Feith's public career began in 1975 when he went to work for Senator Henry "Scoop" Jackson opposing détente, after which he served in the Reagan administration.) Cheney filled key posts on his small but influential staff with prominent neoconservatives such as Libby, Eric Edelman, and John Hannah. The blueprint for the Bush Doctrine announced soon after September 11 was arguably drawn up already in 1992 by then-Secretary of Defense Cheney alongside Wolfowitz and Libby.

133 Rumsfeld, *Known*, pp. 448-49 (criticizing Powell), 503 (criticizing Richard Armitage), 510 (criticizing Paul L. Bremer), 525-27 (criticizing Rice), 621 (criticizing Andy Card).
134 Ibid., pp. 347 (praising Wolfowitz), 423 (praising Feith). The only partial exception is Rumsfeld's passing criticism of neoconservative Kenneth Adelman (without directly naming him in the text) for predicting before the attack on Iraq that it would be a "cakewalk" (ibid., p. 479).
135 Cheney, *Time*, pp. 407-8 (criticizing Powell and Armitage), 410 (criticizing Bush), 416 (criticizing Tenet), 425 (criticizing Powell), 474-77 (criticizing Rice).
136 Ibid., pp. 235 (praising Wolfowitz, Libby and Edelman), 278 (praising Wolfowitz and Libby).
137 Ibid., p. 408.
138 Hans Blix, *Disarming Iraq* (New York: 2004); Andrew Cockburn, *Rumsfeld: His rise, fall, and catastrophic legacy* (New York: 2007), pp. 145-46; Mohamed ElBaradei, *The Age of Deception: Nuclear diplomacy in treacherous times* (New York: 2011), pp. 48-87; Thomas E. Ricks, *Fiasco: The American military adventure in Iraq* (New York: 2007), pp. 50-55, 61, 92; Risen, *State of War*, pp. 102-24 (quote at p. 119). A curious anomaly is Blix, who headed the International Atomic Energy Agency (IAEA) in the 1990s, and subsequently the United Nations Monitoring, Verification and Inspection Commission (UNMOVIC), which was mandated by the U.N. Security Council to assess the status of Iraq's chemical and biological weapons program and long-range missiles. A respected Swedish-born international civil servant, Blix states in his memoir that just before the 2003 attack his "gut-feelings" were that Saddam still possessed WMD, although he had no evidence to prove it. He reports that Iraq was forthcoming on "process"—e.g., not blocking UNMOVIC's access to sites for inspection—but not on "substance," and he quotes approvingly Rumsfeld's pithy phrase, "the absence of evidence is not the evidence of absence." But Blix also incongruously suggests that, because it had no stockpiles and its records might have been destroyed, Iraq *could not* have been more substantive or proven the absence of WMD (*Disarming*, pp. 11, 102, 112, 113, 116, 137, 194, 213, 247, 257, 264). Blix's harsh report on 27 January 2003 to the U.N. Security Council was widely seen as playing into the hands of the Bush administration and making an attack unstoppable. (He toned down his subsequent reports in February and March 2003 but the die was already cast.) One gets the impression that in his memoir Blix wants to justify his skeptical reporting that facilitated the U.S. attack, while at the same time he is

honest enough to admit that it had no basis, and that an impossible burden of proof might have been placed on Iraq. It is also clear that Blix deeply identifies with the West, deploring Saddam's unprecedented tyranny while crediting the U.S.'s good (if mistaken) faith on Iraq's WMD and even finding some redemptive features in the war. By contrast, Mohamed ElBaradei, an Egyptian who succeeded Blix as head of the IAEA and was responsible in the months prior to the U.S. attack for assessing Iraq's nuclear program, suggests in his memoir that Bush et al. should be prosecuted as war criminals. On the personal motives behind Blix's hostile stance toward Iraq, see ElBaradei, *Age*, pp. 70-72.

139 Lustick, *Trapped in the War*, p. 57 (quote); ElBaradei, *Age*, pp. 72-73. Douglas J. Feith's *War and Decision: Inside the Pentagon at the dawn of the war on terrorism* (New York: 2008) is to date the most ambitious attempt to justify the Iraq war. Feith, who served as Under Secretary of Defense for Policy in the Bush administration, alleges that just before the attack it was "generally believed not only by intelligence and policy officials in the United States, but also at the United Nations and around the world at that time" that Saddam possessed WMD. He omits mention not only of the many skeptics outside and even inside the U.S. government, but also, and crucially, of the broad international consensus that there was no urgency to attack and that U.N. inspections should have been allowed to run their course. His prewar belief that Saddam possessed stockpiles of WMD, Feith asserts, "was consistent with assessments from . . . UN inspectors." But, although UNMOVIC reported that not all of Iraq's WMD could be accounted for, it acknowledged the possibility that they had already been destroyed. There is a big difference between saying that you are sure (Feith) and you are not sure (UNMOVIC) (pp. 225, 312, 314, 491, 514). Hans Blix wondered how the likes of Feith could have had "100-percent certainty about the existence of weapons of mass destruction but zero-percent knowledge about their location" (*Disarming*, p. 156). The U.N. inspectors returned empty-handed from all the sites to which U.S. intelligence pointed them. In general Feith's apologia gets tangled in a knot of fatal contradictions. He alleges that September 11 pointed up the urgency of "regime change" in Iraq because it showed that terrorists might resort to mega-killings if they managed to acquire WMD. But why then did neoconservatives like himself also urge the necessity of "regime change" in Iraq *before* September 11? Feith also purports that Bush was open to a diplomatic solution if Saddam had cooperated with U.N. inspections. But he further claims it was immaterial if (as it turned out) Saddam had no WMD because the heart of Washington's charge sheet and the impetus for launching the war lay elsewhere—i.e., the threat Saddam posed to neighboring states, his links with terrorist groups, his tyrannical regime, his intention eventually to acquire WMD. Isn't Feith then saying that the U.S. would and should have attacked Iraq regardless of how the U.N. inspections panned out? Moreover, if Iraq's possession of WMD "was *not* a cornerstone of our rationale for going to war" and not part of the "logic of rationale for regime change," and the motive behind the war was "far broader than the concerns about WMD stockpiles" (his emphasis), then the fear after September 11 that terrorists might acquire WMD from Iraq couldn't have been the critical impetus of the U.S. attack. Likewise,

what Feith called Saddam's "three T's"—"terrorism," "threats to neighbors," "tyranny"—and "the big picture that Saddam was an aggressor, a shredder of Security Council resolutions, a tyrant who had used WMD to kill his own citizens as well as his neighbors, and a megalomaniacal enemy of the U.S." preexisted September 11, so the al-Qaida attack could not have been the war's precipitant (pp. 228, 336, 338, 346, 474, 520). Feith barely mentions Iraq's threat to Israel as a motive for regime change. It might be discretion or, what is more likely the case, it just did not loom large for him.

140 Halper and Clarke, *America Alone*, p. 14; Lustick, *Trapped in the War*, pp. 49, 56.
141 Rumsfeld, *Known*, pp. 354, 382; Cheney, *Time*, p. 373.
142 Patrick Cockburn, *The Occupation: War and resistance in Iraq* (New York: 2006), pp. 2-3. Unger, *Fall*, p. 182, quotes a close aide to the Vice-President saying that Cheney "wanted to 'do Iraq' because he thought it could be done quickly and easily, and because 'the U.S. could do it essentially alone ... and that an uncomplicated, total victory would set the stage for a landslide reelection in 2004.'" The Bush administration, according to Clarke, relished the prospect of exploiting for partisan politics the war on terrorism and an attack on Iraq. "From within the White House, a decision had been made that in the 2002 congressional elections and in the 2004 reelection, the Republicans would wrap themselves in the flag, saying a vote for them was a vote against the terrorists," he recalled. "'Run on the war' was the direction in 2002. Then [Karl] Rove meant the War on Terror, but they also had in mind another war that they would gin up" (*Against All Enemies*, p. 242). The pervasive belief in the Bush administration that the U.S. would win a swift, easy military victory in Iraq has been widely documented. See Fukuyama, *America*, p. 3; Halper and Clarke, *America Alone*, pp. 92-93; Mann, *Rise*, pp. 34-35; Ricks, *Fiasco*, pp. 13, 36; Unger, *Fall*, pp. 267-68, 313; Woodward, *Plan*, pp. 21, 26, 119, 326. Ricks tellingly notes that Washington's preparation for the attack "resembled a banana republic coup d'état more than a full-scale war plan" (*Fiasco*, p. 128). The public assertions of the Bush administration that Iraq possessed WMD and would not recoil from unleashing them cannot easily be squared with its private conviction that the war would be a "cakewalk." Before the attack Rumsfeld composed a memo, later dubbed the "Parade of Horribles," that sketched 20 worst-case scenarios in the event of war. It too casts doubt on the sincerity of the Bush administration's public avowals. Saddam's use of WMD comes in rather low on Rumsfeld's list (fifteenth) and is remarkably understated for a potential catastrophe of this magnitude: "There could be higher than expected U.S. and coalition deaths from Iraq's use of weapons of mass destruction against coalition forces in Iraq, Kuwait and/or Israel." In his memoir Douglas J. Feith's doesn't even bother to include this particular scenario in his abridged version of Rumsfeld's Parade of Horribles. There has been surprisingly little commentary on what the discrepancy between public dread and private complacency says about the Bush administration's alleged fear that Saddam had amassed WMD. The thirteenth possibility, and apparently more worrisome fear, in Rumsfeld's Parade of Horribles was: "US could fail to find WMD on the ground in Iraq and be unpersuasive to the world."

143 Mearsheimer and Walt, *Israel Lobby*, pp. 229-30.
144 Ibid., p. 246. Halper and Clarke also highlight these preconditions in *America Alone*.
145 Mearsheimer and Walt, *Israel Lobby*, pp. 282, 286, 291-302.
146 Ibid., pp. 234, 248.
147 Gary Dorrien, *Imperial Designs: Neoconservatism and the new Pax Americana* (New York: 2004), pp. 3, 205-6 ("consistently," "maximal"); Gary Dorrien, *The Neoconservative Mind: Politics, culture and the war of ideology* (Philadelphia: 1993), pp. 115-32 ("cesspool" at p. 116). Whereas Kristol himself advocated an alliance with Israel on the grounds that it served American interests in the Middle East, Dorrien enters the caveat that "his own passionate commitment to the survival and well-being of Israel revealed a concern for something more than American national interests" (ibid., p. 129). Yet, how is one to square this "passionate commitment" with the fact that, although a prolific polemicist in the post-World War II ideological wars, Kristol did not author a single article on Israel until after its strategic realignment with the U.S. in June 1967?
148 Mearsheimer and Walt, *Israel Lobby*, pp. 129, 238.
149 Robert Kagan and William Kristol, "Preface," in Kagan and Kristol, eds., *Present Dangers*, p. viii; Donald Kagan, "Strength and Will: A historical perspective," in ibid., p. 339.
150 William Kristol and Robert Kagan, "Introduction: National interest and global responsibility," in ibid., p. 22; James W. Ceaser, "The Great Divide: American interventionism and its opponents," in ibid., p. 41; William J. Bennett, "Morality, Character, and American Foreign Policy," in ibid., pp. 294, 304.
151 Fukuyama, *America*, pp. 13, 61 (cf. p. 100).
152 Ricks, *Fiasco*, p. 8.
153 Paul Wolfowitz, "Statesmanship in the New Century," in Kagan and Kristol, eds., *Present Dangers*, pp. 333-34. It is often alleged that Wolfowitz has distinguished himself by promoting democratic values (Mann, *Rise*, pp. 76, 134-35, 257, but cf. pp. 234, 368; Heilbrunn, *They Knew*, p. 234). His actual record however proves otherwise (Noam Chomsky, *Failed States: The abuse of power and the assault on democracy* (New York: 2006), pp. 133-36).
154 Fukuyama, *America*, pp. 63, 117.
155 Elliott Abrams, "Israel and the 'Peace Process,'" in Kagan and Kristol, eds., *Present Dangers*, p. 238. See also Halper and Clarke, *America Alone*, p. 206.
156 Mearsheimer and Walt, *Israel Lobby*, pp. 230, 238-39, 255.
157 See Introduction.
158 On Israeli support for a U.S. attack on Iraq, see Meron Benvenisti, "Hey Ho, Here Comes The War," *Haaretz* (13 February 2003), Uzi Benziman, "Corridors of Power/O What A Lovely War," *Haaretz* (14 February 2003), Gideon Levy, "A Great Silence Over The Land," *Haaretz* (16 February 2003), Aluf Benn, "Background: Enthusiastic IDF awaits war in Iraq," *Haaretz* (16 February 2003), Aluf Benn, "The Celebrations Have Already Begun," *Haaretz* (20 February 2003), and Mearsheimer and Walt, *Israel Lobby*, pp. 234-37. On Israeli support for an attack on Iran, see Mearsheimer

and Walt, *Israel Lobby*, pp. 291-92, 299-300, and Aluf Benn, "Poll: 71% of Israelis want U.S. to strike Iran if talks fail," *Haaretz* (18 May 2007).
159 Mearsheimer and Walt, *Israel Lobby*, pp. 236-37 (Iraq); Robert S. Wistrich, *A Lethal Obsession: Anti-semitism from antiquity to the global jihad* (New York: 2010), pp. 879-927 (Iran).
160 Jeffrey M. Jones, "Among Religious Groups, Jewish Americans Most Strongly Oppose War," *Gallup News Service* (23 February 2007). Among all Americans an invasion was favored by a 57-37 percent margin. An aggregate of surveys conducted by the Pew Research Center from August 2002 to February 2003 found Jews favoring the war by a 52-32 percent margin while among all Americans the margin supporting an attack was 62-28 percent.
161 Jones, "Among Religious Groups." Benn, "Poll," reports that as of May 2007 "59% of Israelis still believe the war in Iraq was justified, while 36% take the opposite view."
162 American Jewish Committee, *2007 Annual Survey of American Jewish Opinion* (6 November-25 November 2007). See also Allison Hoffman, "Wall Street: The man American Jews hate more than Ahmadinejad," *Jerusalem Post* (18 December 2008). The 2007 American Jewish Committee poll found that nearly 60 percent of American Jews opposed a U.S. attack on Iran "to prevent it from developing nuclear weapons" versus only 35 percent supporting it. But the 2010 AJC *Annual Survey* contrariwise found that 59 percent of American Jews supported a U.S. attack versus 35 percent opposing it. (This poll also found that 70 percent of American Jews supported Israel taking military action against Iran if diplomacy and sanctions failed versus 26 percent opposing it.) It is hard to account for this dramatic reversal in opinion except that by 2010 the prospects in Iraq looked less bleak, so fear of a witch-hunt against Jews faded.
163 Arnold Beichman, *Washington Times* (12 March 1996) (Peres); Jeff Cohen, "TV Blowhard Barks at Iran" (27 November 2006; www.CommonDreams.org) (Netanyahu). For Prime Minister Ehud Olmert's equally colorful language, see Mearsheimer and Walt, *Israel Lobby*, p. 299.
164 Jones, "Among Religious Groups." He goes on to say:
As has been well-established, war support is strongly influenced by one's political leanings—Democrats overwhelmingly oppose the war while Republicans favor it by a similarly wide margin. One might assume that the greater war opposition among Jews is attributable to the group being overwhelmingly Democratic. In this sample, 52% of Jewish people identify as Democrats, and another 20% are independents who say they lean to the Democratic Party.
But a closer analysis of the data show[s] that Jewish war opposition goes beyond their basic political leanings. Jewish people are more likely to oppose the war than non-Jews of the same political persuasion. For example, 89% of Jewish Democrats oppose the Iraq war, compared with 78% of non-Jewish Democrats. The departures are even greater when looking at non-Democrats. Sixty-five percent of non-Democratic Jews oppose the war, compared with just 38% of non-Democrats of all other religious groups.

165 Dana Milbank, "Group Urges Pro-Israel Leaders' Silence on Iraq," *Washington Post* (27 November 2002), Dan Izenberg, "Foreign Ministry Warns Israeli War Fuels US Anti-Semitism," *Jerusalem Post* (10 March 2003), Laurie Goodstein, "Threats and Responses," *New York Times* (15 March 2003), Dana Milbank, "For Israel Lobby Group, War Is Topic A, Quietly," *Washington Post* (1 April 2003), James D. Besser and Larry Cohler-Esses, "Iran-Israel Linkage by Bush Seen as Threat," *New York Jewish Week* (2 April 2006), Jim Lobe, "Jewish Community Worried about Iran Backlash," *InterPress Service* (10 May 2006), Ori Nir, "Groups to Bush: Drop Iran-Israel linkage," *Forward* (12 May 2006), Forward Staff, "Groups Fear Public Backlash over Iran," *Forward* (2 February 2007), Ron Kampeas, "As Jewish Groups Huddle, Quagmire in Iraq Undermines Resolve on Iran," *Jewish Telegraphic Agency* (27 February 2007).

166 It was perhaps more than coincidence that as mostly privileged, Ivy League Jews with no record of military service were being blamed in some quarters for the Iraq debacle, Deborah Dash Moore's book, *G.I. Jews: How World War II changed a generation* (Cambridge: 2004), which documents the combat experience of American Jews, was lavishly praised in reviews and garnered many awards.

167 Jones, "Among Religious Groups."

168 Anti-Defamation League, "ADL Commends President Bush's Message to International Community on Iraq Calling It 'Clear and Forceful'" (12 September 2002), American Jewish Committee, "AJC Lauds Bush on State of Union Message on Terrorism" (7 February 2003), Bill Keller, "Is It Good for the Jews?," *New York Times* (8 March 2003), reporting that "most of the big Jewish organizations . . . are backing war," Ori Nir, "Jewish Groups Press for Iran Sanctions," *Forward* (23 September 2005), Ori Nir, "Groups Push for Sanctions, Fear U.S. Will Falter on Iran," *Forward* (2 September 2006), Nathan Guttman, "Activists Set to Push New Sanctions against Iran," *Forward* (9 March 2007). See also Mearsheimer and Walt, *Israel Lobby*, pp. 292-94, 298, 300-1.

169 Norman G. Finkelstein, *The Holocaust Industry: Reflections on the exploitation of Jewish suffering* (New York: 2000; expanded second paperback edition, 2003), pp. 253-55.

170 Norman G. Finkelstein, *"This Time We Went Too Far": Truth and consequences of the Gaza invasion* (New York: 2010; expanded paperback edition 2011), pp. 32-33, 180-86.

171 "America's Place in the World 2005: Opinion leaders turn cautious, public looks homeward," *Pew Research Center for the People and the Press* (17 November 2005), p. 6.

172 Anthony H. Cordesman, "Israel as a Strategic Liability?," Center for Strategic and International Studies (2 June 2010).

173 "Statement of General David H. Petraeus, U.S. Army Commander, U.S. Central Command, before the Senate Armed Services Committee on the Posture of U.S. Central Command" (16 March 2010).

174 "Media Availability with Secretary Gates and Israeli Defense Minister Barak from the Pentagon" (27 April 2010).

175 Haim Malka, *Crossroads: The future of the U.S.-Israel strategic partnership* (Washington, D.C.: 2011), p. 57.
176 Brookings Institution, *D.C.'s New Guard: What does the next generation of American leaders think?* (Washington, D.C.: 2011).
177 Mearsheimer and Walt, *Israel Lobby*, pp. 236-38. The *Forward* reported in mid-September 2002 that Israel's was the "only" government "actively supporting the Bush administration's goal of Iraqi regime change."
178 Anshel Pfeffer, "US Jewish Leader Worried by Thrust of White House Campaigns," *Haaretz* (13 February 2008).
179 "Global Peace Index: Israel hits rock bottom" (20 April 2008; www.ynetnews.com/articles/0,7340,L-3545840,00.html); "Israel Ranked 141 in Global Peace Index," *Jerusalem Post* (3 June 2009); "Israel is World's Fourth Most Dangerous Country, Study says," *Haaretz* (3 June 2009). When the index was expanded in 2011 to 153 countries Israel ranked the ninth most violent (www.visionofhumanity.org/wp-content/uploads/2011/05/2011-GPI-Results-Report-Final.pdf).
180 Shmuel Rosner, "Rosner's Blog: Bush, the divider," *Haaretz* (4 February 2007).
181 Ofira Seliktar, *Divided We Stand: American Jews, Israel, and the peace process* (Westport, CT: 2002), p. 81, citing poll results that "Jews had regularly rated Christian fundamentalists as a group most inimical to them."

INTRODUCTION TO PART III
1 It is also true that, once the media juggernaut gains momentum, and because of the snowballing effect, as well as because of personal, political or professional calculation, otherwise serious scholars will abandon their critical faculties and endorse such pseudo-scholarly literature that they couldn't possibly have read closely, if at all.
2 This writer has played some role in exposing acclaimed pseudo-scholarship, such as Joan Peters's *From Time Immemorial: The origins of the Arab-Jewish conflict over Palestine* (New York: 1984), Daniel Jonah Goldhagen's *Hitler's Willing Executioners: Ordinary Germans and the Holocaust* (New York: 1996), and Alan Dershowitz's *The Case for Israel* (Hoboken, NJ: 2003).

PART III/CHAPTER FIVE
1 Among others, left-wing Israeli lawyers Felicia Langer and Lea Tsemel and Hebrew University chemistry professor Israel Shahak.
2 Benny Morris, *Righteous Victims: A history of the Zionist-Arab conflict, 1881-2001* (New York: 2001), pp. 341-43, 568, 587, 600-1; Tom Segev, *1967: Israel, the war, and the year that transformed the Middle East* (New York: 2007), pp. 475, 517.
3 Amnesty International, *Combating Torture* (London: 2003), section 2.2.
4 Amnesty International, *Report and Recommendations of an Amnesty International Mission to the Government of the State of Israel 3-7 June 1979, Including the Government's Response and Amnesty International Comments* (London: 1980); Amnesty International, *Torture in the Eighties* (London: 1984), pp. 233-34.

5 Norman G. Finkelstein, *Beyond Chutzpah: On the misuse of anti-Semitism and the abuse of history* (Berkeley: 2005; expanded paperback edition, 2008), pp. 144ff.
6 Ibid., pp. 32, 40, 93, 156-58.
7 Human Rights Watch, *Fatal Strikes: Israel's indiscriminate attacks against civilians in Lebanon* (August 2006). See also Amnesty International, *Deliberate Destruction or "Collateral Damage"? Israeli attacks on civilian infrastructure* (23 August 2006).
8 Alan M. Dershowitz, "First Word: What is 'Human Rights Watch' watching?," *Jerusalem Post* (23 August 2006), Abraham Foxman, "No Accident," *New York Sun* (2 August 2006), Martin Peretz, *New Republic* website (6 August 2006). This claque of distinguished apologists also includes liberal icons such as Michael Walzer, who opined during Israel's 2006 offensive, "From a moral perspective, Israel has mostly been fighting legitimately." Ori Nir, "Israeli Military Policy Under Fire after Qana Attack," *Forward* (4 August 2006); see also Michael Walzer, "War Fair," *New Republic* (31 July 2006).
9 Aryeh Neier, "The Attack on Human Rights Watch," *New York Review of Books* (2 November 2006). See also Sarah Leah Whitson, "Armchair Sleuths," *Jerusalem Post* (7 September 2006), and Ian Seiderman, "Right of Reply: Biased against Israel? Not at all," *Jerusalem Post* (11 September 2006).
10 New York: 2006.
11 Michael Ben-Yair, "The War's Seventh Day," *Haaretz* (2 March 2002); Shulamit Aloni, "Indeed, There is Apartheid in Israel" (http://www.ynet.co.il/articles/0,7340,L-3346283,00.html); Roee Nahmias, "'Israeli Terror is Worse,'" *Yediot Ahronot* (29 July 2005) (Aloni); Yossi Sarid, "Yes, It is Apartheid," *Haaretz* (24 April 2008), Meron Benvenisti, "Founding a Binational State," *Haaretz* (22 April 2004); Dinah A. Spritzer, "British Zionists Drop Haaretz Columnist," *Jewish Telegraphic Agency* (8 August 2007) (Rubinstein); Ezra HaLevi, "Haaretz Editor Refuses to Retract Israel Apartheid Statements" (30 July 2008; www.israelnationalnews.com/News/News.aspx/123596) (Rubinstein); Chris McGreal, "Worlds Apart: Israel, Palestine and apartheid" and "Brothers In Arms: Israel's secret pact with Pretoria," *Guardian* (6 February 2006, 7 February 2006) (Tutu, Liel); B'Tselem (Israeli Information Center for Human Rights in the Occupied Territories), *Forbidden Roads: Israel's discriminatory road regime in the West Bank* (August 2004), p. 3; Association for Civil Rights in Israel, *The State of Human Rights in Israel and the Occupied Territories, 2008 Report*, p. 17; "The Problem That Disappeared," *Haaretz* (11 September 2006); "Where Is The Occupation?," *Haaretz* (7 October 2007); "Our Debt to Jimmy Carter," *Haaretz* (15 April 2008); Amos Schocken, "Citizenship Law Makes Israel an Apartheid State," *Haaretz* (28 June 2008); John Dugard, "Apartheid and Occupation under International Law," *Hisham B. Sharabi Memorial Lecture* (30 March 2009). See also Joseph Lelyveld, "Jimmy Carter and Apartheid," *New York Review of Books* (29 March 2007).
12 Gershom Gorenberg, "Road Map to Grand Apartheid? Ariel Sharon's South African inspiration," *American Prospect* (3 July 2003); Akiva Eldar, "Sharon's Bantustans Are Far from Copenhagen's Hope," *Haaretz* (13 May 2003).

13 Norman G. Finkelstein, *"This Time We Went Too Far": Truth and consequences of the Gaza invasion* (New York: 2010; expanded paperback edition, 2011), p. 127.
14 New York: 2006.
15 New York: 1998.
16 *Prisoners*, pp. 13, 23, 25, 154.
17 Ibid., pp. 14-15.
18 Ibid., p. 126.
19 Amnesty International annual reports, 1989, 1990, 1991 (London).
20 *Prisoners*, pp. 120, 173.
21 Ibid., pp. 153, 113.
22 Ibid., p. 145.
23 Ibid., pp. 210-12.
24 Ari Shavit, "On Gaza Beach," *New York Review of Books* (18 July 1991).
25 *Prisoners*, p. 127.
26 Keeping to stereotypes Goldberg depicts only one Sephardic Jew as an appealing personality (ibid., p. 145) whereas the beautiful Israeli is "the blond son of a German Jew" (ibid., p. 118).
27 Ibid., pp. 118, 211.
28 Ibid., p. 131.
29 Amnesty International annual reports, 1991, 1992, 1993, 1994 (London); B'Tselem (Israeli Information Center for Human Rights in the Occupied Territories), *Legislation Allowing for the Use of Physical Force and Mental Coercion in Interrogation by the General Security Service*, position paper (Jerusalem: 2000); Human Rights Watch, *Israel's Interrogation of Palestinians from the Occupied Territories* (New York: 1994). For Israel's "ticking-bomb" alibi to justify torture, see Finkelstein, *Beyond Chutzpah*, pp. 162-63, 165.
30 *Prisoners*, p. 213.
31 Amnesty International, *The Military Justice System in the Occupied Territories: Detention, interrogation and trial procedures* (London: July 1991).
32 *Prisoners*, p. 15.
33 B'Tselem, *The Interrogation of Palestinians during the Intifada: Ill-treatment, "moderate physical pressure" or torture?* (Jerusalem: 1991).
34 *Prisoners*, p. 109; cf. p. 114, where he describes four Palestinians locked "in a space fit, at most, for two small dogs."
35 Ibid., p. 35.
36 Ibid., pp. 117-18.
37 According to Goldberg, Palestinians were "predisposed to martyrdom" only for the "nearest television cameras... in the cause of public relations" (ibid., p. 109).
38 Ibid., p. 140; cf. pp. 106, 160.
39 In passing he acknowledges as a singular exception the "Communist party (true outliers in the Palestinian revolution, because they were committed to nonviolent protest)" (ibid., p. 23).
40 Gene Sharp, "The Intifadah and Nonviolent Struggle," *Journal of Palestine Studies* (Autumn 1989), pp. 3, 7. He estimated "nonviolent forms of struggle" at "85 percent of

the total resistance," and that "the 15 percent or so of the uprising that is constituted by low-level violence involves chiefly stone throwing" (p. 7). Sharp was the director of the Program on Nonviolent Sanctions at Harvard University's Center for International Affairs and president of the Albert Einstein Institution, a research foundation on nonviolence. He is now credited—exaggeratedly, it would appear—with inspiring the nonviolent methods of the Arab Spring.

41 Mary Elizabeth King, *A Quiet Revolution: The first Palestinian intifada and nonviolent resistance* (New York: 2007), pp. 232-33; Zeev Schiff and Ehud Yaari, *Intifada: The Palestinian uprising—Israel's third front* (New York: 1989), pp. 240-66 ("resilient," "spring" at p. 248, "seeds" at p. 250, "outlawed" and "chickens" at p. 251). See also Norman G. Finkelstein, *The Rise and Fall of Palestine: A personal account of the intifada years* (Minneapolis, MN: 1996), pp. 52-53.

42 B'Tselem, *Detained Without Trial: Administrative detention in the Occupied Territories since the beginning of the intifada* (Jerusalem: 1992); Amnesty International, *Military Justice System in the Occupied Territories*.

43 *Prisoners*, pp. 300-1.

44 For the actual circumstances of Corrie's death, see Finkelstein, *Beyond Chutzpah*, pp. 120-21.

45 *Prisoners*, p. 134.

46 Ibid., pp. 101, 109, 130, 161.

47 Sharp, "The Intifadah and Nonviolent Struggle," p. 8.

48 Zeev Maoz, *Defending the Holy Land: A critical analysis of Israel's security and foreign policy* (Ann Arbor: 2006), p. 264; B'Tselem, *Statistics* (http://www.btselem.org/english/Statistics/First_Intifada_Tables.asp), lists 1,162 Palestinians (of whom 254 were minors) killed by Israelis as against 160 Israelis (of whom 5 were minors) killed by Palestinians; Amnesty International annual reports, 1989, 1990 (London). The intifada remained overwhelmingly nonviolent until well into its third year in mid-1990, "and even after that, the uprising did not exhibit organized violence" (King, *Quiet Revolution*, p. 258).

49 *Prisoners*, p. 187.

50 B'Tselem, *The Use of Firearms* (Jerusalem: 1990); Middle East Watch, *The Israeli Army and the Intifada* (New York: 1990); Michal Sela, "The War of Flags," *Davar* (24 October 1990).

51 Amnesty International annual report, 1990 (London); Anne Elizabeth Nixon, *The Status of Palestinian Children during the Uprising* (New York: 1990).

52 *Prisoners*, p. 104. When recalling much later in the book Prime Minister Yitzhak Rabin's assassination Goldberg mentions in passing that Rabin "famously ordered his soldiers to 'break the arms and legs' of the Palestinians" (ibid., p. 180).

53 Ibid., p. 110.

54 B'Tselem, "House Demolitions as Punishment" (http://www.btselem.org/english/Punitive_Demolitions/Statistics_Since_1987.asp); B'Tselem, *House Demolition and Sealing as a Form of Punishment in the West Bank and Gaza Strip, Follow-up Report* (Jerusalem: 1990); *Human Rights Watch World Report 1992* (New York).

55 *Prisoners*, pp. 164-66.

56 The death of a popular Palestinian leader in an internecine feud likewise caused Goldberg to ponder: "How were we supposed to make peace with people who murder so many of their heroes?" (ibid., p. 276). The assassination of Prime Minister Rabin by one of "his own," however, prompts no such musings in Goldberg's mind.
57 Ibid., pp. 33, 105, 133, 169.
58 Ibid., p. 204; emphasis in original.
59 Ibid., p. 160.
60 See Paul Breines, *Tough Jews: Political fantasies and the moral dilemma of American Jewry* (New York: 1990).
61 *Prisoners*, pp. 50-51. ".22s" is an allusion to the slogan of Jewish Defense League leader Meir Kahane, "Every Jew a .22."
62 Ibid., pp. 89-91.
63 Ibid., pp. 8, 244-45.
64 Ibid., pp. 34, 157-58.
65 Ibid., p. 168.
66 Ibid., p. 253.
67 Martin van Creveld, *The Sword and the Olive: A critical history of the Israeli Defense Force* (New York: 1998), pp. 123 ("unique"), 125 ("warrior-settlers," "fighter"), 154 ("military operation"), 273 ("laboratory").
68 Maoz, *Defending the Holy Land*, pp. 581-96 ("key element" at p. 583, "siege mentality" at p. 584, "militarism" at p. 587).
69 *Prisoners*, pp. 7, 167.
70 Ibid., p. 107.
71 Ibid., p. 140. It would appear that Goldberg adapted this argument from Bertrand Russell, who had maintained that nonviolent civil disobedience was a viable strategy in British India but not Hitlerite Germany because, whereas the sensibilities of British officials could never condone the force needed to quell it, the Nazis had no comparable scruples (Bertrand Russell, *Autobiography* (New York: 1998), p. 431).
72 Schiff and Yaari, *Intifada*, p. 117.
73 King, *Quiet Revolution*, pp. 127-64 (Awad); Joel Brinkley, "Majority in Israel Oppose P.L.O. Talks Now, Poll Shows," *New York Times* (2 April 1989).
74 The analogy is quite close, while Goldberg's anti-German slur is groundless. See Norman G. Finkelstein and Ruth Bettina Birn, *A Nation on Trial: The Goldhagen thesis and historical truth* (New York: 1998), pp. 35-54. Popular German opposition to Kristallnacht sprang from both revulsion and embarrassment.
75 Amnesty International, *Combating Torture*, section 2.2.
76 Norman G. Finkelstein, *What Gandhi Says: About nonviolence, resistance and courage* (New York: 2012).
77 *Prisoners*, pp. 268, 271, 300.
78 Ibid., pp. 8, 186, 256-57, 308.
79 Ibid., p. 6.
80 Shlomo Ben-Ami, *Scars of War, Wounds of Peace: The Israeli-Arab tragedy* (New York: 2006), p. 267; cf. Maoz, *Defending the Holy Land*, p. 263. B'Tselem, *Statistics—Fatalities*, 29 September 2000—31 December 2006 (http://www.btselem.org/

English/Statistics/Casualties.asp; for 2006 see http://www.btselem.org/english/Press_Releases/20061228.asp). Finkelstein, *Beyond Chutzpah*, pp. 96-98. The figures on the second intifada refer to the period ending when Goldberg's book was published in 2006. The first Palestinian terrorist attack occurred on 22 November 2000, while the next—which was the first Hamas suicide attack in the second intifada—occurred on 4 March 2001.

81 *Prisoners*, p. 7.
82 Finkelstein, *Beyond Chutzpah*, p. 105. Asked how a pilot felt releasing a one-ton bomb over a residential neighborhood, Halutz replied: "I feel a slight ping in the aircraft, the result of releasing the bomb. It passes a second later, and that's it. That's what I feel."
83 *Prisoners*, p. 275; emphasis in original.
84 Howard Friel and Richard Falk, *Israel-Palestine on Record: How the* New York Times *misreports conflict in the Middle East* (New York: 2007), pp. 48-49 (citing Defense for Children International).
85 Human Rights Watch, *Investigation into the Unlawful Use of Force in the West Bank, Gaza Strip and Northern Israel* (New York: 2000); Amnesty International, *Excessive Use of Lethal Force* (London: 2000); B'Tselem, *Trigger Happy: Unjustified shooting and violation of the open-fire regulations during the al-Aqsa intifada* (Jerusalem: 2002). Yoram Dinstein, *The Conduct of Hostilities under the Law of International Armed Conflict* (Cambridge: 2004), p. 117. The internal quote is from the *International Review of the Red Cross* (emphasis in original).
86 Chris McGreal, "Not Guilty: The Israeli captain who put 17 bullets into a Palestinian schoolgirl," *Guardian* (16 November 2005), Amos Harel, "IDF Officer Cleared in Death of Gaza Girl to Receive Compensation from State," *Haaretz* (22 March 2006).
87 *Prisoners*, p. 281.
88 Human Rights Watch, *Jenin: IDF military operations* (New York: 2002); Amnesty International, *Shielded from Scrutiny: IDF violations in Jenin and Nablus* (London: 2002); Amnesty International, *Under the Rubble: House demolitions and destruction of land and property* (London: 2004). As these reports note, the initial alarums of a large-scale massacre in Jenin were due to the massiveness of Israel's missile assault coupled with its denials of media access and its own military briefings of "hundreds" killed.
89 *Prisoners*, pp. 257, 308.
90 Public Committee against Torture in Israel and LAW (The Palestinian Society for the Protection of Human Rights), *The Assassination Policy of the State of Israel* (May 2002). (See PCATI website, www.stoptorture.org.il/eng, for current statistics.) Amnesty International, *Israel Must End Its Policy of Assassinations* (London: 2003).
91 Human Rights Watch, *In a Dark Hour: The use of civilians during IDF arrest operations* (New York: 2002). B'Tselem, *Human Shield: Use of Palestinian civilians as human shields in violation of High Court of Justice order* (Jerusalem: 2002).
92 *Prisoners*, pp. 17, 183.
93 Maoz, *Defending the Holy Land*, p. 287. Maoz extensively documents how Israel used this strategy of violent provocations to goad Egypt into war in 1956 and to justify its

attack on Lebanon in 1982. Whereas Goldberg asserts that Israel's 1982 invasion of Lebanon "was Israel's first true war of choice" (*Prisoners*, p. 60), Maoz sharply disputes this as well. See Chapter Seven below.
94 *Prisoners*, pp. 106, 135.
95 Ibid., pp. 204, 228.
96 Ibid., p. 196.
97 Ibid., p. 41. Goldberg also claims not to have known "until reaching college" in the 1980s "that blacks and Jews were supposed to despise each other" (ibid., p. 49). It would mean that, although his parents were members of Albert Shanker's United Federation of Teachers in 1968, he never heard about the historic New York City teachers' strike of 1968 that pitted the predominantly Jewish teachers union headed by Shanker against Black activists struggling for community control, shutting down the city's school system for months and poisoning Black-Jewish relations for decades. See Jerald E. Podair, *The Strike That Changed New York: Blacks, whites, and the Ocean Hill-Brownsville crisis* (New Haven: 2002).
98 *Prisoners*, p. 45; emphasis in original.
99 Ibid., pp. 43-46.
100 Ibid., p. 179.
101 Ibid., p. 48.
102 Ibid.
103 Ibid., pp. 64-68.
104 Ibid., pp. 47, 87.
105 Ibid., p. 111.
106 Ibid., p. 27.
107 Ibid., p. 116.
108 Ibid., p. 105.
109 Ibid., p. 109.
110 Ibid., p. 121.
111 Ibid., p. 281. Goldberg notes, however, that this sensibility dulled after a "suicide bomber penetrated the screen of checkpoints around Jerusalem and committed murder." He seems not to have noticed that "virtually all" the checkpoints, blocked roads, etc. are "located *inside* the West Bank—*not between* the West Bank and Israel," and "are imposed on Palestinians *because* they are Palestinians and in order to benefit the Israeli settlers whose presence in the occupied West Bank violates international law" (Amnesty International, *Enduring Occupation: Palestinians under siege in the West Bank* (June 2007), p. 3; emphases in original). See also B'Tselem (Israeli Information Center for Human Rights in the Occupied Territories), *Ground to a Halt: Denial of Palestinians' freedom of movement in the West Bank* (August 2007), which concludes that "chief among [Israel's] objectives is the desire to control and regulate Palestinians' movements so as to separate them from settlers and other Israelis on West Bank roads" (p. 93); Association for Civil Rights in Israel, *The State of Human Rights in Israel and the Occupied Territories, 2008 Report*, pp. 34-35; and United Nations, *The Humanitarian Monitor* (February 2009), p. 1.
112 *Prisoners*, p. 306.

113 Ibid., p. 145.
114 Ibid., p. 311. Again, he quickly enters a caveat, "I recognize that even this would not satisfy the men of Hamas and their rise was unstoppable." But it almost certainly would have affected Hamas operations, insofar as, in Ben-Ami's words, a "fatal symmetry" existed "between settlements and terrorism" (*Scars of War*, pp. 212, 235, 296).
115 *Prisoners*, p. 312.
116 Ibid., p. 150.
117 Ibid., p. 175.
118 Ibid., p. 263.
119 Ibid., p. 275.
120 Ibid., p. 287.
121 Ibid., p. 303.
122 See Chapter Two.

PART III/CHAPTER SIX

1 For another instance of HRW's unprincipled retreat in the face of attacks by the Israel lobby, see Norman G. Finkelstein, *"This Time We Went Too Far": Truth and consequences of the Gaza invasion* (New York: 2010, expanded paperback edition, 2011), pp. 153-56.
2 Benjamin S. Lambeth, *Air Operations in Israel's War against Hezbollah: Learning from Lebanon and getting it right in Gaza* (Arlington, VA: 2011), p. 97.
3 Human Rights Watch, "Israel: Investigate attack on civilians in Lebanon" (17 July 2006). An HRW statement on 24 July regarding Israel's use of cluster munitions merely observed, "They should never be used in populated areas" ("Israeli Cluster Munitions Hit Civilians in Lebanon").
4 Human Rights Watch, "Lebanon: Hezbollah rocket attacks on Haifa designed to kill civilians" (18 July 2006).
5 HRW perhaps calculated that issuing a report after the war was over would not hamper Israel's assault and accordingly not evoke as harsh a reaction from the Israel lobby.
6 An Israeli air strike on a three-story building in south Lebanon left 28 civilians dead, including 16 children.
7 Human Rights Watch, "Indiscriminate Bombing in Lebanon a War Crime" (30 July 2006).
8 Aryeh Neier, "The Attack on Human Rights Watch," *New York Review of Books* (2 November 2006). See Chapter Five.
9 *Report of the Special Rapporteur John Dugard on the Situation of Human Rights in the Palestinian Territories Occupied since 1967* (29 January 2007).
10 Human Rights Watch, "OPT: Civilians must not be used to shield homes against military attacks" (22 November 2006). HRW justified the delay in issuing a report on Lebanon condemning Israel for war crimes on the ground of needing more time to conduct its own on-the-spot investigation. Yet it rushed to condemn Palestinians

of a "war crime" without even the pretext of an investigation, basing itself instead on "media reports." See Norman G. Finkelstein, "Human Rights Watch Must Retract Its Shameful Press Release," *Counterpunch* (29 November 2006; http://www.norman finkelstein.com/article.php?pg=11&ar=705).

11 "Human Rights Watch Statement on our November 22 Press Release" (16 December 2006). Dugard, *Report of the Special Rapporteur*, observed, "It is difficult to categorize such [Palestinian] conduct as a war crime, as originally suggested by Human Rights Watch.... Voluntary, collective action of this kind can at most be categorized as an act of civil disobedience against the occupying Power."

12 *Fatal Strikes*, pp. 1-2.

13 *Why They Died* [hereafter: *WTD*], pp. 90, 175. There was also passing reference in *Civilians Under Assault* [hereafter: *CUA*] that in some cases "Israel deliberately targeted civilians merely because of their political or social association with Hezbollah" (p. 6).

14 *WTD*, p. 18. It noted that in one incident fewer Lebanese civilians were killed than originally reported, and that in a second incident Hezbollah fighters had earlier been nearby a Lebanese village targeted by Israel.

15 HRW provided a minimum figure in *Why They Died* of 1,109 Lebanese deaths, noting that "it is nearly certain that there are many more cases of civilian deaths that are not included in this report or reported elsewhere" (pp. 79-80). Lebanese authorities generally put the total killed at around 1,200 (William Arkin, *Divining Victory: Airpower in the 2006 Israel-Hezbollah war* (Maxwell Air Force Base, AL: 2007), p. 98).

16 HRW cited in *Why They Died* the figure of 250 (pp. 76, 79). A U.S. military study and independent researchers have put the number at about 180; see Mitchell Prothero, "Hizbollah Builds Up Covert Army for a New Assault against Israel," *Observer* (27 April 2008), and Alastair Crooke and Mark Perry, "How Hezbollah Defeated Israel; Part 2, Winning the Ground War," *Asia Times* (13 October 2006).

17 *CUA*, p. 117.

18 Sarah Leah Whitson, director of Human Rights Watch's Middle East and North Africa division, dismissed the lopsided Lebanese death toll on the ground that more Israelis would have died *if* they had not taken shelter; see Hassan M. Fattah, "Rights Group Accuses Hezbollah of Indiscriminate Attacks on Civilians in Israel War," *New York Times* (31 August 2007). But by this logic still more Lebanese would have been killed *if* they had not fled the south *en masse* before Israel indiscriminately assaulted it.

19 Amnesty International, *Deliberate Destruction or "Collateral Damage"? Israeli attacks on civilian infrastructure* (August 2006). Augustus Richard Norton, *Hezbollah: A short history* (Princeton: 2007), reports that "material losses were considerable, totaling approximately $500 million in Israel and about $4 billion in Lebanon, which saw the undoing of fifteen years of post-civil war construction" (p. 142). Arkin, *Divining Victory*, alleges that the media depiction of Israel's assault on Lebanon exaggerated and falsified its destructiveness (pp. 18, 76-77) and that the Hezbollah rocket attacks on Israel were "virtually absent from this picture ... nonexistent" (p. xxi). The latter assertion is patently absurd while he provides scant, trivial evidence of misreporting

(pp. 13-14, 70) and himself concedes that "the accumulation of destruction in Lebanon in just 34 days was unprecedented," and "Israel . . . chose to destroy as much as it could in as short a period of time as possible" (pp. 107, 156). Lambeth, *Air Operations*, mostly recycles Israeli boilerplate, such as "every target selected by the IDF and ultimately struck during the counteroffensive's 34-day course was first double-checked by campaign planners and duly vetted by IAF lawyers to ensure that there was a military justification for attacking it and that all attacks were duly conducted in accordance with binding international laws of armed conflict" (p. 158). He then goes on to observe in passing, however, that "Some Lebanese villages reportedly looked as though they had been hit by an earthquake" (p. 175).

20 *CUA*, p. 47; *WTD*, pp. 11-12. A subsequent HRW study (see below) stated that as many as 4.6 million cluster submunitions were dropped on Lebanon during the war.
21 *CUA*, pp. 5, 49.
22 Ibid., pp. 9-10, 30, 34.
23 Ibid., pp. 9, 49. The passage on p. 49 reads in full:
> In some cases, Hezbollah rockets hit a civilian object, sometimes repeatedly, but the presence in the vicinity of a military objective prevented a conclusion that the civilian object was the intended target. Even so, most of these attacks were indiscriminate in that Hezbollah fired unguided rockets that were incapable of being aimed so that they could distinguish between a military target and civilians. As such, the attacks constituted serious violations of the laws of war.
24 During the 1991 Gulf War, HRW condemned Iraq for Scud missile attacks that struck military targets because "the direct hit does not alter the indiscriminate nature of the weapon used" (Middle East Watch, *Needless Deaths in the Gulf War* (New York: 1991), pp. 382-83, 395-96).
25 *CUA*, p. 62.
26 Ibid., pp. 14-15.
27 *WTD*, pp. 4, 70.
28 HRW justified such an inequity partly on the ground that states would have no incentive to develop precision weapons in the absence of the laws of war prohibiting indiscriminate attacks (*CUA*, p. 15). Leaving aside that this creates an unholy alliance between human rights organizations and munitions-makers (the latter hawking their advanced wares as mandated by the former), states would still have powerful incentives to seek highly discriminate weapons in order to avoid protracted and destructive warfare: for example the U.S.'s precision missile attack to "take out" Saddam Hussein at the start of the 2003 Iraq war to avoid a ground offensive.
29 Ibid., p. 36.
30 Ibid., pp. 80-81, 88. The report of a U.N. "Mission to Lebanon and Israel" likewise concluded, "In the absence of a plausible military target within 1 km of [Nahariya] hospital, this would seem to suggest illegal targeting of a civilian building." Unlike HRW, however, the Mission did not issue a blanket condemnation of all Hezbollah rockets as being indiscriminate weapons, and mere use of any of them in populated areas as a violation of the laws of war. It suggested that the legality of Hezbollah attacks had to

be evaluated on a case-by-case basis, although "Hezbollah's extensive use of Katyusha rockets loaded with lethal anti-personnel ball bearings fired towards heavily populated civilian areas constitutes a clear violation of humanitarian law." "Overall, there emerges a clear picture," the report concluded, "of Hezbollah attacks on Israeli civilians and civilian buildings and infrastructure in violation of the applicable norms of international humanitarian law, and in many instances of the prohibition on indiscriminate attacks and of the principle of distinction." It also concluded that "serious violations of both human rights and humanitarian laws have been committed by Israel ... in many instances, Israel violated its legal obligations to distinguish between military and civilian objectives; to fully apply the principle of proportionality; and to take all feasible precautions to minimize injury to civilians and damage to civilian objects." United Nations General Assembly, *Implementation of General Assembly Resolution 60/251 of 15 March 2006 Entitled "Human Rights Council": Mission to Lebanon and Israel* (2 October 2006), paras. 72-75, 99, 100, 106(b). For further evidence of the accuracy of Hezbollah rockets, see Lambeth, *Air Operations*, pp. 137-38.
31 *CUA*, pp. 95, 105.
32 Contrariwise, HRW alleged that Hezbollah could only aim its unguided artillery rockets with enough accuracy to target "a town or even a neighborhood with some measure of reliability," and that the most common rocket used by Hezbollah was "only accurate within a rectangle of 336 meters by 160 meters" (ibid., pp. 34-35).
33 Ibid., pp. 4, 16-17.
34 Ibid., p. 11.
35 Ibid., p. 10. Mission to Lebanon and Israel, para. 71; Arkin, *Divining Victory*, p. 57.
36 Arab Association for Human Rights, *Civilians in Danger: The location of temporary and permanent military installations close to Arab communities during the Second Lebanon War* (Nazareth: December 2007), pp. 23-24.
37 *CUA*, pp. 10, 30, 95-96.
38 Ibid., pp. 37-44.
39 Ibid., pp. 6, 96 97; for a sampling of what HRW gratuitously called these "self-serving" statements, cf. ibid., pp. 11-14, 97-106, and Mission to Lebanon and Israel, p. 34n86.
40 *CUA*, pp. 7, 24, 104, 106.
41 Jean-Marie Henckaerts and Louise Doswald-Beck, *Customary International Humanitarian Law, Volume I: Rules* (Cambridge: 2005), p. 523. It goes on to enter the caveat that "there appears, at a minimum, to exist a trend in favor of prohibiting such reprisals." Although not in the context of belligerent reprisals, HRW cited in its reports two other standard authorities on the laws of war, A. P. V. Rogers, *Law on the Battlefield*, second edition (Manchester: 2004), and Yoram Dinstein, *The Conduct of Hostilities under the Law of International Armed Conflict* (Cambridge: 2004). Both of these authors also deny the existence of an absolute prohibition on belligerent reprisals against civilians (Rogers, p. 235; Dinstein, p. 226).
42 See however Nasrallah's defense of Hezbollah's belligerent reprisals in Nicholas Noe, ed., *Voice of Hezbollah: The statements of Sayyed Hassan Nasrallah* (London: 2007),

pp. 104-7, 154; see also Naim Qassem, *Hizbullah: The story from within* (London: 2005), pp. 74, 109 (Qassem is the party's Deputy Secretary-General).
43 See http://hrw.org/english/docs/1999/06/26/isrlpa925.htm, and http://hrw.org/english/docs/2000/05/06/isrlpa542.htm.
44 *CUA*, pp. 8, 103.
45 *WTD*, pp. 67-69. For sharp criticism of the Israeli leaflets, see United Nations General Assembly, *Implementation of General Assembly resolution 60/251 of 15 March 2006 Entitled "Human Rights Council": Report of the Commission of Inquiry on Lebanon pursuant to Human Rights Council resolution S-2/1* (23 November 2006) [hereafter: Commission of Inquiry], paras. 28, 149-61. (This report should not be confused with the prior report of the Mission to Lebanon and Israel.)
46 *CUA*, pp. 99-101.
47 Ibid., p. 101.
48 Mission to Lebanon and Israel, paras. 70, 71.
49 Human Rights Watch, *Civilian Pawns: Laws of war violations and the use of weapons on the Israel-Lebanon border* (New York: 1996); see especially the chronology HRW assembled for the period 1993-1996, where a Hezbollah attack on the IDF/SLA (South Lebanon Army, an Israeli mercenary force) was typically followed by an Israeli strike on Lebanese civilians, or an IDF/SLA strike on Lebanese civilians provoked a Hezbollah missile barrage against northern Israel. See also Norton, *Hezbollah*, pp. 77, 86, and Zeev Maoz, *Defending the Holy Land: A critical analysis of Israel's security and foreign policy* (Ann Arbor: 2006), pp. 213-14, 224-25, 252.
50 For the period prior to Israel's May 2000 withdrawal from Lebanon, see Judith Palmer Harik, *Hezbollah: The changing face of terrorism* (London: 2004), pp. 167-68, citing Prime Minister Yitzhak Rabin to the effect that Hezbollah targeted Israeli civilians only after "provocation from the Israeli army," and citing Israeli General Shlomo Gazit, "We bombed and shelled many targets in Lebanon, including some far to the north [of Israel's so-called security zone]. Only then did Hezbollah retaliate by shelling some Israeli localities—with no casualties."
51 According to HRW, "it was not until July 16 that Hezbollah began regularly hitting Haifa." Israel alleged that one Hezbollah rocket hit Haifa on 13 July, causing "no injuries or major damage," but Hezbollah denied it (*CUA*, pp. 54-55, 100-1; Arkin, *Divining Victory*, pp. 14-15).
52 *WTD*, p. 39.
53 See *Civilian Pawns*. Hezbollah's guerrilla war against the occupying Israeli army triggered two major Israeli invasions prior to 2006, Operation Accountability (July 1993) and Operation Grapes of Wrath (April 1996). Israel launched Operation Accountability after the IDF suffered "the highest military casualty toll in southern Lebanon in years." The goals of the attack were "to punish Hezbollah"; "to make it difficult for Hezbollah to continue using southern Lebanon as a base for attacking Israeli forces . . . by deliberately inflicting serious damage on villages in southern Lebanon, through massive shelling which would raise the cost to the population of permitting Hezbollah to live and operate in its midst"; and to generate a refugee

flow that "would put pressure on the central government to rein in the guerrillas." Operation Grapes of Wrath was launched after Israel declared its intention to "act 'tough' against Hezbollah and ignore" a 1993 agreement between Israel and Hezbollah prohibiting attacks on civilians. Israel again carried out "indiscriminate and disproportionate attacks against civilians in what had become virtual 'free-fire' zones across large swaths of the south," and again premeditatedly generated a refugee flight in the hundreds of thousands towards Beirut. "Meanwhile," the HRW report noted, "Hezbollah reprisals, in the form of Katyusha salvos into northern Israel, continued without respite."

54 CUA, p. 107; WTD, pp. 35-36, 53. According to the International Committee of the Red Cross, "the use of human shields requires an intentional collocation of military objectives and civilians or persons *hors de combat* with the specific intent of trying to prevent the targeting of those military objectives" (Henckaerts and Doswald-Beck, *Customary International Humanitarian Law*, p. 340).
55 CUA, p. 108.
56 Ibid.
57 Ibid.
58 Ibid., p. 107.
59 Ibid., pp. 16, 53, 72, 109-10. Failure to take all "feasible precautions" is not in itself a violation prosecutable as a war crime (WTD, p. 54). On a separate issue HRW acknowledged "legitimate questions" from Palestinian Israelis "about whether Israel discriminates against them in terms of the degree of protection it provides them from belligerent attacks" such as the availability of shelters (CUA, p. 110).
60 Arab Association for Human Rights, *Civilians in Danger*, p. 24.
61 WTD, pp. 5, 6, 62.
62 Ibid., p. 62.
63 Ibid., pp. 6, 9, 79.
64 CUA, p. 4.
65 WTD, pp. 71-178 passim.
66 Commission of Inquiry, paras. 14, 21, 25, 81, 117, 125, 128, 135, 176, 191, 211-19, 318, 319, 322, 323, 324, 326, 331, 340(a), 342.
67 WTD, pp. 10, 72-76.
68 On a related note HRW's tacit premise that, in contrast to Hezbollah's rockets, the weapons used by Israel were uniformly discriminate is open to question. HRW itself quoted, for example, an IDF internal investigation after the war that "the Artillery Corps shot approximately 170,000 munitions [shells] during the war, most of it to the approximate direction of the areas of launching," and quoted a senior Israeli officer from the Armored Corps to the effect that "he would be surprised" if even five Hezbollah members were killed. HRW further reported that this apparently indiscriminate artillery fire caused widespread damage in southern Lebanon (WTD, pp. 71, 170). The Navy reportedly fired 2,500 shells. See also Amos Harel and Avi Issacharoff, *34 Days: Israel, Hezbollah, and the war in Lebanon* (New York: 2008), pp. 122, 170, 236, reporting that Israeli artillery batteries "rained" 180,000 shells on "Lebanese

soil, mostly with no significant objectives for attack." To be sure, it is unclear whether these massive indiscriminate attacks sprang from the nature of the weapons used or Israel's heedless use of them, although by HRW's standard they would have constituted serious violations of the laws of war in either case.
69 WTD, p. 6.
70 Ibid., p. 8.
71 Ibid., p. 62.
72 Ibid., p. 63.
73 Ibid.
74 Ibid., p. 66.
75 Ibid., p. 69.
76 Ibid., p. 72.
77 Ibid., p. 76.
78 Ibid.
79 Ibid. In these and other incidents of Israeli attacks on civilians, HRW also partially exculpated Israel by speculating on the flimsiest evidence that Israel used "unreliable or dated intelligence" and "flawed intelligence," or suffered "communication breakdowns," which resulted in "failed targeting" (ibid., pp. 10-11, 74, 78). In still other incidents of manifestly indiscriminate attacks, HRW faulted Israel merely for "failure to take adequate precautions," or for having "failed to take into account the predictable reality that almost all Hezbollah members, military and civilian, had abandoned their homes as soon as the war started" (ibid., pp. 77-78, 94).
80 Ibid., p. 80.
81 Ibid., pp. 7, 63.
82 Ibid., pp. 7, 63-64.
83 Ibid., pp. 13, 72. For incriminating statements by Israeli officials during the attack, see also Lambeth, *Air Operations*, pp. 22, 27.
84 WTD, p. 77.
85 Ibid., pp. 74-75.
86 Ibid., p. 6. Arkin, *Divining Victory*, asserts that the 30 percent of those killed who were children "on the surface ... seems significant, yet the number pretty much matches the percent of children in the Lebanese population at large" (p. 99). He seems not to grasp that this defense of Israel's conduct during the war suggests on the contrary that Israel's attack was indiscriminate.
87 WTD, pp. 9-10.
88 Ibid., pp. 13-14.
89 Ibid., p. 74.
90 Ibid., p. 160.
91 Ibid., pp. 53-54.
92 Ibid., pp. 5, 14, 40-41, 46, 48, 53.
93 Ibid., pp. 14, 45.
94 Ibid., p. 51. A U.S. Army War College study based largely on interviews with Israeli participants in the war also observed:

> Hezbollah is often described as having used civilians as shields in 2006, and, in fact, they made extensive use of civilian homes as direct fire combat positions and to conceal launchers for rocket fire into Israel. Yet the villages Hezbollah used to anchor its defensive system in southern Lebanon were largely evacuated by the time Israeli ground forces crossed the border on July 18. As a result, the key battlefields in the land campaign south of the Litani River were mostly devoid of civilians, and IDF participants consistently report little or no meaningful intermingling of Hezbollah fighters and noncombatants. Nor is there any systematic reporting of Hezbollah using civilians in the combat zone as shields. The fighting in southern Lebanon was chiefly urban, in the built-up areas of the small to medium-size villages and towns typical of the region. But it was not significantly intermingled with a civilian population that had fled by the time the ground fighting began. Hezbollah made very effective use of local cover and concealment . . ., but this was obtained almost entirely from the terrain—both natural and man-made. (Stephen Biddle and Jeffrey A. Friedman, *The 2006 Lebanon Campaign and the Future of Warfare: Implications for army and defense policy* (Carlisle, PA: 2008), pp. 43-44)

The corresponding footnote reads: "We heard no accounts . . . of any significant civilian population on any battlefield south of the Litani, or any systematic effort by Hezbollah to exploit civilian intermingling as a shield." On a related point, the authors reported that "the great majority of Hezbollah's fighters wore uniforms. In fact, their equipment and clothing were remarkably similar to many state militaries'—desert or green fatigues, helmets, web vests, body armor, dog tags, and rank insignia" (ibid., p. 45).

95 Besides "probable" HRW used other locutions expressing varying degrees of certainty: "suggests," "strongly suggests," "may have," "possible," "an act of shielding" (unqualified) (*WTD*, pp. 16, 40, 53).
96 Ibid., pp. 6, 14, 16, 40.
97 Ibid., p. 54.
98 Ibid., p. 45.
99 Ibid., pp. 41-42.
100 Ibid., pp. 56, 62, 63, 73. Arkin, *Divining Victory*, reports, "Beirut's southern suburbs suffered a level of damage unmatched by any other example of bombing in the precision era" (p. xx).
101 *WTD*, pp. 114-16.
102 Ibid., pp. 15, 57-60.
103 Commission of Inquiry, paras. 19, 234-43.
104 Ibid., paras. 26, 244-46, 330. It cautioned however that Hezbollah's firing from "'the vicinity' does not mean from within the [U.N.] bases. . . . The direct targeting by [the] IDF, when they have the advantage of modern precision weapons, remains inexcusable."
105 Ibid., paras. 241, 245, 246. It accused Hezbollah of "an obvious violation of international law," and "illegal and inexcusable" conduct, and Israel of committing a "war crime."

106 Ibid., paras. 26, 330.
107 Human Rights Watch, "Hezbollah Smear Campaign Won't Silence Report: Investigation criticizes wartime conduct" (29 August 2007). See also Fattah, "Rights Group Accuses Hezbollah of Indiscriminate Attacks on Civilians in Israel War."
108 *Flooding South Lebanon* [hereafter: *FSL*], pp. 1, 3, 38. HRW estimated the total of Israeli submunitions fired into Lebanon as ranging from 3.2 to 4.6 million.
109 Ibid., pp. 3, 36-37, 38. The area targeted for the Israeli cluster attacks was approximately 1,400 square kilometers (roughly the size of Rhode Island).
110 Ibid., pp. 39n101, 41.
111 Ibid., pp. 1, 7, 40.
112 Ibid., p. 2.
113 Ibid., p. 1.
114 Ibid., p. 29.
115 Ibid., p. 9.
116 This writer confirmed the point in a phone conversation with Marc Garlasco, senior military analyst at Human Rights Watch (17 March 2008).
117 Meron Rapoport, "When Rockets and Phosphorus Cluster," *Haaretz* (30 September 2006).
118 *FSL*, pp. 2, 19-20, 24, 107.
119 Ibid., pp. 1, 5. Some of the cluster munitions used by Israel dated from 1973, which might in part account for the "exceptionally high dud rates" in Lebanon (ibid., pp. 33, 44-45, 109).
120 Ibid., pp. 6, 7, 8, 11, 41 (soldier), 44, 105, 106.
121 Ibid., pp. 42, 43.
122 Ibid., p. 70.
123 Ibid., pp. 73-74.
124 Ibid., pp. 57, 78.
125 United Nations Mine Action Service, *Annual Report 2009*, p. 62. There are no reliable estimates for the number of Lebanese killed by cluster munitions during the war, but it is assumed that because most Lebanese had fled or were under shelter during the last 72 hours of the war, the bulk of the casualties from cluster munitions occurred after the ceasefire.
126 *FSL*, pp. 91-92.
127 Henckaerts and Doswald-Beck, *Customary International Humanitarian Law*, p. 51 (Rule 15).
128 *FSL*, pp. 1, 9, 10, 16, 23, 68, 104-5.
129 Ibid., p. 107, citing Dinstein, *Conduct of Hostilities*, p. 117.
130 International Court of Justice, *Advisory Opinion on the Legality of the Threat or Use of Nuclear Weapons* (1996).
131 "Dissenting Opinion of Judge Higgins," para. 21; "Dissenting Opinion of Judge Weeramantry," chapter III, "Humanitarian Law," section 10, "Specific rules of the humanitarian laws," (a) "The prohibition against causing unnecessary suffering."
132 *FSL*, p. 1.
133 Ibid., p. 7.

134 Ibid., pp. 8, 104, 105.
135 Ibid., pp. 8-9, 105.
136 Ibid., p. 9.
137 Ibid., p. 10.
138 Ibid., pp. 10, 26, 82, 109.
139 Ibid., p. 10.
140 Ibid., p. 42.
141 Ibid., p. 48.
142 Ibid., p. 49.
143 Ibid., p. 104.
144 Ibid.
145 Ibid., p. 109.
146 Ibid.
147 Ibid., p. 117.
148 The only exception was Israel's targeting of Tebnine Hospital, where HRW spoke of a "strong presumption that Israel attacked the site either knowingly or in reckless disregard of the hospital's presence." Yet, even in this singularly egregious instance it still could not resist speculating that Hezbollah "may have been using" a road nearby the hospital and Israel may have been "targeting Hezbollah combatants using the road" (pp. 11, 63-68, 111, 117). The U.N. Commission of Inquiry categorically concluded that "from a military perspective there was no justification" for this attack on the hospital (paras. 163-65).
149 *FSL*, pp. 101-2. For the Commission of Inquiry findings, see paras. 24, 32, 110, 256, 337, 343 of its report.
150 *FSL*, pp. 6, 44.
151 Ibid., p. 42.
152 Ibid., p. 38.
153 www.democracynow.org/2009/2/16/human_rights_watchs_kenneth_roth_on.
154 Weeramantry, chapter III, "Humanitarian Law," section 3, "Outline of humanitarian law."

PART III/CHAPTER SEVEN
  1 Leon Uris, *Exodus* (New York: 1958). For the impact of *Exodus* on American Jews, see Paul Breines, *Tough Jews: Political fantasies and the moral dilemma of American Jewry* (New York: 1990), pp. 54-56.
  2 Apart from the scholarship itself, a voluminous secondary literature commenting on it has proliferated. As good a place as any to begin is Benny Morris, *1948 and After: Israel and the Palestinians* (Oxford: 1990), pp. 1-34.
  3 See for example Conor Cruise O'Brien, *The Siege: The saga of Israel and Zionism* (New York: 1986), p. 282.
  4 Walid Khalidi, "Why Did the Palestinians Leave?," *Middle East Forum* (July 1959); Erskine Childers, "The Other Exodus," *Spectator* (12 May 1961).
  5 Morris calls it a "partial" ethnic cleansing, and then goes on to assert that this incompleteness was David Ben-Gurion's "fatal mistake. If he had carried out a full

expulsion—rather than a partial one—he would have stabilized the State of Israel for generations." Ari Shavit, "Survival of the Fittest," interview with Benny Morris, *Haaretz* (9 January 2004).

6 Shlomo Ben-Ami, *Scars of War, Wounds of Peace: The Israeli-Arab tragedy* (New York: 2006), pp. 25-26, 42-45.

7 Ibid., pp. 3, 13, 18, 82, 34, 122, 125, 188.

8 For Dershowitz's long history of gross apologetics for Israel, see Norman G. Finkelstein, *Beyond Chutzpah: On the misuse of anti-Semitism and the abuse of history* (Berkeley: 2005; expanded paperback edition, 2008).

9 Alan Dershowitz, *The Case for Israel* (Hoboken, NJ: 2003), pp. 76 (Balance), 91-92 (1967), 100-1 (1973); Alan M. Dershowitz, *Preemption: A knife that cuts both ways* (New York: 2006), pp. 79 (1956), 101-2 (1982).

10 Zeev Maoz, *Defending the Holy Land: A critical analysis of Israel's security and foreign policy* (Ann Arbor: 2006), pp. 36 (1956, 1967), 37 (1973, 1982), 82-93 (1967), 171-82 (1982), 286 (1982), 546 (Balance).

11 Ibid., pp. 252, 388.

12 New York: 2002.

13 Gary J. Bass, "Days That Shook the World," *New York Times* (16 June 2002), Richard Bernstein, "Short Conflict, Far-Reaching Consequences," *New York Times* (17 July 2002), Edward Rothstein, "Six Days of Confusion That Rearranged World Politics," *New York Times* (6 July 2002), Howard Fineman, "Bush Studied '67 Preemptive Strike," *Newsweek* (9 October 2002; www.msnbc.com/news). The back cover of the hardbound edition was studded with advance acclaim from partisan figures such as former Israeli prime minister Ehud Barak and *New Republic* editor Martin Peretz, but also from respected authorities such as historian Wm. Roger Louis and former U.S. ambassador Richard B. Parker.

14 *Six Days*, pp. xiv-xv.

15 He was Senior Fellow at the Shalem Center, a conservative research institute in Jerusalem, and contributing editor to *The New Republic*.

16 Checking Oren's evidence also poses a challenge: an endnote incorporating tens of references frequently corresponds to many paragraphs of text incorporating tens of quotes, making it nearly impossible to match reference against quote.

17 An earlier version of this analysis appeared as an appendix to Norman G. Finkelstein, *Image and Reality of the Israel-Palestine Conflict* (New York: 1995; expanded second paperback edition, 2003). Here, use is made of extensive new material that has since become available, especially volume XIX of the *Foreign Relations of the United States* documentary series, *Arab-Israeli Crisis and War, 1967* (Washington, D.C.: 2004).

18 Oren seems to doubt this on p. 31 of *Six Days*, but see Finkelstein, *Image and Reality*, p. 125, which cites authoritative U.N. sources.

19 After the 1956 Sinai invasion Nasser consented to stationing U.N. peacekeeping forces on the Egyptian side of the border with Israel.

20 *Six Days*, p. 49.

21 Ibid., p. 23.

22 Ami Gluska, *The Israeli Military and the Origins of the 1967 War: Government, armed forces and defence policy* (New York: 2007), p. 40.
23 *Six Days*, pp. 9, 14.
24 Ibid., pp. 23, 48-49.
25 Ibid., pp. 27, 45-46; cf. pp. 29, 42, 44, 64.
26 Finkelstein, *Image and Reality*, pp. 131-32. For background on the DMZs and further documentation, see Muhammad Muslih, *The Golan: The road to occupation* (Washington, D.C.: 1999), chapters 1-2. Oren seeks at one point to discredit Bull on the grounds that he was "ill-disposed toward Israel." He quotes Bull saying in his memoir that, when Israel summoned him on 5 June 1967 to warn Jordan not to attack or else Israel would react in kind, he (Bull) responded: "This was a threat, pure and simple, and it is not the normal practice of the UN to pass on threats from one government to another." Bull does appear grossly derelict from Oren's snippet, yet the very next sentence of his memoir—omitted by Oren—reads: "But this message seemed so important that we quickly sent it . . . and King Hussein received the message before 10:30 the same morning." *Six Days*, p. 184; Odd Bull, *War and Peace in the Middle East: The experiences and views of a UN observer* (London: 1976), p. 113.
27 "Interviews on the Golan Heights and on Jewish Settlements in Hebron, 22 November 1976 and 1 January 1977," reprinted in *Journal of Palestine Studies* (Autumn 1997), p. 145 (the interviews originally appeared in *Yediot Ahronot*). For "Israeli misconduct during border conflict with Syria" being "to a large extent responsible for the process of escalation that evolved into the May-June 1967 crisis," see also Maoz, *Defending the Holy Land*, pp. 82-83, 102-3 (these pages also contain a translation of the Dayan interview), 110.
28 Martin van Creveld, *The Sword and the Olive: A critical history of the Israeli Defense Force* (New York: 1998), p. 172; Tom Segev, *1967: Israel, the war and the year that transformed the Middle East* (New York: 2007), p. 210; Gluska, *Israeli Military*, pp. 100-3 ("massive employment").
29 *Six Days*, p. 46.
30 Ibid., p. 42.
31 John K. Cooley, *Green March, Black September: The story of the Palestinian Arabs* (London: 1973), p. 160. See also Finkelstein, *Image and Reality*, p. 133; Segev, *1967*, pp. 198-201, for apparent confirmation from Rabin; and Maoz, *Defending the Holy Land*, p. 102, for a somewhat similar account. Oren alludes to this explanation on pp. 24, 27 of *Six Days*.
32 The work cited by Oren actually states "between 23 February 1966 and 15 May 1967," and the figures came not from Syria but "Israeli sources" (Moshe Ma'oz, *Syria and Israel: From war to peacemaking* (Oxford: 1995), p. 89; Yacov Bar Siman-Tov, *Linkage Politics in the Middle East: Syria between domestic and external conflict, 1961-1970* (Boulder, CO: 1983), pp. 151-52).
33 *Six Days*, pp. 24, 27, 31, 45, 48, 63; cf. pp. 25, 28, 29, 42, 46, 53.
34 Ibid., p. 81.

35 Yehoshaphat Harkabi, "Fedayeen Action and Arab Strategy," *Adelphi Papers*, no. 53 (London: 1968) n.p. See also Finkelstein, *Image and Reality*, p. 133, and Maoz, *Defending the Holy Land*, p. 110.
36 *Six Days*, p. 317.
37 Finkelstein, *Image and Reality*, pp. 125-27; see also Segev, *1967*, pp. 215-17, and Gluska, *Israeli Military*, pp. 115-18. Both David Ben-Gurion and Moshe Dayan, in the political opposition, blamed the Israeli government's provocative actions and bellicose language for causing the May crisis (*Six Days*, pp. 80-81; Segev, *1967*, pp. 237, 270; Gluska, *Israeli Military*, pp. 104, 126, 144, 265).
38 Maoz, *Defending the Holy Land*, pp. 106-7; see Finkelstein, *Image and Reality*, p. 249n8, for further documentation.
39 "Memorandum from Nathaniel Davis of the National Security Council Staff to the President's Special Assistant (Rostow)" (2 June 1967), *Foreign Relations of the United States, vol. XIX, Arab-Israeli Crisis and War, 1967*.
40 Gluska, *Israeli Military*, pp. 118, 114. Gluska recalls that from summer 1966 "there was a consensus among Israeli generals on the need to impose a 'frontal clash' on Syria that would shake the radical regime, perhaps even cause it to collapse." By early 1967 Israeli Chief of Staff Yitzhak Rabin was referring "to the large-scale clash with Syria as a certain prospect, for which the right pretext must be found," while "the public mood in Israel was ripe for a punitive action against Syria," and Prime Minister Eshkol "too came to the conclusion that what was required was a 'strong blow' which would inflict damage on the Syrian army and regime." On 7 May 1967 the Ministerial Committee on Security conditionally approved an attack on Syria, and during an "extraordinary meeting" of the Knesset Foreign Affairs and Security Committee on 9 May it was unanimously agreed that—in Eshkol's words—"the day of retribution must arrive." It was probably knowledge of this last meeting that caused the Soviets to conclude that an Israeli attack was imminent. In his recital of the steps leading to the Israeli first strike, Alexei Kosygin told the U.N. General Assembly after the war, "On 9 May 1967 the Israeli Parliament authorized the Government of Israel to carry out military operations against Syria." The purpose of the Soviet warning to Nasser, according to Gluska, was to get him to "exert pressure on Israel from the south and thereby prevent Israel from operating in the north . . . there is no evidence that the USSR wanted war, and their conduct in the course of the crisis apparently indicates an attempt to prevent it." Ibid., pp. 74-76, 80, 94-100, 103-6, 114-18; *Official Records of the General Assembly Fifth Emergency Special Session, Plenary Meetings, Verbatim Records of Meetings, 17 June—18 September 1967* (United Nations, New York: 1973), 1526th meeting—19 June 1967, para. 25. For other authoritative sources speculating that the Soviet warning was based on a likely Israeli attack, see Finkelstein, *Image and Reality*, pp. 126-27.
41 *Six Days*, pp. 54-55, 342n52.
42 "Memorandum from the President's Special Assistant (Rostow) to President Johnson" (17 May 1967), "Briefing Notes for Director of Central Intelligence Helms for Use

at a White House Meeting" (23 May 1967), in *Foreign Relations of the United States, vol. XIX, Arab-Israeli Crisis and War, 1967*. See also Finkelstein, *Image and Reality*, p. 127.
43 *Six Days*, p. 72.
44 Ibid., p. 67. Beyond its alleged pro-Egyptian bias, UNEF, according to Oren, inspired "little faith" regarding its "ability to prevent Egyptian-Israeli hostilities," and was viewed "with skepticism" by "Western states disaffected by the UN's increasingly pro-Soviet stance" (ibid.). To sustain these disparaging claims, Oren directs the reader specifically to Brian Urquhart's memoir, *A Life in Peace and War* (New York: 1978). Yet on the cited pages Urquhart says nothing of the sort. For example, recalling the establishment of UNEF after Israel withdrew from the Sinai in 1957, Urquhart writes:

> The Israelis withdrew with a bad grace, destroying roads and railway communications and leaving uncharted minefields in their wake, all of which caused considerable grief and trouble to UNEF. They started a vitriolic campaign about [U.N. Secretary-General Dag] Hammarskjöld's and UNEF's alleged partiality to Egypt. Israel also refused to allow UNEF to be stationed on the Israeli side of the line, a grave weakness for a peacekeeping force. The Israeli attitude to UNEF changed a few months later when they realized that the force, in its impartial way, had achieved peace on what had formerly been their most violent and bloody frontier. (p. 136)

45 Oren dubs U Thant "one of the greatest obstacles to UNEF's survival" and quotes the Israeli Foreign Ministry saying, "it is still unclear what diplomatic consideration or defect of character brought him to make this disastrous move" (*Six Days*, pp. 71, 75). But U Thant's detailed factual accounting (seconded by his U.N. colleagues) makes plain that under the circumstances he had no other option (see Finkelstein, *Image and Reality*, p. 214n10 for references). U Thant comes off very badly in Oren's book—superstitious, "emotionless . . . rather simple-minded" (citing an anonymous source), "anti-American and, perforce, pro-Soviet" and exhibiting "the psychology of the Asian . . . a built-in reaction against the white man" (citing American officials)—no doubt because, like Odd Bull, he preserved on the Arab-Israeli conflict an independent cast of mind (*Six Days*, pp. 71-72, 75). Both U Thant and Odd Bull later speculated that if Israel had agreed to station UNEF on its own side of the border, the June war might have been averted; see also Segev, *1967*, p. 228, for a similar conjecture.
46 *Six Days*, pp. 67ff.
47 Israel's apologists have always strained to reconcile its pretense of having done everything possible to avert war with its refusal to station UNEF on the Israeli side of the border. Then-U.N. ambassador Gideon Rafael later contended that on the Egyptian side of the border UNEF served "as a neutral factor or restraint and a kind of, I would say, shock absorber between the two countries" but on the Israeli side would have served "no purpose whatsoever" (Richard B. Parker, *The Six-Day War: A retrospective* (Gainesville, FL: 1996), pp. 105-6; for Abba Eban's equally contrived rationale, see Finkelstein, *Image and Reality*, p. 128).

48 *Six Days*, p. 74. An integral part of the 1949 armistice agreement, EIMAC was disbanded by Israel after its 1956 Sinai invasion "unilaterally" and "in clear defiance of U.N. resolutions" (U Thant) (for details, see Finkelstein, *Image and Reality*, pp. 127-28). Oren incorrectly refers to EIMAC as the "Mutual Armistice Commission."
49 *Six Days*, pp. 81, 83.
50 Finkelstein, *Image and Reality*, p. 139; Segev, *1967*, p. 235; Gluska, *Israeli Military*, p. 141. For American doubts regarding Israel's economic dependence on the Straits, see "Memorandum of Conversation" (2 June 1967), *Foreign Relations of the United States*, vol. XIX, *Arab-Israeli Crisis and War, 1967*.
51 *Six Days*, pp. 84, 90, 95; cf. p. 166.
52 Finkelstein, *Image and Reality*, p. 139; Segev, *1967*, pp. 240-43; Gluska, *Israeli Military*, pp. 137, 155. Rabin was privy to "top secret" information that "the Egyptians had already decided that ships under American escort would not be stopped," while Eban speculated that Nasser "has not decided to disrupt shipping," but rather "decided to be in a position where he can brandish this sword" at his whim. To be sure, Washington assumed the "probability that the UAR [Egypt] will turn back unescorted tankers (including those of US registry)"; see "Memorandum from the Contingency Work Group on Military Planning to the Middle East Control Group" (4 June 1967), *Foreign Relations of the United States*, vol. XIX, *Arab-Israeli Crisis and War, 1967*. In addition to the sources cited in Finkelstein, *Image and Reality*, the absence of a blockade in the Straits is documented in "Telegram from the Mission to the United Nations to the Department of State" (22 May 1967), "Memorandum for the Record" (26 May 1967), "Telegram from the Department of State to the Embassy in the Soviet Union" (28 May 1967), "Memorandum from Secretary of State Rusk and Secretary of Defense McNamara to President Johnson" (30 May 1967), "Telegram from the Department of State to the Embassy in Israel" (1 June 1967), in ibid. The editors of the *Foreign Relations of the United States* volume refer on p. 80 to the "purported closing of the Gulf of Aqaba to Israeli shipping." Oren also contends that in 1957 Israel had won "international recognition of its right to act in self-defense if the Straits were ever blockaded," and that the U.S. "pledged" to "regard any Egyptian attempt to revive the Tiran blockade as an act of war to which Israel could respond in self-defense" (*Six Days*, pp. 81, 12). Although Israel did obtain from the U.S. and other maritime states support for its right of "free and innocent" passage in the Straits, Washington still stipulated that "any recurrence of hostilities or any violation by any party" be referred back to the United Nations. U.S. officials and legal scholars as well as U.N. secretaries-general Hammarskjöld and U Thant all conceded it was a "complicated" jurisdictional dispute. Oren makes passing reference (p. 141) to the "murky legal waters of Tiran."
53 "Telegram from the Embassy in Portugal to the Department of State" (2 June 1967), and "Memorandum of Conversation" (2 June 1967), *Foreign Relations of the United States*, vol. XIX, *Arab-Israeli Crisis and War, 1967*.
54 Segev, *1967*, pp. 273, 296, 330; Gluska, *Israeli Military*, pp. 158-59, 164, 167, 168, 172, 181, 190, 226; "Memorandum for the Record" (1 June 1967), *Foreign Relations of the United States*, vol. XIX, *Arab-Israeli Crisis and War, 1967*.

55 Basing himself on the wholly unreliable memoir of Israel's U.N. representative, Gideon Rafael, and the recollection 25 years later of U Thant's aide, Brian Urquhart, Oren suggests that Egypt suddenly reneged on the terms of the moratorium at the end of May and that consequently the proposal was not submitted to Eshkol (*Six Days*, p. 126). Yet U Thant's meticulous account of these negotiations running through early June reports Rafael's explicit rejection and makes no mention of an Egyptian volte-face on the moratorium's terms (on the contrary, he was still citing Nasser's support on 1 June), while Urquhart's own memoir closely follows U Thant (see Finkelstein, *Image and Reality*, p. 129 and sources cited on p. 215n16 for U Thant's account and Urquhart's memoir, as well as supplementary U.N. documentation and Rafael's unreliability; and Parker, *Six-Day War*, pp. 94-95, for Urquhart's apparently mistaken later recollection). For Israel's rejection at the end of May of a two-week moratorium on both Israeli flagships using the Straits and Egyptian interference with non-Israeli vessels, see "Telegram from the Mission to the United Nations to the Department of State" (27 May 1967); for U.S. support of "a two or three week even-handed moratorium which would enable a high-level representative of the Secretary-General to visit the area and study the situation," see "Telegram from the Department of State to the Embassy in Israel" (28 May 1967), *Foreign Relations of the United States, vol. XIX, Arab-Israeli Crisis and War, 1967*. See also Gluska, *Israeli Military*, p. 186.
56 *Six Days*, pp. 126, 144; Finkelstein, *Image and Reality*, p. 129 and sources cited.
57 *Six Days*, p. 145.
58 Dean Rusk, *As I Saw It* (New York: 1990), pp. 386-87. See also Finkelstein, *Image and Reality*, p. 251n18, and *Six Days*, p. 196.
59 Daniel Dishon, ed., *Middle East Record, 1967* (Tel Aviv: 1971-77), p. 199; see also Finkelstein, *Image and Reality*, p. 252n19. For Nasser's possible openness to a "political compromise" in early June, see also "Memorandum from the Deputy Assistant Secretary of Defense for International Security Affairs (Hoopes) to Secretary of Defense McNamara" (2 June 1967), *Foreign Relations of the United States, vol. XIX, Arab-Israeli Crisis and War, 1967*.
60 Maoz, *Defending the Holy Land*, pp. 87, 93.
61 *Six Days*, pp. 92-97, 119-21.
62 For historians who credit Operation Dawn (the planned date of attack was allegedly 27 May) but attach slight significance to it, see Finkelstein, *Image and Reality*, p. 218n37, and Avraham Sela, *The Decline of the Arab-Israeli Conflict: Middle East politics and the quest for regional order* (Albany: 1998), p. 90; for an historian who altogether doubts its existence, see Benny Morris's review of Oren's book in the *Jerusalem Report* (21 August 2002). Even assuming an Egyptian attack was planned, and leaving aside that the alleged plan was aborted long before 5 June when Israel attacked, it could only have influenced the Israeli decision to strike first if Israeli officials knew about it. But whereas Tel Aviv did convey fears of an impending Egyptian attack to Washington at this time, officials such as Eshkol explicitly conceded in private that these communications were designed "to create an alibi" for an Israeli first strike, while both at the time and in his later mem-

oirs Eban emphatically dismissed all talk of a planned Egyptian attack as "hypochondriac frivolities" and a "cheap trick" to justify an Israeli first strike. Neither British and American nor for that matter Israeli intelligence could detect in late May any evidence of an imminent Egyptian attack (for U.S. intelligence estimates, see Table 2 below). According to Segev, "the most current Israeli research" concludes that, although "the Egyptian military did authorize a plan for an air attack on the southern Negev on May 27," a study by the Israeli Ministry of Defense found it "extremely questionable" that Israeli officials were aware of these plans. See *Six Days*, pp. 102-3, 107-8, 110, 114-15, 122; Finkelstein, *Image and Reality*, pp. 134, 219n37; Segev, *1967*, pp. 255-59.

63 *Six Days*, pp. 92, 95, 120. Historians who credit Operation Dawn argue on the basis of the Egyptian memoirs that it was Amer's secret brainchild and that Nasser almost immediately cancelled the plan upon learning of it. Oren manages to prove otherwise through tortured reasoning and by playing fast and loose with the already problematic evidence. For example he reports an alleged statement by Amer complaining that his first-strike plan had been leaked abroad, but omits Nasser's alleged reaction conveying that he knew nothing of this plan: "Why is Amer upset? Does he think that we shall start the war?" (*Six Days*, p. 120; Parker, *Six-Day War*, p. 45). For a devastating critique of Oren's rendering of Operation Dawn, which "is neither [supported] by available documentary evidence nor . . . reconcilable with the chronology of events," see Roland Popp, "Stumbling Decidedly into the Six-Day War," *Middle East Journal* (Spring 2006), pp. 295-98. Oren additionally asserts that the alleged "Egyptian first strike" posed a "potentially greater threat" to Jordan than an Israeli attack because an unsuccessful Egyptian offensive would be blamed on Jordan, undermining Hashemite rule, while a successful Egyptian offensive might "continue onward to Amman." "The predicament, as defined by royal confidant Zayd al-Rifai," Oren continues, "was mind-boggling: 'Even if Jordan did not participate in a war . . . it would be blamed for the loss of the war and our turn would be next'" (*Six Days*, p. 128; the ellipsis is Oren's). But in the original source cited by Oren, we read that King Hussein feared an *Israeli* attack in the event of a regional war "no matter what Jordan did." In order to document Jordan's worry, the original source quotes al-Rifai: "Even if Jordan did not participate directly in a war *that was started by Israel* it would not only be destroyed by the Arab world and even blamed for the loss of the war but our turn would be next" (Samir A. Mutawi, *Jordan in the 1967 War* (Cambridge: 1987), pp. 100-1; my emphasis). It would seem that the "predicament" posed by an "Egyptian first strike" to Jordan would not have been quite so "mind-boggling" if Oren had not excised the phrase "that was started by Israel." For Hussein's fear that Jordan was "likely a target in the short run" by Israel and "an inevitable one in the long run," see also "Telegram from the Embassy in Jordan to the Department of State" (18 May 1967), *Foreign Relations of the United States, vol. XIX, Arab-Israeli Crisis and War, 1967*.

64 *Six Days*, p. 158.

65 Ibid., pp. 158, 167, 160, 169; cf. p. 99.

66 Gluska, *Israeli Military*, pp. 200, 214, 226-27; Segev, *1967*, p. 323.

67 "Memorandum for the Record" (1 June 1967), *Foreign Relations of the United States, vol. XIX, Arab-Israeli Crisis and War, 1967*. See also "Telegram from the Embassy in Israel to the Department of State" (30 May 1967), ibid.
68 Sela, *Decline of the Arab-Israeli Conflict*, p. 91.
69 For Begin and further supporting documentation, see Finkelstein, *Image and Reality*, pp. 134-35. The UNEF commander quoted by Oren on Egypt's imminent attack, Major-General Indar Jit Rikhye, reports elsewhere in his memoir that Egyptian troops were in fact ambiguously positioned, and concludes that "the Egyptian armed forces had eventually accepted the final decision of Nasser not to attack" (*The Sinai Blunder* (London: 1980), p. 168).
70 "Memorandum from the President's Special Assistant (Rostow) to President Johnson" (25 May 1967), "Memorandum for the Record" (26 May 1967), "Memorandum from the Central Intelligence Agency's Board of National Estimates to Director of Central Intelligence Helms" (26 May 1967), in *Foreign Relations of the United States, vol. XIX, Arab-Israeli Crisis and War, 1967*. See also "Memorandum of Conversation" (25 May 1967), "Message from President Johnson to Prime Minister Wilson" (25 May 1967), "Memorandum of Conversation" (26 May 1967; document 69), "Special Report of the Watch Committee" (26 May 1967), "Memorandum of Conversation" (26 May 1967; document 77), "Telegram from the Department of State to the Embassy in the United Kingdom" (27 May 1967), in ibid.
71 *Six Days*, pp. 153, 86, 87, 90, 97, 147, 149, 150-51; cf. pp. 100, 106, 156, 157, 164, 168, 210.
72 Ibid., pp. 110, 139, 146, 147, 122, 133-34, 151, 87, 99; cf. pp. 104, 152, 159, 165, 172. "Memorandum of Conversation" (26 May 1967; document 69) (Eban), "Memorandum of Conversation" (26 May 1967; document 77) (Johnson), in *Foreign Relations of the United States, vol. XIX, Arab-Israeli Crisis and War, 1967*. For Peled and Weizman, as well as sources asserting Israel's steadily improving and Egypt's steadily deteriorating military situation, and the certainty of an Israeli victory, see Finkelstein, *Image and Reality*, pp. 135-36.
73 "Memorandum Prepared in the Central Intelligence Agency" (23 May 1967; emphases in original), "Memorandum for the Record" (26 May 1967), "Intelligence Memorandum Prepared in the Central Intelligence Agency" (26 May 1967), "Memorandum of Conversation" (2 June 1967), "Memorandum from Robert N. Ginsburgh of the National Security Council Staff to the President's Special Assistant (Rostow)" (3 June 1967), in *Foreign Relations of the United States, vol. XIX, Arab-Israeli Crisis and War, 1967*. See also "Memorandum of Conversation" (26 May 1967), "Draft Briefing by Director of Central Intelligence Helms for the President's Foreign Intelligence Advisory Board" (14 June 1967), in ibid.
74 Van Creveld, *Sword and the Olive*, pp. 172, 176-77. For Israeli leaders' confidence of victory, see also Segev, *1967*, pp. 256 (Rabin), 333 (Dayan), 337 (Allon). To enhance the Arab threat, Oren gestures to Jordan's "twenty-four Hawker Hunter" aircraft and "eleven brigades" (*Six Days*, p. 137). In fact the Jordanian army was a "kind of showpiece" serving primarily as a "palace guard" while the Jordanian air force was "not a threat at all" (Eric Hammel, *Six Days in June: How Israel won the 1967 Arab-Israeli war* (New York: 1992), pp. 285-87).

75 Segev, 1967, pp. 296, 300.
76 See Chapter Four.
77 Segev, 1967, pp. 276, 307, 310, 323, 326, 336.
78 Finkelstein, *Image and Reality*, p. 141.
79 Segev, 1967, p. 334.
80 For a similar conclusion but based on different reasoning, see Ersun N. Kurtulus, "The Notion of a 'Pre-emptive War': The Six Day War revisited," *Middle East Journal* (Spring 2007).
81 For this argument, see esp. Gluska, *Israeli Military*, pp. 159 ("in the long run"), 254 ("from hour to hour the possibility of offensive Egyptian, Jordanian, and Syrian initiative is growing," quoting Yariv), 255 ("thousands of additional Israeli casualties," quoting Dayan).
82 Maoz, *Defending the Holy Land*, pp. 89, 92.
83 Gluska, *Israeli Military*, pp. 155-56, 164, 167, 190, 192, 197, 202, 224, 225.
84 Segev, 1967, p. 293, my emphasis.
85 Maoz, *Defending the Holy Land*, p. 91.
86 Gluska, *Israeli Military*, p. 224; Finkelstein, *Image and Reality*, pp. 141-43.
87 *Six Days*, pp. 311-12, 259-60; cf. p. 291. For Benny Morris and the Palestinian refugees, see Finkelstein, *Image and Reality*, chapter 3.
88 *Six Days*, pp. 187, 190-91, 195, 232, 253, 260-62, 276, 279.
89 Israel initially feigned it was Egypt that opened armed hostilities—further proof of how feeble its pretext for "preemptive" war was.
90 *Six Days*, pp. 184-87.
91 Ibid., pp. 229-31, 260, 262, 276, 278, 291. Van Creveld, *Sword and the Olive*, p. 188. Van Creveld reports that Syria "scarcely lifted a finger while their allies were being pulverized," and that "any talk of a [Syrian] offensive was absurd, given that by the evening of June 6 most of their air force had been destroyed by the IAF" (p. 191), while Maoz reports that "the Syrians and Jordanians did their absolute minimum to help the Egyptians during the war" (*Defending the Holy Land*, p. 310).
92 Segev, 1967, pp. 239, 299-300.
93 *Six Days*, pp. 211, 155, 154, 302; cf. p. 284.
94 Ibid., pp. 81, 87, 90, 91, 122, 133, 155, 187, 208, 153; cf. pp. 88, 152.
95 Ibid., p. 122.
96 Michael Brecher, *Decisions in Crisis: Israel, 1967, 1973* (Berkeley: 1980), p. 100.
97 *Six Days*, p. 314.
98 For the West Bank and Sinai, see Finkelstein, *Image and Reality*, p. 143, and sources cited, and van Creveld, *Sword and the Olive*, pp. 105, 151. See also Chapter Ten below.
99 For the congruencies between the build-ups to the respective wars, see Finkelstein, *Image and Reality*, p. 142.
100 *Six Days*, pp. 135, 155, 192, 257, 191, 253-55.
101 Ibid., pp. 122, 228-29, 261; cf. pp. 23, 280.
102 "Interviews on the Golan Heights," p. 145; Maoz, *Defending the Holy Land*, p. 626n22.

103 Segev, 1967, pp. 175-80, 184, 300. Segev also observes that once Jordan opened hostilities, "Israel could have responded by defeating the Jordanian army without taking the West Bank and Jerusalem" (ibid., p. 345; cf. Maoz, *Defending the Holy Land*, p. 518). On Israeli territorial designs prior to the June attack, see also Gluska, *Israeli Military*, pp. 16-21, 70, 76, 220; nonetheless Gluska echoes Oren's untenable position that Israeli territorial conquests during the June war were "never contemplated" (ibid., pp. 146-48, 218).

104 *Six Days*, p. 312.

105 Michael Walzer, *Just and Unjust Wars: A moral argument with historical illustrations* (New York: 1977), p. 292; Alan Dershowitz, *Preemption: A knife that cuts both ways* (New York: 2006), passim.

PART III/CHAPTER EIGHT

1 New Haven: 2007.

2 For recent mainstream scholarship on Soviet intentions before and during the June war, see Galia Golan, "The Soviet Union and the Outbreak of the June 1967 Six-Day War," *Journal of Cold War Studies* (Winter 2006).

3 *Foxbats*, p. 9.

4 Ibid., p. 7.

5 They speculate that "perhaps out of reluctance in Israel to acknowledge the close call it had faced, and in the United States to admit that it had done little to thwart the Soviet plan, the official narrative and academic convention in both countries discarded any reference to the deliberate Soviet instigation of the crisis" (ibid., p. 13). It will surely come as news in Israel, where its prospects on the eve of the June 1967 war have been typically compared to a "second Holocaust," and its subsequent victory called a "miracle," that it has been in denial about "the close call it had faced."

6 Ibid., p. 6.

7 Ibid., p. 9.

8 Ibid., pp. 24-25.

9 Ibid., p. 26.

10 Ibid., p. 32.

11 Ibid., pp. 35-36.

12 Ibid., pp. 36-37.

13 Ibid., p. 50.

14 Ibid., pp. 34-35, 43, 56, 75, 133.

15 Ibid., pp. 43-44.

16 Ibid., pp. 50-51; cf. p. 81.

17 Ibid., p. 72.

18 Ibid., pp. 79, 237n4. Erwin Weit, *Ostblock intern: 13 Jahre Dolmetscher für die polnische Partei- und Staatsführung* (Hamburg: 1970), p. 164.

19 *Foxbats*, p. 59.

20 Ibid., pp. 65-67.

21 See Chapter Seven.
22 *Foxbats*, p. 69.
23 Ibid., p. 76. For the Israeli retaliatory raid in the Jordanian village of Samu, see Chapter Seven.
24 *Foxbats*, p. 74.
25 See Chapter Seven.
26 Ibid.
27 *Foxbats*, pp. 90, 102, 103.
28 Ibid., p. 90.
29 See Chapter Seven.
30 *Foxbats*, p. 103.
31 Ibid., pp. 95-97.
32 Beyond the "single phrase" revelation, the authors also allege that Brezhnev's speech contained many more "crucial factual disclosures" and "startling statements." But, alas, we will never really know because the text was "almost certainly revised" before being distributed to other Communist parties. They further allege that another "key phrase" confirming the Kremlin plot, although not in Brezhnev's speech, "was more likely included" in another text. Ibid.
33 Ibid., p. 105.
34 Ibid., p. 77; cf. p. 68. For the Egyptian troop movements, removal of UNEF and declared blockade of the Straits of Tiran, see Chapter Seven.
35 Or, alternatively, that an Egyptian plan was implemented with "Soviet consent . . . if not instigation" and "Soviet collusion."
36 *Foxbats*, pp. 77, 105-6, 109-10, 236n47, 244n27.
37 For this "conventional narrative," see Golan, "The Soviet Union," p. 10.
38 *Foxbats*, pp. 113-16, 119-20.
39 Ibid., pp. 113-14.
40 Ibid., pp. 116, 142.
41 Ibid., p. 121, and Isabella Ginor and Gideon Remez, "The Soviet Military Role in the Arab-Israeli Conflict: Research update I—The full story," *Progressive Conservative, USA* (24 October 2007).
42 *Foxbats*, pp. 11, 27, 120, 137. The authors also speculate in passing, and without evidence, that the purpose of the overflights was to test the missile defense around Dimona (ibid., p. 133).
43 Ibid., pp. 127-29. At the time Israel assumed Egyptian-piloted MiG-21s had overflown Dimona.
44 Ibid., pp. 85-86, 131-33.
45 It was not possible to check sources such as "Report of a preliminary talk with Vybornov for a television production, provided to Isabella Ginor, who acted [as] a consultant, on 6 July 2006" (ibid., p. 239n43; cf. p. 248, nn31, 34). This writer did request from the authors information on many of their alleged sources and initially they were cooperative, but when confronted with egregious misrepresentations in their citations, they ceased corresponding.
46 George Mellinger, *Yakovlev Aces of World War II* (Oxford: 2005), p. 77.

47 *Foxbats*, pp. 174-75.
48 Ibid., p. 86; cf. pp. 131, 158. The article, V. Vakhlamov, "Aleksandr Vybornov," *Zhurnal As* (1993), is posted at http://airaces.narod.ru/all3/vyborn_ai.htm.
49 In an email I queried the authors, "Did you ask Nachumi and McFarland whether Vybornov was referring to his 'Egyptian exploits' during the June 1967 war?" (23 February 2008). The words quoted in the text are from their reply (24 February 2008).
50 Email dated 25 February 2008.
51 Email dated 25 February 2008.
52 *Foxbats*, p. 86.
53 After publication of their book, the authors announced yet another "extraordinary disclosure": the current spokesperson of the Russian air force publicly acknowledged that "in 1967" a Soviet pilot executed a "combat operation in Egypt," and "reconnaissance flights over the territory of Israel in a MiG-25RB aircraft." However, in the cited source the spokesperson did not state that the combat operation occurred during the June 1967 war, he did not state that reconnaissance flights occurred before the June 1967 war, and he did not state that these flights were over Dimona. The pilot himself reportedly denied all the allegations. David Horovitz, "Russia Confirms Soviet Sorties over Dimona in '67," *Jerusalem Post* (23 August 2007).
54 *Foxbats*, p. 133.
55 Ibid., pp. 136-37.
56 Ibid., pp. 107, 135.
57 Ibid., pp. 144-45, 157.
58 Ibid., p. 98.
59 They point to "memoirs" written by a Donetsk school administrator for a "local newspaper, followed by interviews with us, which he supported with photographs" (of his family?) as the "first published evidence" that the planned naval invasion was a "historical fact." They also acclaim a 2003 interview in a Belarussian Defense Ministry newspaper with a former Soviet soldier, who alleged that his marine artillery company was attacked while crossing the Suez Canal, as "the first direct confirmation" and "striking corroboration," albeit "short on specifics," of a Soviet naval landing. The soldier refused to be interviewed by the authors, but this reticence only proves that "the decades-long cover-up continues." To demonstrate Leonid Brezhnev's personal involvement in this naval invasion, they gesture to a description in his World War II memoir of a Soviet naval landing in the Black Sea that "corresponds neatly to the Soviets' planned Mediterranean operation in 1967." And, to prove Brezhnev's complicity in the grand plot, it is noted that he described the Israeli attack in June 1967 as "treacherous"—"an epithet traditionally used in Soviet parlance for the German invasion of the USSR in 1941." Was Hitler's attack also a Soviet conspiracy? (Ibid., pp. 150, 176-77)
60 Here's a proof of the planned nuclear blast and of its cover-up:
   An electrician's mate on the nuclear sub K-125, then in Alexandria, claimed in 1992 that his captain was instructed: "If Israel drops an atomic bomb on Egypt or Syria—nuclear missiles should be fired on it [Israel] in order to obliterate it."

But when we contacted this former sailor a decade later, he retracted his version, claiming that a newspaper reporter had misunderstood him (she, however, recorded the interview and stands by its accuracy). He professed fear for the safety of his family, despite their present domicile in Israel—fears that, even if unfounded, indicate the extent of the Russian cover-up as impressed on the servicemen involved. (ibid., p. 140)

Where to begin?

61 Ibid., p. 24.
62 Golan, "The Soviet Union," pp. 14-15.
63 An Israeli joint air and sea assault on 8 June 1967 killed 34 American servicemen and wounded at least 173 on the U.S.S. *Liberty*.
64 *Foxbats*, pp. 180-81, 185.
65 Ibid., pp. 134-35, 181, 184, 188; cf. p. 201 for Israel's alleged cover-up of its imprisonment of Soviet soldiers. Although "Israeli officialdom ... flatly denied" holding Soviet prisoners, the authors know otherwise because two former Mossad chiefs issued the denials while "wearing broad grins."
66 All the quotes except the last come from the Yale University Press webpage. Lustick's quote is from "U.S. Policies toward Israel and Iran: What are the linkages?," *Middle East Policy* (13 July 2010).

PART III/CHAPTER NINE

1 Jimmy Carter, *Palestine Peace Not Apartheid* (New York: 2006), pp. 208, 216.
2 Quincy Wright, "The Middle East Problem," in John Norton Moore, ed., *The Arab-Israeli Conflict, Readings and Documents*, abridged and revised edition (Princeton: 1977), p. 722 (originally published in *American Journal of International Law*, vol. 64, no. 2, April 1970).
3 Julius Stone, "Peace and the Palestinians," and "No Peace—No War in the Middle East," in Moore, ed., *Arab-Israeli Conflict*; Julius Stone, *Conflict through Consensus: United Nations approaches to aggression* (Baltimore: 1977); Julius Stone, *Israel and Palestine: Assault on the law of nations* (Baltimore: 1981).
4 Stone anchored his defense of Israel's occupation in many dubious (if still recycled) historical claims and legal-moral judgments, among them that: (i) although Israel was created at the expense of the Arabs in Palestine, the interests of these Palestinians were "merely ... peripheral" and "marginal" ("Peace," pp. 138-42); (ii) the primary beneficiaries of the "distribution of territory after World War I" in the Middle East were the Arab people, whereas "the Jews of the world," the other "principal" and "proper claimant" to Middle East territory, got much less; consequently it was Arabs who bore the "duty of redress for wronged marginal interests" of the Palestinian Arabs (ibid.; *Israel*, pp. 13, 25, 71); (iii) "it was the understanding of the Jewish and Arab leaders not merely that there should be a Jewish home in Palestine but that Palestine should be the Jewish homeland" (*Israel*, pp. 18, 184n12); (iv) a "distinctively Palestinian national self-recognition ... emerged on the scene—if at all— ... in 1966," and insofar as it did not previously exist and the Arab people as a whole received a "vast territorial allocation" in the Middle East, the "allocating

to the Jewish people" of "a minute fraction of the area . . . in no way impaired any right of self-determination of any other nation" (*Israel*, pp. 12, 15, 17, 25, 125). Stone also asserted that "Jewish settlement [in Palestine] was accompanied by substantial immigration from surrounding Arab countries," and a "significant number" of the Palestinian refugees "never lived in that part of Palestine which is now Israel" ("Peace," pp. 144-45). Judging from this last claim, it appears that the "revelations" Joan Peters trumpeted to much fanfare in *From Time Immemorial* (1984) were not only counterfeit but also common currency (for Peters, see Norman G. Finkelstein, *Image and Reality of the Israel-Palestine Conflict* (New York: 1995; expanded second paperback edition, 2003), chapter 2).
5 Stone, *Israel*, pp. 51-53; cf. Stone, *Conflict*, pp. 57-65, 125-27.
6 Stone, "No Peace," p. 325; Stone, *Israel*, p. 119.
7 Stone, *Israel*, pp. 22-25, 71-72 (quote); Stone, "Peace," pp. 144-49.
8 Stone, *Israel*, pp. 116-23 (quote at p. 116), 132.
9 Ibid., pp. 123, 180.
10 Ibid., pp. 67-69, 128 (quote).
11 See Chapter Seven.
12 Stone, *Israel*, pp. 46, 53, 117-18.
13 *Official Records of the General Assembly Fifth Emergency Special Session, Plenary Meetings, Verbatim Records of Meetings, 17 June—18 September 1967* (United Nations, New York: 1973).
14 Resolution A/L. 519. The full text of the resolution can be found in *Official Records of the General Assembly Fifth Emergency Special Session*, 1526th meeting, para. 82; for the vote, see 1548th meeting, para. 170.
15 *Official Records of the General Assembly Fifth Emergency Special Session*, 1527th meeting, para. 33. A recent study by one of the U.S.'s leading Middle East negotiators falsely asserts that "In the 1967 war President Lyndon Johnson fingered Egypt as the aggressor" (Aaron David Miller, *The Much Too Promised Land: America's elusive search for Arab-Israeli peace* (New York: 2008), p. 138).
16 *Official Records of the General Assembly Fifth Emergency Special Session*.
17 Ian Brownlie, *International Law and the Use of Force by States* (Oxford: 1963), pp. 408-9. He allowed for a single exception in the case of a "war of sanction" conducted "in the name of the international community."
18 R. Y. Jennings, *The Acquisition of Territory in International Law* (Manchester: 1963), p. 55.
19 D. W. Bowett, "International Law Relating to Occupied Territory: A rejoinder," *Law Quarterly Review* (July 1971), pp. 473-75.
20 Sharon Korman, *The Right of Conquest: The acquisition of territory by force in international law and practice* (Oxford: 1996), p. 200. She cites a raft of legal authorities finding that annexation in wars of self-defense was already prohibited as far back as the League of Nations Covenant (pp. 182-92). Both Article 2(4) and Article 51 of the U.N. Charter bar, according to Korman, such annexations. Although Article 51 allows for self-defense in the event of armed attack, it "is limited to the necessities of defense and by the principle of proportionality, and as such does not include the right to deprive

the attacker of its territory with a view to preventing future aggression" (pp. 205-10; quote at pp. 207-8). Nonetheless Korman contrives that, because Israel was the "victim of an attack," resolution 242 allowed for "at least minor acquisitions of territory by Israel" (pp. 210-11; cf. pp. 203, 250; but cf. also pp. 256-57). Both premise ("victim of...") and conclusion ("at least minor...") are unfounded, while within the broader context of Korman's analysis they amount to special pleading.
21 John Dugard, *Recognition and the United Nations* (Cambridge: 1987), pp. 113, 155-56.
22 Stone, *Israel*, pp. 54-55.
23 Brownlie, *International Law*, p. 153.
24 See Korman, *Right of Conquest*: "But just as potential criminals in most civilized national societies are not threatened with robbery as punishment for robbery, or with the death penalty as punishment for murder, so international society in the era of the United Nations, by abolishing conquest or territorial dismemberment as a legitimate punishment for the crime of aggression, seeks to transcend the morals of an earlier and barbarous age reflected in such primitive principles as the lex talionis—'an eye for an eye, a tooth for a tooth'—or the title by conquest" (p. 216). She further notes that Stone's interpretation is contrary to the practices of the United Nations, pointing to the U.N.'s preservation of Iraq's territorial integrity after evicting it from Kuwait in 1991 (pp. 214-16).
25 Stone also asserted that (1) the "inadmissibility" clause was introduced merely "by way of consolation to the Arab States," which could not win the principle of full Israeli withdrawal, and (2) only the Arab states proposed that this "Delphic," "eloquently ambiguous and conciliatory" and "superficially ambiguous" prohibition "should be taken literally in its widest ambit," while in actuality it was only meant to bar the acquisition of territory in an "unlawful war" (Stone, *Israel*, pp. 53-54; Stone, *Conflict*, pp. 57, 59, 63, 65).
Even if Stone were right that the "inadmissibility" clause was a token verbal gesture to placate the Arabs, his claim would be irrelevant to the interpretation of resolution 242. The resolution says what it says, and its wording matters, regardless of whether it was crafted to gain votes or avoid vetoes or for any other reason. In the withdrawal clause, for example, the omission of the word "the" before the phrase "territories occupied in the recent conflict" was a verbal gesture to placate the Israelis. But one does not hear Israel's defenders argue that the missing "the" is of no consequence. Quite the opposite. I am grateful to Frank J. Menetrez for this point.
26 "Introduction to the Annual Report of the Secretary-General on the Work of the Organization, 16 June 1966—15 June 1967," *General Assembly Official Records: Twenty-Second Session. Supplement No. 1A* (United Nations, 15 September 1967), para. 47. U Thant continued, "It would lead to disastrous consequences if the United Nations were to abandon or compromise this principle" (ibid.); cf. para. 49, "it is indispensable to an international community of States—if it is not to follow the law of the jungle—that the territorial integrity of every State be respected, and the occupation by military force of the territory of one State by another not be condoned." The president of the General Assembly noted in his synopsis of the debate at the Special

Session, "[T]here is virtual unanimity in upholding the principle that conquest of territory by war is inadmissible in our time and under the Charter. The affirmation of this principle was made in virtually all statements and—I should add with some emphasis—by none more emphatically than all of the big Powers.... In this sense, virtually all speakers laid down the corollary that withdrawal of forces to their original position is expected" (*Official Records of the General Assembly Fifth Emergency Special Session*, 1549th meeting, para. 11).

27 *Official Records of the General Assembly Fifth Emergency Special Session*.
28 The U.S. early on in the debate submitted a draft resolution (A/L. 520) that vaguely called for "disengagement and withdrawal of forces" but, ostensibly due to lack of support, did not put it to a vote. For the text of the U.S. draft, see *Official Records of the General Assembly Fifth Emergency Special Session*, 1527th meeting, para. 39; for the U.S. withdrawal of the draft from consideration, see 1548th meeting, para. 175.
29 Draft resolutions by the Soviet Union (A/L. 519) and Albania were also submitted for a vote (A/L. 521) but they received little support. For the texts of the Soviet and Albanian drafts, see *Official Records of the General Assembly Fifth Emergency Special Session*, respectively, 1526th meeting, para. 82 and 1535th meeting, para. 67; for the votes, see, respectively, 1548th meeting, paras. 171-74 and 1548th meeting, para. 176.
30 To be precise, the General Assembly was split on whether full Israeli withdrawal should be conditional on an *explicit* commitment by Arab states to a *simultaneous* termination of belligerency (Latin American draft) or whether full Israeli withdrawal should be conditional on an *implicit* commitment by Arab states to an *eventual* termination of belligerency (Non-Aligned draft). Although the arguments on both sides were compelling, it must be said that the warning of the Iraqi representative proved prescient. He predicted that Israel would exploit any condition put on the Arab states as a pretext for avoiding full withdrawal:

> [I]t is necessary to avoid the pitfalls of adopting a resolution full of loop-holes, one which will enable Israel to have the excuse it wants to procrastinate on withdrawal and to prolong its occupation. One way to do this is to insist that all outstanding questions have to be resolved and settled before withdrawal is completed. This approach conforms entirely with the policies of Israel and its plans. Since the discussion of all these complex and varied questions is likely to take time and their settlement is not foreseeable in the immediate future, the linking of withdrawal to final and definite settlement of all issues will enable Israel inevitably to maintain its occupation, hoping with the passage of time that occupation will be transformed into permanent annexation. This is no fanciful excursion into the future. It is solidly based on past experience. Let us not forget that 40 percent of the territory which Israel controlled before 5 June was first occupied under the terms of a temporary cease-fire.
>
> ...
>
> All Israel has to do is make exorbitant demands which it knows beforehand the Arabs will not accept, and then, arming itself with that refusal, continue its occupation of Arab territories, gradually making changes, such as those it has

already made in Jerusalem, with a view to the ultimate annexation of those territories. (1545th meeting, paras. 60-61, 71)

When the Security Council convened in November 1967, the Non-Aligned countries joined with the Latin American countries on the basis of the original Latin American draft resolution making Israel's full withdrawal conditional on the Arab states' explicit and simultaneous termination of belligerency. For the text of this joint draft, which was submitted to the Security Council, see *United Nations Security Council*, S/8227.

31 For the full text of the Non-Aligned draft (A/L. 522/Rev. 3), see *Official Records of the General Assembly Fifth Emergency Special Session*, 1540th meeting, para. 78, 1543rd meeting, para. 157, 1545th meeting, paras. 28-33.
32 For the full text of the Latin American draft (A/L. 523/Rev. 1), see *Official Records of the General Assembly Fifth Emergency Special Session*, 1544th meeting, para. 7 and 1548th meeting, para. 58. The Latin American countries first introduced into the General Assembly debate the legal principle barring acquisition of territory by force. See Arthur Lall, *The UN and the Middle East Crisis, 1967* (New York: 1968), chapter 9. This principle was inscribed in many treaties among Latin American countries predating World War II (see Brownlie, *International Law*, pp. 92-102, 410-13, and Korman, *Right of Conquest*, pp. 234-38).
33 The vote on the Non-Aligned resolution was 53 in favor and 46 against, with 20 abstentions, while the vote on the Latin American resolution was 57 in favor and 43 against, with 20 abstentions. See *Official Records of the General Assembly Fifth Emergency Special Session*, 1548th meeting, paras. 167, 177. Neither resolution garnered the necessary two-thirds vote to be adopted. The only member states that neither voted for one of these resolutions nor expressly endorsed the principle of full withdrawal during the General Assembly debate were Israel, Kenya, Laos, Niger, Portugal, Rwanda, Singapore, and South Africa.
34 *Official Records of the General Assembly Fifth Emergency Special Session*, 1554th meeting, para. 91; see also 1546th meeting, paras. 3, 9, 10, 32.
35 *Official Records of the General Assembly Fifth Emergency Special Session*, 1547th meeting, para. 92. On the isolation of Israel's position, see also Lall, *UN and the Middle East Crisis*, p. 180.
36 *United Nations Security Council*, S/PV. 1381.
37 *United Nations Security Council*, S/PV. 1382.
38 Lord Caradon et al., *United Nations Security Council Resolution 242: A case study in diplomatic ambiguity* (Washington, D.C.: 1981), p. 13; for Caradon's position, which has been grossly distorted by Israel's apologists, see also Lall, *UN and the Middle East Crisis*, pp. 226, 252.
39 See Chapter Four.
40 "Telegram from the President's Special Assistant (Rostow) to President Johnson" (24 October 1967), "Telegram from the Mission to the United Nations to the Department of State" (26 October 1967), "Telegram from the Mission to the United Nations to the Department of State" (4 November 1967), "Telegram from the

Department of State to the Embassy in Israel" (5 November 1967), "Telegram from the Department of State to the Embassy in Israel" (30 November 1968), "Memorandum from Secretary of State Rusk to President Johnson" (n.d. [Document 513]), in *Foreign Relations of the United States, 1964-1968, vol. XIX, Arab-Israeli Crisis and War, 1967* (Washington, D.C.: 2004). See also Nina J. Noring and Walter B. Smith II, "The Withdrawal Clause in UN Security Council Resolution 242 of 1967" (U.S. State Department; classified), which is excerpted in Finkelstein, *Image and Reality*, pp. 147-48; see also ibid., p. xvii.

41 "Telegram from the Embassy in Israel to the Department of State" (16 August 1967), "Telegram from the Mission to the United Nations to the Department of State" (4 November 1967), in *Foreign Relations of the United States, vol. XIX, Arab-Israeli Crisis and War, 1967*. See also Finkelstein, *Image and Reality*, p. 257n63.

42 Lall, *UN and the Middle East Crisis*, p. 254.

43 "Declaration of Principles of International Law Concerning Friendly Relations and Co-operation among States in Accordance with the Charter of the United Nations," *UN General Assembly Resolution 2625* (XXV), 24 October 1970 (see Korman, *Right of Conquest*, pp. 209, 243). Stone, *Conflict*, pp. 60-61, also denies the unambiguous meaning of these words in the 1970 resolution.

44 The recent versions of the resolution read: "The withdrawal of Israel from the Palestinian territory occupied since 1967, including East Jerusalem."

45 Resolution 194 (III) affirmed the right of the Palestine refugees to return or to compensation. In recent years the resolution has been calling for a "just resolution" of the refugee question "in conformity with" 194.

46 An authoritative opinion on the legal status of General Assembly resolutions repeatedly affirmed by resounding majorities was rendered by Judge Hersch Lauterpacht in the 1955 South-West Africa Voting Procedure case before the International Court of Justice. A "State may not be acting illegally," he wrote in an oft-cited separate opinion,

> by declining to act upon a recommendation or series of recommendations on the same subject, but in doing so it acts at its peril when a point is reached when the cumulative effect of the persistent disregard of the articulate opinion of the Organization is such as to foster the conviction that the State in question has become guilty of disloyalty to the Principles and Purposes of the Charter. Thus, a ... State which consistently sets itself above the solemnly and repeatedly expressed judgment of the Organization, in particular in proportion as that judgment approximates to unanimity, may find that it has overstepped the imperceptible line between impropriety and illegality, between discretion and arbitrariness, between the exercise of the legal right to disregard the recommendation and the abuse of that right, and that it has exposed itself to consequences legitimately following as a sanction. (*South-West Africa—Voting Procedure, Advisory Opinion of 7 June 1955, ICJ Reports 1955*, p. 120)

It would be hard to dispute that Lauterpacht's strictures apply to Israel's "persistent disregard" of the overwhelming judgment of the General Assembly.

47 *Legal Consequences of the Construction of a Wall in the Occupied Palestinian Territory, Advisory Opinion* (Int'l Ct. of Justice July 9, 2004), 43 IL M 1009 (2004) [hereafter: *ICJ*]. See the Appendix for further discussion of the ICJ opinion.
48 *ICJ*, para. 87, quoting the 1970 General Assembly resolution "Declaration of Principles of International Law ..."; cf. paras. 74, 75, 117.
49 Ibid., para. 99, quoting Security Council resolution 446 (1979); the ICJ also cited (para. 120) Security Council resolutions 452 (1979) and 465 (1980), the last of which condemned Israeli settlement practices as a "flagrant violation" of the Fourth Geneva Convention.
50 Ibid., paras. 117-20.
51 Andrew C. Esensten, "Dershowitz Advises Israel on Wall Dispute," *Harvard Crimson* (24 February 2004).
52 See the note in the Appendix on the separate opinions of Higgins and Kooijmans. In an earlier defense of Israel, Higgins (who is Jewish) had questioned the applicability of the "inadmissibility" principle to the Israeli-occupied territories because Israel supposedly "responded to a threat of annihilation" (Rosalyn Higgins, "The June War: The United Nations and legal background," in Moore, ed., *Arab-Israeli Conflict*, p. 552).
53 He is both Jewish and a survivor of the Nazi holocaust.
54 "Human Rights Watch Urges Attention to Future of Palestinian Refugees" (21 December 2000; www.hrw.org/en/news/2000/12/21/human-rights-watch-urges-attention-future-palestinian-refugees); "Israel, Palestinian Leaders Should Guarantee Right of Return as Part of Comprehensive Refugee Solution" (21 December 2000; www.hrw.org/en/news/2000/12/21/israel-palestinian-leaders-should-guarantee-right-return-part-comprehensive-refugee-). Amnesty International, *The Right to Return: The case of the Palestinians*, policy statement (London: 29 March 2001).
55 Adam Roberts, "Prolonged Military Occupation: The Israeli-occupied territories 1967-1988," in Emma Playfair, ed., *International Law and the Administration of Occupied Territories: Two decades of Israeli occupation of the West Bank and Gaza Strip* (Oxford: 1992), p. 84; Antonio Cassese, *Self-determination of Peoples: A legal reappraisal* (Cambridge: 1995), p. 230.
56 From the dovish to the hawkish extreme, the full gamut of leading Israeli legal scholars has rejected many of these established principles and applications of international law. See, e.g., Eyal Benvenisti and Eyal Zamir, "Private Claims to Property Rights in the Future Israeli-Palestinian Settlement," *American Journal of International Law* (1995) (rejecting Palestinian right of return); Yoram Dinstein, *War, Aggression and Self-Defence*, fourth edition (Cambridge: 2005), pp. 40-41 (disputing "inadmissibility" principle in defensive wars), and 192 (asserting Israel acted in "self-defence" in June 1967); Yoram Dinstein, *The Conduct of Hostilities under the Law of International Armed Conflict* (Cambridge: 2004), pp. 232-33 (disputing illegality of Israeli settlements); Yoram Dinstein, *The International Law of Belligerent Occupation* (Cambridge: 2009), pp. 240-41 (asserting legality of some Israeli settlements); Michla Pomerance, "The ICJ's Advisory Jurisdiction and the Crumbling Wall Between the Political and

the Judicial," *American Journal of International Law* (January 2005), p. 38 (disputing "inadmissibility" principle in defensive wars); David Kretzmer, "The Advisory Opinion: The light treatment of international humanitarian law," ibid., p. 91 (disputing illegality of Israeli settlements); Yaffa Zilbershats, "International Law and the Palestinian Right of Return to the State of Israel," in Eyal Benvenisti, Chaim Gans and Sari Hanafi, eds., *Israel and the Palestinian Refugees* (Berlin: 2007) (rejecting Palestinian right of return). On the other hand, soon after the June 1967 war the Israeli Foreign Ministry's legal counsel, Theodor Meron, privately opined that the international law prohibition on building civilian settlements in the Israeli-occupied territories was "categorical." Meron, who left Israel and later became a distinguished jurist and president of the U.N. tribunal on war crimes in the former Yugoslavia, recently reaffirmed this opinion on the settlements' illegality. Gershom Gorenberg, *The Accidental Empire: Israel and the birth of the settlements, 1967-1977* (New York: 2006), pp. 99-102; Donald Macintyre, "Secret Memo Shows Israel Knew Six Day War Was Illegal," *Independent* (26 May 2007); www.soas.ac.uk/lawpeacemideast/resources/ (English translation of Meron's 1967 memorandum).
57 New York: 2004.
58 The subsequently published accounts of Ross's key aides echoed his version of events. See Miller, *Much Too Promised Land*; Martin Indyk, *Innocent Abroad: An intimate account of American peace diplomacy in the Middle East* (New York: 2009).
59 *Missing Peace*, p. 14.
60 Ibid., p. 773.
61 Ibid., p. 106.
62 For comprehensive accounts of Camp David based on eyewitnesses, see Charles Enderlin, *Shattered Dreams: The failure of the peace process in the Middle East, 1995-2002* (New York: 2002); Clayton E. Swisher, *The Truth About Camp David: The untold story about the collapse of the Middle East peace process* (New York: 2004); and Jeremy Pressman, "Visions in Collision: What happened at Camp David and Taba?," *International Security* (Fall 2003).
63 *Missing Peace*, p. 775.
64 Ibid., p. 189.
65 Ibid., p. 356; cf. p. 359.
66 Ibid., pp. 131-32, 362, 400, 416, 418.
67 Ibid., p. 307.
68 Ibid., pp. 42 ("Palestinian resentment"), 190, 265 ("Palestinian rioting"), 359, 362, 376-77, 379, 409.
69 Ibid., p. 411.
70 Ibid., pp. 417, 419.
71 Ibid., pp. 90-94.
72 Ibid., p. 776. This one-sided focus on Palestinian violence is echoed in Miller, *Much Too Promised Land*, pp. 261-71 passim, and Indyk, *Innocent Abroad*, pp. 70-71.
73 *Missing Peace*, p. 781.
74 Amnesty International, *Five Years after the Oslo Agreement: Human rights sacrificed for "security"* (1998); B'Tselem (The Israeli Information Center for Human Rights in

the Occupied Territories), *Oslo: Before and after* (1999); Human Rights Watch, *Israel's Record of Occupation: Violations of civil and political rights* (1998). Unless otherwise indicated, the quoted statements in the text come from these reports.

75 B'Tselem, "Statistics: Fatalities in the first intifada" (www.btselem.org/english/Statistics/First_intifada_Tables.asp).
76 Martin van Creveld, *The Sword and the Olive: A critical history of the Israeli Defense Force* (New York: 1998), p. 349.
77 For the settler's fine, see Palestinian Society for the Protection of Human Rights and the Environment, *Five Years of Oslo: A summary of human rights violations since the Declaration of Principles* (1998).
78 *Missing Peace*, p. 366.
79 See Chapter Five.
80 In addition to publications already cited, see Amnesty International, *Palestinian Authority: Prolonged political detention, torture and unfair trials* (1996), and Human Rights Watch, *Palestinian Self-Rule Areas: Human rights under the Palestinian Authority* (1997).
81 *Missing Peace*, p. 189.
82 Shlomo Ben-Ami, *Scars of War, Wounds of Peace: The Israeli-Arab tragedy* (New York: 2006), pp. 191, 211.
83 Andy Levy-Ajzenkopf, "Sharansky on Tour Promoting Identity, Freedom," *Canadian Jewish News* (1 July 2008).
84 Graham Usher, "The Politics of Internal Security: The PA's new intelligence services," *Journal of Palestine Studies* (Winter 1996), p. 28; *The B'Tselem Human Rights Report* (Spring 1994).
85 In addition to above-cited sources on the PA's human rights record, see esp. Amnesty International, *Trial at Midnight: Secret, summary, unfair trials in Gaza* (1995).
86 *Missing Peace*, p. 193. Miller likewise reports that the U.S. "tolerated Arafat's state security courts . . . largely to keep the peace process going, and partly because Israelis tolerated it . . . as well" (*Much Too Promised Land*, p. 326).
87 B'Tselem (Israeli Information Center for Human Rights in the Occupied Territories), *Land Grab: Israel's settlement policy in the West Bank* (May 2002).
88 *Missing Peace*, p. 491; cf. p. 380.
89 Ross alleges that if Palestinians had accepted the 1978 Camp David autonomy plan, they "could have vetoed" further settlement expansion (ibid., p. 692). Yet, the autonomy plan made no mention of the Israeli settlements, let alone a Palestinian veto on their expansion. Moreover, if Palestinian acceptance of the Oslo Accord failed to halt settlement expansion, it is unclear why their acceptance of Camp David would have.
90 Ibid., p. 89.
91 At one point Ross alleges that Arafat tacitly acquiesced in settlement expansion (ibid., p. 195; for the identical claim, see Indyk, *Innocent Abroad*, pp. 71-72, 118-19). Why Arafat would be indifferent to Israel's dismemberment of the territory he aspired one day to govern goes unexplained.

92 *Missing Peace*, p. 354.
93 Ben-Ami, *Scars of War*, pp. 212, 215-16 (extended quote), 235, 296. Elsewhere in the book Ben-Ami referred to Israel's "increasingly unbearable colonialist system of domination and land grab" in the West Bank (p. 230).
94 *Missing Peace*, pp. 117-18, 190, 354.
95 His account focuses primarily on the minutiae of negotiations, which fall outside the scope of this chapter and which future historians will require a Rosetta stone to decipher. Consider this hieroglyphic from Ross's text:
> In our secure call the next day, Bibi [Netanyahu] raised my original bridging idea—not so much the notion of 11+2 as his being able to say he had done something less than 13, and Arafat and Clinton being able to say it was a 13 percent transfer of territory. But now Bibi said he did not know how to actually do this. There needed to be an area of special status that would make up the difference between what he was doing for the further redeployment and the total we were asking for. I saw an opening here and probed: Is the problem that roads or an economic zone can't cover sufficient territory to reach the 13 percent given the size of the FRD [further redeployments] you can do? Yes, was the answer, and he could simply not increase the size of the B area—an area where Israelis retained the security responsibility but the Palestinians had the civil responsibility. Previously, I had raised the idea of creating what might be termed a "B-" area—an area that gave the Palestinians more authority than in the C areas, but less than a full-fledged B area. Bibi had explored it, but also said it was not doable. I revisited this idea now but with a slightly different twist. What if we created an area that you could say was a "C" and they would be able to say was a "B"? (ibid., p. 390)

Shortly after the 1995 Oslo II Accord was signed, this writer observed, "With its multiple, chapter-length annexes and appendices and multitude of pettifogging, obscure, ambiguous and mutually contradictory details, Oslo II presages, not the emancipation, but the emasculation of Palestine" (Finkelstein, *Image and Reality*, p. 176). This excerpt of Oslo-in-action suggests the prediction was not off the mark.
96 *Missing Peace*, p. 775.
97 Ibid., p. 42; cf. pp. 200, 686.
98 Ibid., pp. 35 ("eyes...responsible"), 42 ("It was theirs"), 44 ("Israel's presence," "land was theirs"), 55 ("rightfully theirs"), 82 ("outrage," "considered to be theirs"), 195 ("considered to be theirs"), 332 ("believed was theirs"), 763 ("land is 'theirs'"), 765 ("perceived to be theirs").
99 Arafat "flew into a rage" and "ranted for several minutes" after seeing the Oslo map, Ross similarly observes, because of the "appearance" that the Palestinian areas comprised "isolated islands that are cut off from each other" (ibid., p. 205). In fact the Oslo map did shatter the Palestinian territory into a maze of fragments. For an identical dismissal of the "Palestinians' sense of entitlement to all the territories in the West Bank and Gaza occupied by Israel in 1967," and the "particular Palestinian mind-set" that "all of historic Palestine was rightfully theirs and had been taken away from them by force.... Now they argued it was unfair to be expected to bargain over the 22

percent that encompassed the West Bank and Gaza," see Indyk, *Innocent Abroad*, pp. 295, 311.
100 *Missing Peace*, p. 43.
101 According to Ross, U.N. resolution 242 did "not necessarily mean withdrawal from all the territories captured in 1967" (ibid., p. 815). In support of this claim he cites the authority of U.N. Ambassador Arthur Goldberg, and the Washington Institute for Near East Policy monograph *UN Security Council Resolution 242: The building block of peacemaking* (Washington, D.C.: 1993). However, as already shown and quoting Goldberg, the consensus of the Security Council (and General Assembly) was that 242 called for full Israeli withdrawal from the territories it occupied in June 1967 apart from minor and mutual border adjustments. The quality of the monographic evidence Ross relies on can be gathered from statements such as "the Arab population of the West Bank and the Gaza Strip" is "often wrongly called 'The Palestinians,'" and 242 "does not require the Israelis to transfer to the Arabs all, most, or indeed any of the occupied territories" (WINEP, *UN Security Council Resolution 242*, pp. 6, 18-19).
102 Eyal Benvenisti, *The International Law of Occupation* (Princeton: 1993), pp. 145-46, 215-16; cf. p. 187.
103 Security Council resolution 338, passed during the October 1973 war, called for implementation of resolution 242.
104 Norman G. Finkelstein, *The Rise and Fall of Palestine: A personal account of the intifada years* (Minneapolis, MN: 1996), pp. 53-56.
105 Dinstein, *War, Aggression and Self-Defence*, p. 302; David Cortright and George A. Lopez, *The Sanctions Decade: Assessing U.N. strategies in the 1990s* (Boulder, CO: 2000); Marc Weller and Barbara Metzger, *Double Standards* (Negotiations Affairs Department, Palestine Liberation Organization: 24 September 2002).
106 *Missing Peace*, pp. 47 ("throughout," "naught"), 115 ("agenda," "redefinition"), 127 ("painful"), 759-60 ("irreversible," "*new* consensus"; my emphasis), 766 ("failed"), 767 ("threshold").
107 Noam Chomsky, *Fateful Triangle: The United States, Israel and the Palestinians*, updated edition (Boston: 1999), chapter 3; Norman G. Finkelstein, *Beyond Chutzpah: On the misuse of anti-Semitism and the abuse of history* (Berkeley: 2005; expanded paperback edition, 2008), pp. 292-97.
108 Yehuda Lukacs, ed., *The Israeli-Palestinian Conflict: A documentary record, 1967-1990* (Cambridge: 1992), pp. 477-79.
109 Yehoshaphat Harkabi, *Israel's Fateful Hour* (New York: 1988), p. 101. It is a measure of how deeply the facts have been buried that even an Israeli Mossad chief appears genuinely unaware of this Saudi peace plan. Efraim Halevy, *Man in the Shadows: Inside the Middle East crisis with a man who led the Mossad* (New York: 2006), p. 141.
110 Avner Yaniv, *Dilemmas of Security: Politics, strategy and the Israeli experience in Lebanon* (Oxford: 1987), pp. 20 ("Zionist state"), 22-23 ("political move"), 50-54 ("cabinets," "moderates," "radical," "deliberately"), 67-70 ("civilians," "peace offensive"), 87-89 ("inflexibility"), 100-1 ("*raison d'être*"), 105-6, 113, 143 ("destroying"),

294n46 ("doves"). In his capsule summary of the sequence of events just reviewed, Indyk writes: "In 1982, Arafat's terrorist activities eventually provoked the Israeli government of Menachem Begin and Ariel Sharon into a full-scale invasion of Lebanon" (*Innocent Abroad*, p. 75).
111 *Missing Peace*, p. 49. For excerpts from the Algiers political communiqué, see Lukacs, *Israeli-Palestinian Conflict*, pp. 415-20.
112 For the text see M. Cherif Bassiouni, ed., *Documents on the Arab-Israeli Conflict: The Palestinians and the Israeli-Palestinian peace process* (Ardsley, NY: 2005), vol. 2, pp. 879-81.
113 Ben-Ami, *Scars of War*, pp. 203-4 ("encouraged," "disarray," "amenable"), 207 ("accommodating," "oblivion," "vital"), 210, 211. Ben-Ami occasionally ascribes the Oslo Accord's silence on critical Palestinian rights to the bungling of PLO negotiators (ibid., pp. 212, 230). Yet, corrupt as it was the PLO acquiesced in Israeli demands not from incompetence but, as Ben-Ami himself acknowledges, because of its "circumstantial weakness": "If the Oslo Accords fell short of Palestinian expectations, it was because the agreement was the result of the balance of power" (ibid., pp. 204, 211). The insider account of Israeli negotiator Uri Savir confirms that at every stage in the Oslo and post-Oslo negotiations the Palestinian team, if forced to accept the wrong answers, nonetheless did pose the right questions (*The Process: 1,100 days that changed the Middle East* (New York: 1998), esp. pp. 69-70, 72, 185, 196, 200-1, 211, 213). On the official PLO leadership being more pliable than grassroots Palestinian representatives, see also *Missing Peace*, p. 103.
114 *Missing Peace*, p. 91.
115 Meron Medzini, ed., *Israel's Foreign Relations: Selected documents, 1995-1996* (Jerusalem: 1997), p. 323.
116 Ben-Ami, *Scars of War*, pp. 220, 233. Ross himself concedes that Barak went "way beyond" Rabin, "who would have found [Barak's] ideas on the borders and Jerusalem almost impossible to stomach" (*Missing Peace*, p. 715). Israeli strategic analyst Zeev Maoz confirms that Rabin's "vision of the final status settlement with the Palestinians ... was very narrow, consisting of Israeli military presence along the Jordan Valley and the establishment of a Palestinian entity that was less than a state" (*Defending the Holy Land: A critical analysis of Israel's security and foreign policy* (Ann Arbor: 2006), p. 462). Indyk purports that, at a dinner party just before his death, Rabin came out in support of a Palestinian state, but he still concedes that the state Rabin had in mind would have comprised no more than 80 percent of the West Bank and "Palestinian sovereignty in any part of Jerusalem was out of the question" (*Innocent Abroad*, pp. 2-3, 313).
117 Halevy, *Man*, p. 46.
118 *Missing Peace*, p. 42.
119 Jerusalem Media and Communications Center (JMCC) poll no. 30, "On Palestinian-Israeli Peace Index" (1999); cf. JMCC, in cooperation with Tami Steinmetz Center for Peace Research, Tel Aviv University (1999), poll no. 35, "On Palestinian and Israeli Attitudes Towards the Future of the Peace Process" (1999), p. 5.

120 Three distinct phases marked off the Israeli-Palestinian negotiations of 2000-1: the Camp David summit in July 2000, the parameters President Clinton proposed in December 2000, and the Taba negotiations in January 2001. Ross's narrative covers the first two phases, Taba getting barely a mention. For convenience's sake *Camp David* will denote both the summit and Clinton proposals. However, where the distinction needs to be made *Camp David summit* will denote the first phase and *Clinton Parameters* the second.
121 *Missing Peace*, pp. 685-86 ("tendency to pocket"), 693 ("said no"), 705 ("not presented"), 708, 749-50, 767 ("could not compromise"), 768, 775 ("illusion"), 808 ("Arafat legacy").
122 Ibid., p. 663.
123 *ICJ*, paras. 78, 87.
124 Ibid., paras. 119-20; cf. para. 99.
125 See above.
126 *Missing Peace*, pp. 635, 640, 667, 673-75, 723, 724-25, 768 ("meaningful concessions"). The delineation by lead Israeli negotiator Gilead Sher of "real 'core' Palestinian positions" yet again shows that all the concessions at Camp David came from the Palestinian side: "most of the territory occupied in 1967, . . . plus land swaps, less a small percentage of the land, which Israel would continue to retain"; "in return for Israeli flexibility on formulations that could have satisfied the Palestinian needs for appearances, the Palestinians would not have demanded the actual exercise of the Right of Return into Israel"; "with regard to Jerusalem . . ., explicit sovereignty over 'Al-Haram al-Sharif,' the areas around the mosques, two Quarters in the Old City, and over the majority of Arab neighborhoods outside the walls." Gilead Sher, *The Israeli-Palestinian Peace Negotiations, 1999-2001: Within reach* (New York: 2006), pp. 62-63. Ross occasionally suggests that it was Palestinian negotiators rather than Arafat himself who offered these compromises: "We had continually moved toward [Arafat]; while his negotiators moved, he had not moved at all" (*Missing Peace*, p. 708). However, Ross neither adduces evidence to support this distinction nor is it plausible that the positions articulated by Arafat's hand-picked negotiators significantly differed from his own. Even after his death in late 2004, Arafat's successors still hewed to the course he mapped out in the Oslo negotiations. Ross also seems unaware that, were he correct, his book would make little sense: What point would there be in minutely detailing the positions of Palestinian negotiators if they represented no one except themselves? After noting that "Palestinian negotiators conceded that a majority of the settlers would remain in settlement blocs that would be annexed to Israel," and that "there would have to be a residual Israeli security presence" in the West Bank, Indyk specifically goes on to acknowledge, "Arafat also made some important concessions . . . : that the Palestinians would recognize Israeli sovereignty in all the newly built Jewish suburbs of East Jerusalem all the way from Givat Zeev in the north to Giloh in the south and Maale Adumim in the east; that Israel would have sovereignty over the Jewish Quarter of the Old City and that the Wailing Wall would remain in Israel's hands" (*Innocent Abroad*, pp. 337-38).

127 *Missing Peace*, pp. 674-75, 677. Echoing his Israeli counterpart, Ross also declares that "the Palestinians had come more to maneuver in the souk than to negotiate a deal" (ibid., p. 675). Although the metaphor is right, they apparently got the subject wrong. According to Ron Pundak, not the Palestinians but "Barak dragged his feet and treated the talks like a Persian market. Abu Mazen [Mahmoud Abbas]—the Palestinian architect of the Oslo accord ...—repeatedly recommended that the general principles guiding the Permanent Status Agreement be established at the outset.... But Barak, fearing he would 'expose' his position too early in the game, rejected this proposal." Ron Pundak, "From Oslo to Taba: What went wrong," *Survival* (Autumn 2001), p. 39. Pundak is Director-General of the Peres Center for Peace in Tel Aviv and participated in Israeli-Palestinian negotiations during the Oslo years.
128 Cited in Ron Pundak, "Camp David II: Israel's misconceived approach," p. 7 (www.peres-center.org/media/Upload/229.pdf).
129 *Missing Peace*, p. 743.
130 Compare these passages from Ross:
   In the first meeting on territory and borders, Abu Ala tried a new tack. Whereas previously he would not discuss security until the Israelis accepted the Palestinian concept of their eastern border, now he added the condition that he would not discuss possible modifications to meet Israeli needs on the western border unless he knew that the total size of the Palestinian territory would remain unchanged. As he put it, so long as the Palestinian state would comprise the 6,500 square kilometers that currently made up the West Bank, Gaza, and East Jerusalem, he could consider modifications to meet Israeli needs; if not, he could not. This was Abu Ala's way of trying to get the Israelis to concede both the eastern border and equal swaps of territory as conditions for considering Israeli needs. This was, of course, a prescription for going nowhere. (Ibid., pp. 663-64)
   Shlomo ... persuasively argued it was time for both sides to give up their myths. Israel was giving up its myths: being in the Jordan Valley forever and not dividing Jerusalem. These myths were as central to Israel's belief system as the right of return was to the Palestinians. It was time for both sides to accept reality and surrender their myths. (Ibid., p. 721; cf. p. 4)
In the first instance Ross deems the Palestinian tack a nonstarter because it demands from Israel the impossible "concessions" of recognizing the internationally sanctioned Palestinian border and compensating Palestinians for the Palestinian territory Israel covets, while in the second instance he puts on the same plane of unreality Israel's claim on the Jordan Valley and all of Jerusalem, and the Palestinian right of return, even if the former claim has no legal basis whereas the latter one does, and leaving aside that Palestinians did in effect surrender it.
   In like fashion Indyk puts forth this prescription for resolving the conflict:
   Ideally, Israeli and Palestinian leaders would have the courage to stand in front of their people and explain that in order to achieve peace both have bitter pills to swallow: Palestinians would have to give up their claim to a right of return to Israel in return for the implementation of that right in their Palestinian home-

land; Israelis would have to concede their claim to Arab parts of Jerusalem. (*Innocent Abroad*, p. 413) He depicts the relinquishment of Israeli control over the Arab parts of East Jerusalem as a reciprocal concession, yet Israel has no legal claim to any of East Jerusalem. This ideal solution seemingly based on mutual compromise in fact requires Palestinians to make the double concession of the right of return and the illegal Jewish settlements in East Jerusalem, while it requires Israel to make none.

131 Israeli and other official American accounts of the negotiations also resort to this needs framework. Sher rebukes Palestinians for attempting to "hide behind the veil of international legitimacy ... UN resolutions"; for having "presented the traditional Palestinian moral demand for 1967 borders and implementation of UNSCR 242"; for putting forth "the familiar Palestinian narrative regarding Jerusalem: 'We have given up our justified demand for the western part of the city. In all the remaining parts you have nothing to look for, everything should be turned over to us'"; and for being "stuck in their comfortable cradle of international legitimacy." He favorably contrasts Israel's diplomatic posture that "does not demand more than accommodating its most basic needs," while "satisfying" these Israeli needs would constitute a "reasonable" settlement "guided by feasible solutions, not by a perceived notion of 'justice.'" Sher, *Israeli-Palestinian Peace Negotiations*, pp. 40 ("veil"), 43 ("most basic needs"), 68 ("moral demand"), 71 ("turned over"), 75 ("satisfying," "reasonable"), 84 ("cradle"), 191 ("feasible"). "What stands in the way of a solution," according to Miller, "is the absence of political will and leadership on both sides to understand what's necessary to meet the other side's needs and to take the political decisions to move forward." In order to break out of this impasse, he counsels, the Palestinians must be told, "Fine, you want your hundred percent; here's what Israel needs. Now get serious" (Miller, *Much Too Promised Land*, pp. 363, 370).

132 *Missing Peace*, pp. 667-68.
133 Ibid., p. 55.
134 See Finkelstein, *Image and Reality*, pp. 157-71.
135 *Missing Peace*, p. 636.
136 Ibid., p. 654.
137 Ibid., p. 734.
138 Ibid., p. 762.
139 Ibid., p. 763.
140 Ibid.
141 Ibid., p. 771.
142 Ibid., p. 726.
143 Enderlin, *Shattered Dreams*, p. 202.
144 *Missing Peace*, p. 639.
145 Ibid., p. 655. In fact the military value of the Jordan Valley is nil. Ben-Ami dismisses it as a "mythological strategic asset," while Maoz deems it a "fairly ridiculous" Israeli demand that was "meaningless in terms of strategy," and a "strategic burden rather than a strategic asset" (*Scars of War*, p. 270; *Defending the Holy Land*, pp. 477, 493, 539, 646n50). "Even the IDF [Israel Defense Forces] acknowledged that

the eastern border in the Jordan Valley and along the river," Ross himself reports, "was less significant than historically thought," it was one of "Israel's myths" that it "could never surrender the Jordan Valley lest it give up its essential security border" (*Missing Peace*, pp. 636, 774; but cf. p. 616).

146 *Missing Peace*, pp. 681-82. Indyk quotes Clinton stating on Jerusalem, "We've got to get the functions right and then the packaging. The Israelis will have to let Arafat have some of the symbols [of sovereignty]" (*Innocent Abroad*, p. 316; bracket in original).

147 *Missing Peace*, p. 726. Some 1.4 million Gazans live on 365 square kilometers of land or 4,000 Gazans per square kilometer as compared to an Israeli population density of 300 Israelis per square kilometer. Ross was hardly unaware of these grim realities when he calculated that Palestinians could make do with less territory, for he himself quotes Palestinians on this point:

> Saeb spoke of enlarging the size of the swap area adjacent to Gaza to relieve the terrible population density there. Dahlan was especially poignant on this subject, observing that we were asking for 8 percent annexation of the West Bank to accommodate 80 percent of Israel's 200,000 Israeli settlers. He pointed out that they were asking us to increase the size of the swap area to relieve the pressure on 1.2 million Palestinians living in Gaza—an area roughly equal in size to the area we now said the Israelis would need to annex for the "comfort" of their settlers in the West Bank. (Ibid., p. 724)

148 Ibid., pp. 748-49. When Barak first proposed allowing for some Palestinian rights in East Jerusalem, Indyk, another impartial American arbiter, recoiled: "Personally, I considered Barak's offer a mistake; he was moving too far, too fast" (*Innocent Abroad*, p. 322). In his epilogue Ross seems to sanction Israel's annexation of a much higher percentage of the West Bank in the event of a unilateral Israeli withdrawal. Putting aside the veracity of the various percentage-offers he cites, the basis of his revised calculation perplexes. After asserting that Israel would need to annex 15-20 percent of the West Bank to absorb about 75 percent of the settlers, he continues: "At Camp David and again in the Clinton ideas we spoke of three settlement blocs that could accommodate 80 percent of the settlers. But we were focused on an agreement that would annex these areas to Israel and for which there would be some territorial compensation to the Palestinians" (ibid., p. 798). The Clinton Parameters called for Israeli annexation of about 5 percent of the West Bank. If Israel could absorb 80 percent of the settlers on the basis of a 5 percent annexation, why would it need to annex 15-20 percent of the West Bank to absorb 75 percent of the settlers?

149 *Missing Peace*, pp. 655, 726. Going by Barak's calculations, it would seem that he shared Ross's conception of Palestinian needs. Just prior to the Camp David summit Barak estimated that in the event of a peace settlement Israel "would need $23 billion to meet security and resettlement needs" and an additional "$10 billion in loan guarantees," whereas "he saw the Palestinians needing $5 billion" (ibid., p. 500).

150 In fact Israel was unmovable even after Palestinians forfeited the substance of their rights. The December 2000 Clinton Parameters recognized a formal Palestinian

Right of Return but in practice allowed for only symbolic repatriation. Although Clinton inferred from their response that Palestinians understood "they would have to concede the 'Right of Return,'" Israel nonetheless insisted that it "did not intend to grant the Palestinians the Right of Return to Israel, neither *formally* nor practically." Throughout the negotiations Israel emphatically rejected "moral, legal or political responsibility for the creation of the refugee problem." The conviction of Palestinians that "Israel had to recognize its responsibility for forcefully uprooting refugees and taking over their property, in the course of the 1948 war, and for preventing their return" was, according to Sher, a "radical position." Such a "radical position" also happens to coincide however with the broad consensus among historians, as Sher himself obliquely acknowledges ("They [Palestinian negotiators] relied heavily on the writings of Israel's 'new historians' to prove their case"). Sher, *Israeli-Palestinian Peace Negotiations*, pp. 17-18 ("moral, legal"), 59, 101, 102 ("radical position," "relied heavily"), 138, 203 ("neither formally"; my emphasis), 210 ("have to concede"), 211. The Israeli reservations to Clinton's proposals, according to Ross, were "within the parameters, not outside them," whereas Palestinian reservations were "deal-killers" (*Missing Peace*, pp. 755, 756). It is hard to make sense of this distinction. Apart from its rejection of Clinton's proposal on the Palestinian refugees, Israel's allegedly "within the parameters" reservations also repudiated Clinton's proposals for total or partial Palestinian sovereignty over al-Haram al-Sharif/ Temple Mount, Palestinian sovereignty over Arab neighborhoods in Jerusalem, and minimal annexation of Palestinian land. Sher, *Israeli-Palestinian Peace Negotiations*, pp. 5, 203-7, 211; for Palestinian demands, which departed in roughly equal degree from Clinton's parameters in the other direction, but still made significant concessions on their *rights*, see ibid., pp. 216-17. Indyk also repeatedly alleges that it was Arafat's rejection of the Clinton Parameters that torpedoed them, but his only source is Ross (*Innocent Abroad*, pp. 5, 370). A White House spokesman announced on 3 January 2001, "Both sides have now accepted the president's ideas with some reservations" (Swisher, *The Truth*, p. 402), while Clinton himself told the Israel Policy Forum on 7 January 2001, "Both Prime Minister Barak and Chairman Arafat have now accepted these parameters as the basis for further efforts. Both have expressed some reservations" (Pressman, "Visions in Collision," p. 20).

151 Ross's contempt for Palestinians is of a piece with his treatment of Arafat, who must not disappoint Big Daddy in the White House. He warns Arafat that "there better not be any surprises tomorrow. No holdups, no questions, no reluctance to sign. Any of that takes place and you lose President Clinton. Understood?" (*Missing Peace*, p. 207); impresses on Arafat that "it is remarkable that the President took time out from campaigning to call you" (ibid., p. 286); scolds Arafat to "not let Clinton down" (ibid., pp. 301, 416); threatens Arafat before an encounter with Netanyahu, "Don't just come to the meeting, make sure you give me a gift from that meeting that I can take to President Clinton" (ibid., p. 302); wows Arafat that "President Clinton was prepared to assume the 'risk and responsibility' of launching an American initiative to save the peace process. These words, I said, should convey great meaning to you" (ibid., p. 341); chides Arafat that "he had disappointed President Clinton . . . there

were costs for him in disappointing Clinton" (ibid., p. 372). It is almost certain that Ross did not speak in this tone to President Hafez al-Assad during parallel negotiations on the Syrian track, and the reason is not hard to find. "Barak was also far more attracted to dealing with Hafez al-Assad than to dealing with Yasir Arafat," Ross reports. "In his eyes, Assad was everything Arafat wasn't. He commanded a real state, with a real army, with thousands of tanks and hundreds of missiles" (ibid., p. 509; cf. p. 90). Like Barak, Ross evidently respected Assad: the Syrian strongman disposed of real military might whereas Arafat did not. In the moral calculus of those who only understand the language of force, only he who commands force deserves respect.

152 *Democracy Now!*, Transcript (14 February 2006) (Ben-Ami); Maoz, *Defending the Holy Land*, p. 476; cf. p. 493.

INTRODUCTION TO PART IV
1 See Chapter Four.

PART IV/CHAPTER TEN
1 Benny Morris, *1948 and After: Israel and the Palestinians* (Oxford: 1990), p. 6.
2 David Remnick, "Blood and Sand: A revisionist Israeli historian revisits his country's origins," *New Yorker* (5 May 2008).
3 Shlomo Ben-Ami, *Scars of War, Wounds of Peace: The Israeli-Arab tragedy* (New York: 2006).
4 Norman G. Finkelstein, *Image and Reality of the Israel-Palestine Conflict* (New York: 1995; expanded second paperback edition, 2003), chapter 3.
5 The designations used throughout this chapter of "old" Morris and "new" Morris do not correspond to a precise cut-off date. Especially in his middle period it is not always easy to mark off the "old" from the "new" Morris.
6 New York: 1987.
7 New York: 1993.
8 New York: 1999.
9 London: 2003.
10 New York: 2008.
11 New Haven: 2009.
12 See Chapter Eight.
13 Morris, *Righteous Victims*, pp. 652-54, 61.
14 Shabtai Teveth, *The Evolution of "Transfer" in Zionist Thinking* (Tel Aviv: 1989), p. 17.
15 Ibid., pp. 2, 6. Anita Shapira, *Land and Power: The Zionist resort to force, 1881-1948* (Oxford: 1992), pp. 285-86. See also Finkelstein, *Image and Reality*, p. 103 and sources cited.
16 Morris, *Birth*, p. 25.
17 Morris, *Righteous Victims*, p. 139.
18 Benny Morris, "Revisiting the Palestinian Exodus of 1948," in Eugene L. Rogan and Avi Shlaim, eds., *The War for Palestine: Rewriting the history of 1948* (Cambridge:

2001), p. 40. The British proposed in 1937, and the Zionists seconded, transfer alongside partition to resolve the Palestine conflict.
19 Benny Morris, *The Birth of the Palestinian Refugee Problem Revisited* (Cambridge: 2004).
20 Ibid., p. 60.
21 Morris, *Righteous Victims*, pp. 37, 46, 49.
22 Ibid., p. 653.
23 It could still be argued, and it is Morris's contention, that although creating a Jewish state necessarily entailed the ethnic cleansing of Palestine, the establishment of a Jewish state was nonetheless a greater moral good. Even in his original, liberal phase, Morris put both moral and historical culpability for the creation of the Palestinian refugee problem on the Arabs because inter alia they rejected the U.N. Partition Resolution and initiated the 1948 war. See Benny Morris, "The Eel and History," *Tikkun* (January-February 1990), Morris, *Road*, p. 236, and Finkelstein, *Image and Reality*, pp. 81, 222n8.
24 Morris, *1948*, p. 407; Benny Morris, "Fallible Memory," *New Republic* (3 February 2011).
25 Morris, *Birth... Revisited*, p. 43.
26 Benny Morris, "And Now for Some Facts," *New Republic* (28 April 2006).
27 Morris, *1948*, p. 407.
28 Morris, "Fallible Memory."
29 Morris, *One State*, p. 68.
30 Ibid., p. 67.
31 Ibid., p. 105.
32 Morris, *1948*, p. 409.
33 Ibid., p. 408.
34 Morris, *One State*, p. 179.
35 Morris, *1948*, pp. 393, 394; Morris, *One State*, p. 90. In one place he does grant albeit grudgingly that Arab opposition to Zionist settlers resulted not only from the "threat to the 'Arab-ness' of their country" but "perhaps, down the road, to their very presence in the land" (ibid., p. 37).
36 Morris, *1948*, p. 393.
37 Morris, *One State*, pp. 188-89.
38 Ibid., p. 19.
39 Morris, *Righteous Victims*, p. 136.
40 Morris, *1948*, pp. 394-95.
41 Ibid., p. 395.
42 Morris, *One State*, pp. 53-54; Morris, *1948*, pp. 395-96.
43 Morris, *Righteous Victims*, p. 123.
44 Morris, *1948*, p. 395.
45 Morris, *One State*, p. 106.
46 Yehoshua Porath, *The Palestinian National Movement: From riots to rebellion* (London: 1970), pp. 91-92, 165-66, 297.
47 Morris, *Righteous Victims*, pp. 570, 573, 574, 577-79.
48 Ibid., p. 562.

49 Ibid., pp. 564, 567-68.
50 Ibid., p. 662 (from supplementary chapter to 2001 paperback edition).
51 Morris, *One State*, p. 52.
52 *Palestine Royal Commission Report* (London: HMSO, 1937), pp. 76, 94, 110, 131, 136, 363.
53 Morris, *One State*, p. 109.
54 Daniel Jonah Goldhagen, *Hitler's Willing Executioners: Ordinary Germans and the Holocaust* (New York: 1996).
55 Norman G. Finkelstein and Ruth Bettina Birn, *A Nation on Trial: The Goldhagen thesis and historical truth* (New York: 1998), pp. 9-10, 25-26.
56 Morris, *Righteous Victims*, pp. 9-12.
57 New York: 1984.
58 Morris, *1948 and After*, pp. 14-16; Morris, *Road*, pp. 148-49.
59 Morris, "And Now for Some Facts" (my emphasis).
60 Morris, *1948*, pp. 399-400, 405-6; see also Morris, "And Now for Some Facts," where he estimates the number of Palestinians killed at 8,000.
61 "Benny Morris responds," *Tikkun* (March-April 1989).
62 See below.
63 Morris, *Birth*, pp. 85-86.
64 Benny Morris, "Response to Finkelstein and Masalha," in *Journal of Palestine Studies* (Autumn 1991), p. 105. For Morris's disingenuous reporting of Israeli atrocities in 1948, see also Finkelstein, *Image and Reality*, pp. 54-56, and Saleh Abdel Jawad, "Zionist Massacres: The creation of the Palestinian refugee problem in the 1948 war," in Eyal Benvenisti, Chaim Gans and Sari Hanafi, eds., *Israel and the Palestinian Refugees* (Berlin: 2007), pp. 59-127.
65 Zeev Maoz, *Defending the Holy Land: A critical analysis of Israel's security and foreign policy* (Ann Arbor: 2006), pp. 47-79.
66 Morris, *Border Wars*, pp. 85, 271-72, 427.
67 Ibid., pp. 178-79; cf. pp. 229-30.
68 Ibid., pp. 279-80. For specific Israeli forays designed to "provoke war with Egypt, using retaliatory strikes that would push Egypt into counter-attacking," cf. ibid., pp. 358, 364-65, 391.
69 Ibid., p. 85. In light of the new Morris's assertion, cited below, that, except for a subsequent Egyptian arms deal with the Soviet bloc, Israel's February 1955 raid on Gaza "probably had very little to do with the substance of [Nasser's] policies" after the attack, it merits quoting several more representative passages from *Border Wars*: "March 1955 witnessed a radical change in Egyptian policy towards Israel" (ibid., p. 91); "The available evidence overwhelmingly suggests that Nasser and the RCC [Revolutionary Command Council] were genuinely shaken by the raid, and that the regime radically changed course in its wake.... The raid apparently had an immediate and profound effect on Nasser.... He no longer believed in Israel's professions of peacefulness.... Egypt, Nasser said, could not 'afford to sustain another [such] defeat' without retaliating" (ibid., pp. 328-29); "within three weeks [of the raid] the Egyptians began to take a 'low-profile' revenge along the Gaza border" (ibid., p. 331);

"Before 28 February 1955, attacks across the Gaza frontier into Israel had been local and sporadic, not state policy; thereafter they were promoted and directed by Cairo. Before 28 February, Cairo generally had pursued a 'policy of restraint'.... After Gaza, everything changed" (ibid., p. 334); "Systematic murder and sabotage raids, organized from Cairo by the Egyptian army, began only in the wake of the Gaza Raid" (ibid., p. 338); "after the Gaza Raid Nasser had promised that no more IDF attacks would go unanswered" (ibid., p. 345); "The IDF raid on Gaza triggered a qualitative and quantitative rise in the level of Israeli-Arab, and specifically Israeli-Egyptian, hostility and violence. Egypt responded to the raid by a policy of low-level harassment along the frontiers" (ibid., p. 355); "Israel's raid on the Egyptian military camp in Gaza on 28 February 1955 clearly resulted in a major policy switch in Cairo. Egyptian soldiers and military intelligence agents unleashed a continuous revenge-oriented campaign of sabotage and murder along the Gaza Strip frontier" (ibid., p. 413); "Ben-Gurion's return to the Cabinet and the Gaza raid killed 'the [Nasser] policy of restraint'.... Before the raid, there was no confrontational policy of harassment and guerrilla warfare. Afterwards, there clearly was" (ibid., pp. 426-27).
70 Ibid., p. 428.
71 Ibid.
72 Ibid., pp. 46-54, 137 ("5,000"), 411-12 ("vast bulk"), 416.
73 Ibid., pp. 166-72 ("state-authorized," "overall attitude" at p. 166), 407-9 ("massacres").
74 Ibid., pp. 97-100, 412, 415.
75 Morris, "Fallible Memory."
76 Morris, *Righteous Victims*, p. 509; see also ibid., p. 512.
77 Ibid., p. 501; see also Morris, *Road*, p. 236, "the IDF's Operation Litani of March 1978, in which [Israel] briefly occupied southern Lebanon and killed, captured or drove out hundreds of Palestinian gunmen."
78 Human Rights Watch, *Civilian Pawns: Laws of war violations and the use of weapons on the Israel-Lebanon border* (New York: 1996). Still higher figures are cited in other authoritative sources (see Chomsky and Fisk below).
79 Morris, *Righteous Victims*, pp. 523 ("reluctant," "avoid"), 525 ("care"), 533 ("massive," "traumatized," "pinpoint").
80 Noam Chomsky, *Fateful Triangle: The United States, Israel and the Palestinians*, updated edition (Boston: 1999); Robert Fisk, *Pity the Nation: The abduction of Lebanon* (New York: 1990).
81 Dov Yermiya, *My War Diary: Lebanon, June 5–July 1, 1982* (Boston: 1984), pp. 3 ("machine"), 10 ("hospital"), 18 ("Thousands"), 26 ("permeated," "retaliation"), 27 ("practice"), 28 ("Auschwitz"), 52 ("overtaken"), 68-69 ("game"), 75 ("disgusting"), 80-81 ("step"), 122 ("firepower"), 123 ("barrages").
82 Morris, *Righteous Victims*, p. 523; Yermiya, *War Diary*, pp. 122-23.
83 Fisk, *Pity the Nation*, pp. 314-15 (his emphasis).
84 Maoz, *Defending the Holy Land*, pp. 206, 630n15.
85 Morris, *Righteous Victims*, p. 639.

86 Amnesty International, *Unlawful Killings during Operation "Grapes of Wrath"* (London: July 1996).
87 Morris, *Righteous Victims*, p. 601.
88 Ibid., pp. 340-43, 568.
89 Ibid., p. 561; see also ibid., p. 580.
90 Ibid., p. 588.
91 Ibid., pp. 587, 591, 599.
92 Finkelstein, *Image and Reality*, pp. xxix-xxx.
93 Morris, *Righteous Victims*, p. 327; see also ibid., p. 338.
94 Morris, *One State*, p. 70.
95 Ibid., p. 123.
96 Morris, *Righteous Victims*, pp. 342, 592, 596, 601.
97 Ibid., (supplementary 2001 chapter), pp. 665 ("extreme," "television"), 668 ("collateral"), 669 ("cautious"); Benny Morris, "Peace, No Chance," *Guardian* (21 February 2002) ("great restraint," "virtual," "straight"); Benny Morris and Ehud Barak, "Camp David and After—Continued," *New York Review of Books* (27 June 2002) ("torrent"); Benny Morris, "This Conflict is about Israel's—Not the Arabs' Survival," *Guardian* (8 February 2006) ("discrimination"); Morris, "And Now for Some Facts" ("avoid," "armed"); Morris, *One State*, p. 151 ("great care," "Arab and Western").
98 *The Mitchell Report* (4 May 2001), section heading "What Happened?". The report was submitted by a committee convened to investigate the causes of the second intifada. It was chaired by former U.S. Senator George Mitchell.
99 Ben Kaspit, "When the Intifada Erupted, It Was Finally Clear to All: Israel is not a state with an army but an army with a state," *Maariv* (6 September 2001).
100 Morris, *One State*, p. 140.
101 Amnesty International, *Excessive Use of Lethal Force* (London: 2000), pp. 5-6.
102 Human Rights Watch, *Investigation into the Unlawful Use of Force in the West Bank, Gaza Strip and Northern Israel* (New York: 2000), p. 1.
103 Morris, *Righteous Victims*, p. 664 (supplementary 2001 chapter).
104 B'Tselem (Israeli Information Center for Human Rights in the Occupied Territories), *Trigger Happy: Unjustified shooting and violation of the open-fire regulations during the al-Aqsa intifada* (Jerusalem: 2002), p. 16.
105 Morris, *Righteous Victims*, p. 665 (supplementary 2001 chapter).
106 B'Tselem, *Trigger Happy*, p. 7.
107 Morris, *One State*, p. 151.
108 Amnesty International, "No One Is Safe: The spiral of killings and destruction must stop," press release (29 September 2003; my emphasis).
109 Alex Fishman and Sima Kadmon, "We Are Seriously Concerned about the Fate of the State of Israel," *Yediot Ahronot* (14 November 2003).
110 Morris, *Righteous Victims*, p. 667 (supplementary 2001 chapter); Morris, *One State*, p. 151.
111 Amnesty International, *Israel Must End Its Policy of Assassinations* (London: July 2003), pp. 4-6.

112 Morris, *Righteous Victims*, p. 668 (supplementary 2001 chapter).
113 B'Tselem (Israeli Information Center for Human Rights in the Occupied Territories), *Israel's Assassination Policy: Extrajudicial executions*, position paper (Jerusalem: 2001); Public Committee against Torture in Israel (PCATI) and LAW (The Palestinian Society for the Protection of Human Rights), *The Assassination Policy of the State of Israel* (2002), p. 76. See also Norman G. Finkelstein, *Beyond Chutzpah: On the misuse of anti-Semitism and the abuse of history* (Berkeley: 2005; expanded paperback edition, 2008), pp. 131-41.
114 Lily Galili, "Reserve Pilots to Refuse Liquidations," *Haaretz* (19 September 2003); Amos Harel and Lily Galili, "Air Force to Oust Refusenik Pilots," *Haaretz* (23 September 2003).
115 Morris and Barak, "Camp David and After—Continued."
116 Human Rights Watch, *Jenin: IDF military operations* (New York: 2002); Amnesty International, *Shielded from Scrutiny: IDF violations in Jenin and Nablus* (London: 2002).
117 Tsadok Yeheskeli, "I Made Them A Stadium in the Middle of the Camp," *Yediot Ahronot* (31 May 2002).
118 Jessica Montell, "Operation Defensive Shield: The propaganda war and the reality," *Tikkun* (July-August 2002).
119 Morris, "And Now for Some Facts"; Peter Bouckaert, letter, *New Republic* (19 June 2006).
120 Uzi Benziman, "Until Proved Otherwise," *Haaretz* (18 June 2006). B. Michael, "Of Liars and Hunters," *Yediot Ahronot* (3 September 2005); B. Michael, "Stop the Lying!," *Yediot Ahronot* (5 September 2008).
121 Morris, *One State*, p. 203n1.
122 See Chapter Five.
123 Quoted in Yermiya, *War Diary*, p. 149.
124 In one of the first studies by an Israeli new historian, Simha Flapan sought to qualify this Palestinian opposition to partition but subsequent scholarship has not borne out his research (*The Birth of Israel: Myths and realities* (New York: 1987), pp. 55-79). For the rationale behind Palestinian rejection of the 1947 Partition Resolution, see esp. Walid Khalidi, "Revisiting the UNGA Partition Resolution," *Journal of Palestine Studies* (Autumn 1997).
125 Shabtei Teveth, *Ben-Gurion and the Palestinian Arabs: From peace to war* (New York: 1985), pp. 187-88.
126 Morris, *1948 and After*, p. 9 (my emphasis).
127 Uri Ben-Eliezer, *The Making of Israeli Militarism* (Bloomington, IN: 1998), pp. 150-51 ("not final" is the author's paraphrase); Ben-Ami, *Scars of War*, p. 34.
128 Ben-Ami, *Scars of War*, pp. 36-38.
129 Morris, *Border Wars*, pp. 11-13, 401, 410-11 ("expansionist" at p. 410); Morris, *Road*, pp. 210-11 ("sections").
130 Morris, *Border Wars*, pp. 179, 229-30, 278-79, 332, 427; Morris, *Righteous Victims*, p. 280.

131 Morris, *Righteous Victims*, pp. 289-90; see also Maoz, *Defending the Holy Land*, pp. 70-71.
132 Morris, *Righteous Victims*, p. 298; Ben-Eliezer, *Making*, pp. 221-22.
133 Morris, *Righteous Victims*, p. 299.
134 Morris, *Border Wars*, p. 428.
135 Morris, *One State*, pp. 35, 38, 64.
136 Ibid., pp. 74-75 (my emphases); see also ibid., pp. 30-31, 161-62.
137 Ibid., p. 78.
138 Ibid.
139 Morris, *Righteous Victims*, p. 242.
140 Morris, *One State*, pp. 78-79.
141 Ibid., p. 79.
142 Morris, *Righteous Victims*, pp. 314, 321-25.
143 Ibid., p. 314.
144 Ibid., p. 321.
145 When citing the scholarship of others, Morris's purpose is almost always to ridicule it. See Norman Finkelstein, "Rejoinder to Benny Morris," *Journal of Palestine Studies* (Winter 1992), pp. 65-66.
146 See Chapter Nine.
147 See Chapter Seven.
148 Morris, *One State*, pp. 81-87. The only exception he allows for is a brief period after the June 1967 war.
149 See Chapter Nine. Morris asserts that the two-state settlement is "espoused by the international community, spearheaded by Washington" (*One State*, pp. 26-27). But judging by the documentary record, the two-state settlement "espoused by the international community" has been consistently *blocked* by Washington.
150 Morris, *Righteous Victims*, pp. 338, 562, 608-9.
151 Morris, *One State*, pp. 26, 75, 79, 85.
152 Ibid., p. 139.
153 See Chapter Nine.
154 Morris, *Righteous Victims*, p. 673, my emphasis (supplementary 2001 chapter).
155 Morris, *One State*, p. 128; my emphasis.
156 www.jewishvirtuallibrary.org/jsource/Politics/labor.html.
157 www.knesset.gov.il/elections/knesset15/elikud_m.htm ("west of the Jordan river" refers to the pervasive Zionist belief that Jordan is already a Palestinian state).
158 Morris, *Righteous Victims*, pp. 596, 606-8, 611, 621, 629.
159 For example, the PNC "annulled the clauses in the Covenant that called for the destruction of Israel but failed to promulgate a new covenant from which these statements were absent" (ibid., p. 638; cf. p. 645).
160 Ibid., p. 668.
161 Morris, *One State*, p. 167 (my emphasis).
162 Among those Morris accuses in *One State* of "mendacity" or being "mendacious" are Rashid Khalidi (p. 114; he is also accused on p. 169 of "pure invention"), Palestinians

generally (p. 131), Virginia Tilley (p. 182; she is also accused on p. 181 of a "whopper of truly gargantuan dimensions," on p. 182 of the "sheer quantity of untruths ... even by Tilley-land standards," and on p. 220n17 of "nonsense"), and John Mearsheimer and Stephen Walt (p. 217n188), while Ali Abunimah is accused of "hogwash" and "liberal blather" (pp. 168, 219n2), and Henry Siegman of being one among many "wishful thinkers and naifs" (p. 219n9). If such epithets were used by Israel's critics—with far more justice—to describe its defenders, would Yale University Press have allowed them to pass?

163 Ibid., pp. 120, 126.
164 Ibid., p. 132. Morris later asserts however that the text of the 2003 draft Palestinian constitution "subverts the interpretation that the PNA [Palestinian National Authority] was positing a Palestinian Arab state restricted to the West Bank, Gaza, and East Jerusalem and living alongside Israel in its post-1948 borders" (ibid., pp. 152-54). According to the leading American authority on this draft constitution, Professor Nathan Brown of George Washington University, Morris's rendering of its context is "inaccurate" and his rendering of its content "extremely strained" (email correspondence of 12 June 2009).
165 Morris, *One State*, pp. 193-94.
166 Ibid., p. 195.
167 Ibid., pp. 133-50.
168 Ibid., p. 135.
169 Ibid., p. 173.
170 Morris, *Righteous Victims*, p. 659 (supplementary 2001 chapter).
171 See Chapter Nine.
172 Morris, *Righteous Victims*, p. 663 (supplementary 2001 chapter). It bears passing mention how the new Morris renders the Israeli offer at Camp David. In a famous 2002 presentation by Barak and Morris, they jointly made the Israeli case for why negotiations broke down. Although putting the best possible face on the Israeli offer at Camp David, Barak conceded that he did call for the West Bank to be bisected by a "razor-thin Israeli wedge running from Jerusalem through from [sic] Maale Adumim to the Jordan River." Benny Morris and Ehud Barak, "Camp David and After: An exchange," *New York Review of Books* (13 June 2002). But the new Morris alleges, "It is not clear whether, at the end of the summit, Israel still insisted on retaining [a] thin strip of territory running from Jerusalem through Maale Adumim to the Jordan River" (*One State*, p. 137). Is Morris now suggesting that Barak and he himself were guilty of "mendacity"?
173 Morris, *One State*, p. 154.
174 Ibid., pp. 154-60.
175 Ibid., p. 176.
176 Paul Scham and Osama Abu-Irshaid, "Hamas: Ideological rigidity and political flexibility," United States Institute of Peace Special Report (June 2009), pp. 2-4. For extensive documentation, see also Norman G. Finkelstein, *"This Time We Went Too Far": Truth and consequences of the Gaza invasion* (New York: 2010; expanded paperback edition, 2011), pp. 44-45.

177 Morris, *One State*, pp. 165-66 (my emphases).
178 Giora Goldberg, Gad Barzilai and Efraim Inbar, *The Impact of Intercommunal Conflict: The intifada and Israeli public opinion* (Jerusalem: 1991), p. 21. The other options were non-state (autonomy, annexation, etc.).
179 Asher Arian, *Israeli Public Opinion on National Security 2003* (Jaffee Center for Strategic Studies, Tel Aviv), p. 12; Jerusalem Media and Communication Center, poll no. 35, *On Palestinian and Israeli Attitudes towards the Future of the Peace Process* (in cooperation with Tami Steinmetz Center for Peace Research, Tel Aviv), p. 5.
180 Arian, *Israeli Public Opinion 2003*, p. 33 (tabulating Israeli support for U.S. President Bill Clinton's territorial parameters, which are the closest approximation to the international consensus for which poll data are available).
181 Morris, *One State*, pp. 71-72.
182 Morris, *Border Wars*, pp. 163-64 ("entire nation" quoting head of the Military Government); Morris, *Righteous Victims*, p. 598.
183 Arian, *Israeli Public Opinion 2003*, pp. 30-31; Asher Arian et al., *The 2007 Israeli Democracy Index* (Jerusalem: 2007), pp. 68, 107. See also references in Chapter Two above.
184 Morris, *One State*, pp. 166, 174-75, 204n5.
185 See Chapter Nine.
186 For further references and analysis, see Finkelstein, "*This Time,*" pp. 45-49.
187 Morris, *One State*, p. 165.
188 Ibid., pp. 199-200.
189 Ibid., p. 201.
190 Ibid., pp. 90 ("catchphrases"), 169 ("Western liberals"), 170 ("no respect").
191 John L. Esposito and Dalia Mogahed, *Who Speaks for Islam?: What a billion Muslims really think* (New York: 2007), chapter 2.
192 Benny Morris, "What Egyptians Really Want," *National Interest* (11 February 2011). Morris was also not averse to lecturing Westerners who *have* lived in the Arab world that they did not "observe the deep complexities in Arab societies" and "never actually witnessed the viciousness, the intolerance, and the illiberalism that characterized the Muslim Middle East" in countries such as Saudi Arabia, Sudan and Iraq—of which he presumably had personal, first-hand knowledge, without ever having lived in these places (Morris, "Fallible Memory").
193 Morris, *One State*, p. 187.
194 Ibid., pp. 220-21n18.
195 Ari Shavit, "Survival of the Fittest," *Haaretz* (1 January 2004). In the interview he said:

> My turning point began after 2000. I wasn't a great optimist even before that. True, I always voted Labor or Meretz or Sheli [a dovish party of the late 1970s], and in 1988 I refused to serve in the territories and was jailed for it, but I always doubted the intentions of the Palestinians. The events of Camp David and what followed in their wake turned the doubt into certainty. When the Palestinians rejected the proposal of Barak in July 2000 and the Clinton

proposal in December 2000, I understood that they are unwilling to accept the two-state solution. They want it all. Lod and Acre and Jaffa.
196 The Clinton Parameters are discussed in the notes to Chapter Nine above.
197 Baruch Kimmerling, "Benny Morris's Shocking Interview," *History News Network* (26 January 2004; www.hnn.us/articles/3166.html).
198 Morris, "The Eel and History."
199 Ibid.
200 See Chapter Five.
201 Shavit only turned against the Gaza massacre in the last days when international outrage peaked. Ari Shavit, "Gaza Op May Be Squeezing Hamas, But It's Destroying Israel's Soul," *Haaretz* (16 January 2009).
202 A. B. Yehoshua, "An Open Letter to Gideon Levy," *Haaretz* (16 January 2009).
203 Finkelstein, *Beyond Chutzpah*, pp. 14-15.
204 Finkelstein, *"This Time,"* p. 93.
205 Benny Morris, "Why Israel Feels Threatened," *New York Times* (30 December 2008). See also Finkelstein, *"This Time,"* pp. 35-36.
206 Benny Morris, "A Second Holocaust?: The threat to Israel" (2 May 2008; www.mideastfreedomforum.org/de/node/66); Benny Morris, "Obama's Nuclear Spring," *Guardian* (24 November 2009); Benny Morris, "When Armageddon Lives Next Door," *Los Angeles Times* (16 April 2010); Benny Morris, "On Iran, a Stark Choice," *Los Angeles Times*, 14 February 2012. Speaking in Berlin, Morris said:
Realistic leaders in Washington and Jerusalem cannot allow Teheran to have the Bomb. And, in the coming months or year, must do what is necessary to halt and destroy the Iranian nuclear project. And if this involves a protracted, conventional air assault on the Iranian nuclear facilities—then so be it. The Iranians will have brought that assault on their own heads. And, if conventional weapons cannot do the job—and if Israel is forced to go the course alone, it is doubtful that its conventional capabilities will be sufficient to destroy the Iranian nuclear project—then non-conventional weaponry will have to be used to stymie the project. And many innocent Iranians will die. But the Iranians will have brought this upon themselves by bringing to power and leaving in power a leadership that will have forced Israelis to do what was necessary in order to survive. ("A Second Holocaust")

CONCLUSION
1 In response to pressing political developments, this writer completed in the interim three manuscripts, *"This Time We Went Too Far": Truth and consequences of the Gaza invasion* (New York: 2010; expanded paperback edition, 2011), *Goldstone Recants: Richard Goldstone renews Israel's license to kill* (New York: 2011), and a forthcoming book on resolving the Israel-Palestine conflict.
2 Daniel Septimus, "Reading between the Lines: Satire and the Shoah," *Jerusalem Post* (3 May 2007); Tom A. Peters, "An Acerbic Look at the Holocaust Industry," *Christian Science Monitor* (29 May 2007). See also Alvin H. Rosenfeld, *The End of the Holocaust* (Bloomington, IN: 2011).

Notes for pages 301–310   439

3   Alan Dershowitz, *The Case for Israel* (Hoboken, NJ: 2003), p. 204. To be sure Dershowitz now whistles a different tune when among Jews (see Chapter Two above).
4   On Israel's use of white phosphorus in Gaza, see Finkelstein, *"This Time,"* pp. 81-82.
5   Ari Shavit, "Survival of the Fittest," interview with Benny Morris, *Haaretz* (9 January 2004).
6   In a recent survey of American Jewry the mean score for neoconservatives on a scale of 0 (unfavorable) to 100 (favorable) was 23.6 ("J Street National Survey of American Jews," 29 June—3 July 2008).

APPENDIX

1   A shorter version of this appendix appeared in Norman G. Finkelstein, *Beyond Chutzpah: On the misuse of anti-Semitism and the abuse of history* (Berkeley: 2008).
2   For a comprehensive review of Israel's human rights record in the West Bank and Gaza, see ibid., part II.
3   See David Kretzmer, *The Occupation of Justice: The Supreme Court of Israel and the Occupied Territories* (Albany: 2002).
4   For the relevant body of international law and the legal positions of the respective parties to the wall dispute, see Harvard Program on Humanitarian Policy and Conflict Research, *The Separation Barrier and International Humanitarian Law* (July 2004).
5   A 20 July 2004 U.N. General Assembly resolution (ES-10/15) supporting the ICJ opinion was adopted by 150 votes in favor (including all European Union countries) and six against (Israel, United States, Australia, Marshall Islands, Micronesia, and Palau). The major human rights organizations also found that the wall's construction inside occupied Palestinian territory violated international law. See Amnesty International, *The Place of the Fence/Wall in International Law* (19 February 2004); B'Tselem (Israeli Information Center for Human Rights in the Occupied Territories), *Behind the Barrier: Human rights violations as a result of Israel's separation barrier* (April 2003); Human Rights Watch, *Israel's "Separation Barrier" in the Occupied West Bank: Human rights and international humanitarian law consequences* (February 2004); International Committee of the Red Cross, *West Bank Barrier Causes Serious Humanitarian and Legal Problems* (18 February 2004); Oxford Public Interest Lawyers (OXPIL) for the Association for Civil Rights in Israel (ACRI), *Legal Consequences of Israel's Construction of a Separation Barrier in the Occupied Territories* (February 2004); United Nations, *Concluding Observations of the Human Rights Committee: Israel* (21 August 2003).
6   *Legal Consequences of the Construction of a Wall in the Occupied Palestinian Territory, Advisory Opinion* (Int'l Ct. of Justice July 9, 2004), 43 IL M 1009 (2004) [hereafter: *ICJ*], part 1. For background to the ICJ deliberations, see Ray Dolphin, *The West Bank Wall: Unmaking Palestine* (London: 2006), chapter 4. The January 2005 issue of the *American Journal of International Law* [hereafter: *AJIL*] contains many articles on the advisory opinion.
7   The ICJ deliberated on whether the proper terminology was *fence*, *barrier*, or *wall*. Noting the inadequacies of each term, the Court elected "to use the terminology employed by the General Assembly" (*ICJ*, para. 67)—hence, following the Court, the adoption of *wall* in this appendix as well.

8 Ibid., para. 87; cf. paras. 74-75, 117, where the illegality of Israel's annexation of East Jerusalem is also recalled. See Chapter Nine above for the 1970 U.N. General Assembly resolution.
9 *ICJ*, paras. 89-101, citing inter alia the consensus of international opinion on the applicability of the Fourth Geneva Convention to the occupied Palestinian territory.
10 Ibid., paras. 102-13, citing inter alia the authoritative opinion of the U.N. Human Rights Committee.
11 Ibid., para. 57.
12 Ibid., para. 58.
13 For a comprehensive summary of the ICJ's findings, see Geoffrey R. Watson, "The 'Wall' Decisions in Legal and Political Context," in *AJIL*, pp. 6-26, and Pieter H. F. Bekker, "The World Court Rules that Israel's West Bank Barrier Violates International Law," in *The American Society of International Law* (July 2004).
14 As of 2010 projections, 80 of the 149 illegal Jewish settlements and over 85 percent of the total settler population will be located on the "Israeli" side of the wall.
15 For the international consensus on these settlements, see Harvard Program on Humanitarian Policy and Conflict Research, *The Legal Status of Israeli Settlements Under International Humanitarian Law* (2004), pp. 6-7, reporting that the United Nations, the European Union, the International Committee of the Red Cross, and the High Contracting Parties to the Fourth Geneva Convention, have all affirmed their illegality. See also Eyal Benvenisti, *The International Law of Occupation* (Princeton: 1993), pp. 140-41. Violations of Article 49 of the Fourth Geneva Convention constitute "grave breaches" that must be investigated and prosecuted pursuant to Articles 146-48. Not long after the June 1967 war, both Theodor Meron, legal counsel to the Israeli Foreign Ministry, and Defense Minister Moshe Dayan privately acknowledged the illegality of building settlements in the Israeli-occupied territories (Gershom Gorenberg, *The Accidental Empire: Israel and the birth of the settlements, 1967-1977* (New York: 2006), pp. 99-102, 173).
16 *ICJ*, paras. 119-20; cf. para. 99.
17 Ibid., paras. 121-22.
18 Ibid., paras. 123-31.
19 Ibid., paras. 132-34.
20 Ibid., paras. 135-36.
21 To qualify as an act of military necessity, it must be "the only way for the State to safeguard an essential interest against a grave and imminent peril" (quoted from Article 25 of the International Law Commission's *Articles on Responsibility of States for Internationally Wrongful Acts*; for full reference, see Watson, "The 'Wall' Decisions," *AJIL*, p. 15n80).
22 *ICJ*, para. 137.
23 Ibid., para. 140; cf. paras. 141-42.
24 Among her criticisms of the majority opinion Judge Higgins purported that it should have pointed up the "tragedy" that each side refused to be the first to meet its respective obligations under international law for resolving the conflict. Thus, Palestinians allegedly would not recognize that "Israel is entitled to exist, to be

recognized, and to security" before Israel was forthcoming, while Israel would not recognize that "the Palestinian people are entitled to their territory, to exercise self-determination, and to have their own state" before Palestinians were forthcoming (*ICJ*, "Separate Opinion," paras. 18, 30, 31; cf. "Separate Opinion of Judge Owada," paras. 26-28). Higgins was apparently unaware that already decades ago the Palestinian side had met all its obligations to recognize Israel, whereas Israel only just recognized the Palestinians' right to self-determination and statehood, and only on an undefined *part* of "their territory" (see Chapter Nine above). Both Judge Higgins (*ICJ*, "Separate Opinion," para. 19) and Judge Kooijmans (*ICJ*, "Separate Opinion," para. 13) suggested that the advisory opinion took insufficient note of the terrorist attacks against Israel. Yet one might just as well have faulted the advisory opinion for referring one-sidedly to "the fact ... that Israel has to face numerous indiscriminate and deadly acts of violence against its civilian population," and for equating Israeli and Palestinian human rights violations even though Israel has overwhelmingly been the main perpetrator of these violations (*ICJ*, paras. 141, 162).

25 *ICJ*, "Separate Opinion of Judge Higgins," paras. 24, 35, 40.
26 *ICJ*, "Separate Opinion of Judge Owada," paras. 22-24.
27 *ICJ*, "Separate Opinion of Judge Kooijmans," paras. 28-30, 34.
28 *ICJ*, "Declaration of Judge Buergenthal," para. 1.
29 Ibid., paras. 3, 7.
30 Ibid., para. 5.
31 Ibid., para. 9, my emphasis.
32 HCJ 2056/04, *Beit Sourik Village Council v. The Government of Israel* (30 June 2004), 58(5) P.D. 807 [hereafter: *HCJ I*].
33 Ibid., para. 3; but cf. paras. 12, 29.
34 Ibid., paras. 1-3.
35 See Chapter Five above. For the Israel High Court's approval of these gross human rights violations, see Finkelstein, *Beyond Chutzpah*, pp. 207-20. For a yet more lopsided presentation than the High Court's, see Ruth Wedgwood, "The ICJ Advisory Opinion on the Israeli Security Fence and the Limits of Self-Defense," *AJIL*, pp. 55-57, where the "fraught context" of the ICJ deliberations consisted only of Israeli suffering. In like fashion Hebrew University Professor of International Law Michla Pomerance, "The ICJ's Advisory Jurisdiction and the Crumbling Wall Between the Political and the Judicial," *AJIL*, opposed ICJ intervention because it bore on "matters impinging so crucially on [Israel's] existence, its territorial rights, and the defense of its citizens from a continuing daily terrorist onslaught" (p. 31). On this basis, however, wouldn't the ICJ's intervention have been warranted on the petition of Palestinians, who faced far graver threats from Israel to their "existence" and "territorial rights," and from Israel's "daily terrorist onslaught"?
36 *HCJ I*, paras. 9-11.
37 Ibid., paras. 16-19; cf. para. 54.
38 Ibid., para. 22, cf. para. 69; one resident of Mevasseret Zion supported the proposed route.

39 Ibid., paras. 23-24. Besides the provisions in the Hague Regulations and Fourth Geneva Convention cited in the ICJ opinion, the HCJ also cited, controversially, article 23 (g) of the Hague Regulations. However, in its second judgment the HCJ set aside the relevance of this article, stating that the HCJ's findings still stood on the basis of the articles cited by the ICJ. In addition, the Court assumed the application of international human rights covenants in its second judgment.
40 Ibid., paras. 28-29.
41 Ibid., para. 30-31.
42 Ibid., para. 32.
43 Ibid., para. 46.
44 Ibid., para. 47.
45 See Meron Rapoport, "A Wall in the Heart," *Yediot Ahronot* (23 May 2003), and Dolphin, *West Bank Wall*, p. 51.
46 Cf. *HCJ I*, para. 56: "From a military standpoint, there is a dispute between experts regarding the route that will realize the security objective. As we have noted, this places a heavy burden on petitioners, who ask that we prefer the opinion of the experts of the Council for Peace and Security over the approach of the military commander. The petitioners have not carried this burden. We cannot—as those who are not experts in military affairs—determine whether military considerations justify [the wall's route].... [T]here is no justification for our interference in the route of the separation fence from a military perspective." Leaving aside that petitioners could not have "carried this burden" in light of the Court's reflexive deference to the military commander, shouldn't the "heavy burden" of proof have been on the state, not petitioners?
47 Ibid., para. 47.
48 Ibid., para. 12.
49 In fact, it appears that the state showed "little consideration" for Palestinian lives in tracing the wall's route, although it was at pains not to harm "Gilboa irises" and "Egyptian antiquities" (Rapoport, "Wall in the Heart").
50 *HCJ I*, para. 16; cf. paras. 50, 53, 64, 70.
51 Ibid., para. 13. The Court made this same self-contradictory argument in its second judgment. See B'Tselem (Israeli Information Center for Human Rights in the Occupied Territories), *Not All It Seems: Preventing Palestinians' access to their lands west of the Separation Barrier in the Tulkarm-Qalqiliya area* (Jerusalem: 2004), p. 4, "This willingness [of the State] to make changes, which resulted from the sharp worldwide criticism relating to the barrier, undermines Israel's official position that no less harmful routes exist that would meet security needs." On Israel's rerouting of the wall due to international pressures, not least the impending ICJ decision, see also Dolphin, *West Bank Wall*, pp. 56-58, 60, 77, 156-57, 200, and Isabel Kershner, *Barrier: The seam of the Israeli-Palestinian conflict* (New York: 2005), pp. 18, 63-64, 110.
52 *HCJ I*, para. 36.
53 Ibid., paras. 41-42.
54 Ibid., para. 57.
55 Ibid., para. 58.

56 Ibid., paras. 60-61. Cf. ibid., para. 71, which states that, to diminish the injuries on the local population, "the proposals of the Council for Peace and Security—whose expertise is recognized by the military commander—may be considered."
57 Ibid., para. 85.
58 As already shown, several judges in the ICJ majority, although supporting a proportionality test, did not believe the wall could pass it.
59 Watson, "The 'Wall' Decisions," *AJIL*, praised the High Court's "three-part test of 'proportionality' that rivals the most intricate constructions of American constitutional law" (pp. 24-25), apparently unaware that two of the three prongs lacked—at any rate, as applied by the Court—real content, while the third was standard. For a multi-prong test of the wall's legality comparable to the High Court's but reaching the ICJ's conclusions, see Ardi Imseis, "Critical Reflections on the International Humanitarian Law Aspects of the ICJ Wall Advisory Opinion," *AJIL*, pp. 109-14.
60 B'Tselem, *Behind the Barrier*, pp. 28-31.
61 The U.N.'s Office for the Coordination of Humanitarian Affairs (OCHA) attached little overall significance to the reroutings of the wall ordered by the Court:

[T]he impact of these re-alignments is negligible compared to projected Barrier construction around the major settlement blocs: in particular, the Qedumim and Ariel "Fingers," which will eviscerate the Qalqiliya and Salfit governorates; the encirclement of Ma'ale Adumim settlement, which will compound the separation of East Jerusalem from the rest of the West Bank; and construction around the Gush Etzion bloc, which will sever the Bethlehem urban area from its agricultural hinterland and stymie its potential for residential and urban development. (*Five Years after the International Court of Justice Advisory Opinion: A summary of the humanitarian impact of the barrier* (July 2009), p. 31)

62 HCJ 7957/04, *Zaharan Yunis Muhammad Mara'abe v. The Prime Minister of Israel* (15 September 2005) [hereafter: *HCJ II*].
63 *HCJ II*, para. 18.
64 Ibid., paras. 18-19.
65 Ibid., para. 19.
66 Ibid., paras. 19-20.
67 Ibid., paras. 21-22.
68 Hebrew University Professor of Law David Kretzmer, "The Advisory Opinion: The light treatment of international humanitarian law," *AJIL*, muddied the waters by characterizing the ICJ's position as "a theory that posits that the fact that civilians are living in an illegal settlement should prevent a party to the conflict from taking any measures to protect them." Such a theory, he continued, "would seem to contradict fundamental notions of international humanitarian law" because "the measures may be needed to protect civilians (rather than the settlements in which they live)" (p. 93). The question posed to the ICJ, however, was not "any measures," but only whether *building a wall around settlements* to protect them could be justified. To reckon by Kretzmer's characterization, the ICJ must also have opposed evacuation because it too constituted a measure to protect settlers. In addition, Kretzmer took issue both with the consensus interpretation of the Fourth Geneva Convention

barring any transfer of population by a state to occupied territory, and Buergenthal's affirmation that a wall for protecting settlements was illegal. On the latter point Kretzmer perplexingly asserted that the ICJ "failed to find . . . that building a fence around settlements involved ipso facto a violation of international humanitarian law." Yet, (1) the court majority manifestly did hold such a wall to be illegal ("the route chosen for the wall gives expression *in loco* to the illegal measures taken by Israel with regard to Jerusalem and the settlements"), (2) Buergenthal in his declaration was plainly underscoring agreement with the court majority on this point, and (3) on Kretzmer's bizarre reading, it would mean that Buergenthal staked out the position most critical of Israel (pp. 92-94). It is telling that, although hawkish if judged by international legal opinion, Kretzmer stands prominently at the dovish extreme of mainstream Israeli legal opinion, just as it is telling that the Israel High Court leaned heavily on Kretzmer's reasoning to support its findings. (See paras. 16, 20 of *HCJ II* for explicit references to Kretzmer. Many other passages in the Court judgment echo Kretzmer in style and content; see, e.g., pp. 100-1 of Kretzmer and para. 70 of *HCJ II*.) Even critical mainstream Israeli legal opinion appears to fall outside the international consensus, while the spectrum of mainstream Israeli legal opinion, ranging from Kretzmer to the Israel High Court to the state attorney, appears to be rather narrow, differing more on matters of detail than substance.

69 On the operative legal principle, *ex injuria non oritur jus* ("no legal title can be derived from an illegal act"), as it applies to the wall and settlements, see Iain Scobbie, "Words My Mother Never Taught Me—'In defense of the International Court,'" *AJIL*, p. 84.

70 See *Israeli-Palestinian Interim Agreement on the West Bank and the Gaza Strip* (28 September 1995), Article XXXI, para. 6: "Neither Party shall be deemed, by virtue of having entered into this Agreement, to have renounced or waived any of its existing rights, claims or positions."

71 *HCJ II*, para. 57.

72 Ibid., para. 61.

73 Pomerance, "The ICJ's Advisory Jurisdiction," denied the applicability of the non-acquisition principle in instances of self-defense against aggression. In her view, states had legal title to territory conquered in defensive wars (p. 38). Setting aside the dubiousness of Israel's claim to self-defense in June 1967 when it occupied the West Bank (see Chapter Seven), Pomerance's assertion finds no support in U.N. resolution 242, on which she relied (see Chapter Nine). Reflecting the consensus of mainstream opinion, Paul J. I. M. de Waart, "International Court of Justice Firmly Walled in the Law of Power in the Israeli-Palestinian Peace Process," *Leiden Journal of International Law*, 18 (2005), opined that "the illegality of territorial acquisition resulting from the threat or use of force has become a peremptory norm of international law" (p. 483). More generally Pomerance implied that the findings of the ICJ in its advisory opinion sprang from its "dependence" on the General Assembly "for its budget, and of its members for reelection to the bench," and its consequent "rubber-stamping [of] UN resolutions" (pp. 40-41). Yet, this accusation is difficult to sustain in light of the lopsidedness of the ICJ vote in its advisory opinion combined with the manifest independence of judges in the majority writing separate opinions, and the comparable

findings of major human rights organizations, all of which suggests not a "rubber-stamping" Court but rather the flagrance of the wall's illegality: the fundamental questions posed by the wall were simply not controversial, which might also explain the resounding General Assembly support for the advisory opinion. See Pieter H. F. Bekker, "The World Court's Ruling Regarding Israel's West Bank Barrier and the Primacy of International Law," *Cornell International Law Journal*, 38 (2005): "It really is a clear and shut case" (p. 559).
74 *ICJ*, paras. 118, 122. Earlier on the High Court took oblique notice of these ICJ conclusions in its abstract of the advisory opinion (see *HCJ II*, paras. 48-49).
75 *HCJ I*, para. 27.
76 The sole exception was the High Court's use of *West Bank* and *occupied areas* when citing from Palestinian petitions. Striking an Orwellian note, the High Court used the phrase *territories of the area* to designate those parts of the West Bank not incorporated by the wall (see *HCJ II*, para. 7).
77 Elsewhere in the judgment the High Court made a couple of fleeting references to this critical ICJ finding (see ibid., paras. 19, 49).
78 Ibid., para. 18; cf. paras. 1, 3.
79 Ibid., para. 63.
80 Ibid., quoting from the advisory opinion.
81 Ibid., para. 65. For similar censure of the ICJ for expending "no effort to consider any of the facts that might have justified Israeli defensive measures," see Sean D. Murphy, "Self-Defense and the Israeli Wall Advisory Opinion: An ipse dixit from the ICJ?," pp. 70-75, *AJIL*. Murphy also took the ICJ to task for making "no explicit reference to the widely known history of Israel's vulnerability in the Middle East, which has entailed repeated armed conflicts with neighbors and an enduring exposure to terrorist attacks, particularly since the second intifada broke out." He was curiously silent, however, on the "widely known history" of the vulnerability of neighbors to Israeli aggression and terrorist attacks.
82 *HCJ II*, paras. 100-1.
83 Dolphin, *West Bank Wall*, p. 46. On the questionable utility of the wall for averting terrorist attacks, see OXPIL for ACRI, *Legal Consequences*, para. 93, and B'Tselem, *Behind the Barrier*, pp. 29-30.
84 *HCJ II*, para. 68.
85 Ibid., para. 70.
86 This was also the official position of the Israeli government which, in its submission to the High Court, criticized the "factual infrastructure" of the ICJ opinion as "superficial and wanting," being based on erroneous and outdated information. Gary Fitleberg, "Israel Disagrees with International Court of Justice," *TruthNews* (23 February 2005).
87 Of the ICJ data itemized by the High Court as erroneous (*HCJ II*, para. 67), some are indisputably mistakes or outdated, while other errors alleged by the High Court seem to be matters of judgment and interpretation. In addition, it appears that data on which the High Court relied were likewise flawed; see *Report of the Special Rapporteur of the Commission on Human Rights, John Dugard, on the situation of human rights in the Palestinian territories occupied since 1967* (17 January 2006), paras. 17-20; see also

Report of the Special Rapporteur of the Commission on Human Rights, John Dugard, on the situation of human rights in the Palestinian territories occupied since 1967 (27 September 2006), paras. 33-42 for revised data on the wall.
88 See Bekker, "The World Court's Ruling," p. 562n38.
89 *ICJ*, para. 151; cf. the opinion's title, "Legal Consequences of the Construction of a Wall in the Occupied Palestinian Territory"—my emphasis.
90 For this topographic argument justifying the wall's route, cf. *HCJ II*, para. 99.
91 *HCJ I*, para. 18. Paraphrasing the Council's affidavit, the Court reports:
  In the opinion of the council members, the separation fence must achieve three principal objectives: it must serve as an obstacle to prevent, or at least delay, the entry of terrorists into Israel; it must grant warning to the armed forces in the event of an infiltration; and it must allow control, repair, and monitoring by the mobile forces posted along it. In general, the fence must be far from the houses of the Palestinian villages, not close to them. If the fence is close to villages, it is easier to attack forces patrolling it. Building the fence in the manner set out by respondent [the State] will require the building of passages and gateways, which will engender friction; the injury to the local population and their bitterness will increase the danger to security. Such a route will make it difficult to distinguish between terrorists and innocent inhabitants. Thus, the separation fence must be distanced from the Palestinian homes, and transferred, accordingly, to the border of the area of Judea and Samaria. In their opinion, the argument that the fence must be built at a distance from Israeli towns in order to provide response time in case of infiltration, can be overcome by the reinforcement of the obstacle near Israeli towns. Distancing the planned route from Israeli towns in order to seize distant hilltops with topographical control is unnecessary, and has serious consequences for the length of the separation fence, its functionality, and for attacks on it. In an additional affidavit . . ., members of The Council for Peace and Security stated that the desire of the commander of the area to prevent direct flat-trajectory fire upon the separation fence causes damage from a security perspective. Due to this desire, the fence passes through areas that, though they have topographical control, are superfluous, unnecessarily injuring the local population and increasing friction with it, all without preventing fire upon the fence.
  For the Council's criticism on this score, see also Dolphin, *West Bank Wall*, pp. 48-49.
92 *HCJ I*, para. 47. It was also unclear how significant topographical advantage was in tracing the wall's route. U.N. Special Rapporteur John Dugard reported that "the wall seems to have been built without regard to security considerations in many areas (for instance, in some areas the wall is built in the valley below Palestinian villages)" (*Israeli Practices Affecting the Human Rights of the Palestinian People in the Occupied Palestinian Territory, Including East Jerusalem*, 18 August 2005; para. 16). See also B'Tselem (Israeli Information Center for Human Rights in the Occupied Territories) and Bimkon (Planners for Planning Rights), *Under the Guise of Security: Routing the Separation Barrier to enable Israeli settlement expansion in the West Bank* (September 2005), pp. 17, 26, 50, 60, and B'Tselem, *Not All It Seems*, p. 3.

93 *HCJ II*, para. 101.
94 Ibid., para. 75.
95 Ibid., para. 111.
96 Ibid., para. 112. In point of fact, petitioners did not ignore the settlers' security concerns. According to the Court's own paraphrase earlier in the judgment, petitioners proposed, "To the extent that Alfei Menashe needs a separation fence, such a fence can be built around that community, on the basis of the existing fence around it" (ibid., para. 83).
97 Ibid., para. 113.
98 Ibid., para. 114.
99 Ibid., para. 116.
100 See ibid., para. 80: "First it is contended [by petitioners] that respondents [the State] have no authority to erect the fence around the enclave, both due to the lack of security necessity and due to the creation of de facto annexation of the enclave territory to the State of Israel. . . . Petitioners further argue that the enclave was not created for military or national security reasons, and not even for the security needs of Alfei Menashe residents. The construction of the fence around the enclave was intended to put Alfei Menashe west of the fence, and make it territorially contiguous to the State of Israel. It is an act whose entire purpose is to move the effective border of the state, and it is not legal according to the laws of belligerent occupation. . . . The fence creates a long term change, whose meaning is practical annexation of the lands in the enclave to an area in absolute control of the State of Israel."
101 Ibid., para. 9.
102 On this point, see also OXPIL for ACRI, *Legal Consequences*, para. 94.
103 *HCJ II*, para. 22.
104 While not fully consistent, survey data suggest that most settlers would voluntarily evacuate if financially compensated. Even among those settlers who could not be financially coaxed into repatriation, only a small minority, perhaps as few as one percent, would forcefully resist an official evacuation order, and probably not for very long.
105 B'Tselem, *Behind the Barrier*, p. 33. To protect roads from terrorist attacks, resort could be made to road-protection walls, not to mention restrictions on Palestinian access to them.
106 The state's decision in the case of some settlements to trace the wall's path so as not to leave them outside it appears to have been dictated neither by the strategic concern of annexing major blocs nor by security but rather by the lobbying clout of local settler organizations. Kershner, *Barrier*, pp. 21-22, 62.
107 B'Tselem and Bimkon, *Under the Guise of Security*, p. 39. See also B'Tselem, *Not All It Seems*, pp. 3, 23.
108 *HCJ II*, para. 86.
109 Ibid., para. 90.
110 Ibid., para. 31.
111 *HCJ II*, para. 16.

112 Ibid., para. 100. On a secondary point, the Court maintained in both judgments that Israel offered to pay compensation for this temporary taking of possession (*HCJ I*, para. 8; *HCJ II*, paras. 5, 16). However, a University of Oxford study reported: "While land owners are entitled to demand compensation, the vast majority have not done so (on the urging of the Palestinian Authority), so as not to legitimize the Israeli seizure. In any case, the amount of compensation offered has been well below the real value of the land"—in Qalqiliya, for example, only 10 percent of the actual value (OXPIL for ACRI, *Legal Consequences*, paras. 123, 220).
113 *HCJ II*, para. 39.
114 B'Tselem, *Behind the Barrier*, p. 19. During the wall litigation, the State Attorney's Office "admitted that temporary seizure orders were also used to erect permanent structures and that they may be extended indefinitely." B'Tselem concluded: "The permanent nature of the barrier, together with past experience with Israel's 'temporary' seizures of land, leads to the conclusion that 'taking control of land' is in fact expropriation" (ibid., pp. 37-38; cf. p. 40). See also Amnesty International, *The Place of the Fence/Wall*, pp. 10-11, and Human Rights Watch, *Israel's "Separation Barrier,"* p. 4.
115 *ICJ*, para. 121.
116 *HCJ II*, para. 71. For the *risk* of the wall's permanence itself constituting a violation of international law, see Jean-François Gareau, "Shouting at the Wall: Self-determination and the legal consequences of the construction of a wall in the Occupied Palestinian Territory," *Leiden Journal of International Law*, 18 (2005), pp. 515-16, arguing that the alleged "temporary nature of the structure is irrelevant, insofar as the mere possibility of an annexation (be they actions that may facilitate a land grab, or a creeping acquisition of barter chips for future negotiations) or of enforced demographic shifts places Israel in breach of its obligations to respect the Palestinians' right [to self-determination]; as it has a duty to do nothing that might impede the enjoyment thereof, skewing the terms of the negotiation in such a fashion violates the principle."
117 B'Tselem, *Behind the Barrier*, p. 33; cf. pp. 18-19, 41; Human Rights Watch, *Israel's "Separation Barrier,"* p. 4; Amnesty International, *Israel Must Immediately Stop Construction of the Barrier* (7 November 2003); see also OXPIL for ACRI, *Legal Consequences*, paras. 116, 290-91.
118 Yuval Yoaz, "Justice Minister: West Bank fence is Israel's future border," *Haaretz* (1 December 2005). For an earlier, if more elliptical, acknowledgment by Livni, see Kretzmer, "The Advisory Opinion," p. 92n32; see also Human Rights Watch, *Israel's "Separation Barrier,"* pp. 3-4.
119 Yoaz, "Justice Minister."
120 Rapoport, "A Wall in the Heart."
121 The one kernel of truth in the High Court's claim of the wall being "inherently temporary" is that, as Jewish settlements east of the wall expand, Israel will probably use this proclaimed temporariness to reroute the wall, further encroaching on the West Bank, in order to protect—with the Court's blessings, no doubt—these settlers' "human dignity" and creation in "God's image."

122 Zeev Maoz, *Defending the Holy Land: A critical analysis of Israel's security and foreign policy* (Ann Arbor: 2006), p. 557.
123 United Nations—Office for the Coordination of Humanitarian Affairs (OCHA), *The Humanitarian Impact of the Barrier: Four years after the advisory opinion of the International Court of Justice on the barrier* (July 2008); United Nations—Office for the Coordination of Humanitarian Affairs (OCHA), *Five Years After*. In his recent defense of the wall's legality and the HCJ decisions, Yoram Dinstein, Israel's leading authority on international law, alleged that the ICJ opinion, besides being faulty, had been superseded and effectively rendered obsolete by the re-demarcations Israel has since made in the wall's path, which have supposedly "radically altered" and "thoroughly recast" it, and thereby mitigated the "disproportionate" injuries wrought by it (Yoram Dinstein, *The International Law of Belligerent Occupation* (Cambridge: 2009), pp. 247-59). In fact, whereas the amount of West Bank land encompassed by the wall has been reduced by approximately one-third (Dinstein incorrectly states that it will now incorporate only 7.8 percent of the West Bank), in crucial respects the situation today is worse than it was expected to be when the ICJ issued its opinion. For example, Israel has not lived up to many of the pledges it made at the time, such as promising easy movement of Palestinians trapped on either side of the wall. In general, it would be hard to exaggerate the real and potential damage wrought by the wall on Palestinian life, as the OCHA reports and others have documented. See also World Health Organization, *The Impact of the Barrier on Health* (July 2010).
124 International Crisis Group, *The Jerusalem Powder Keg* (2 August 2005); Jerusalem and Ramallah Heads of the Mission for the European Union, *Report on East Jerusalem* (November 2005) (unpublished report of the European Union), available at http://holyland-lutherans.org/05%20Nov%20EU%20Jerusalem.doc.

INDEX

A
Abbas, Mahmoud, 23, 425n127
Abunimah, Ali, 436n162
Adelman, Kenneth, 377n134
administrative detention, 103, 109, 225, 272
African-Americans, 5–7, 14, 38, 43, 356n4, 358n33, 389n97
Ajami, Fouad, 100
Albright, Madeleine, 228
Alfei Menashe, 328–49, 447nn96, 100
Allon, Yigal/Allon Plan, 172, 178, 281–82, 284, 292
Aloni, Shulamit, 99
Amer, Abd al-Hakim, 169, 406n63
American Israel Public Affairs Committee (AIPAC), 72, 74, 246, 374n98
American Jewish Committee, 39
American Jews
  compared to Israeli Jews, 12, 14–15, 88–89, 251, 302
  disenchantment with Israel, vii, xiii, xv–xix, 3, 8–17, 20, 23, 26–30, 33, 85–89, 93–94, 99–102, 120–22, 123, 160–61, 180–81, 217, 220–21, 248, 251, 297, 299–304, 305, 309, 353, 356n9, 364n48
  and dual loyalty, xiii, xiv, 8, 33–43, 45–89, 300, 366n13, 373n81, 376nn123, 130
  and electoral politics, 5, 54, 56, 59, 63–64, 66, 356n7, 369–70n25, 370–71n43
  and ethnic bond to Jewish state, vii, xiii–xiv, xviii–xix, 3, 26–28, 33, 35–37, 40–43, 300, 303, 376n123
  and Gaza invasion (2008–9), 16, 27–28, 301–2
  identity and relationship to Israel, xv–xvi, 3–46, 55, 62–63, 83–89, 93–94, 99–122, 123, 160–61, 180–81, 217, 220–21, 248, 251,

297, 299–304, 305, 309, 353, 355n1–368n28
intellectuals, xiv, 28–29, 37–43, 367n20
and Iran, 85–89, 381n162
and Iraq, 85–89, 381n160, 382n166
leadership, 22, 29, 36–37, 61, 66, 67, 72–74, 86, 88, 366n13
and Lebanon invasions, xvi, 16, 24, 301
liberalism of, vii, xiii–xix, 3–17, 23, 25–30, 33, 42, 67, 85, 89, 93–94, 99–100, 119–22, 123, 217, 248, 251, 299–304, 305, 353, 356n9, 367n25, 384n8
making *aliyah*, 9, 36, 100, 120
Orthodox, 27, 29, 300
and other ethno-religious groups, xv, 5–7, 14, 38, 89, 356n4, 358n33, 383n181, 389n97
poll data, xiii, xvi, xviii, 6, 15, 22–28, 36, 55, 299–300, 355n4, 364n48, 381nn160, 162, 164, 383n181
significance of June 1967 war for, xiv, 3, 5, 8–9, 33, 39–43, 45, 180, 301–4
and U.S. national interest, xiii, 33, 41, 45–46, 84, 300, 303, 367n20
younger generations, vii, xiv, xviii, 21, 28–29, 36, 38, 42, 68, 89, 112, 301–2, 367n27
Amit, Meir, 170, 172
Amnesty International, xvii
on checkpoints, 389n111
on Israel's criminalization of Palestinians' political activity, 109–10
on Israel's use of force, 110–11, 116–18, 224, 274–77
on Israeli impunity, 224
on Operation Defensive Shield (2002), 117, 276–77, 388n88
on Operation Grapes of Wrath (1996), 271
on Palestinian Authority, 226–27
on Palestinian detainees, 97, 103, 106, 109–10
on Palestinian refugees, 220, 239, 292
on West Bank wall, 351
Ansar Three (prison). *See* Ketziot
Ansar Two (prison). *See* Gaza Beach camp
anti-Arab/anti-Muslim animus, xiii, 12–15, 30, 39, 70–71, 121, 259, 272, 293–94, 358–59n35, 359n37, 361n8
Anti-Defamation League (ADL), 13, 98, 360n4, 364n58
anti-Semitism
actuality of, xix, 7–8, 19, 61, 86, 112, 115, 119, 262, 264, 361n8, 376n123
alleged source of Israel-Palestine conflict, 257–65, 286–89, 296–97
misuse of term, xviii, 7–8, 19, 25, 28, 43, 82, 86, 98, 119, 257–65, 287, 289, 296–97, 301, 364n58
apartheid, 25, 99, 278

Arab Association for Human Rights, 130–31, 134
Arab League, 234
Arab-Muslim world, 45–89, 113, 257–65, 286–89, 293–97, 437n192
Arab Revolt (1936–39), 262
Arab Spring (2011), 34, 46, 52, 65, 84, 87, 89, 293, 386n40
Arafat, Yasir, 223–29, 232–41, 247, 273, 278, 286–88, 420nn86, 91, 421nn95, 99, 423n110, 424n126, 427n146, 427–28n150, 428–29n151
Arendt, Hannah, 38
Ariel, 443n61
Arkin, William, 391–92n19, 396n86, 397n100
Armitage, Richard, 377nn133, 135
al-Assad, Bashar, 369n17
al-Assad, Hafez, 429n151
Association for Civil Rights in Israel (ACRI), 13, 99, 226
Australia, 20, 218, 361n9, 375n116, 439n5
Awad, Mubarak, 114

B

Bacevich, Andrew J., 80
Baker, James, 376n123
Balfour Declaration (1917), 53, 365n5
Barak, Aharon, 308, 353
Barak, Ehud, 236–40, 275–76, 288–89, 294, 297, 400n13, 423n116, 425n127, 427nn148, 149, 428n150, 429n151, 436n172, 437n195
Begin, Menachem, 159, 170, 179, 423n110

Beinart, Peter, 29, 299, 364–65n58
Beirut, 133, 139–44, 269–71, 395n53, 397n100
Beit Sahour, 109
Beit Sourik, 317–29, 333–37
Bekker, Pieter H. F., 445n73
belligerent reprisals, 132–33, 393n41, 393–94n42
Bellow, Saul, 37
Ben-Ami, Shlomo, xvii, 115, 156–57, 225, 228, 235–36, 248, 254, 278, 390n114, 421n93, 423n113, 426n145
Ben-Gurion, David, 10, 16, 36, 56, 156–58, 174, 255, 259, 266, 278–81, 366n13, 371n47, 399–400n5, 402n37, 432n69
Bennett, William, 71, 80
Benvenisti, Eyal, 231, 418n56
Benvenisti, Meron, 99
Ben-Yair, Michael, 99
Benziman, Uzi, 277
Berrigan, Reverend Daniel J., 19
Bethlehem, 353, 443n61
Blix, Hans, 377–78n138
Bolton, John, 71
Bowett, D. W., 209
Bremer, Paul L., 377n133
Brezhnev, Leonid, 188–92, 410n32, 411n59
Britain, 373n83
and Africa, 58
and Arab-Muslim world, 47–48, 53–60, 158, 267, 279, 370n38, 375nn116, 117, 118
and India, 53, 108, 260, 387n71

Jews, 21–22, 365n5
  and public opinion, 20–23, 361n9, 363n39
  and Zionist-Arab/Israel-Palestine conflict, 20–23, 53, 56, 64, 215, 280, 365n5, 365–66n6, 406n62, 430n18
Bronner, Ethan, xvii
Brown, Nathan, 436n164
Brownlie, Ian, 209, 413n17
B'Tselem (Israeli Information Center for Human Rights in the Occupied Palestinian Territories), xvii, 226, 273
  and apartheid analogy, 99
  on detainees, 98, 106, 109
  on freedom of movement, 389n111
  on human shielding, 118
  on Israel's use of force, 224, 274
  on Israeli courts, 225
  on Operation Defensive Shield, 277
  on political liquidations, 275
  on settlements/settlers, 224, 347, 350, 389n111
  statistics, 386nn48, 54, 387–88n80, 420n75
  on West Bank wall, 347, 442n51, 448n114
Buergenthal, Thomas, 220, 314–316, 331–32, 352, 444n68
Bull, Odd, 163, 401n26, 403n45
Bundy, McGeorge, 62–63
Bush, George W./Bush administration, 45, 51–52, 73–89, 161, 260, 369n21, 373nn82, 83, 375n106, 376–77n132, 378nn138, 139, 379n142, 383n177
Bush, George H. W. (Bush Sr.), 376nn123, 132
Buthelezi, Mangosuthu, 235

C

Camp David, 244, 420n89
  2000 summit, 222, 229, 233, 237–48, 288–89, 294, 419n62, 424nn120, 126, 427nn148, 149, 436n172, 437n195
Canada, 20–21, 23, 166, 361n9, 363n39
Caradon, Lord, 64, 215
Card, Andy, 377n133
Carter, Jimmy, 19, 25–26, 75, 99, 203, 217
Cassese, Antonio, 221
Ceaser, James W., 80
Center for Strategic and International Studies, 88
Chamberlain, Neville, 86
Chavez, Cesar, 119
checkpoints, 108, 120, 327, 343, 345, 389n111
Cheney, Dick, 52, 74–78, 375nn113, 117, 376n127, 130, 376–77n132, 377n135, 379n142
Chicago Council on Global Affairs, 24–25, 363n39
Childers, Erskine, 155
Chomsky, Noam, 360n5, 380n153
Christian fundamentalists, 7, 43, 71, 102, 260, 383n181
Churches, 21, 25

Civil Rights Movement. *See* African-Americans
Clarke, Jonathan, 380n144
Clarke, Richard, 74, 379n142
Clifford, Clark, 54–55
Clinton, Bill, 222, 238, 240–47, 294, 376n123, 421n95, 424n120, 427nn146, 148, 427–28n150, 428–29n151, 437n180
Clinton Parameters (2000), 244–45, 247, 294, 424n120, 427n148, 427–28n150, 437n180, 437–38n195
closure policy, 227, 228, 318
cluster munitions, 128, 145–54, 301, 390n3, 392n20, 398nn109, 119, 125
Cockburn, Patrick, 78
Cohen, Steven M., xv, 26–27, 364n48, 368n28
Cold War, 36, 45–49, 65, 83, 199–200, 367nn19, 25, 409n2
collective punishment, 120, 210, 228, 307
Commentary, 37–39, 67, 366nn14, 15
Communism/Communist parties, 40, 43, 49, 166, 188, 190, 410n32
 American, 67, 301
 Israeli, 186–88, 365–66n6
 Palestinian, 385n39
 Soviet, 40, 166, 183–201
Conference of Presidents of Major American Jewish Organizations, 61, 89, 366n13
Congress, 23–24, 60, 379n142
conservatism, 3, 5–7, 24, 27, 251
Cordesman, Anthony H., 87
Corrie, Rachel, 110, 386n44

Council for Peace and Security, 319–28, 342, 442n46, 443n56, 446n91
Creveld, Martin van, 113, 174, 408n91
curfews, 114, 118, 318

D

David versus Goliath myth, 157, 161, 265
Dawidowicz, Lucy, 38
Dayan, Moshe, 16, 158, 163–64, 171, 176, 178–79, 189, 244, 266–67, 279–82, 402n37, 440n15
Decter, Midge, 37, 367n27
Defense for Children International, 116
Deir Yassin, 38
Democratic Party, 5–7, 23, 54, 67, 85, 371n43, 381n164
Dershowitz, Alan M., xvii, 25, 28, 30, 98, 157–59, 180, 220, 301, 383n2, 400n8, 439n3
Deutscher, Isaac, 360n5
Dimona nuclear facility, 183–201
Dinstein, Yoram, 116, 148, 153, 393n41, 418n56, 449n123
Dobrynin, Anatoly, 63
Dubai, 86
Dugard, John, 99, 126, 209, 391n11, 446n92
Dulles, John Foster, 56–59

E

Eban, Abba, 11, 64, 172, 180, 186, 403n47, 404n52, 406n62

Edelman, Eric, 377nn132, 136
Eden, Anthony, 58
Egypt, 53, 87, 260, 263, 289, 293, 370n38, 375n116, 378n138, 442n49
   and Gaza Raid (1955), 266–68, 431–32n69
   and June 1967 war, 48–49, 94, 158, 162–79, 183–201, 203–16, 244, 282, 368n9, 403nn44, 47, 402n40–409n103, 410n35–411n60, 413n15
   and October 1973 war, 70, 159
   "Operation Dawn" (1967), 169, 405–6n62, 406n63
   peace treaty with Israel, 244, 292
   and Sinai invasion (1956), 37, 41, 54, 56–60, 158, 266–68, 279–80, 366n13, 371nn47, 50, 389n93, 400n19, 403n44, 404n48, 431n68, 431–32n69
Egyptian-Israeli Mixed Armistice Commission (EIMAC), 167, 169, 404n48
Eichmann, Adolf, 38
Eisenhower, Dwight D., 54–60, 366n13, 370–71n43
ElBaradei, Mohamed, 378n138
Erdogan, Recep Tayyip, 87
Eshkol, Levi, 37, 165, 169, 171–74, 179, 402n40, 405n55
Europe, 54
   and anti-Semitism, 61
   and international law, 84, 439n5, 440n15
   and Nazi holocaust, 229, 258
   and public opinion, 20–21, 360–61n8
Exodus (Uris), vii, 8, 93, 112, 155, 253, 296, 301, 399n1

F
Fatah, 164–65, 275
Feinberg, Abe, 370n25
Feith, Douglas, 71, 373n82, 377nn132, 134, 378–79n139, 379n142
Finkelstein, Norman G., xviii, 101, 299, 383n2, 421n95, 438n1
Fisk, Robert, 270–71
Flapan, Simha, 434n124
Ford, Gerald, 75, 376n132
Fourth Geneva Convention, 107, 204–5, 220, 309–13, 316, 319–20, 331–34, 418n49, 440nn9, 15, 442n39, 443–44n68
Foxbats over Dimona (Ginor and Remez), 183–201, 254, 409n5, 410nn32, 35, 42, 45, 411nn53, 59, 411–12n60, 412n65
   praise for, 198–201
Foxman, Abraham, 13, 30, 98, 364n58
France
   and Algeria, 371n46
   and Ben-Gurion, 279, 281
   and public opinion, 20–21, 361nn8, 9
   and Sinai invasion (1956), 54, 56, 58–59, 158, 267, 279
Freedman, Lawrence D., 199
Freedom House, 12
Friedman, Thomas, xvii, 100

Fukuyama, Francis, 67, 80,
    373–74n83

G
Gandhi, Mahatma, 108, 112–13, 260
Gareau, Jean-François, 448n116
Garlasco, Marc, 398n116
Gates, Robert, 88
Gaza Beach camp (prison), 103–6
Gaza Freedom Flotilla attack (2010),
    15, 21, 24, 28, 86, 87
Gaza Strip
    blockade of, 21, 24, 361n14
    invasion of (2008–9), 16, 21–22,
        24, 26–28, 296, 297, 301–2,
        360n60, 438n201
    occupation of (since 1967), 16, 70,
        94, 97–122, 126, 159, 176–79,
        203–48, 261, 268, 271–74, 278,
        283–91, 296, 335, 421–22n99,
        422n101, 425n130, 436n164,
        439n2
    population density, 247, 427n147
    pre-1967 history of, 166–67,
        176–78, 191, 266–68, 279–81,
        283, 431–32n69
    raid (1955), 266–68, 431–32n69
    withdrawal of Jewish settlers from
        (2005), 331, 346
Gazit, Shlomo, 394n50
Gelb, Leslie, 376n130
Gerecht, Reuel Marc, 50–51
Germany, 21, 108, 113–14, 190, 363n39,
    375n117, 385n26, 387n74
    Nazi era, 7, 25, 67, 85, 108, 113–15,
        260, 264, 367n27, 373n83,
        387nn71, 74, 411n59
    and public opinion, 20, 21, 23,
        361nn8, 9
Gilad, Amos, 49
Gilbert, Martin, 201
Ginor, Isabella. See *Foxbats over
    Dimona*
Glazer, Nathan, xv–xvi, 36
Gluska, Ami, 166, 190, 402n40,
    409n103
Golan Heights, 163, 176–79, 231, 282
Goldberg, Arthur, 62–63, 372n66,
    422n101
Goldberg, Jeffrey, xvii, 93, 99–122,
    385nn26, 37, 386n52, 387n56,
    387nn71, 74, 389nn93, 97, 111
Goldhagen, Daniel Jonah, 264, 383n2
Goldmann, Nahum, 366n13
Gomulka, Wladislaw, 188
Gore, Al, 277
Great Depression, 5
Grechko, Andrei, 185, 196–97
Greenberg, Stanley, 23
Greenwald, Glenn, 29
Gromyko, Andrei, 63, 186, 191
Gush Etzion, 443n61

H
Ha'am, Ahad, xix
Hague Regulations, 310–13, 319–20,
    329, 334, 349, 442n39
Halutz, Dan, 116, 388n82
Hamas, 24, 26, 115–18, 261, 275, 290,
    388n80, 390n114
Hammarskjöld, Dag, 403n44, 404n52
Hannah, John, 377n132
Hannity, Sean, 302,
al-Haq, 273

Harel, Amos, 369n17, 395–96n68
Harel, Isser, 187–88
Harkabi, Yehoshaphat, 165
Harman, Avraham, 171
Hartman, Rabbi David, 100
Hass, Amira, xvii
Hebron, 114, 179
Herzog, Isaac, 14
Hezbollah, 51, 70, 394nn49, 50, 394–95n53
  and 2006 Lebanon war, 24, 51–52, 86, 125–54, 391nn13, 14, 19, 392n23, 392–93n30, 393n32, 393–94n42, 394n51, 395n68, 396n79, 396–97n94, 397nn104, 105, 399n148
Higgins, Rosalyn, 148, 314, 418n52, 440–41n24
Hijazi, Rafiq, 101
Himmelfarb, Milton, 356n7
Histadrut, 9
Hitler, Adolf, 7, 59, 85, 174, 387n71, 411n59
Hoagland, Jim, 201
hoaxes, xvii, 39, 94, 183–201, 254, 383n2, 413n4
Hoenlein, Malcolm, 61, 88
Holocaust, xviii, 25, 360n1
  actual historical event, vii, 37, 41, 104, 229, 258, 264, 270, 367n27, 418n53
  ideological instrumentalization of historical event, 7–8, 19, 25, 38, 264, 297, 301, 367n27, 409n5, 438n206
  "second," 7, 297, 409n5, 438n206

house demolitions, 109, 111, 118, 227, 318
human rights organizations, significance of, xvi–xvii, 123, 248, 307, 318
Human Rights Watch (HRW), xvii, 392nn24, 28, 395n59
  and Beirut press conference (2007), 144–45
  on Israel-Lebanon conflict, 124–54, 269, 390nn3, 5, 10, 391nn15, 16, 18, 392nn20, 30, 393nn32, 39, 41, 394nn49, 51, 394–95n53, 395–96n68, 396n79, 397n95, 398n108, 399n148
  on Israel-Palestine conflict, 106, 117–18, 126, 220, 226, 239, 274, 276–77, 292, 350–51, 390–91n10, 391n11
  pressured by Israel lobby, 98, 124, 126, 127, 132, 145, 154, 390nn1, 5
human shielding, 117–18, 126–27, 134, 142–44, 270, 395n54, 397n94
Hungarian revolt (1956), 39–40, 59
Hussein, King, 176, 189, 282, 372–73n72, 401n26, 406n63
Hussein, Saddam, 50–51, 74, 111, 373n82, 392n28

I
Imseis, Ardi, 443n59
India, 23, 53, 88, 108, 215, 387n71
Indyk, Martin, 420n91, 421–22n99, 422–23n110, 424n126, 425–26n130, 427nn146, 148, 428n150

International Atomic Energy Agency, 377n138
International Committee of the Red Cross, 132, 395n54, 440n15
international community, xvi, 79, 160, 221, 231–32, 309–10, 413n17, 414n26, 435n149
International Court of Justice (ICJ), xvii
  on Israel-Palestine (2004), 218–21, 238–39, 284, 302, 307–17, 326–53, 418n49, 439nn5, 6, 7, 440–41n24, 441n35, 442nn39, 51, 443nn58, 59, 443–44n68, 444–45n73, 445nn74, 77, 81, 86, 87, 449n123
  on legal status of U.N. General Assembly resolutions (1955), 417n46
  on nuclear weapons (1996), 148–49, 153–54
  and Straits of Tiran dispute, 168–69
intifada
  first (outbreak: 1987), xvi, 98, 100–21, 224–25, 235, 261–62, 271–73, 284, 291, 386n48
  second (outbreak: 2000), 100–21, 262, 272–78, 291, 318, 388n80, 433n98, 445n81
Iran
  coup (1953), 60, 370n38
  end of Shah regime (1979), 52
  "nuclear threat" posed by, 49–51, 85, 88, 297, 375n106, 438n206
  and public opinion, 20, 24, 85–86, 88, 363n39, 380–81n158, 381n162
  as regional power, 49–52, 71, 131
  threats against, 24, 71, 85–86, 88, 297, 363n39, 438n206
  war against Iraq (1980–88), 50
Iraq, 111, 263, 279, 368n6, 370n38, 373n82, 437n192
  and U.N. inspections, 377n138, 378n139
  U.N. representative (1967), 415–16n30
  U.S. attack of 1991, 51, 120, 145, 230–32, 235, 243–44, 392n24, 414n24
  U.S. attack of 2003, 45, 50, 51, 68, 73–89, 142, 161, 375n106, 376n121, 377n134, 377–78n138, 378–79n139, 379n142, 380n158, 381nn161, 162, 164, 382n166, 383n177, 392n28
  war against Iran (1980–88), 50
Islamic fundamentalism, 49, 78, 83, 113, 257, 259–65, 287, 289, 297
Islamic Jihad, 261, 275
Israel
  credibility of state authorities, 277, 338
  "delegitimization," 30
  deterrence capacity, 175
  diplomatic intransigence, xvii, 62–66, 87, 160, 166–69, 203–48, 284–85, 289, 299–304, 307–53, 366n13, 371n47, 403n47, 404n48, 405n55,

460 INDEX

412n1–428n150, 436n172,
439n4–449n123
human rights record, xv–xvii,
xix, 3, 8–9, 15–17, 20–21, 30,
93–154, 220–21, 224–27, 239,
248, 269, 273–77, 292–93,
300–53, 385n34–399n148,
439n2–449n123
infiltration into (1948–1956),
162, 164–65, 167, 266–68,
431–32n69
intelligence agencies, 49, 66, 71,
75, 103–6, 138–39, 164–66,
170–72, 175, 187, 196, 236, 274–
75, 277, 323, 376n121, 396n79,
406n62, 412n65, 422n109
laws, 11–13, 330, 358n28, 359n37
as nuclear power, 38, 50, 183–201,
297, 438n206
political establishment, xiii, xvi,
10–16, 28, 30, 36–39, 49–53,
64, 72, 85, 89, 97, 99, 111, 113–
17, 122, 139, 157, 160, 163, 170,
175, 180, 206, 214, 221, 225–27,
236–37, 251, 253–97, 305–9,
351, 353, 373n82, 375n106,
383n177, 386n52, 388–89n93,
403n47, 409n5, 418–19n56,
423n116, 429n151, 440n15,
444n68
political parties, xvi, 12, 15, 36,
172, 179, 226, 227, 235–36, 282,
284–85, 351, 437n195
public image, vii, xiii–xviii, 3, 8–17,
19–30, 36–43, 87–89, 93–102,
112, 120–23, 155–61, 180–83,
198–99, 203, 221, 248, 251,
253, 297–307, 353, 357–58n22,
360–61n8, 361n9, 361–62n21,
363n39, 365–66n6, 367n25,
383n179
society, xv, xviii, 8–15, 52–53,
88–89, 114–15, 120–22, 237,
251, 269, 271, 290–91, 294–97,
303–4, 305–9, 357n19,
358–59n35, 359n41, 362n23,
381n161, 437n180
as target of boycott, divestment
or sanctions, 21, 22, 25, 109,
230–32, 371n47
territorial ambitions, xv–xvi, 34,
62, 81, 156–57, 162–64, 176–80,
203–48, 278–83, 307–53,
409n103, 412n1–429n152,
436n172, 439n4–449n123
terrorism against, 21, 25–26, 43,
159, 222–24, 227–28, 267–68,
270, 275, 315–27, 336–48, 352,
388n80, 390n114, 423n110,
441nn24, 35, 445n81, 445n83,
446n91, 447n105
Israel Defense Forces (IDF), xvi, 42,
47, 70–71, 103–19, 123–54, 155–81,
253–97, 301–2, 317–53, 386n48–
390n114, 390n1–399n148,
399n5–409n103, 426–27n145,
430n23, 431n64–438n206,
439n2–449n123
bulldozer operator, 276
"hooliganism" (Montell), 277
impunity, 224, 272
martial prowess, 86–87
pilots' protest, 275
position in Israeli society, 113

"purity of arms," 9, 41, 93, 265–66
war crimes, 98, 117, 125–54,
    276–77, 302, 390n1–399n148
Israel Democracy Institute, 13
Israel High Court
    and human rights violations
        during second intifada, 318,
        441n35
    judgments on West Bank wall,
        305–53, 441n35–449n123
    liberalism of, 115, 226, 307–9, 333,
        351–53, 443n59, 444n68
    partial ban on torture (1999), 16,
        115
Israel lobby, 20, 45–89, 215, 246,
    363n39, 368n1–383n181
    and ethnic bond to Jewish state,
        46, 61, 66–73, 82, 84, 373n81,
        376n123
    *The Israel Lobby and U.S. Foreign
    Policy*. *See* Mearsheimer; Walt
    and Israel-Palestine conflict, xix,
        25–26, 34, 46, 53, 56, 62–66,
        81–84, 87–88, 215, 364n58,
        390n1
    pressuring critics of Israel, 25–26,
        123–28, 132, 145, 154, 302,
        364n58, 390nn1, 5
Israel Policy Forum, 22, 428n150
Israel Project, 23, 363n39
Israeli Democracy Index, 10
Israeli-Syrian Mixed Armistice
    Commission (ISMAC), 162
Israelis
    children, 116, 317, 357n19, 386n48
    founding generation, 9–10, 15–16,
        36
    killed or wounded, 26, 41, 110,
        115–17, 127–28, 131, 162, 164–65,
        223–24, 228, 267–68, 275,
        317–18, 394n53
    left-wing, 100, 121, 157, 275, 285,
        295–96, 383n1
    legal scholars, 418–19n56, 443–
        44n68, 444n73, 449n123
    Palestinian minority among, xv,
        12–16, 130–31, 134, 144, 291,
        358n34, 358–59n35
    public opinion, 10–14, 88–89, 114–
        15, 237, 290–91, 358–59n35,
        359n41, 362n23, 381n161,
        437n180
    Sephardic Jews, 385n26
    settlers, 108, 223–25, 227, 289,
        329–33, 338, 345–52, 389n111,
        424n126, 427n147, 427n148,
        440n14, 443n68, 447nn96,
        104, 106, 448n121
    women, 8, 317
Issacharoff, Avi, 369n17, 395–96n68

J

Jabotinsky, Zeev, 255
Jackson, Henry "Scoop," 377n132
Jenin, 117, 178, 276–77, 388n88
Jennings, R. Y., 209
Jerusalem (East), 62, 177–79, 204–5,
    217, 219, 231–47, 279–92, 308–11,
    314, 335, 349, 353, 389n111,
    409n103, 416n30, 417n44,
    423n116, 424n126, 425–26n130,
    426n131, 427nn146, 148, 428n150,
    436n164, 440n8, 443n61, 444n68
Jewish Agency, 247

Jewish Defense League, 387n61
Jewish Diaspora, 7–10, 21–22, 28, 30, 120, 365n5
  assimilation, xviii–xix, 35, 40–43
  critics of Israel, 22, 38–39, 367n25
  Islamic world, 264
  "self-hatred" among, xviii, 301
Jewish People Policy Planning Institute, 28, 247
Johnson, Lyndon B./Johnson administration, 48, 62–63, 172, 413n15
Jordan (Kingdom of), 48, 62, 158, 162, 164, 173, 176–79, 189, 193, 199, 205, 279, 281–82, 284, 289, 368n6, 370n38, 372–73n72, 401n26, 406n63, 407n74, 408nn81, 91, 409n103
  peace treaty with Israel, 292
  proposed national home for Palestinians, 204, 235, 268, 284, 290, 292–93, 435n157
Jordan River, 178–79, 244, 279, 285, 435n157, 436n172
Jordan Valley, 243, 423n116, 425n130, 426–27n145
Judaism, xviii–xix, 8
Judt, Tony, 364–65n58
June 1967 war
  aftermath, 9, 16, 52–53, 62–66, 97, 113, 157, 160–61, 203–21, 229, 230–34, 237–38, 243–44, 256, 272–73, 283–85, 291–92, 301–4, 367nn25, 27, 372nn66–70, 372–73n72, 409n103, 412n4–419n56, 421–22n99, 422n101, 424n126, 426n131, 435n148, 440n15, 444n73
  borders, 22, 62–66, 203–21, 230–34, 237–38, 243–44, 281–85, 291–92, 320, 372nn66–70, 372–73n72, 409n103, 412n4–419n56, 421–22n99, 422n101, 424n126, 426n131, 444n73
  build-up to and events during, 48, 94, 158, 162–80, 183–201, 203–21, 272–73, 281–84, 297, 368n9, 401n26–409n103, 409n2–412n65, 444n73
  significance for U.S.-Israel relations, xiv, 3, 5, 8, 20, 33, 36–41, 45, 47–48, 52–53, 83, 301–4, 366n14, 367n27, 380n147

K
Kafr Kassem, 38
Kagan, Robert, 80
Kahane, Meir, 120, 387n61
Katz, Mark N., 199
Kedourie, Elie, 264
Kennedy, John F., 48
Kerry, John, 89
Ketziot (prison), 100–20
Kfar Saba, 339, 341
Khalidi, Rashid, 435n162
Khalidi, Walid, 155
kibbutzim, 9, 100, 121, 359n51
Kibya, 38
Kiernan, V. G., 374n91
Kimmerling, Baruch, 295
King, Martin Luther, 112–13, 119
Kirkpatrick, Jeane, 71
Kissinger, Henry, 76, 376n132

Kooijmans, Pieter, 314–15, 441n24
Korman, Sharon, 209, 413–14n20, 414n24
Kosygin, Alexei, 197, 402n40
Krauthammer, Charles, 51, 70
Kretzmer, David, 419n56, 443–44n68, 448n118
Kristol, Irving, 35, 67–68, 79, 380n147
Kristol, William, 80
Kurtzer, Daniel C., 200
Kuwait, 60, 88, 230–31, 243–44, 379n142, 414n24
Kuznetsov, V. V., 64

L

Lambeth, Benjamin S., 392n19
land swaps, 216, 239–47, 288, 424n126, 425n130, 427n147
Langer, Felicia, 383n1
"language of force," 70, 72, 81, 157, 374n91, 429n151
Latin America, 214–15, 415–16n30, 416nn32, 33
Lauterpacht, Hersch, 417n46
League of Nations, 209, 413n20
Lebanon, 139, 164, 279
    1958 U.S. intervention in, 60, 370n38
    1978 invasion of, 150, 268–69, 432n77
    1982 invasion of, xvi, 16, 150, 159, 231–32, 234, 266, 268–71, 360n60, 389n93, 423n110
    1993 invasion of, 394–95n53
    1996 invasion of, 271, 394–95n53
    2006 invasion of, 16, 51, 98, 123–54, 301, 360n60, 390n3–399n148
    casualty figures, 16, 127–28, 139–40, 147, 269, 360n60, 390n6, 391nn14–18, 398n125
    cluster munitions fired at, 128, 145–54, 301, 392n20, 396n86, 398n108–399n148
    occupation of South (1982–2000), 70, 159, 232, 394nn49, 50, 394–95n53
Ledeen, Michael, 70
Lenin, Vladimir, 10, 68, 374n83
Levy, Gideon, xvii, 296
Lewis, Bernard, 201
Libby, Lewis "Scooter," 76–77, 376–77nn132, 136
Lieberman, Avigdor, 11, 15, 122
Liel, Alon, 99
Limbaugh, Rush, 302
Livni, Tzipi, 28, 351, 448n118
Lukács, Georg, 35
Lustick, Ian, 201

M

Maale Adumim, 424n126, 436n172, 443n61
Malcolm X., 119
Mandela, Nelson, 235
Mandelbaum, Michael, 201
Mao Tse-tung, 65
Maoz, Zeev, xvii, 70, 113, 118, 157–60, 165, 169, 175, 189, 248, 351, 388–89n93, 408n91, 423n116, 426n145
Marshall, George, 56
McFarland, David, 195, 411n49

McNamara, Robert, 172–73
Mearsheimer, John J., xiv, 45–53, 60–87, 369n12, 373n82, 376n121, 380–81n158, 436n162
media (U.S./Western), xvii, 23–26, 66, 93–95, 99, 122, 126, 139, 161, 183, 198–201, 301, 383n1, 388n88, 391–92n19
Meir, Golda, 76
Menetrez, Frank J., 414n25
Meron, Theodor, 419n56, 440n15
Mevasseret Zion, 319, 441n38
Michael, B., 277
Miller, Aaron David, 376nn123, 130, 413n15, 420n86, 426n131
Mitchell, George/Mitchell Report (2001), 273–74, 433n98
Montell, Jessica, 277
Moore, Deborah Dash, 382n166
Mormons, 89
Morris, Benny, 16, 156, 176, 201, 251–297, 302, 399–400n5, 405n62, 408n87, 430n23, 431–32n69, 435–36n162, 436nn164, 172, 437n192, 438n206
Moyers, Bill, 26
Mubarak, Hosni, 89, 293
Murphy, David, 200
Murphy, Sean D., 445n81
Muslims, vii, 49, 53, 62, 68, 72, 87, 100, 113, 257–65, 286–89, 293–97, 361n8, 437n192
Mussolini, Benito, 59

N
Nablus, 179, 277
Nachumi, Amir, 195, 411n49
Narkiss, Uzi, 172, 179
Nasrallah, Sayyed Hassan, 132–33, 393n42
Nasser, Gamal Abdel, 48–49, 56–59, 62, 83, 94, 158, 165–77, 188, 191–93, 197–98, 266–68, 368nn6, 9, 371nn46, 47, 50, 400n19, 402n40, 404n52, 405nn55, 59, 406n63, 407n69, 431–32n69
National Brands Index, 20
National Security Council (U.S.), 47, 57, 63, 165–66, 174
Native Americans, 8, 181, 258, 296
Neier, Aryeh, 98
neoconservatives, xiv, 5, 30, 35, 37, 42–43, 50, 67–72, 75–84, 251, 367n27, 373n82, 375n106, 376–77n132, 377n134, 378n139, 380n147, 439n6
Netanyahu, Benjamin, 15, 30, 85, 122, 223, 373n82, 421n95, 428n151
Netanyahu, Benzion (Netanyahu Sr.), 30
New Deal, 5
"new historians," 253–97, 428n150, 434n124
New Left, 43, 67
New Republic, 28, 29, 98, 367n25, 400nn13, 15
Nixon, Richard, 75–76
Non-Aligned Countries, 214, 415–16n30, 416n33
nonviolence, 70, 103, 108–10, 114–15, 126, 318, 385–86n40, 386n48, 387n71
Norway, 21

O

Obama, Barack, 15, 23, 89, 222
O'Brien, Conor Cruise, 399n3
October 1973 war, 70, 159, 230, 422n103
oil, 54–58, 62, 65, 74–75, 167, 244, 374n103
Olmert, Ehud, 381n163
Open Society Institute, 98
Operation Accountability (1993). *See* Lebanon
Operation Ajax (1953). *See* Iran
Operation Cast Lead (2008–9). *See* Gaza Strip
"Operation Dawn" (1967). *See* Egypt
Operation Defensive Shield (2002). *See* West Bank
Operation Grapes of Wrath (1996). *See* Lebanon
Operation Iraqi Freedom (2003). *See* Iraq
Operation Litani (1978). *See* Lebanon
Operation Peace in the Galilee (1982). *See* Lebanon
Oren, Michael, xvii, 93, 161–81, 400nn16, 18, 401nn26, 31, 32, 403nn44, 45, 404n52, 405nn55, 62, 406n63, 407nn69, 74, 409n103
Orwell, George, 445n76
Oslo Accords, 223, 225, 228–29, 232–33, 235–37, 241, 262, 284–85, 330, 332, 420n89, 421n95, 421–22n99, 423n113, 424n126, 425n127
"Oslo years" (1993–2000), 100–22, 221–48
Owada, Hisashi, 314, 441n24

P

Pahlavi, Mohammad Reza. *See* Shah of Iran
Pakistan, 20, 50
Palestine
    occupation of. *See* June 1967 war; settlement of Israel-Palestine conflict
    partition of (1947). *See* United Nations
    refugee camps, 109, 117–18, 261, 276–77
    self-determination/statehood, 21–24, 88, 109, 203–48, 261, 284–93, 308, 335, 353, 413n4, 420n91, 423n116, 425n130, 435n149, 438n195, 441n24, 448n116
Palestine Liberation Organization (PLO), 159, 225, 232–36, 268–70, 286, 289, 423n113
    Algiers Declaration (1988), 234–35, 237, 285
Palestine National Council, 234, 285–87
Palestinian Authority, 107, 225–27, 273, 436n164, 448n112
Palestinian National Charter, 286
Palestinians
    children, 26, 103–5, 110–11, 116–18, 266, 272–75, 386n48
    Christians, 260, 262
    citizens of Israel. *See* Israel
    collaboration with Israel, 110, 225–27, 235, 271
    due process denied, 103–9, 225–27, 272, 318, 420nn85, 86

"eliminationist" mindset (Morris), 264–65
ethnically cleansed in 1948, 16, 156, 399–400n5, 430n23
human rights violations by fellow Palestinians, 103, 106–7, 110–11, 225–27, 387n56, 420n86
human rights violations by Israel, xv–xvii, xix, 8–9, 16–17, 26, 30, 93–124, 126, 223–25, 227–29, 273–78, 292, 299–353, 385n29–390n114, 390–91n10, 391n11, 421n93, 439n2–449n123
killed or wounded, 16, 26, 38, 105, 109–11, 115–19, 224–25, 227, 265–77, 318, 360n60, 431n60
national identity, heritage under assault, 109–10, 277
poverty inflicted upon, 227–28
public opinion of, 237, 287–88, 290–92
and recognition of Israel, 232–37, 240–41, 286, 291–92, 440–41n24
refugees, vii, 16, 23, 39, 117–18, 155–56, 164, 176, 205, 217, 220, 235, 238–41, 244–45, 247, 254, 256, 267, 269–70, 276–77, 283, 285, 288, 291–92, 413n4, 417n45, 418–19n56, 424n126, 425–26n130, 427–28n150, 430n23
women, 118, 266, 275
Palmer Report, 361n14
Partition Resolution (1947). *See* United Nations

Pedatzur, Reuven, 200
Peel Commission (1937), 262–64, 278, 280
Peled, Mattityahu, 172
Peres, Shimon, 85, 233, 236–37, 284, 286
Peretz, Martin, 28, 30, 98, 367n25, 400n13
Perle, Richard, 373n82, 376n132
permanent status issues, 205, 217, 238, 246, 285, 425n127
Peters, Joan, 39, 264, 383n2, 413n4
Petraeus, David H., 88
Pickering, Thomas R., 201
Pipes, Daniel, 199
Podhoretz, Norman, 37–40, 43, 67, 76, 367n19, 376n131
pogroms, 119, 259–60
Poland, 188, 190, 375n116
political liquidations, 114, 117–18, 275, 318
Pollard, Jonathan, 356n9
Pomerance, Michla, 418–19n56, 441n35, 444n73
Porath, Yehoshua, 261
Powell, Colin, 75, 77, 377nn133, 135
Public Committee Against Torture in Israel (PCATI), 117, 275
Pundak, Ron, 425n127
Pushkin, Alexander, 119

Q
al-Qaida, 379n139
Qalqiliya, 338–41, 443n61, 448n112
Qana, 125, 271, 390n6
Qedumim, 443n61

R

Rabin, Yitzhak, 10, 170–71, 174–79, 223–27, 233–37, 284, 286, 386n52, 387n56, 394n50, 401n31, 402n40, 404n52, 423n116
Rafael, Gideon, 403n47, 405n55
Rapoport, Meron, 351
Reagan, Ronald, 75, 367n27, 373–74n83, 377nn132
Remez, Gideon. *See Foxbats over Dimona*
Remnick, David, 29–30, 299
Reporters Without Borders, 12
Republican Party, 5, 7, 67 68, 379n142, 381n164
Rice, Condoleezza, 74–77, 375n118, 377nn133, 135
al-Rifai, Zayd, 406n63
"right of return" (Palestinian refugees), 23, 220, 238–41, 244, 288, 291–92, 418–19n56, 424n126, 425–26n130, 427–28n150
"right to exist" (Israel), 232, 234, 286, 440–41n24
Rikhye, Indar Jit, 407n69
Roberts, Adam, 220–21
Rodinson, Maxime, 360n5
Roosevelt, Eleanor, 56
Roosevelt, Franklin D., 5
Roosevelt, Theodore, 296
Rosenberg, M. J., 22, 27
Ross, Dennis, xvii, 93, 221–48, 288, 376n123, 420nn89, 91, 421nn95, 99, 422n101, 423n116, 424n126, 425n127, 425–26n130, 427nn145, 147, 148, 149, 427–28n150, 428–29n151

Rostow, Walt W., 48, 63
Roth, Kenneth, 98, 126, 153
Rove, Karl, 379n142
Rubin, Barry, 49
Rubinstein, Danny, 73, 99, 278
Rumsfeld, Donald, 74–78, 375n116, 376n130, 376–77n132, 377nn133, 134, 138, 379n142
Rusk, Dean, 62, 64, 168
Russell, Bertrand, 387n71
Russia, 21, 37, 50, 64, 76, 88, 166, 183–201, 280, 302, 361n8, 411n53, 412n60

S

Sabagh, Hamutal, 294
Sadat, Anwar, 184
Said, Edward, 295
Salfit, 443n61
Samu, 162, 166
Sarid, Yossi, 99
Sarna, Jonathan, 17, 41
Saud, King Ibn, 55
Saudi Arabia, 48, 50, 54, 55, 57, 60, 88, 234, 368n6, 422n109, 437n192
Save the Children, 111
Savir, Uri, 423n113
Schiff, Zeev, 109, 114
Schindler, Alexander, 61
Scobbie, Iain, 444n69
Segev, Tom, 174, 177, 179–80, 406n62, 409n103
Sela, Avraham, 170
September 11, 2001 attacks, 65, 79, 83, 110, 145, 296, 377n132, 378–79n139
settlement of Israel-Palestine conflict, xiv, xvii, 8–9, 21, 89, 113–14,

119–20, 156–60, 231, 235, 259, 285, 387n56
Arab initiatives, 157, 160, 234, 422n109
international consensus on two-state settlement, xvi, xix, 17, 66, 84, 203–48, 284, 290–92, 309, 332, 372n66, 414–15n26, 417n46, 418–19n56, 435n149, 437n180, 440n15, 442n101, 444nn68, 73
"peace process," xvi, 25, 30, 93–94, 101, 109, 205, 217, 221–48, 254, 262, 286–88, 330, 351, 419n62–429n151
struggle for, xix, 25, 27, 72, 109–10, 160, 225, 303–4
settlements, 108, 204–5, 223–24, 227–29, 235, 238–39, 241, 244, 262, 285, 288–89, 389n111, 390n114, 420nn89, 91, 421n93, 427n147
evacuation of, 23, 120, 331, 338, 345–47, 443n68, 447n104
illegality of, 217–20, 229, 231, 239, 241, 243, 288, 302, 307–53, 389n111, 418n49, 418–19n56, 439n2–449n123
political clout of settler organizations, 447n106
and public opinion, xiii–xiv, 15, 21, 23, 25, 84, 87, 302, 355n4
and U.S., xiii, 23, 25, 84, 87, 227–28, 231–32, 239–44, 424n126, 427n148
Shah of Iran, 49, 52
Shahak, Israel, 383n1
Shamir, Yitzhak, 286

Shanker, Albert, 389n97
Sharansky, Natan, 225
Sharett, Moshe, 36
Sharon, Ariel, 16, 99, 159, 172, 175, 321–22, 423n110
Sharp, Gene, 385–86n40
Shavit, Ari, 103–6, 296, 438n201
Sher, Gilead, 424n126, 426n131, 428n150
Siegman, Henry, 436n162
Sneh, Moshe, 186–87
Socrates, 373n83
Solomon, Barbara Probst, 39
South Africa, 99, 363n39, 416n33
Soviet bloc, 158, 431n69
Soviet Union, 36, 39–41, 46–83, 120, 158, 165–66, 176, 183–201, 205–6, 215, 301, 365–66n6, 367nn19, 20, 368n9, 372nn68, 70, 373–74n83, 402n40, 403nn44, 45, 409nn2, 5, 410nn32, 35, 411nn53, 59, 412n65, 415n29, 431n69
Stalin, Joseph, 43, 67, 260, 280, 302
State Department, 54, 59, 371n50
state security courts, 226–27, 420n86
Stone, I. F., 367n25
Stone, Julius, 204–17, 221, 412–13n4, 414nn24, 25, 417n43
Straits of Tiran, 166–69, 191–92, 279, 404n52, 405n55
Students for Justice in Palestine, 302
Suez Canal, 56–59, 158, 173, 178–79, 371n50, 411n59
Suez crisis (1956). *See* Egypt
suicide bombings, 21, 101, 115–18, 228, 327, 338–39, 388n80, 389n111
Sullivan, Andrew, 24

Sweden, 21
Syria, 51, 60, 131, 159, 162, 164, 189, 203, 205, 231, 263, 368n6, 369n17, 370n38, 375n106, 376n127, 429n151
  and June 1967 war, 158, 162–66, 173, 176–79, 189–92, 199, 282, 401nn27, 32, 402n40, 408nn81, 91, 411n60
Szold, Henrietta, 37

T
Taba (2001 negotiations), 424n120
Tabenkin, Yitzhak, 179
targeted assassinations. *See* political liquidations
Tenet, George, 75, 377n135
Teveth, Shabtai, 255
Third World, 43
Tilley, Virginia, 436n162
torture, 16, 97–98, 105–8, 111, 115, 119, 225–28, 270, 271–72, 293, 307, 318, 385n34
Transparency International, 357–58n22
Trotsky, Leon, 67, 280
Truman, Harry S., 53–56, 60, 369–70n25
Tsafrir, Eliezer, 49
Tsemel, Lea, 383n1
Turkey, 87
Tutu, Desmond, 99
two-state settlement. *See* settlement of Israel-Palestine conflict

U
Unger, Craig, 74, 379n142

United Nations, 43, 132, 176, 180, 186, 314, 414n24, 414–15n26, 440n15
  Charter, 63, 209, 216, 310–11, 349, 372n67, 413–14n20, 415n26, 417n46
  Declaration of Principles (1970), 216
  deliberations after June 1967 war, 62–65, 205–16, 402n40, 413n13–417n43, 418n52
  Emergency Force (UNEF), 162, 166–67, 169, 191–92, 400n19, 403nn44, 45, 47, 407n69
  General Assembly, 63–64, 205–8, 210–19, 231, 234, 238, 246, 278, 284, 292, 309–10, 372n66, 402n40, 414–15n26, 415nn28, 29, 415–16n30, 416nn32, 33, 417nn43, 46, 418n48, 422n101, 439nn5, 7, 444–45n73
  Human Rights Committee, 440n10
  and Iraq, 377n138, 378n139, 414n24
  and Israeli invasions of Lebanon, 133, 135, 144, 145, 152–53, 271, 392–93n30, 394n45, 398n125, 399n148
  Office for the Coordination of Humanitarian Affairs (OCHA), 443n61, 449n123
  Palestinian statehood bid at (2011), 21, 23–24, 88
  Resolution 181 ("Partition Resolution," 1947), 53–56, 157, 278, 280–84, 370n26, 430n23, 434n124

Resolution 194 (1948), 238, 417n45
Resolution 242 (1967), 63–65, 203–4, 215–16, 229–32, 286–87, 372n70, 414nn20, 25, 422nn101, 103, 426n131, 444n73
Resolution 338 (1973), 230–32, 286–87, 422n103
Resolution "Peaceful Settlement of the Question of Palestine," 217–18
Security Council, 63–64, 204, 210, 215, 219, 229–33, 246, 286, 309–11, 372n70, 377n138, 379n139, 416n30, 418n49, 422nn101, 103
Special Rapporteur, 126, 391n111, 445–46n87, 446n92
and Straits of Tiran dispute, 166–68, 404n52, 405n55
U.S. stance on Israel at, xix, 23–24, 54, 62–66, 218, 230–34, 246, 370n43, 372nn66–68, 413n15, 415nn26, 28, 422n101, 435n149, 439n5
United States
college and university campuses, vii, xviii, 25, 28, 180, 299, 302, 364n45
intelligence agencies, 48, 50, 56, 59–60, 75, 77, 88, 170–73, 175, 200, 371n50, 375nn115–18, 378n139
international hostility toward, 62, 87–88
and Israel, xiii–xix, 9, 20, 22–25, 33–34, 35–43, 45–89, 165–78, 184, 186, 198, 203–48, 275, 280–81, 288, 290, 297, 300, 303, 356n9, 362n23, 363n39, 365–66n6, 366n13, 368n1–383n181, 404nn50, 52, 409n5, 412n63, 413n15, 415nn26, 28, 419n58–429n151, 435n149, 438n206, 439n5
and Middle East, 34, 40, 45–89, 165–78, 184, 186, 191, 193, 198, 203–16, 230–32, 243–44, 246, 280–81, 297, 363n39, 366n13, 367n20, 368n6–383n177, 392n28, 404n52, 405n59, 409n5, 413n15, 415nn26, 28, 429n151, 438n206
and Palestinian Authority, 225–27, 420n86
public opinion, xvi, 6, 19, 20, 22–25, 66, 93, 100, 156, 203, 217, 296, 361–62n21, 363n39, 366n13, 370n26, 375n106, 381nn160, 164
terrorism against, 51, 62, 65, 78
and Vietnam war, 41
Uris, Leon, 8, 112, 155
Urofsky, Melvin I., 366n13
Urquhart, Brian, 403n44, 405n55
U.S.S. *Liberty*, 198, 412n63
U Thant, 166–68, 210, 403n45, 404nn48, 52, 405n55, 414n26

V

Vybornov, Aleksandr, 194–97, 411n49

W

Waart, Paul J. I. M. de, 444n73
Wachsman, Nachshon, 223
Walt, Stephen M., xiv, 45–53, 60–87, 369n12, 373n82, 376n121, 380–81n158, 436n162
Walzer, Michael, 28, 180, 384n8
War of Attrition, 194
"War of Independence" (1948), 15–16, 36, 38, 41, 54–56, 155–60, 162, 176–80, 256, 265–67, 269, 278–84, 289, 291, 293, 367n25, 370n36, 399–400n5, 428n150, 430n23, 431nn60, 64, 436n164
War on Terror, 65, 260, 379n142
Washington Institute for Near East Policy (WINEP), 246–47, 422n101
water resources, 178–79, 279, 308, 312, 436n172
Watson, Geoffrey R., 443n59
Wedgwood, Ruth, 441n35
Weeramantry, Christopher, 148, 153
Weiss, Philip, 29
Weizman, Ezer, 172–73, 179
Weizmann, Chaim, 53
Westad, Odd Arne, 200
West Bank, 16, 25, 70, 94, 97–99, 106–22, 157, 159, 176–80, 203–48, 253–97, 307–53, 372–73n72, 389n111, 409n103, 421n93, 421–22n99, 422n101, 423n116, 424n126, 425n130, 427nn147, 148, 436nn164, 172, 439n2–449n123
 Operation Defensive Shield (2002), 117, 276–77, 388n88
wall, 218–20, 307–53, 439n2–449n123
Wheeler, Earle, 171, 173
white phosphorus, 301–2
Whitson, Sarah Leah, 391n18
Wiesel, Elie, 30, 36
Will, George, 71
Wilson, Woodrow, 369n25
Wolfowitz, Paul, 71, 75–76, 80–81, 367n27, 376nn121, 130, 376–77n132, 377nn134, 136, 380n153
Woodward, Bob, 74
Woolsey, James, 71
World War I, 412n4
World War II, 19, 35, 67, 367n27, 373n83, 380n147, 382n166, 411n59, 416n32
World Zionist Organization, 366n13
Wright, Quincy, 203
Wurmser, David, 373n82

Y

Yaari, Ehud, 109, 114
Yale University Press, 183, 198–201, 254, 292, 412n66, 436n162
Yaniv, Avner, 234
Yariv, Aharon, 164, 170–71
Yehoshua, A. B., 438n202
Yemen, 368n6
Yermiya, Dov, 269–70
Yglesias, Matthew, 29
Yodfat, 279

Z

Zakheim, Dov S., 200

Zamir, Eyal, 418n56
Zgheir, Kamal, 117
Zilbershats, Yaffa, 419n56
Zionism, xiv, xviii–xix, 5, 9–10, 13, 15–17, 28–29, 36–43, 53–60, 67, 69, 100, 112, 119–21, 155–56, 166, 183, 234–35, 255–97, 300, 365–66n6, 366nn13, 14, 368n28, 370n36, 430nn18, 35, 435n157
    associated with "the Jews," 261, 263
    goal of "transfer," 15–16, 156, 255–59, 263, 291, 430n18
Zionist Organization of America, 366n13

www.ingramcontent.com/pod-product-compliance
Lightning Source LLC
Chambersburg PA
CBHW021426080526
44588CB00009B/443